Heine's Jewish Comedy

Heine's Jewish Comedy

A Study of his Portraits of Jews and Judaism

S. S. PRAWER

'[A people] demands its history from the hand of the poet rather than that of the historian. It does not ask for faithful reporting of naked facts; what it wants is to see these dissolved again into the original poetry from which they sprang. The poets know this, and they secretly take a malicious pleasure in remodelling, in whatever ways they see fit, what the people's memory has preserved; as a means, perhaps, of pouring scorn on historians proud of their dryness and on state-archivists as desiccated and dull as the parchment of their documents.'

Heine, *A Journey from Munich to Genoa*, Chapter 7

CLARENDON PRESS · OXFORD

Oxford University Press, Walton Street, Oxford OX2 6DP

Oxford New York Toronto
Delhi Bombay Calcutta Madras Karachi
Kuala Lumpur Singapore Hong Kong Tokyo
Nairobi Dar es Salaam Cape Town
Melbourne Auckland
and associated companies in
Beirut Berlin Ibadan Nicosia

Published in the United States by
Oxford University Press, New York

First published 1983
Reprinted (new as paperback) 1985

British Library Cataloguing in Publication Data
Prawer, S. S.
Heine's Jewish comedy: a study of his portraits
of Jews and Judaism
1. Heine, Heinrich—knowledge—
—Jews   2. Jews in literature
I. Title
831'.7   PT2339
ISBN 0-19-815834-3

Typeset by
Wyvern Typesetting Ltd, Bristol
and printed in Great Britain by
Biddles Ltd, Guildford and King's Lynn

CONTENTS

Contents

ABBREVIATIONS

B	*Heinrich Heine. Sämtliche Schriften*, ed. K. Briegleb *et al.*, Munich 1968–76.
E	*Heines Sämtliche Werke*, ed. E. Elster, Leipzig and Vienna, 1887–1890.
HAD	*Heinrich Heine. Historisch-Kritische Gesamtausgabe der Werke* (Düsseldorfer Ausgabe), ed. M. Windfuhr *et al.*, Hamburg 1973 ff. (in progress).
H-Jb	*Heine-Jahrbuch* 19 (1980).
HSA	*Heinrich Heine. Säkularausgabe*, ed. Nationale Forschungs- und Gedenkstätten der klassischen deutschen Literatur in Weimar and Centre National de la Recherche Scientifique in Paris, Berlin and Paris 1970 ff. (in progress).
L	*Der Prosanachlaß von Heinrich Heine*, ed. E. Loewenthal, in *Heines Werke in Einzelausgaben*, ed. G. A. E. Bogeng, Vol. 12, Hamburg 1925.
Lyr. Int.	*Tragödien nebst einem lyrischen Intermezzo von H. Heine*, 1823.
M	Heinrich Heine: *Zeitungsberichte über Musik und Malerei*, ed. M. Mann, Frankfurt a.M. 1964.
W	*Heinrich Heine: Atta Troll. Ein Sommernachtstraum*, ed. W. Woesler, Stuttgart 1977.
Werner-Houben:	*Begegnungen mit Heine. Berichte der Zeitgenossen. In Fortführung von H. H. Houbens 'Gespräche mit Heine'*, ed. M. Werner, Hamburg 1973.

ACKNOWLEDGEMENTS

To keep annotations to a minimum, Heine's letters have generally been identified by recipient and date only; for other works references are given, wherever possible, to the Hanser edition, edited by K. Briegleb. I have, however, consulted and compared the two critical editions still in progress, as well as editions and compilations by Elster, Walzel, Kaufmann, Mann, Houben, and M. Werner. Prose quotations are given in English; I have made my own versions in all but a few acknowledged cases, but have consulted with profit existing translations by C. G. Leland, A. Werner, F. Ewen, M. Hadas, E. M. Butler, P. Branscombe, A. Elliot, L. Untermeyer and others. Verse quotations appear in the original German, with literal, line-by-line versions appended. Other works consulted will be noted only occasionally; I have preferred to use the space at my disposal to let Heine speak for himself, and to state my own views, rather than to engage in polemics with other scholars. That I owe a debt to many such scholars goes without saying; the works I have found of greatest use in my special, limited context are listed in the Select Bibliography. I am particularly grateful to the Humanities Research Centre of the Australian National University and its director, Professor Ian Donaldson, to the Tauber Institute of Brandeis University and its director, Professor Bernard Wasserstein, and to Professor Harry Zohn, for enabling me to write and think without undue distraction in congenial surroundings and stimulating company during two terms of sabbatical leave. Thanks are due also to the staff of the Taylor Institution Library (Oxford) and the Goldfarb Library (Brandeis) for keeping me supplied with reading material, and to that of the Heinrich Heine Institut (Düsseldorf) for patiently answering my questions. The greatest debt of all is expressed in the Dedication.

Waltham, Mass. December 1981

For
HELGA

PROLOGUE
A Comet Lights the Diaspora

(i)

Heine's work is full of verbal snapshots, portraits, and caricatures of Jews actual and imagined, historical and contemporary, famous and obscure, single and in groups, ex-Jews, and Jews who remained within the community to which their fathers had belonged. This book collects such portraits and caricatures together and presents them in chronological order, in the context of Heine's own spiritual, intellectual, and artistic development. The gallery so established depicts pedlars, old clothes men, pawnbrokers, corncutters,[1] shopkeepers, brokers, speculators of various kinds, bankers, scholars, rabbis, synagogue cantors and beadles, university students, poets, musicians, painters, impresarios, journalists, society hostesses, and Jews in many other walks of life—all seen from the perspective of a nineteenth-century German poet who was born a Jew but who thought it necessary to pay the price of baptism for his entry into the wider cultural community of the West. 'Modern poetry', Heine said in one of his works, echoing Hegel but speaking very much out of his own experience, 'is no longer objective, epic, and naïve; it is subjective, lyrical and reflective'.[2] The portraits are therefore coloured by the poet's mood, by his own changing problems and purposes; they are often parabolic, exaggerating aspects of an individual's outer appearance in order to portray what Heine called the 'signature' of his inner being, or using his name and aspects of his personality in order to characterize a whole group. He frequently invents incidents in order to bring out what he considers essential traits, and uses dream and fantasy as readily as realistically described action in pursuit of this same purpose. 'History', he wrote in 1828, in defence of his method, 'is not falsified by the poets. They faithfully convey its meaning even when they invent figures and incidents'.[3] For Heine, every true historian must have something of the poet in him; but he must also have something of the philosopher. The highest compliment he could pay to a historian he admired was to say that he combined the talents and insights of a philosopher with those of a great artist (letter to Jules Michelet, 20 January 1834).

While Heine was ever anxious to champion the imaginative writer's approach against that of professional historians, to urge the claims of Sir Walter Scott against those of David Hume and his own against those of Leopold von Ranke, he was also perfectly well aware of temperamental quirks and weaknesses which impaired the clarity of his own view of men and events.

> It is part of my character, or rather my sickness, that in moments of ill humour I do not spare even my best friends, going so far as to mock and maltreat them in the most hurtful way.
>   (Letter to Joseph Lehmann, 26 June 1823)

Heine's utterances have to be seen in their particular context (at whom are they directed? what purpose is the poet pursuing? what provocation has he had? what censorship does he seek to circumvent?); and they have to be held and weighed against other evidence. Nevertheless, he does convey certain aspects of nineteenth-century experience more powerfully than any other writer—and among these aspects the Jewish experience looms large, not in spite of but just because of the feeling, expressed in a letter to Rudolf Christiani dated 7 March 1824, that what water was to the fish, German-ness was to him. He just could not live outside the element of the German language and German culture. Heine was a poet truly alive in his own time and place, sensitive to social and intellectual currents, aware of the historical forces which had made Europe what it was and were transforming it into what it was yet to become. And being a poet meant that he was not only sensitive and aware, but also able to express himself more fully than others, able to use words 'to sharpen his awareness of his ways of feeling, so making these communicable.'[4] These qualities are well to the fore in his depiction of what the present book calls his 'Jewish Comedy'.

The choice of this title should serve to remind the reader that

Dante was one of Heine's literary heroes—he often glanced towards him for confirmation of his own personality and art, assenting to his description of the miseries and humiliations of exile, and calling the author of the *Inferno* 'the public prosecutor among the poets'.[5] In the final stanzas of *Germany. A Winter's Tale (Deutschland. Ein Wintermärchen)* he compares his own work with the *Inferno*: whoever has once been consigned to these 'melodious flames' is doomed to stay there for eternity—no saint and no saviour can release him for as long as there are men to read and respond to the poet's words.[6] And if the wealth of sharply etched figures in Heine's writings does indeed recall the *Divine Comedy*, from which they differ in so many other fundamental respects, then the recurrence of many of these figures in one work after another recalls the technique of the *Human Comedy* of Balzac, whom Heine knew personally and who dedicated one of his stories to him.[7] The 'Jewish Comedy' of my title should therefore recall aspects of both Dante and Balzac. It should also remind us of the sharp and often cruel eye for the *comic* which Heine demonstrated in his depiction of other men, including the many Jews who appear in his pages; but his 'Comedy' can no more be restricted to the merely comic than can those of his great predecessor and contemporary.

What a tragic story is the history of the Jews in modern times! And if one tried to write about this tragic element, one would be laughed at for one's pains. That is the most tragic thing of all.[8]

This inextricable intertwining of the comic and the tragic gives his Jewish Comedy its sharply distinctive flavour, and helps to make it an important part of that *comédie intellectuelle*, that drama of the human mind, which Paul Valéry saw in all literature.[9]

Among the famous who appear in these pages are the Rothschilds, Meyerbeer and his family, Ludwig Börne, the Mendelssohns, Achille Fould, and many others; they are intermingled with fictional characters like the corn-cutter Hirsch-Hyazinth, and little Samson, the champion of a God who works no miracles through him. Biblical characters and characters from Jewish history are presented in a new light by a poet deeply concerned with the problems of his own time; and we find depictions of the Jews as a people, a kinship group, a religious-social community, and a cultural subgroup, which place the individual portraits into a wider, developing context. From his own existential vantage point, of which this book tries at all times to keep the reader aware, Heine looked out at other men and women, including many of Jewish origin, and created out of what he saw a fascinating portrait gallery whose description and analysis will be my main concern.

When one speaks of 'portraits' in this context one is, of course, applying a metaphor from the visual to the verbal arts. Heine himself constantly sought such metaphoric illumination, and in the course of his life he described his own writings in terms of at least four distinct visual forms. One of these is the early photograph, the daguerreotype, whose development Heine viewed with fascination though also with some misgivings: in one of his last works he speaks of the scenes from Parisian life which he first published in the 1840s and then radically revised in the 1850s as 'honest daguerreotypes' significantly arranged by the artist.[10] The second of the visual forms for which Heine saw analogies in his own writings is that of painting in general and realistic painting in particular[11]—an art which, however faithfully it seeks to match the superficies of life, is of necessity more selective, and more expressive of the artist as well as the ostensible subject, than a photograph. We shall find him presenting himself to his readers, more than once, as a guide through a picture-gallery. Thirdly, perhaps most important of all, Heine not infrequently speaks of some of the contemporaries whom he introduces into his writings as *Fratzen* or *Karikaturen*.[12] The second of these terms reminds us that his later works were composed in a Paris that saw an unprecedented flowering of the art of caricature in the cartoons and lampoons of Charles Philipon, in Grandville's scenes from 'animal' life, and above all in the superb drawings and lithographs of Honoré Daumier. When Heine introduces a thumb-nail sketch of an obscure moustachioed contemporary into one of his letters from Paris, or when he merges Meyerbeer's activities as an orchestral conductor with his alleged activities as an orchestrator and conductor of his own fame, then we cannot but recall the cartoons and caricatures that were so prominent feature of French life, entertainment, and social comment in the mid-nineteenth century: an age in which no Parisian could look at Louis Philippe's head without being at once reminded of Philipon's pear. Most of Heine's portraits could be ranged along a scale whose end-points are suggested by Fielding in his Preface to *Joseph Andrews*: the scale, let us say, between Hogarth at one end and Gillray at the other. One is constantly reminded of the *portrait-charge* or loaded likeness which dominated French caricature from Philipon to André Gill, and of Daumier's caricature maquettes: little clay busts which depicted in the round the lawyers and politicians that people his lithographs. Heine in fact uses the image of the portrait statue—*ein ikonisches Standbild*[11]— when he talks of his depiction of Ludwig Börne: an attempt, surely, to counteract the two-dimensional suggestions adhering to his other images from the visual arts, and to suggest a greater multiplicity of possible angles of vision from which the same portrait might be seen.

One must not, however, think of the literary portrait, as it is found in Heine's works, too exclusively in terms of the visual arts. The historical portraits he found in the works of historians he read—particularly such French contemporaries as Thiers, Mignet, Michelet, and Thierry—were a powerful influence; here he could find confirmation of his own penchant for subordinating visual to intellectual and moral elements, for characterizing by description and evocation of activities, thoughts, and verbal expressions, rather than those of peculiar features of face and body. Nor is it only *contemporary* historians, in Germany as well as France, who are assimilated in this way. There is an illuminating remark in Theodor Creizenach's recollections of a conversation he had with Heine when he visited him in 1846. Creizenach found the poet reading J. M. Jost's history of the Jews; and he tells us that Heine said to him: 'If I were certain of another ten years of life, then I too would write Jewish histories. As preparation, however, it would be necessary to read no book but Herodotus for a whole year.'[14] Herodotus's cosmopolitan interest in states and individuals beyond his own Dorian front door; his scepticism, again and again overwhelmed by delight in Arabian Nights' and travellers' tales; his powerful sense of the mythic; his love of digressions to embellish his central themes, and his deliberate intermingling of the great and the small; his handling of the Ionian language, so easy and fluent, yet at the same time so consummately polished—all these features may be found again, *mutatis mutandis*, in Heine's verbal portraits, sketches, and cartoons of historical and contemporary figures. Above all, Herodotus would seem to have offered him what he also saw in the work of writers like Michelet and Thierry: a combination of curiosity about life with an artist's command of language, a union, in short, of poetry and history. But Heine had not been a pupil of Hegel's for nothing; poetry and history had also to be informed, in his view, by philosophy. The letter to Jules Michelet of 20 January 1834 to which I have already referred, is particularly illuminating in this respect; for it shows clearly what he missed in Herodotus as well as what he found there.

You are the true historian, because you are at the same time a philosopher and a great artist. You are a Herodotus who is not credulous, you are a Tacitus who does not despair. . . . You believe in progress and in providence. In that belief we are at one.

Heine ends his letter with an admiring reference to Michelet's style, which he dare not comment on further because of what he feels to be his own imperfect command of the French language.

   Throughout his life, Heine read and assimilated a great deal of literature, and literary traditions, actual and nascent, play a powerful part in all his works. He saw himself in many ways as the heir of Aristophanes: in both authors vigorously character-ized personages become symbols or indices of social, political, and aesthetic forces and conditions. The 'character' tradition too, running from Theophrastus via La Bruyère into many European literatures, Menippean satire, the 'characterizations' of Friedrich Schlegel, and the European novel, from his beloved *Don Quixote* to the writings of Scott and the young Dickens, all helped to shape his way of seeing and his manner of expression, as did the pen-portraits of contemporaries which he found in the journals he so avidly read until paralysis made it impossible to frequent Parisian *cabinets de lecture*. For all his assimilation of such varied elements he retains his distinctive voice—a voice never drowned by the voices of his predecessors and contemporaries whose echoes are still audible as we listen, with our inner ear, to what Heine has to tell us.

Heine more than once deplored the use of documents a poet had not himself intended for publication; and the stress in this book will be on works that first appeared before the general reading public in a form the poet himself sanctioned. We would lose a great deal, however, if we disregarded other material that became public property after his death—his letters, jottings, and conversations with others. Such material will therefore be considered in the 'Intermezzi' which follow each of the four main parts into which the present book is divided. Heine's portraits and caricatures of Jews and Judaism will be brought before the reader in chronological sections, and in the context of his development as a man and as a poet; this Prologue, however, will introduce the material and methods to be used by following one such depiction all the way through his work and then through all the letters and conversations that have been preserved.

(ii)

The extent and the (severe) limitations of Heine's knowledge of Torah and Talmud, of Jewish ritual and folklore, of the Hebrew language and contemporary Yiddish, have been exhaustively documented and examined—most recently by Ruth L. Jacobi in her book on Heine's Jewish heritage (*Heines jüdisches Erbe*, 1978) and by Jeffrey L. Sammons in *Heinrich Heine. A Modern Biography* (1979). Professor Sammons describes very well how Jewishness became and remained a significant part of the poet's cultural consciousness. At the age of six, he tells us, Heine

was placed in a communal Hebrew school run by a distant relative of the family named Rintelsohn. It is not easy to say how much he learned in this school. One of the deepest students of his Jewish environment thinks it probably was not much and that the time would have been taken up largely by relating Midrashic legends, which would have suited young Heine perfectly. In the greatest of his late 'Hebrew Melodies' he ascribes to the poet Jehuda ha-Levi a youthful preference for the homiletic and parabolic narratives of the Talmud to its legal disputation, which very likely reflects his own boyhood inclination. It is doubtful that he ever learned to read Hebrew with any facility. He knew some words and phrases, naturally; he could remember part of a verb paradigm, which he built into a joke in *The Book of LeGrand*, and he could write the cursive script, which he employs very occasionally for a word or two in his letters. But his transliterations of Hebrew phrases are often wildly faulty and, when he needed a translation of sections from the Passover service, he had to ask a friend to do it for him.

This raises, for Professor Sammons and for us, the question of the quality of Jewish life in Heine's paternal home. His mother had become hostile to orthodox Judaism after early clashes with the Jewish community in Düsseldorf, though she never formally abandoned the faith into which she had been born. Her son soon found himself, to quote Professor Sammons yet again, 'on one side of a rather rapid generational transition'.

His father appears to have been conventionally if sincerely pious, though at the end of his memoir-fragment Heine tells us that his father advised him against the appearance of atheism because it would be bad for business; furthermore, Samson Heine was apparently a Freemason, which he certainly could not have been if this orthodoxy had still been intact. Uncle Salomon was certainly strongly committed to the Jewish community, which he supported generously and to which he left a variety of significant legacies in his will. But in that same document he excused his son from all memorial rituals, including the 'kaddish' which, of course, he had no right in Jewish law to do. The ambitious social climbing of the family naturally presupposed conversion to Christianity by all hands, and Salomon must have regarded this circumstance with equanimity, though in fact his own son resisted it. There are anecdotes indicating that Heine was raised to keep the Sabbath, and his evident familiarity with the Passover 'seder', so effectively described in *The Rabbi of Bacherach*, suggests the probability that it was celebrated in his home. Heine remarked there that even renegade Jews are moved in their hearts when they hear the melody of the Passover ritual; very likely he was thinking of himself. There is no other evidence that the family was observant. Heine nowhere mentions celebrating any holy days and there is no indication that he ever had a bar mitzvah or was even exposed to the rites and customs of the observant Jew. In fact he makes errors in simple Jewish matters of a kind that would not be usual for one with a traditional upbringing. During his student days he undertook an extensive study of Jewish history and tradition, and it is likely that most of what he knew derived from that experience rather than from his boyhood. It is true that he was very firm in the Bible—in Luther's translation, of course—and that his interest in it increased as the years went by. But Luther's Bible has always been a fundamental resource for German writers, and Heine differs from the usual pattern perhaps only by a somewhat greater emphasis on the Old Testament.[15]

I hope that a chronological survey of Heine's portrayal of Jews and Judaism will help to trace, among other things, the evolution of his attitudes to a community to which his immediate family never ceased to belong, and to throw some light on the way in which Jewishness remained a significant factor in his thought and feeling even after his formal acceptance into the Protestant Church.

But one important caveat must now be entered. Into Heine's many and varied writings portraits of Jews intrude surprisingly often—as contemporary friends and enemies were quick to notice. Nevertheless, they form only one strand in a most varied tapestry; and though I shall try, throughout, to place the portraits I isolate into their full context, the very fact of focusing on just one set of details is bound to lend these a prominence that is not theirs in the original design. For every single portrait of a recognizably Jewish figure there are many portraits or sketches of Germans and Frenchmen, Englishmen and Italians, men and women of past and present, which have no overt connection with Jews or Judaism. We also find, of course, many portraits of those whose connection with Judaism was that they were implacably hostile to it and to all those who professed it. Historians who want to trace the development of Jew-hatred from primitive xenophobia and religious intolerance to modern racial anti-Semitism can find many relevant pages in Heine's works—some of these, indeed, seem to anticipate the holocaust of the present century. This context too I shall try to keep before the reader. Nevertheless, as I have said, isolation of a single group of portraits is bound to lend that group a prominence which the author did not intend. I am encouraged, however, by my experience with some volumes issued many years ago by the curators of the

British National Gallery under the title: *100 Details from Pictures in the National Gallery* and *More Details from Pictures in the National Gallery*. These treasured volumes have helped me, over the years, to appreciate the National Gallery collection more fully than I would have done without their help. Need I say that I hope the reader of the present book will have the same experience when he returns to Heine's own works and reintegrates into their original context the passages I have transferred into mine?

(iii)

Heine's attitudes developed and changed, and the portraiture this book discusses developed and changed with them. Moreover, his portraits of individuals usually occur in contrasting or supportive groups—as when Mendelssohn-Bartholdy and Meyerbeer are compared and contrasted with Rossini, when Ludwig Börne is shown in the midst of his admirers and disciples, when James de Rothschild is held against the Foulds or the Péreires. The same holds good of fictional portraits: Gumpelino and Hirsch-Hyazinth need one another like Don Quixote and Sancho Panza, and by the time Heine begins to write the third chapter of the incomplete *Rabbi von Bacherach* the pious Ashkenazic rabbi has come to need a worldly, Sephardic foil and complement (see Chapter 8 below). Before launching into a chronological discussion of such portraits and portrait groupings I would like to look in some detail at just one developing portrait: that of Eduard Gans (1797–1839), a pupil and editor of Hegel who became a professor of law in the University of Berlin.

Heine first met Gans in the early 1820s. They came together in Berlin, where Gans had helped to found a Society for the Culture and Science of the Jews (*Verein für Cultur und Wissenschaft der Juden*), which Heine himself joined on 4 August 1822. The *Wissenschaft* of this title denoted an ideal of scholarly discipline which sought to apply carefully thought-out critical-philological methods to the source materials that speak to us of the past, without the need to pronounce 'superior' value-judgements on the ages and cultures whose 'essence' was to be disengaged.[16] The genitive construction *Wissenschaft der Juden* implied that this discipline was to be *applied to* the products of Jewish culture and to be *spread among* the Jews. One of the sub-organizations of this Society was an institute for the scholarly, *wissenschaftlich* study of Judaism, whose results were to be published in a journal: the term used to describe both institute and journal, *Wissenschaft des Judentums*, was to have a great future in Jewish scholarship. There was also an education section in which Heine lectured on German history and institutions to young Jews from the Polish provinces. Since most of the younger members of the Society had come under the influence of Hegel, their conception of science and scholarship tended to have a Hegelian slant; but among the older members there was at least one confirmed Kantian, Lazarus Bendavid. It is also worth noting that the fullest statement of the Society's aims and philosophy, formulated by I. Wohlwill with help from the others, alluded to Leibniz's monadology in one of its key sentences—an allusion Heine seems to have found highly amusing.

Gans was born in the same year as Heine; like Heine he received his secondary education in a Gentile *Gymnasium*; like Heine again, he refused to consider a business career (traditional in both their fathers' families) and studied law at the universities of Göttingen and Berlin; like Heine he hoped to take advantage of the more tolerant attitudes that seemed to be developing in Germany in order to obtain a professorship at a German university. What drew the two men together into the Society for the Culture and Science of the Jews was a feeling that the Jewish communities of Germany were failing to realize their full cultural potential; that scientific (*wissenschaftlich*) study of all the manifestations of Jewish life (*Kultur* in the all-embracing sense) was necessary in order to show actualities and possibilities—to make Jews aware of what they had been, what they were, and what they could be in nineteenth-century German society. It was also hoped that 'scientific' study of Jewish culture would dispel prejudices among Germans and would lead, through the absorption of Jewish energies in matters other than trade and money transactions, to a better integration of Jews into German society. The Society's aim, therefore, was threefold:

  (i) to spread modern science and scholarship, a spirit of *Wissenschaft* whose chief philosophical representative was thought to be Hegel, among German Jews, in order to enable them to take their proper place in German society once full civil rights had been granted them;

 (ii) to study, in a scholarly, 'scientific' way, Jewish cultural achievement in all fields, in order to disengage—in Hegelian fashion—the 'essence' of Judaism; this would help to define the nature of the contribution Jews had made throughout the ages to religion, philosophy, history, law, literature, and civic affairs;

(iii) to inform Jews and Gentiles alike of the results of these studies, by means of scholarly publications and lectures, in order to acquaint the Jewish world with its own inner essence and the Gentile word with the valuable contributions Jews had made, and could continue to make, to the sum total of human culture.

The Society did not find wide support, and was disbanded after a few years for lack of money and membership; but through the scholarly labours of Leopold Zunz it exerted a powerful influence on Jewish scholarship and Jewish self-definition in Germany long after it had ceased to exist.

   Gans and Heine met outside the framework of the Society too; but there were some temperamental clashes, and each therefore tended to visit circles in which they were both received only at times when he knew that the other would not be there. Both Heine and Gans accepted baptism for the sake of their careers rather than out of conviction that Christianity was the only true faith. 'If the state is so stupid', Gans is reported to have said to Felix Eberty, 'as to forbid me to serve it in a capacity which suits my particular talents unless I profess something I do not believe—and something which the responsible minister *knows* I do not believe: all right then, it shall have its wish.'[17]

   The reader of Heine's works meets Gans first in a series of *Letters from Berlin* (*Briefe aus Berlin*) in which the young poet sought to convey his experience of city life to the readers of a provincial newspaper. The writer of these *Letters* encounters

Gans in the street, and at once asks him for news—'petty news
of the town', *armselige Stadtneuigkeiten*, such as provincial
readers will lap up. But Gans is not in a mood for gossip: 'He
shakes his grey reverent head and shrugs his shoulders.' The
questioner therefore deserts him abruptly and collars another
informant, a musician who 'always has a pocketful of news'
and who, once he starts unpacking these, goes on without
stopping, like a mill-wheel.[18]

This brief first glimpse of Gans (in the context of many other
figures or institutions) suggests that he is known as a gossip,
but that he is also moody; that despite his youth (he was just
twenty-five years old at the time) he can give the impression of
being an old man; that the shrug is a gesture characteristic of
him. The young-old man shrugging his shoulders: a Jewish
caricature is in the making.

Gans next surfaces, for a moment, in one of the fictional
dreams that are so important a structural feature of *The Hartz
Journey* (*Die Harzreise*, 1826). Having climbed the 'Brocken'
mountain, famed for its association with witches and devil-
worship, the narrator finds himself troubled by 'chaotic,
frightening, fantastic visions'—'Dante's *Inferno* arranged for
the piano'—which culminate in the performance of a dream
opera entitled *Falcidia*. That opera, the narrator tells us, had a
legal text by Gans, something to do with the laws of
inheritance, and music by Berlin's most fashionable Italian
composer, Gasparo Spontini. *Erbrechtlicher Text von Gans*:[19]
here *The Hartz Journey* adds three further items to the
developing portrait-caricature. First, a piece of information:
the subject which Gans had made his special study was the Law
of Inheritance, of which the Roman *lex Falcidia* was an
important component. Secondly, a pun: *érbrechtlich* means
'pertaining to inheritance'; but if the stress is slightly shifted
(*erbréchtlich*) it looks as though the word were an absurd
Yiddishism, cognate with *sich erbrechen* ('to be sick') and
meant 'sick-making'. We know from other evidence that
Heine did not think highly of the style in which Gans's early
works were written. Lastly, an atmosphere: is there not
something theatrical, bombastic, Italian opera-like about
Gans?

A later 'travel picture', *Ideas. The Book of LeGrand* (*Ideen.*

Das Buch LeGrand, 1827) introduces Gans yet again in a brief
but significant passage. Heine mocks the pedantic habit of
excessive quotation to which German scholars are particularly
prone—and he illustrates this with the case of the man who in
early editions is simply designated as 'my friend G. in Berlin'.

My friend G. in Berlin is, so to speak, a little Rothschild in the matter
of quotations. He'll be glad to lend me a few million, and if he
happens not to have that many in store, he can easily get them
together for me with the help of a few cosmopolitan bankers of the
spirit [*bei einigen kosmopolitischen Geistesbankiers*].[20]

Here, for the first time, we have a public hint that Gans is of
Jewish origin—through the juxtaposition with Rothschild in a
sentence whose speech rhythms (*ist so zu sagen ein kleiner
Rothschild*) resemble those Heine will employ later when
characterizing the speech of Jewish figures like Hirsch-
Hyazinth (*The Baths of Lucca,* 1830). The mention of
Rothschild alongside Gans fulfils, once again, at least three
purposes. It suggests, first of all, that men of Jewish origin now
play a significant part in the intellectual as well as in the
financial life of Europe. Secondly, the juxtaposition serves to
convey that even though Gans may now be baptized, he is still
categorized with his former co-religionists by friend and foe.
Thirdly, the mention of Rothschild leads to the notion of
'cosmopolitan bankers of the spirit'—a notion which suggests,
among other things, that excessive quoting is connected with a
commercialization and mechanization of the intellectual and
spiritual life. The word here translated as spirit, *Geist,* was of
course a keyword in Hegelian philosophy, and serves to
remind us that Gans, whose father was a court Jew well known
for his banking transactions, had become one of Hegel's most
eminent disciples.

What neither Gans nor the contemporary reading public
could know, was that Heine had written a poem, after hearing
of Gans's baptism, which gave bitter expression to his sense
that the President of the Society for the Culture and Science of
the Jews had deserted his post in an irresponsible manner.
Gans is not named, but later documents make it quite clear that
he is meant.

O des heil'gen Jugendmutes!
Oh, wie schnell bist du gebändigt!
Und du hast dich, kühlern Blutes,
Mit den lieben Herrn verständigt.

Und du bist zu Kreuz gekrochen,
Zu dem Kreuz, das du verachtest,
Das du noch nor wenig Wochen
In den Staub zu treten dachtest!

Oh, das tut das viele Lesen
Jener Schlegel, Haller, Burke—
Gestern noch ein Held gewesen,
Ist man heute schon ein Schurke.

[O for youth's sacred courage!
How speedily you are tamed!
Now your blood has cooled somewhat, you have
come to an arrangement with the gracious lords.

You have humbled yourself before the cross
the very cross that you despised,
that only a few short weeks ago
you sought to tread into the dust!

That's what comes of all that reading
Of people like Schlegel, Haller, and Burke—
the man who but yesterday was still a hero
has turned into a knave today.][21]

Heine never published this poem, but he did not destroy it either—he must, therefore, have reckoned with its ultimate appearance, even if only posthumously, in his collected works. It alludes, prominently, to its protagonist's assumption of Christianity; but what it really deplores (as Klaus Briegleb has well said) is a decay of the fighting spirit, a decay of strength. The reading of conservative philosophers has led, the poet tells us, to an unprincipled abandonment of the fight for emancipation—emancipation from the tutelage of those who used the religion of the cross to rule over others. The poem characterizes its protagonist as a man who seemed courageous but crumbled into cowardly submission when the test came; it never names Gans, however, as it moves inexorably towards that impersonal construction of the final line which gives it a wider application and an especially bitter note. One remembers, suddenly, that Heine's own baptism, his own 'crawl to the cross', had *preceded* Gans's by several months. In venting his rage against Gans he is raging against himself. The portrait of Gans is becoming more than just the portrait of an individual: it is the portrait of a generation to which Heine also belonged, a generation of young Jews who had abandoned the ways of their rabbinically trained forefathers (who would have deplored not only the reading of Friedrich Schlegel, Haller, and Burke, but that of Hegel too!) and had lost the strength and authenticity single-minded adherence to Jewish traditions might have lent them. Emancipation from the tyranny of the rabbis—one of the planks in the platform of the Society for the Culture and Science of the Jews!—had led to submission to another kind of tyranny.

The bitter mood of this poem is absent from a bibulous section of *The North Sea* (*Die Nordsee* II) which, for the first time in Heine's work, brings Gans into proximity with Hegel, the great teacher to whom Gans owed the philosophical framework within which he thought and wrote. The speaker of the poem, who is refreshing himself at an inn after an arduous sea voyage, looks into his glass of wine and sees all history there:

> Alles erblick ich im Glas,
> Alte und neue Völkergeschichte,
> Türken und Griechen, Hegel und Gans,
> Zitronenwälder und Wachtparaden,
> Berlin und Schilda und Tunis und Hamburg . . .

> [In my glass I see everything:
> ancient and modern history,
> Turks and Greeks, Hegel and Gans,
> lemon groves and military parades,
> Berlin and Gotham and Tunis and Hamburg . . .][22]

The great and the little, the admirable and the contemptible, are as inextricably commingled in the drinker's mind as they are in life; and the reader is deliberately left in doubt whether the relationship between Hegel and Gans is analogous to that between Turkey and Greece, or that between poetic Italian landscapes and prosaic Prussian parade-grounds . . . or any of the other relationships suggested by the parallel pairs. Unlike the unpublished 'renegade' poem, this *North Sea* poem is content to suggest an intellectual and spiritual relationship and to leave judgement on it in abeyance. We may be quite sure, however, that in the context of Heine's developing work an affinity with Hegel is more respectable than an affinity with Schlegel, Haller, and Burke.

Heine's portrayal of Gans's philosophical affinities, and his place within the constellation of German intellectual life, is carried on by a fantastic passage in *The Baths of Lucca* (1830) in which an Italian professor of law is credited with some very strange notions. The Italian had heard of F. K. von Savigny, the leader of the conservative 'historical school of law' (*historische Rechtsschule*) in Prussia, and of Heine's own equally conservative teacher, the Göttingen professor Gustav Hugo. He has also heard of their more liberal opponent in Heidelberg, A. F. J. Thibaut, and Thibaut's protégé and pupil Eduard Gans. Somehow, however, he has transmogrified their relationship into that between participants in a ball—a ball at which Gans had asked Savigny to be his partner, but had been refused and had then become Savigny's enemy. Many of Heine's contemporary readers would here have recognized an allusion to the anti-Jewish Savigny's unswerving opposition to Gans's appointment at the University of Berlin, where Savigny himself occupied a chair of law. In that sense Savigny had indeed refused to become Gans's partner. The narrator of *The Baths of Lucca* then recounts how he tried to disabuse the Italian professor of his error.

'Your information, sir, is incorrect . . . Signor Gans does not dance, he loves mankind too much for that—for if he did dance, there might be an earthquake. The invitation to a dance of which you have told me is probably a misunderstood allegory. The historical and the philosophical schools of law are presented as dancers; and in this allegorical sense a quadrille of Hugo, Thibaut, Gans, and Savigny may be conceived. And in this same sense it may perhaps be said that Signor Ugone [= Hugo], although he is the *diable boiteux* of jurisprudence, dances as daintily as Lemière, while Signor Gans has recently attempted some high leaps that have made him the Hoguet of the philosophical school.'[23]

The quadrille Heine describes in this transparent allegory had begun to interest the German public in 1814. In that year Thibaut had published his pamphlet *On the Necessity of a Common Civil Law for Germany (Über die Notwendigkeit eines allgemeinen bürgerlichen Rechts für Deutschland)*, which was favourable to the spirit that had produced the Declaration of the Rights of Man and the Code Napoléon. Savigny had countered in the same year with *The Vocation of Our Time for Legislation and Jurisprudence (Vom Beruf unserer Zeit für Gesetzgebung und Rechtswissenschaft)*, arguing for a law that was not rationally constructed according to general principles but had grown up historically within a given people. In the spirit of Romanticism, Savigny and his school 'rejected the idea of a universal source of law and justice and a universal sanction for laws—i.e. natural law—and claimed the national spirit and the unique national history to be the source of all laws, and the idea of justice prevailing in any nation.'[24] By partnering Gans with Thibaut in the 'philosophical' school and opposing him to such formidable 'historicals' as Savigny and Gustav Hugo, Heine not only defines Gans's position on the politico-intellectual map of Germany but also leaves no doubt of Gans's importance. Identification with M. F. Hoguet, one of the most celebrated dancers and choreographers of the day, whose leaps and turns he had already converted into political allegory in *The Hartz Journey*, again suggests the outstanding position Gans had now gained in the intellectual world. At the same time, however, portrait is once again passing over into caricature. Gans's physical clumsiness and lack of grace is suggested by the remark that if he were to dance in a literal rather than an allegorical sense, he would cause an earthquake; and the observation that Gans had tried some high leaps in recent times ('daß Signor Gans in der neuesten Zeit einige große Sprünge versucht') alludes obliquely to Gans's notorious desire to shine, to be the centre of attention, in any company in which he found himself. This last suggestion is strengthened by the reaction of the Italian professor after his error had been dispelled: he takes up his guitar and sings of the loud trumpetings, the 'Tarar', with which Gans's name resounds through the world.

> Es ist wahr, sein teurer Name
> Ist die Wonne aller Herzen.
> Stürmen laut des Meeres Wogen,
> Droht der Himmel schwarz umzogen,
> Hört man stets Tarar nur rufen,
> Gleich als beugten Erd und Himmel
> Vor des Helden Namen sich.

> [It is true, his well-loved name
> is the joy of every bosom.
> Though the ocean waves be stormy,
> though heaven threatens with black clouds,
> all we hear is a trumpeted 'Tarar',
> as though heaven and earth bowed down
> before the mighty hero's name.][25]

The 'Tarar' that outroars wind and waves represents at once the trumpetings of fame and Gans's own booming voice. The passage thus mingles, characteristically, admiration of Gans's achievements, approval of his intellectual position, with irritation at his fame, his maladroitness, and his lack of reticence and tact.

In the 'travel picture' which followed *The Baths of Lucca*, entitled *The Town of Lucca* (1831), Gans's name is not mentioned; but his figure nevertheless appears in one of those allegories which we can recognize by now as an integral part of Heine's literary portraiture. The narrator tells us of a conversation he purports to have had with some grey lizards he encountered in the Apennine mountains, and he comments:

Nature has her history too—one that differs from the 'natural history' taught in schools. It would be good to appoint one of the grey lizards that have been living in the clefts of the Apennine rocks for thousands of years to an extraordinary associate professorship [*als ganz außerordentliche Professorin*] at one of our universities—then we would hear extraordinary things. But this would offend the pride of some gentlemen of the faculty of law, who would protest against such an appointment. One of them is already secretly jealous of poor *Fido savant* and is afraid that he might one day supplant him as a fetcher and carrier of learning at his masters' command [*im gelehrten Apportieren*].²⁶

Heine's allusion to the unwillingness of German professors to accept members of a thousands-of-years-old species as colleagues at their universities is an unmistakable allegorization of their attitude to the Jews; and his reference to the faculty of law makes it obvious that he is attempting to call up in his readers' minds the *cause célèbre* of Eduard Gans, who had invoked the tolerant Prussian edict of 1812 in vain, had seen the edict modified in the Jews' disfavour, and had received his associate professorship, his *Extraordinariat*, only after submitting to baptism. This initial submission, Heine suggests, may lead Gans on to become a *Fido savant*—just another academic retriever ready to obey his Prussian master's voice. And it is precisely this, Heine tells us, which has roused the deepest apprehensions of other academic retrievers in ordinary: what they are afraid of now is not that their new colleague would introduce alien and subversive notions into university life, but that he would become too good at what they themselves were doing and would thus threaten their cherished monopoly. The sound-link between 'Fido savant' and 'Savigny' is surely not fortuitous; it seems well calculated to make subliminal connections.

In one respect Heine's caricature is well on target. Gans did exhibit some *Fido savant* tendencies after obtaining his long-desired professorship. His opposition to Savigny lessened (though Savigny would never have anything to do with him) and he declared himself against allowing Jews unlimited freedom to take law degrees at German universities.²⁷ Nevertheless Gans remained, for his own part, an adherent of the Hegelian Left, a thorn in the conservatives' side, and an opponent of political reaction. He was never an advocate of Friedrich Schlegel, Karl Ludwig Haller, or Edmund Burke. When he died, however, at the early age of forty-two, the successor chosen to replace him was none other than Friedrich Julius Stahl—a convert from Judaism who had become one of the principal theoreticians and apologists of Prussian conservatism. Stahl was precisely the sort of person whom Heine (borrowing the voice of irritated competitors) had caricatured as *Fido savant*; precisely the sort of person, too, who would support his political and social views by appealing to the authority of Haller and Burke. Yet by a final irony we can find Heine himself, when he sketched out a preface for a new edition of *Pictures of Travel* IV in 1834, quoting Stahl with approval:

O what fools they are who allow their vanity to impel them to become leaders in revolutionary times! 'Do you know what the leader of a party is?' Friedrich von Stahl has asked; 'He is a man who stands at the very edge of an abyss while his followers constantly push him forwards from behind.'[28]

Always torn between his suspicion of revolutionaries and his desire for social amelioration, the poet had more sympathies with Stahl's views than were ever shown by Eduard Gans. It is equally characteristic of his attitudes in the 1830s that he penned the passage just quoted and that he forbore to make it public.

(iv)

In 1831 Heine moved to Paris; he was never again to set eyes on Gans, but he did not dismiss him from his mind or his work. He learnt that Gans had been giving very successful lectures on modern history, whose positive evaluation of the French Revolution of the previous century had filled the Prussian authorities with suspicion and alarm. This information the poet used in his reworking of the Tannhäuser legend, in which Tannhäuser is made to traverse Germany on his way from Rome back to his Parisian Venusberg.

> Zu Potsdam vernahm ich ein lautes Geschrei—
> ‚Was gibt es?' rief ich verwundert.
> ‚Das ist der Gans in Berlin, der liest
> Dort über das letzte Jahrhundert.'
>
> [At Potsdam I heard loud yelling—
> 'What is it?' I asked, with astonishment.
> 'It's Gans in Berlin—he is lecturing there
> on the history of the last hundred years.'][29]

This stanza unites, in Heine's best manner, the physical and the spiritual, the literal and the metaphoric. Gans's loud voice was notorious among his acquaintances; but he had now acquired a voice that carried—*eine weithin hallende Stimme*, as Heine once proudly said of himself—in another sense. The reverberations of his lectures were heard in the traditional stronghold of Prussianism, Frederick the Great's Potsdam, and the *großes Geschrei* Tannhäuser purports to have heard, may well be the cries of consternation among Prussian conservatives swelling the noise made by Gans's pronouncements. Gans himself, it should be remembered, took this passage in good part as a caricature of his own loud voice: 'Dear Heine,' he wrote on 7 June 1838, 'we have not heard from one another since you recognized me by those loud yells at Potsdam . . . Let me hear from you again, dear friend; and if vocal chords are capable of perfection, I might soon be audible as far as Paris.'[30]

For some five years after his early death, Eduard Gans appears only peripherally and anonymously in Heine's works. One of the comic bear's tirades in *Atta Troll*, for instance, first published in 1843, seems to contain an allusion to Gans's last published treatise—a refutation of Savigny's views on property rights (*Das Recht des Besitzes*, 1803) entitled *Über die Grundlage des Besitzes. Eine Duplik* (1839)—along with an allusion to the slogan 'La propriété est le vol' from Proudhon's *Qu'est-ce que la propriété?* of 1840.

> "Ja, das Erbe der Gesamtheit
> Wird dem Einzelnen zur Beute,
> Und von Rechten des Besitzes
> Spricht er dann, von Eigentum!
>
> "Eigentum! Recht des Besitzes!
> O des Diebstahls! O der Lüge! . . ."
>
> ["The community's heritage
> becomes the prey of an individual
> who then speaks of the right of possession,
> of property.
>
> Property! Right of possession!
> Shame on such theft and on such lies!"][31]

In 1844, however, Gans surfaces with a vengeance, when the poet took the death of Ludwig Marcus, who like Gans and like Heine himself had been a prominent member of the Society for the Culture and Science of the Jews, as his opportunity to look back on his friends and associates in the hopeful years he had spent in Berlin.

The first thing we hear of Gans in *Ludwig Marcus* (later revised and entitled *Ludwig Marcus. Words in his Memory*) is loud laughter. The naïve savant Marcus, a man of tiny physical stature, had written a work on the history of Abyssinia which touched on the subject of female circumcision. Heine tells us:

How heartily the late Eduard Gans laughed when he showed me the sentence in Marcus's essay in which the author expressed the wish that someone better up to it than he was himself might devote his labours to this subject [*es möchte jemand diesen Gegenstand bearbeiten, der demselben besser gewachsen sei*].[32]

An appreciation of linguistic *doubles ententes*, especially those which involved sexual allusions, was something Gans clearly shared with Heine. The possible double meanings Gans is made to point out in Marcus's innocent sentence centre on the words *bearbeiten* and *besser gewachsen*; the humorous implications perceived in this last word, derived from *wachsen* ('to grow'), refer not only to a presumed sexual inadequacy, but also to little Marcus's stunted growth. It is a joke which Heine will turn against Gans later in this same obituary.

The turn comes very soon, in fact. Having made Gans ostentatiously demonstrate his undoubted superiority in intelligence, knowledge of the world, and physical stature over poor little Marcus, Heine proceeds to characterize the Society for the Culture and Science of the Jews to which all three of them belonged, and comments:

The obituary of the late Ludwig Marcus has insensibly led me to an obituary of the Society of which he was a most honourable member and as whose president Eduard Gans, whom I have already mentioned and who has also departed this world, made his influence felt. This highly gifted man is the last person one could praise for his modest self-sacrifice and anonymous martyrdom. Though his soul opened itself readily to all questions concerning the welfare and the salvation of mankind, enthusiasm never intoxicated him to the point of leaving his own immediate interest out of account. A witty lady with whom Gans often took his tea in the evenings rightly observed that even in the most heated discussion and despite his great absent-mindedness Gans always managed, when he reached for the plate that held the sandwiches, to get hold of those which had fresh salmon on them rather than those with ordinary cheese.'[33]

With the help of Rahel Varnhagen—for she, surely, is the 'witty lady' referred to in the last sentence I have just quoted—Heine here brings together once again the physical and the moral, the apparently random detail and the essence of a character. He evokes the complexity of Gans—his combination of self-seeking and altruism, professorial absent-mindedness and expert gourmandise, great gifts and petty habits, idealism and an eye for the main chance—with a completeness that surpasses all his previous portrayals.

The dualism of presentation now analysed continues in the passage that follows.

How much German scholarship owes to the late Eduard Gans is widely known. He was one of the most active apostles of the Hegelian philosophy, and he vulgarized Hegel's writings in an elegant way—in so far as he understood them himself.[34]

Heine believed, as we know from his *Towards a History of Religion and Philosophy in Germany*, that he had understood better than Hegel's more orthodox pupils certain elements of the movement in German philosophy which culminated in the Hegelian system—but that except for Hegel and God, no one had ever fully understood the Hegelian system and its implications. As for 'vulgarizing'—he himself had often been accused of that; but it was a charge he saw as a compliment rather than an insult. He took pride, in fact, in what he thought to be his ability to disengage the kernel of a doctrine from its shell or husk and to make his insights generally accessible in a style as unlike as possible to the ponderous periods of German academics. If Gans could 'vulgarize' in this positive way, he must have transcended that clumsiness of style, lightened that impenetrability of utterance, which Heine had once laid to his charge. The epithet 'elegant', with which Heine here dignifies Gans's 'vulgarizations', would have seemed to him wholly inappropriate as a description of Gans's early writings. The later Gans, it would seem, had come nearer to Heine's own mode of excellence; and it is significant that he now praises his dead comrade in arms for making Hegel's thought fruitful in German jurisprudence in a way that Heine believed unequivocally beneficial.

In jurisprudence he fought and annihilated those lackeys of Roman law who, having no inkling of the spirit that animated the law-givers of the ancient world, busied themselves with brushing the dust out of the garments they had left behind, freeing them from moths, or even patching them up for use in modern times. Gans scourged such servility even when it wore the most elegant livery . . .[35]

In 1854, when *Ludwig Marcus* was reissued, Heine added a sentence which made his meaning crystal clear:

How the poor soul of Herr von Savigny whimpers as it feels Gans's kicks!

So Gans did not, after all, become a mere *Fido savant*. On the contrary: even in his professorial capacity he remained a fighter against obscurantism and blind worship of the past. That showed itself in his lectures even more than in his writings.

More even by his words than by his writings Gans furthered the development of the German idea of liberty and the desire for it [*des deutschen Freiheitssinnes*]. He unshackled the most carefully fettered thoughts and tore the mask from the face of liars. He was a nimble, fiery spirit; the sparks of his wit kindled splendid fires or—at the very least—spread glorious illumination all around.

Wit; furthering the conception of liberty and the desire for it; unmasking hypocrisy; saying what the authorities did not want to be said—the virtues Heine here detects in Gans's lectures are precisely those which he himself strove to realize in the poetry of the 1840s. As so often, the lineaments of a self-portrait shine through the portrait Heine is painting of his contemporary and early associate.

   This is true also of the negative accentuation that marks the next stage of his description of Gans. Taking his cue from a 'gloomy saying' in Goethe's *Faust, Part II*, Heine contemplates the relationship between genius and virtue, *Genialität* and

Tugend, in a way which must irresistibly remind readers of Börne's charges against Heine himself—charges which we shall see the poet attempt to counter and refute in *Ludwig Börne. A Memorial* and in *Atta Troll*. Genius and virtue, he now declares, with regard to Eduard Gans,

live in perpetual enmity and sometimes turn their backs on each other. I grieve to report that in respect of the Society for the Culture and Science of Judaism [*sic*] . . . Gans did not behave virtuously at all; that he was, in fact, guilty of the most unforgivable felony. His defection was all the more revolting because he had played the agitator and had taken on specific duties as president of the Society. Traditionally it is the duty of the captain to be the last to leave his floundering ship—but Gans saved himself first. When it comes to moral stature, surely, little Marcus towered above the great Gans, and he in turn might have regretted that Gans was not more 'up to' his task.

And so we have come full circle. Once again the great President of the Society for the Culture and Science of the Jews confronts its tiniest member, but the proportions are inverted in this moral context: Marcus is the great and Gans is the little one. Heine himself, whose baptism had after all *preceded* that of Gans, is invisibly present at this moral measuring: 'I had not taken on any presidential duties, I had not helped to found the Society, I was not the captain', we seem to hear him say; nevertheless it is only too plain that, on the moral scale here set up, the poet himself stands much nearer to the negative pole of Gans than to the positive one of Ludwig Marcus.

   This brings us to the ultimate paradox and the real point of the comparison. Marcus is morally far superior to Gans—but Gans has been more useful to the world. Where Marcus's researches have not led to anything Heine thinks permanently valuable, Gans has advanced the cause of truth, and the emancipation not just of Jews but of Gentile Germans too, through his championship of the 'philosophical' against the 'historical' school of law, his exposition and development of Hegel's doctrines in a liberal sense, his research into the historical basis and social significance of the laws of inheritance, his unstuffy views on the history of Germany, and his fight for more adequate conceptions of freedom and progress.

(v)

It has of late become clear that Heine's work is all of a piece, that the procedures of his poetry are not abandoned in his prose *Pictures of Travel*, his attempts at narrative fiction, and his journalistic reports. The mosaic portrait our investigations have so far constructed confirms this; its materials have been gathered from all these sources, and have fitted together perfectly. There is also, as one might expect, a good deal of continuity between Heine's published work on the one hand and his letters and recorded conversations on the other, a continuity which will enable us to gather further significant fragments for our mosaic. In these letters and conversations Heine speaks to a more limited public, of course, than in his writings for publication; but except in a few letters to his immediate family Heine is as careful in his formulations, as conscious of the need to project a persona, as he is when addressing the public at large.

On 1 September 1833 we find Heine writing to a Potsdam lawyer, E. C. A. Keller, in order to persuade him to support a new legal journal which Gans and Heine were attempting to establish. Since this project had to be made as attractive as possible to Keller, Heine emphasizes the qualities which fitted Gans for the post of editor.

A few weeks before leaving Berlin I made the acquaintance of Dr Gans, and found in him an honourable and energetic young man, who deserves my respect in every way and who is, I am sure, worth more than any of the gentlemen who display their Christian charity by maligning him because of his Mosaic affiliation [*die ihn, den Mosaisten, gehörig anfeinden*]. I value his stalwart, virtuous disposition; his learning is not in the common mould, if my judgement of human knowledge can be trusted; for Dr Gans has complete command of his materials, penetrates science and scholarship with the sharp eye of a man who thinks for himself, and constantly promotes new and striking views of the things he discusses.

In emphasizing the qualities that make Gans an ideal journalist as well as a scholar to be taken seriously—his sharp and quick penetration, his promotion of new and striking ideas based on sound knowledge of the facts—Heine is at pains to counteract unfavourable aspects of the Jewish stereotype which might prejudice the non-Jew Keller against Gans. Hence the stress on his 'stalwart, virtuous disposition', on that *Tüchtigkeit in der Gesinnung* which German Gentiles so often assumed to be present in themselves but absent in their Jewish fellow citizens. The very terms *Jude* and *jüdisch* had come to denote unadmirable qualities in popular usage. Heine's letter therefore follows, for once, the practice of many of his contemporaries in avoiding these terms; his choice of *Mosaist* (rather than *Israelit*) was perhaps influenced by the thought that a Christian lawyer might be presumed to have some respect for Moses the Lawgiver. At the same time his dig at what Christian charity had come to mean in practice reminds the Gentile world, in the person of the recipient of the letter, that it might do better to look to its own faults instead of projecting them all on to the Jews.

When he writes to his Jewish friends in Berlin, Heine does not, of course, have to adopt these particular strategies. There he engages in good-humoured banter about Gans's scholarly habit of quoting authorities and sources for his slightest remarks, praises his work on the laws of inheritance from which Heine himself has derived many important insights, and describes a dream in which Gans knocks at the window while his fellow Hegelians are trying to reduce the poet himself to a Hegelian *Idee*.

> But I leapt about the room in my rage and called out: 'I am not an Idea, I know nothing of an Idea, all my life long I have never had an Idea'—it was a horrible dream, I remember how Gans yelled even louder than I; little Marcus sat on his shoulder and shouted the relevant quotations with an uncanny hoarse voice, smiling the while with such ghastly friendliness that I awoke with terror.
>
> (to Moses Moser, 23 May 1823)

This dream-vision caricatures Gans and Marcus in ways we have already observed in Heine's published work—but the element of the grotesque is strengthened when the little man is put on the bigger man's shoulder like an organ-grinder's monkey and made to supply, in a shout toned down by hoarseness, the quotations Gans could never do without. The passage also suggests, for the first time in Heine's writings, that he felt an element of the demonic in Hegel's generalizations and abstractions. This may help to explain why towards the end of his life, when he tried the experiment of 'returning' to the God he had once declared dead, he made Hegel rather than the Saint-Simonians responsible for the hubris of his earlier years.[36]

Another aspect which Heine omitted from his public portrayals of Gans is the interest both Gans and Heine took, during their brief collaboration, in Jewish emigration from Germany to a homeland of their own. This interest was kindled by a project for settling Jews on Grand Island in the State of New York put forward by M. M. Noah in the early 1820s. The idea was soon abandoned; but in Heine's mind the Grand Island project became so firmly identified with Gans that he could imagine no name but 'Ganstown' for the capital of the hoped-for settlement.

When, one day, Ganstown will be built and a happier generation than ours blesses its palm branches and chews its unleavened bread [*Lulef benscht und Matzes kaut*] by the Mississippi—the mercantile and Stock Exchange expressions we use today will become part of poetic language . . .

(to Moser, 23 May 1823)

With self-torturing humour Heine here adopts the Gentile stereotype of what a Jewish poet would be like—he had earlier used a metaphor taken from financial transactions and asked his Jewish correspondent Moser: 'Does this image not make you appreciate that I am a Jewish poet?' (Ibid.) In another letter to Moser he describes his vision of a Jewish exodus from Berlin not to the new American colony, but to Jerusalem: 'It was a great Jewish army, and Gans ran from one man to the next in order to bring some order into it.' (20 July 1824.) What is highlighted here, besides the discontent with life in Germany which could lead to a Jerusalem nostalgia of which Gans himself showed no sign, is Gans's energy and organizing talent.

Other letters of the 1820s dwell mainly on Gans's faults: his indiscreet love of gossip:

If I had anything to say to him, I might just as well publish it in the *Berlin Advertiser* . . .

(to Joseph Lehmann, 26 June 1823);

his excessive love of quotations; his desire to hear himself talked about:

How is Gans? Does he still consult his servant-girl Molly[37] when he considers, each morning, whom he should quote in the course of the day—and does he still take stock of his fame each evening?

(to Moser, 25 October 1824);

and the rebarbative style of his earlier writings. After reading an issue of the journal put out by the Society for the Culture and Science of the Jews, Heine writes to Leopold Zunz:

I have studied all kinds of German: Saxon, Swabian, Franconian—but our Journal-German I find the most difficult of all. If I did not happen to know what Ludwig Marcus and Dr Gans want to say, I would not understand a word of what they have written.

There are other complaints of this kind; but one day after the letter just quoted Heine writes to tell Moser of his joy at hearing that the King of Prussia had granted Gans a stipend which would enable the latter to devote himself to his studies for two years. The joy was not unconfined, however, for the stipend was only a consolation prize for the professorship Gans had been denied because he was a Jew. We have already seen that in later days Heine would distinguish sharply between Gans's style and Marcus's, and would acknowledge that the former was far more effective—beneficially effective—than the latter.

The next glimpse we have of Gans in Heine's letters is, however, the most disenchanted yet. It occurs in the course of an epistle in which Heine laments that the Jews of Hamburg, most of whom he dislikes, should think Gans a mere clown:

Gans is considered a fool in Hamburg, and I am not surprised . . . I deeply regret that Gans's silly behaviour, his gossiping with friend and enemy, could have put me off my stroke for even a minute. It serves him right if the Jews abuse him and make him responsible for every ill; why does he talk so much about what he is going to do, why must he always make promises and arouse expectations? I also intend to do things, perhaps I am doing something significant merely by being the man I am; but in future I shall take what steps I can to protect myself from the kind of publicity Gans doles out—one that is wholly incompatible with my activities.

(to Moser, 23 August 1823)

Gans here acts as a warning example while also constituting a danger to Heine's own reputation in Germany. Nevertheless, the poet adds, his strictures on Gans do not arise from motives of personal spite or pique; they are due, rather, to 'love for our good cause', the cause of those emancipatory struggles to which the subject of these strictures was as devoted as the writer and recipient of the letter in which they were made. His love, therefore, extended also to Gans, to whom he won't write directly 'for fear he could tell too many of his dearest friends, in strict confidence of course, what I candidly tell him'.

In the future you will always see how dear he is to my heart, how highly I esteem his generous nature, and how much I count on him.

And why does he still harbour such affection for Gans? 'Not', Heine says to Moser on 30 September 1823, 'because of the fat books he writes, not even because of the nobility of his actions—but only because of the funny way in which he used to pull me about when he was telling me something, and because of the good-natured childlike expression that came over his face when he encountered hostility or when something bad happened to him.' I hope most of my readers will agree that Heine has here made a significant contribution to our understanding of the way in which sympathy may arise between human beings, and has made Gans's gestures and expressions vividly present to posterity.

On 20 July 1824 a huffy note may be heard again: Gans, it appears, had shown his displeasure with Heine by failing to transmit greetings to him when such greetings might have been expected. Might Gans not be poisoning the poet's relations with other friends? Has Gans's prattle, perhaps—Heine asks Moser, who was famous for a cloak that made him resemble Schiller's Marquis Posa—'managed to make a hole in your beautiful Posa cloak?' The image of malicious gossip rending the cloak of magnanimous friendship is at once allegoric and surrealistic—an earnest of what Heine could do in conversation too when he improvised symbolic anecdotes about Gans's odd behaviour.

When, one evening, he and Gans came from the *Tiergarten* [a large park in Berlin] to Mendelssohn-Bartholdy's house, he told the company there, among other things: 'We bought some pinks on the way; I plucked mine to pieces and threw them into the water, and Gans'—he continued in a weary, melancholy tone—'has *eaten* his!' This recitation, perfect and rounded in itself like a little poem, so expressive of Gans's bad habits, worked like magic: everybody at that gathering was beside himself with delight.[38]

Gans was not slow to rib Heine in return— no wonder that the two of them avoided meeting each other in public whenever they could! 'Is it not annoying', Heine asks Moser on 25 June 1824, in a letter in which respect far outweighs contempt,

that one of the greatest thinkers of our time gives so little thought to himself and what he looks like to others? It is wrong of me to pull his leg, I know, although I never hurt him, and although he unconsciously provokes such leg-pulling; it would be better if I had told him the strict truth every time he made a public exhibition of his weaknesses and caused them to be talked about by all the world. His friends should always do this. Just the other day I was told some typical anecdotes about Gans which are fit only for the ears of those who appreciate his intelligence, and those who know how lovable he is in reality. But all the world sees of this comet is his trailing tail.

The image of the comet, which Heine uses in that passage, has been plausibly linked with Jean Paul; but it also has its place in a series of 'light' metaphors which Heine used in respect of Gans and of himself: 'I am a pale will o' the wisp; but Gans is a light, a light of exile.' (To Moser, 28 November 1823.) 'Light of Exile', or 'Light of the Diaspora'—*Meor ha-Golah*—was, we must remember, a traditional Jewish title; it had been most notably applied to Rabbi Gershom ben Yehuda of Mainz, who lived from *c.*965 to 1028.

When he applies Rabbi Gershom's title to his eminent contemporary, Heine places the latter's career in an unmistakably Jewish context—the context of Jewish history in the Diaspora; and when he next takes up the 'comet' image again, as he does in an important letter to Moser dated 8 October

1825, he places it in the context of Gans's baptism, which had been preceded (we must again remember) by the poet's own. Now that Eduard Gans has officially divested himself of the Jewish equivalent of his first name, 'Eli', Heine plays on it in a passage dominated by the Hebrew-Yiddish terms *Goim*—often transliterated '*Goyim*'—and *Reshoim*. The first of these means 'non-Jews' and the second 'evil-doers' (or simply 'anti-Semites').

I await Gans's return with great suspense. I believe he will return with new Eli-gance. I also believe that although according to the way Zunz classified the Society's library the first part of his *Law of Inheritance* qualifies fully as a source of Jewish history, that part of the work which will appear after his return from Paris will no more be a source for Jewish history than the writings of Savigny and other *Goyim und Reschoim* [sic]. In short—Gans will return from Paris as a Christian, in the most watery sense of that term. Sugar-Cohn, I fear, will become his Carl Sand.

The Hamburg sugar broker, Gustav Gerson Cohn, who favoured the reform of Jewish modes of worship but detested apostasy from Judaism, is here likened to Carl Sand, whose disapproval of August von Kotzebue's political activities led him to assassinate the object of his detestation. Works which Gans—and, as the poet often reminded Jewish correspondents, Heine himself too—would write after the apostasy that drew the wrath of more faithful Jews on his head, could no longer count as unsullied 'sources' of Jewish history. How deeply Gans's baptism stirred up remorse about his own appears clearly in one of the bitterest letters Heine ever wrote. It is addressed, once again, to his friend and confidant Moses Moser.

I don't know what to say; Cohn tells me Gans is preaching Christianity and seeking to convert the children of Israel. If he does this out of conviction, he is a fool; if he does it out of hypocrisy, he is a blackguard. I won't ever stop loving Gans, but I must confess that I would have been happier if instead of the above news I had been told that Gans had stolen silver spoons.

I just cannot believe, dear Moser, that you should be of the same opinion as Gans, although Cohn assures me that this is so and that he has it from your own mouth. I would be particularly sorry if you should see my own baptism in a favourable light. I assure you that if the laws had allowed the stealing of silver spoons, I would not have had myself baptized. I'll tell you more when I see you.

(19 December 1825)

Nowhere else does Heine make it so clear that the betrayal of the fighting, oppositional spirit, which was all he could see in Gans's acceptance of the religion of the Cross, was but the mirror image of his own apostasy. 'We spoke of Gans,' he adds a little later in this same letter; 'Can one speak of anything else in this world nowadays? Everyone sees him, everyone hears him. Hallelujah.' The appointment to an associate professorship of law in the University of Berlin, with which Prussia rewarded Gans's conversion, increased his fame and ensured (as Heine says in another letter) that posterity would have a chance to understand Gans's style better than Heine himself felt able to do in the third decade of the nineteenth century (to Moser, 24 February 1826).

In this same year of 1826 Heine dates a letter to Moser 'Hamburg, the 23rd of the month Gans', immediately adding the following ironic disclaimer:

But, you changeable, inconsistent month of April, pardon me the wrong I did you when I juxtaposed you with Dr Gans. That you have not deserved! (I am speaking of the month.) It is a manly, consistent month, a decent, orderly month . . .

In calling April an *ordentlicher Monat* Heine is not only suggesting that baptism had brought disorder into Gans's life, but he is also punning on the *Extraordinariat* or *außerordentliche Professur*, the associate professorship, which he received in payment. The next paragraph of the letter to Moser which I have here begun to cite again refers to this *Extraordinariat*:

Give my regards to our 'extraordinary' friend and tell him that I love him. I say this in all seriousness—it comes from my soul. His image is still dear to me, though it is not the image of a saint, an image one can worship and expect to perform miracles.

Now comes an especially revealing sentence:

I often think of him, because I do not want to think of myself;

after which Heine continues:

This night I thought: what kind of a face would Gans make if he came

to stand before *Moshe Rabbenu*, supposing the latter appeared again
on earth? And Moses, surely, is the greatest jurist that ever lived—the
laws he gave have endured until our present day.

It is not only Professor Gans, then, but also Dr Heine, who has
to confront the greatest practitioner of the subject in which
both won their academic laurels: the prophet who proclaimed
the Jewish God from Mount Sinai and first welded the
Israelites into a people. The use of the Hebrew phrase for 'Our
Teacher Moses', which Heine actually writes out in Hebrew
letters, underscores the poet's sense that he, and Gans too,
cannot simply wash away his past allegiances, his early history,
in the water of the baptismal font. And as so often, the
emotional turmoil into which thoughts of Gans now threw
Heine gives birth to a dream-picture in which Gans appears in
familiar surroundings but uncharacteristic silence. The scene is
Strahlau, a place near Berlin famous for its fishing and scenic
beauty, a favourite spot for excursions, at which some
anti-Jewish riots had recently occurred.

I . . . dreamt that Gans and Mordecai Noah came together in Strahlau
and Gans was—*mirabile dictu*—silent as a fish. Zunz stood by,
smiling sarcastically, and said to his wife: 'Now do you see, little
mouse?'

Noah had appointed Gans his representative in Germany, not
knowing that the man he wished to help him establish a Jewish
settlement in America had abjured Judaism. Zunz and his wife
(the *Mäuschen* endearment at the end is characteristic of their
affectionate relationship) are introduced as a kind of chorus.
They had remained Jews, though even Zunz had at one time
considered baptism; and Zunz can now smile sarcastically at
the absurd human spectacle the confrontation of Gans and
Noah offers. Later Heine introduces another as yet unbaptized
member of the (now defunct) Society for the Culture and
Science of the Jews into his dream-vision—the writer and
editor Joseph Lehmann, who is made to mouth slogans of the
Enlightenment and of Hegelian philosophy, which provide the
background against which Gans's, and Heine's, abandonment
of Judaism must be seen. That Gans remains uncharacteristi-
cally silent may be regarded, not just as caricature *e contrario*,
but also as a sign of guilt or of doubt.

The imagined confrontation of Gans with Moses, with Mordecai Noah, and with Leopold Zunz is capped, in Heine's letter to Moser of 14 October 1826, by a confrontation with the spirit of Judaism itself. Moser had compared the Jewish people to Christ crucified, and Heine borrows this image as he punningly connects Gans's Hebrew name 'Eli' with the words from the Cross attributed to Christ in Matthew 27: 46.

Give my regards to Gans too. I do hope that Gans, who is still a freshman in Christianity, is not already beginning to talk in pious Christian accents. No, Clumsy Cohen has surely lied to me about that. But if ever Gans should do so, then the Judaism you have presented as the crucified Saviour of the World would call out to him, full of grief: 'Dr Eli! Dr Eli! lama sabachthani!'

Heine adds to this his usual protestation that he still loves Gans and that he will always remain his friend.

The only letter to Gans himself which editors of Heine have ever been able to unearth belongs to this period. It was written in May 1826 and accompanied the first volume of Heine's *Pictures of Travel*. The poet begins by distancing himself from any theological views Gans's baptism might have entailed.

Dear Gans! Valued Colleague!
The word 'colleague' refers to jurisprudence and not to theology. The word dear, however, refers to my heart, which still loves you dearly, loves you heartily—*quand même*—perhaps I would not write to you at all if there were no *quand même*. You don't understand me; what I want to suggest is that it offends me to the depths of my soul to think that our books are no longer *sources*; that because of this I am angry with you and angry with myself; and that because of this anger, I feel I must say to you that I love you just the same, that I love you *quand même*.

Heine then proceeds to belittle the book he is sending to Gans, and draws attention to the dedication of one of its sections to Rahel Varnhagen.

This name, which is dear to me, I have nailed to the doorpost of my book, and this had made it more homely [*wöhnlich*] and more safe for me. Books too must have their *mezuzzah*. Farewell, and love me still, me

Your friend
H. Heine

H. G. Reissner, to whom we owe the fullest account so far of Gans's life and work, has perceptively remarked on the 'height of irony' reached by the passage just quoted.[39] Here we find the Christian convert Heine explaining to the Christian convert Gans, by means of an image taken from Jewish ceremonial, why he dedicated the poems of *The Homecoming* (*Die Heimkehr*) to the Christian convert Rahel Varnhagen! Notwithstanding his baptism, Gans could still be expected to respond to the symbolism of the *mezuzzah*, the ritual capsule containing a Hebrew prayer which is affixed to the right-hand doorpost of a house inhabited by Jews. Such a capsule, Heine confesses, makes a house more *wöhnlich* for him—an unusual term which forms part of Heine's poetic vocabulary and denotes the sensation of being safely at home, of feeling at ease in one's surroundings. The water of baptism, the poet here reminds Gans, cannot wash away one's Jewish feelings and one's Jewish history.

The *quand même* which Heine sounds in this revealing letter to Gans was often heard in this period. Originally one of the battle cries of the Restoration—being for king and royalty *quand même*, despite everything that had happened—it was frequently converted to other uses by men who could not be said to belong to the conservative camp. The note struck by this *quand même* continues to resound through Heine's letters when he speaks of Gans. We find him constantly re-iterating that he is annoyed by something or other that Gans has done but that at the bottom of his heart he loves him very much (for example, to Joseph Lehmann, 26 May 1826). In the autumn of 1826 he seems to have reread some of Gans's writings and felt confirmed in his liking; he now calls him the *Oberhegelianer*, Chief of the Hegelians, and on 9 June 1827 he sends him greetings, via Moser, in unusually warm terms. A few months later another letter to Moser speaks of Heine's plans for a journal he will edit in Munich, entitled *New Political Annals* (*Neue politische Annalen*). He asks him not to say anything about this to Gans, because 'apos-tates are unsuitable'—presumably unsuitable to further the cause of Jewish emancipation which Heine intends to champion. He then strikes out the remark about the unsuit-ability of apostates, reflecting, perhaps, that it did not come well from himself; but he never did ask Gans to contribute to his journal.

An especially revealing passage is to be found in a letter to Moser, date 9 June 1827, in which the poet describes the popularity he now believes himself to have attained in Germany.

I now have a voice that sounds far into the land [*eine weitschallende Stimme*]. In years to come you will often hear it thunder against the policing of men's thoughts and the suppression of their fundamental rights. I shall obtain a quite extraordinary professorship in the university of the intellectual and spiritual élite [*in der Universitas hoher Geister*].

The metaphors Heine here uses to portray his own literary achievements and aspirations are clearly derived from his portrait of Eduard Gans. Moser could not possibly have missed the significance of his references to a voice that carries far into the distance, and to that *Extraordinat* at a prestigious university which Gans had finally attained but which was forever to elude Heine himself—at least in the literal sense.

Soon there came a time in which he felt dire need of the support which the now 'established' Gans might give him by wielding his pen. In *The Baths of Lucca* Heine had savagely attacked a fellow poet who had reviled him for being a Jew; and he felt that by doing this, by making August von Platen an example, he had performed a valuable service for other men and women of Jewish origin. Few of the latter agreed with him; the upwardly mobile members of his own family were shocked and incensed; but from Gans Heine hoped for understanding and support. A last brush-stroke is now added to his developing portrait.

[Ludwig] Robert, Gans, Michael Beer, and others have all shown Christian patience when they were attacked as I was. They chose to keep wisely silent—I am different, and that is a good thing. It is good if the wicked find the right man for once, the man who will ruthlessly and unsparingly take revenge for himself and others.

(to Varnhagen von Ense, 4 January 1830)

Since the revenge he had taken was on Gans's behalf as well as his own, he thought Gans morally obliged to champion his cause.

It is Gans's most sacred duty to do battle on my behalf; please ask him to do so, in my name. He must now fulfil his promise to have my book immediately reviewed in the *Yearbooks for Scientific Criticism*; if not, I'll cut off his ears and thus inflict what is for him the ultimate punishment: he won't be able to hear himself talk any more. But whatever he elects to do, he must do soon.

(Ibid.)

Nothing happened, of course: neither now nor when Heine appealed for help against attacks in French journals would Gans allow himself to be drawn into the polemics stirred up by the poet's attacks on Count Platen in *The Baths of Lucca*. He still tried to keep up friendly relations with him however; in 1838 he sent him a note, brought to Heine by that very Gasparo Spontini whose name the poet had linked with Gans's in *The Hartz Journey*, expressing the hope that they would meet again. They never did; but Gans's name crops up occasionally in Heine's conversations in Paris; and whenever he enumerates interesting acquaintances whom he intends to portray in his memoirs, Gans figures in the list.

(vi)

Lichtenberg says very justly that we may not only love ourselves but also hate ourselves in other people. And so I quarrelled recently with our friend Gans. If you see him, tell him what I said and give him my most friendly greetings. I love him very much and I thought of him when I wrote the opening of the Göttingen chapter of my *Hartz Journey*.

(to Varnhagen von Ense, 14 May 1826)

Here Heine, with the help of Lichtenberg, says it himself: his portrait of Gans is really a double portrait; the love-hate it exhibits is directed towards the portrayer as well as the portrayed. Heine too, like Gans, had believed for a time that Judaism could be lightly abandoned; but what he has to say about Gans's baptism and his conduct afterwards shows clearly that he soon learnt to think differently. A characteristic letter to Moser shows the poet looking back nostalgically to the heyday of the Society for the Culture and Science of the Jews.

That was a much warmer time. If I am not mistaken, Gans was not yet baptized then and wrote long speeches for the Society, and sported the device: *Victrix causa diis placuit, sed victa Catoni*—the conquering cause was pleasing to the gods, but the conquered one to Cato . . .

Heine tells Moser to speak freely about the baseness of Jews who have themselves baptized to gain some material advantage. He need not spare either Gans or Heine himself:

As Solon said that no one should be called happy before his death, one could also say that no one should be called an honest man before his death.

(23 April 1826)

The quotation at the head of this paragraph also shows how deeply hidden Heine's references to contemporaries may be—for without his hint, who would have suspected the presence of Gans in the opening section of *The Hartz Journey*? It may parody, once again, Gans's fondness for quotations, or embody reminiscences of Gans's own student days recalled when Heine met him in Göttingen in July 1825. Or might Heine be referring to the *Falcidia* dream? There are bound to be hidden references which later readers can no longer catch.

Nor is this the only way in which the portrait of Gans that I have tried to reconstitute from Heine's writings will seem incomplete. We miss descriptions of his appearance, of the kind we find in the reminiscences of Friederike von Hohenhausen, for instance:

Eduard Gans, whose strikingly handsome head with its fresh colouring, its proudly arched eyebrows over dark eyes, recalled a spiritual Antinous;[40]

or Laube's more sober portrait of Professor Gans at a somewhat later time:

This man of medium height, fleshy, ruddy and healthy-looking with protuberant blue eyes and curly black hair receding from his high forehead . . .
This man who went about his business, most of the time, in a formal

dark coat, who bowed calmly and confidently, who came over to you slowly and with self-assurance . . .

or Laube again, recalling Gans just before his premature death:

He was portly and overweight, and this caused the blood to rise to his head. His face was very red, his eyes were protuberant. 'Apoplectic', said those who knew about such things . . .[41]

We learn from Heine that he was in the habit of ribbing Gans in company; but he tells us nothing of the 'biting sarcasm', the jokes about the poet's 'vanity and lechery', with which, according to I. H. von Fichte, Gans used to regale Heine in return. None the less we do get, from Heine's writings, a clear if complex picture of the man whom Fanny Hensel once called a cross between a man, a child, and a savage. We see and hear Gans with his shoulder-shrugging, his precociousness, his good-natured expression, his habit of pulling his partner about when he was telling him something, his loud voice, his hearty laughter, his jokes, his effective lecturing technique, his organizing talent strangely yoked with lack of tact and discretion, the sometimes clumsy style of his early writing, his Hegelizing, his effective opposition to the historical school of law, his self-regard and inordinate desire for fame, and his happily never fully-realized potential for metamorphosing from a rebel sympathetic to the aspirations of 'Young Germany' into a *Fido savant*, a poodle of the establishment. A man stands before us, with all his contradictions, in a difficult historical situation: a German and a Jew, at once Light of the Diaspora and swiftly vanishing Comet, a renegade from Judaism who, for all his baptism and his subsequent refusal to engage himself in Jewish causes, nevertheless remained a Jew in the eyes of his friends and foes. And Heine conveys all this now in realistic, now in almost surrealistic scenes; now in exhortations and direct statement, now in humorous or uncanny dream-visions which convey in subtle and nuanced ways the impression Gans had made on a poet whose own fate was bound up with his in so many ways. The letters and conversations complete and round out in important ways the double portrait which emerges from Heine's published works and which is surely of interest, not only to the literary critic, but to all who concern themselves with the troubled social history of countries in which Jews and Gentiles try to live together.

As we saw in the case of *The Hartz Journey*, Gans may be implicitly present even where Heine does not explicitly mention him. When the poet speaks of the obstacles the Prussian State put into the path of its Jewish intellectuals; when he glances at the ideological function of Roman law and, especially, the 'historical school of law' in German life and German thought; when he speaks of the comfort German liberals could derive from penetrating to the essence of Hegel's political and social philosophy; when he anlyses the legal implications of the story told in *The Merchant of Venice*; when he has one of his characters remark that no democratic victory can be of use unless it leads to reforms of *Erbrecht*, laws of inheritance—in all these cases and many more he voices opinions which contacts with Gans, and reflections on Gans's career, had helped to shape. In that way he could present his influential contemporary not only as a reflection of himself and his own problems as a Jew born on German soil, but also as a fellow worker and fellow fighter in the cause of man's emancipation from outworn laws, inhumane conventions or restrictions, and noxious privilege. In the same way Leopold Zunz may be present, by implication, when the poet dwells on the cultural achievements of the Jewish past, or Uncle Salomon Heine when he speaks of Jewish bankers and plutocrats, or Giacomo Meyerbeer when he satirizes the manipulation of fame made possible by a venal press. By their very nature such presences are often intangible—yet we must remain conscious of them if we want to assess the full extent to which Heine's experience of Jews and conception of Judaism affected his work.

Having recognized such presences, we must, however, beware of over-simplification. Certainly Gans (and Moses Moser) helped Heine to interpret Hegel—but Heine attended Hegel's own lectures on the philosophy of world history throughout the summer semester of 1823, and probably sampled those on the philosophy of history and the philosophy of law in 1821–2. He also encountered many other Hegelians on his life's way. It would therefore be absurd to see only Gans's influence when we look at Heine's belief in the

importance of world-historical individuals; his faith in ideas
which must precede and inform actions if these are to further
true progress; his search for the 'spirit' of individual peoples
and his long-held conviction that the 'spirit' of Judaism was
one of abstraction and denial of sensuality; or, indeed, his
fascination with 'dying' or 'exiled' or 'degraded' gods which
has clear connections with Hegel's views on the necessary rise
and decline of religions. Certainly Gans helped Heine to see
the reactionary dangers inherent in the 'historical' school of
law, and Gans's career helped Heine to see the hostility to
Jewish aspirations inherent in Savigny's social attitudes—but
Heine had had a close look at representatives of the 'historical'
school as a law student in Göttingen and had been taught
opposition to them in the University of Bonn before he had
ever heard of Gans. Certainly Gans helped Heine to see the
necessity for tearing down the cultural wall that divided Jew
from Christian, the Jewish world from the non-Jewish world,
without abolishing totally the substance of Judaism (*aufgehen*,
Gans said like a true Hegelian, does not mean *untergehen*)—
but that was a conclusion at which he could well have arrived
without Gans's help, in opposition, perhaps, to the liberal
Professor Georg Sartorius whom he had come to admire in
Göttingen but who opined that once Jews had been educated
to German citizenship they should accept baptism as a
preliminary to losing their Jewish identity altogether. Certain-
ly Gans helped him to appreciate the importance of *Erbrecht*,
the law of inheritance, in the affairs of men—but he could
easily have gathered this from his own law studies or from his
later contacts with the Saint-Simonians, who popularized the
device: 'Plus d'héritage'. In the pages that follow we shall
therefore try to see what Heine himself has to say, and what he
has to show, without penetrating too deeply into that labyrinth
of 'influence' studies in which so many good men and sound
scholars have lost their way.

PART I
German-Jewish Dilemmas

CHAPTER 1
Israel and Edom

(i)

Eduard Gans is not the only Jewish figure that crowds on to
the canvas of Heine's *Letters from Berlin*. In the very first of
these letters the tourists' guide—for as such the author or
narrator presents himself to his original readers and to
us—leads us to the steps of Berlin's cathedral. Characteristical-
ly, he not only *shows*, but emphasizes the *act* of showing.
Should we enter, he asks, to look at the painting by Karl Begas
which King Frederick William III had just donated to the
cathedral of his capital? No, he answers in our name; let us stay
outside, for once inside we would probably be subjected to
snide and sly attacks on the (increasingly popular) rationalist
theory of E. G. Paulus.

Look, rather, to the right of you, at the milling mass of humanity
crowding a square courtyard girded with iron railings. That is the
Stock Exchange. There the adherents of the Old Testament and those
of the New are haggling away. Let us not get too close to them. God,
what faces! Avarice in every muscle. When they open their gobs I
seem to hear them yelling at me: 'Hand over your money!' They will
have scraped quite a bit together by now. The richest among them
must be those whose pasty faces show the deepest imprint of
discontent and ill humour. How much happier is some poor devil
who couldn't tell you whether a louis-d'or is round or square! The
Berliners are right to have little respect for businessmen . . .[1]

This passage is clearly written from the point of view of a man
with scant affection for the life of the merchant and
money–manipulator to which history had condemned so
many Jews, but who is also anxious to show that among the
pasty-faced speculators whose way of living he rejects German
Christians are at least as prominent as Jews. Money-making,
and the highwayman ethics that in our guide's view seem to go
with it, breed unhappiness and ill-temper; and our recognition

of this leads us to share the disrespect Berliners are said to have
for those who choose to spend their time in so alienating a way.
But the commercial spirit which makes its devotees ugly,
avaricious, and discontented knows no religious or ethnic
frontiers. It cannot therefore be used as an argument for
denying Jews the right to become full and equal members of
civil society. The passage just cited illustrates what we shall
soon come to recognize as one of the constant methods of
Heine's verbal portraiture; we might call it the method of
superimposition. To convey a vivid image of the Stock
Exchange speculators who are his subject and, at the same time,
suggest an attitude to them, Heine speaks of them in terms
appropriate to *highwaymen*—just as in visual caricature a
prime minister might be portrayed as a pedlar or a business
tycoon as a shark. He combines this with another of the
caricaturist's favourite devices: the suffusion of the whole face
by one ruling trait, one dominant passion.

'Superimposition' is one of several techniques Heine tried
out on his public in *Letters from Berlin*. Among the others are
presentation through contrast, and an apparently passionless
narration that lends itself to irony. All these were to stand him
in good stead in later, more mature works. And in a passage
which appears to belittle the portraits he introduced into his
Berlin townscapes, he characteristically induces in the reader a
sense of their real importance.

People don't look at the painting which I am lightly sketching out;
what they do look at are the little figures which I have drawn into it
for the sake of animation. They may even come to think these little
figures my main concern! One can produce a painting without
figures, I suppose, just as one can eat one's soup without salt . . .[2]

As so often afterwards, Heine forces his readers into active
collaboration, keeping them alert by means of different
gradations of irony. It will soon become obvious that his
concern, throughout his life, was with human beings rather
than landscapes, with character–drawing rather than the
evocation of a physical environment.

Not long after our encounter with the Jews and Christians of
the Stock Exchange we hear of Jews again—this time outside
the buildings of Berlin University. The guide points to

students emerging from a lecture, bids us watch the fashion of their clothes, and tells us that the student corporations, whose fascination with the mores of an older Germany had been responsible for many eccentricities of dress at German universities, have recently been dissolved. This dissolution has meant, among other things, that there have been fewer duels among the students—but, the guide continues, there was one duel recently that had a most unhappy outcome.

During a symptomatology lecture two medical students, Liebschütz and Febus by name, quarrelled over a trifling matter—they both claimed seat no. 4. What they did not know was that the auditorium contained *two* seats bearing the same number, the number 4 each of them had been assigned by the professor. One called the other a silly ass [*dummer Junge*] and that ended the brief exchange. The next day they fought a duel, and Liebschütz ran his opponent's rapier right through his own body. He died a quarter of an hour later. Since he was a Jew, some of his student friends took him to the Jewish cemetery. Febus, also a Jew, had fled, and— But I see that you are not listening to what I am saying, and are admiring the lime trees instead. Yes, these are the famous *Linden* of Berlin, of which you have heard so much . . .[3]

Medicine was one of the few professions which Jews had been allowed to practise in Prussia without changing their religion; it is not, therefore, surprising that both the students involved should turn out to be Jewish. What Heine here shows us is the extent to which Jewish students had taken on the manners, and observed the codes, of the academic corporations, the *Burschenschaften*, whose German nationalism frequently took on an anti-Jewish as well as an anti-French colouration. Even when the *Burschenschaften* have been dissolved, Jewish students, over-eagerly one might think, stick to their codes: codes which in this case conflict with traditional Jewish abhorrence of such needless endangering of human lives. In recounting this episode Heine may also be concerned, as he was in his personal behaviour throughout his life, to rebut charges of physical cowardice that some of their enemies often brought against Jews. Indeed, duelling and challenges to duels played a not inconsiderable part in his own life, and the fitness of Jews to 'give satisfaction' according to German duelling codes constitutes the central theme of a play to which Heine returned many times in his younger days and from which he was to choose a motto for one of his *Pictures of Travel*: Ludwig Robert's *The Force of Circumstances* (*Die Macht der Verhält-nisse*).

Two further points clamour for notice in this instructive passage of the *Letters from Berlin*. The two young men involved were clearly clumsy duellers—there can have been few instances in which a contestant speared himself on his opponent's rapier in the way described—though there is a special piquancy in remembering that Heine himself, in a duel he fought in the early 1820s, ran his hip on to the tip of his opponent's weapon without such fatal results.[4] The second point to notice is that sad stories about Jews were plainly not of absorbing interest to the (largely non-Jewish) audience to which the poet addressed himself. The guide's charges become distracted, cease listening to his story, and cause him to pass on to another subject.

A third encounter with a Jewish figure in the first of these *Letters from Berlin* has already been described in the Prologue of the present book. The encounter is, of course, with Eduard Gans. In him Heine shows his readers another type of Berlin Jew in the period of assimilation, without, however, drawing attention to his Jewish origins: not the dedicated money-maker of the Stock Exchange or the medical student clumsily imitating the manners and mores of the predominantly Gentile and often anti-Jewish student corporations, but a man about town who may be expected to know what is going on in Berlin's social and intellectual life, even if—in his scholarly distraction—he refuses to stop for gossip. Heine here brings before us, affectionately, not only Gans's characteristic gestures, but also that air of stupendous learning which makes him seem old and venerable before his time. One last important encounter takes place *in effigie* rather than in person:

If you want to delight your eyes, look at the pictures exhibited in [this] glass showcase . . . Here you may see hanging side by side Auguste Stich the actress, the theologian Neander and the violinist Boucher . . . How absent-minded Neander looks again! He must be turning the gnostics over in his mind—Basilides, Valentinus, Bardesanes, Carpocrates, and Marcus . . .[5]

The theologian whose notorious absent-mindedness is here recalled along with the work which had made him famous— *Genetic Development of the Principal Gnostic Systems* (*Genetische Entwicklung der vornehmsten gnostischen Systeme*, Berlin 1818)—was a scion of the Mendel family of Hamburg who had taken on the name Neander ('new man'!) at his baptism. It is noteworthy that the loquacious guide refrains from hinting at this eminent Christian theologian's Jewish origins, and that he has at least looked into his standard work on the gnostics: the names he lists are all mentioned in the opening paragraphs of that book. Whether the framing of Neander between an actress and a fiddler has any significance beyond that of evoking the odd accidental collocations characteristic of big city life is hard to determine. One should remember, however, that some of these collocations serve an unmistakably satirical purpose in *Letters from Berlin*—as when Gans's Judaeophobic antagonist Savigny is made to appear in the company of mountebanks.

The veteran violinist Alexandre-Jean Boucher, whose portrait had appeared alongside that of Neander in the first of these *Letters from Berlin*, is credited in the second with calling the Prussian capital *la capitale de la musique*. Yes, our guide agrees, taking up a theme on which Heine was to play many variations in later works, the city has been drowning in music this last season, one concert following hard on the heels of another, and Weber's bridal chorus pursuing one everywhere. Nevertheless, he adds, everyone is eagerly looking forward to the concert announced by the flautist L. F. P. Drouet because that is expected to be the occasion on which the young Felix Mendelssohn-Bartholdy will be playing in public for the first time. Mendelssohn, then barely thirteen years old, did not in fact make his expected début at Drouet's concert; but he did appear before an enthusiastic public for the first time in the month in which this second 'Letter from Berlin' was written, and thus began a career on which Heine was to comment more than once in the years to come.

Our guide would clearly have failed to do his duty if he had omitted to mention the cult of Goethe among poets and intellectuals of the 1820s. In Berlin the high priestess of that cult was a Jewish-born hostess to whose salon Heine had recently been admitted: Rahel Varnhagen, née Levin. Heine's own veneration of Goethe remained this side of idolatry; but he thought him a great poet and as such divinely superior to the burghers of his native Frankfurt whose project for raising a statue to Goethe he had recently ridiculed in a sonnet. After quoting this satirical sonnet, the guide of *Letters from Berlin* continues (in a passage that again conspicuously employs superimposition effects):

As is well known, the great man himself put an end to all discussion of the project by returning his Frankfurt citizenship papers to his compatriots with the terse comment that he was not a Frankfurter.

Such citizenship papers are said to have, since then, dropped 99 per cent below par—to adopt the language they speak in Frankfurt; with the result that Jews now have a better chance of making this desirable acquisition. But—to speak like a Frankfurter once more—have not the Rothschilds and the Bethmanns stood at par for a long time? A businessman's religion is the same all the world over. His counting-house is his hassock, his ledger is his Bible, his stock-room is his sanctuary, the Stock Exchange bell is the knell that summons him to prayer, his gold is his god, and credit is his faith.[6]

Now we understand better why in the first of the *Letters from Berlin* our guide had turned our attention to the Stock Exchange after deflecting it from the cathedral. For the men of money, who dominated so much of the life Heine knew, the Stock Exchange had taken the cathedral's place. This applied to the Christian Bethmanns as much as the Jewish Rothschilds— money worship was endemic in modern business life, and should not have been used as an excuse for discriminating against Jews. Among those who discriminated most notoriously and obviously in Heine's day were the non-Jewish citizens of Frankfurt, money-grubbers *par excellence* in Heine's eyes; and the poet gleefully seizes on the rebuff Goethe had recently administered to his native city to remind the good burghers of Frankfurt that there was nothing so grand, nothing so universally valued, about the rights they proudly and unjustly denied the Jews that lived amongst them.

The disquisition on the Jews and non-Jews of Frankfurt takes us back, according to a principle of association of ideas proclaimed at the very beginning of the *Letters from Berlin*, to the Berlin Stock Exchange; and this in turn leads our guide to offer further remarks on Jewish affairs.

I now see my chance to speak of two recent events. The first of these is the opening, a few weeks ago, of the new Stock Exchange building, arranged and furnished on the model of its sister institution in Hamburg; and the second is the old project, now newly warmed up, for converting the Jews. But I shall pass both of these by, for I have not yet been inside the new building, and the Jews are too sad a subject. I shall, however, have to return to the Jews in the end, when I come to speak of their new mode of worship, which originated mainly in Berlin. As yet I cannot do this because I keep missing my chances to attend the new 'Mosaic' services. Nor do I want to discuss the new liturgy which has long been in use in the Berlin cathedral—for if I did, my letter would swell into a book. The liturgy has many enemies. The chief of these is said to be Schleiermacher . . .[7]

The Jews are a sad subject, *ein gar zu trauriger Gegenstand*, not because they refuse the blandishments of the Society for the Promotion of Christianity among the Jews, but because of what history had done to so many of them. To make them better able to take their rightful place in German society was one of the objects kept in view by the Society for the Culture and Science of the Jews in which Heine was active in the early 1820s. Several of the members of that Society (but decidedly not Heine himself) also belonged to those who sought to reform synagogue ritual in a way that would bring it nearer to the ritual of Protestant churches (itself recently reformed); these 'Reformers' were foremost among those who sought to avoid the stigma that popular use had attached to the words *jüdisch* and *Jude* by substituting such terms as *mosaisch* and *Mosaist*.

Soon after this excursion into inner-Jewish affairs, our guide allows us, in the midst of a great deal of miscellanous information, a brief glimpse of Jewish involvement in the cultural affairs of Germany and Europe.

Michael Beer has written a new tragedy, *The Brides of Aragon*, in Italy, and a new opera by Meyerbeer is now being performed in Milan. Spontini is now setting Koreff's *Sappho* to music . . .[8]

The physician and writer David Ferdinand Koreff, a friend of E. T. A. Hoffman, of Jewish birth but baptized into the

German Lutheran Church, has attracted Berlin's foremost Italian composer to a work of his which is based on a theme from ancient Greece; while the brothers Michael Beer and Meyerbeer, of whom a great deal more will be heard in Heine's writings, are bringing together Spain, Italy, and Germany in yet another cosmopolitan mix.

Koreff's name had appeared twice before in these *Letters from Berlin*. In the first Letter the guide had referred to a rumour that Koreff had chosen a subject from Prussian history for the subject of his latest libretto, and that this was to be set to music by Spontini,[9] while the second Letter had talked at greater length of his collaboration with a German composer, G. A. Schneider, on an opera based on the thirteenth-century romance of Aucassin and Nicolette.

> . . . as composer of Koreff's *Aucassin and Nicolette* [Schneider] has been the subject of general conversation from 26 February right up to the present hour. For at least eight days everyone talked of Koreff and Schneider, Schneider and Koreff. On one side stood dilettantes with pretensions to genius who denigrated the music, on the other a crowd of bad poets who made pedantic criticisms of the text. I for my part found this opera extraordinarily enjoyable. I was entertained by the colourful tale which this gifted poet unfolded with such charm and childlike simplicity; I was delighted by the charming contrast between a serious occident and a gay orient;

(Is it fortuitous that orient and occident should come together in this way when a Jewish-born librettist collaborates with a Gentile German composer? This is not a question our guide raises, for he never adverts to Koreff's Jewishness at all—let him therefore continue in his own way:)

> and as the strangest, most loosely connected images played about me, the Romantic spirit flowered and stirred within my heart. The performance of a new opera in Berlin always causes great commotion; on this occasion it was all the greater because *Musikdirektor* Schneider and *Geheimrat* Ritter Koreff are so widely known. We shall soon be losing the last-named since he has long been making preparations for a great journey abroad. That is a loss for our city, for this man distinguishes himself by his sociable qualities, his pleasant personality, and his generosity of spirit.[10]

This unusually warm praise of Koreff is compounded by the

appearance, in a journal called *The Spectator* (*Der Zuschauer. Zeitschrift für Belehrung und Aufheiterung*, 14 March 1822), of a sonnet Heine had dedicated to him. Koreff's libretto for *Aucassin and Nicolette* is there described as a woven carpet or tapestry with many brightly-coloured figures, depicting battles between Christians and Muslims together with the loves and sufferings that accompany them.

> Freundlich ergötzt die bunte Herrlichkeit:
> Wir irren wie in märchenhafter Wildnis,
> Bis Lieb' und Licht besiegen Haß und Nacht.
>
> Du, Meister, kanntest der Kontraste Macht,
> Und gabst in schlechter, neuer Zeit das Bildnis
> Von Liebe aus der alten, guten Zeit!
>
> [The multicoloured splendour delights and pleases:
> we seem to stray through a fabulous wilderness
> until love and light overcome hatred and night.
>
> You, O master, understood the power of contrast,
> and in a bad new age you provided the image
> of love and life as it had been in the old, good days.][11]

In later years Heine was to think somewhat differently about Romantic orientations towards an 'alte, gute Zeit'; but he always retained his liking for the colourful, the extravagant, the fairy-tale elements of Romanticism, just as he was to continue to believe that the secret of effective communication lay in a proper understanding and use of contrast. By praising Koreff in the way he did Heine's narrator or 'lyric I' indirectly demonstrates that men of Jewish origin could enter into the spirit of German Romanticism and make significant contributions to it. The poet is clearly speaking *pro domo* here—but this does not make his tribute to Koreff any less genuine. The gossipy guide tactfully omits to mention, therefore, what was then the talk of the town—that Koreff was leaving Berlin under a cloud, charged with many indiscretions; and the tributary poem says nothing about the tepid reception *Aucassin and Nicolette* had in fact been accorded by the opera-going public.

One last Jewish figure that flits across our attention in this second letter derives from British fiction rather than German social life. The guide tells his provincial charges of the enormous success the novels of Sir Walter Scott were then enjoying in Berlin and takes the opportunity of slipping in a compliment to Elise von Hohenhausen, to whose salon the young Heine had recently been granted admission. Frau von Hohenhausen, he tells us, had shown herself an admirably precise translator from Byron; the translation of *Ivanhoe* on which she was then engaged would prove even more admirable because her feminine sympathies would go out more readily to the figures invented by Scott than to those of the gloomy creator of Childe Harold.

The fair and tender Rebecca could fall into no more fair and tender hands than those of this sensitive poetess who in this case need only translate with her heart.[12]

Here the heart of a Romantically-minded aristocratic German lady is depicted as fully and unreservedly in sympathy with a Jewish figure created by a Scottish aristocrat. Rebecca is the only figure from *Ivanhoe* that the guide sees fit to mention.

The last of these *Letters from Berlin*, dated 7 June 1822, then shows our guide returning to the subject of the Stock Exchange, which he had throughout linked with that of the Jews living in the Prussian capital.

I have seen the new Stock Exchange. It is splendidly appointed. A large number of spacious, lavishly decorated rooms. Everything is on the most generous scale. I have been told that the noble, artistic son of the great Mendelssohn, Joseph Mendelssohn, is the real begetter of this institution. Not only businessmen, but civil servants too, and scholars, and men from all walks of life, visit the Stock Exchange building. The reading room is particularly attractive; I found over a hundred journals there, from Germany and abroad. Our *Rhenish-Westphalian Gazette* is also there, as I saw for myself. Dr Böhringer, a man who has had a thoroughgoing scholarly training, is in charge of this reading room and knows how to put visitors in his debt with obliging courtesy. Josty [a famous Berlin restaurateur of the day] manages the restaurant and the café. The attendants all wear brown liveries with gold braid, and the hall porter is particularly imposing by reason of his large marshal's baton.[13]

There is nothing ironic in the adjective 'great' which Heine here has his guide apply to Moses Mendelssohn, the pious Jew who became the friend of Lessing, the philosopher whose German writings were read with a respect and admiration which materially advanced the cause of Jewish emancipation in Germany. The compliment to Moses's 'artistic' (*kunstsinnig*) son is less straightforward, however. What are we to think of a 'nobility' and an artistic taste which expresses itself in a Stock Exchange building furnished like a palace and accoutres its porter like a field marshal? Heine leaves it to his readers to supply the answer.

The Mendelssohn family appears again in the last scene of the *Letters from Berlin* to include a glimpse of a Jewish-born figure.

It is very quiet in the musical world. The *capitale de la musique* fares like every other capital: it consumes what is manufactured in the provinces. Except for young Felix Mendelssohn whom the experts unanimously pronounce a musical prodigy capable of becoming a second Mozart, I cannot find a single musical genius among autochthonous Berliners who actually live here . . .[14]

What our guide here reports of Felix Mendelssohn he has clearly learnt at second hand; but he does suggest that Moses Mendelssohn's grandson is thought capable, by all the competent judges, of bringing to the Prussian capital an honour and a renown it would otherwise sadly lack—despite its newly won reputation of being *la capitale de la musique*. The guide draws no moral from this—he simply reports; he nowhere identifies himself with Jews or suggests that his interest in the Jewish community of Berlin may be other than that of a detached, fair-minded observer.

Before leaving these *Letters from Berlin* it is worth while casting a last look at the guide who has been escorting us. Three features of his self-presentation are of especial interest in the context of Heine's Jewish Comedy. The first of these is his combination of love of Germany, delight in the colourful variety he finds in the life of the Prussian capital, and attitudes that can best be described as cosmopolitan, supra-nationalist:

I love Germany and the Germans; but I love no less the inhabitants of the rest of this earth, whose number is forty times greater—and it is surely love which gives a man his true value. I am therefore—God be thanked!—worth forty times more than those who cannot pull themselves out of the swamp of national egotism and who love none but Germany and the Germans.[15]

That is said in the context of a hostile caricature of a young Teutomaniac who thinks even the French language an index of Babylonian corruption. Shortly afterwards the guide tells us about a royal wedding and takes the opportunity to stress the social divisions of Berlin and his own humble place there.

I am not of noble rank, nor am I a high official in the civil service, nor am I an army officer—this means that I cannot appear at court and that I was not therefore able to attend in person the wedding festivities in the royal palace.[16]

The third bit of self-characterization is surely the most significant of all. The guide tells his charges of the one occasion on which this system of exclusions, these marked distinctions of rank, cease to operate: and that is the masked ball at the Berlin Opera House.

What does it matter who is beneath the mask? The quest is enjoyment, and for that one only needs human beings. Nowhere can one be a human being more fully than at a masked ball, where the waxen mask hides our usual mask of flesh, where a simple *Du* restores the intimate familiarity of a pristine society, where a costume covers all pretensions and brings about the most beautiful equality and the most beautiful freedom—the freedom conferred by masks, *Maskenfreiheit*.[17]

We shall have many occasions to watch Heine avail himself of the *Maskenfreiheit* here praised by the guide of *Letters from Berlin*. Not for nothing has he been dubbed, by one of his most perceptive critics, the 'elusive' poet.

Soon after writing the *Letters* with which this chapter has so far been concerned, Heine left Berlin for a tour of that part of Poland which was then under Prussian administration; and here he encountered a group of Jews very different from the bankers, merchants, and Stock Exchange speculators, the rising lawyers and brilliant hostesses, patrons of the arts and musical virtuosos, on whom the guide had focused our attention in Heine's account of life in the Prussian capital. It has to be remembered that in the course of his work for the Society for the Culture and Science of the Jews, the poet had come into close contact with a few Jews from Poland—especially some indigent young hopefuls such as J. L. Braunhardt, whom he taught German history and geography from a patriotic German standpoint while advising them at the same time that they should consider seeking their fortunes in tolerant America rather than prejudice-ridden Germany. Nothing, however, had prepared him for his encounter with Polish Jews in their surroundings during a journey through part of Poland in 1822. His account of that confrontation, published in *On Poland* (*Über Polen*) in 1823, is so instructive that it demands to be quoted in full despite its length. To put this long passage into its proper perspective one has to remember the social context Heine had sketched in at the very beginning of the essay in which it occupies a prominent place:

Though my body moved in the higher spheres of society, in the charmed circle of *chateaux* owned by the Polish nobility, yet my spirit roamed among the huts of the common people.[18]

One has to remember, too, the political and social creed he seeks to communicate to his readers:

Men should bow down only before their king; except for this point of my creed I subscribe unreservedly to the North American catechism. I will not deny that I love the trees of the forest better than family trees, that I respect the Rights of Man more than the rights enshrined in canon law, and that I esteem the dictates of reason more highly than the abstractions of short-sighted historians . . .[19]

One has to remember, lastly, that when Heine shows us Jews in the context of Prussian Poland's larger cities, he wants us to see them only as one element in a colourfully varied throng:

I don't want to write a great deal about the city folk of Prussian Poland: it is a blend of Prussian officials, German *émigrés*, Polonized West Prussians, military men, and so on.[20]

The passage now to be quoted, however, is triggered off by another kind of experience—a first encounter with Jews in a *shtetl*, a small town in which they formed the majority of the inhabitants.

The Jews stand, in Poland, between the peasant and the nobleman. They make up more than a quarter of the population, engage in all trades, and may fittingly be called Poland's third estate. Our

compilers of statistics, who measure everything by German or at
least by French standards, are therefore in error when they tell us that
Poland has no *tiers état*—just because this estate is more rigidly
separated from the others, because its members delight in misunder-
standing the Old Testament, and because in externals they still differ
sharply from that ideal of a comfortable bourgeoisie whose prettified
Sunday-best image we may find in those descriptions of philistine life
in the imperial cities of yore with which women's keepsakes
published in Nuremberg have made us so familiar. You may see,
therefore, that by reason of their number and position the Jews of
Poland perform a more important function in the economy of the
state than they do with us in Germany; and that, in order to say
something useful about them, one needs to do more than just poke
one's grand nose into a pawnshop, as is the wont of sentimental
north-German novelists, and one needs something more, too, than
those profundities of Schellingian philosophy which are the
stock-in-trade of intellectual shop assistants in the German south. I
have been told that in the Grand Duchy of Poland the Jews stand on a
lower cultural level than their co-religionists farther east; I will
therefore avoid making sweeping statements about Polish Jewry as a
whole and will refer you instead to David Friedländer's book *On the
Improvement of the Israelites (Jews) in the Kingdom of Poland*,
Berlin 1819. It is probable that the condition of Jews has not
materially altered since the appearance of this book, which is written
with a rare love of truth and humanity—except for its unjust
misrepresentation of the merits and the moral importance of the
rabbis. It is said that there was a time in the history of the Grand
Duchy, as in that of the rest of Poland, in which all handicrafts were
practised solely by Jews; but now one sees many artisans emigrating
from Germany, and Polish peasants too seem to find handicrafts and
other trades more to their taste than hitherto. It is strange, however,
that the ordinary Pole usually becomes a shoemaker or a brewer or a
distiller. In one of the suburbs of Posen I found every second house
ornamented with a shoemaker's sign, which put me in mind of the
town of Bradford as it appears in Shakespeare's *The Pinner of
Wakefield*. In Prussian Poland, however, Jews are admitted to all
such positions because this is thought beneficial. One may note in
passing that the arsenic in the mines there has not yet been refined
into a hyper-pious philosophy and that the wolves in the ancient
Polish forests have not yet been trained to howl historical citations.

It would be a good thing if our government found suitable means
to instil greater love of agricultural pursuits into the Jews of the
Grand Duchy, for it is said that at present there are only very few
Jewish farmers. In Russian Poland they are found frequently. The

dislike of the plough among Polish Jews is believed to be due to the excessively sorry appearance which the peasant serf used to present; if the peasantry now raises itself from that degradation, then the Jews will also take to the plough.

With very few exceptions all the inns of Poland are in Jewish hands, and the many distillers attached to them do great harm to the country because they tempt Polish farmers to drunkenness. But drinking brandy, as I have tried to show earlier on, is part of the peasant's idea of bliss.

Every nobleman has a Jew in the village or the city whom he calls his 'agent' and who sees to all his commissions, purchases, sales, enquiries, and so on. This characteristic arrangement is a clear indication of the Polish nobleman's love of ease and comfort.

The external appearance of the Polish Jew is terrible. A shudder runs down my spine when I remember my first experience (just beyond Meseritz it was) of a Polish village inhabited mainly by Jews. Not even the *Berlin Weekly* under Wadzeck's editorship, stewed, physically, into a porridge, could have nauseated me as utterly as the sight of those filthy and ragged apparitions. Not even the high-minded orations of a fifth-former enthused by thoughts of gymnastic exercises and the fatherland could have hurt my ears as excruciatingly as the jargon spoken by Polish Jews. But compassion soon shouldered out disgust when I took a closer look at the way these people lived; when I saw the pigsty-like hovels which they inhabit and in which they jabber [*mauscheln*], pray, haggle, and are miserable. The language they speak is a kind of German shot through with Hebrew and decked out with Polish. They immigrated into Poland in very early times because of religious persecution in Germany—in such cases the Poles have always been distinguished by their tolerance. When hyper-pious counsellors advised the Polish king to force Polish Protestants to convert back to Catholicism, he answered: 'Sum rex populorum sed non conscientarum!'—I am King of my peoples but not of their consciences.

It was the Jews who first brought industry and trade to Poland, and King Casimir rewarded them with large privileges. They seem to have stood much nearer the nobility than the peasantry; there is, in fact, an old law by which Jews were raised to the nobility by the mere fact of conversion to Christianity. I do not know whether and why this law has sunk into abeyance—nor do I know for certain what it is that may have fallen in value.

In those early days the Jews must, surely, have stood far above the nobleman in intellectual and spiritual cultivation, for the nobility then practised only the rough arts of war and lacked, as yet, the French polish of later times. At the very least, however, the Jews always pored over their Hebrew books of learning and religion, for the sake of which they had left their fatherland and their creature comforts behind. They failed, clearly, to keep pace with European civilization, and their spiritual world sank into a morass of unedifying superstition squeezed into a thousand grotesque shapes by a super-subtle scholasticism. And yet, and yet . . . Despite the barbarous fur cap that covers his head and the still more barbarous ideas that fill it, I value the Polish Jew much higher than many a German Jew who wears his hat in the latest Simon-Bolivar fashion and has his head filled with quotations from Jean Paul. In rigid seclusion that Polish Jew's character became a homogeneous whole; when breathing a more tolerant air it took on the stamp of liberty. The inner man did not become a composite medley of heterogeneous emotions, nor did it atrophy through being constrained within the walls of the Frankfurt ghetto, ordinances decreed by the high, wise, and mighty city fathers, and disabilities charitably decreed by law. I for my part prefer the Polish Jew with his filthy fur, his populated beard, his smell of garlic, and his jabbering jargon, to many another who stands in all the glory of his gilt-edged securities.[21]

One thing is sure about this revealing passage—whatever we go to Heine for, it should not be accurate factual and statistical information. Though in the urban Poland of his day the Jewish population exceeded 20 per cent in some cases, in the country as a whole they made up perhaps one-fifteenth of the total number, and certainly not the quarter which Heine claimed.[22] Similar doubts may be and have been cast on other 'facts' reported in Heine's essay: the quantitative relation between Polish, Jewish, and German craftsmen, for instance, and hence the claim of Jews to be considered Poland's third estate. Other statements are simply Utopian. While rightly linking the depressed state of Jewry in Prussian Poland with the depressed state of the peasantry, Heine underestimates the obstacles that would confront Jews ready and willing to desert commerce for agriculture even when the Polish farmer's lot had been made more tolerable. How willing, for instance, would such a farmer be to accept a Jew into the farming community? As the Israeli experience has shown, Heine was quite correct in his surmise that once Jews decided to become farmers, they would make a brilliant job of it; but in European conditions the kind of redeployment and resettlement he and many of his contemporaries had in mind would come up against more obstacles than he was ready to allow—obstacles which his own brother Gustav would encounter not long afterwards.

What we can go to Heine for, however, is at least as valuable as accurate statistics: dramatizations of states of mind and attitudes characteristic of the time in which he wrote. His group-portrait of the Polish Jews he encountered in the course of his brief journey is clearly meant to render the impression an intelligent, liberal, open-minded German might form on such a journey; and it is set into the context of other possible attitudes and states of mind which are at once evoked and criticized.

Heine's description of Polish Jewry is deliberately calculated, from the outset, to demolish five propositions: (1) that all Jews are rich; (2) that a social group as sharply divided from the rest as the Polish Jews still are in matters of culture and life-style cannot fulfil the functions that the 'third estate' traditionally fulfilled in Germany and France; (3) that the acceptance of 'erroneous' interpretations of the Old Testament (Heine does not signal great faith in rabbinical commentaries here) thrusts a group outside the pale of citizenship; (4) that no one can be a good middle-class citizen who fails to conform to Romantic ideals propagated by the popular keepsake, the *Frauentaschenbuch*, published in Nuremberg under the editorship of Friedrich de la Motte Fouqué; (5) that Jews *are* what the stereotypes in the heads of German writers and readers make them out to be. Heine goes on to say that one cannot gain an accurate impression of contemporary Jews if one meets them only in pawnshops and if one is too bemused by Romantic German philosophy to see what goes on before one's eyes.

The compliment to David Friedländer which follows this proposition is more than simply an acknowledgement of important source material. It pays tribute to an honoured older member of the Society for the Culture and Science of the Jews to which Heine belonged; to the humanitarian ideals of Moses Mendelssohn, whose disciple Friedländer had been; and to the kind of enlightenment that Mendelssohn had tried to foster. But as Philipp Veit has well said, Heine could not believe, as Friedländer so often showed himself prone to do, that 'self-effacing and self-degrading conformity was a responsible solution for the problem of a Jew in an inimical environment'.[23]

He therefore corrects Friedländer in two significant respects. He does not feel it incumbent upon himself to hide the appellation 'Jews' behind the biblical euphemism 'Israelites'; he accordingly adds the terms 'Juden' in brackets after 'Israeliten' in the title Friedländer had given his pamphlet on Poland (*Über die Verbesserung der Israeliten im Königreich Pohlen*, Berlin 1819). Above all, however, he could not go along with Friedländer's concrete ideas on the 'improvement' (*Verbesserung*) of Jews, and he therefore dissented from the diatribes against rabbis and Talmudists of which Friedländer's work is so full. The devaluing of orthodox rabbis, explicit in Friedländer's pamphlet and implicit in Heine's own remark about Jewish 'misinterpretation' of the Old Testament, needs severe qualification; one must not, the poet now asserts, allow such views to obscure the rabbis' 'merits and moral importance'. Early nineteenth-century Russians, he tells his readers, with obvious polemical intent, believed that a people that followed the teaching of these rabbis was fit to compete on equal terms for administrative positions in the Russian part of Poland—a belief that Prussia under Frederick William III clearly did not share. Heine's brother Maximilian was indeed to carve out a prestigious and lucrative career in the medical service of the Russian army; but those who know the history of Russia's dealings with its Jewish population in the nineteenth century will not think Heine's polemical point at all well taken.

His main aim in this passage is not, however, the buttering up of Russia; he seeks rather to attack those whom he considered the principal enemies of Jewish equality of opportunity in post-Napoleonic Germany: all-too-pious Christians (*Frömmler*), and reactionary academics, particularly those of the historical school of law. He does this by following associations triggered in the mind of German readers when Russia was mentioned: the *mines* in which political and other prisoners were made to toil, and the *wolves* that still howled in the Russian forests. These images Heine now superimposes on the German conditions he wants to satirize to suggest a series of contrasts and parallels between the physical hardships of Russia and the spiritual hardships of Germany. In Russia they dig arsenic out of the bowels of the earth—but they do not refine this arsenic into the poisonous hyper-piety which

would force Jews to abandon their religion if they wanted full
civil rights. In Russia the forests are full of wolves—but these
are more harmless than the academic wolves of Germany, the
followers of Savigny and others who justify their reactionary
cruelty by quoting historical precedents and examples.

One charge that opponents of civil equality constantly
levelled at Jews was that they had made no contribution to
agriculture and that their ubiquitous dram-shops did harm to
the Polish farming community. Heine's answer to this implies
that Jews must be given the opportunity to enter walks of life
hitherto barred to them; he does not spell this out, however,
and stresses, instead, that if the life of the peasantry were made
more agreeable, more Jews would seek to share it, and fewer
dram-shops would be needed in which the downtrodden and
ill-paid peasantry could drown its sorrows. As things were,
Polish Jews found themselves drafted into the service of the
aristocracy, providing goods and services needed to minister to
their ease and comfort—a characteristic variant of the
traditional function of the 'court Jew' of an earlier age.

The Jews may be the *tiers état* of Poland: but their fate is
closely bound up, in Heine's account, with that of the Polish
peasantry, who, like the Jews, are financially dependent on the
nobility. How can one expect Jews to divest themselves of their
traditional middleman pursuits if the agricultural life presents a
horrifying picture of poverty and servitude? But the economic
function of Polish Jews as Heine here describes it implies that
they are not likely to be active agents in the emancipation of the
peasantry—even though their own emancipation may be
closely bound up with it.[24]

Now comes the shock. For the first time we are made to
look, through Heine's fastidious eyes, at the external
appearance of the poorer Jews of Poland. The very memory of
this encounter brings a shudder of revulsion. *Das Äußere des
polnischen Juden ist schrecklich. Mich überläuft ein Schauder
. . .* But as Heine evokes the 'subhuman' conditions in which
this indigent populace is forced to live, we remember his
similar description of the Polish peasantry and reflect on the
difference which enlightened reforms, enlightened legislation
and administration could make. And as so often, he now
surprises his readers with a 'superimposition' or 'contrast'

effect. Two groups are seen together, and each becomes a standard by which the other is judged. The ragged and filthy apparitions he encountered in Poland provide a measure of Heine's dislike of the contents and editorial policy of a Berlin newspaper, run, no doubt, by impeccably clean and respectably dressed Germans—a dislike made the more memorable by the almost surrealist image of stewing a copy of the paper into a pap and ingesting the result. Revulsion inspired by the language spoken by Polish Jews is then measured, in the same way, against revulsion inspired by another, very different phenomenon: the antics of German patriotic societies which mingled gymnastics with high-sounding phrases redolent of hated for Frenchmen and Jews.

Here Heine shows, for once, limitations of appreciation and understanding which he shared with most of the German Jews of his day. Yiddish, for him, is not a language in its own right, but spoilt German—he shows scant appreciation of its vigour and charm, its wit and poetry, and has no feeling for its latent literary possibilities.

For all his defence of the rabbis against the strictures of would-be reformers such as David Friedländer Heine does feel, as he looks at the indigent Polish Jews, that they have been left behind by the progress of European civilization; that the religion on which their culture is based has become superstition moulded by scholastic hyper-subtleties. That, of course, was the premise on which the Society for the Culture and Science of the Jews based its educational policies. But Heine is far too sceptical of 'enlightened' European Jews and the bourgeoisie on which they tried to model themselves to rest content with the proposition that they had reached a desirable state to which the 'unenlightened' Jewish masses had to be elevated. In the most remarkable passage of his essay on Poland he shows that the revulsion and pity he felt for the Polish Jews he encountered can coexist with profound admiration. Admiration, first, of a moral and intellectual civilization that antedates by far the culture of the nobleman who now lords it over the Jews; admiration, secondly, of a courage and steadfastness which shows itself in the sacrifices these Jews and their ancestors have made for the sake of their sacred scriptures and books of traditional wisdom; admiration, lastly, of a 'wholeness' or authenticity of character which contrasts with the self-division, the *Zerrissenheit*, Heine was to diagnose so frequently in his contemporaries and in himself.

Here Heine has broached, in a Jewish context, a theme of enormous importance in the cultural debates that were carried on in eighteenth- and nineteenth-century Germany. How could one be a whole man, an integral human being, in modern society? For Heine and his readers Polish Jews furnish one answer to this question, show one way in which this could be done: through *schroffe Abgeschlossenheit*, a rigid seclusion from the culture of the outside world—though one would have to ask, of course, as Heine makes us ask, whether freedom and wholeness of *that kind* might not be too dearly bought. The tone of his description certainly suggests that he thinks the price too high.

As so often, Heine makes his principal points and explores the implications of his subject through a series of contrasts. The unified world-view of the tradition-bound Polish Jews is contrasted with the heterogeneous and frequently conflicting emotions and values of his more 'assimilated' German co-religionist. The Polish community's pride in its exclusive Jewishness is contrasted, to its advantage, with the stunting effect of aspiring to equal the mentality of members of a city council which *forces* Jews to live in a ghetto—the Frankfurt council, for instance, whose conventional appelation *hochweis* ('wise to the highest degree', 'high and wise') is a mockery and whose benevolence is a hollow sham. Besides his portrait of the Polish Jew Heine now places a rapid sketch of an enlightened German Jew, the man who wears a hat of the latest fashion rather than the 'barbarous' fur cap of his Polish counterpart, and whose head is filled with quotations from the (then widely read) novels of Jean Paul Richter rather than the precepts and sayings of the rabbis. He piles up, in this concluding passage, all that his fastidious eye, ear, and nose found most revolting about the Jews he encountered in Poland—and yet, uncompromisingly, he opts for their 'wholeness', their authenticity, rather than the in-between state of the fashionably-dressed German Jew, preferring the Polish Jew's pride in his heritage (out of tune with the time though it be) to the gilt-edged securities that enabled Westernized Jews to adopt a Gentile life-style. Once again, we see, Heine is criticizing the values implicit and explicit in Friedländer's pamphlet on the 'improvement' of Poland's Jews.

It should not be forgotten, all this while, that the conditions Heine is describing in his essay are conditions in *Prussian* Poland, and that his description of the material misery in which Polish peasants and many Polish Jews have to live are therefore criticisms of the Prussian administration. And even where he seems to be concentrating on Polish conditions, a whole network of allusions, comparisons, and oppositions enables him, as Klaus Pabel and E. J. Krzywon have shown, to write obliquely about Germany: to speak of the Polish aristocracy and imply something about the German nobility, to measure the fate of Polish Jewry and the Polish peasantry against that of their German equivalents. To convey his concern with emancipation and advance, his struggle to have the essential dignity and rights of all human beings recognized and assured, Heine evolved a characteristic style whose early manifestation in *On Poland* has been well described by Krzywon:

Through his use of Polish motifs Heine worked out for himself a dialectical mode of expression based on techniques of opposition and contrast. This helps us to perceive and understand realities that seemed incapable [in the German conditions of Heine's day] of being directly expressed. Between configurations of reality which confront one another in Heine's writings other realities appear, neither sayable nor said, which the reader can nevertheless give body to with the help of the associations and contrasts the poet has provided. Here Heine created for himself a sophisticated means of depicting his world which censorship regulations could not reach—a new style that relied, in the main, on a perpetual process of unveiling.[25]

One item is missing from this perceptive description: the relativization which Heine's use of contrast, his 'perpetual unveiling', brought with it. This is what makes so much of his writing double-edged and invites games of 'deconstruction' which the present study forbears to play beyond the danger line. Instead I shall quote just one example, from the essay on Poland, of the sort of game in which Heine involves his German readers. The subject at the back of his mind is clearly an arrogant German nobility and its negative attitude towards Jewish emancipation.

The Poles know nothing of proud aristocratic disdain of the middle classes; this can only come into being in countries that have a powerful middle class [*Bürgerstand*] putting forward claims of its own. Pride of birth will not stir the Polish nobleman until the Polish peasant starts buying estates and the Polish Jew stops showing deference. Such stirrings of pride would therefore be a sign that the country was on its way up. Because the Jews are here on a higher social plane than the peasants, they will be the first to come into collision with such new pride—but the clash will then, no doubt, be given a more religious name.[26]

The multiple ironies of this passage—class divisions and arrogance of birth as a sign that a country is on its way *up*, the dressing-up of anti-Jewish feelings determined by class interest in a time-honoured religious garb—should be obvious without further analysis.

One last factor governing the ambivalances and complexities of the 'Poland' essay has been stressed by Maria Grabowska. Like so many of his contemporaries, Heine had been affected by the novels of Sir Walter Scott, with their preference for characters whose physical and spiritual features were in some way marked by a colourful past and who, by virtue of this, escaped what was felt as the 'banality' of modern life. Grabowska rightly sees this preference as an element in Heine's contrast between Polish and German Jews—though she also recognizes that it is *only* an element, and that it does not, therefore, cancel out the negative features Heine's portrayal impresses upon us. Heine was always fascinated by contradictions, and Grabowska quotes a Polish critic, M. Kofta, who said of him that he tended to bring out the positive *and* the negative elements of phenomena that came under his scrutiny, and that this inhibited unqualified enthusiasm as well as unqualified negation.[27] That Heine was capable of overcoming such inhibitions the later chapters of this book will have ample cause to show; we shall find his enthusiasm for the poet Yehuda Halevi as unqualified as his distaste for everything he saw—or thought he saw—in the life and work of the composer and impresario Joseph Dessauer.

(ii)

Heine's confrontation of *shtetl* Jews in Prussian Poland with their more westernized co-religionists in Berlin and Frankfurt is shot through with sometimes implicit, sometimes explicit criticism of the social policies pursued by those who controlled the secular destinies of post-exilic Jewry. The resentments that fuelled such criticism may well have played a part in Heine's choice of Belshazzar's Feast as the subject of his first exercise in the art of the ghostly ballad, the *Schauerballade*, which had played so powerful a part in German folk poetry and had been given a new lease of life, and a new direction, by Bürger, Herder, and Goethe. The tyrant in Heine's *Belshazzar* [*Belsatzar*][28] is killed by his own servants, and not, as in the Book of Daniel, by enemies breaking into his kingdom and his palace; and this change brings a suggestion of social revolution, the revolt of slaves against their arrogant masters, into the tale of Jehovah's vengeance upon those who defy him. One should not overestimate the Jewish content of a ballad that shows Heine's assimilation, not only of the Bible, but also of German *Schauerballaden* and Byron's *Hebrew Melodies*. Nevertheless it is well attested that the inspiration for this ballad came to Heine from a post-biblical Jewish source—from a hymn recited at the Passover ceremonies in Jewish homes which has as its refrain the words 'And it happened in the middle of the night'.[29] Heine's opening words bear traces of this refrain:

> Die Mitternacht zog näher schon . . .

> [Midnight was already approaching . . .]

The Passover hymn in question, it should not be forgotten, mentions the fate of Belshazzar among other miracles that the Lord performed on behalf of his people.

There are further indications that it will not do to see this ballad as an out-and-out secularization of the biblical narrative. The prominence given to the ineffable name 'Jehovah', and the shudders inspired by the moving finger writing letters of fire that presage punishment of the blasphemer, inject into the poem a numinous quality akin to that which may be found in the Book of Daniel. As for the elimination of both Daniel himself and the actual wording of the fiery writing—that only throws into relief Heine's stark confrontation of blasphemer and weird apparition. *Something* breaks in from outside, something connected with the Jewish God Whom Belshazzar had sought to defy; and what we learn of the blasphemer's end is fully consistent with divine punishment, with punishment by a God who chooses to work—as the biblical Jehovah chooses to do—through history.

(iii)

The young Heine's most elaborate series of Jewish portraits may be found in a work in which Jews and Judaism are not overtly mentioned at all. *Almansor*, a play written between 1820 and 1822, ostensibly deals with the adjustment of Mohammedan Moors to the Christianization of Spain under Ferdinand and Isabella in the sixteenth century. The relevance of this play to the situation of Jews in nineteenth-century Germany, and in particular to Heine's own situation, has, however, been authoritatively demonstrated by Hartmut Kircher, who has rightly pointed to Heine's experience of overt and latent anti-Semitism (anti-Jewish riots in 1819, anti-Jewish pamphlets by eminent German academics, regressive policies by Frederick William III making baptism mandatory for aspirants to academic and civil service positions in Prussia) as among the most powerful factors determining the anti-Christian tone of many of the speeches given to sympathetic characters in *Almansor*.[30]

Kircher has also isolated the various types of motivation and adaptation which Heine observed among Jewish converts to Christianity, and which he then transferred to a Spanish-Muslim setting in his play. First there is the heroine, Zuleima: like many Jewish ladies of Heine's day—Dorothea Veit, for instance, the daughter of Moses Mendelssohn who became first the mistress and then the wife of Friedrich Schlegel—Zuleima is presented as a convert to Christianity who genuinely feels the attractions of that religion, and becomes its eloquent advocate. The naïvety with which she accepts what the clergy tell her may make her touching faith suspect, however, in Heine's context.

Zuleima is surrounded, in the play, by converts of a very different stamp. There is her father, for instance, once called Aly but now known as Don Gonzalvo, whose reasons for abandoning his Muslim religion along with his old name had been less straightforward than those of his daughter. He has no real inner relation to the Christian faith. He feels, rather, the attractions of a dominant culture that is condemning his own Muslim culture to stagnation; the attraction of being allowed to stay and take his place in society in the land in which he was born, even if that means forswearing the faith of his forefathers; the attraction, lastly, of the distant prospect of a better order, an order born from bloody conflict, when civil and religious tyranny will be toppled, when from the flames of prisons and castles there would arise what the play calls the eternal Word, the Word that was in the beginning, the glorious Word that transcends all the faiths of this earth. A chorus introduced for this one purpose opens the prospect in the form of a vision:

> Und rote Bäche flossen, Glaubenskerker
> Und Zwingherrnburgen stürzten ein, in Glut
> Und Rauch, und endlich stieg, aus Glut and Rauch,
> Empor das ewge Wort, das urgeborne,
> In rosenroter Glorie selig strahlend.[31]

Gonzalvo's servant, Pedrillo, who has been baptized along with his master, shows little understanding of the new faith and the culture that goes with it; he keeps slipping into vocabulary more appropriate to the days when he was still called Hamahma:

> Beim Barte des Propheten—ich wollte sagen
> Der heiligen Eli- Elisabeth . . .
>
> [By the beard of the prophet!—I mean
> By Saint Eli- Elizabeth . . .][32]

Hamahma-Pedrillo is clearly a first sketch of Hirsch-Hyazinth in *The Baths of Lucca*, where Heine no longer deems it necessary to dress up his Jews as Mohammedans. Contrasted with Pedrillo is another servant, Hassan, who stubbornly clings to the ancient faith, refusing all compromises and lip-service; he pours scorn on the 'traitors' that fail to follow his example. It is Hassan who speaks the two lines from the play which are so often quoted for their historic insight, which use the lessons gained from the course of the Inquisition to formulate a chilling prophecy whose truth the twentieth century has experienced to the full:

> ALMANSOR: Wir hörten, daß der furchtbare Ximenes
> Inmitten auf dem Markte, zu Granada—
> Mir starrt die Zung im Munde—den Koran
> In eines Scheiterhaufens Flamme warf!
> HASSAN: Das war ein Vorspiel nur, dort, wo man Bücher
> Verbrennt, verbrennt man auch am Ende Menschen.

> [ALMANSOR: We heard that Ximenes the Terrible
> in Granada, in the middle of the market-place,
> —my tongue refuses to say it!—cast the Koran
> int the flames of a burning pyre!
> HASSAN: That was only a prelude, Where they burn books
> They will, in the end, burn human beings too.][33]

The most interesting attitude, from Heine's point of view, is that of the eponymous hero the play, Almansor, whose name means 'The Defender'. Conscious of his 'Muslim' cultural heritage, but not deeply attached to the religion of his fathers, he easily adopts the outward behaviour and modes of speech characteristic of the dominant Christian culture. He is full of rage, however, at the suppression of an important part of his identity, a part that continues to live a submerged life. In such circumstances the Christian persona becomes a mask.

> Die Schlangenhaut, die schützet wider Schlangen;
> So wie die Wolfsfellhülle schützt das Lamm,
> Das wehrlos fromm die Waldungen durchstreift.
> Trotz Hut und Mantel bin ich doch ein Moslem,
> Denn in der Brust hier trag ich meinen Turban.

[The snakeskin I wear protects me against snakes
as the wolf's hide protects the lamb
that roams the world without defence.
For all my hat and coat I have remained a Muslim:
I wear my turban here, in my heart.][34]

Not surprisingly it is Almansor in whose mouth we find the
most anti-Christian speeches of Heine's play. He feels, it is
true, an immediate and instinctive sympathy for Jesus of
Nazareth; the thought of Jesus's martyrdom causes a tear of
sorrow to drop into his cup of joy;[35] but he is no less
immediately and instinctively repelled by what he regards as
the blood cult of those of Christ's followers who converted the
religion of love which he sought to found into an instrument of
tyranny and oppression.[36] In the very last words of the play,
however, the consolatory power of Jesus Christ is invoked by
Aly, now called Gonzalvo, deeply shaken by the deaths of
Almansor and Zuleima:

Jetzt, Jesu Christ, bedarf ich deines Wortes,
Und deines Gnadentrosts, und deines Beispiels.

[Now, Jesus Christ, I have need of your word,
the consolation of your grace, and your example.][37]

At every point Heine's play about the Christianization of
Muslims in sixteenth-century Spain recalls the experience of
Jews in ancient and (especially) in modern times. The
'Mohammedan' institutions and customs to which the charac-
ters refer constantly mirror Jewish ones: they range from the
veneration of a sacred scroll of the Law to the custom of tearing
one's garments when mourning, and the prohibition of pork.[38]
Echoes of Jewish history can be heard, not only in the lines on
the burning books and men which I have already quoted, but
also in descriptions of voluntary exile and banishment as
alternatives to baptism, in evocations of humiliating treatment
that echo one of the speeches of Shylock:

ALMANSOR: ich seh den span'schen Hund!
Dort spuckt er meinem Bruder in den Bart,
Und tritt ihn noch mit Füßen obendrein . . .
[ALMANSOR: I see the Spanish cur!
There he spits into my brother's beard,
and, for good measure, spurns him with his foot.]

And in such details as the assumption of a new name at baptism:

> Dorten vertauscht man dir den alten Namen,
> Und gibt dir einen neu'n; damit dein Engel,
> Wenn er dich warnend ruft beim alten Namen,
> Vergeblich rufe.

> [There they take away your old name
> and give you a new one in exchange; so that your guardian angel,
> when he warns you by calling out your old name,
> should call in vain.][39]

Disappearance of the old names, the character once called Hamahma but now called Pedrillo suggests, often goes with the disappearance of old virtues:

> Und was die alte Gastlichkeit betrifft,
> So ist das eine jener Heidensitten,
> Wovon dies christlich fromme Haus gesäubert.

> [As for our ancient hospitality—
> that is one of those pagan customs
> of which this pious Christian house has been cleansed.][40]

When Heine then shows us how the worldly-wise claim to recognize ex-Muslims by the over-ostentation of their dress, how the daughters of neo-Christians are besieged by Christian adventurers for the sake of their money, how the rich neo-Christians themselves seek 'respectable' Christian sons-in-law, how baptized Moors banish Mauresque music from their entertainments for what is explicitly called 'political' reasons, how neo-Christian veneer constantly peels off to reveal the old 'Muslim' beneath[41]—then we cannot but draw parallels with what we know of Jews who bought the entrance ticket of baptism in order to gain admittance to European culture and society in the nineteenth century.

Almansor is preceded by a motto that warns us not to take the play for pure fantasy;[42] and in a letter to his friends Friedrich Steinmann and J. B. Rousseau, Heine glossed this by saying: 'Into this play I have cast my own self, with my paradoxes, my wisdom, my love, my hatred, and all my craziness.'[43] Among these paradoxes the problems caused by

Heine's Jewishness loom large: his lack of deep attachment to the Jewish religion counteracted by reluctance to embrace another and by hatred of those who faced him with the necessity of doing so; his desire to be a full and useful citizen of a state that thought of itself as Christian, coexisting with a deep-rooted wish not to deny a Jewish origin and heritage which had, inevitably, helped to make him what he was; the attraction which the dominant European culture undoubtedly exerted on him countered by cherished cultural memories connected with Judaism. All this has been externalized, projected, in the figure of Almansor himself: a protagonist who, as Hartmut Kircher has shown, combines *desire* to be accepted as a full member of the dominant Christian community with *revulsion* at the betrayal of his own origins forced upon him by outside pressures and with *hatred* of institutions that demand such betrayal as the price of acceptance.

(iv)

The word *Jude*, Jew, which is pointedly absent from *Almansor*, features all the more prominently in the poem *Donna Clara*, written in 1823. This marks a new departure for Heine; for in his early verse he had carefully avoided references which might reveal that its author was Jewish. At the very outset of his career as a poet he had written to Christian Sethe:

Besides the fact that in this huckster city of Hamburg not the slightest feeling for poetry is to be found—except, perhaps, for occasional verses in celebration of weddings, funerals, or Christmasses, specially commissioned and paid for in cash—it has also been noticeable, for some time, that an oppressive tension exists between baptized and unbaptized Jews. All Hamburgers I call 'Jews'; those whom I call 'baptized' in order to distinguish them from the circumcised are what the vulgar call 'Christians'. In this climate it may easily be predicted that Christian charity is not likely to leave unscathed love-songs written by a Jew.[43]

Some of his earliest poems were published under a pointedly Germanic pseudonym; and even when he wrote affectionate sonnets in praise of his mother there was no hint to suggest that she might be Jewish. (These sonnets are just the kind of tribute that the proverbial Jewish mother dreams of receiving from her child—redolent of love and admiration, and at the same time breathing feelings of guilt at not having been able to reward maternal love sufficiently.)

> Ich bin's gewohnt, den Kopf recht hoch zu tragen,
> Mein Sinn ist auch ein bißchen starr und zähe.
> Wenn selbst der König mir ins Antlitz sähe,
> Ich würde nicht die Augen niederschlagen.
>
> Doch, liebe Mutter, offen will ichs sagen:
> Wie mächtig auch mein stolzer Mut sich blähe,
> In deiner selig süßen, trauten Nähe
> Ergreift mich oft ein demutvolles Zagen.
>
> Ist es dein Geist, der heimlich mich bezwinget,
> Dein hoher Geist, der alles kühn durchdringet,
> Und blitzend sich zum Himmelslichte schwinget?
>
> Quält mich Erinnerung, daß ich verübet
> So manche Tat, die dir das Herz betrübet?
> Das schöne Herz, das mich so sehr geliebet?
>
> [I am used to bearing my head high;
> my disposition is somewhat stubborn and unyielding;
> even if the king were to look into my face
> I would not cast down my eyes.
>
> But I will openly confess, dear mother,
> however powerfully my pride and my courage may swell,
> in your blessed, sweet, familiar presence
> I am often seized by a humble timidity.
>
> Is it your spirit that softly conquers me,
> your lofty spirit that pierces through all things
> and mounts towards heaven on glittering wings?
>
> Am I tormented by the memory of having committed
> many an act that grieved your heart—
> that beautiful heart which loved me so much?][45]

A second sonnet then caps this effusion by showing the poet searching for love throughout the world and only finding it when, in Byronic gloom, battered and sick, he returns to his mother's house.

In *Donna Clara* Heine throws to the winds all the caution he had so far shown in talking about Jewish affairs in his poetry—though he does, characteristically, ask Moser to be discreet and not to let non-Jews see the poem before he himself published it.[46] Behind the poem are readings in Jewish history which Heine undertook during the time of his membership of the Society for the Culture and Science of the Jews, often under the guidance of Leopold Zunz—and behind it, too, are some painful experiences of his own of which he speaks to Moser in the same letter dated 6 November 1823.[47] 'I wanted to convey', Heine says of this poem in his letter to Ludwig Robert of 27 November 1823, 'something that happens to an individual and is at the same time universal, world-historical . . . I wanted to do this in a simple, non-tendentious, epically impartial manner. The whole conception was serious and sad rather than comic; the poem was even to be the first part of a tragic trilogy.'[48]

Donna Clara introduces into Heine's poetry a hero of a special kind: a man who can pass for the flower of Christian chivalry, who is accepted as such, but who, in the end, reveals that he belongs to a group that is hated and despised. Like *Almansor*, whose hero has some points of resemblance with that of *Donna Clara*, the poem is set in Christian Spain. As the hero walks in the garden with the Christian lady of his heart, who has no idea that he is a Jew, he hears from her lips again and again words that recall the arguments of anti-Semites in nineteenth-century Germany.[49] Her words reveal, first of all, that she sees Jews as long-nosed subhumans akin to noxious insects; then that she hates in them the cruel and treacherous murderers of Christ; and lastly that she loathes in them the representatives of a people whose blood is alien to her own. The knight at the centre of the poem then takes a Heinesque revenge; after the lady has given herself to him, without any suspicion of his origins, he satisfies her curiosity about his name by revealing his identity:

> 'Ich, Sennora, Eur Geliebter,
> Bin der Sohn des vielbelobten,
> Großen, schriftgelehrten Rabbi
> Israel von Saragossa.'

[I, señora, your lover,
am the son of the celebrated
great and learned rabbi
Israel of Saragossa.][50]

Long delayed, the main stress of this stanza falls heavily on the word Israel—deliberately chosen by Heine, for the only rabbi of Saragossa he knew about was called Abraham. If 'Israel' recalls the Jewish people as a whole, the sonorous name 'Saragossa' recalls the great days of Spanish-Jewish culture which Heine had studied in various historical works and which he was later to celebrate in his poem *Jehuda ben Halevy*. The adjectives that precede and retard the climactic revelation of Rabbi Israel's name eloquently assert the fame, the greatness, and the learning of the rabbis in periods and countries in which Jewish culture flourished, just as the appearance and bearing of the knight himself bespeak the potential nobility of the stock from which he sprang. Yet even at the end, after the final revelation, the knight remains incognito—the lady had asked for *his* name, but the only name he vouchsafes her is that of his *father*. He remains as nameless at the end of Heine's poem as he had been at the beginning.

The problems posed by the kind of masked Marrano existence led by the knight of *Donna Clara* were to have been treated in two further poems that would have combined with *Donna Clara* into a tragic trilogy. The son he begot in the night of love of the first poem was to have been brought up, in the second poem, knowing nothing of his father and his origins—he was to be shown scorning his father without any inkling of their relationship. The same son was then to join the Dominican order and was to have been seen, in the final poem, having his Jewish brethren tortured to death.[51] Heine never completed this trilogy, however, and the impression left by *Donna Clara* is therefore comic rather than tragic. 'This often happens to me,' Heine told Moser on 28 November 1823; 'I try to tell my grief, and it all becomes comic!'[52]

One of the ambitions Heine nursed during the time of his membership of the Society for the Culture and Science of the Jews was to write a historical novel: a novel which would do for the Jews what Walter Scott was doing for the Scots and the English. He began to write such a novel, hoping that it would become the poetic chronicle of the life of medieval Jewry in Germany and perhaps in Spain too; and during the writing two poems came to him, poems that try to express feelings aroused in him by his concentrated study of Jewish history, particularly the voluminous work of the eighteenth-century French historian Jacques Basnage (*L'Histoire et la religion des Juifs depuis Jésus-Christ jusqu'à présent*). The first of these poems is entitled *To Edom!* [*An Edom!*]—'Edom' being here the name traditionally given to the Jews' enemies. It is an acrid reflection on the theme of imperfect tolerance; a tolerance which consists in the Jews' case of patient submission to oppression and abuse while Gentiles are asked to do no more than allow their Jewish fellow citizens to breathe the common air. Only sometimes—*Manchmal nur, in dunkeln Zeiten*—a strange mood comes over Edom, and forces him to colour his pious claws (*die liebefrommen Tätzchen*) with Jewish blood. But, the poem concludes, we are not living in such dark days now; there has been a *rapprochement*, a friendship that is becoming firmer, a friendship which is making the Jews abandon their traditional badge of sufferance and begin to rage almost like Edom himself:

> Jetzt wird unsre Freundschaft fester,
> Und noch täglich nimmt sie zu;
> Denn ich selbst begann zu rasen,
> Und ich werde fast wie Du.[53]

No work of Heine's had ever adopted the persona of a Jew more unequivocally than this bitter parody of emancipation and integration in which we see Israel taking on not the virtues but the vices, or the raging madness, of Edom. But as yet—so the wording of the last two lines proclaims to all who have ears to hear—Israel has not gone as far as Edom down the slippery slope. The process is only beginning; Israel is almost—almost but not quite—coming to resemble those whose friendship it is so fervently seeking.

What is missing from *To Edom*, with its stress on murder, rage, and madness, is the expression of that particularly Jewish grief which Börne had called *ungeheurer Judenschmerz*—the grief that seizes the Jew when he contemplates the history of his people's persecution.[54] This omission Heine tries to make good in a poem beginning

Brich aus in lauten Klagen,
Du düstres Martyrerlied . . .

[Break out in loud lamentations,
dark songs of martyrs . . .][55]

The 'dark song' of which Heine here speaks is, first and foremost, the novel he had begun to write, a novel to be entitled *The Rabbi of Bacherach*. His evocation of a 'thousand-year-old grief', the poet hopes—not without mockery of a young man's unreasonable expectations, of Romantic conceits and pathetic fallacies—will move to tears not only the men and women who read his words but all of nature too, from the flowers to the stars. The tears that flow so freely in the love-plaints of Heine's early poems are now to be shed at the fate of Israel:

Und alle die Tränen fließen
Nach Süden, im stillen Verein,
Sie fließen und ergießen
Sich all in den Jordan hinein.

[And all these tears will flow
southward, in silent union,
they will flow, and pour themselves
into the river Jordan.]

The poet himself describes these verses (and well he might!) as less significant, *unbedeutender*, than *To Edom*.[56] He was always deeply conscious of the tragic dimension of Jewish history; but this did not mean that its chronicles had to be sentimentally tearful. Heine would surely have been the first to applaud Salo Baron's later strictures on the lachrymose view of Jewish history!

As a holiday from such lachrymose exercises Heine allowed himself some high-spirited improvisations, one of which has come down to us in a report by Eduard Wedekind, a fellow student at Göttingen University. The report dates from 1824. Confined for some minor misdemeanour in the university's own place of detention, the *Karzer*, Wedekind consoled himself by scribbling on to the wall a little poem Heine had dashed down shortly before.

Als König Pharao ins rothe Meer
Hineinfiel mit seinem großen Heer,
Da kamen die Töchter Israel
Und wollten ihn ziehn aus der rothen Well
Und zogen und zogen und schrien und schrien nicht wenig:
Wir haben ihn, wir haben ihn, wir haben den rothen König.

[When King Pharaoh fell into the Red Sea
with his great army,
the daughters of Israel came
and wanted to pull him from the red waves.
They pulled and pulled and yelled with might and main:
'We have him, we have him, we have the red king!']⁵⁷

The last of these playful lines would seem to hold at least three
meanings: a biblical one, made absurd by the notion that the
Red Sea actually turned people red; a ludic one (the king of
hearts or diamonds in a card game); and a scatological one. The
poem is interesting, in our context, because it shows Heine
ready to make ironic, indeed ludicrous, use of the Passover and
Exodus story that provides so serious a background in his
Rabbi of Bacherach.

There are other poems of these early years in which Heine
draws on his Jewish heritage or into which he introduces
Jewish figures. *To a Renegade*, prompted by Eduard Gans's
apostasy from Judaism, has already been discussed; but there is
also a poem called *Almansor*, written in 1825, three years after
the play of the same name, and ultimately reprinted, in the
Book of Songs (*Buch der Lieder*, 1827), just before *The
Pilgrimage to Kevlaar*, Heine's most reverent evocation of
Roman Catholic piety. He wanted to make sure, as a note to an
earlier reprint of this sequence pointed out explicitly,⁵⁸ that
Almansor would be taken as a *persona* adopted for the purposes
of a literary work and not as a spokesman for Heine himself.

The poem *Almansor*⁵⁹ begins with an evocation of the
splendours of Cordoba cathedral—a building that had once
been a mosque but is now dedicated to Christian worship.
Almansor ben Abdullah addresses the massive pillars of this
cathedral: since they, he tells them, bear the burden of the new
faith so patiently, he, weaker than they, must not agonize too
much over doing what the times would seem to demand.

Und sein Haupt, mit heiterm Antlitz,
Beugt Almansor ben Abdullah
Über den gezierten Taufstein
In dem Dome zu Corduva.

[And with a gay, serene countenance
Almansor ben Abdullah bends his head
over the ornamented baptismal font
in the cathedral of Cordoba.][60]

These lines end the first section of the tripartite poem on a note reminiscent of Heine's euphoric feeling, soon to be belied, that submitting to baptism was easier than having a tooth pulled.

The second section brings us the now 'Christian' knight, his hair still damp from the baptismal font, emerging from the cathedral and riding gaily through a beautiful countryside. He is shown as happy and at ease:

Dorten jagt der lustge Ritter,
Pfeift und singt, und lacht behaglich,
Und es stimmen ein die Vögel
Und des Stromes laute Wasser.

[There the joyous knight courses along,
whistles, sings, and laughs at his ease,
and the birds join in,
and so do the stream's purling waters.]

The goal of this happy journey is a festive castle where Clara de Alvarez is living it up during her father's absence in the wars. Almansor joins the gay throng of dancing knights and ladies, murmuring sweetly flattering words to one lady after another, and proudly pointing to the golden crosses embroidered on his coat:

Er versichert jeder Dame:
Daß er sie im Herzen trage;
Und 'so wahr ich Christ bin!' schwört er
Dreißigmal an jenem Abend.

[He assures each lady
that he bears her in his heart;
and he swears 'as sure as I am a Christian'
some thirty times that evening.]

The third and last section of the poem then shows the festivities over, the guests departed, and the lamp throwing its fitful light on Almansor, his post-baptismal euphoria gone, resting his head in Doña Clara's lap. From a golden flagon the lady pours attar of roses on Almansor's head and kisses it gently while her tears flow. The lips of the now sleeping Almansor twitch and curl as he dreams

> er stehe wieder
> Tief das Haupt gebeugt und triefend
> In dem Dome zu Corduva,
> Und er hört viel dunkle Stimmen.
>
> All die hohen Riesensäulen
> Hört er murmeln unmutgrimmig,
> Länger wollen sies nicht tragen,
> Und sie wanken und sie zittern;—
>
> Und sie brechen wild zusammen,
> Es erbleichen Volk und Priester,
> Krachend stürzt herab die Kuppel,
> Und die Christengötter wimmern.

> [. . . he is standing once more,
> his head bowed and dripping,
> in Cordoba cathedral,
> and he hears many low voices.
>
> He hears the lofty gigantic pillars
> murmur with anger and rage;
> They want to bear it no longer!
> They stir, they shiver,
>
> and they break in wild confusion.
> The people and the priests grow pale,
> The dome crashes down,
> and the Christian gods whimper.]

The psychological pattern of this poem, which ends with a bang *and* a whimper, is in no way invalidated or obscured by Heine's denial that he is here speaking *pro domo*. Its central character is clearly a man without deep conscious commitment to the religion he is abandoning. He therefore thinks conversion an easy matter. 'I must bow to the time', he says to himself, 'as those who are stronger than I have also done.' The first results seem to prove him right. Happily and gaily he takes his place among Christian knights and ladies; he flaunts his new status, and swears by it constantly. Here, however, the first discordant note may be heard. When, on the very day of his baptism, he asks Isabella, Elvira, Leonora, and the rest in turn to accept his word *as a true Christian* as guarantee that *each* of them is the lady of his heart, we may well feel that both the Christianity and the affection are shown in a very dubious light. Then comes the reaction: gaiety and overbold wooing are followed by sadness and melancholy as tears and attar of roses fall on the head that had bowed over the font. And most important of all—what had been lightly accepted in waking life is felt as nightmarish humiliation in the subconscious mind, or the soul, that speaks in our dreams. In these dark dreams of abasement and revenge the very pillars that Almansor had cited as examples of submission are seen to rebel. They take upon themselves the task once assumed by the biblical Samson and crash about the heads of their new masters.

The poem *Almansor* seems to me the most complete depiction, in all Heine's published work, of the hopes he had placed in baptism and the traumatic shock it had unexpectedly turned out to be.

(v)

The poems considered in the preceding section have already brought us into the orbit of *The Rabbi of Bacherach*, a historical novel set in the fifteenth century for which Heine collected material in the early 1820s. He excerpted books on Jewish history, and consulted fellow members of the Society for the Culture and Science of the Jews on details of history, ritual, and folklore. Some of his excerpts from such historians as Schudt, Basnage, and Mignet have been preserved.[61] Above all, however, Heine could not embark on a historical novel in the 1820s without following in the footsteps of Sir Walter Scott, to whose *Waverley* he was to attribute, twenty years later, a formal perfection that was at the same time unsurpassable and fruitful:

While entertaining the crude masses with material that is bound to interest them, the novel delights educated readers by means of a formal construction whose inimitable simplicity Scott yet unfolds in the richest way imaginable . . .

We know that Heine read *Ivanhoe* in 1821 and may surmise that this reading was still fresh in his mind when he began his own tale of the sorrows and joys of the Jews in late medieval times. His principal female character continued that tradition of sympathetic Jewesses which Scott had so notably furthered; but for the rabbi himself, for the sympathetic male Jew, he would have to look elsewhere. He began his work in earnest, with high hopes, in 1824; in the following year, however, with only the first chapter completed, it ran aground, and was put aside for later continuation. The story of that continuation, and of the circumstances which led Heine to publish his still fragmentary tale, will be told in Chapter 8 below; but the first section, as we now have it, belongs essentially to the 1820s and must therefore be considered here.

Ivanhoe seems to have provided the model for Heine's opening paragraphs. Beginning with a description of the Rhine landscape and the change it undergoes around the town of Bacharach, he conducts the reader into the town as he knew it in his own time and thence into the much more lively bustle of the same time in the Middle Ages. (Heine always writes Bacherach; I have left that spelling in the title of his novel-fragment, but adopt the more usual spelling Bacharach elsewhere.) From this opening description the reader moves to a general survey of the conditions under which German Jews lived in medieval times, and to a vivid evocation of the ring of popular hatred which surrounded medieval Jews, who were accused of poisoning wells, desecrating the host, and slaughtering Christian children in order to use their blood for festival rituals.

On their feast-day the Jews, already sufficiently hated because of their faith, their wealth, and their lists of debtors, were wholly in the hands of their enemies, who could all too easily work their destruction by spreading the rumour that a child had been murdered for the purpose described, or perhaps even by smuggling the bloody corpse of an infant into the house of one of these outlawed Jews and then falling upon his praying family during the night. A riot of murder, pillage, and forcible baptism would follow, the dead infant found in the Jew's house would work great miracles, and would even, perhaps, be canonized by the Church.[63]

The narrator, whose tone and mode of expression leaves no doubt throughout this long expository passage that his sympathies are on the Jewish side, then tells us that St. Werner was a saint of this kind and that an abbey was built in his honour which has now become one of the most beautiful ruins to be seen on the Rhine, whose Gothic glory delights us 'when we sail past on some happy green summer's day *and do not know its origins.*' (my italics.) Other churches were also built to St. Werner in the thirteenth century—one of them at Bacharach; their inauguration was marked by the slaughter or maltreatment of innumerable Jews. For two hundred years after that, however, the Jewish community of Bacharach was spared such extreme accesses of popular rage, though they were still besieged by enmity and threats.

We have now been given the physical setting within which, and the historical background against which, Heine's story of fifteenth-century Jewish life is to be told. From the ring of hatred around the Jews, whose manifestations and whose economic base we have been taught to recognize, we are ready to move in upon the Jewish community in one German town and on one small family group in its midst.

The more [the Jews of Bacharach] were pressed by hatred from outside, the more close and comforting became their home life, the more deep-rooted became their piety and fear of God. The Rabbi of Bacharach was the very model of a man who walked in the way of the Lord; his name was Rabbi Abraham, he was still young, but the fame of his learning was spread far and wide.[64]

The portrait of the rabbi that now follows traces his origin in a family of poor scholars, and tells us of the wealth he acquired by betrothing himself—for love, in an impetuous betrothal scene in which Heine somewhat misrepresents Jewish custom and law—to the beautiful Sarah, daughter of a dealer in precious stones, of his years of study in Spain, where he came into contact with the highest manifestations of Jewish culture, and of his return from there as a man at once learned, cultured, and confirmed in his faith.

The rabbi's way of life since his return from Spain had been exceedingly pure, pious, and serious. With meticulous scruple he practised even the most petty customs enjoined by the Jewish faith. He went without food every Monday and Thursday, ate meat and drank wine only on the sabbath or other festivals. His days were spent in prayer and study; during the day he expounded the divine law in the circle of the pupils his fame had attracted to Bacharach, and by night he gazed at the stars or into the eyes of his beautiful Sarah. The rabbi's marriage had remained childless; but there was no lack of life and bustle around him . . .[65]

This portrait of a passionate nature subduing itself by ascetic practices and strict devotion to duty is followed by a description of the 'life and bustle' that could be discerned in the rabbi's childless house. It evokes powerfully the activities of a spiritual leader who lives close by the synagogue, teaches there and at home, keeps open house, and practises the virtue of charity.

The narrator who tells us all this is not content with giving us observable facts; he also retails rumours, and for this purpose introduces a chorus of male gossips whom he calls *die Fuchsbärte*, the men with foxy beards. These insinuate that the rabbi married for money rather than for love, and that his sojourn in Spain led him to activities and thoughts more fit for Christians than medieval Jews. The narrator discounts such rumours and suggests that even the owners of these foxy beards spread them more for the love of *médisance* than for any genuine belief in their truth and substance.

Having thus conveyed something of the atmosphere of the rabbi's house and his community, having flashed a suggestion of Sephardic Spain into his Ashkenazic tale, having suggested a biblical *figura* and a symbolic dimension by naming his protagonists *Abraham* and *Sarah*, Heine has his narrative voice launch into a description of the Passover festival which is rightly regarded as one of the high points of his work. From this description the Gentile reader will gain an admirable introduction to the *Seder*, the service celebrated in the home, with its ritual objects and foods, its prayers, its stories, its lived detail (the family *Haggadah*, the book of prayers and songs, has ancient wine stains on it from previous *Sedarim*). The illustrations of the *Haggadah* afford Heine the opportunity to introduce Old Testament figures into his medieval narrative, with an affectionate irony that is far removed from the bitter irony so characteristic of his tone elsewhere. We are shown these boldly-drawn and colourful pictures from the perspective of the rabbi's wife, who remembers how she loved to study them when the family *Haggadah* was brought out for the *Sedarim* of her childhood.

They depicted all sorts of Bible stories, such as Abraham smashing his stone idols with a hammer; the angels visiting him; Moses slaying the *Mitzri* [Egyptian]; Pharaoh sitting on the throne in all his splendour; the frogs won't leave him alone even when he is eating; he is drowned, thank God; the children of Israel step carefully into the Red Sea; they stand before Mount Sinai, open-mouthed, with their sheep, cows, and oxen; the pious King David plays his harp; and at last—here is Jerusalem with the towers and battlements of its temple bathed in the light of the sun!

Sarah's brief lament at her childless state gives the poet an opportunity to focus on one of the scenes in this list:

The rabbi did not reply, but merely pointed to a picture on which the *Haggadah* happened to be open at that moment: a most charming depiction of the three angels coming to Abraham in order to announce that a son will be born to him by his wife Sarah who meanwhile, with female slyness, stands behind the entrance to the tent in order to hear what the angels and her husband might be talking about.

Later on in the story, when Sarah follows her husband on his precipitate flight, these loved illustrations will take on the tonality of her fear:

It was as if the Rhine were murmuring the melodies of the *Haggadah*, and its pictures arose from the waters, large as life and distorted into crazy images: the patriarch Abraham smashes the idols, only to find them growing whole again; the *Mitzri* puts up a terrible fight against the enraged Moses; Mount Sinai belches forth lightning and flames; King Pharaoh swims about in the Red Sea, holding his crenellated crown between his teeth; frogs with human faces swim after him as the waves foam and roar, and a dark gigantic hand rises out of their midst.[66]

Such grotesque images of fear are alien, however, to the 'melancholy gaiety, serious playfulness, and fairy-tale mystery' which Heine detects in the *Seder*, where 'the traditional chanting of the *Haggadah* by the head of the household, with occasional choral support from the assembled company, makes an appeal so eerie and so inward, so motherly in its lullaby effects and then, suddenly, so rousing, that even Jews who have deserted the faith of their fathers and have gone running after alien joys and honours are stirred to the very depths when, by chance, the old familiar Passover sounds reach their ears.' It will not have escaped the reader's notice that the Jews who have 'gone running after alien joys and honours' are likely to belong to a later period than the medieval one here evoked, and that the celebration of the *Seder*, which has remained essentially unchanged for many centuries, constitutes a link between the period Heine describes and that in which he and his first readers lived.

Nor is the Passover the only festival celebrated in Jewish homes whose atmosphere *The Rabbi of Bacherach* attempts to capture and reproduce. There is the sabbath too, whose loving evocation in this fragmentary novel reminds one of the atmosphere and furnishings of Moritz Kaufmann's genre paintings of nineteenth-century Jewish life rather than the fifteenth century in which the story is set. Sarah recalls how she would sit, on the Jewish sabbath,

on the little stool in front of the velvet armchair reserved for her father, who stroked her long hair with his soft hand and comfortably rocked to and fro in his voluminous dressing-gown of blue silk . . . The flowered cloth had been spread over the table, all household appurtenances had been washed and polished till they shone like mirrors, the white-bearded beadle of the Jewish community sat next to her father, chewed raisins, and talked in Hebrew, and little Abraham came in lugging a huge tome and modestly asked his uncle for permission to expound a paragraph of Holy Scripture . . .

Here we have a flashback to Rabbi Abraham's boyhood, marked, like that of so many Jewish children, by a precocious ability to discourse learnedly on the Old Testament and its traditional commentaries, an ability which gives Heine the opportunity to introduce another set of biblical characters which may serve as *figurae* for the characters of his tale.

The little fellow laid the book on the broad armrest of the easy chair, and expounded the story of Jacob and Rachel: how Jacob had lifted up his voice and wept aloud, when he first saw his little cousin Rachel, how he talked to her so familiarly at the well, how he had to serve for her during seven years, how quickly these years sped by for him, how he married Rachel and loved her for ever and ever . . .

The festival of Tabernacles, *Succoth*, also figures in these reminiscences. Sarah sees in her mind's eye

how she and her little cousin who had now grown so big and had become her husband, played in the leafy tabernacle [*Succah, Lauberhütte*] when they were children, how they enjoyed themselves there, looking at coloured tapestries, flowers, mirrors, and gilded apples, how little Abraham was always tender with her until gradually he grew older and more severe, and was at last grown up and very severe indeed . . .[67]

Such severity is lightened, however, during the festival of Passover with whose memorable evocation *The Rabbi of Bacherach* opens.

Heine's detailed description of the domestic Passover service affords him a welcome opportunity to let his narrative voice praise the beauty, not only of Sarah, but of other Jewish women like her.

Her face was touchingly beautiful, and the beauty of Jewish women is generally of a peculiarly touching kind. Their consciousness of the profound misery, the bitter disgrace, and the dire perils, in which their relatives and friends have to live, suffuses their lovely features with a certain inward suffering, and an anxiously watchful affection, that cast a strange spell over our hearts.[68]

Heine seems well on the way here to doing for the Jewish people what Scott did for the Scottish and English peoples, and, incidentlly, providing a counterweight, with his dignified rabbi, to Scott's portrayal of Isaac of York, who, in Scott's own words, 'perhaps owing to . . . hatred and persecution, had adopted a national character in which there was much, to say the least, mean and unamiable' (*Ivanhoe*, Chapter 5). While the rabbi's wife may be seen, at least in intention, as a more matronly version of Scott's Rebecca, Rabbi Abraham is consciously presented as everything that Isaac of York is not: cultivated, brave, dignified, humorous, and tolerant even towards Jews who leave the fold of traditional Jewish pieties. As a German rabbi who has spent years of study in a Spain where Jewish culture and Jewish poetry were then at their highest point of development, he represents, or is meant to represent, a fusion of all that is best in the *Ashkenazic* and the *Sephardic* traditions.

Throughout this chapter of *The Rabbi of Bacherach*, the narrator's perspective is close to that of his Jewish characters: and from their point of view, in particular from that of Sarah, we now see the entry of two strangers. These 'tall pale men muffled in very wide cloaks' declare themselves travelling co-religionists who want to accept the invitation extended to all such strangers by the time-hallowed formula recorded in the *Haggadah*: 'Come and celebrate Passover with us.' They are welcomed, and the rabbi continues his reading and commentary. At one point, as we have seen, he comforts his as yet childless wife by pointing to a picture of the biblical Sarah hiding behind a tent-flap as she listens to the annunciation that a son will be born to her and her husband, the Patriarch Abraham. Soon afterwards, however, we watch, from the perspective of the rabbi's wife, a sudden, terrifying alteration. The rabbi's face appears distorted with horror, but only for a moment; he regains mastery over himself, and allows the serene joyfulness he had shown so far to shade over into hilarity, indulging in pranks that make the rest of the company laugh but inspire in Sarah, who knows her husband better, anxiety and fear. When the ceremony is interrupted for the ritual handwashing before the evening meal, the rabbi signals to his wife to follow him; he drags her out of the house and through the dark town until they reach the road along the Rhine which leads to Bingen. There, in the eerie moonlight, the rabbi climbs on to a jutting rock and casts into the waters the silver hand basin his terrified wife had still been holding in her hand. With a cry of 'Shaddai full of mercy!' Sarah sinks at her husband's feet and asks him to solve the sinister riddle of his unusual behaviour.

It now transpires that the strangers who had entered the family circle were enemies who had smuggled a dead child under the rabbi's table in order to accuse him of ritual murder. Having discovered this plot after looking beneath the table-cloth, the rabbi had concealed his knowledge under a hideous forced gaiety. His uncanny joking and clowning at this point relates to the much-discussed theme of 'masks', of appearance deliberately assumed to disguise reality, in Heine's work, and indicates something of the tragic background which so often offsets the foreground frivolity of Jewish humour. Under the cover of such gaiety the intended victim escapes his persecutors. 'Cunning has saved us,' the rabbi now tells his wife; 'praised be the Lord'. As for their friends and relatives, he continues, she need have no fear; the wicked accusers only thirsted after his, the rabbi's, blood, and they would content themselves, once they found he had escaped, with seizing his goods and chattels. 'Come with me, beautiful Sarah, to another land; we will leave misfortune behind, and so that misfortune should not pursue us, I have cast into the waves my last possession, the silver basin, as atonement. The God of our fathers will not desert us.'[69]

Heine has here begun to interweave, with the Jewish folklore he so convincingly introduced into the earlier portions of his story, ceremonies and legends from other sources. There are no Jewish precedents for the rabbi's sacrifice of the silver basin; such appeasement of the gods belongs to ancient Greece rather than Judaea, the world of Polycrates rather than that of Father Abraham. In the passage that follows, which shows Sarah being rowed to safety by the rabbi with the help of a fair-haired deaf-and-dumb boy known as *der stille Wilhelm*, German legends of the Rhine merge, in Sarah's imagination, with tales and pictures from the Passover *Haggadah*. Throughout this concluding passage of the opening chapter of *The Rabbi of Bacherach* the location of the centre of consciousness in the tired and frightened Sarah enables Heine to introduce flashbacks to earlier incidents in the life of his two protagonists: the sabbaths of their childhood, a *Sukkoth* celebration, their irregular betrothal, young Abraham's departure for his rabbinical studies, the anger of Sarah's father at his daughter's betrothal without his consent, and that father's prophecy, before his death, that after the rabbi's seven years of study the young couple's union would be followed by seven years of beggary. A nightmare sequence follows, in which the Rhine seems to murmur *Haggadah* melodies and throw up dreadful visions, partly inspired by the *Haggadah*'s pictures and stories; but then, as Sarah murmurs a Jewish night prayer whose half-remembered wording haunted Heine all his life ('ten thousand at his right, ten thousand at his left, to protect the king against the terrors of night'),[70] another *Haggadah* image suddenly puts the nightmare vision to flight. Sarah sees Jerusalem miraculously restored to its ancient glory, its splendid forecourts and chambers peopled by her long-dead father and by the friends and relatives of whose safety her husband had sought to assure her; King David kneels in the Holy of Holies in his purple cloak and glittering crown, chanting his psalms and accompanying himself on some stringed instrument; and with a smile Sarah sinks at last into sleep.[71]

On this comforting note the opening chapter of *The Rabbi of Bacherach* ends. Heine had completed it by 1825 and then left it among his papers. We do not learn on what information the rabbi bases his confident prediction to Sarah that the family and congregation they had abandoned in Bacharach would not be touched by their persecutors; but the prophecy of Sarah's father that the couple would have to beg their way through life for seven years may be seen as foreshadowing some kind of punishment for the rabbi's desertion of his post. There is clearly a meaningful relation between the exodus into freedom celebrated by the Passover ceremonies and the flight from persecution into the unknown that ends a chapter in which these ceremonies had been so memorably described. This becomes particularly clear when the chapter culminates in a smiling vision of that Jerusalem for whose restoration Jewish prayers of the Diaspora so fervently plead. We take our first leave of the rabbi and his wife on a note of exaltation and hope after nightmare terrors.

The opening chapter of *The Rabbi of Bacherach* seems to me one Heine's finest works. The periodic but never cumbersome style he here adopts shows itself admirably suited throughout to its varying narrative functions. The point of view from which his narrative voice tells its story, sometimes alongside his Jewish characters, sometimes within Sarah's consciousness, conveys directly to the reader the Jewish community's enclosure within a richly satisfying family and religious life and its sense of being menaced by shadowy representatives of a hostile outside world. The poet shows Jewish folklore in the process of assimilating the folklore of this outside world with which some contact was inevitable. This chapter can be read by Christian readers as an admirable introduction to traditional Jewish life which is not seriously impaired by a few inaccuracies and anachronisms, and by Jewish readers as a confirmation of traditional Jewish values threatened by the assimilation movements of a later age. The uneasiness caused by the rabbi's desertion of his flock is somewhat assuaged by our hope that he will turn out to be right in his prediction that his community will be safe—particularly if we remember that the story is set in the fifteenth century, and that history does not record a massacre of the Jews of Bacharach at that period. The massacre mentioned in a passage from Schudt's *Jewish Memorabilia (Jüdische Merkwürdigkeiten)* from which Heine took excerpts belongs to an earlier age. Nevertheless, the spectacle of the captain deserting his ship is a disquieting one; and most readers will look beyond the hopeful mood of the chapter's ending to see the rabbi visited by some sort of punishment—perhaps that foretold by Sarah's father for a different and less heinous offence. Here Heine had to face a problem for which a solution would have to be found if his novel was ever to be brought to an artistically and morally satisfying conclusion. How he tackled this task, will be seen below, in Chapter 8.

Heine did a great deal of reading for *The Rabbi of Bacherach*, and some of his notes on this have been preserved. In these notes and excerpts he laid stress on the problem of renegades—Jews who abandoned their Judaism and not infrequently turned against their erstwhile co-religionists.[72] The poet was clearly weighing the implication of his own baptism. At the same time the tenor of these excerpts suggests that the confrontation of orthodox rabbi and de-Judaized Jew, which we shall observe in the much later Chapter 3 of the *Rabbi* fragment, was planned from the beginning, and that there was to be further elaboration of the themes broached in *Almansor* and *Donna Clara*. Indeed, the rabbi's abandonment of his congregation makes him a renegade too, though in a different sense from those who abjured the Jewish religion by submitting to baptism. And at this point we must remind ourselves that the poem *Donna Clara*, as we now have it, is also a fragment; that Heine thought of elaborating it, as we have seen, into a tragic trilogy in whose final part the son of a Jewish father, brought up as a Christian, becomes the persecutor and torturer of his Jewish brothers. Heine's Jewish Comedy could hardly be deemed complete without the spectacle of Jewish anti-Semitism and self-hatred.

(vi)

While the chapter of *The Rabbi of Bacherach* which has just been examined was not published until the 1840s, the play *Almansor* appeared in print in 1823, when it joined another play (*William Ratcliff*) and a cycle of poems in a volume entitled *Tragedies; with a Lyrical Intermezzo* (*Tragödien nebst einem lyrischen Intermezzo von H. Heine*). In so far as the love-plaint of the 'lyrical intermezzo' has any roots in the poet's personal experience, a Jewish girl (his cousin Amalia) would seem to be involved; and one may, I suppose, attach some biographical significance to the poem in which a Northern pine tree yearns for an Eastern palm (*Lyr. Int.* 33)—but none of this has any overt Jewish colouration, nor could one find in it any such thinly-veiled, easily detectable allegories of the Jewish condition as we have traced in *Almansor*. The poem *To a Singer* (*An eine Sängerin*) which had appeared in his first collection (*Gedichte*, 1822), and the sonnets to his mother in that same volume, had also given no indication that the persons celebrated were in fact Jewish.[73] As a lyric poet Heine chooses to address his growing public, for the most part, with the voice of Edom rather than that of Israel.

CHAPTER 2
The 5,588 Years' War

(i)

In 1826 Heine published the first volume of a collection of writings in which he made full literary use of the journalistic experience he had gained while composing his *Letters from Berlin* and *On Poland*. The title he chose for this collection was *Reisebilder* (*Pictures of Travel*), and he opened the volume with an account of a journey, on foot, from the university town of Göttingen, where he had matriculated as a law student, to the Brocken mountain, famous for its view and its witches. *The Hartz Journey* or *Journey to the Hartz Mountains* (*Die Harzreise*), a carefully composed mosaic of things seen and heard, dreams, and reflections, presented, for the most part, in a humorous vein, reminds us that Heine had received his early education in a school whose very buildings spoke of the Christian world in which he grew up. It does so in a passage which describes the narrator of *The Hartz Journey* watching some children as they stream out of school.

These charming little boys, nearly all of whom were red-cheeked, blue-eyed, and flaxen-haired, jumped about and shouted jubilantly, awakening in me the memory, wistful and cheerful at once, of myself as a little chap who had to sit all through the long morning on wooden benches from which I was not allowed to rise, in the dark Catholic monastery school in Düsseldorf. I had to endure such a deal of Latin, beating, and geography there! I too used to cheer and rejoice beyond measure when the old Franciscan bell struck twelve at long last. The children saw by my knapsack that I was a stranger and greeted me most hospitably. One of the boys told me that they had just had Religious Instruction, and he showed me the Royal Hanoverian Catechism that was used to test them in Christianity. The little book was very badly printed; this meant, I fear, that from the first the doctrines of their faith were likely to make an unpleasing, blotting-paper-like impression on the children's minds. I was also shocked to find the multiplication tables, which conflict so dangerously with the doctrine of the Holy Trinity, printed between the same covers as the catechism, on the last page of the book. This could easily mislead these children into sinful doubts. We do these things more intelligently in Prussia; in our zeal to convert the people who understand arithmetic so well we take good care never to print the multiplication tables after the catechism.[1]

Here Heine confronts the doctrine of the Trinity with Jews whose training in the counting-house might be thought to predispose them to look on such doctrines in a sceptical manner that boded ill for the success of that Society for the Conversion of the Jews whose missionary fervour in Prussia Heine ridiculed on more than one occasion. It becomes clear that the narrator of *The Hartz Journey* is himself little inclined to subscribe to Christian dogma in its orthodox form—a well-known later passage of the work will, in fact, offer a reinterpretation that transforms the Holy Ghost into the spirit of social and political liberation:

> Dieser tat die größten Wunder,
> Und viel größre tut er noch;
> Er zerbrach die Zwingherrnburgen
> Und zerbrach des Knechtes Joch.
>
> Alte Todeswunden heilt er,
> Und erneut das alte Recht:
> Alle Menschen, gleichgeboren,
> Sind ein adliges Geschlecht.
>
> Er verscheucht die bösen Nebel,
> Und das dunkle Hirngespinst,
> Das uns Lieb und Lust verleidet,
> Tag und Nacht uns angegrinst.
>
> [This performed the greatest wonders,
> and will perform even greater miracles;
> it broke down the despots' castles.
> and smashed the yoke of servitude.
>
> It heals old wounds that once were mortal,
> and renews man's ancient right:
> all men are born equal,
> they all belong to a noble race.

It drives away the mists of evil,
and the dark phantasm
which spoilt our love and our happiness,
grinning at us by night and day.]²

Only in this form can the narrator of *The Hartz Journey* subscribe to the doctrine of the Trinity—but in this form he can adopt it enthusiastically enough to present himself as a Knight of the Holy Ghost. So presented, the notion of the Holy Ghost will also do some good, we may suppose, to the sceptical Jews who frustrate the efforts of the Society dedicated to their conversion by professing themselves unable to reconcile the doctrine of the Trinity with the laws of arithmetic. One need hardly stress that Catholic theologians like Ignaz Döllinger were less than delighted by Heine's reinterpretation of one of the central doctrines of the Christian faith.³

The Jewish stereotype lightly evoked in the reference to 'people who understand arithmetic so well' is given further definition a paragraph later, when the narrator tells of a visit to some refining works that process silver, and to a mint in which the silver so processed is transformed into coin of the realm. The passage turns on an untranslatable pun: *Silberblick* means both 'glint of silver' and 'financial good luck'.

As so often in life, I missed the *Silberblick* when I visited the refinery. I was luckier, however, in the mint, and was able to see how money is made. But alas—that's as far as I ever got. My part on such occasions has always been that of a mere onlooker; I truly believe that if ever thaler were to rain from the sky all I would come away with would be a hole in the head, while the Children of Israel would merrily gather up the silver manna.⁴

The 'manna' image from the Book of Exodus, humorously appropriate here, is complemented towards the end of this same paragraph by an image from St. Luke: the narrator describes his vision of silver coins coming to rest in Abraham's bosom (*im Schoße Abrahams*). The Jewish stereotype here suggested by the conjunction of silver coinage with the name Abraham is then reinforced by another name from the Old Testament a few pages later, when the narrator mentions furniture 'which is of no interest to us because it is new, or because it belongs to Hans today and to Isaac tomorrow.'⁵ This passage, which sets property that has merely exchange value against things that take on value by being lived with for a long time, affords us a brief glimpse of the Jewish dealer in second-hand goods—a type through which many Germans gained their first contact with the Jews that lived amongst them.

Before it took its place in the first volume of *Pictures of Travel*, Heine's *Hartz Journey* had appeared, in somewhat shorter form, in a journal called *The Good Companion* (*Der Gesellschafter*). That earlier version, whose publication stretched over January and February 1826, had introduced an autobiographical note into the passage about the silver workings in Clausthal which the poet later found it prudent to delete. 'I just had to see', Heine had written, with his own uncle Salomon clearly in mind, 'how this metal grows and is processed—this magic-working metal of which an uncle often has too much and a nephew too little.' 'I soon found out,' he added, in words which Uncle Salomon would have cause to adapt to his nephew's case, 'that spending silver thalers is easier than hewing them out of mountains, smelting them, and minting them into coin.'⁶

The conjunction of Jews with the mathematical spirit necessary for success in the counting-house, and with materialist opposition to the more mystical parts of Christian doctrine, which has been so marked a feature of *The Hartz Journey* so far, comes to a head in a dream the narrator purports to have had in the city of Goslar. Heine's account of this dream plays, once again, on the complex meanings of the word *Geist* (at once spirit, reasoning faculty, and spectre) in order to introduce a portrait-caricature of Dr Saul Ascher, a Berlin bookseller recently deceased, many of whose writings have been recognized in our own day as distinctive and important contributions to the self-definition of German Jewry in the early nineteenth century.⁷ Among Germans he was notorious as a resolute opponent of Romantic Teutomania—his *Germanomanie* (1815) was one of the books burnt by patriotic youths at the Wartburg Festival of 1817, with solemn imprecations against the Jews: 'Woe upon the Jews that cleave to their Judaism and defame our German nationhood (*unser*

Volkstum und Deutschtum)!' Ascher's work on Christianity to which we shall hear Heine's narrator refer was published two years after the Wartburg Festival under the title *Some Opinions on the Future of Christianity (Ansichten von dem zukünftigen Schicksale des Christentums)*.

'Reason is the highest principle,' I said soothingly to myself as I slipped into bed. But it availed me nothing. I had just been reading in Varnhagen von Ense's *German Tales*, which I had brought with me from Clausthal, that terrible tale of a son who is about to be murdered by his own father and is warned in the night by the ghost of the mother. The vivid way in which this story is told caused a cold shudder of horror to go through all my veins while I was reading it. Ghost stories thrill us with additional terrors when we read them on a journey, especially at night, in a city, a house, a room where we have never been before. Involuntarily we think: How many terrible things may have happened on this very spot? To make matters worse, the moon shone into the room in a doubtful, suspicious-making way, all sorts of uncalled for shadows quivered on the walls, and when I sat up in bed to find out what was happening, I saw—

There is nothing more uncanny than catching sight of one's own face by moonlight in a mirror. At the same instant a clumsy, yawning bell struck so slowly, and in so long drawn out a manner, that I firmly believed it had been striking for twelve long hours, and that it was now time to begin all over again. Between the penultimate and the last stroke another bell chimed in, very rapidly, with an almost scolding shrillness, annoyed perhaps by the slowness of its friend. As the two iron tongues fell silent, and deathlike stillness pervaded the house, I suddenly seemed to hear, in the corridor outside my room, a hesitant dragging of feet, like the unsteady steps of an old man. At last the door opened, and there entered, slowly, the late Dr Saul Ascher. A cold fever shook my bones, I trembled like an aspen leaf, I hardly dared look at the ghost. He appeared much as he had done in life: the same transcendentally grey frock-coat, the same abstract legs, and the same mathematical face; the latter was a little more yellow than usual, and the mouth, which formerly described an angle of $22\frac{1}{2}$ degrees, was pinched together, while the circles around the eyes had a larger radius. Tottering, and supporting himself on his malacca cane as usual, he said courteously, in his customary drawling manner of speech: 'Do not be afraid, and do not believe that I am a ghost. Your imagination is playing you a trick if you think that you are seeing me as a ghost. What is a ghost? Can you give me a definition? Can you deduce for me the conditions under which a ghost would be possible?

What reasonable connection could such an apparition have with Reason itself? Reason, I say, Reason . . .' And now the ghost proceeded to an analysis of Reason, citing Kant's *Critique of Pure Reason*, Part II, Section 1, Book 2, chapter 3, on the distinction between phenomena and noumena, and then proceeded to construct a hypothetical system for the belief in ghosts, piling one syllogism on top of the other and concluding with the logical demonstration that the existence of ghosts is absolutely impossible. Meanwhile the cold sweat ran down my back, my teeth chattered like castanets, and from the very depths of dread I nodded unconditional assent to every proposition by means of which the spectral doctor proved the absurdity of fearing ghosts. He was so absorbed in his demonstration that at one time, in a moment of abstraction, he drew a handful of worms out of his waistcoat pocket instead of his gold watch; noticing his error he thrust them back again with comically anxious haste. 'Reason is the highest . . .' Here the clock struck one, and the ghost vanished.[8]

What a splendid invention! Heine's sceptical ghost (whose Jewishness is proclaimed by his name) demonstrates his own impossibility by quoting from a philosopher whose dealings with the question of spectres, in *Dreams of a Ghost-Seer*, had included much more hedging of bets than those here attributed to Dr Ascher. The latter's way of suppressing the evidence of the grave-worms he pulls out of his pocket instead of his watch is one of Heine's happiest conceits. For its full effect, however, the vision of Saul Ascher's ghost depends on the description of the living Ascher that precedes it in *The Hartz Journey*.

What is fear? Does it stem from reason or from the imaginative faculties? This was a problem I often disputed with Dr Saul Ascher when we accidentally came across one another in the Café Royal of Berlin where for quite a long period I used to take my midday meal. He always maintained that we feared things which reasonable proof taught us to recognize as fear-inspiring. Only Reason was an active power in man—not the imaginative sensibility [*Gemüt*]. While I ate and drank to my heart's content, the doctor constantly demonstrated to me the advantages of Reason. Towards the end of his demonstration he would frequently look at his watch, and he always concluded with the sentence: 'Reason is the highest principle!' I still see him before me, this Dr Ascher, with his abstract legs, his tight, transcendentally grey frock-coat, and his stark, freezingly-cold face, a face that would have served very well as frontispiece to a geometry textbook. This man, well into his fifties, was a personified straight line. In his striving for the positive the poor man had philosophized everything beautiful out of his life—all sunshine, all faith, and all flowers, until nothing remained to him but the cold, positive grave. He had a particular grudge against the Belvedere Apollo and Christianity. Against the latter he even wrote a pamphlet, demonstrating that it was unreasonable and untenable. Altogether he wrote a whole pile of books, in all of which Reason boasted of her excellence. The poor doctor meant every word he said in full earnest, and to that extent he deserved our respect. The great joke, however, was precisely this: that he pulled such an earnestly foolish face when he showed himself incapable of understanding what every child understands just because it is a child. I visited the reasonable doctor in his own house a few times, and found him in the company of pretty girls; for Reason does not prohibit sensuality. Once, however, when I called again, his servant told me that the 'Herr Doktor' had just died. I did not experience much more emotion at hearing that news than if he had said that the 'Herr Doktor' had just gone out.[9]

What Heine here evokes for his readers is the image of a Jew who eagerly embraces German philosophy (there were many Kantians among the Berlin Jews of Ascher's generation, just as there were to be many Hegelians in the generation that followed his) while rejecting the Christianity of the German Romantics along with the Apolline classicism of Winckelmann and the mature Goethe. The devotion to arithmetic with which the poet had credited Jews in earlier passages has now given way to a rationalism that transforms Ascher's very form into a geometrical shape. The reference to Ascher's relations with pretty females alludes to some gossip that had gone round Berlin—for the rest, however, the historical Ascher is reduced to just one facet of his complex character.[10] That facet—an unimaginative rationalism yoked to an admiration of Kant—is clearly what had impressed Heine most in the brief contacts he had with the man and his work; and in the true caricaturist's manner he therefore subordinated his whole presentation (including his description of Ascher's physical appearance) to bringing it out, before launching into the delightful fantasy already quoted.

From the first description of Ascher's appearance to his ghostly vanishing after 'demonstrating' the impossibility of ghosts, the reader is left in no doubt that Ascher is ridiculous, and that anyone so devoid of imagination, and so utterly unable to inspire affection in his acquaintances, is much to be pitied. By the very fantasy he weaves around him the author of *The Hartz Journey* demonstrates how far *he* is from the imaginative deficiencies he has diagnosed. And yet—is there not an element of self-caricature here? Had not Heine himself just written what some might well have called 'a book against Christianity'—a play and a poem, both called *Almansor*, which threw a lurid light on proselytizing Christendom and the ill effect that conversion could have on those newly recruited to the Christian Church? Had he not introduced jokes about the irreconcilability of orthodox Christian doctrine with the rules of mathematics into the very work in which Dr Ascher makes his unforgettable appearance? Did he not himself possess, as many of his works were to show, a rationalist, anti-Romantic streak? Was he not himself indebted to the Enlightenment, to that *Aufklärung* whose greatest representative in Germany, Lessing, had an incalculable influence on his work? The portrait of Saul Ascher, like that of Eduard Gans, is thus in part a caricature of tendencies within Heine himself.

Once we have realized that, we will not be in danger of overlooking one of the most striking aspects which the vision of Dr Ascher's ghost presents to the attentive reader. By carefully showing us that the narrator had just been reading a collection of ghost stories, by commenting on the disorientating effect of sleeping in a strange bed in a strange room in a strange town, by discoursing on the moonlight and the strange shadows it throws, on the narrator's fright when he suddenly catches sight of his own face in the mirror, on the sudden stillness after the two contrasting bells that had ushered in a midnight hour which popular superstition has given over to ghosts—by all this Heine signals to us that Dr Ascher is, in a way, right. There *are* no ghosts; or at least—the ghost of Dr Ascher never appeared to the narrator in the same sense in which, say, the children coming out of school appeared to him. He is a product of the narrator's imagination and ultimately, therefore, of Heine's ability to give imagined creatures life. It is this ability, and not the capacity of superstitiously believing in spectral apparitions, which ensures the narrator's, and Heine's, superiority over the dry, unimaginative creature to whom the name Saul Ascher is attached in *The Hartz Journey*. The historian is bound to point out that the real Ascher was a much more complex and a much more interesting figure than a reading of *The Hartz Journey* would suggest. But Heine makes no pretence of giving his readers a fully rounded portrait. What he offers instead is a brilliant caricature, heightening just one feature, and a symbolic representation of anti-Romantic tendencies in nineteenth-century intellectual life which Heine knew by introspection as well as by observation of others.

The caricature of Saul Ascher holds much else that is interesting and important in our context. The passage describing the ghostly vision at Goslar begins with words that have not yet been quoted:

> The night I spent at Goslar brought me a very strange adventure. I still cannot think back on it without fear. It is not that I am timid by nature—but of ghosts I am almost as afraid as the *Austrian Observer*.[11]

Why the *Austrian Observer* (*Österreichischer Beobachter*)? One reason should be obvious: Heine is suggesting that the fear of subversion behind officially inspired articles in this conservative journal derived from superstition. The editor's gloss in the Düsseldorf edition (*HAD* VI, 608) speaks of 'the ghosts of revolution'. But Heine's reference is more specific than that. In 1811 Saul Ascher had made himself (not for the first time!) *persona non grata* in Prussia by candid correspondences in various newspapers about Prussian financial policies. No. 201 of the *Austrian Observer* published an official *démenti* of one such correspondence with the following gloss:

> This article is the work of a completely misinformed Jewish correspondent who, one year ago, was taken to the State prison because of similar calumnies and, as has been proved, was regrettably discharged far too early.[12]

Heine had a retentive memory for glosses of this kind, glosses with an anti-Jewish bias, and he is subtly preparing the ground for Saul Ascher's spectral apparition by a reference to the paper that had attacked him.

Another detail appears only in the magazine version and not in the book version of *The Hartz Journey*. Saul Ascher, it will be recalled, is described in both versions as a personified straight line: 'and this', Heine had originally written, 'made him a contrast to me, who at that time lived in accordance with Hogarth's wavy line.' The serpentine line commended in Hogarth's *Analysis of Beauty* (1753) played a prominent part in the aesthetics of the day and is well fitted to convey the flexibility the narrator attributes to himself in contrast with the rigidity he finds in Ascher's mental life. The passage may, in addition, contain a private joke—for Eduard Gans had (if we can believe the testimony of Heine's first scholarly biographer, Adolf Strodtmann) used the Hogarthian term *Wellenlinie* to describe Jewish assimilation processes. The poet may well have decided to delete the reference to Hogarth because he felt that the point he wanted it to make was too private and obscure.

Dr Ascher is not the last of Heine's Jewish contemporaries to be caricatured in *The Hartz Journey*. Another unflattering portrait appears in a passage in which the narrator speaks of the close attention German theatre directors had recently been paying to the historical accuracy of costumes worn by actors in historical plays. Such accuracy, he assures his readers ironically, had become indispensable:

For if Mary Stuart were to wear an apron belonging to the time of Queen Anne, then Christian Gumpel the banker would rightly complain that such inaccuracy destroyed all illusion; and if it should happen that Lord Burleigh slipped, by mistake, into the hose of King Henry IV, then Frau von Steinzopf née Lilienthau, wife of an exalted official in the war ministry, would not take her eyes off this anachronism for the whole evening.[13]

Gumpel, here introduced for the first but by no means the last time into Heine's writings, was a Hamburg banker, a business rival of Heine's uncle Salomon, who seems to have relished jokes at Gumpel's expense. His first name was Lazarus, not Christian; Heine savours the incongruity of attaching the name 'Christian' to a Jewish businessman, and suggests at the same time that once rich German Jews became drawn into the scene of conspicuous cultural consumption, baptism—with its consequent change of name—will not be far away.

But here, of course, lies the real irony: it was not Lazarus Gumpel and his sons who left the Jewish fold and assumed the inappropriate name 'Christian'—it was the poet himself who did exactly that. On 28 June 1825 Harry or Heinrich Heine officially became Christian Johann Heinrich Heine. The last of these three given names he continued to use with reasonable frequency (though he preferred 'H. Heine' on the title pages of his books). The middle one he occasionally employed in fun, signing himself 'Hans'; Jeanette Wohl, before Heine became her enemy, also refers to him at times as 'der Hans' in her correspondence with Börne. The name 'Christian', however, he never used at all; he preferred to bestow it on one of his butts.

It should also be remembered that Uncle Salomon was himself a well-known patron of the Hamburg theatre; he often attended performances, and responded generously to appeals from local Thespians in need of financial support. The poet may therefore have been casting a sly side-glance at his uncle as well as that uncle's business rival when he made Gumpel an assiduous frequenter of playhouses. The satiric point of the passage is, of course, that such visits failed to provide an asthetic education: the money-making bourgeois, the poet would have us believe, responds only to the crudest stimuli. He is bound to fasten on externals—and it is no accident that these externals happen to be, in Gumpel's case, the way an actress is dressed. The sexual implications of this become even more obvious in what follows; for the anachronism that so fascinates Kriegsrätin von Steinzopf that she can't take her eyes off it turns out to be a male actor's tights. Again there has been a significant change of name—but this time it has not been caused by an act of baptism, although such an act will almost certainly have preceded it. Fräulein Lilienthau has married into the Prussian aristocracy, which Heine characterizes by the speaking name 'von Steinzopf'. *Zopf* is the pigtail worn in the old Prussian army and the word was frequently used, in Heine's day, to designate the age that had just passed away (*Zopfzeit*), while *Stein* suggests rigidity, petrification. 'Lilienthau', on the other hand, is a characteristic example of the names Jews took on when German laws required them to conform, in respect of first names and surnames, to the nomenclature customary in Western Europe. Henceforth Jews would have two names, a Hebrew one used in the synagogue and a German one used elsewhere—a symbol of a dual identity which Heine eagerly seized on. We have already heard him reminding Eduard Gans of his Jewish roots by calling him 'Dr Eli' immediately after his baptism. In later works he would show a continuation of this name-changing process; even the German name 'Hirsch', he suggests, came to sound too 'Jewish' and had to be replaced by something more 'classical'.

The brief glimpse Heine's *The Hartz Journey* allows us of German theatres and their patrons suggests that Jews were beginning to constitute a significant and visible part of the audience, and that Jewish women were beginning to marry into Christian families that included the Prussian aristocracy. The suggestion that the moral and aesthetic problems raised by the play being presented—Schiller's *Maria Stuart*—are the last things to interest Gumpel and Frau von Steinzopf satirizes the contemporary theatre public in general, not just its Jewish sector; but Heine's focusing on just these two figures does suggest that he considers recent arrivals in 'respectable' society to be in danger of becoming caricatures embodying the least admirable traits of that society.

All this while, it must be remembered, the word 'Jew' (*Jude* and its cognates) had not occured in *The Hartz Journey*. Heine had either suggested a Jewish context by speaking in Old Testament images modified to bring out their new symbolic content (the Children of Israel gathering up their *silver* manna) or had allowed what his contemporaries would have recognized as 'Jewish' names to do their work unaided (Saul Ascher, Lilienthau). Such reticence is abandoned, however, when Heine brings an anti-Semite on to his stage. In the *Brockenhaus*, a mountain hotel, the narrator finds himself sharing a room with a young businessman.

He hailed from Frankfurt am Main, and consequently he spoke at once of the Jews, declaring that they had lost all feeling for what is beautiful and noble, and that they sold English goods at 25 per cent under the manufacturers' prices.[14]

Here Heine is looking back on his own time as an *apprenti millionnaire* at Frankfurt and on his own family's commercial connections with England; and he uses these reminiscences to expose, with economy and wit, a mechanism of anti-Jewish prejudice that had, of necessity, been left out of *Donna Clara*. That poem, we recall, had portrayed religious, nationalistic, and biological/racial objections to Jews; here, in *The Hartz Journey*, we can watch envy of Jewish flair dress itself up as objection to cultural deficiencies, objection to the alleged 'atrophy' of such feelings as Jews may have had in remote biblical times for the beautiful and the noble. No one, Heine's context suggests, could be less qualified to pronounce on the beautiful and the noble than the Frankfurt businessman who levels such charges at his Jewish fellow citizens.

One characteristic detail must not go unnoticed. The businessman complains that the Jews are selling English goods at 25 per cent *under* the manufacturers' prices—a commercial paradox that caricatures brilliantly the kind of sales talk one can still hear from a certain kind of market cheapjack in our own day. Only stolen goods, or 'loss-leaders', or goods subsidized by an exporting country to a ruinous degree, could possibly be sold in the way the Frankfurt Jew-hater is here made to suggest. It will be the first of these possibilities, no doubt, which will be uppermost in the businessman's mind. Heine may therefore be attempting, in this passage, to conjure up what later ages learnt to know as the Fagin syndrome—the image of the Jew as receiver and dealer in stolen goods—which has proved so ineradicable from Gentile minds even in our own day and age.

The encounter with the Frankfurt Jew-hater holds no suggestion that we are to imagine the narrator of *The Hartz Journey* as being himself of Jewish birth. Before the work ends, however, Heine does introduce a passage that suggests, in symbolic fashion, how closely the narrator may be identified, in this respect, with the recently baptized author. This passage may be found at the climax of the narrator's account of how he ascended the Ilsenstein—a mountain-peak crowned with a cross made of iron.

My advice to anyone standing on the very top of the Ilsenstein is not to think of the Emperor and the Empire, nor of the beautiful Ilse, but only of his own feet. For as I stood there, lost in thought, I suddenly heard the subterranean music of the enchanted palace, and I saw the mountains all around stand themselves on their heads, and the red-tiled roofs of Ilsenburg began to dance, and the green trees flew about in the blue air until everything went green and blue before my eyes. Overcome by giddiness I would surely have plunged in the abyss if I had not, in my soul's dire need, clung fast to the iron cross. For doing this in the awkward position in which I found myself no one, surely, will blame me.[15]

Here Heine's narrator takes up again the theme of conversion and baptism lightly brushed in earlier portions of *The Hartz Journey*; but this time he does not stand outside as a mere observer, this time he is himself forced to cling to the cross by force of circumstances. The earlier version of the work from which I have already quoted introduces a significant variant here. Recounting his clinging to the cross, the narrator adds: 'No one, surely, will blame me for doing this, since I had such weighty reasons; *and up to this moment I have not regretted it.*'[16] (My italics.) The omission of the italicized phrase in the *Pictures of Travel* version may serve to suggest once again how deeply Heine came to regret a baptism of convenience which never did him any good.

The Hartz Journey makes a first parodistic use of a biblical image that was to turn up in Heine's later writings over and over again. Describing a man in green whom he had encountered at an inn, the narrator tells us that he looked 'as King Nebuchadnezzar did in his latter years, when, as the legend has it, he became like the beasts of the forest and ate nothing but salad.'[17] In the fullness of time Heine would see his own fate prefigured in that of Nebuchadnezzar and even sign a letter with that monarch's name.

The first of Heine's *Pictures of Travel* is also the first of his works which presents itself to the reader as a fragment. It is, however, perfectly balanced within itself; it has satisfactorily broached and developed a number of important themes; and its open-endedness is therefore partly an illusion, partly a deliberate stylistic device. The German Romantics, we must remember, had made a special feature of the *Fragment*; in this respect, as in so many others, Heine remained under the spell of Romanticism.

It does seem, however, as if Heine had thought, at one time, of writing a continuation of *The Hartz Journey*. In the sketches he made for that continuation he has his narrator tell the story of a fourth-century Jew who was believed to have found the true cross and who became bishop of Jerusalem after his conversion to Christianity. Heine adds:

Whoever does not believe me when I say that we owe the finding of the Cross and the concept of serving the cross to a Jew, may look the story up for himself . . . How much we owe to the Jews! I will not here mention that we owe Christianity itself to them, for up to now little use has been made of it. But the invention of bills of exchange, commercial premiums, and the Cross! Is not our deepest gratitude due to them? And yet—their German stepfatherland won't even allow them to become barristers or advocates in Prussia, as a change from dealing in cast-off trousers. Long live the Jew . . . Long live the Empress Helena! Long live the cross on the Ilsenstein![18]

Here Heine adds further touches to his portrait gallery of the Jewish community he knew: the ubiquitous old-clothes man alongside the intending barrister and civil servant thwarted by illiberal laws; the manipulators of premiums and bills of exchange (not, of course, actually *invented* by Jews as Heine claims here and elsewhere); and the long procession of men and women of Jewish origin who helped to found and shape the Christian religion and who—from the time of the Empress Helena (225–330) onwards—chose to abandon Judaism in the service of other nations and other gods.

Very soon after this, in the last of these fragments which he himself never actually published, Heine adds another tiny but characteristic touch. The narrator has been visiting some caves, one of which had been dubbed, by a humorous superintendent, 'the Jewish Temple' (*der Judentempel*). Heine seizes on this appellation with evident delight. On entering the cave, his narrator pretends to see 'petrified Jews' all around him, including 'one of special note': 'a sugar broker with a three-cornered hat and a reform face.'[19] The reference here is to the Temple Society (*Tempelverein*) which sought to reform Jewish religious rites in Berlin, Hamburg, and elsewhere, and which called its houses of worship 'temple' instead of 'synagogue'. Among the prominent members of the Hamburg branch there was indeed, as we have already seen, a sugar broker, Gustav Gerson Cohn, whom Heine had met and whom he intended to commemorate in this somewhat equivocal but essentially good-humoured way.

If the broker in question ever saw this passage, he would probably not have felt hurt by it. Another Jewish businessman, however, thought himself mortally insulted by a passage in the published text of *The Hartz Journey*. In the offending episode the narrator evokes the bliss which the coming of spring brings to Hamburg, and adds: 'Even on the black commission agent who has so far escaped the hangman's noose, who bustles about with a rascally face that resembles the goods he peddles, the sun shines down its most tolerant rays.'[20] No name is mentioned, nor is there any hint (beyond the word 'tolerant', embodying a concept frequently evoked in contemporary debates on Jewish emancipation) that the commission agent is a Jew. Nevertheless one Joseph Meyer Friedländer, who was connected with the Heine family by marriage, thought that the cap fitted him, and made a great outcry about it in public and in private. Such quarrels are now of little interest; what is of moment, however, is the way in which here, as in the passage about Saul Ascher, Heine evolves a method of verbal caricature in which a man's personal appearance is made to reflect his habitual preoccupations. Just as Saul Ascher's face and figure are constantly described in mathematical terms, so the commission agent's face is a *Manufakturwaren-gesicht*, a reflection of the goods he deals in; and the adjective 'black' with which he is characterized suggests at once dark clothes, a swarthy complexion, and a rascally or sombre soul.

(ii)

The poems that make up a large part of the *Pictures of Travel* volume in which *The Hartz Journey* appeared include *Donna Clara* and *Almansor*, as well as a number of others that refer peripherally to members of Heine's family or contain evocations of other figures which may or may not have had Jewish originals. Not infrequently critics have sought allegories of Heine's relation to Jews and Judaism in his early poems. The young woman whom the lyric I of *Sea-Spectre* (*Seeges-*

penst) has been seeking throughout the world (for five thousand years, the poet adds, in a variant he later deleted) and whom he now thinks he has found in a ghostly city beneath the sea—this young woman has been taken by some to be a representation of the Jewish people.[21] The ceremony described in the poem *Purification* (*Reinigung*), in which the poet describes himself as casting his sins, pains, and follies into the ocean, shows analogies with the *Tashlikh* ceremony of the Jewish New Year which are probably no more fortuitous than the echoes of the sixth chapter of Genesis in *A Night at the Sea-shore* (*Die Nacht am Strande*) in the same cycle, *The North Sea* (*Die Nordsee. Erster Zyklus*).[22] Another cycle, entitled *The Homecoming* (*Die Heimkehr*), contains charming reminiscences of childhood games the poet seems to have played with his sister Charlotte. Persistent legends associate No. 47 ('Du bist wie eine Blume'—'You are like a flower') with a Jewish girl, and the poet's wish to lay his hand on her head in blessing with Jewish domestic ritual.[23] Many have also tried to read references to Heine's cousin Therese into the story of unrequited love *The Homecoming* appears to tell.[24] As in the case of *Lyrical Intermezzo*, however, the impartial observer is not likely to find any overt Jewish colouration in the poems Heine chose to include in the *Homecoming* cycle. Even Rahel Varnhagen, to whom the cycle is dedicated, appears in the full splendour of her post-baptismal panoply of names and titles: 'Frau Geheime Legationsrätin Friedrike Varnhagen von Ense'.[25] The poems of *The Hartz Journey*, however, do present us with one figure which no examination of Heine's Jewish portraits can afford to leave out of account.

In the longest and most elaborate of these poems, it will be remembered, Heine had made his central protagonist dub himself a 'Knight of the Holy Spirit'—a spirit that would sweep away antiquated disabilities and lead men to the recognition that they all belonged to the same aristocratic lineage. The knight of this poem received the call to proclaim the new gospel only after passing through a series of stages reminiscent of those sketched out by Lessing in *The Education of Mankind* (*Die Erziehung des Menschengeschlechts*, 1780). First, the narrator tells an ardent listener, he had come to believe in God the Father, Who had made this beautiful earth and Who ruled it justly. After that he had learnt to revere God the Son,

> der liebend
> Uns die Liebe offenbart,
> Und zum Lohne, wie gebräuchlich,
> Von dem Volk gekreuzigt ward.

> [who lovingly
> revealed Love to us,
> and was in return, as is usual,
> crucified by the populace.][26]

This opposition of great man and incomprehending populace, so characteristic of Heine, stands in piquant contrast to the notion, proclaimed just three stanzas later, that all men are equal in the sense that they are all born aristocrats:

> Alle Menschen, gleichgeboren,
> Sind ein adliges Geschlecht.

Be that as it may, the figure of Jesus Christ is one that had a constant attraction for Heine. It returns in the poem *Peace* (*Frieden*) which ends the cycle of *North Sea* poems included in the first volume of *Pictures of Travel*. This poem evokes a vision of what has been well termed an 'irenic' Christ—a peace-bringing figure towering over the whole world.[27] It is probable that Moses Moser's symbolic interpretation of the Christ figure, his vision of Judaism itself as a Christ suffering vicariously for all mankind,[28] helped to inspire Heine's poem; but what we read in most editions of the poet's works is only half of what he had originally written. The vision of peace which now constitutes the whole of the poem was originally followed by a long address to a sycophant who would give anything to have conceived and penned that visionary scene—for it would have brought him pecuniary rewards and social advancement. 'As you can see,' Heine seems to be telling his readers, 'I can write "Christian" poems with the best of them; but don't you dare think of me as a pious, peaceful lamb or a mercenary purveyor of uplift! Of those German literature already has more than enough.' There was such an outcry, however, against the *Stimmungsbruch* represented by this second part of the poem, that Heine decided to alter the whole tone and tenor of the work by deleting the offending lines. In this final, truncated version Christ as a bringer of peace, the 'irenic' Christ, represents a religious principle that all men of goodwill may revere. It still remains true, however, that Heine saw in Jesus of Nazareth a figure that Jews may claim as theirs with as good a right (he sometimes thought: with better right) than those who called themselves Christians. In a later work he even has a Swabian girl innocently remind her fellow Christians of the surest sign of Jesus's Jewishness: his circumcision.

(iii)

The first volume of *Pictures of Travel* was followed, within a year, by a second volume which included another cycle of poems entitled *The North Sea* as well as a related prose work headed *The North Sea: Third Section* (*Die Nordsee. Dritter Teil*). One poem in the cycle contains what some commentators have seen as an allusion to the *Pirke Avot*, or Sayings of the Fathers, which occupy a prominent place in the sabbath liturgy.[29] In our context, however, another poem is more significant: that entitled *Sea-Sickness* (*Seekrankheit*), which Heine chose to delete when he transferred *The North Sea* poems to his *Book of Songs* (*Buch der Lieder*) in the late 1820s. *Sea-sickness* not only contains the first of Heine's jocular references to the drunkenness of Lot, but it also casts a jaundiced—or rather sea-sick—look at Jewish emancipation. The poet lists what he sees as the defects of his German fatherland, for whose firm earth he longs as his ship is stomach-churningly tossed by the waves; and among these defects the Federal Diet and other deliberative assemblies take pride of place.

> Mag immerhin deine Schneckenversammlung
> Sich für unsterblich halten
> Weil sie so langsam dahinkriecht,
> Und mag sie täglich Stimmen sammeln
> Ob den Maden des Käses der Käse gehört?
> Und noch lange Zeit in Beratung ziehn,

Wie man die ägyptischen Schafe veredle,
Damit ihre Wolle sich bessre
Und der Hirt sie scheren könne wie andre,
Ohn Unterschied—

[Let your assembly of snails
Think itself immortal
because it crawls along at so slow a pace.
Let it collect votes, every day, to settle
      the question
whether the maggots in the cheese are the
      owners of the cheese.
Let it go on deliberating, for a long
      time yet,
the question of ennobling Egyptian sheep
so as to improve their wool,
so that the shepherd can sheer them along
      with the others
without discrimination . . .][30]

The 'Egyptian sheep' of these last lines are a transparent allegory of the Jews whose 'ennobling' was so often demanded as a prerequisite of full emancipation—an emancipation which would confer on them the privilege of being exploited by those in control in exactly the way other citizens were. We shall have many later occasions to see Heine use such terms as 'Egyptian', 'Arab', and 'Bedouin' as periphrases, or satirical-symbolic counters, for 'Jews'.

The North Sea: Third Section is the prose account of a vacation happily spent on the Frisian island of Norderney. The narrator details his encounters and reflections and feels moved, at one point, to explain why he could never take pleasure in the aristocratic sport of hunting:

A sense of what is noble, beautiful, and good may often be imparted by education; but a taste for hunting is in the blood. When a man's ancestors have been shooting roebucks from time immemorial, his descendant will also take pleasure in this hereditary pastime. My ancestors, however, belonged to the hunted rather than the hunters; and if I am asked to blaze away at the offspring of their erstwhile colleagues, my blood rebels. I know from experience that I find it easier to confront the hunters themselves in a duel, where I can let fly at one of these sportsmen who sigh for the good old days when men too counted as big game. Thank God—those times are past! If such sportsmen take it into their heads to hunt men nowadays, they have to pay cash for the privilege . . .[31]

Jews are not overtly mentioned in this passage; but it must have been clear to most of Heine's readers who the 'hunted' people were that the reluctant sportsman here claims as his ancestry. The phrase about the rebelling of his 'blood' is particularly interesting: we shall have other opportunitites to find Heine claiming 'blood-kinship' with his Jewish forebears without detriment to his official Protestantism. What would be clearer to German readers than it can be to those who read their Heine in translation is the devaluation of the hunting nobility implied by the phrase I have inadequately rendered as 'shooting roebucks'. *Böcke schießen* was and is, of course, a common idiom for 'making gross blunders'. The descendant of a hunted people thus insinuates his intellectual superiority over the hunters while at the same time asserting his social equality by alluding to his power of facing them in a duel. The final words of the passage I have just quoted then touch on the change from the oppressive power of hereditary privilege to the no less oppressive power of money—a theme on which Heine will play many variations in his later writings.

The narrator of *The North Sea: Third Section* is not the only descendant of a hunted people to appear in that work. The first version contained a reference to the political beliefs of a thinker whom Heine, playing on the German term for a fellow believer or co-religionist, *Glaubensgenosse*, calls *mein Unglaubens-genosse Spinoza*—'Spinoza, my companion in unbelief'.[32] That, it would seem, did not fit the persona Heine here wanted to project and was therefore sacrificed. Later editions of these *Pictures of Travel* also sacrificed Heine's tribute to a contemporary for whom he always retained a personal liking. After castigating the German theatre in general, the first version had dwelt on a light at the end of this dramatic tunnel: 'a splendid satire which really hits its mark, Ludwig Robert's *Bird of Paradise (Der Paradiesvogel)*'.[33] Here Heine may have come to feel that he was doing his friend Robert too much honour—one of his letters leaves no doubt that he could no longer enjoy *The Bird of Paradise* when he set it against a

masterpiece of world literature like Aristophanes' *The Birds*.[34]
There is one reference to a contemporary of Jewish antecedents
which Heine did not, however, remove from any edition of his
work:

I often think of the lovely familiar old tale of the fisherman's boy who
had watched the nocturnal dance of the water-nixies by the shore and
who afterwards wandered all over the world with his fiddle and
enchanted the hearts of all men when he played them the nixies'
waltz. This tale I was first told by a dear friend when, at a concert in
Berlin, we heard the playing of another boy endowed with such
wondrous power—I mean Felix Mendelssohn–Bartholdy.[35]

Many of Heine's readers would know the story of how Felix
Mendelssohn's grandfather, the great Moses Mendelssohn,
had to pay toll, on entering Berlin, along with pigs and cattle.
Now only the images of Germanic fairy-tale are powerful
enough to suggest the aesthetic delights with which Moses's
grandson charmed his German audiences. The stone the
builders sought to reject has become a corner-stone.

Despite his knowledgeable reference to 'rabbinical syna-
gogues', however, and the patent irony of *obiter dicta* like
'God knows that I am a good Christian',[36] the narrator of *The
North Sea: Third Section* consistently seeks to present him-
self as a Protestant. He therefore explains a long diatribe
against the Roman Catholic hierarchy by claiming that even
when—like a good Romantic—he wanted to praise the medi-
eval Church and its influence, he was prevented from doing so
by the Protestant zeal to which he had become accustomed—
der angewöhnte protestantische Eifer.[37] If I am to be called
a Protestant, Heine appears to be saying, I might as well
protest!

(iv)

The glory of this second volume of *Pictures of Travel* is
undoubtedly *Ideas. The Book of LeGrand* (*Ideen. Das Buch
LeGrand*), one of the most complex and fascinating works in
the canon of Heine's writings. Here again portraits and

caricatures of Jews constitute a significant element of Heine's narrative.

The first glimpse the reader has of Jewish figures in *Ideas. The Book of LeGrand* occurs in the course of a humorous vision of hell, deliberately designed to counter that of *The Divine Comedy*.

Dante's description is a little too mild, too poetic on the whole. Hell appeared to me as a great kitchen in a bourgeois household, with an endlessly long stove on which were placed three rows of iron pots, and in these sat the damned and were being cooked. In one row sat Christian sinners, and, incredible as it may seem, their number was anything but small, and the devils fanned the flames beneath them with especial zeal. In the next row sat Jews, who kept on shrieking and were occasionally teased by the devils; it was very droll to hear a fat, wheezing pawnbroker complain of the excessive heat and see a little devil pour several buckets of water over his head so that he might realize what a refreshing benefit baptism could be. In the third row sat the heathens who, like the Jews, could have no part in salvation, and must burn forever . . .[38]

How constantly the notion of *baptism* comes to Heine's mind and pen when he thinks of Jews in these years! What he says of hell in this passage is hardly an advertisement for a doctrine that would deny salvation even to Socrates, nor is it calculated to increase one's respect for the practical effects of subscribing to Christian precepts—witness the large number of Christian sinners. Heine mitigates considerably the fate Dante had prepared for usurers in the seventh circle of his inferno; but there is some characteristic *schadenfreude* in his depiction of what awaited Jewish pawnbrokers in an imagined afterlife. Before long we shall meet such pawnbrokers again, in their more familiar, this-worldly role.

In *The North Sea: Third Section* the descendant of a hunted people had, it will be remembered, conquered his dislike of deadly weapons sufficiently to face the descendants of the hunters on the duelling field. *Ideas. The Book of LeGrand* introduces a different attitude.

When, in the nether world, Odysseus casts his eyes on Achilles, leader of heroes in the land of the dead, and extols Achilles' renown among the living along with his glory even among the shades, the latter replies:

> 'My lord Odysseus, spare me your praise of death. Put me on earth again, and I would rather be a serf in the house of some landless man, with little enough for himself to live on, than king of all these dead men that have done with life.'

Yes, and when Major Duvent challenged the great Israel Löwe to fight with pistols, and said to him, 'If you do not meet me, Mr Löwe, you are a dog,' the latter replied, 'I would rather be a live dog than a dead lion (*Löwe*)—and he was right. I have fought duels often enough, dear Madame, to have earned the right to say this. God be praised. I am alive![39]

The verse from Ecclesiastes 9: 4 ('. . . for a living dog is better than a dead lion') gives birth, in Heine's German version (*Lieber ein lebendiger Hund . . . als ein toter Löwe*) to a Jewish figure whose brave name (*Löwe* = lion) belies his timid disposition. His opponent also has an etymologically meaningful name—'Duvent' suggest a braggart whose words are not worth fighting over. To refrain from fighting in such cases is commendable, even if it does raise the stereotype image of a Jewish hyper-timidity that contrasts amusingly with a predilection for such 'savage' names as 'Löwe' or 'Wolf'. A touch of Israel Löwe's realism would have prevented the needless death of the Jewish student described in *Letters from Berlin*; the verse from the Old Testament can therefore be reinforced with a quotation from Homer; Greek and Hebrew can join together in a paean to life. Achilles absolves Israel Löwe—but this very juxtaposition suggests the narrator's detachment from Major Duvent's timid opponent which is an essential element in the complex humorous effect of this passage. The adjective 'great' applied to a character we have never heard of before introduces an unmistakable element of parody which is wholly absent from the reference to Achilles.

'The great Israel Löwe' would seem to be an invented character, born from verbal suggestions in the German version of the Old Testament verse; but the next Jewish character to confront us in *The Book of LeGrand* belongs once again to the population of Hamburg among whom so many of Heine's grotesques originated. The narrator describes how historical events may be recalled by the sight of present-day acquaintances.

When I encountered my tailor, I thought at once of the Battle of Marathon; when I encountered the banker Christian Gumpel, dressed to the nines, I thought at once of the destruction of Jerusalem; when I caught sight of a Portuguese friend who was heavily in debt, I thought of Mahomet taking flight; and when I saw the university proctor, whose strict probity is well known, I thought at once of the death of Haman.[40]

Gumpel, whom we first encountered in *The Hartz Journey*, is now well on the way to becoming one of Heine's stock butts. His narrator's reference to the destruction of Jerusalem holds at least four suggestions: (i) that Gumpel, despite the name 'Christian' with which Heine has once and for all endowed him, is Jewish; (ii) that the banker's ornate dress contrasts incongruously with the sackcloth and ashes which the association brings to mind; (iii) that men such as Gumpel are little inclined to heed the Psalmist's warning against 'forgetting Jerusalem'; (iv) that for such prosperous bankers exile from the traditional Jewish homeland has not been an uncomfortable experience. The 'Portuguese friend' mentioned in the same passage may be a member of Hamburg's prestigious community of Sephardic Jews; Heine himself, as Philipp Veit has pertinently reminded us, was sufficiently alive to the prestige and historic importance of this community to adopt, at times, what Veit calls 'the Marrano pose'. He even signed a letter to Charlotte Heine, dated 30 March 1824, 'Your Portuguese brother'. There would thus be a special piquancy in imagining a member of that dignified clan forced to take to his heels in order to escape his creditors—an undignified exit which Heine heightens mock-heroically by comparing it to the hegira. In a later passage of this same work the poet will return to Mohamet's flight and will associate it with that of one of the most honoured personalities in Hispano-Jewish history: 'Rabbi Jizchak Abarbanel', or Isaac ben Judah Abarbanel (1437–1508), whose distinguished career Heine had studied in preparation for *The Rabbi of Bacherach*.[41] As for that proctor (*Universitätsrichter*), he, no doubt, is first cousin to those who summoned Heine before them on a memorable occasion in the

University of Göttingen. Haman, it will be remembered, is the archetypal enemy of the Jews, the man who sought (according to the Book of Esther) to destroy the exiled Jewish people and was hanged for his pains—a fate Heine more than once wished on his enemies.

When Jews come into view once more in *The Book of LeGrand*, they do so in the by now familiar guise of pawnbrokers. The narrator recalls the difficulty he experienced when he was trying to learn Greek:

Hebrew I found easier, for I have always had a great predilection for the Jews, even though they have always, up to this very hour, crucified my good name; but I could not get as far in Hebrew as my watch, which had much intimate commerce with pawnbrokers and thus fell into Jewish ways—for instance, it did not work on Saturdays. It learnt the sacred language, too, and later studied its grammar; in sleepless nights I was often astonished to hear it ticking away to itself: *katal, katalta, katalti—kittel, kittalta, kittalti—pokat, pokadeti—pikat, pik, pik* . . .[42]

In expressing his 'predilection' for Jews, the narrator distances himself from them; he sees himself a victim of their gossiping tongues, and evokes the stereotype of the crucifying mob to express his sense of outrage; yet when he speaks of Hebrew as 'the sacred tongue' and invokes the verbal paradigms by whose means so many Jewish children have learnt to read and speak it, he indicates his affinity with the very pawnbrokers whose customer university students were so often forced to be. But this is not to be thought of as religious affinity—for very soon afterwards the narrator expresses his unequivocal preference for the gay gods of the ancients as against 'our' Trinity and 'our' monotheism.[43] This is the contrast Heine will later elaborate into one between 'Hellenes' and 'Nazarenes': the Nazarene camp contains both Judaism and Christianity.

Having established his perspective, Heine can now go on to introduce some well-known German Jews into his narrative. The beginning of this passage we have met before, since one of the figures so introduced is Eduard Gans.

My friend G. in Berlin is, so to speak, a minor Rothschild in respect of quotations and will be glad to lend me a few million; if, by any chance, he should not have enough of them in stock he can easily collect the requisite number by going to a few other cosmopolitan bankers of the intellect. Should some wealthy scholar—Michael Beer, for instance—want to purchase this secret from me, I shall be glad to part with if for 19,000 thaler; I might even be prepared to go down a bit.[44]

Heine's narrator here draws a significant parallel between cultural-intellectual exchange in nineteenth-century Germany, and money transactions. Jews, once confined only to the latter, now play a significant part in the former. As he does so, he brings into view three Jewish circles with which Heine had personal contact: (i) wealthy bankers, headed by the Rothschild family; (ii) scholars such as Eduard Gans, striving, with some success, to become part of the academic establishment; and (iii) wealthy dilettantes such as the dramatist Michael Beer, who were able to indulge their tastes because of the riches an earlier generation had amassed by means of financial and commercial acumen. Calling Beer 'a great scholar' (*ein großer reicher Gelehrter*) is of course an additional irony. The caricatures of Gans and Beer are then matched, in the final sentence, by the narrator's self-caricature: the traffic in cultural goods exemplified by well-placed quotations and allusions appears, in the satirist's case no less than in that of his butts, a continuation of the old huckstering in a new sphere.

The chapter which affords its readers these glimpses of Gans, Rothschild, and Beer continues its high-spirited disquisition on the use of quotations and references in a passage which again brings in Jews ancient and Jews modern.

I could dilate at length on the food of the ancient Hebrews and descend from there by degrees to Jewish cookery in the most recent times. This would give me the chance to quote the whole of the Steinweg [a street in Hamburg inhabited largely by Jews]. I could also cite the humane pronouncements of many Berlin scholars on the subject of Jewish food, and could go on from there to other excellences and pre-eminences of the Jews, to inventions we owe to them, like bills of exchange, or Christianity. But stop! We won't give them too much credit for the last-named, because we have not, as yet, made much use of it. I think the Jews themselves have profited less from this than from the invention of bills of exchange. Apropos Jews I could cite Tacitus—he said that they worshipped asses in their temples. Apropos asses—what a vast field of possible citations here

opens up before me! How many notable facts could be quoted anent ancient asses as opposed to modern ones! The former were so sensible, and the latter—alas—are so stupid. Take Balaam's ass, for instance—how reasonably it speaks,
vide Pentat. Lib.————————
Madame, I have not the book by me and will therefore leave a hiatus that can be filled at a convenient opportunity.[45]

This Sternean passage, which utilizes some of the material Heine had wanted to include in a continuation of *The Hartz Journey*, enshrines the first of Heine's many public tributes to Jewish cookery, of which he once said that it had done more for the cohesion of the Jewish people than all the religious reform movements put together. Here, however, the humorous sally is directed, not at Jews who are more impressed by mother's cooking than by Jewish conceptions of God and morality, but rather at non-Jews whose 'humane' attitude consists in allowing themselves to be lavishly wined and dined. Heine likes to remind his readers of the Jewish origin of Christianity (an 'invention' that has recoiled on the Jews with greater force than their alleged invention of bills of exchange); and he is also becoming increasingly fond of using Old Testament stories—like that of Baalam and his ass—for modern satiric purposes. By mentioning the *Steinweg* he achieves local colour (Hamburg features prominently in *The Book of LeGrand*) and also reminds his readers that even where there is no enforced ghetto, Jews do like to cluster together, to live in close proximity to one another. In later writings the word *Steinweg* becomes a shorthand term evoking the Jewish quarter of Hamburg together with its inhabitants and eating-places. And among these inhabitants the 'black commission agent" whom he had briefly caricatured in *The Hartz Journey* and who had chosen to identify himself publicly as Joseph Meyer Friedländer, makes another pseudonymous appearance. In his letters Heine usually refers to him as 'the black one', *der Schwarze*; he therefore becomes, *e contrario*, 'Herr von Weiß' in *Ideas. The Book of LeGrand*.

If one can't actually hang people, one has to brand them. Once again I am speaking figuratively—I brand people *in effigie*. Herr von Weiß, it is true (he who is as white and as pure as a lily), has been kidded into believing [*hat sich weiß machen lassen*] I had spread it about Berlin that he was branded in literal fact: the fool has therefore had himself looked over by the civic authorities and obtained a certificate attesting that his back bears no such armorial device. This negative heraldic attestation he regards as a diploma which ought to gain him admittance to the best society. He was therefore astonished to find himself thrown out on his ear, and he now goes about crying murder against poor me whom he intends to shoot down with a pistol as soon as he can discover where I might be found.[46]

Such fools, the narrator declares, are cash and meat and drink to him—all he has to do is to put people like Herr von Weiß into a book and then use the royalties to buy himself a cask of Rüdesheimer of the best vintage, or some other delicacy of that kind.

In the fifteenth chapter of *The Book of LeGrand* the narrator once again hints at his own Jewish origins.

Madame, I notice a faint cloud of disapproval on your lovely brow, and you seem to be asking: is it not wrong of me to dress fools in this way, stick them on the spit, carbonado them, baste them, and even butcher many that I cannot possibly swallow, who must therefore be left a prey to the sharp beaks of other humorists [*Spaßvögel*] while widows and orphans howl and lament—
Madame, c'est la guerre! I will solve the whole riddle for you: I am not by any means one of the reasonable and rational men, but I have joined their party, and for 5,588 years we have been at war with the party of fools.[47]

'For 5,588 years'—Heine is writing in 1827, and 5,588 is the equivalent of that year in the Jewish calendar established by Hillel II in the fourth century. More clearly than in the early version of *The North Sea* cycle, where the lyric I of *Sea Spectre* had sought his lost love 'for five thousand years', Heine here signals to his readers that despite his baptism he still feels himself part of the Jewish people. The warfare between folly and reason in which the protagonist of *The Book of LeGrand* seems himself involved is complicated by Jewish-Gentile dichotomies.

Heine's hint at Jewish origins and allegiances at the beginning of this important chapter lends a special interest and significance to a passage near its end, where Heine identifies with his narrator and casts an ironic glance at Christian allegorizations of the Song of Songs.

I cannot help my unhappy passion for Reason. I love her though she does not return my love. I give her everything and she gives me nothing. Yet I cannot tear myself from her. And as, once upon a time, the Jewish King Solomon, in his Song of Songs, sang of the Christian Church, using the image of a passionate black maiden so that his Jews should not suspect what he was driving at—just so have I, in countless poems, sung the very opposite: I have celebrated Reason in the image of a cold, white virgin that attracts and repels me. Now she smiles at me, now she shows her anger, and finally she turns her back on me . . . Read my *Ratcliff*, my *Almansor*, my *Lyrical Intermezzo*—Reason, Reason, nothing but Reason!—and you will be terrified by the heights my folly has reached. In the words of Agur, the son of Jakeh, I can say of myself: 'Surely I am more foolish than any man, and have not the understanding of a man.'[48]

The multiple ironies of this characteristic passage contain two ingredients relevant to our present context: a mocking view of the way in which Christian theologians have dealt with Hebrew texts; and that delight in using the wording of the Scriptures for secular purposes which Margaret Rose has described and 'placed' in her book on Heine's biblical parody. But though Heine introduces the words of the Bible in what may be thought frivolous contexts, he never devalues them—never wavers in his respect for the Book for whose sake the Jewish people endured so much, the Book which helped that people to survive when other ancient peoples perished.

   Respect for the Bible entails respect, then, for the people that created and cherished it; but this does not prevent Heine's ambivalent feelings about the Jews of past and present from rising to the surface on many occasions. Let us recall one sentence in which he cites one of the multitude of anti-Jewish pronouncements, by respected writers of antiquity and modern times, which he had met in his reading and which constantly come to his mind when he thinks about the people with which his destiny was indissolubly linked:

Apropos Jews—here I could cite Tacitus—he said that they worshipped asses in their temples. Apropos asses—what a vast field of possible citations here opens up before me![49]

Taken literally, such Gentile charges against Jews are absurd—who, Heine suggests, could now seriously share Tacitus's perverse notion of what went on in Jewish houses of worship? Yet the pervasive irony of *The Book of LeGrand* suggests that symbolically Tacitus may have a point. As for the 'vast field of possible citations' which opens up before the narrator—here we cannot but recall, once again, that the habit of dragging in quotations from every possible source on every possible occasion was one which Heine associated above all with Eduard Gans. The portrait of Gans is developed, and its symbolical import is probed, even when Heine does not overtly mention the contemporary who presented such an uncomfortable mirror image of himself.

Ideas. The Book of LeGrand contains many autobiographical passages, and there can be little doubt that Heine worked into this Sternean composition part of those 'memoirs' of which he had spoken in a letter to Ludwig Robert dated 4 March 1825. 'A kind of *Wahrheit und Dichtung*' he had called them, with an allusion to the title of Goethe's autobiography, and he had added that they would not appear before the public until a much later date. *The Book of LeGrand* is, in fact, full of deliberate parallels with Goethe's *Poetry and Truth*, and the descriptions it contains of the narrator's school-days in Düsseldorf, and of Napoleon's triumphal entry into that city, dovetail very well with the fragment of Heine's *Memoiren* which will be discussed below in Chapter 15. We find passing allusions to Heine's academically trained grandfather and uncle;[50] and Philipp Veit has convincingly argued that the 'Evelina' mentioned in the dedication of *The Book of Le-Grand*, as well as the unnamed 'she' of its eighteenth chapter, have a closer connection with the poet's cousin Amalie than many more recent critics have been willing to concede. After Amalie's early death on 9 June 1838 Heine copied a French version of Chapter XVIII into Cécile Furtado-Heine's autograph album and added the words: 'Le héros de cette vieille histoire vit encore; ayez pitié de lui. L'héroïne est morte; priez pour son âme!'[51] The disappointed wooing which warped Heine's later love-life and helped to poison his relationship with the Hamburg branch of his family also plays a considerable part in the often so sad Jewish Comedy that disengages itself from his works.

CHAPTER 3
Jewish Emancipation and Gentile Culture

(i)

The third volume of *Pictures of Travel* takes the wanderer for the first time beyond the frontiers of Germany. The goal is Italy—but anyone who expects an account of that country comparable to Goethe's *Italian Journey* is bound to be disappointed. 'Nothing is more tedious', Heine's narrator warns the reader, 'than reading an account of travel in Italy—except, perhaps, the writing of such an account. The only way in which an author can make the whole exercise tolerable is to speak of Italy itself as little as possible.'[1] Small wonder, then, that German concerns constantly intrude—and that the Jews whom we meet in these accounts all turn out to be German Jews.

The first of these pieces, *The Journey from Munich to Genoa* (*Die Reise von München nach Genua*) had begun life as a serial in Cotta's *Morning Chronicle* (*Morgenblatt für gebildete Stände*) in 1828. It had there borne the title *Journey to Italy* (*Reise nach Italien*), and its opening instalment had included a conversation between the narrator and a typical Berliner who had extolled Berlin at the expense of Munich. Among the delights Berlin had to offer, this Prussian patriot listed the humorist M. G. Saphir—'the one and only Saphir', he had called him in his Berlinese dialect, *Saphir, den eenzigen Menschen*.[2] This reference was deleted when the work appeared again, in *Pictures of Travel III*, in 1829. Other Jewish figures are allowed to remain, however: among them Heine's own brother Maximilian, who is shown accompanying the narrator part of the way; and, more significantly, 'Rothschild I', who appears alongside Wellington, the Grand Mufti, the Pope, Metternich, and a whole motley crew of carpet knights, stockjobbers, and clerics, all of whom think that by backing

Turkey against the Russians they are defending the status quo.[3] This image of Rothschild as the financial prop of reaction and of the power politics of the established order was conventional among German liberals of the day, and we shall see Heine modify it considerably in his later work. *The Journey from Munich to Genoa* is most notable, however, for another appearance of a Jewish figure who would engage Heine's attention again and again the years to come: the composer Giacomo Meyerbeer, the brother of that Michael Beer whom Heine had gently ridiculed in *The Book of LeGrand*. 'Italy', a pale Milanese patriot is made to say, in answer to a florid Briton who had accused the Italians of indifference to politics 'sits on its ruins; and if it sometimes awakes with a sudden start and leaps up at the memory of some song or other, then its enthusiasm is due, not to the song itself, but to ancient memories and feelings roused by that song, memories, and feelings which Italians have ever borne in their hearts and which now break out tempestuously—that is the real meaning of the frenzied jubilations you heard at La Scala last night.' The narrator then adds, in words that end the chapter:

This confession may help to explain the enthusiasm aroused everywhere on the Italian side of the Alps by the operas of Rossini or Meyerbeer. If I have ever seen real human frenzy, then it was at a performance of Meyerbeer's *Crociato in Egitto*, whenever the music modulates, as it sometimes does, from a soft, melancholy air to one of jubilant grief. The Italians call that kind of frenzy *furore*.[4]

By bracketing Meyerbeer with Rossini, and describing the enthusiastic reception of his work in the very land of opera, Heine would seem to pay him the highest possible compliment. There is only one slight rift in this lute of praise: the pale Italian's remark that what moved his countrymen to enthusiasm was *not the music itself*, but rather 'ancient memories and feelings', memories and feelings associated with a freer Italy which are stirred up by Meyerbeer's compositions.[5]

The bracketing of Meyerbeer and Rossini, with their very different national and ethnic origins, is one of many signs of the perspective which Heine deliberately adopts in *The Journey from Munich to Genoa*. This perspective becomes unmistakable when the narrator tackles the problem of 'emancipation' which was of such burning concern to the Jews of early nineteenth-century Europe.

No one knew better than Heine the apprehension many of his contemporaries felt when they thought that national peculiarities might be lost in a common European culture. But need they really fear this? Might not the different national and ethnic groups continue to make their distinct contributions to enrich this common culture? On the social and political front, in any case, the logic of the time seemed to demand a united Europe.

Gradually, day by day, foolish national prejudices are disappearing; all harsh differentiations are lost in the generality of European civilization; there are no more nations in Europe, only parties; and it is marvellous to see how these parties, for all their varying colouration, recognize one another and how they understand one another, despite many differences in language. . . . Our age hastens towards its great task.

But what is this great task of our own age? It is emancipation. Not only the emancipation of Irishmen, Greeks, Frankfurt Jews, West Indian blacks, and other such oppressed peoples, but the emancipation of the whole world, and more especially that of Europe: a Europe which has come of age and is breaking out of the strong leading-strings held by the privileged, by the aristocracy.[6]

In his 1978 Leo Baeck Memorial Lecture Felix Gilbert has cited this very passage and has defined what it means by 'emancipation': 'the abolition of all those privileges, regulations and laws which established a hierarchy among social classes, restricted the economic activities which the individual could pursue, and gave members of the superior class the right to command the services of those of lower status. Emancipation implied full equality of every member of the state—every citizen—before the law . . .' By evoking this key concept Heine is making again a point he had already hammered home in his essay on Poland: that fighting for *Jewish* emancipation just isn't enough; the Jews could only be fully and truly emancipated along with the rest of oppressed humanity. Nor is it at all fortuitous that the Jews here appear between the Greeks and the West Indian blacks. Like the Greeks, then still under Turkish rule, they are fighting for political emancipation, though not, of course, for national liberation in the same sense; like the blacks, they are still being treated as second or third-class citizens because of their ethnic identity. Like the Greeks again, they have made an essential contribution to European culture and civilization. 'As the Greeks are great through the idea of Art', Heine tells us, 'and the Hebrews through the idea of an All-Holy God, so the Romans are great through the idea of their eternal city of Rome.'[7] Heine never abandoned his Hegelian search for 'idea' and 'spirit', the *Idee* and the *Geist* informing all phenomena and working themselves out in history. Indeed, we shall see that he came to regard the Jews as 'the people of the spirit'. Nor did he ever, despite the mockery of *Ideas. The Book of Le-Grand*, lose his respect for ideas or his belief in their transforming power. His praise of the distinctive contribution the Jews have made to the concert of ideas in Europe is neither hollow nor ironic, even though for his own part he said many irreverent things about the All-Holy God of Abraham, Isaac, and Jacob.

It will have been noticed that the passage about emancipation speaks, specifically, of *Frankfurt* Jews. This too is not fortuitous; Frankfurt had come to stand, in many minds, as the prime example of a modern German city which strove to perpetuate the medieval, pre-Napoleonic segregation of its Jewish inhabitants. Ludwig Börne, a native of Frankfurt, led the fight against such attitudes, and never tired of pillorying the city fathers who had driven him into exile. Here as elsewhere Heine ranges himself alongside Börne in that struggle: even his view of Rothschild (which he was later to modify) is at this time essentially that of Börne.

The volume of *Pictures of Travel* devoted to Italy bears a motto from Goethe's *West-Easterly Divan* which in Heine's context carries an anti-clerical image. 'Hafiz', it declares, 'and Ulrich von Hutten had to take up arms against monkish cowls in brown and blue. My targets dress like ordinary Christians.'[8] *The Journey from Munich to Genoa*, in this same volume, has also acquired a motto it had lacked in its earlier version published in the *Morning Chronicle*:

"What you never reckon with is nobility of spirit—your wisdom founders on that." (He opens his desk, takes out two pistols, one of which he places on the table while loading the other.)[9]

This quotation comes from Ludwig Robert's play *The Force of Circumstances*, where the speaker is a young Jew insulted by an aristocrat, a Jew who does indeed show the nobility of spirit or disposition, *the edles Gemüt*, with which his Christian adversary refuses to credit him. By means of these mottos the Italian travel pictures are placed in a context that includes anti-aristocratic as well as anti-clerical sentiments—and *The Journey from Munich to Genoa* reminds its readers of a noble-spirited Jew whose image may continue to linger in their minds when they come to the undignified ex-Jew who takes the centre of the stage in *The Baths of Lucca* (*Die Bäder von Lucca*).

(ii)

We have seen in Chapter 2 how Heine twice introduces into his *Pictures of Travel* quick caricature sketches of his uncle's Hamburg business rival Lazarus Gumpel, replacing that worthy's inappropriate first name (should it not have been 'Dives'?) with the even less appropriate 'Christian'. Thus groomed for stardom, Gumpel comes to dominate the travel picture Heine included in the same volume as *The Journey from Munich to Genoa*: the ever controversial *Baths of Lucca*, in which passages of fine sensibility and imaginative power co-exist with some crudities and puerilities unworthy of a great poet.

Heine uses the figure of Gumpel, in *The Baths of Lucca*, to satirize the attempts of *nouveau riche* Jews to assimilate a culture for which neither their education nor their everyday occupation has fitted them. Gumpel has now assumed the style and title of an aristocrat, and calls himself, while taking the baths at Lucca, 'Marchese Christophoro di Gumpelino'; but a lady he visits in that style can see in him only a lord of misrule, a peer in the realm of folly.[10] She warns the narrator that the Marchese's nose is liable to give offence, tells of his love for an English lady, and adds that he has some excellent qualities: a great deal of money, for instance, along with a portion of healthy good sense in the midst of follies and affectations that lead him to take up every fad of the time. When the person so described actually enters, the narrator recognizes his old friend, Gumpel the banker, with his moneyed smile, a belly that is fair in the sight of the Lord, and broad shining lips that nuzzle the lady's hand. Here, for the first time, we see Heine attempting an elaborate verbal caricature of a wealthy Jew's outer appearance—a caricature that culminates in a long reflective passage on that favourite organ of cartoonists, the 'Jewish' nose. The Marchese's nose, we are told, is so prominent that it nearly poked the narrator's eye out when he embraced him. Its noble form, Heine continues, in his broadest satiric manner, showed how justified the Marchese was in assuming the style and title of a nobleman—for it announced to all and sundry that his lineage was ancient indeed, was so noble that the Lord himself, *der liebe Gott*, could contract a union within that family without fear of misalliance. In recent times, however, Heine continues, the members of this family have come down in the world:

so that since the reign of Charlemagne they have had to scratch a living, in the main, by trading in old trousers and Hamburg lottery tickets; but this has in no way diminished their pride in their ancestry or induced them to give up hoping that they would, one day, come into their property again, or that at the very least they would be awarded damages for having been forced to emigrate. This would happen, they thought, when their old legitimate sovereign would make good his promise of restoration, a promise with which he has been leading them by the nose for two thousand years. Is this being led by the nose the reason, perhaps, why their noses have grown so long? Or are these long noses a kind of uniform, by which the divine old king Jehovah recognizes his palace guards even when they have deserted? The Marchese Gumpelino was a deserter of this kind, but he still wore his uniform, and it was a brilliant one: it was sprinkled all over with little crosses and stars of rubies, a miniature version of the Order of the Red Eagle, and other such honorific decorations.[11]

Heine's amusing aria on the Jewish nose has three serious purposes. It suggests, firstly, some of the ways in which men project their earthly relationships on to their relationship with God. Questions of legitimate sovereignty, emigration, restoration, and compensation all had topical importance for Heine's contemporaries in the post-Napoleonic period. The passage throws doubt, secondly, on the possibility of leaving Judaism by an act of baptism—Jehovah's uniform is in the flesh, and can never be wholly discarded. Judaism implies a *family* connection, a link by common descent, that cannot be simply wished away. And lastly: in the sentence that speaks of an ancient nobility reduced to peddling second-hand trousers, Heine conveys in hilarious vein (think of Jews offering worn pantaloons to Charlemagne and his knights!) not only a sense of historical degradation[12] but also a social scale along which men like the Marchese and his ancestors may be ranged.

One of the characters of *The Baths of Lucca*, it will be remembered, credits the Marchese with some good qualities; but whatever these may be, they do not fit him easily and naturally into polite European society. His malapropistic compliments to Lady Mathilde go as ludicrously awry as his wooing of her friend Lady Maxwell. He is a long way removed from the cultural *savoir faire* of Heine's narrator, the 'Herr Doctor' who tells us of his encounters with Gumpelino.

Not surprisingly, analysts of self-lacerating Jewish humour have seen Heine's disquisition on Gumpelino's Jewish nose as an important piece of evidence. Sig Altman, for instance, whose *The Comic Image of the Jew* is one of the most intelligent treatments of this complex subject, has remarked on the many characteristics of the archetypal Jewish joke which it has managed to combine.

There is the playful language as such, the "dialectical" style, the crass metaphors. Then there is the two-edged sword extended towards the Jews: one one side the adoption of anti-Semitic cadences in connection with the nose, on the other the resentment of assimilation, characterized here as desertion; then there is an ambiguous mixture of irony and bitterness in the remark concerning the "ancient nobility" and God's failure to keep His promise. There is finally the sideswipe at Christianity in the reference to God's liaison with that family, which Christians do not even consider worthy of toleration.[13]

The line from Heine to Philip Roth or Woody Allen or Mel Brooks may be a long one, but it runs reasonably straight.

When we next encounter Gumpelino, he is dragging his considerable bulk up the hills beyond Lucca, advertising his baptized status by exclaiming 'Jesus!' at every step. Having reached the summit he finds enough breath to eulogize the circle of English and Irish ladies in which he has been moving—and he does so, significantly enough, in terms of the theatrical stage.

> I never met a woman like that in ordinary life. Only in plays could you find anything like it: Julie Holzbecher would perform this part admirably . . .[14]

It is clear from this, as well as his later quotations from Schlegel's translation of *Romeo and Juliet*, that Gumpelino had become an assiduous patron of the German theatre—and we remember at once that *The Hartz Journey* too had stressed the noticeable presence of Jewish men and women in the playhouses of Berlin. We then hear Gumpelino talk on a subject he really knows something about—the exchange value of louisd'or—and have just time to learn that he has engaged an Italian Catholic chaplain to officiate at his devotions before we meet the character who will now upstage him. That character is his valet, a man whom he calls 'Hyazinth' but in whom the narrator recognizes an old acquaintance bearing a different name. He looks up and discerns

> a scarlet livery-coat overloaded with gold braid which gleamed in the sunlight. From all this crimson splendour a sweating little head emerged and nodded at me in a way that I knew well. And really—when I looked more closely at the pale, worried little face and the busily winking little eyes I recognized someone I would have expected to see on Mount Sinai rather than on the Apennines . . .[15]

The reference to Mount Sinai leaves no doubt about the Jewishness of this new figure, who bears to Gumpelino some of the relation that Sancho Panza bears to Don Quixote—except that in the present case it is the master who is fat and the servant who is lean. The flowery name 'Hyazinth' turns out to disguise the more characteristically German-Jewish name 'Hirsch', and the bearer of both names stands revealed as a man who once earned his living in Hamburg by selling lottery tickets, cutting corns, and appraising jewelry. This *Luftmensch* has now been taken into Gumpelino's service, and the change of name, about which he is anything but happy, has been imposed on him by Gumpelino—another sign of the Marchese's doomed attempt to put his Jewishness behind him, as well as his veneer of 'classical' learning.

Adolf Strodtmann, in an early but still valuable biography of Heine, claimed that when the poet heard of a poor lottery agent named Isaak Rocamora, he exclaimed: 'Rocamora. What a charming title for a book! Before I die, I shall write a poem called "Rocamora"!' No such poem was ever written; but on the strength of this passage Rocamora—who is not otherwise known to fame—has been claimed as a model for Hirsch-Hyazinth. It has also been maintained, by Philipp Veit, that some of the same character's traits were based on traits Heine had observed, and caricatured, in the Berlin Reformer David Friedländer. But why, then, is there no allusion to the name Rocamora (which had so charmed the poet) or that of Friedländer? 'Gumpelino', after all, is clearly based on 'Gumpel'. J. A. Kruse's excellent book on Heine's Hamburg years supplies what I believe to be a vital clue. Basing himself on the work of Gustav Karpeles, another of the poet's early biographers, and on other sources, Kruse tells us that Salomon Heine 'held up the successful businessmen Hirsch and Gumpel' as models his nephew would do well to copy.[16] There we have them both. Aaron Hirsch, who turns up sporadically in Heine's letters right up to the end of his life, was Uncle Salomon's bookkeeper before striking out on his own; and Heine may well have borrowed his name along with that of Gumpel in order to make fun of the 'models' his uncle had seen fit to hold up to him.

Be that as it may—Heine was surely right in regarding Hirsch-Hyazinth as his most successful character creation. He stands on his own feet, independent of any original in the Hamburg society of his day, and engages his creator's sympathies far more than his employer and foil, Gumpelino. Heine constantly allows him to present his own views in his own language, without interposed authorial comment. The very first words we hear him speak, however, are designed to show that he is not easily at home in standard German, that he is prone to malapropisms, that he is never quite certain which language register he ought to use. 'I am expecting', he declares in a phrase more appropriate to a pregnant woman than to a lottery agent turned valet, 'that you still know me': *Ich bin guter Hoffnung daß Sie mich noch kennen.* Unlike Gumpelino, however, he is not at all anxious to partake of such delights of a Gentile culture as Italy has to offer. He thinks back nostalgically to his round as a lottery agent in what he calls, in a delightful variation on the German word for the homeland, his little stepfatherland, *Stiefvaterländchen*, Hamburg. He expresses this nostalgia in a series of expressive distortions of the German language which include the viewing of *Papogoyim* in the Hamburg Zoo: a coinage which takes in both the parrots in the cages (*Papageien*) and the non-Jewish fathers (*Papa + Goyim*) who have brought their children to see them. Not all Hirsch's malapropisms, it should be said, offer such harmless delights— some of them carry, for the reader, a scatological meaning of which the little man remains blissfully unaware.

Though Hirsch-Hyazinth is anything but delighted at being dragged around Italy in quest of culture, he is quite as conscious as his master of the necessity for education and self-cultivation, *Bildung*. He is sensible, too, of the honour that can be gained by the acquisition of the dominant majority's culture. Here Heine has indeed seen truly. He has seen the respect which even the simplest Jews traditionally have for learning along with the desire to gain honour, not just riches, in European society.

Gumpelino soon packs Hirsch-Hyazinth off with a message to the lady of his heart and takes the occasion to boast that his servant's livery has forty thalers' worth of gold braid more than the livery of Rothschild's footmen. The Rothschilds, we see, set a standard, a pattern that wealthy Jews try to emulate or exceed. At the same time, however, Gumpelino is made to broach a subject which allows us to see his pathetic obsession with European culture in a new light.

'I take an inward pleasure in seeing how this man is perfecting himself in my service. Now and then I myself give him lessons in refinement and self-cultivation. I often say to him: "What is money? Money is round and rolls away, but culture remains." Yes, Herr Doctor, if I should, God forbid, lose my money I would still be a great connoisseur of art . . .'[16]

What follows is designed to show how ludicrously inadequate Gumpelino's connoisseurship in fact is; but this does not devalue his feeling that there is something of more permanent worth in an ability to appreciate the arts than in the possession of material riches. What Heine here conveys, through the mouth of the otherwise farcical Gumpelino, is the value Jews traditionally attach to cultivation of spirit and intellect, together with their feeling of insecurity: money rolls away, the acquisition of riches is not enough, one must have something more to rely on, something more to show for one's endeavours ... In the passage that follows, however, in which we hear Gumpelino recite inappropriate verse by Matthisson while the narrator is lost in the contemplation of a sunlit landscape, Heine shows no less clearly that a talent for the acquisition of money does not necessarily imply an equal talent for the acquisition of culture—that its corollary is more likely to be a defective aesthetic sensibility. Gumpelino, for his part, is irritated by the narrator's superior attitude and puts it down to the Herr Doctor's self-division, a Byronic *Zerrissenheit* in the face of which he asserts his own wholeness, his ability to enjoy himself without excessive introspection.[18]

Heine is here playing a significant variation on the theme of 'wholeness' which he had broached in his essay on Poland and its Jews. In confronting Gumpelino with a narrator persona whose heart is agitated by the multitudinous conflicts and contradictions of his age, he shows up Gumpelino's claim to 'wholeness' for what it is: an index of spiritual and intellectual limitations. That kind of 'wholeness' depends on an inability to respond adequately to nature, to religion, to the culture of one's time. The price one has to pay for it is much too high; a sensitive and intelligent being, aware of what is going on in the world, would have to prefer his self-division, his *Zerrissenheit*, to the Marchese's self-satisfied totality.

Gumpelino's speech about the relative value of money and culture has a somewhat sharper tone in a manuscript version that has been preserved.

If only I had Rothschild's money! But what use is it to him? He lacks culture, and understands as much about music as an unborn calf, about painting as a cat, about poetry as Apollo—that's the name of my dog. When men like that lose their money, they cease to exist.[19]

This speech characterizes Gumpelino, of course, with his envy of the Rothschilds and his deluded pride in a cultivation that expresses itself in naming his dog Apollo; but it is also Heine's device for having a go at the Rothschild family without seeming to do so. In the event he thought it more diplomatic to omit this passage when *The Baths of Lucca* came to be printed. He also omitted part of the 'lesson' which Gumpelino claims to have taught Hirsch-Hyazinth:

'As an example [of the superiority of culture over money] I often show him his friend Adolph Goldschmidt *nebbish* [a Yiddish expression denoting pity]; that fellow earned some money and wanted to have more—wanted to have as much as Rothschild; he lost it all again and has shrunk back into an ordinary man. Now he is nothing but a corpse that wants to fool people into believing that there is some life left in it. At night he stands in front of his mirror and tells himself how many millions he once owned—for there is no one else who would be prepared to listen to that old tale any more.'

The narrator, Heine's *alter ego*, agrees:

'Yes, Marchese, when such an Icarus comes too near the sun of Rothschild he burns his gilt-edged, government-secured wings and plunges down into the sea of nothingness.'

The Marchese then concludes his disquisition with that characteristic expression of self-satisfaction which also surfaces, as we have seen, in the published version of *The Baths of Lucca*.

'When people like that lose their money, they also lose their honour and their character. But if I, God forbid, should lose my money, I would still remain a great connoisseur of painting, music, and poetry.'[20]

In the narrator's interposition the mock-heroic tone and mythological imagery which had been such prominent features of the poems in *The North Sea* cycle are impressed into the service of a satire directed at the values of those who make money their god, while Gumpelino's speeches in this deleted passage are a significant experiment in the art of hitting two targets at once—the person attacked by the speaker, and the speaker himself. In the event, however, Heine seems to have felt that the chapters of *The Baths of Lucca* in which he took a savage revenge for anti-Semitic attacks made on him by his fellow poet August von Platen would bring enemies enough about his head; he therefore omitted the passages that would have given equal offence to the Rothschilds and the Gold-schmidts.

We have now seen the Marchese name his servant 'Hyacinth' and his dog 'Apollo'. The most obvious purpose of this in-appropriate nomenclature is to show the ludicrously inadequ-ate use Gumpelino makes of the cultural information that filters through to him; but there is more to it than that. Heine here broaches, obliquely but unmistakably, his constant theme of the degradation of the gods and heroes of the ancient world—a theme connected, in his mind, with the advent of Christianity. When Apollo becomes a dog and Hyacinthus a Jewish corn-cutter, both in the service of a baptized Jewish parvenu, they may indeed be thought to have fallen from their ancient glory. We shall hear a late poem in Heine's *Romanzero* play that theme to its ultimate conclusion.

The fifth chapter of *The Baths of Lucca* shows us Gumpelino taking his place among the admirers of an Italian lady of ample though faded charms, to whom he pays homage, at one point, 'in the name of all Germany'.[21] The spotlight of this chapter, however, falls not on him, but on another beau, the old professor of law whose conversation with the narrator about the intricacies of legal scholarship in Germany gives Heine the opportunity to contrast, by simple juxtaposition, the place Eduard Gans occupies in the world of European culture and learning with that of Gumpelino and Hirsch (see the *Prologue* above). In the chapter that follows, the Marchese takes the centre of the stage again; his exploits are glossed with compar-isons from the Old Testament, he is shown rapidly calculating costs on his fingers, and a gallant speech he makes to a lady leads the narrator to a psychological analysis of some subtlety.

The Marchese approached and made a long speech in his respectful manner, a manner that was ironically expansive and formed a puzz-ling contrast with the short, sharp way which he adopted as soon as he turned to business affairs, and with the insipid vapidity of his sentimental vein. Yet this manner was not unnatural; it had grown on him, perhaps, because he was not bold enough to proclaim openly the power to which he believed himself entitled by virtue of his money and his intellect. He therefore tended, in a poor-spirited way, to hide his sense of superiority behind exaggeratedly humble words.

There was something disagreeably amusing about his smile on such occasions; it was hard to know whether to beat or to applaud him.[22]

This mixture of assertiveness and self-distrust, of commanding assurance in one field and feelings of inadequacy in another, of genuine diffidence and ironically disguised superiority, has been well observed and bears an interesting relation to the contrast, drawn in the previous chapter of *The Baths of Lucca*, between Eduard Gans's intellectual penetration and his social clumsiness. It adds an essential element to Heine's satiric portrait of German Jewry in the age of emancipation.

In Chapter 8 the spotlight shifts from Gumpelino to his servant. In mock-heroic vein Heine shows us Hirsch-Hyazinth under a laurel tree with Gumpelino's dog Apollo—Daphne, we see, has now joined Hyacinthus and Apollo 'in exile'—engaged in making a list of those who have used his services as a lottery agent. The narrator too, it appears, was among his customers.

'If only you had played the number 1365 instead of 1364 the last time you had a flutter with me in the lottery, you would now be worth 100 000 marks and wouldn't have to run about here in Italy! You could be sitting quietly and contentedly on your sofa in Hamburg and let other people tell you what it's like in these Italian parts. As God is my judge, I would never have made the journey here if I had not done it as a favour to Herr Gumpel. The heat I've had to stand, and the danger, and the tiredness! Wherever there is some crazy fad, there he has to be, and I have to tag along. I'd have left him long ago if he could do without me. But who could then tell the folks back home of all the respect and all the culture he enjoyed abroad? And to tell you the truth, I'm beginning to see that there's a lot *in* all this culture. In Hamburg, thank God, I don't need any; but it *might* just come in handy in some other place. The world has changed such a lot. And people are right—a bit of culture does a man credit . . .'[23]

While keeping an ironic distance between Hirsch and the reader, Heine is nevertheless beginning to use him as a spokesman, as an unconscious but sharp-eyed purveyor of a satiric view of the German-Jewish world. Hirsch's presentation of the impecunious intellectual who secretly longs for the quiet life of the rentier, his blithe assumption that culture is the last thing one needs in money-grubbing Hamburg, his lively sense of the social changes that are completely transforming the world in which he has to live—all these lend weight to Freud's assertion, in *The Joke and its Relation to the Unconscious*, that Harry or Heinrich Heine and Hirsch-Hyazinth have more in common than just their initials and their change of name.

At the same time, however, the simple Hirsch is made to exemplify attitudes to poetry which Heine had often encountered among members of his own family and their acquaintances. This is made clearer in a passage Heine shortened considerably before publication. When the narrator thinks he has caught Hirsch in the act of writing poetry (suggested, no doubt, by his presence under the laurel bough in the presence of a canine Apollo), the little man throws up his hands in horror.

'Poetry? God protect me from poems and from thinking for the sake of thinking! I am a practical man, a man of the world. Pardon me, I forgot: you are a poet yourself, you write beautiful poems, I have read them to find a few mottos for my lottery tickets, but, to tell you the truth, there are not many ideas in them that I can use. My brother-in-law Mendel and my brother Moritz have helped me to read them, and they often said to me: "If that Dr Heine would only use his brains a bit better and start a decent business, he could become a great man." And honestly now: why must you always write about the sea? I have been to Cuxhaven myself, and have looked at the sea. What is there to say about it? It's nothing but water . . .[24]

'There is some truth in your words, Mr Hyazinth', the narrator replies; 'and on the other side of the Jordan there are many people who think just like you.' 'The other side of the Jordan' holds the Jewish community of Hamburg, including Heine's own uncle Salomon whose views are not unfairly represented in the words Hirsch here attributes to his brother Moritz and his brother-in-law Mendel.[25] The poet probably deleted the passage just quoted from *The Baths of Lucca*—a passage, be it noted, in which the narrator is actually given Heine's own name!—because it seemed too directly autobiographical for his more oblique purposes.

Among the humble avocations by means of which Hirsch-Hyazinth made his living before being drawn into Gumpelino's cultural orbit we find that of a cutter of corns, and it is with great pride that he recalls how he once had the honour to relieve the feet of one of the Rothschilds of such unwanted excrescences.

'This happened in his inner sanctum while he sat on his green armchair as though it were a throne. He spoke like a king, with courtiers standing all around him; he ordered them about and sent messages to all the kings of the world; and while I was cutting his corns, I thought to myself: what you now have in your hand is the foot of the man whose own hands hold the whole world. Now *you* are somebody too: if you cut too deep down below he'll lose his temper up above and he'll cut the kings more sharply. That was the greatest moment of my life.[26]

Hirsch's speech conveys very well the sense of social upheaval and mobility engendered by a money economy, along with the pride less wealthy Jews were apt to feel at the achievements of Europe's greatest bankers. The Rothschilds, shouldered out of an earlier chapter along with the Goldschmidts, now come into clearer view—not quite clear enough for the narrator, however, who asks Hyazinth whether the financier on whose lower extremities he had been permitted to operate was 'that noble-hearted Briton, the man in Lombard Street, who has opened a pawnshop for emperors and kings'. New banker, the ironic question would seem to suggest, is but old pawnbroker writ large; the former would find 'noble-heartedness' as little an asset in his business dealings as the latter. The narrator's question elicits from Hirsch-Hyazinth an answer which is worth quoting in full.

'Of course, Herr Doktor, that's understood; I mean the great Roth-schild, the great Nathan Rothschild, Nathan the Wise, with whom the Emperor of Brazil has pawned his diamond crown. But I have also had the honour to make the acquaintance of Baron Salomon Rothschild in Frankfurt; and though I was not so intimate with his foot as with that of the other Rothschild, he did know how to value me. When Marchese Gumpelino told him I had once been a lottery agent, the Baron said very wittily: "I am something like that myself, I am the chief agent of the Rothschild lottery, and my colleague shall not take his meal with the servants, he shall sit next to me at my table." And as God is my judge, Herr Doktor, I did sit next to Salomon Rothschild, and he treated me quite like his equal, quite *famillionaire* . . .'[27]

Ganz famillionär—Freud has made that coinage the corner-stone of his analysis of jokes, and has shown how much of Heine's own resentments, as a poor relation in a family grown rich by financial operations, Hyazinth is made to convey in his naïve pride.[28] But several other features of this passage are worthy of note. First, how Heine here supplements the pawn-broker image with that of the lottery collector to describe the Rothschilds' operations—suggesting that what they do on a global scale humbler Jews do more modestly in their German backyards. By making Rothschild himself recognize this, Heine conveys, secondly, something of Jewish solidarity: the pride poor Jews take in the achievements of their rich co-religionists is supplemented by the rich Jews' feeling—strong even in the midst of 'famillionaire' condescension—that the poor were their brethren and had a right to be treated as such. The last and perhaps the most masterly stroke is the reminis-cence of Lessing's *Nathan the Wise* which Heine makes his Hirsch-Hyazinth introduce at this point. This was the work which had done more than any other piece of writing to prepare German minds for civic emancipation of the Jews. The ironic superimposition of Lessing's noble Jew on to the 'noble-hearted' Briton Nathan Rothschild serves to suggest that what brought about the Gentile world's increasing 'tolerance' was not so much the humanitarianism of Lessing as the logic of economic development, the power of money which brought respectability—if not always a reputation for 'noble-heartedness'—in bourgeois society. The best, however, is still to come. Hirsch-Hyazinth continues:

'I was in Salomon Rothschild's house when he gave the famous children's ball of which you have read in the papers. Never in all my born days will I see such a grand show again. I have, after all, been to a ball in Hamburg which cost 1500 marks and 8 shillings—and that was nothing but a few chickens' droppings compared to a real dungheap. The gold and silver I saw there, and the diamonds! Such stars and orders! The Order of the Falcon, the Order of the Golden Fleece, the Order of the Lion, the Order of the Eagle—and there was even a child, I assure you, a tiny tot, that wore the Order of the Elephant! The children wore lovely fancy dress and they played at making loans. They were dressed up like kings, with crowns on their heads; but there was one of the bigger lads who was dressed exactly like old

Nathan Rothschild. He played his part very well, kept both hands in his trouser-pockets, rattled his money, and shook with bad temper when one of the little kings wanted to borrow off him—only the little lad with the white coat and the red trousers got a kindly pat on the cheek and was praised: "You're my boy, my pet, I'm proud of you; but your cousin Michel had better keep away from me, I'll give nothing to a fool like that who expends more men in a day than he has coming in in a year; he'll make some trouble yet in the world and spoil my business." As true as the Lord shall help me, the boy played his part wonderfully well, especially when he helped a fat child dressed in white satin with real silver lilies in its efforts to walk and said to it occasionally: "Now, you, behave yourself, make an honest living, and see that they don't chase you out again, or I'll lose my money." I assure you, Herr Doktor, it was a pleasure to listen to that lad; and the other children too—dear sweet children they all were—played their parts extremely well—until the cake was brought in and they all started fighting for the best piece, tore the crowns off one another's heads and some of them even . . .'[29]

Hyazinth's anecdote provides the reader not only with a physical caricature of Nathan Rothschild—the stance with his hands in his pockets was a gift to contemporary cartoonists—but also with an ironic commentary on the history of Europe and the Rothschilds' involvement with the newly-established order. As Peter von Matt has rightly said: to look through Hirsch Hyazinth's eyes is to acquire a clear eye for the economic foundations of power, and for the role played by great banking houses in at once consolidating and diminishing the monarchical systems of Europe. The reader's pleasure is enhanced, however, by the way in which the narrator winks at him over Hyazinth's head; by the perception, that is, of symbolic meanings hidden from the little man who cannot himself see, for instance, that the fat child with the silver lilies stands for the king of France after the Restoration. For author and reader Hyazinth's 'naïve' tale constitutes a sophisticated satire on the social power of money, on European politics in the age of the Holy Alliance and its congresses, and on the veneer of civilization which peels off when men's appetites and acquisitive instincts are aroused.

In the manuscript version of *The Baths of Lucca* Hirsch-Hyazinth's account of his dealings with the Rothschilds is followed by a long passage about the 'fear' the narrator pretends to have of them.

I am not used to being afraid . . . I protect myself from stupid princes by keeping away from their territories and thus giving them no opportunity to try their tricks on me—but before Nathan Rothschild I tremble with fear. Before you can say Jack Robinson, he could send a few kings, stockbrokers, and policemen to my rooms and have me carried to the nearest fortress prison . . .[30]

Such are the realities of power! To avoid the fate he has envisaged for those who offend the Rothschilds, the narrator promises, with obvious irony, to write a book in praise of that great family's merits. What such a book might be like is revealed by another passage in this same manuscript, a passage also deleted before *The Baths of Lucca* went into print.

When I think about political economy in these our latter days it becomes ever more clear to me that without the Rothschilds' help the financial embarrassment of most states would have been exploited by subversives wanting to mislead the populace into upsetting whatever order or disorder constituted the status quo. Revolutions are generally triggered off by deficiency of money; by preventing such deficiencies the Rothschild system may have served to preserve peace in Europe. This system, or rather Nathan Rothschild, its inventor, is still providing firm foundations for such peace: it does not inhibit states from making war on one another exactly as before, but it does make it difficult for the people to overthrow established authority . . . Religion is no longer able to guarantee to governments that the people will remain peaceful; the Rothschild system of loans can perform that task much better, it possesses the moral force or power which religion has lost, it can act as a surrogate for religion—indeed, it *is* a new religion, and when the old religion finally goes under it will provide substitutes for its practical blessings.

Heine then adds, in words that reveal more clearly than any so far his equal dislike of the Christianity he had so recently embraced and of what he was henceforth so often to call the new 'religion' of money:

Strangely enough, it is once again the Jews who invented this new religion . . . Murdered Judaea was as cunning as the dying Nessus, and its poisoned robe—poisoned with its own blood—consumed the strength of the Roman Hercules so effectively that his mighty limbs grew weary, armour and helmet fell away from his withered body, and his voice, once so mighty in battle, dwindled to a prayerful whine. Miserably, in a death-agony that dragged on through a thousand years and more, Rome dies by the Judaic poison.[31]

It is not difficult to guess the considerations which induced Heine, when he came to publish *The Baths of Lucca*, to omit this anti-Christian passage with its double-edged compliment to Jewish financial flair and the Jews' alleged capacity for subtle revenges. It was all too close to the stereotype of the Jews in the minds of their enemies—to charges levelled against them by those who wished them ill, from Seneca to Voltaire.

Chapter 9 of the *Baths of Lucca* shows Gumpelino at home, at his devotions before what Hyazinth calls 'the Primadonna with the Christ-child'. As so often, Hirsch's malapropism is apt beyond his intention: for there is indeed little difference between the Marchese's devotion to opera and his devotion to Roman Catholic ceremony. This gives Hirsch the clue to reveal his own religious philosophy. Roman Catholicism, we find, is too irrational for his sober nature, Protestantism too dry and unimaginative; and as for *die altjüdische Religion*, Judaism of the old observance, that, in the Christian dispensation, brings those who profess it only misfortune and disgrace. What about the new 'reformed' Judaism, then, whose professors attend a 'temple' instead of a *shool* or synagogue and call themselves 'Mosaic' rather than 'Jewish'? In his letters Heine himself had used such euphemisms when writing to non-Jews; but for the religious reformers he had always had very imperfect sympathies. Here is what Hirsch has to say about the 'Mosaists' and their 'temple':

'I can make do for a while with the new Israelite Temple; I mean the pure Mosaic worship, with orthographical German prayers and uplifting sermons and a few little sentimentalities that a religion just can't do without. As God is my judge, I don't ask for a better religion than that—it's well worth supporting. I mean to do my bit, and when I get back to Hamburg I'll go to the new Temple every Saturday except those on which the lottery results are declared. There are, I am sorry to say, people who give this new Israelitish faith a bad name and say—if you'll forgive the expression—that it may lead to schisms. But I give you my word it's a good clean religion, a little too good perhaps, for the common man, for whom the old Jewish religion is,

perhaps, still quite serviceable. The common man must have some-
thing stupid to make him happy . . .'[32]

Hirsch's malapropism—*Mosaik-Gottesdienst* for *mosaischer
Gottesdienst*—is as appropriate as ever: it transforms a religious
service devised for those who follow the laws of Moses into
one put together from all sort of little bits and pieces instead of
being carved from a monolith. 'A thing of shreds and patches'
would convey the same thought by means of a different image.
Hirsch's naïvely expressed determination to visit the Temple
only on those Saturdays on which no lottery business is con-
ducted shows the erosion to which the laws of Moses (they
forbid business dealings on the sabbath!) were subject in the
age of 'mosaic' worship under the pressure of economic ne-
cessity. His stress on the 'cleanliness' of the new religion, on
the other hand, conjures up by contrast the lack of personal
hygiene with which reformed Western Jews so often charged
their more orthodox East-European brothers. Heine's essay
On Poland had played on the same contrast. The essay on
Poland is equally recalled by the justly famous passage which
now follows in *The Baths of Lucca*, a passage which transposes
into Hirsch's 'epic' idiom that respect for the 'wholeness' of
orthodox Judaism which Heine had expressed in his own voice
and manner in the earlier work. The excerpt is particularly
remarkable in our context because it introduces, in a most
sympathetic way, the commonest guise in which rural non-
Jews would encounter Jews in Heine's day: as pedlars carrying
their packs of miscellaneous wares. By permission of the late
Professor William Rose, I adapt the translation he published in
Heinrich Heine. Two Studies of his Thought and Feeling,
Clarendon Press, Oxford 1956:

There lives in Hamburg . . . a man named Moses Lump, who is also
called Moses Lümpchen, or briefly Lümpchen; he runs about the
whole week in wind and weather with his bundle on his back to earn
the few marks he needs; now when he comes home on Friday evening
he finds the lamp lit with its seven candles, a white cloth on the table,
and he lays down his bundle and all his cares, and sits down at table
with his mis-shapen wife and even more mis-shapen daughter, par-
takes with them of fish cooked in a tasty garlic sauce, sings the most
splendid psalms of King David, rejoices whole-heartedly at the ex-
odus of the Children of Israel from Egypt, rejoices also that all the

miscreants who behaved wickedly towards them died in the end, that King Pharaoh, Nebuchadnezzar, Haman, Antiochus, Titus and all such people are dead, while Lümpchen is still alive and eating fish with his wife and child—And I tell you, *Herr Doktor*, the fish is delicious, and the man is happy, he does not have to worry about culture, he sits wrapped contentedly in his religion and his green dressing-gown like Diogenes in his tub, he looks cheerfully at his candles, which he does not even have to snuff himself—And I tell you, when the candles begin to burn a little dimly and the *Schabbes-frau* whose task it is to snuff them is not at hand, and if Rothschild the Great were to enter with all his brokers, discounters, dispatchers and *chefs de comptoir* with whom he has conquered the world, and he were to say: 'Moses Lump, ask me a favour; whatever you wish shall be granted'—*Herr Doktor*, I am convinced, Moses Lump would calmly reply: 'Snuff my candles!' and Rothschild the Great would exclaim in astonishment: 'Well, if I weren't Rothschild I should like to be such a Lümpchen!'[33]

The irony of this passage—it is, after all, the simple Hirsch-Hyazinth who comments on the 'foolishness' that makes possible the felicity of Moses Lump—cannot blind us to its underlying seriousness. The life of the poor, sincerely religious Jewish pedlar excites admiration, even envy; but such emotions are tinged with the knowledge that once Jews have bitten the apple of European culture they can never return to anything like this uncomplicated contentment. The speaking name 'Lump' ('rascal', 'ragged scamp') does not fit the character of the man who bears it; it indicates, rather, the contempt in which the world generally holds such unassuming men. Jews often owed undignified names to the crude humour of government officials, exercised when German and Austrian laws forced Jews to abandon their ancient style of name-giving and assume European names instead.

The imagined intrusion of Rothschild into the simple life of Moses Lump is of especial interest. The humble little Jew, secure in his religion and his ancient customs, is here confronted by the Jew who influences the counsels of monarchs—a fairy-tale monarch himself who can make wishes come true by the magic of money. These two extremes of Jewish society have something in common, something that distinguishes them at once from Hirsch-Hyazinth, whose story brings them together, and from the narrator of *The Baths of Lucca*, whose

Byronic self-division had been highlighted in an earlier chapter. Rothschild and the poor pedlar, the servant of Mammon and the servant of Jehovah, are not divided within themselves—they are at rest in their own world, they have an inner security which contrasts with modern *Zerrissenheit*. That is why the great financier can, at the end, express his admiration of the pedlar's sabbath bliss by saying that he would wish to be this 'Lümpchen' *if he were not Rothschild*. So, at least, Hirsch-Hyazinth sees it; whether the Rothschilds would, in real life, have concurred, is a question Heine wisely leaves unanswered.

Between them, the fictional creations Gumpelino, Hirsch-Hyazinth, and Moses Lump, suggest a social hierarchy of German Jewry. Klaus Pabel, in an illuminating study of the *Pictures of Travel*, has described this as 'a typology of Jewish fate in the Diaspora ranging from orthodox identity and poverty to loss of identity and wealth'. Originally they all belonged to that 'sound nobility' of which Heine speaks near the beginning of the *Baths of Lucca*: a family with which God once formed an alliance but which has, since then, come down in the world. Now they have developed a scale of differentiated attitudes and self-images. This begins with Moses Lump, who rests content with his inherited Jewish religion, his lowly economic function, and his alienation from the Gentile people on whom he largely depends for his livelihood. Next comes the more adaptable Hirsch-Hyazinth, whose devotion to the religion of his father is less unquestioning, who has come to look on Judaism as a 'misfortune', but who nevertheless keeps his loyalty to the people into which he was born. It is he, therefore, who tells us of the unbroken existence of 'Lümpchen', which he admires but cannot share. In his endeavours to better his social position he has been drawn into the service—and to a not inconsiderable extent manages the life—of the Marchese Gumpelino, whose wealth acts as a propellant that makes him aspire away from the bourgeoisie towards the aristocracy, away from Judaism towards fashionable Christianity, away from complete absorption in money-making towards the acquisition of European culture. His aristocracy, his Christianity, his culture are all depicted as unauthentic. True emancipation, as Heine conceives it, must take other paths, paths that may, perhaps, lead to something like the narrator figure in *The Baths of*

Lucca, the 'I' which is not to be identified with the author's empirical 'I' but which has clearly derived many of its features from Heine's actuality and aspirations.[34] Whether that is a recipe for happiness is another question again; for the narrator of *The Baths of Lucca* must perforce share the self-division, the *Zerrissenheit*, that was the lot of so many intelligent and culti-vated Europeans of the nineteenth century.

From the poetic heights of Hyazinth's presentation of the life of Moses Lump Heine brings us down with a characteristic bump to a narrative of Gumpelino's misfortunes in love in which a dose of salts plays a wearisome part. The salts are supplied by Hirsch, who turns out his pockets to find them, and this action enables Heine to add some realistic details designed to root Hirsch even more firmly in Jewish life. The salts (*Glaubersalz*, malapropized by their owner into *Glauben-salz*, which leads to various puns or ambiguities involving *Glauben*, religious faith) were given to him by his lady love, fat Gudel who lives on the *Dreckwall*. Here we have another street name from the Hamburg Jewish quarter to match the *Steinweg* Heine had earlier used as shorthand for the whole district and its inhabitants, a speaking name which could easily be made to characterize the unhygienic conditions that often pertained to the crowded urban dwelling-places of the Jewish poor. In Hirsch's pocket is also found a black-bound book containing the Psalms of David (*Tehillim*, often used as in-cantations in times of danger), a list of debtors, and a flat piece of bread, like a ship's biscuit, with a hole in the middle. On this last item Heine makes no comment; but those in the know will take it for a sign that Hirsch celebrates Passover in the tradi-tional way, for it is a custom in many communities to save a small piece of the unleavened bread which has been used in the *Seder* ritual from one year to the next. The small hole enabled a piece of string to be passed through this piece of *matzah*, which could then be hung up or even worn as an amulet. Rothschild also comes into view once more, since he is never far from the little man's mind: the powders Hirsch hands to Gumpelino are said to have the democratic property of making Rothschild and the humblest little commission-agent feel the same natural effects.

Chapter 10 of *The Baths of Lucca* keeps us in the company of familiar characters but takes a new turn—a turn prepared for, thematically, by hints in earlier chapters (such as a symbolic incident involving a tulip) and, indeed, by the defiant prominence given to Jewish figures throughout. Heine is now preparing to settle his accounts with Count Platen for anti-Semitic insults against himself. Platen's poetry turns out to be part of the cultural curriculum Gumpelino and Hirsch have to absolve; but before he launches into his savage attack, Heine takes time out to explain why his portrait of Gumpelino may seem to lack full individual definition. The narrator addresses his 'dear reader' in the following terms.

I hope you will be sharp-witted enough to understand a negative character without too much positive individuation. If I indulged in the latter, I might find myself involved in an action for libel or in things even worse than that. The Marchese is powerful by reason of his money and his connections. He is also the natural ally of my enemies, he supports them with his subsidies, he is an aristocrat, an ultra-Papist, only one thing is lacking—well, that too he will allow himself to be taught, he has the manual in his hands, as you will see.[35]

In the proximity of Platen Gumpelino becomes a more sinister figure than he seemed before. His hankering after social recognition makes him the ally of aristocrats by birth, his change of religion fills him with a convert's zeal to advance the cause of Catholicism—he is even in danger of taking on the homosexuality of Platen, whose poems he is holding in his hand. Hyazinth, whole pale little businessman's face we now see for the last time, is not affected by this ominous turn in *The Baths of Lucca*; he departs in a blaze of glory as he tells the story of his honest dealings with a non-Jewish greengrocer, who won 50 000 marks in the lottery for which Hyazinth was an agent in circumstances that would have made it easy for Hyazinth to pocket the money himself. The receipt for this he always carries with him.

'When I die', Hyazinth said, with a tear in his eye, 'let the receipt be put into the grave with me; and when, up there, on the Day of Judgment, I have to account for my deeds, I will stand forth before the Almighty's throne with this receipt in my hands; and when my evil angel has recited the wicked actions I have performed in this world, and my good angel gets ready to read off the list of my good actions, I shall calmly say: "Be quiet!—All I ask you is: Do you find this receipt correct? Is this the handwriting of Christian Hinrich Klotz? Then a tiny angel will come flying up and will say that he knows little Klotz's handwriting perfectly, and he will tell the story of my honest action. The Eternal Creator, however, the All-Knowing One from Whom nothing is hidden, remembers the story and praises me in the presence of the sun, the moon, and the stars; and straight off He reckons out in His head that when my wicked actions are deducted from 50 000 marks worth of honesty, I shall still have a balance in my favour; and then He says: 'Hirsch! I hereby create you an Angel of the First Class; you are entitled to wear wings with red and white feathers.'[36]

That counteracts admirably the newly sinister portrait of Gumpelino, and at the same time subverts Gentile stereotypes of Jewish sharp dealing with men of another faith. The humorous anthropomorphization of Jehovah—at once a Jewish god who does sums in his head and a German God who hands out to his angels the equivalents of Prussian titles and decorations—adds the finishing touch to Heine's tender portrait of an unpretentious little German Jew, a portrait of which, as his letters of the time attest, he was justifiably proud.

The later French version of *The Baths of Lucca*, in which Heine had a hand, draws its readers' attention to a point that might easily be missed by Germans as well as by Frenchmen unacquainted with German conditions. The lottery for which Hirsch works, the French version explains, is that of Altona, not that of Hamburg. 'À Hambourg il n'existent d'autres loteries que les loteries de lots et de séries qu'on tire tous les trois mois, tandis qu'à Altona on a conservé la loterie française toujours ouverte et accessible aux classes les plus pauvres.'[37] Klotz is probably one of these poorer customers, and Hyazinth takes pride in having helped him to a modest fortune. That Heine shows such familiarity with the ways of lotteries need not surprise us; not only did he enjoy a flutter himself, but his father had, at one time, tried to augment his income by acting as a lottery agent. *The Baths of Lucca* convey the harried life of such an agent very well by designating the wearisome routes by which Hirsch trudged across Hamburg in his attempts to make a living before the Marchese took him into his service.

The time has now come to settle accounts with August von Platen, who had dared to make his fellow poet's Jewishness a shame and a reproach. Heine has the narrator of *The Baths of Lucca* speak as a Protestant who uses the right to protest which is enshrined in the very name of his religion, and he does so in the person of Heine himself, the 'baptized Heine' whom Platen had attacked in his play *The Romantic Oedipus*.

Yes, dear reader, you are not mistaken: he means me. You can read for yourself in *Oedipus* that I am a real Jew who, after writing love-songs for a few hours, sits down to clip or circumcise coins; that on the sabbath I squat down together with long-bearded Yids to chant the Talmud; that on Passover eve I slaughter an immature Christian and that, out of pure malice, I always choose some unhappy writer for that purpose. No, dear reader, I won't lie to you, you will not find such admirably developed images in *Oedipus*, and that precisely is what I object to. Count Platen has the best subjects sometimes and has no idea how to treat them. If only he had a little more imagination, he would at the very least have depicted me as a secret pawnbroker; what comic scenes would then have offered themselves! It hurts me deeply to see how the good count misses one opportunity after another for a good joke. What splendid use he could have made of Ernst Raupach [a dramatist whom Platen wrongly believed to be Jewish] as the Rothschild of tragedy from whom the Prussian royal theatres get their loans! . . .[38]

One might take a passage such as this as a variation on John Stuart Mill's prayer: 'Lord enlighten Thou our enemies, sharpen their wits, give acuteness to their perceptions and consecutiveness and clearness to their reasoning powers; we are in danger from their folly, not their wisdom: their weakness is what fills us with apprehension, not their strength.' But it is surely more curious than that. After exhibiting, in the figures of Gumpel and Hirsch, his undoubted power to concentrate his observation of contemporary Jewish traits into portrait-caricatures in which anti-Jewish stereotypes are both used and subverted, Heine now takes a self-lacerating delight in projecting such stereotypes on to himself. Jews, one remembers, have often shown themselves surprisingly ready to be amused by jokes and caricatures that exploit their enemies' view of them. In Heine's case, the startlingly masochistic exhibition we have just been examining forms the prelude to an attack on Platen which ridicules that poet's tragic homosexuality and even, *horribile dictu*, his poverty. This distasteful performance may best be characterized with an image Heine himself used in another connection—the image of patients in a hospital who expose their own diseases in the process of mocking those of others.[39] Let us draw a veil over the Platen chapters of *The Baths of Lucca* and pass on to the work in which the hospital image may be found.

(iii)

The work just mentioned, *The Town of Lucca* (*Die Stadt Lucca*), follows *The Baths of Lucca* in *Pictures of Travel* and was clearly intended as its sequel. Heine planned, at first, to reintroduce Gumpelino and Hirsch-Hyazinth, but such traces of this attempt as still survive[40] show so feeble a repetition of what had been done with these characters in the earlier work that it comes as no surprise to find it soon abandoned. Jewish characters and Jewish problems, so central in *The Baths of Lucca*, are now assigned to the periphery again. An attack on rabbis, for instance—rare in the early Heine, whose respect for the logic of strict orthodoxy is well attested—is only incidental to a general indictment of the clergy, though it is noticeable that once the Jewish theme has been touched on, Heine cannot help elaborating it. The following passage from *The Town of Lucca* shows the mechanism clearly:

It is a common observation that the whole world over the faces of priests—rabbis, muftis, Dominicans, church commissioners, popes, Buddhist monks, in short, the whole of God's diplomatic corps—show a certain family resemblance; the kind of resemblance one always finds in people that ply the same trade. All over the world tailors are noted for their slender limbs, butchers and soldiers have the same ferocious appearance, Jews have the same distinctively honest expression—not because they are descended from Abraham, Isaac, and Jacob, but because they are businessmen. A Christian businessman in Frankfurt resembles a Jewish businessman in Frankfurt as one bad egg resembles another . . . Therefore ecclesiastical businessmen, people who make their living by religion, also take on a certain facial resemblance.[41]

Rabbis, we see, are still the first that spring to Heine's mind when he thinks of God's diplomatic corps; and that soon triggers off thoughts of secular Jews. The observation that these 'have a distinctively honest expression' is ironic, of course; Heine intends to bring to his readers' minds the stereotype of the cunning Jew who cheats you in business dealings. He only does this, however, in order to discredit the stereotype. What those who operate with it object to, he argues, is not 'Jewishness' at all, but a business mentality which pervades all walks of life and respects no religious or ethnic frontiers.

Heine continues his attack on the Gentile stereotype of the Jew elsewhere in *The Town of Lucca*. A procession of Italian monks, for instance, gives him an opportunity to glance at objections to Jewish modes of speech—what Germans deprecate as *mauscheln*, a singsong jargon with a nasal or throaty accent.

The foremost monks walked with their arms crossed, in solemn silence; but [others] chanted so nasally, and with such slurps and gurgles, that if the majority of the population had been Jews and their religion the dominant religion of the state, this kind of chant would have been termed *mauscheln*.[42]

The charges levelled against Jews, whether religious or moral or aesthetic, can be levelled equally well at their non-Jewish contemporaries. Heine therefore takes special delight in treating *aristocrats* with the kind of disdain which German anti-Semites reserved for Jews: 'a sneaking crew of noble bugs', he calls them in *The Town of Lucca*, 'that nestle in the cracks of ancient thrones'.

It is not unnatural for a traveller in Italy to reflect on the relation of classical antiquity to a Christian culture; and if the traveller happens to be Heine, he will extend that reflection to take in the Jewish origin of Christianity. This is what we find in *The Town of Lucca*. The sixth chapter of that work begins with a quotation from the *Iliad*—ironically ascribed to the Vulgate, to indicate its biblical status for the narrator—which speaks of the happy life of the Greek gods.

Then suddenly there came panting in a pale Jew, dripping with blood, a crown of thorns on his head and a great wooden cross on his shoulders; and he threw the cross down on the high table of the gods so that the golden goblets trembled, and the gods fell silent and grew pale, and became ever paler, until finally they dissolved altogether into mist. And now a sad time followed, in which the world grew grey and dark. The happy gods were gone, and Olympus became a lazar-house where gods who had been flayed, roasted, and turned on the spit slunk tediously about, dressed their wounds, and sang dismal songs. Religion no longer gave joy; it gave consolation instead. It was a mournful, bloodstained religion for delinquents.

But perhaps it was necessary for a sick and downtrodden humanity? If one sees one's god suffer, one bears one's own pains with greater ease. The happy gods of former times, who themselves felt no sorrow, had no notion how a poor, tormented human being could feel . . . In order to be loved whole-heartedly, one must suffer. Pity is the final consecration of love, perhaps it is love itself. Of all the gods that have ever been, Jesus is therefore the one who has been most loved. Especially by women.[43]

It was the Jews, then, who brought forth the pale Galilean at whose breath the world grew grey; it was the Jews who gave humanity the religion of love, charity, and pity which it needed at a precise moment in its history. When Jesus appears in Heine's pages, he does so as a Jew, reared in the religion of Israel, drawing on the Israelite heritage for help in performing his world-historical task. He also appears as a *bon dieu citoyen*, a true democrat whom the narrator professes to love beyond any other god. 'Truly,' he adds, 'if Christ were no god as yet, I would elect him to that office; and instead of an absolute god forced upon me I would much rather serve him, an elected god, the god of my choice.'[44] Heine is here playing his game of outwitting the censor by disguising a political statement as a religious-confessional one. What he is commending, clearly, is in line with the principle established by the 1830 revolution in France: the substitution of election by the people for an unquestioned dynastic succession. We may also, however, see in this tribute to a freely 'elected' Christ an attempt to justify, *ex post facto*, the baptism which had caused Heine so much anguish.

All this gives added point to Heine's satire, in *The Town of Lucca*, on the activity of rich Christians who proselytize among poor Jews. Here is a typical onslaught, put into the mouth of an Anglo-Irish lady:

'These rich people now, Herr Doctor, whom we see [as Presidents, Vice Presidents or Secretaries of Societies for the Conversion of the Heathen] making every effort to render some mouldy old Jewish beggar fit for heaven, thus ensuring that they will enjoy his company in the world to come—I have always wondered why it is that they never think of letting him share in their delights here on earth. They would never, for instance, invite him to their country houses for the summer, where, I am sure, dainties will be served that the poor fellow would enjoy just as much there as he would in heaven itself.'

To which the narrator, the 'I' that speaks in *The Town of Lucca*, answers:

'The explanation, dear lady, is very simple. Heavenly enjoyments cost nothing, and our pleasure is doubled when we can make our fellow man happy without charge.'[45]

What Heine here has in mind—as his letters attest—is above all the Society for the Conversion of Jews which operated in Berlin. That city, indeed, and its Jewish inhabitants, are never far from Heine's thoughts—as becomes obvious from a later conversation between the narrator of *The Town of Lucca* and an Italian lady. The name 'Berlin' suggests 'bears'; and that in turn suggests the name of that wealthy Jewish family which included the dramatist Michael *Beer* and his more famous brother Giacomo Meyer*beer*.

'Many bears live in the city itself: it has even been said that Berlin owes its inception to bears and that its real name is Bear-lin. The city bears, by the way, are very tame, and some of them are so well educated that they write the most beautiful tragedies and compose the most glorious music.'[46]

The calculated reference to 'tameness' in this passage would seem to reduce the rousing potential attributed to Meyerbeer's music in *The Journey from Munich to Genoa*, just as its 'glory' is somewhat dimmed when it is yoked with an appreciation of the 'beauty' of Michael Beer's feeble plays. 'Are the Berliners Christians then?' the Italian lady asks, when given this information about the bears (Beers) that inhabit it; and her question elicits the following characteristic answer.

Their position with regard to Christianity is very peculiar. At bottom they lack it altogether—they are much too rational to practise it seriously. Since they know, however, that Christianity is necessary to the state, to ensure obedience to authority and to keep thieving and murdering in reasonable bounds, they expend much eloquence on at least converting their fellow men to Christianity. They seek, as it were, to provide substitutes for themselves in the practice of a religion that they would like to keep up but whose tenets and injunctions they find too troublesome for their own part. In this awkward situation they turn to the poor Jews, who are always so ready to be of service. These now become Christians in their stead; and since money and kind words can persuade this people to allow anything at all to be done to it, the Jews have thrown themselves into Christianity with such a will that they have begun lamenting the decay of faith in modern times, defending the doctrine of the Trinity to the death, even believing in the Trinity when the weather gets hot. They rage against rationalists, creep about the country as missionaries and religious spies handing out edifying tracts, show great talent in turning up their eyes in church, pull the most sanctimonious faces, and they are drawing upon themselves, by their practices, so much applause from the highest quarters that professional jealousy has begun to rear its ugly head, and that the older masters of the craft have already begun to complain, secretly, that Christianity has fallen altogether into the hands of the Jews.[47]

This bitterly satiric passage brings a notable addition to Heine's growing gallery of caricature-portraits: the convert from Judaism who not only practises his new religion but who also goes out to proselytize among non-Christians. The poet may well have Neander in mind here. The Jewish origins of such men are never forgotten, though, by their new co-religionists who (Heine insinuates), resent their competitive presence in much the same way as Christian businessmen resented Jewish traders and conservative professors of law the zeal of baptized ex-Jews among their colleagues. Even the most spiritual of professions are mindful of their privileges and the economic advantages they confer! Contemporary readers would no doubt be reminded, by Heine's satiric passage, that no less an authority than Friedrich Schleiermacher had voiced disquiet at the danger of a 'Judaicization' of Christianity.

Heine's depiction of the Jewish proselyte is placed in a wider context by a conversation between the narrator and an emancipated British lady which again reverts to the Jewish origins of Christianity. The narrator explains, in words Heine himself clearly endorses, that he sees the different religions as conglomerations of loved traditions, sacred stories, feasts of remembrance, which have come down to the various peoples of the world as sacred heirlooms bequeathed by their ancestors, and which should never be forced on to men of another faith. The Greeks, he alleges, understood this very well:

But then a people came out of Egypt, the homeland of crocodiles and of priests, and besides skin diseases and stolen vessels of gold and silver it brought with it a so-called positive religion, a so-called church, a framework of dogmas one had to believe in and sacred ceremonies one had to perform—the model of all later state religions. Now there arose that spirit of smelling out faults in other people (*die Menschenmäkelei*), of proselytizing, of forcing men to profess positive beliefs, and all those sacred atrocities that have cost humanity so much blood and so many tears."

"Damn this people and its original sin!"

"O Mathilde, it has been damned long ago and now drags the anguish of its damnation through the centuries. O that Egypt! Its manufactures defy the tooth of time, its pyramids stand unshakeably, its mummies are as indestructible as ever—and just as indestructible is that mummy of a people which roams the earth wrapped in its ancient lettered mummy-cloth, a petrified piece of world history, a ghost that makes its living by peddling bills of exchange and cast-off trousers. Do you not see, my lady, that old man over there, the man with the white beard whose tip seems to be growing black again, the man with those spectral eyes . . .?"

"Isn't that the place where there are ruins of ancient Roman tombs?"

"Yes indeed, that is where the old man is sitting; and perhaps, Mathilde, he is just saying his prayers, eerie prayers in which he laments his sorrows and accuses nations that have long vanished from the earth and only live on in old nursery tales—but he, in his anguish, hardly notices that he is sitting on the graves of the very enemies for whose destruction he is praying to heaven."[48]

One wonders how seriously Heine means his readers to take this account of Judaism. The 'skin disease' charge refers to the old chestnut, well known to classical antiquity and much used by Voltaire, that the group which became the Hebrew nation was segregated and finally expelled by the Egyptians because of some contagious disease. But what of this 'so-called Church' and that 'framework of dogmas'? These are features ancient Judaism conspicuously lacked, especially when compared with Christianity—as, indeed, Moses Mendelssohn and others had pointed out often enough by Heine's day. One cannot help feeling that here as elsewhere Heine is using the old Voltairean trick of getting at Christianity by pretending to scourge Judaism. Such rejection of dogma and Church should be seen, however, in the context of that other view of religion which Dolf Sternberger has rightly connected with Heine's interest in the Society for the Culture and Science of the Jews and his endeavours to recapture the Passover atmosphere of his childhood in the opening chapter of *The Rabbi of Bacherach*. 'In ancient times', the narrator of *The Town of Lucca* explains, '. . . religion was a beloved tradition, hallowed tales, festival of remembrance and mysteries handed down from one's forebears; a people's *Familiensakra*, as it were—a sacred family inheritance.' And he adds, in words that bitterly reflect once again on Heine's own conversion: 'An ancient Greek would have . . . thought it inhuman to force or trick anyone into giving up the religion in which he was born and adopting another.'[49]

The passage which saddles the Jews with the blame for making religion an affair of state, quoted earlier in this chapter, is chiefly remarkable because here for the first but by no means the last time Heine introduces the figure of the Wandering Jew to convey his vision of the Jewish people as a whole. In German, it should be remembered, that figure is known as the Eternal Jew, *der ewige Jude*. Despite the resentment of Israelite conceptions of state religion, despite the humorous touches in the account of the Exodus from Egypt and in the quaint notion of a ghost dealing in old clothes, Heine presents his Wandering Jew as a tragic figure, lamenting wrongs and sorrows that belong to the distant past and crying vengeance on long-dead enemies. His position at the Roman tomb, and the strange image of the white beard rejuvenated by time and growing dark again at the tip, are symbolic details that make the figure unforgettable. He does indeed convey something of the ghetto sense of history: the *presentness* of Edom, and Haman, and Nebuchadnezzar, in the consciousness of Jews leading their separate corporate existence in the midst of an often hostile Gentile world. Are not such attitudes, we are led to ask, anachronistic in the nineteenth century? Is it not time to look out into the world instead of brooding over the same sad stories, and the same old stories of triumph over enemies long since gone? Heine therefore merges his variation on the folk image of the Wandering or Eternal Jew—a Gentile creation, we should remember, reworked and reinterpreted by a poet who was never unconscious of his roots in the Jewish people—with another image, one that has become dear, in more recent times, to the makers of horror movies: the image of the mummy miraculously enabled to walk the earth. He does this not only in order to convey a sense that orthodox Judaism had become an anachronism in the modern world, but also to suggest that just as Christianity derived from Judaism, so Judaism itself was influenced by Egyptian cults. This last notion was to be taken up and seriously developed by Freud in *Moses and Monotheism*.

The humorous touches which characterize the passage just quoted are typical of the way in which religion is discussed throughout *The Town of Lucca*. We find Jewish 'in-jokes', for instance, when a formula from the Passover service listing the plagues the Lord visited on the Egyptians (which comes out as *Dem Zefardeyim Kinnin* in Heine's somewhat garbled version) is presented as an Arabic formula for transforming men into asses. The kinship of Jews and Arabs is an established fact in the poet's mind. We find flippant listings of the more disreputable incidents in the Old Testament, along with sexual innuendo and irreverent reinterpretations of Mosaic laws, when Lady Mathilde parodies the Creed:

I already believe the main things in the Bible: I believe that Abraham begat Isaac and Isaac begat Jacob and Jacob, in his turn, begat Judah; and I also believe that Judah came in unto his daughter-in-law by the way to Timnath. I also believe that Lot had a drop too much in the company of his daughters. I believe that Potiphar's wife kept pious Joseph's garment in her hand. I believe that the elders who surprised Susannah in her bath must have been *very* old. I believe, in addition, that the patriarch Jacob cheated first his brother and then his father-in-law, that King David arranged a good posting for Uriah, that Solomon got himself a hundred wives and complained afterwards that all is vanity. I also believe in the Ten Commandments and even keep most of them: I do not covet my neighbour's ox or his maidservant or his cow or his ass. I do not labour on the Lord's sabbath; and to make quite sure—for no one can know exactly which day of the week the Lord rested on—I often remain idle the whole week through . . .⁵⁰

The New Testament, needless to say, does not fare much better on Mathilde's wicked tongue—her interpretation of 'love your enemies' in Matthew and Luke is hardly less scandalous than her dealings with the Books of Moses, the Books of Kings, and the Apocrypha. The narrator himself, however, is apt to use Old Testament imagery for more serious purposes; as when he tells the reader that he does not want 'to emulate Ham by uncovering the nakedness of his fatherland'.⁵¹

Mathilde's strictures on the Jewish religion and on the *Urübelvolk* which brought it out of Egypt are clearly not meant to characterize her as an anti-Semite; in her exchanges with the narrator there is something of the tolerant spirit of Lessing which shows itself, on occasions, in deliberate paraphrase or quotation. The term *Menschenmäkelei*, for instance, which occupies an important place in a passage already cited, derives directly from *Nathan the Wise*. But anti-Semites or Judaeophobes were, at one time, to have found a place in *The Town of Lucca*; for in Heine's manuscript draft one may read a passage about German nationalists who sit down with Teutonic thoroughness (*gründlich*, *kritisch*, *historisch*) to determine what degree of non-German descent was necessary to qualify a man for execution when their 'new order' was established.⁵² Heine did not in the end use this passage in *Pictures of Travel*, though its substance was to appear more than once in his later writings. In view of what happened to German Jews in our own century we may well think his vision uncannily accurate. He was able to detect tendencies in his time whose full unfolding would not come until well over a century later.

In the Gumpelino of *The Baths of Lucca*, it has been said, Heine gave German literature its first full-length caricature of the moneyed bourgeois. How strongly Heine's Hamburg experiences had endowed this whole type with Jewish features for him appears again in a dream-vision of *The Town of Lucca*;

a vision that confronts the narrator with Heine's principal
bêtes noires.

I see those dreadful mask-like faces: the visages of noble lackeys
baring their teeth [the German aristocracy], the threatening noses of
bankers [the moneyed bourgeoisie], the death-dealing eyes that dart
sinister glances from cowls [the Catholic clergy] . . .[53]

The 'threatening noses' with which the bankers are endowed in
this passage will be recognized as an all too familiar part of the
Jewish stereotype on which Heine himself had recently played
so many variations in his portrait of the Marchese Gumpelino.
Because of his family circumstances, Heine's personal contact
with bankers throughout his life was almost totally confined to
contact with the heads and employees of Jewish-owned firms.

(iv)

In 1828, before his Italian journeys, the poet had moved to
Munich to take up the post of co-editor of a journal founded
and owned by the firm of Cotta, the most respected publishing
house in Germany. In that journal, *New Political Annals* (*Neue
allgemeine politische Annalen*), he printed some accounts of
experiences he had had in England during his brief stay there in
1827. Among these experiences, a speech made in the House of
Commons by an MP named Spring-Rice figured prominent-
ly—a speech which introduced the topic of civil rights for Jews
into the context of a debate on Catholic emancipation. Heine
translated this from Hansard, and printed his (edited) version
in *New Political Annals* in order to shame Germans with the
matter-of-fact way in which members of the British House of
Commons put forward the principle of Jewish emancipation.
Spring-Rice's speech rehearses, to the accompaniment of loud
laughter, the absurd arguments adduced by previous genera-
tions to exclude Jews from the rights of citizenship. Arguments
that sensible Englishmen laugh out of court, Heine would
seem to be telling his German readers, were still being solemn-
ly served up in Germany as the third decade of the nineteenth
century drew to its close.[54]

Heine's articles on England also included an account of William Cobbett's views on the National Debt, translated and adapted from the *Weekly Political Register*, in which the latter's notorious Judaeophobia surfaces for a moment.[55] Speaking of the way in which the British nation is eaten up—as he sees it—by its creditors, Cobbett feels constrained to add: '. . . these creditors are generally Jews, or Christians resembling Jews.' Heine tones this down in his translation: '. . . von ihren Kreditoren, die gewöhnlich Juden sind, oder besser gesagt, Christen die wie Juden handeln'. By adding the words 'oder besser gesagt', the poet seems to suggests that *none* of these creditors are in fact Jews: that they are all Christians who trade, or act, in the way Jews are generally said to trade and to act.

When, in 1831, these English reminiscences were republished, under the title *English Fragments* (*Englische Fragmente*), in the same fourth volume of *Pictures of Travel* that also contained *The Town of Lucca*, Heine deleted his adaptation of Cobbett's remark about the Jews (had he remembered the Rothschilds, perhaps?) along with Spring-Rice's speech to make the score even. In making this latter deletion he may well have reflected that it was apt to give a misleading impression of the state of things in England, where no unbaptized Jew could take a seat in the House of Commons until the 1850s, and where full emancipation had to await the Promissory Oaths Act of 1871 and its supplementation in 1890.[56] *English Fragments* did offer, however, some welcome opportunities to raise the whole subject of equality of civil rights—most obviously in the section that deals with the Catholic Emancipation Bill and the debates it occasioned in the British Parliament. Heine must have been well aware that the very term 'emancipation', which he used so frequently when he wanted to plead the cause of contemporary Jewry, gained its currency in the modern world through the struggles of British Catholics for a repeal or amendment of the Test and Corporations Act. Here, inevitably, the cause of the Jews was also debated and such debates led Heine once again to raise the question of how the civic status of Jewish communities like those of Frankfurt am Main could be improved. The poet is very careful, however, to deflect suspicions of sectarian obsession by placing the Frankfurt issue in a world-wide perspective.

The urge to oppress others is one of the ingredients of human nature, and when we complain, as constantly happens these days, about civil inequalities, we only look upwards towards those whose privileges offend us; we never look downwards, never think of raising to our level those whom traditional injustice dubs our inferiors. When we see those below struggling to climb up, we are annoyed and hit them on the head. The Creole demands the rights of the European, but falls into a rage when he sees the mulatto aspiring to become his equal. The mulatto behaves in the same way towards the mestizo, and the mestizo towards the negro. The Frankfurt philistine is enraged by the privileges of the nobility; but he is even angrier when he finds himself asked to emancipate the Jew. I have a Polish friend who is an enthusiastic champion of liberty but who has not yet freed his peasants from their serfdom.[57]

Jews and Jewish problems are deliberately being presented as just one small item in the large concerns of the nineteenth-century world. The task of emancipating them fully is only part of the wider task of emancipating *all* the oppressed and underprivileged.

The important third chapter of *English Fragments* opens with yet another view of a Stock Exchange—that of London, this time, in which Jews may be observed alongside other 'nations'. The passage offers a rare example of Heine using the German term *Nation* when speaking of the Jews—a term normal in the eighteenth century which champions of Jewish emancipation tended to avoid in the nineteenth so as not to revive the spectre of 'a nation within a nation' which had been raised by Fichte and other Germans opposed to giving Jews full civic rights.

Under the archways of the London 'Change each nation has its appointed place, and notices have been affixed on which one may read their names: Russians, Spaniards, Swedes, Germans, Maltese, Jews, Hanseatics, Turks, and so on. In days of old each dealer stood beneath the notice designating his nation; but now this is no longer so. Mankind has advanced—Dutchmen now stand where Spaniards once stood, the Hanseatic League has replaced the Jews, where one seeks Turks one now finds Russians, the Italians stand in the place once occupied by the French, and even the Germans have made some progress.

What happened at the 'Change happened elsewhere in the world too. The old notices have stayed where they were, but the people underneath have been pushed away and their places supplied by others whose new heads sort but ill with the old superscription. The stereotyped characterizations of different peoples which we still find in learned compendia and alehouses have become useless to us; they can only lead us into hopeless errors.[58]

Heine calls the Jews a 'nation' in the context of a passage that unequivocally condemns ahistorical national stereotypes— hostile stereotypes propagated by German university teachers and their beer-swilling students or by solid citizens *in gelehrten Kompendien und Bierschenken*. The remark that the place once occupied by the Jews is now taken by the Hanseatic League suggests not only the powerful urge, experienced by Jewish intellectuals such as Heine himself, to break away from the Stock Exchange and all it stood for, but also the mercantile talents of Hamburg citizens who prided themselves on their unimpeachable Christian ancestry. It also, of course, undermines the racial stereotyping of peoples by listing the 'Hanseatics' among the 'nations', along with Jews, Turks, and Russians. At the same time Heine acknowledges that Jews were present among the many dealers he found in the Stock Exchange he visited in 1827. Indeed, he had already had personal dealings with its most prominent Jewish member; for Uncle Salomon had given him an introduction to Nathan Rothschild in the form of letters of credit which the poet had hastened to convert into cash by an unauthorized manœuvre that his uncle would hold against him for the rest of his life. Nathan Rothschild is not actually named in *English Fragments*; but a passing mention of a 'fat Jew in Lombard Street, St. Swithin's Lane', for whose protection England had evolved (and applied) harsh property laws, would be taken by many as an oblique reference to him.[59]

The principal point made in the Stock Exchange section of *English Fragments* is unobtrusively reinforced by a later chapter headed 'The New Ministry'. Here Heine comments on the change from a Whig to a Tory government:

Now as of old [the Tories] will once again administer the fruits of the people's industrious labour in such a way that these find their way into their own pockets. These governing corn–Jews will drive up the price of their grain . . .[60]

Kornjuden had often formed targets of resentment for farmers and purchasers of grain bewildered by the activities of middle-men who advanced money, bought futures, and manipulated prices in accordance with demand. By applying this term to the English Tories of 1827 Heine suggests that Jews were being used as whipping-boys or scapegoats for practices in which Gentile aristocrats and landowners indulged on a larger scale and with greater impunity. It must be remembered that the leader of the Tories Heine knew was the Duke of Wellington; but by listing the young Disraeli's *Vivian Grey* among the fashionable novels of the day[61] the poet just flashes into view a later leader who took a defiant pride in his Jewish ancestry. In later years the editor of an English journal, *The Critic*, was to interview Heine and hear him recollect reading Disraeli's *Contarini Fleming*—a strange, wild book, he called it, of a kind which he might have written himself.[62]

English Fragments ends with a chapter entitled 'Liberation'; and the liberation here envisaged is one that would free men from ecclesiastical as well as political tyranny. In analysing the connection between these two, Heine once again glances at the Jews, though he does not name them. As in *The Town of Lucca* they are seen as links between ancient Egypt and modern Europe.

When I find time, once again, for scholarly investigations which don't have to yield immediate positive results I shall prove, with all due tediousness and thoroughness, that the caste system was born in Egypt and not in India. For two thousand years this system has assumed the garb of every country. It may well be dead now—but it still keeps the appearance of life and walks among us, evil-eyed and wreaking havoc, poisoning our spring time with its odour of decay, sucking blood and light from the hearts of the nations like the medieval vampire that it is. It was not only crocodiles and their famous tears that emerged from the mud of the Nile—priests that know how to weep just as artfully emerged from this same mud, as did that warrior caste with its hereditary privileges which outdoes the crocodiles in murderousness and greed.[63]

These priests and that warrior caste belong to *Christian* states—and in the struggle to liberate the nations from them, Heine avers, the Bible has always played an essential part.

Heine demonstrates what he means by this in a paean to Protestantism and the printing press.[64] This leads him to speak once more of the new religion, the religion of his own time, a religion of liberty proclaimed above all by France; among the high priests of that religion Jesus Christ again, inevitably, appears.[65] And now, as he prepares to announce the new religion more solemnly than ever before, Heine finds in the Old Testament a repository of figures, locations, and slogans with which to describe the new 'Gospels'.

The French are the chosen people of the new religion, its first Gospels and dogmas are in their language, Paris is the new Jerusalem, and the Rhine is the Jordan which separates the hallowed land of freedom from the country of the philistines.[66]

If the Jews brought the disease from Egypt they could also—as the very vocabulary of this passage would seem to suggest—provide an antidote.

(v)

The *New Political Annals* that Heine co-edited from 1827 to 1828 contained little from his pen besides the first version of what later became his *English Fragments*. He did, however, see to it that the readers of his journal were kept up to date on the struggle for Jewish emancipation in Bavaria and Württemberg; and he contributed a review of Wolfgang Menzel's history of German literature (*Die deutsche Literatur*) in the course of which he quoted Fichte's dictum that Spinoza's works had to lie fallow for more than a century before someone said something worthwhile about them. Of greater interest in our context is another review, published in Cotta's *Morning Chronicle* (*Morgenblatt für gebildete Stände*) during the time of Heine's editorship of the *New Political Annals*. This dealt with Michael Beer's play *Struensee* in a laudatory tone lightened by some characteristic *caresses perfides*. The piece was written to curry favour, and Heine was ashamed of it, but he seized the opportunity it offered to show how dramatists of Jewish extraction treated the theme of the social underdog: they used it to plead the cause of freedom from censorship, and to raise again the burning question of emancipation.

The idea of human equality rouses our time to enthusiasm . . . Works in which this idea is prominent are therefore sure of a rapturous welcome. After Goethe's *Werther* it was Ludwig Robert who first brought this idea on to the stage. In *The Force of Circumstances* Robert produced a true *tragédie bourgeoise*; with a skilful hand he ripped the prosaic cold compresses from modern humanity's burning heart . . . France and Germany found the same garb for the same sorrow, when both Casimir Delavigne and Michael Beer gave us a *Pariah*.[67]

Ludwig Robert's play, already mentioned in *The Hartz Journey* and about to furnish a motto for *The Journey from Munich to Genoa*, shows a delicate sense of honour in its bourgeois Jewish hero which makes him morally more than a match for the aristocratic Gentile officer who despises him. Heine's review in a way continues the work that play had begun: just as Robert had sought to convince his audience that his August Weiss deserved to be taken as seriously as his Colonel von Falkenau, Heine tries to show that it is not unreasonable to discuss Ludwig Robert and Michael Beer alongside writers of impeccably Gentile provenance. Goethe is mentioned in connection with Robert, Delavigne in connection with Beer.

In 1828 Heine also drafted a curious little journalistic account of the adventurer Wit von Dörring (1800–63), whose uncle Ferdinand von Eckstein he was to savage in his later years in Paris. He says nothing, however, of the Jewish antecedents of Wit himself when he presents him as a man who cannot be appreciated by anyone with a rigid sense of honour and propriety. Morally, it would seem, Wit stands at the opposite pole of Ludwig Robert's Jewish hero.

Let sentimental souls blame him for ceasing to play the Mortimer of liberty—[that Schillerian character] with his enthusiasm, his black coat, and his long hair. One does not need Thomas Parr's 130 years of experience to see that such Mortimers, with their daggers, were harmful rather than useful to poor Liberty languishing in goal. I leave it to others to blame him for switching to the role of Lord Leicester—the man who wants to continue making eyes at his erstwhile beloved, Liberty, while publicly denying her and throwing himself into the arms of a crowned harridan. This is not what theatre folk call a "thankful" part, it's not even conducive to good notices; and one can hardly blame some honest Hans von Birken or some other German reviewer for giving way to his feelings rather than using his reason and belabouring Wit with crude earnestness. We, however, have finer sensibilities; what we criticize is not the role but the way it is played; and from that point of view we declare Johannes Wit von Dörring to be a rare master. We praise his deftness and his boldness, his excellent command of language, his equal talent for charm and malice, the art with which he assumes plumes borrowed from elsewhere, as well as the bright wing-feathers of his intellect which he can use to fly with as well to dazzle.[68]

In the end Heine deemed it wiser not to publish this eulogy of a disreputable character, and his tribute to Wit remained in manuscript until after his death. Psychologically, however, the essay is of the greatest interest. In this political adventurer who, after paying lip-service to the cause of freedom, had become a kind of press agent to one of the most notorious autocrats of the day, Heine saw, as Jeffrey L. Sammons has rightly said, 'in some perverse way . . . a mirror of himself'. Sammons has seen in the Wit affair an example of one of the poet's most curious strategies: confessing his own ethical weaknesses by lauding them in others. Sammons also sees in this dubious relationship an example of the way in which Heine's apparent shrewdness tended to backfire and injure his reputation instead of advancing it.[69] Yet Heine *was* shrewd enough, it would appear, to make no public reference to Wit at all—he left in the limbo of unpublished drafts not only the essay from which I have already quoted, but also a passage in *The Town of Lucca* in which the narrator confesses himself attracted to Wit's memoirs because 'he compromises everybody there, and that makes them a very good book.'[70] Whether some of Heine's sympathy for Wit may have been due to feelings of common origin must remain a matter for speculation. He himself preserves complete silence on this subject even in his private letters and recorded conversations.

The last of Heine's works to be published before their author left Germany in order to settle in Paris was an Introduction to a book by Robert Wesselhöft entitled *Kahldorf on the Nobility* (*Kahldorf über den Adel, in Briefen an den Grafen M. von Moltke*, 1831). Here we find him protesting against applying in the human sphere views appropriate only to animal husbandry. The notion that when the nobility engenders offspring 'better blood' is produced than when commoners do the same he calls 'bestial and absurd', 'an obscene joke deriving from the Middle Ages'. He also revives those hunting metaphors which we have heard him apply before to the relation between the classes and between Christians and Jews in Europe. 'The whole history of our time', he now writes, 'is nothing but an exalted hunting expedition against liberal ideas; high and mighty ladies and gentlemen show greater ardour than ever in the pursuit of their prey; their uniformed huntsmen shoot at every honest heart in which liberal ideas have taken refuge; and there is no lack of learned hounds to retrieve wounded words dripping with blood . . .'[71] One cannot read a passage such as this without remembering how the narrator of *The North Sea: Third Section* had sought his ancestors among the hunted rather than the hunters, and how Heine himself, in a letter to Immermann, had opined that Prussian noblemen aware of his origins would like nothing better than to see him reduced to the status of a dog. Specifically Jewish resentments thus mingle and merge with the resentments characteristic of a rising third estate.

FIRST INTERMEZZO
'Will God be strong in the Weak?'

The sketches, portraits, and caricatures of Heine's published works, styled to suit a wide reading public embracing different classes and creeds, are supplemented by those in Heine's letters and conversations, styled to suit one particular recipient. The earliest such documents which have been preserved date from 1815–16. They include an extravagant compliment to Friederike, one of the daughters of that uncle Salomon Heine who plays such an important and baneful part in Heine's life:

The angels must be like that . . . O Lord! let me enter a celestial realm that holds such angels!

(17 February 1815);

an equally extravagant appeal to a schoolfriend, Christian Sethe, to help an ostracized Jewish boy who also attended the Düsseldorf *Lyzeum*:

I must ask you to befriend poor Levy. It is the voice of humanity that speaks to you. I implore you, by all you hold sacred, to help him. He is in direst need. My heart bleeds. I cannot say much. The words are burning in my veins . . .

(6 July 1816);

and the first of many attempts, in face of rising anti-Semitism, to transcend the usual divisions into 'Jew' and 'Christian', or 'Jew' and 'Gentile', while retaining the associations Gentile abuse had woven around the term 'Jew':

In this huckstering city of Hamburg not the least feeling for poetry is to be found—unless it be occasional *carmina* for weddings, funerals, and baptisms which have been expressly ordered and paid for in cash; and added to this there has now been, for a considerable time, an oppressive tension between baptized Jews and unbaptized ones. When I say 'Jews' I mean *all* the inhabitants of Hamburg; 'baptized

Jews' as distinct from circumcised ones are what the vulgar call 'Christians'.

(to Sethe, 20 November 1816)

The young Heine knew, however, that his readiness to redefine the word 'Jew' in this way was not shared by his Christian contemporaries; and he therefore expressed his fear that if his identity became known, his poems would not be well received by the German public for whom they were intended. No wonder, then, that he chose a pointedly Germanic pseudonym under which to publish his earliest poems!

In the letter to Sethe from which I have just quoted, the fateful figure of 'Molly' moves onto the centre of the stage. This is the name by which Heine knows Amalie, another daughter of Salomon Heine—the archetype, for him, of the woman loved but not loving in return, the first stage in the creation of his own personal Lorelei myth. Five years later we meet her again, watching the poet's grotesque agonies with 'aqua tofana eyes':

Up there in the corner, in a box just by the stage, sits a beautifully dressed-up little doll in whose manufacture the celestial master turner has outdone himself. I don't want to make this charming little face break into a laugh—but I would welcome a few crystal tear-drops from these death-dealing aqua tofana eyes. That is the cliff on which my reason has suffered shipwreck and which I would never-theless like to cling to in a fearful embrace. It is an old story . . .

(to Heinrich Straube, March 1821)

An old story indeed—images from the *Odyssey* mingle with images from Goethe's *Torquato Tasso* and German Romantic poetry. In Heine's case, as all readers of the *Book of Songs* (*Buch der Lieder*) will know, the story had a social and finan-cial twist—the preferred suitor is richer and more at home in the beloved's social ambience than the poor poet. In the *Book of Songs* that suitor turns up as the dream-image of a little man with white linen and a dirty soul (*B* 1, 24); in the letters he is a moustachioed hare.

. . . when I was a little monkey by the banks of the Oronoco and my love a little long-tailed monkey with soft paws, she often used me extremely ill: my chest bore the imprint of her nails, and she threw herself at last into the arms of some filthy hare because he had taken part in the war of liberation against the foxes and sported mighty whiskers. I for my part was not allowed to wear such whiskers because I had just accepted an associate professorship of aesthetics among the monkeys . . .

(to W. Smets, 24 December 1821)

The reference to Amalie Heine's husband John Friedländer, who had indeed served in the army during the Wars of Liberation against Napoleon, is plain to see in this bitter animal fable. Heine ever afterwards took a malicious delight in mocking Jews and ex-Jews who sported martial moustaches.

Heine's sketch of the 'beautifully dressed-up doll' from Uncle Salomon's side of the family is set off, in the letter to Straube written in March 1821, by swift sketches of his own immediate family: the father, Samson Heine, sunk in melancholia, the mother, Betty Heine, afflicted by blinding headaches to which the poet was also subject, a sister, Charlotte, who 'sings like an angel', and two brothers, Maximilian and Gustav, writing bad verses while preparing themselves for careers in medicine (long open to Jews in most German states, and traditional in Heine's maternal family) and in agriculture (long closed to German Jews, either *de jure* or *de facto*). None of these, as we shall see, were truly receptive to the young Heine's literary work—they either dismissed it outright or damned it with faint praise.

What appears clearly from Heine's earliest letters is that despite his attempts at transcending the usual distinctions he was himself always conscious of the ethnic and religious affiliation of those he dealt with. A passage from a letter to Fritz von Beughem shows this habit of mental classification particularly clearly. From Bonn, where he had gone at Uncle Salomon's expense to study law, Heine writes to his erstwhile schoolfriend on 15 July 1820:

Steinmann, a Jew, a poet, Prince Wittgenstein, and the latter's tutor make up my whole social circle at this moment.

'A Jew' is all the characterization Heine deems necessary to indicate the ingredient in his social mix represented by his fellow student Isaak Coppenhagen.

(ii)

Heine's letters of the 1820s again and again look at Jews in the context of anti-Semitism: they commend a Gentile lawyer for his willingness to 'help poor Ikey, trodden underfoot like a worm, to climb on to the bench of humanity' (*den wurmartig zertretenen Mauschel auf die Menschenbank hinauf hilft*—to E. C. A. Keller, 1 September 1822); and they cry a plague on both houses in a letter from Lüneburg, where the poet's parents had gone to live:

> The Jews here, as everywhere, are intolerable hucksters and draggle-tails, the Christian middle class is unedifying, with an unusual amount of *Rishess* [Jew-hatred]; to the higher social ranks the same applies in higher degree. Our little dog is sniffed at and ill-treated in the street in such a pointed way as to make clear that the Christian dogs are filled with *Rishess* against the Jewish dog . . .
>
> (to Moses Moser, 18 June 1823)

The vocabulary of the last-quoted letter makes it clear that Heine is writing to a Jewish correspondent, to whom he can venture criticism of their fellow Jews in terms that might be misunderstood by Gentiles.

At Göttingen University Heine had learnt to know at first hand the logic of anti-Semitism, a logic he applied to Christian friends in bitter parody and mockery. "All that is German', he writes to Christian Sethe on 14 April 1822, 'is repellent to me—and you, alas, are a German.' One has only to substitute the words 'Jewish' and 'Jew' for the word 'German' in that sentence to understand the lesson Heine had been taught by anti-Jewish *Burschenschaftler*. It is highly significant that the letter to Sethe in which this passage occurs goes on to describe something like persecution mania: 'I can hardly sleep at nights. In my dreams I see my so-called friends whispering, hissing into one another's ears observations and gossip about me—and this drips into my brain like molten lead. During the day I am constantly haunted by mistrust—everwhere I hear my own name pursued by gales of derisive laughter.' Such feelings of persecution and derision were undoubtedly strengthened by anti-Jewish publications not only from the vulgar and lunatic fringe, but from respected university professors such as J. F. Fries and C. F. Rühs, whose views Heine cites more than once as proof that he is not regarded as a true German by those who form and control public opinion in his native land. 'If I were a German—and I am *not* a German, see Rühs, Fries, *passim* . . .' (to Moses Moser, 23 August 1823). The unkindest cut of all, in Heine's eyes, was that such views were held by German liberals as easily as German conservatives. This materially influenced his political attitudes.

> Although I am a radical in England and a carbonaro in Italy, I don't adhere to the demagogues in Germany; for the quite accidental reason that if the latter were to be victorious, a few thousand Jewish throats—and the best ones at that!—would be slit.
>
> (to Moritz Embden, 2 February 1823)[1]

From here it is only a short step to the conception, implicit in Heine's early essay on Romanticism, that the German language could become the fatherland of those whom Teutomaniacs denied full citizenship of the German lands into which they had been born—a conception which would become of particular importance when the poet had settled in France. There, however, it was supplemented by another, no less powerful, conception of which the present book will have to speak in a later chapter: that of a book, *the* book, the Bible, as the 'portable fatherland' of the Jews.

Heine's journey to Poland, and his encounter with Polish Jews, also find expression in his letters. 'I went there', he tells Joseph Lehmann on 26 June 1823, 'to hunt for pure, healthy human dispositions, which I am able to ferret out particularly well because I am so intimately acquainted with impurity and sickness. I have always found the healthiest dispositions among Jewish women . . .' He adds, characteristically, that God must share his admiration, for He had chosen a Jewish woman to bear His son. But as we already known from his essay on Poland, Heine also shuddered away from the unhygienic poverty and squalor he observed in the home of these *gesundeste Naturen*, a squalor that gave birth to a revolting image which first turns up in a pointedly anti-*Christian* context in a letter to Immanual Wohlwill, where Heine speaks dismissively of 'families of ideas that make their nest in the interstices of the old world, in the bedstead of the Divine Spirit, as families of bedbugs make their nests in the bedstead of a Polish Jew' (1 April 1823). The pure healthy dispositions and high morality of Jewish women, and the image of 'bugs from the well-known bedsteads' (*Wanzen aus den wohlbekannten Bettstellen*), will turn up sporadically in Heine's writings ever afterwards. The tension between them is not accidental.

Another observation which Heine's early letters add to his portrayal of nineteenth-century Jewry is that of the Jewish bush telegraph. We hear of a group of Jews passing through Hamburg on their way back from the Brunswick trades fair and bringing gossip and news to their co-religionists: it is through them that 'all Israel' comes to hear of the failure of Heine's tragedy *Almansor* at its one and only staging (to Moser, 30 September 1823). A similar cultural news service may be observed in action when Heine, on his travels through Germany, goes to a Jewish money-changer in Celle in order to obtain some current coin. There he is told of the success which Michael Beer's play *The Pariah* had in Berlin. The money-changer, Heine tells Moser on 21 Janary 1824, in words that glance ironically and punningly at commercial valuations of art,

had heard this news from a corn-cutter, who had come directly from Berlin, and who had there convinced himself that the *Pariah* stood at *par* with the work of Goethe and Schiller.

Heine's letter shows how proud simple Jews could be of successes by German Jews in the cultural field, and, incidentally, points to corn-cutting as a not uncommon occupation among such Jews. There was at least one Jewish corn-cutter in Hamburg too, with whose calling Heine was later to endow his archetypal 'little Jew', Hirsch-Hyazinth. He was also, as we shall see in a moment, to use corn-cutting as a symbol for the operations would-be reformers such as David Friedländer sought to perform on the body of historical Judaism.

The news Heine heard at Celle gives rise, in the letter to Moser from which I have just quoted, to a consideration of prime importance for our understanding of his Jewish portraits. He objected violently to the way in which Beer suggested some parallel between Jews and Indian Pariahs—a parallel Max Weber was later to elaborate, but one which Heine rightly thought misleading and potentially damaging; and he objected even more strongly to a speculation Beer had put into his pariah's mouth: the speculation that his ancestors might have brought about his present social ostracism through some bloody misdeed. 'This allusion to Christ', he adds,

> may please some people, particularly since it comes from the mouth of a Jew . . . who is not yet baptized . . . I would rather see Michael Beer baptized and speak his mind about Christianity boldly, in the true manner of Almansor, than timidly suppressing criticism or even flirting with it in the way I have just indicated.
>
> (to Moser, 21 January 1824)

Heine is here 'prophetically' objecting not only to the notion of the Jew as pariah, which has haunted sociological and historical thinking from Max Weber to Hannah Arendt and has been so decisively rejected (in Heine's spirit) by Salo Baron, but also to Freud's speculations, in *Moses and Monotheism*, that some 'crime' performed in the dim-distant past, long before the execution of Jesus, in some way affected the present consciousness and the present fate of the Jewish people.

The 'flirting with Christianity' which Heine scourged in Michael Beer he also detected in the activity of a group of Jews who moved into the centre of his attention again and again in the 1820s: men who wished to reform Jewish ceremonial in ways that would make it resemble the ceremonial of German Protestants. What he most objected to here was the weakening of Judaism by reducing it to a rationalistic Deism. For reasons whose social grounding will, by now, have become apparent, he expresses his concern by means of the metaphor of 'corn-cutters' who venture, with disastrous results, into fields usually reserved to physicians or barber-surgeons.

> A few corn-cutters (Friedländer & Co.) have sought to cure the body of Judaism from the vexatious ulcer that is disfiguring its skin by bleeding it; and because of their lack of skill and their cobweb-like bandages of reason Israel must bleed to death. Let us hope for a speedy dispelling of the delusion that the most glorious thing to do is

to dissipate what strength and power we have, to negate one-sidedly, to adopt Auerbachian idealizations.

(to Immanuel Wohlwill, 1 April 1823)

Despite his reservations about Friedländer's over-conciliatory stance *vis-à-vis* German society and his over-eager rejection of rabbinical orthodoxy, Heine continued to respect this disciple and friend of Moses Mendelssohn. The other 'Reformer' he names in his letter to Wohlwill, however, Isaac Levin Auerbach, became for him the symbol of all that weakens and debilitates. He used his name as a kind of shorthand by saying that the thermometer had dropped down to Auerbach (to Moser, 23 April 1826) or advised Moser, ironically, to take lessons from Auerbach on how to make watered-down, deadly-dull speeches (19 March 1824). 'Will God be strong in the weak', he asked the same friend seven months later, on 25 October 1824, 'in Auerbach and his crew?'

Heine saw the Reform movement, as Jeffrey Sammons has well said, 'as an accommodation to the philistine values of the dominant society, reinforcing and joining its regressive structures rather than emancipating them; . . . his intellectual's and poet's temper was uncongenial to compromise and the levelling of human authenticity.'[2] This applied to the Reformers he met at Hamburg at least as much as to those he met in Berlin—and his unconcealed opposition to them did not help to endear him to Uncle Salomon, whose circle was, on the whole, pro-Reform. Heine particularly disliked Dr Eduard Kley, who had been tutor to Michael Beer in Berlin and had then been called to Hamburg, where he combined the offices of director of the Jewish Free School and preacher at the New Jewish Temple; one suspects that this personal dislike, and Heine's dislike of the Reform movement generally, was due in no small measure to his observation that Reform Judaism appealed above all to the *wealthier* section of the community. He could not really warm to the Reformers' chief Hamburg opponent, Rabbi Dr Isaac Bernays, either.

I visited Dr Gotthold Salomon, and did not wholly dislike him—but he is an Auerbachian just the same. Kley I did not visit; you know that I could never stand him . . . I heard Bernays preach; he is a charlatan, none of the Jews understands what he is saying, there is no strength of will in him, he is never likely to play a more significant part than he does at present—but he is intelligent and he has more spirit than Dr Kley, Salomon, Auerbach the First, and Auerbach the Second. I did not pay him a visit, although I had occasion to do so. My respect goes out to him insofar as he manages to cheat the rogues of Hamburg—but the late robber-chief Cartouche I respect far more.

(to Moses Moser, 23 August 1823)

The attitudes towards 'reformed' and 'orthodox' congregations which Heine here describes in a private letter will be conveyed to a larger public, in later years, by means of the final section of his poem *Der Tannhäuser*. At this point it is worth noting, however, that these letters from Hamburg leave no doubt that Heine attended acts of worship in synagogue and 'Temple'—however vehemently he might later deny ever having done so. Not that this made him love the Jewish religion! He was committed, he explained to Moser, to fight for Jewish civil rights, but

the born enemy of all positive religions will never champion a religion that first thought of discrimating between man and man in ways that now bring us such anguish; and if, in a peculiar manner, I do appear as its champion, then there are special reasons: sentimental attachment [*Gemütsweichheit*], obstinacy, and a calculated desire to have an antidote ready.

Since Heine's own Hamburg relatives were involved in the Reform movement which led to the opposition of the new 'Temple' to the old synagogue, he found that the expression of his sentiments did not win him friends at his uncle's court. He could not, however, bring himself to be diplomatic.

In spite of all extraneous considerations I could not pay homage to a weakness I loathe, nor could I heap abuse on strength. I am referring to my heretical opinions about Kley and Bernays. If you know me at all you will realize that my whole nature was bound to be revolted by the former while thinking the stronger Bernays, though he lacks the negative 'Temple' virtues, worthy of respect. My predilection for the consistent and rigorous attitude of orthodox rabbis was formed years ago as a result of historical studies—it is not an a priori assumption, nor does it arise from the sort of pragmatic calculation which is characteristic of G. G. Cohn . . . Because I am . . . a *whole* man (although you will never admit that) I could not find favour in Hamburg. I soon noticed that and kept my distance from the Jewish

rabble. And yet this mob takes it upon itself to pronounce on me!
People of whose very existence I know nothing have told my brother
that I have talked to them and said God knows what. I am beset by
loathsomenesses of this kind—typically Jewish ones, or rather, pos-
sible only in Israel . . .

(to Moser, 5–6 November 1823)

The 'loathsomenesses' of which Heine here complains are
associated in his mind with the mercantile life he had decisively
rejected for his own part, but with whose language registers he
still likes to play. It is a register he associates with Jews:
perhaps because he had seen his own father and uncle learning
to use it in their dealings with fellow merchants. 'I have re-
ceived your letter of 8 October', he writes to Moser on 28
November 1823, 'with which my letter crossed. 'Crossed' is a
commercial expression which I remember from the days in
which I was set on going into trade . . . I still know many such
expressions, and could write a devotional manual for
Israelites.'

Heine's feelings of superiority over the Jewish hucksters of
Hamburg took a hard knock, and the 'wholeness' he had
arrogated to himself in his letter of 5–6 November 1823 dis-
appeared for ever, at the time of his baptism. He even came to
look on the Reform party in the Hamburg community with
less jaundiced eyes.

Last Saturday I attended the [Hamburg] Temple, and had the plea-
sure of hearing with my own ears how Dr Salomon inveighed against
baptized Jews and taunted them with 'allowing themselves to be
tempted into breaking faith with the religion of their fathers by the
mere hope of obtaining *a position*' (*ipsissima verba*!). The sermon, I
assure you, was a good one, and I intend visiting the man who
preached it in the near future.

(to Moser, 14 December 1825)

In this letter, which informs Moser that if the law had permit-
ted the stealing of silver spoons Heine would have done that
rather than go through the baptism ceremony, he commends
Moser's friend G. G. Cohn, the President of the *Tempelverein*
whose pragmatism he had so recently reviled, for showing
forgiveness by feeding the apostate with *Kuggel*, a sabbath dish
he loved:

He heaps glowing *Kuggel* on my head, and with contrition I eat this sacred national dish which has done more for the preservation of Judaism than all three issues of our journal. But then: it has had a greater circulation!

The 'journal' to which Heine refers in the passage just quoted is the short-lived organ of the Berlin Society for the Culture and Science of the Jews which appeared under the title *Journal for the Science of Judaism* (*Zeitschrift für die Wissenschaft des Judentums*) in 1822. Here members of the Society sought to publish the results of their twin endeavour to find, in Jeffrey Sammons's words, 'a formula that would reconcile the leading edge of modern scholarship and philosophy with Jewish identity, and . . . a program of action that would lift ordinary Jews up to their own level of intellect and insight, thus making it possible for them to take an honoured place within the German nation while keeping Jewish consciousness and community intact.' 'Heine', Sammons adds, 'took the opportunity of the *Verein* to explore the boundaries of his Jewish self and test the options available to a person in his situation.'[3] He intended, as he told Moser on 9 January 1824, to write a really good article for the *Journal*; at the very least he would examine the resources of the Göttingen library to see if a worth-while bibliography of writings concerning the Jews could be put together for the *Journal*'s benefit. In the event, no contribution arrived from Heine; but the *Journal* was in any case so short-lived that even a completed article might have arrived too late to see the light of print.

The opening chapter of the present book has already looked at Heine's dealings with the Society's chief begetter, Eduard Gans, and we have had glimpses of its oldest member and link with the generation of Moses Mendelssohn: David Friedländer. It is now time to look, in some detail, at the sketches of other members which Heine introduces into his letters.

(iii)

Pride of place must go to Moses Moser, bank official, scholar, and disciple of Hegel. Recipient of Heine's confidences, in long conversations and unusually frank letters, Moser was charged with drawing Heine's attention to reviews of his works and hostile (particularly anti-Semitic) references to him in the German press; writing friendly reviews whenever opportunity offered; relieving the poet of an irksome duty by writing a review of an Indological volume; supplying him with quotations and references from Hebrew sources; lending him money; looking after his brothers when they visited Berlin; sending him news of the Society for the Culture and Science of the Jews; running various errands for him—a stream of commissions great and small, in return for which Moser received many assurances of the poet's love and friendship. But alas—here too Heine thought himself, in the end, misunderstood and unappreciated:

With Moser I have had constant misunderstandings for some time now. I no longer write to him about my intentions, still less about my actions, least of all about my poetry. The latter seems to bore him and (who knows?) he may be right. Thinking is his true element, and a short while ago he has completely rethought himself—by which I mean that he has made himself into a new man by the exercise of his thinking powers. People like us remain what we were, and that, perhaps, is a good thing.

(to Joseph Lehmann, 26 May 1826)

Despite such complaints Moser emerges from these letters as a generous, noble-hearted, and highly intelligent man. Heine depicts him as punctilious, order-loving, to an almost philistine degree—though his bachelor lodgings occasionally suggested a more bohemian life-style. His nickname, 'Marquis Posa', derived from an impressive (though rather worn) cloak which he wore on cool days, but it was deemed appropriate in other respects because the character in Schiller's *Don Carlos* from whom the name derived had become a symbol, in Germany, of self-sacrificing friendship and concern with the welfare and liberties of all mankind. Moser is a *necessarius*, a friend to be constantly employed, and as such Heine found him, on more than one occasion, a reproach to himself by virtue of his selflessness and steadfastness. 'Yes, great Moser,' the poet writes on 30 September 1823, 'H. Heine is very small . . . Do not measure me by the standards of your own great soul.' On 15 December 1825, when relations were already cooling, Heine calls Moser 'a piece of myself', *ein Stück von mir selbst*—though at the same time Moser's philosophical constructions and Hegelian terminology provoked Heine to parody. Moser comes alive in Heine's letters in a delightful way. We re-experience the wintry walks the two friends took together, with Moser wrapped in his Marquis Posa cloak, admiring Heine's works, making grandiloquent speeches in a Schillerian vein even when following a call of nature. We meet Moser in his modest bachelor's lodgings ('your intellect becoming ever more brilliant and your dressing-gown ever more tattered') and learn how he mutters Homer to himself 'as our ancestors muttered the *Tosaphot Yomtob*' (8 September 1825). Homer, we see, has replaced the rabbinical commentary to which Heine here, as in his later poem *Disputation*, refers under its Ashkenazic name *Tausves Jomtov*. This did not mean, however, that Moser had put by his Jewish heritage.

I remember that you were particularly good at reciting the psalm 'By the rivers of Babylon'; and you did this so beautifully, so movingly, that I am still inclined to weep when I think of it, and not only at the psalm. You had some very good ideas about Judaism in those days, about the baseness of Christians who made proselytes and the baseness of Jews who accepted baptism not only because they wanted to remove obstacles but also because they wanted to profit by it as though baptism were a business—there were other such ideas too, which you ought to write down some time.

(23 April 1826)

When he penned these words, both he himself and Eduard Gans had already become nominal Christians—a fact to which the following passage of the letter plainly refers.

You are independent enough to dare to say all this despite Gans's baptism; and as for me—you need not mind me at all. As Solon said that no one should be called happy before his death, so it might be said that until he is dead no one should be called an honest man.

I am glad the elder Friedländer and Bendavid are full of years and will soon die; these we have safe, and our times cannot, therefore, be charged with having failed to produce a single blameless person.

Forgive my ill humour, it is directed chiefly against myself. I get up occasionally in the night, stand in front of my mirror and scold myself. Perhaps, as I write this, I see my friend's soul as just such a mirror; but I have the impression that it is no longer as clear as it once was.

That last phrase plainly shows the cooling of what had been Heine's warmest friendship. At a time when the poet first contemplated and then enacted what he felt to be a base compromise, Moser had been cast in the dangerous part of conscience or super-ego. This had contributed to the characteristic literary stylization already referred to: it was not only his *cloak* that made Moser the Marquis Posa of Heine's Don Carlos! The complex of self-sacrificing friendship, high idealism, humanitarian rhetoric, and machiavellian indirection suggested by the Posa image was overlaid by other literary stylizations as the friendship with Moser waned. Moser then becomes Antonio, the courtier-statesman who gives reasonable but unwelcome advice to the poet-hero of Goethe's *Torquato Tasso* (to Moser, 24 February 1826); and four days later, at the nadir of their relationship, he even likens his friend to Pantalone, the garrulous old man of the *commedia dell' arte*. After that, friendly intimacy with Moser was over for good; but the extent to which Heine retained his respect for him will be seen when we come to his obituary of Ludwig Marcus in a later chapter. What must be stressed here, however, is that Heine showed himself particularly anxious to impress on Moser that even after baptism he had not forgotten his Jewish provenance. He demonstrates this in many ways—as when he refers to 'our teacher Moses', *Moshe rabbenu*, in his letter of 23 April 1826, and uses the Hebrew alphabet to spell out this time-hallowed formula.

Ludwig Marcus, as the opening chapter of this book has already shown, also appears among the members of the Society for the Culture and Science of the Jews portrayed in Heine's letters. We find the poet organizing financial help for the 'good

Marcus' and protesting to Moser that his appreciation of the little man's virtues are not 'tinged with contempt': 'How wrong you are when you say that I mock Marcus! By God, I am better than you think. I have written the poor little man an affectionate letter today . . .' (28 November 1823). What is always in the foreground of Heine's attention is Marcus's exceedingly small stature—either as a standard of smallness generally, as when religious reformers are accused of wanting to constrain a statue of Hercules into Marcus's little brown jacket, or as a point of contrast, when those who exceed Marcus in stature are shown to be beneath him in greatness of soul. Eduard Gans, as we saw, is subjected to this contrast—but so is Heine himself. 'Truly', he writes on 30 September 1823, '"little Marcus" is greater than I!' But when Marcus joins Moser and other members of the Society for the Culture and Science of the Jews in applying Hegelian terminology to everything and reducing live beings to the status of an idea, Heine feels moved to protest, in a passage which characteristically suggests that there was a female member of Marcus's household with whom Heine was more intimately and vitally concerned than with the little man himself.

And we? Do we exist? For heaven's sake, don't tell me again that I am just an idea! I am madly annoyed by this. You can all become ideas, I don't care about that; but don't bother me with such stuff. Just because you and old Friedländer and Gans have become ideas, you want to lead me astray and turn me into an idea too. All credit to Rubo, whom you could not persuade to play along. Lehmann would like to become an idea, but he can't. What do I care for little Marcus and his demonstration that I am an idea—his servant-girl knows better than that! With Jewish tears in her eyes, Dr Zunz's wife complained to me that they wanted to turn her husband into an idea too, and this was robbing him of all his strength and sap; Jost had withdrawn from the Society for that reason, and it had made Auerbach sick . . .

(to Moser, 18 Kune 1823)

This *jeu d'esprit* caricatures most of the members of the Society, including the historian I. M. Jost, who came to reject its endeavours as the hubris of inexperienced and arrogant young men, Julius Rubo, and others we have already met or are about to meet in these pages. It drastically suggests the Hegelian fervour which had superseded the deism of earlier Jewish intellectuals, and playfully connects it with the wrath of Jehovah Heine feels to be directed against him at the very moment in which he is preparing to glorify the traditions of Judaism in the pages of *The Rabbi of Bacherach*. Could it be that He too had become infected by new cosmopolitan philosophies and is prepared to abandon His erstwhile champions? Beware of Spinoza, Heine warns,'le petit juif d'Amsterdam', who whispers into the Lord's ears: 'Entre nous, monsieur, vous n'existez pas!'

The Bible, whose sanctity this irreverent passage about the Jewish God deliberately assails, was for Heine—as the present book will often have cause to show—a source of richly individualized characters, general human types, significant incident, and poetic utterance. He knew it, in the main, in Luther's translation; but during his association with the Society for the Culture and Science of the Jews, he heard some of it in Hebrew: notably that Psalm 137, the song of the Babylonian exile, which will resound like a leitmotif through his later work. It was, as we have seen, Moses Moser who recited that psalm to him; and it is therefore on Moser that he tried out one of his bitterest Bible parodies, ending his vision of a future Jewish Republic, ironically named 'Ganstown', with the vision of a new poetry dominated by images which the Germans of Heine's day associated above all with the Jews who lived in their midst. Little Marcus, it will be noted, again puts in an appearance, though only vicariously this time.

When . . . a new Jewish literature shall come to flower, the mercantile expressions of today's Stock Exchange will become part of the language of poetry, and a poetic grandson of little Marcus, arrayed in prayer shawl and phylacteries [*in Talles und Tefillin*] will sing before the whole Ganstown community [*Kille*]: 'By the waters of the Spree they sat down and counted banknotes; then came their enemies and said: Give us Bills of Exchange on London, the course standeth high . . .'

But enough of this self-persiflage. Keep your affection for me!

(23 May 1823)

What this self-mocking Bible parody unmistakably suggests is that any legacy left by the Berlin Diaspora will not be as richly poetic as that left by an earlier generation of Jewish exiles.

Whatever disrespect the recollection of Berlin Jewry inspired in Heine did not extend to the great scholar Leopold Zunz. True enough, he caricatures him, along with his wife, in such letters as that of 18 June 1823; but the caricature is affectionate, and Heine's respect and admiration shine through again and again. 'I send a thousand thanks to Dr Zunz', Heine writes to Moser on 25 October 1824, 'for his message about the Jews in Spain. Although very brief, it was an intelligent hint, of more use to me than any number of hefty tomes—without knowing it, Zunz will have influenced *The Rabbi of Bacherach*.' Zunz helped Heine to learn about important and interesting Jews of the past; when Heine came to read the twelfth-century Travel Notes of Benjamin ben Jonah of Tudela, he felt an urgent desire to see Benjamin's work edited and translated by Zunz (to Moser, 25 June 1824). Many times Heine refers to Zunz's theories on what constitutes a 'source' for the historian of the Jewish people, expressing the hope that his own *Rabbi of Bacherach* will prove to be such a source. Baptism, he felt, had disqualified him to some extent—a feeling he conveyed in characteristically veiled and parodistic form in the dedication to Zunz which he sent with a copy of his *Pictures of Travel* in May 1826. The reference to 'Ararat', in that Dedication, is another of Heine's many references to M. M. Noah's scheme for a Jewish settlement on Grand Island, New York.

To Dr Zunz, Judge designate of Israel, Vice-President of the Society for the Culture and Science of the Jews, President of the Institute for the Science of Judaism, Editor of the Society's Journal, Member of the Committee for Agriculture, Librarian . . .

I shall stop at this last title, for I am sending you herewith a copy of my latest book for the Society's library. Should the Society and its library have already been transferred to Ararat, I request that said copy should be handed to Frau Dr Zunz for use in the kitchen. The greater part of the book is a 'source' and is therefore indispensable for a history of our Jews. I, however, remain with unaltered love and friendship,

   Your friend
    H. Heine
   Dr. iur. and member of the Society for the Culture and Science of the Jews in the Eighteenth century.

'In the *eighteenth* century'! For the nineteenth century the Society's endeavours already seemed a lost cause. 'If civil disabilities and community apathy played a role in the demise of the *Verein*', Michael Meyer has rightly said, 'so did its own ideology. Though its leaders were concerned with giving expression to their consciousness of themselves as Jews, they failed to develop a rationale for continued Jewish identification. Their conception of the future did not provide any incentive for the Jew to remain a Jew.'[4] But even if Heine could now envisage success only for the historical endeavours of the Society (the endeavours, that is, which had found their doughtiest champion in Zunz), even if he thought his own writings unfit to serve as an unsullied source of Jewish history after his baptism, he remained conscious of the value his brief association with the Society had been to his efforts at self-definition. His friendship and admiration for Zunz was genuine, and survived all the fun he had had at the expense of this great scholar and his devoted wife. 'Zunz-jokes', *Zunzwitze*, constituted a sub-genre for which he retained his taste (to Moser, 8 October 1825). What amused and touched him particularly was the patent love Mrs Zunz bore her physically not very prepossessing husband. We have already seen something of this in the mock complaint Heine puts into her mouth: that other members of the Society for the Culture and Science of the Jews were trying to reduce her husband's corporal being— along with so much else in the physical world!—to a Hegelian Idea. Heine's letter to Wohlwill of 1 April 1823 supplements this in a wholly characteristic way.

[Mrs Zunz] takes greater delight in her husband every day. She maintains that his pockmarks are little spittoons of the amoretti. I too like him very much, and I am deeply grieved to see this excellent man so misunderstood because of his rough, repellent exterior. I expect a great deal from his sermons which are soon to appear in print; not, to be sure, pious edification and soothing plasters for the soul, but something much better: something which will arouse dormant strength and power. *That*'s what is lacking in Israel.

After his baptism Heine's respect for Zunz's scholarship, and for the kind of inner strength which his life and work constantly exhibited, remained unimpaired—and even in his final days in Paris he showed himself overjoyed when Zunz and his wife visited him. He laughed and he cried, he reminisced about Berlin, he discussed Hebrew poetry and the Kabbalah, he spoke Yiddish and a little Hebrew, and he was as reluctant to let these old friends go their ways as he was eager to see other visitors leave.[5]

Immanuel Wohlwill (originally called Wolf) is another member of the Society whose portrait peeps out at us from the pages of Heine's correspondence. Wohlwill, after discussion with Gans, Zunz, and others, had formulated the programme of the Society and published his formulation in the opening number of its journal; and because of a Leibnizian image in his otherwise characteristically Hegelian article Heine constantly referred to him as 'the Monad' or 'the fat Monad-worshipper'. The adjective in that last appellation was no figure of speech— a reference to Wohlwill's embonpoint appears, along with an allusion to his change of name, in the bantering letter appropriately dated 1 April 1823 from which I have already quoted.

Although in this cold winter many a friendship has frozen to death, your beloved portly image has not yet been able to squeeze out of the postern of my heart, and the name Wolf—Wohlwill, I should say— lives warmly in my memory.

Heine then talks of his conversations with Moser, in which Wohlwill figured, and remarks—in true cartoonist's fashion— on his friend's physical likeness to two Chinamen who were being exhibited in Berlin at that moment. After comments on Gans, Zunz, orthodox and reforming Jews, and Heine's own relation to Judaism, the letter ends with a warning about Hamburg, where Wohlwill was staying when he received it:

Have you seen my sister in Hamburg? She is a dear sweet girl. Do you get into much female company there? Be careful; Hamburg women are beautiful. But in your case this does not matter much— you are a quiet, orderly, inwardly happy man, and when you take fire, it is in the cause of all mankind. I am differently constituted. On top of that you have the good fortune to be a moral man; you look before you leap, you consider ethical pros and cons, you are contented, you are well-behaved, you are virtuous—and just because you are such a dear good boy, I have written you this long letter.

When one reads a passage such as this, one is reminded of

Heine's confession to Immermann that he could understand things best by looking at their contraries—that he understood his own nature only when he compared and contrasted it with that of human beings of a different temperament and cast of mind (10 June 1823). Heine's portrayal of the placid, good-natured, unexciting, philistine Wohlwill, with his fondness for philosophical jargon, thus becomes indirectly another essay in self-definition. The portrait is rounded out, in every sense, by stray references elsewhere: in a letter to Moser of 27 September 1823, for instance, in which Heine quoted Cervantes ('a fat man, hence a good man') as a characterization of Wohlwill, and adds, after speaking of his friend's temporary dejection: 'I like [Wohlwill] very much. He has a good deal of feeling, but alas—his feelings have no backbone.' 'I love him', he had explained to Moser a month before, on 23 August 1823, 'and would like to cure him of the sentimentality into which he has lied himself and which is now spoiling his temperament.'

We have already heard Heine's sly remark that Joseph Lehmann, who was to earn universal respect as an editor and journalist of rare integrity, 'would have liked to become an idea but could not [manage it].' In the great dream-vision of the letter to Moser dated 23 April 1826, in which Gans and Mordecai Noah meet in Strahlau and Gans shows himself, for once, silent as a fish, Lehmann also appears, along with Zunz and his affectionate wife:

Zunz stood by with a sarcastic smile and said to his wife: 'Now do you see, little mouse?' I think that Lehmann made a long speech, in full voice and larded with terms like 'Enlightenment', 'changing circumstances of the time', 'progression of the world-spirit'; but instead of sending me to sleep his words did just the opposite: they woke me from my dream.

This view of Lehmann as a cliché-spouting bore did not, however, prevent Heine from writing him friendly letters, making use of his journalistic contacts in various ways, and keeping up sporadic contact with him throughout his life. For all his intellectual limitations, Lehmann appeared to Heine an honest man worthy of a kind of respect that the poet withheld from more brilliant and sparkling contemporaries. Into a copy of the *Book of Songs* (*Buch der Lieder*) which he sent to him

shortly after its publication in 1827 he wrote the words: 'To his
dear and well-tried friend Joseph Lehmann the author sends
this book as a token of his friendship' (*HSA* XX, 305).

Another characteristic dream-vision recorded in Heine's
letters to Moser also brings before us members of the Society
for the Culture and Science of the Jews. It can be found in a
letter from Göttingen dated 20 July 1824:

In spite of a plethora of work, and anguish, and complications of all
sorts, I think of you continually. Last night, the night that has just
passed, I dreamt of you. I saw you riding in ancient Spanish costume
on an Andalusian steed in the midst of a great swarm of Jews
journeying to Jerusalem. Little Marcus with his great maps and travel
books went ahead to show the way; Zunz, *en escarpins*, carried the
Society's *Journal*, bound in red morocco; his wife ran by his side as a
vivandière, carrying a cask of kosher holiday brandy on her back. It
was a great Jewish army, and Gans ran from one end to the other to
see that everything was in order. Lehmann and Wohlwill carried
banners that bore the shield of David and the maxims of Bendavid.
Cohn the sugar broker led the adherents of the reformed Temple.
Past pupils of the Society's school carried the bones of Saul Ascher.
All baptized Jews followed as army suppliers. There were many
carriages in the rear of the train. In one these sat Oppert the VD
specialist, as medical officer, and Jost, as historian of the deeds that
were yet to be accomplished. In another coach sat Friedländer with
Frau von der Recke; and in one of the most splendid of all the
carriages of state sat Michael Beer, as *corps de génie*, with the actors
Wolf and Madame Stich by his side—they were to perform Beer's
Pariah in Jerusalem and harvest a well-earned fame . . .

Pages of commentary could not exhaust the allusive riches of
this *jeu d'esprit*. It tells us that thoughts of emigration were
never far from the minds of these young Jewish intellectuals
unable to find the right careers open to their talents in Ger-
many. Its Spanish colouring, due in part to Moser's reputation
as a Schillerian Marquis Posa, reminds us of the Society's
interest in the Hispano-Jewish culture of the Middle Ages—an
interest with a contemporary relevance, for might not the kind
of symbiosis that had proved possible in Spain be possible also
in Germany? It glances at Ludwig Marcus's absorption in
Oriental geography; at Zunz's activities as an editor and his
wife's splendid combination of orthodox piety, house-keeping

talents, loving devotion to her husband, and generous hospitality; at Gans's organizational ability; at Reform Judaism; at Saul Ascher's pioneering efforts to redefine Jewishness which qualified him to have his relics transferred to Jerusalem like those a Jewish saint; at the schools the Society ran for the benefit of poor immigrant boys; at Jewish doctors like Samuel Oppert, who had already figured in another dream reported to Moser in March 1823, where again he had sat in a carriage that seems to have made an indelible impression on Heine:

Dr Oppert, the clap-specialist, rode up to my lodgings in his carriage, entered my room in the splendour of his decorations and his white silk stockings, and told me in confidence that he was a cultured man.

(I forbear to speculate why Heine should dream, or should say that he dreamt, of a doctor known for his treatment of venereal disease.) Lazarus Bendavid also has his meed of notice in Heine's letters—writing to Zunz on 27 June 1823, he says of Bendavid's contribution to the Society's journal that it was suitable neither to the time when nor to the place where it appeared. So much, then, for the maxims on the banners carried, in Heine's dream vision, by Lehmann and Wohlwill, neither of whom Heine considered an intellectual giant. The progression from David to Bendavid could hardly be considered an advance! And then there is Michael Beer and his *Pariah*, whom we have met before. Beer, Heine felt, could be useful to him and had to be buttered up on occasions; but this set up resentments which come out in passages such as the following:

The Muses . . . are curious creatures. They are old maids who were beautiful in their younger days, when they had the right of domicile in Athens; in the summer they lived in Thessaly, and they turned down the most advantageous matches. When they grow older, and the whole world gained the Athenian *connubium*, no one wanted to marry them; now we find them gadding about the world, and one of them, in her despair, recently agreed to marry a rich Jew, who contracted the match only in order to gain renown. But that marriage, I now hear, is off again.
Is Michael Beer back from Paris yet?

(to Moser, 25 June 1824)

One further element in the dream-vision of 20 July 1824

deserves more than a brief glance: the proximity of David Friedländer and the Gentile aristocrat Elise von der Recke. To understand what is involved here we must remind ourselves of Heine's scorn of the feeble compromises which he thought proponents of a rational reform of Judaism all too ready to make.

We no longer have the strength to wear a beard, to fast, to hate, and to find in hatred the power to endure—that's what impels us to "reform". One faction owes its education and enlightenment to players in the theatre: and so it aspires to new set-decoration for Judaism, wants the prompter to wear ecclesiastical bands instead of a beard, tries to pour an ocean into a pretty papier mâché bowl and to dress Hercules in little Marcus's wee brown jacket. Another faction wants to found an evangelical Christianity trading under the name 'Judaism'; its adherents make themselves a prayer shawl from the wool of the Lamb, a jacket from the feathers of the Holy Ghost, and underpants from the spirit of Christian love.

The faction caricatured at the end of this passage is that associated with David Friedländer, whose notorious offer to subscribe to a 'Christian' creed if doctrines irreconcilable with Judaism were omitted from it had been contemptuously dismissed by Schleiermacher and refused with scant thanks by W. A. Teller, the Prussian theologian to whom Friedländer had addressed his epistle. Heine therefore continues, using commercial metaphors that have an obvious relevance to the occupations of most of the Berlin 'reformers':

They then became insolvent and their successors call themselves: "God, Christ & Co." Fortunately this house will not go on trading for long; the bills of exchange it has drawn on philosophy are bouncing back unhonoured, and in Europe it is going bankrupt, even though its commission–houses in Africa and Asia, established by missionaries, may keep going a few centuries longer.

(to Wohlwill, 1 April 1823)

The special animus here revealed derives in part from the Prussian government's refusal to allow unbaptized Jews to become university professors or enter the civil service and judiciary—a refusal that faced Heine, as we know, with the necessity of outwardly subscribing to a Christian creed. While admiring strength and power he felt more and more that he, for one, belonged to the party of the weak.

I too lack the strength to wear a beard, to let them call "Ikey Mo" after me in the street, to fast, and so on. I haven't even the strength to eat *Matzot* [unleavened bread prescribed for Passover] properly; for here I am lodging in a Jew's house, opposite Moser and Gans, and instead of bread I am given *Matzot* to eat, and I am breaking my teeth on them. But I comfort myself by saying that we are, after all, in exile (*wir sind ja im Gohles*). My needling of Friedländer must not be taken too seriously either, for I recently ate the most marvellous pudding at his house, and he is living opposite me and

—now watch Heine lauching into a rapid caricature of a Jew who has gained entry to a non-Jewish salon where he feels constantly called upon to justify his very existence against attacks by anti-Semitic academics—

there he is, at his window, sharpening his quill pen; any minute now he will write to Elise von der Recke: 'Most high and well-born lady, I am not really as intolerable as Professor Voigt says . . .'

The conjunction of David Friedländer and Elise von der Recke recurs elsewhere in Heine's letters (see his letter to Moser, dated 20 July 1824), and it has a precise contemporary significance. In 1820 Friedländer had published a pamphlet couched in the form of an open letter to Elise von der Recke (*Ein Sendschreiben an die Frau Kammerherrin von der Recke, geb. Gräfin von Medem*) which had complained of the persecution of nineteenth-century Jews by German writers (*Beitrag zur Geschichte der Verfolgung der Juden im neunzehnten Jahrhundert durch Schriftsteller*). One of Friedländer's exhibits had been Professor Johannes Voigt's biography of his Königsberg colleague Christian Kraus, in which Voigt had alleged that Kraus found 'even esteemed and educated Jews like David Friedländer in Berlin almost wholly intolerable'. Such revealing indications of Gentile German reactions to Jews were never lost on Heine. He knew that the fight against the discouraging effect of such attitudes needed all the strength that German Jews could muster; and it should therefore not surprise us to find him taking up the theme of inner strength once again in the tribute to his uncle Salomon which he added as a postscript to his letter of 1 April 1823. 'Have you seen him?' he asks Wohlwill, and he continues: 'He is one of the people I respect most; he is noble, and he has inborn strength. This last item, as you know, ranks highest with me.'

(iv)

The younger Heine firmly believed that his career as a writer had put other authors of Jewish provenance under an obligation to him. 'The axiom', we find him writing to Moser on 9 January 1824, 'that a tragedy must needs be bad if its author is a Jew can now no longer be brought forward unchallenged. For this Michael Beer can never thank me enough.' If nevertheless Beer's *Pariah*, he adds, had been rejected by the spectacled Brahmins and epauletted Shustras of Berlin—the intellectual and military men who frequented the theatres of the Prussian capital—then let Beer seek consolation for such oppressive effects of the caste spirit in the arms of a *Bayadère* . . . And Heine goes on to cite the section of Gans's *Law of Inheritance* in which such open unions may seek their sanction. Eduard Gans, we see, is never long absent from Heine's thoughts in these early days. His letters allow us many other valuable glimpses of Jewish-born contemporaries who were making a name for themselves as writers in the German language: Moritz Saphir, for instance, whom Heine, punning on his name, dismisses at first as 'unpolished' (to Moser, 1 July 1825), but whose jokes grow on him in the course of the 1820s. In a letter to Joseph Lehmann dated 26 May 1826, Heine claims to have detected literary promise in Saphir's poems many years ago; he sees him as a wit capable of rising to heights of true humour; but he feels hurt that Saphir allowed him to be insulted in a journal he was then editing by an insalubrious Jewish reviewer who—here, as so often, comes the cartoonist's stereotype!—seemed to have a vocation for dealing in old clothes rather than for judicious assessment of literary works. That was wrong of Saphir, Heine concludes; choice spirits should make common front against the rabble.

Among the choicer spirits Heine seems to have counted, at this time, a descendant of Frederick the Great's court Jew

Daniel Itzig—a lawyer who had taken on the name Eduard
Hitzig after his baptism, and who had become the friend
and confidant of a number of writers associated with the
Romantic movement in Germany. Hitzig is encoun-
tered in Heine's letters as an intermediary who helped the
young poet in his relations with publishers, and as an ex-
perienced adviser who counselled him to give up thoughts of
making a living as a lawyer or civil servant and to devote
himself to literature instead. The two men did not often meet
face to face; for the most part Heine had to rely on the reports
of others. 'I hear', he writes to Immermann on 24 February
1825, 'that Hitzig is directing many literary manœuvres and
that he has founded a poet's club in Berlin.' Such a man, clearly,
could be useful to him; Heine therefore asked Moser to keep
Hitzig well-disposed towards him and was delighted to hear
that Hitzig took an interest in his fortunes (to Moser, 11
January and 22 July 1825; to Hitzig, March 1825). The poet
was furious, however, when a rumour reached him that his
friends had approached Hitzig with the request that he should
find a position for Heine in Berlin. He took this as a slur on his
honour and immediately wrote an angry letter to Moser for-
bidding any unsolicited interference in his life (24 February
1826). For the rest, Heine showed himself an assiduous reader
of Hitzig's publications, but declared himself distressed by the
'suppurating matter' exhibited in his life of Zacharias Werner.
As for Hitzig's meritorious edition of the posthumous works
of E. T. A. Hoffmann—Heine claims to have found these so
full of caricatures and distortions that he began to feel queasy
(to Ludwig Robert, 27 November 1823). A strange reaction
indeed from a man who was to become a master of the grotes-
que portrait-sketch and the verbal cartoon!

Ludwig Robert, the recipient of these strictures on Hitzig's
Hoffmann edition, was also a prominent purveyor of reading
matter for the middle classes. He was, in fact, the brother of
Rahel Varnhagen, and his original family name, like hers, had
been Levin. We have already seen the important part played by
Robert's drama *The Force of Circumstances* in Heine's writings
of the 1820s; in the letters, he diplomatically avoided critical
comment on Robert's comedy *The Baboon*, preferring to use
its German title, *Der Pavian*, for a series of puns that became a

standing joke between him, Robert, and Robert's beautiful non-Jewish wife Friederike. They can hardly have taken amiss his remark that Robert's talents as a comedy writer were inferior to those of Aristophanes! For his own part he was glad when the Roberts approved of his writings; he agreed to contribute to almanachs edited by them (with often frustrating results), and he seems to have respected Ludwig Robert as a man of integrity. 'I like him very much,' he told Moser on 28 November 1823; 'he has not shown himself petty in his dealings with me, and that, in this age of egoism, means a great deal.' As for understanding Heine, however—of that he thought Robert no more capable than the rest of his acquaintances, with the possible exception of Rahel Varnhagen. When Heine was temporarily estranged from Rahel's husband, he asked Moser to report to him any comments Robert might make on the rights and wrongs of this estrangement, and added: 'God knows, these people know me very little and the little they know they misunderstand.' (January 1824.)

Ludwig Robert's sister, the celebrated Rahel, gained Heine's respect and affection by standing no nonsense from him and yet showing a generous appreciation of his good qualities as a writer and as a man. He showed occasional pique—his letter to Rahel of 1 April 1829 is a strong example; but this passed, and to the end of his life he treasured his memories of her in a way he treasured few others. 'The most intelligent lady, *die geistreichste Dame*, I have ever met', he calls her in a letter to Immermann dated 14 January 1823. To Ludwig Robert he writes, on 27 November 1823, about 'the dear, good little woman with the great soul', adding that he has been reading Goethe to please her.

Tell her that she is rarely absent from my thoughts. The whole of last week I was busy with her, for I read Mme de Staël's *Corinne*—a book I could never have understood before that great epoch in my life in which I came to know your sister.

To Moser he protests his affection for Rahel, the German Corinne, whom he now terms, with a fervour highly unusual in his comments on contemporaries, 'that glorious woman' (*die herrliche Frau*, 28 November 1823); and on 14 May 1826 he sends a book to Varnhagen with the request that it be transmit-

ted to 'our dear, good, noble Friedrike'. Fried[e]rike it should
be remember, was the name Rahel had adopted at her baptism.
True, he correctly divined Rahel's psychological need for con-
stant expressions of affection and regard; but he would not
have pandered to that need, or spoken so warmly of Rahel after
her death, if he had not responded so favourably to her perso-
nality and intellect. When writing to her, he cultivated a prose
style that has a close affinity—in its half-mocking, half-serious
tone—with that of his lyric poetry.

When, after a few centuries perhaps, I shall have the pleasure of
seeing you again as the most beautiful and glorious of flowers in the
most beautiful and glorious of heavenly valleys, then, please, greet
me graciously, as an old acquaintance, with your friendly glance and
sweet breath. I shall be a prickly holly—or perhaps, even, something
worse. I am sure you will do this; for you did something just like it in
1822 and 1823, when you treated me—at a time that found me sick,
bitter, cantankerous, poetic, and insufferable—with a courtesy and
kindness which I had done nothing to deserve in this present life; I
can only ascribe it to benevolent memories of acquaintance in some
earlier existence.

(12 April 1823)

Heine's playfulness cannot hide his genuine feeling of obliga-
tion—of gratitude to an intelligent and cultured lady who saw
his faults, criticized them openly and constantly, and yet
showed, in word and deed, that she valued him for what he was
and (even more) for what he could yet become.

(v)

The stimulating atmosphere of Berlin and its literary coteries
contrasted sharply with that of Hamburg, where Heine's Un-
cle Salomon kept court as head of the family and one of the
most respected members of the Jewish community, and where
the poet himself hoped at one time to establish himself as a
lawyer employed by the local government. He kept in touch
with Moser and other Berlin friends by means of a lively
correspondence in which we hear a good deal of a friend and
business associate of Moser's, the sugar broker G. G. Cohn.

'In coming to know Cohn', Heine assures Moser on 11 July 1823, 'I have come to know a very good man'; and again, on 23 August of the same year: 'Cohn has proved a very good friend to me in Hamburg, and I have come to like him very much.' But, he continues, this set Cohn apart from the rest of his Hamburg acquaintances, whom Heine dismisses as a 'miserable rabble' in whom one can take an interest only if one keeps one's distance from them (to Moser, 23 August 1823). The bitterness of this remark is increased by its context—after attacks on the Jews and unqualified rejection of their demands for emancipation by Professors J. F. Fries, C. F. Rühs, and others, Heine felt alienated alike from his co-religionists and from his country. Even with G. G. Cohn relations grew troubled—first by quarrels about Reform Judaism, which Cohn supported and Heine deplored, and then by malicious gossip among Uncle Salomon's entourage in which Cohn had some part. Though the matter was patched up and Cohn showed himself generous towards Heine, their friendship was never re-established; Cohn, the man who had heaped glowing *Kuggel* on the poet's head after his baptism and who might have become Gans's Carl Sand, dwindled to *Zuckerkohn*, a minor item in Heine's stock of cartoon figures.

When Heine turns to look at the Hamburg Jews around his Uncle Salomon, the ideas of 'money' and 'guzzling' at once present themselves to his mind; but he did not think that the average Hamburg Gentile was any better. The vices of Hamburg Jews were those of their society as a whole, aggravated by traits that derived from the special disadvantages against which they had to make their way. One such trait Heine pin-points, in a letter to Rudolf Christiani, by means of a typical pun:

I paid a visit to your friend Dr Halle. He is very affable, very obliging (*zuvorkommend*), and he is a veritable Jew. His very first question showed him jumping ahead (*zuvorkommend*) in the Jewish way: 'I hear', he said, 'you are to be my colleague?'

(6 December 1825)

Dr Adolf Halle, it should be noted, was baptized in 1816. Heine here exhibits a mechanism that operated in the same way against him: he refers to the Jewishness of nominal Christians as though their baptism had never taken place at all. One remembers what Börne wrote to Jeanette Wohl about Heine himself after his baptism:

Heine is a perfect *Bacher* [young Jew; especially one who studies the intricacies of the Talmud at a *Yeshiva* or religious seminary]! How he came to be that, or rather stay that way as a Jew by birth, I cannot explain to myself . . . His way of making jokes is typically Jewish . . .

As for the question that Dr Halle asked Heine, and of which he complains in his letter of 6 December 1825—that touched a very sore spot indeed, for it was more than doubtful whether the Hamburg city fathers would be willing to grant the poet the sort of employment in their judiciary that they had bestowed on the serviceable Adolf Halle. That the latter was allowed to wed Uncle Salomon's daughter Therese, whom Heine himself might have liked to wed after his disappointment over Amalie, could only confirm his low estimate of the values by which the Hamburg branch of his family lived.

The head of that family inspired in Heine, as his letters amply document, a good deal of respect. We have seen some of this already in his letter to Wohlwill dated 7 April 1823; here is another testimony, in a letter to Friederike Robert dated 12 October 1825.

Salomon Heine . . . is a remarkable man, who unites the greatest merits with great faults. We live, it is true, amidst constant differences of opinion, but I love him to an extraordinary degree, almost more than I am myself aware of. We are much alike in our essential being and our character. The same headstrong boldness joined with an unfathomable softness of sentiment and incalculable caprice—the only difference is that fortune made him a millionaire and me the exact opposite: a poet; and so there has been a mighty divergence between our outward development, the development of our opinions and ways of life.

But though Uncle Salomon could show himself, on important occasions, gracious and generous, Heine came to feel more and more humiliated by the way in which that generosity was exercised. 'Everything he does for me', Heine reported to Moser on 1 April 1825, after his uncle had agreed to keep him at the University of Göttingen for a further six months, 'he does in a disagreeable way.'

This did not prevent Heine, however, from paying his uncle's immediate family a charming compliment: an occasional poem, written in 1825 in the manner of the first *North Sea* cycle, and pasted into a copy of *Pictures of Travel* I in company with a prose preamble:[6]

The following poem, which I wrote on the island of Norderney last September, in honour of an aunt whose birthday I wanted to celebrate, is so much part of the preceding cycle of Sea Pictures that I must, at least, inscribe it into this copy of the book.

The poem that follows, entitled 'Sunrise' (*Sonnenaufgang*), envisages the sun surveying the world and resting its gaze on 'uncle's villa in Ottensen'. There it finds, gathered around the breakfast table,

> die schöne Tante
> Und den Oheim, den fürstlichen Mann,
> Und die lieben Mädchen,
> Und Carl, den göttlichen Jungen
> Dem die Welt gehört,
> Und den vornehmherrlichen Herrmann,
> Der jüngst aus Italien gekommen,
> Und vieles gesehn und erfahren,
> Und jetzt erzählt . . .
>   [my comely aunt,
> and uncle, the princely man,
> and the dear girls,
> and Carl, the divine boy
> to whom the world belongs,
> and gloriously gentlemanly Hermann,
> who recently returned from Italy
> where he saw and experienced much—
> and he now tells his tale . . .][7]

There is irony in this passage, and some resentment, especially in its evocation of Heine's cousins Carl and Hermann; but on the whole the mock-heroic tone is sustained without malice. *Castle Contumely* (*Affrontenburg*), a poem to be discussed later, will conjure up a considerably more sinister impression of the atmosphere at Ottensen.[8]

If Heine's feelings towards his uncle remained mixed, those towards that uncle's entourage deepened more and more into downright hatred. 'Steinweg' and 'Dreckwall', two Hamburg streets inhabited by Jews, became terms of opprobrium with Heine—the suggestions of stones and mud in their very names facilitated such ideographic use. When his sister Charlotte was pregnant, he advised her, with obvious satiric intent, not to look at too many 'Steinwegfaces' (8 May 1824); and in other letters, the Hamburg Jewish quarter is described as full of donkeys (for example to Moser, 9 January 1824). The donkeys are joined by dogs elsewhere: 'A pack of curs hostile to me is crouching around my uncle', he writes to Moser on 18 June 1823; though at that time Hamburg still seemed to him, despite a detested crew of male and female Hamburgers speaking their Jewish German (*Societät mauschelnder Hamburger und Hamburgerinnen*), as compounded of Elysium and Tartarus at once (to Moser, 23 August 1823). When he spoke of Jewish contemporaries as 'curs', Heine was well aware that he was seeing them in a guise that he himself assumed, all too easily, in the eyes of ill-disposed non-Jews. In a letter to Karl Immermann dated 10 June 1823, we find him inveighing against German aristocrats who wished to reduce him to the status of a dog. He showed unceasing sensitivity to allusions that glanced at his Jewish descent, and indulged in bitter self-persiflage—as when, in a letter to Moser of 23 May 1823, he compared his correspondent's feelings to *gold* and his own to *paper-money*, and added:

Has this image not shown you that I am a Jewish poet? But why should I be embarrassed? We are among ourselves, and I like to use our national images.

Heine was to essay many variations on such 'national images', juxtaposing poetry and money, the world of Apollo and that of Mercury, in ways that play a calculated game with his readers' knowledge of Jewish stereotypes. In this spirit we find him writing, again to Moser, on 23 August 1826: 'I would like to pawn the golden hooves of my Pegasus with a Jew in order to borrow some good sense—to pawn gold in order to borrow some pennies of ready cash.'

In his own immediate family, especially with his mother, Heine did find the affection so woundingly denied him in Hamburg; but he never found intellectual stimulation and literary encouragement there:

. . . my mother has read my poems and tragedies, but did not find them particularly to her taste; my sister just tolerates them, and my father has not read them at all.

(to Moser, 23 May 1823)

Nor could Heine warm to his sister Charlotte's husband, Moritz Embden, though he had initially welcomed the match:

Impelled by the well-deserved contempt I showed him, my sister's husband has sought revenge by maligning me everywhere and inciting Cohn, among others, to speak of my 'dissolute' way of life in my uncle's house. This was intended to encourage my uncle to send me away from Hamburg—for my own good, of course!

(to Moser, 24 February 1826)

Because of Embden's attitude and behaviour, Heine lamented, he had lost a sister. His younger brothers, on the other hand, induced him to play a fatherly role at this time; he did what he could to help and advise them in their choice of careers. The youngest brother, Maximilian, followed in the footsteps of earlier members of the van Geldern family and trained to become a physician. The other brother, however, whose experiments with a commercial career were fated to be no more successful than Heine's own, wanted to get away from traditional German-Jewish callings and devote himself to agricultural management. Might not Moser help here by approaching Israel Jakobsohn, one of the few Prussian Jews who owned agricultural estates? Heine asked him to try, anyway, explaining his request as follows:

My brother, who has had several years of practical training in agriculture and is able to take on the tasks of an agricultural supervisor, has not secured a post. The reason for this, he tells me, is partly that he is circumcised, partly that farming is in a depression at the moment and workers are being laid off—most of all, however, it seems to be his Jewishness that has stood in his way.

(to Moser, 30 September 1823)

Jakobsohn's answer seems to have been such that the poet resolved, for the future, to do anything rather than again ask a favour from a wealthy co-religionist. His tragedy, of course, was that throughout his life he was never able to do without such favours for long. Nor did the budding agronomist Gustav ever achieve his ambition to help with primary food production: after his failure in business (which earned him the family sobriquet 'oil merchant') he achieved worldly success in that growing profession of *journalism* into which so many Jews were to drift in the course of the nineteenth century. He joined the opposite party from that of his famous brother, however, and earned his social ennoblement by faithfully toeing the conservative line in Metternich's Vienna.

Despite his abuse of the Jews of Hamburg Heine did not become that all-too-well-known phenomenon, the Jewish anti-Semite. 'Do you think', he asks Moser on 9 January 1824, 'that the cause of my brethren is less dear to me than before? Then you are mightily mistaken ... "May my right hand wither if ever I forget thee, Yerushalaim".' He reads much history, in preparation for *The Rabbi of Bacherach*, and derives from this, as he tells Moser on 25 June 1824, 'a plenitude of instruction and anguish.' 'The spirit of Jewish history', he continues, in Hegelian vein, 'reveals itself to me more and more fully, and this spiritual armour will be very useful in times to come.' And when he followed what he believed to be the call of the time and became, nominally, a Protestant on 28 June 1825, he felt this action to be a desertion, an unworthy relinquishing of an essential part of his heritage. 'Beneath my dignity, and a stain on my honour' Heine had called the step towards which Prussian illiberality was pushing him (to Moser, 27 November 1823); and afterwards we find him again and again impelled to such self-torturing remarks as that in a letter to Moser dated 18 December 1825: 'I am becoming a true Christian; I am sponging on rich Jews.' Such *obiter dicta*, of which there are many, lend credibility to what Heine's not always reliable cousin Hermann Schiff reports after his visit to the poet in 1827, a time of great physical and mental stress. 'How are you, Heine?' Schiff asked; and the great German poet, now officially called Christian Johann Heinrich Heine, is said to have replied: 'Allen Meschumodim soll zu Mute sein wie mir'—'All apostates should feel as wretched as I do!'[9]

(vi)

> I am now hated by Christian and Jew. I very much regret having been baptized; I see no sign that things have gone better with me since then. On the contrary: I have experienced nothing but misfortune from that day onwards.
>
> (to Moser, 9 January 1826)

Even if Heine's Jewish feeling had been less strong than it in fact proved to be, his German contemporaries constantly reminded him of origins his baptism should have made them forget. 'Isn't it absurd', he writes to Moser in the letter just quoted, 'I am no sooner baptized, than I am abused as a Jew.' On 28 July of the same year, the same correspondent is told:

> I feel the urge to say goodbye to the German fatherland. It's not because I have a particular desire to tramp about the world: what drives me away is, rather, the torment of the situation in which I now find myself. The mark of the Jew, for instance, can never be washed off.

It was becoming clear to Heine that in his case baptism would not smooth the way towards honourable and profitable employment as easily as in that of Eduard Gans; and as this dawned on him, the figure of the Wandering Jew assumed a new importance in his mind.

> How well founded and deep is the myth of the Wandering Jew! In the silent woodland valley a mother tells her children this eerie tale; the little ones, frightened, draw nearer to the fire; outside it is dark night—the posthorn sounds—Jewish traders are travelling to the Leipzig fair. We are the heroes of the tale and do not know it. No barber can shave off the white beard whose tip rejuvenating time turns dark again.

The strange visual detail of the white beard which turns dark again at its tip would henceforward always come to Heine's mind when he thought of the Wandering—or Eternal—Jew and his own kinship with him. And from this Christian vision of his people's destiny he turned, by a natural progression, to Christ himself, whose divine mission he had so recently acknowledged. The Jesus who appears in his letters is not, however, the Son of God who had doomed the Wandering Jew to a life that would not end until the Second Coming. Under the influence of a paper Moser had read to the Society for the Culture and Science of the Jews, Jesus became, for Heine, yet another representative of the Jewish people and yet another exemplification of its sufferings.

I often think of the image you presented to the Society: the gigantic Christ with his crown of thorns, who walks through the world for thousands of years. You are milder than I, and better, and therefore your images are more beautiful, gentle, and consoling.

This passage comes again from the letter to Moser dated 28 July 1826; and on 14 October of the same year Heine reminds his friend of his conception of Jews and Judaism, *das Judentum*, 'crucified for the salvation of the world.' It should not surprise us, in view of these unorthodoxies, to find the poet speaking of his own fate in Christological terms. 'My honest name is still being crucified in Hamburg,' he writes to Moser on 14 April 1828; '"they know not what they do."' From here it is but a short step to Heine's presentation of the fate that awaited gifted writers in contemporary Germany:

After the publishers' scorn and spitting in the face comes the tea-party scourging, the crowning with the thorns of would-be clever praise, the crucifixion in literary magazines between two critical thieves—none of this could be borne if one did not keep in mind the Ascension that must come in the end!

(to Immermann, 14 January 1823)

Parodistic use of the Bible always came naturally to Heine—he compares himself as readily to Nebuchadnezzar as to Christ (see his letter to Friederike Robert dated 11 March 1829); but this did not mean that he regarded the book, sacred to observing Jews and Christians, without admiration and respect. He had nothing but scorn for those who fastened on 'errors' and inconsistencies in order to discredit biblical narratives. Did not these prove the very opposite of what the demystifiers thought they proved? 'The minor contradictions to be found in the Bible', he writes to Immermann on 26 December 1829, 'are for me an assurance that it has not been put together with some definite ulterior purpose. Bad faith is always careful about details.' And when, depressed, thwarted in his plans for a permanent post in Germany, he retires to Wandsbek to think out his position and his future action, he communes only, as he tells Varnhagen on 5 April 1830, with Adolphe Thiers and with the Good Lord: 'I am reading', he tells his correspondent, 'the History of the French Revolution by the first of these authors, and the Bible by the other.' God as a fellow author: that was a conceit Heine would often use in the years to come. His interest in the Bible as an authentic historical source did not mean, however, that his concern with more recent Jewish history had abated. With his appetite whetted by the conception of Jesus to which Moser had introduced him, he showed himself eager to learn what his friend thought the role of Moses Mendelssohn to have been in the life of German and European Jewry, and asks him, in a letter of 13 October 1829, to send him the text of a paper Moser had written on that subject.

Heine's correspondence of the 1820s has an important feature which has been analysed and illustrated by Rutger Booß. In letters to Jewish correspondents, particularly members of the Society for the Culture and Science of the Jews, he uses a number of Hebrew and Yiddish words and idioms most (but not all!) of which refer to features of Jewish ritual. Booß lists the following: *benschen, goi, go(h)les, jonteftig, Kille, Kugel, Lulef, Matzes, Mauschel, meschugge, Mesusse, nebbisch, Rischeß, Rosche, Talles, Tefillim*. Such words do not occur, in this period, in letters to his immediate family, whom he clearly wants to impress with his assimilated Germanness. Nor do any patently Yiddish words appear in Heine's published work before the 1830s, though Hebrew ones do, for special effects and local colour—one remembers the Hebrew paradigms in *Ideas. The Book of LeGrand*, for instance. In face of such material, however, and of Heine's angry reaction to anti-Jewish pronouncements by Germans of all political persuasions, one must never overlook the truth he formulated in a letter to Rudolf Christiani on 7 March 1824:

I am one of the most German of creatures . . . At bottom I love what is German more than anything in the world . . . If my muse assumed, out of displeasure with Germany, a somewhat foreign garb occasionally . . . it did so for good and sufficient reason, out of a just annoyance. . . .

Nothing could more distort the picture of Heine's Jewish Comedy than to leave out of account this love—so often thwarted, yet never eradicated—of Germany, its people, its language, and its cultural treasures.

(vii)

We have already seen how Heine's arrival in the Munich of 1828 coincided with debates in the Bavarian legislature on the question of Jewish emancipation—debates conducted outside the House of Representatives (*Ständeversammlung*) by journalists of various persuasions and parties. A letter to Moser of 14 April 1828 attests the eager interest with which Heine followed these debates, in the course of which strong anti-Jewish prejudices found an airing, prejudices that surfaced in attacks on Heine himself in *Eos* and other contemporary journals. When his hopes of a professorship at Munich University were dashed, he felt himself victimized by an aristocratic and clerical cabal against candidates of Jewish ancestry; and wrongly seeing a manifestation of this cabal in the clumsy anti-Jewish passages of August von Platen's *The Romantic Oedipus* (1829), he felt constrained, as his letters protest, to pay Platen back not only for his own sake, but also for the sake of other men and women whose history resembled his own. 'Read Count Platen's *Romantic Oedipus*,' he tells Moser on 15 June 1829; 'it is directed against *you*.' After his baptism, it would appear, Heine felt more strongly than ever that Judaeophobic attacks on one person of Jewish origin touched, and should concern, other Jews too.

Heine did not exactly improve his image of respectability by his sneaking regard for suspicious characters like Wit von Dörring. His letters confirm that he was fascinated by Wit, and reveal that he hoped to use Wit's association with the notorious reactionary Duke of Brunswick for some personal advantage—perhaps a decoration to pin to his coat. He had no illusions about Wit's trustworthiness, but he clearly enjoyed his company. Wit and he, he writes to Campe on 1 December 1828, had in common an interest in wine and in the theatre; a statement in which the word 'wine' is perhaps to be taken metaphorically for other delights, as a reference to *die lange Mahle*, one of the prostitutes Heine frequented in Hamburg, might seem to indicate. After reading Wit's *Memoirs* he tells him, on 12 December 1828:

> If your pen served a better cause, everyone would agree that you are the best political writer of our time. But write whatever you like; I am big enough, despite the howls of execration that rise up against you, to sign myself
>
> Your friend
> H. Heine.

To Varnhagen he writes, on no less than two occasions, that if he, Heine, were in power, he would have Wit hanged; but he admits being so charmed by his company that in his presence he could forget all the defects of his character. What a lot of fun one could have with Wit! (Letters of 12 February and 1 April 1828.) In indignant letters to her husband dated 11 and 13 March 1829 Rahel Varnhagen reports that Heine defended the 'good-for-nothing' Wit against her strictures and proclaimed him Germany's most talented political writer. He even compared him with Varnhagen himself! Neither here nor anywhere else, however, is there any allusion to Wit's Jewish connections.

Heine clearly preferred the company and conversation of an unscrupulous soldier of fortune like Wit von Dörring to that of rich Jewish dilettantes who used the leisure their inherited wealth afforded them to compose literary works. In Heine's own circle of acquaintances the principal example of such a dilettante was Michael Beer. In 1828 Beer swam into his orbit again because he had struck up a mutually advantageous friendship with that very Eduard von Schenk on whose patronage Heine's academic prospects in Bavaria seemed to depend. We therefore find Heine writing to Wolfgang Menzel on 2 May 1828 in a vein that was to become familiar in European literature through Balzac's *Lost Illusions*. In a single sentence he evokes, for Menzel's benefit, the milder German equivalent of those corruptions of the literary life to which Balzac would introduce his Lucien de Rubempré in the Paris of a later day.

The *Literary Gazette* you are editing has printed a review of Schenk's *Dürer* which flowed from the pen of Michael Beer (I read some of this last night); in return, Eduard Schenk will scratch Beer's back in the *Evening Journal*—Cotta will publish the literary works of both of them—and that's how our literature marches on.

What he felt to be most galling was that he himself was drawn into this unworthy game: as we know, he published a review of Beer's play *Struensee* which did not reflect his real, low estimate of that work and for which he felt obliged to apologize, privately, to several of his friends. The memory of this undignified episode—he had sought to curry favour with Schenk, of course—set up resentments in Heine which were later discharged against a more famous member of the Beer family, Michael's brother Giacomo Meyerbeer. Michael himself, however, did not escape unscathed. Alexander Weill reports that Heine once told Beer that if he really wanted *Struensee* to succeed on the stage, he would have to ask the actors to *improvise* their lines; while the always reliable Rahel Varnhagen reports to her husband that Heine said to her, apropos Michael Beer: 'He'll be immortal as long as he lives.'[10] No wonder that Rahel described Heine as a mud-stained harlequin or executioner in a letter of 11 March 1828—personae the poet would show himself very ready to adopt in many a work of his own.

   That relations between two such sharp (and similar!) characters as Rahel and Heine would remain for ever untroubled was not to be expected; there was indeed a tiff in March 1829, when it seemed to Heine that Rahel did not sufficiently appreciate his company. But the cloud passed remarkably quickly. Heine could never expel from his heart the woman whose intelligence and wit he had once commended by calling her *die geistreichste Frau des Universums* (to Varnhagen, 14 May 1826); on whom he had showered adjectives like 'dear', 'good', and 'noble' as well as 'witty'; to whom he had dedicated one of his works, and of whom he had said:

I confess that no one understands and knows me like Frau von Varnhagen. When I read her letters, it is as though I had risen in my sleep, in the midst of a dream, had positioned myself before a mirror and had there held converse with myself, occasionally boasting a little. What is so particularly good is that I don't need to write Frau von Varnhagen long letters. As long as she knows that I am alive she also knows what I feel and think. She has, I surmise, guessed more fully than I did myself why I dedicated one of my works to her. It would seem that I wanted to signify, in this way, that I belonged to somebody. As I course wildly about the world, I sometimes encounter people who want to make me their property—but these have always been people I don't care for particularly; and so long as that is the case, my collar shall ever bear the device: "J'appartiens à Mme Varnhagen."

> (to August Varnhagen von Ense, 29 July 1829)

The dog persona again, we see; this time, however, it has been assumed by the poet himself, of his own free will, as an extreme rhetorical sign of devotion.

In May 1829 we find Heine once again enjoying the hospitality and stimulating company he always found at the Varnhagens, and taking his usual lively interest in Rahel's affairs.

I kiss Frau von Varnhagen's hand and assure her that I have not yet recovered from the fright her illness last winter gave me . . .

> (to Varnhagen, 4 February 1830)

When I was ill the letter you and Frau von Varnhagen wrote to me did me a great deal of good . . .

> (to the same, 27 February 1830)

My brain is tired, else I would say a great deal to Frau von Varnhagen, who has fought for the truth, suffered, battled, and even lied for it. How I delight in every line she writes!

> (ibid., postscript dated 28 February)

Rahel can hardly have been wholeheartedly pleased at being praised for having *lied* in the cause of truth; she may have reflected, however, that this was her friend's backhanded way of admitting her to the company of the poets she admired but could never emulate. Be that as it may, Heine's last letters from Germany breathe an affection unusual with him, as he speaks of 'our precious Rahel', 'my dear friend', and 'loving, unshakeable friendship', as though no cloud had ever appeared on the horizon of their platonic relationship. Even a complaint about Rahel's scarcely legible handwriting turns into the prettiest of compliments which includes the observation that it resembled Heine's own and therefore indicated, on the physical plane, their mental affinity.

As I strew . . . sand on this page in order to turn it, I notice that my handwriting is becoming very like that of Frau von Varnhagen. At bottom it would be against nature if my writing were different. Our thoughts, after all, are as alike as one star is to the other—I mean, especially, stars that are many millions of miles away from the earth. If I now go on to say that a letter by Frau von Varnhagen sometimes resembles the Milky Way, I allude to the lament of astronomers that the bright throng of constellations in that Milky Way prevents them from picking out and looking at individual stars with sufficient distinctness. They ruin their eyes, as I do when, as at this moment, I have one of Frau von Varnhagen's letters before me. But never mind: dear Frau von Varnhagen, do write me, soon, another of those celestial epistles which ruin my eyes and refresh my heart.

(to Varnhagen, 5 April 1830)

As his time in Germany drew to a close, Heine came more and more to see in Rahel and her husband friends he wanted to keep for the rest of his life. In a letter of 16 June 1830 he excuses himself to Varnhagen for his habit of dropping into superlatives—'a written grimace', *eine Schreibgrimasse*, he calls this stylistic tic; and he finds that only the rhetorical device of aposiopesis, of falling silent, is adequate to convey the depth of his affection for Rahel. 'Farewell,' he writes, 'and you especially, Frau von Varnhagen, go on loving me . . . I love you both very much; I have not enough paper to say *how* much . . .' Everything Heine will subsequently say about Rahel Varnhagen suggests that such protestations were more than empty flourishes. He genuinely respected her, and needed to feel her approval and her affection even when they could no longer meet.

One of the many bonds between the younger Heine and Rahel Varnhagen was their common regard, this side of idolatry, for Ludwig Börne, satirist, social critic, German patriot, and fighter for Jewish emancipation. Heine first mentions Börne, in his letters, when he had felt repulsion at the shallow punning jokes of Moritz Saphir, and had begun to reflect on the qualities that make wit and humour worth while. 'In its isolation', he had written to Moser on 1 July 1825, 'wit is worth nothing at all. I find it bearable only when it rests on a foundation of seriousness.' What a strong, bright light this remark throws on Heine's Jewish Comedy! But let him continue: 'That is why the wit of Börne, Jean Paul, and the Fool in *King Lear* is so powerfully effective.' In May 1826 he sent the man whom he had here placed in the company not only of Jean Paul Richter, but also in that of Shakespeare, a copy of his first *Pictures of Travel* volume, with an inscription that assured Börne of the author's 'veneration and heartfelt love'. Eighteen months later we find him, at last, face to face with Börne and conversing with him on equal terms. 'In Frankfurt', he reports to Varnhagen on 28 November 1827,

I lived with Börne for three days. We talked a good deal about Frau von Varnhagen. He is busy collecting his scattered essays into three volumes. The first of these contains his writings on the theatre. I would never have thought that Börne had so high an opinion of me: we were inseparable right up to the moment in which he accompanied me to the stage-coach.

That Börne appeared to have a high opinion of Heine was, of course, a commendation; it made Heine think that in him he found the ideal reviewer of his recently published *Book of Songs*. We therefore find the poet, in letters of increasing urgency (12 January and 2 May 1828), asking the influential journalist and editor Wolfgang Menzel to commission a review from Börne without delay. Nothing came of that, however; and the last glimpse we have of Börne, in the letters Heine wrote before settling in Paris, where he would see more of Börne that he wished, occurs in a letter to Varnhagen dated 1 April 1828. 'I hear that Börne is now with you', he writes. 'He likes me very much. He is much better than I . . .' An ominous note may be detected here: is Börne 'better' than Heine because the latter cannot wholeheartedly return his predilection? Heine caps that 'better' with another, even higher compliment: 'he is much greater . . .' This time, however, the sting comes immediately; *viel größer*, he says of Börne, *aber nicht so großartig*. The quality which he attributes to himself in fuller measure than Börne ranges from the 'grand' and 'imposing' to the 'magnificent', the 'lofty', the 'sublime'. Börne's qualities, Heine would seem to be telling his correspondent, are fine human ones; but they are not the qualities of genius, the qualities of the true poet. His description then comes to rest on a physical ailment with which Börne was afflicted—an ailment that so often has the effect of isolating the sufferer and making him bad company: 'His deafness will, I am sure, embarrass Frau von Varnhagen considerably. It is a grievous affliction . . .' The outlines of Heine's later, unflattering portrait of Börne are already discernible.

(viii)

With Moses Moser, recipient of so many of the young Heine's confidences, he came to feel less and less kinship in the last years he spent in Germany. This closest of all his friends is demoted, in ways we have already seen, from Posa to Antonio and thence to Pantalone. His advice now seems worse than narrow-minded—narrow-*hearted*, *engherzig* (to Moser, 14 February 1826). In his office, in the bank that employs him, Moser seems insulated from the storms to which his friend feels exposed; phrases like 'you in your well-protected office have no idea . . .' and 'you in your idyllically restful office . . .' (30 September 1829) occur more and more frequently. 'My friend Moser', Heine writes to Varnhagen on 27 February 1830, after Moser had signified his disapproval of *The Baths of Lucca*; 'but can I continue to call that man a friend who does not sympathize with me in the main things that affect my life?' 'All this is odious', he adds, 'and I have determined to do without friends of that kind.' Nor could Heine look to Hitzig for any support; as early as 1 January 1827 he had treated Hitzig, in a letter to Friedrich Merckel, as a fit subject for irony—though he could not afford, as yet, to joke about him in public. That stage in their relationship was not to come until the 1850s, though there has been speculation that the portrait of the Christianizing Berlin councillor which ended the first cycle of *The North Sea* in *Pictures of Travel*, 1826, may have owed some of its traits to this baptized scion of the Itzig family.[11]

With his own family too—always excepting his mother—

relations grew less and less cordial. His brother Gustav annoyed him by gossiping and indiscretions (to Merckel, 31 December 1827). His complaints about Salomon Heine, whom he addressed as 'dear, good, generous, stingy, noble, infinitely beloved uncle' in a letter dated 15 September 1828, multiplied—he had even committed to paper, in a letter to Varnhagen of 12 February 1828, the sentence: 'My uncle, the Hamburg millionaire, has acted towards me in the most villainous manner.' But that may have been partly a projection of Heine's own bad conscience, for he had made unauthorized and unethical use of some letters of credit his uncle had given him for his journey to England in 1827, and must have felt that on this occasion at least his uncle had a strong case against him. It was around this time that Heine seems first to have said to his uncle that the best thing about Salomon Heine was that he bore his, Heine's, name,[12] a saying that uncle never forgot, and one to which he alludes more than once in his later correspondence with his famous nephew. But something of the old respect always remained, and Uncle Salomon, the lion of the family, seemed royal indeed when compared with his entourage and competitors—even if they bore, as one prominent Hamburg family did, the imposing name of Leo.

Salomon Heine's entourage comes in for increasingly heavy irony in Heine's letters.

Give my regards to Moritz Oppenheimer. It is true that I do not love him, although as a Christian I am bound to love my enemies; but then, I am only a young beginner in Christian charity. Moritz Oppenheimer, however, is a Christian of longer standing, and he should love me, and not smile me out of the respect of other men.
(Draft of a letter to Salomon Heine, 15 September 1828)

Another draft of the passage just quoted, with its bitter reference to Heine's own baptism, shows him compounding his irony at the expense of Oppenheimer's senior Christianity by associating with him the stereotype of the Jewish nose.

Give my regards to Mme Heine, but keep them as cool as possible, for I know she does not feel too warmly about me. When I was last in Hamburg something she said—a single syllable!—showed where the wind was blowing from. I am not petty enough to make a secret of it; I therefore confess, in all honesty, that the wind seemed to blow from

Moritz Oppenheimer's nose. Since then I have hated that nose, although, as a Christian. I am obliged to love all noses, even when they sniffle evil against me. I am only a young beginner, and it will be a long time before I can come to love Moritz Oppenheimer's nose. He, as a Christian of longer standing, should love me all the more.

Bitter jokes about the requirement of Christian charity imposed on him by his baptism are not infrequent in Heine's writings. The following characteristic note has been found among his papers:

Peaceable disposition. Wishes: a humble cottage, thatched roof, but a good bed, good food, milk and butter (very fresh), flowers before my window, and a few fine trees in front of my door—and if the Good Lord wants to make my happiness complete, he will grant me the joy of seeing six or seven of my enemies hanged on these trees. With a deeply moved heart I will, before their death, forgive them all the wrong they did me in their lifetime—yes, one must forgive one's enemies, but not before they have been hanged . . .

Freud, who quotes a slightly altered version of this fragment in *Civilization and its Discontents*, adds the comment: 'A great imaginative writer may permit himself to give expression, jokingly at all events, to psychological truths that are severely proscribed.'[13]

Heine's letters and conversations increasingly reveal that his published work was multiplying his enemies in the Jewish community. This applied particularly to those who thought themselves personally insulted. We have seen how his reference to a 'dark broker who has so far escaped the gallows' in *The Hartz Journey* had brought the wrath of one Joseph Friedländer down on Heine's head. The tone of Heine's references to this member of the Friedländer family (to which the 'timid rabbit', the preferred suitor of the poet's beloved Amalie also belonged) may be gauged from passages such as the following:

Have you heard whether the black fellow whom they haven't hanged yet [*der schwarze Ungehenkte*] has been spreading more lies about me? I would be glad to know for certain to whom he has boasted that he would have me beaten up. That is very important to me . . .
(to Friedrich Merckel, 6 October 1826)

When writing to Jewish correspondents he felt free to adopt

the very language of German anti-Semites to denigrate his 'dark broker':

You will have heard that some smelly Jew in Hamburg has been spreading lies all over the place about having me beaten up. The pig-dog attacked me in the street . . . but he in fact barely got hold of my coat-tails, and even that much he denied when I complained to the police . . . A pack of infamous villains have made use of this story. But why do I bother to write to you about such filth . . .

(to Moser, 14 October 1826)

Rosa Maria Assing records in her diary on 15 June 1826 that Heine gave her his version of this incident in which he called Friedländer *einen jüdischen Mauschel* and added: 'What can I do about all this? In the end the fellow can accuse me of having stolen silver spoons, and all I shall be able to do is to keep silent.'[14] Incidents like this, which occasionally made the gossip columns in contemporary newspapers, rendered the wealthier members of the Heine clan progressively more wary of their dangerous Harry and no doubt helped to confirm their determination to do something, when occasion arose, to prevent too much dirty linen being washed in public.

The unpleasantness provoked by a comparatively harmless squib in *The Hartz Journey* (in which Friedländer was not expressly named) was compounded by *The Baths of Lucca*, where the ridiculous aspirant to the status of a cultured European was given the surname, though not the first name, of the Hamburg banker, Lazarus Gumpel. Uncle Salomon seems to have been mildly amused (though horrified by the unbridled attack on Count Platen); but the Gumpel family, not surprisingly, showed itself less than delighted. 'There is, once again, a fool around here' Heine reports to Varnhagen from Hamburg on 3 January 1830, 'who pretends that *he* is the Marchese Gumpelino; he is jumping about in the most dangerous way . . .' And again, three days later, to the painter Johann Peter Lyser: 'Funnily enough there is a young man here, one Gumpel, who runs about in a rage, gives himself out for Gumpelino, and swears to have me killed.' No wonder that the Jewish community of Hamburg showed little eagerness to have Dr Heinrich Heine settle in its midst. They would, no doubt, have heard other versions of a pronouncement by Heine which

Ludwig von Diepenbrock-Grüter entered in his diary on 20 November 1826.

In social life I seek to make my enemies appear merely ridiculous, even if I could relate evil actions they have performed. If you have made a man ridiculous, you have stoned him to death. . . .[15]

That Heine professed an ability to look at himself as objectively as he looked at others did little to mollify Diepenbrock's disapproval. 'How can a man', he wrote in his diary on Christmas Day 1830, after another conversation with Heine, 'respect others if he has so little respect for himself?' Fear of Heine's satiric vein was becoming widespread, even well beyond Berlin and Hamburg. When he visited a relative by marriage, the delightful Charlotte Moscheles, in London during the spring of 1827, the latter stipulated that when he came to write up his London experiences he would not mention her husband, the pianist Ignaz Moscheles, at all—for Heine, she said, knew little of music, and was bound to discover some personal weakness or foible on which to exercise his satiric pen. The future would prove her only too right.[16]

The poet was capable, however, of more generous responses towards fellow artists and writers. He had come to know August Lewald, who in 1827 was in the employ of the Hamburg municipal theatre, and had confided in him enough to tell him what a deep hurt the death of his father had been to him: 'my father', he said to Lewald, 'was an unhappy man who never really succeeded in anything his whole life long.'[17] Just before leaving Germany, he did his very best to help Lewald's career as a writer. On 9 December 1830 he sent a letter to Wolfgang Menzel (whom he was soon to regard as his bitterest enemy), asking him to review Lewald's fiction in order to promote recognition of its worth as soon as possible; and on 17 January 1831 he wrote in similar terms to the influential novelist and editor Wilhelm Häring (Willibald Alexis).

One of my friends, A. Lewald, asks me to send you the enclosed Novelle, which is to appear in the second volume of his collection and which should therefore go into print straightaway if you could see your way to fulfilling his wish to have it published in *Der Freimüthige*. I think you will like this Novelle; it will enable you to recognize its author's great talent for narrative fiction. He knows how to tell a story and how to present characters in the round; and I have prophesied that he will one day belong to the most widely popular writers in this genre. I have only just come to know him through his writings; you need not therefore ascribe my favourable predisposition to personal partiality. I do hope, my dear Häring, that you will read the first volume of Lewald's *Novellen* which has recently appeared, and would be glad if you could write an effective review in *Der Freimüthige* . . . The book deserves rapid recommendation—if only to convince its author that his real vocation is narrative fiction and not the theatre, on which he is at present wasting his talent . . .

Lewald was to show himself a loyal friend to Heine in later years.

(ix)

As the nineteenth century moved into its fourth decade, Heine decided that the time had come to strike his tents in Germany and move to Paris—the Paris whence had come not only the heady news of the July Revolution but also the economic-social-religious doctrine of Saint-Simon which found a ready response in the hearts and minds of many young German (and German-Jewish) intellectuals. To find the means for his emigration and resettlement he had to look around for funds that would supplement the allowance from Uncle Salomon on which he continued to rely; and one of those on whom he counted for help was his uncle's wealthy acquaintance and co-religionist Hartwig Hesse, the head of the firm *Hesse, Newman & Co.* We find him, therefore, on 10 February 1831, writing to Hesse one of those accomplished begging letters which will henceforth punctuate his correspondence. He begins by quoting from the *Doctrine de Saint-Simon* which he had apparently discussed with Hesse shortly before:

. . . *mendier* n'est-il pas le lot nécessaire de ces êtres vraiment divins, qui, entièrement absorbés dans la vaste pensée qui les domine, sont incapables d'appliquer un seul instant leur prévoyance à leurs besoins personnels? Le dernier degré de leur sublime dévouement, n'est-il pas cette vertu même qui leur donne le courage d'aller *mendier*, auprès la richesse insouciante ou hautaine, les moyens de soutenir une existence dont eux seuls connoissent le prix pour l'humanité?

The doctrine of Saint-Simon, Heine explains, is now his new Gospel; and in order to pursue the great interests of mankind that depend on its propagation and realization, he asks Hesse for any, even the least, sum he can spare.

Ich bitte. I cannot imagine that an extraordinary man like you can fail to understand the extraordinary self-confidence which fills my soul at this moment with something of a *religious* pride. *Ich bitte* ...
He who is commended to your protection,
H. Heine.

The spectacle of a neophyte Protestant poet of German-Jewish origins asking a wealthy businessman of similar antecedents for the means to propagate the 'Gospel' (*Evangelium*) of Saint-Simonism—and doing so in tones curiously reminiscent of Israel Zangwill's *King of the Shnorrers*—surely deserves a place (even if it is only a modest one) in Heine's Jewish Comedy.

The poet was not, however, to leave Germany without experiencing once more the forces that militated against full Jewish emancipation in Germany. In 1822, if we can believe his cousin Hermann Schiff, he had said that anti-Jewish disturbances would not occur again in Germany, if only because 'the Press is a weapon, and there are now two Jews who can wield the weapon of a serviceable German style. I am one of these; the other is Börne.'[18] If Heine did indeed say this, he was due for a rude awakening. In September 1830, just after his return from Heligoland where news of the July Revolution in France had reached him, Heine experienced for himself a series of anti-Jewish demonstrations in Hamburg in the course of which windows were smashed, Jews chased out of places of public resort and maltreated, and the old taunting cry of Jew-baiters, '*Hep Hep*', heard once more in the streets. Heine had already begun to think of eventually writing his memoirs, and he made some notes for this purpose whose general drift is clear enough, even though they were intended only for his own later use.

First evening. It was not only the mob, but that respectable bourgeoisie which in Paris too played such an active part; the shopkeepers who stand in the doorways in their slippers and conduct business in comfort, unlike the [Jewish] pedlars. Motif: Glosses on the age—*Morning Chronicle* [*Morgenblatt*]—perhaps there was a poem of mine in it.[19]

Here Heine is clearly concerned to distance himself from contemporary observers who saw the Hamburg riots as the work, simply, of an undisciplined mob, a *Lumpenproletariat* of some sort. He interpreted them, rather, as reflecting the resentments of tradespeople who felt their livelihood threatened by the numerous Jewish pedlars who undercut them in and around their city, pedlars whose hard lot he contrasts with the bourgeois comforts enjoyed by the shop-keepers that feared their competition. He goes on, in the note just quoted, to consider a possible motif (*Vorwurf*) for his memoirs or some other work: perhaps that Cotta's *Morgen-blatt* attracted anti-Semitic hostility because it contained one of Heine's poems. The word *Vorwurf*, one remembers, can mean 'reproach' as well as 'motif'. He then continues:

Second evening. A Jew defends himself, but as at the battle of Navarino the Cross and Christian heroism carried the day. Twelve men overpowered the Jew. The open ham sandwiches shone with joy at this defeat of the national enemies of pork and Christianity.

This bitter note evokes scenes recorded by several observers of the Hamburg riots: men armed with sticks and other weapons entered restaurants and other places of public resort and roughly ejected any Jews they found there. The effects Heine aimed at by bringing in a reference to the recent battle of Navarino, at which England, France, and Russia overcame the Mohammedan Turks, and by the zeugma that joins pork and Christianity, are obvious enough. Having glossed the *cowar-dice* of these rioters in his satirical note, Heine goes on to suggest their *inhumanity* in another jotting—he imagines him-self in a Hamburg menagerie during the riots and finds the animals looking like human beings while the human beings raged with animal fury. Yet another jotting links the anti-Jewish disturbances of 2–5 September 1830, not only with grievances against the Hamburg Senate, but also with the resentment good Christian burghers felt against marginal figures other than the Jews who earned their living in ways that did not meet their standards of respectability.

A prostitute standing by the Dammtor said: 'If the Jews are insulted today, then it will be the turn of the Senate next, and after that it will be our turn.' Cassandra of the Red Light District, how soon your words were to be fulfilled!

The last sentence just quoted refers to the fact, noted by several contemporary observers, that during the riots one of the many Hamburg brothels was sacked by an angry mob.

Heine's ironies at the expense of the nominally Christian rioters did not mean, however, that he saw the Jews of Hamburg in a heroic light. One of his jottings suggests a joke not yet fully worked out:

The list of victims of the revolutionary battles includes Herr M. He remained on the Steinweg . . .

Er ist auf dem Steinweg geblieben—the phrase Heine uses could mean that Herr M. gave his life on the field of battle, but suggests strongly that what he did in fact was to stay prudently at home, in the street which the poet so often used as a short-hand symbol for the Jewish district. The most telling thrust of all goes well beyond the Hamburg community, however, and well beyond the riots of 1830:

One Jew said to the other: 'I was too weak.' This saying commends itself as a motto for the history of Judaism.

A saying such as this derives its force and conviction from Heine's experiences with the Jewish Reform movement in Berlin and Hamburg, with the activities (and the rapid demise) of the Society for the Culture and Science of the Jews, and with the many volumes of Jewish history he had read in preparation for *The Rabbi of Bacherach*. But the thought of present and past Jewish weakness also brought recollections of Jewish stubbornness and strength of purpose—a stubbornness and a strength which had helped to preserve Judaism throughout the centuries in spite of worse persecutions than any seen in 1830. 'The Jews', we therefore read in a note belonging to the same context as the jottings about the Hamburg riots, 'were the only people that preserved their freedom of worship when all of

Europe became Christian.' The proud and stiff-necked Jew, keeping his freedom and independence by defying all attempts to convert him, is an important ingredient in the Jewish Comedy traced in these pages, a comedy which necessarily shows so much of human weakness, half-heartedness, and voluntary or involuntary servitude.

For his own part Heine seems to have thought, at this time, that his newly-found faith in Saint-Simonism cancelled out the traumatic effects of his baptism. During a meal at the house of the painter Moritz Oppenheim he was heard to declare, in response to a question by a fellow guest, that he 'found it more difficult to have a tooth drawn than to change his religion'.[20] That was sheer bravado, as Heine's letters, and more than one of his early works, may serve to prove. He was to find, in later years, that the trauma remained, and that a change of religion did not necessarily bring with it a corresponding change in social status or a significant diminution of Jewish self-consciousness and ethnic identity.

PART II
Parisian Perspectives

CHAPTER 4
Philistines and Culture Heroes

(i)

In 1831 Heine moved to Paris, where he was to live as a freelance writer and occasional foreign correspondent until his death in 1856. He now saw and presented himself as a German author living in voluntary exile in the freer atmosphere of France, whose writings might help to ameliorate political and social conditions in a native land that still had his love and his loyalty. He hoped, at the same time, to further international understanding and friendship by interpreting the intellectual and cultural life of Germany to the French, and that of France to the Germans.

The first work in which Heine tackled his self-imposed task was *French Painters* (*Französische Maler*)—an elaborate account of the Paris salon of 1831 written in the first instance for the readers of Cotta's *Morning Chronicle*. He used this series of articles on what would have seemed a non-political subject to smuggle all sorts of social and political observations past the censors, employing such apparently innocuous symbols as rays of spring sunshine and the extinguishing of a night-light to suggest the dawn of a new era which would follow on tyrannicide. I take this example from Heine's description of Horace Vernet's painting of Judith and Holofernes. Here the poet depicts Vernet's Judith in terms that deliberately contrast with his depiction of Ary Scheffer's Gretchen at the beginning of the previous chapter of *French Painters*. Judith is a dark Semitic beauty, caught in a moment of action, of incipient death-dealing movement, her left hand holding the sword that will slay Holofernes: 'a little butcher-like, yet enchantingly lovely'. Oxymora, expressions of mixed feelings whose very complexity fascinates, dominate Heine's description.

Her head is wondrously comely and uncannily lovable; black curls, which do not hang down but rear themselves up like short snakes, have a fearful grace. The face is a little in the shadows, and a sweet savagery, a dark loveliness and a sentimental rage animate the noble features of this death-bringing beauty. Her eyes especially sparkle with sweet cruelty and the voluptuousness of revenge; for she has also to avenge the insult the ill-favoured heathen has inflicted on her own body . . .[1]

'She has *also* to avenge . . .' What is unspoken here, but would not escape any reader familiar with the biblical story, is the political aspect of Judith's deed: she is liberating her country from a tyrant as well as avenging her own violation.

There she stands, this charming figure, at the frontier of virginity which has just been crossed: divinely pure yet stained by the world, like a desecrated host.[2]

Heine's use of the phrase *wie eine entweihte Hostie* to describe one of the national heroines of the Jewish people shows that he is moving towards an idea of 'spiritualism' or 'Nazarenism' which unites Jews and Christians, and which contrasts with the 'sensualism' represented in Horace Vernet's painting by the sleeping Holofernes, on whose not very comely features the satisfaction of his sexual encounter with Judith is still visible. 'Is it irony on Horace Vernet's part that the rays of spring sunshine flood the sleeper as if transfiguring him, and that the night-light is about to be extinguished?'[3] The irony, Irmgard Zepf has said, in her useful analysis of *French Painters*, lies in a whole series of contradictions: Judith represents at once Nazarenism and revolution, Holofernes is at once a tyrant, a barbarian oppressor, and a 'Hellenic' sensualist; the alluring Judith has given sensual pleasure without receiving any, the ugly Holofernes has received pleasure but given only a sense of desecration; the delicate and beautiful woman is about to deal out death, the warrior Holofernes is blissfully and peacefully asleep . . . Yet in the end the 'I' of *French Painters* yearns for the fate of Holofernes, about to die by the hand of the Semitic beauty he has enjoyed and violated: 'When it comes to be my turn to die', he apostrophizes whatever gods there be, 'let me die like Holofernes!'[4] Irmgard Zepf describes this as a confession of sensualism, an identification with the Saint-Simonians' desire to vindicate sensual enjoyments, a challenge to ascetic ideals, a challenge also to the German reading public and its devotion to late Romantic literature—but it seems to me that there is a pronounced element of non-'Hellenic' masochism in such adoration of a dark, death-dealing beauty, and that this prepares us for the fascination of Heine's Herodias figure in *Atta Troll* and that of the many Salome figures in the European *décadence* from Gustave Moreau to Oscar Wilde. Such figures contrast with, and significantly complement, the sad and submissive Jewish beauties Heine had apostrophized in the opening chapter of *The Rabbi of Bacherach*.

Just as Heine saw himself as an eminent representative of German literature in Paris, so he now presented Giacomo Meyerbeer as a representative of German music-making. In his account of a concert devoted to the compositions of Ferdinand Hiller, a Frankfurt composer and pianist who was born a Jew but converted to Christianity (*F. Hillers Konzert*, first published in Cotta's *Morning Chronicle* in December 1831), the unbaptized Meyerbeer and the baptized Hiller are both treated as Germans *tout court*, with not the slightest perceptible glance at their Jewish origins. *Robert le Diable* in fact turns out to be the chief example Heine cites on the 'German' side when he comes to speak of the contest between adherents of the German and adherents of the Italian school of music for the favour of Parisian music-lovers.[5] The same opera plays a prominent part in *Conditions in France (Französische Zustände)*, a series of articles Heine contributed to the *Augsburg Gazette (Augsburger Allgemeine Zeitung)* early in 1832 and republished in book form in December of the same year. Here Heine resumes his familiar role of cicerone and conducts his German public around France. At Rouen he points out the castle of Robert, the second Duke of Normany, and comments: 'There, in that castle, Robert the Devil once dwelt—the same Robert who has been set to music by Meyerbeer.' When describing a cholera epidemic in Paris, he tells his readers: 'So many people went to the Morgue, they had to form a queue—just as they do at the Paris Opera when *Robert le Diable* is on the programme';[6] and when he comes to characterize the balls given by the rich bourgeoisie, he once again bids his audience recall the same widely acclaimed composition.

These people were dancing for their dividends; the more moderate they were politically, the more passionately did they dance, and the fattest, most moral bankers danced the infamous waltz of the nuns from the celebrated opera *Robert le Diable*. Meyerbeer has brought off an unprecedented coup: he has enthralled the flighty Parisians for a whole winter! They are still flocking to the Académie de Musique to see this opera; but I hope Meyerbeer's enthusiastic champions will forgive me if I express my belief that what is proving so attractive is not only its music but also its political meaning.[7]

There follows a tongue-in-cheek exegesis of this popular work which depicts it as an allegory of social and political forces in Louis Philippe's France.

The image of bankers dancing to some particularly eerie music Meyerbeer had composed for the *corps de ballet* of the Paris Opera is just the sort of image that would attract a cartoonist; and we find these reports from Paris moving even further in the direction of caricature when they come to discuss the Stock Exchange. This phenomenon clearly fascinates the cicerone of *Conditions in France* as much as it had fascinated his predecessor in *Letters from Berlin*—not least because of the contrast between what he thinks one of the noblest buildings in Paris and the less than noble pursuits to which it is dedicated.

Here, in this lofty vaulted hall . . . the trade in state securities throws waves like a rushing, roaring sea of self-interest. Out of the wildly agitated ocean of humanity the great bankers snap their jaws like sharks. Here one monster swallows the other; and if you look up to the gallery you will even spy speculating ladies, like birds of prey waiting to swoop from a rock jutting out of the sea. It is here, however, that we must look for the interests which, in our day and age, determine peace and war.[8]

This passage applies most effectively what one might call the Grandville method of caricature: the depiction of human types in the guise of symbolically appropriate animals. No distinction is made between Jewish and Gentile speculators: they are all at one in their pursuit of the same golden prey.

The cholera epidemic already mentioned provides some of the most memorable pages of *Conditions in France*. The rich, Heine reports, were able to escape from its worst effects by leaving Paris for the country:

M. Aguado, one of the wealthiest bankers and a knight of the Legion of Honour, was the field marshal who led this great retreat. This knight is said to have constantly peered from the window of his coach, out of his wits with fear, and to have taken his blue-liveried footman, who was mounted behind, for the very figure of Death, for the Cholera itself.

There were bitter murmurings among the populace when it saw the rich take flight to healthier regions, carrying their physicians and apothecaries with them. The poor saw with dismay that money could now protect even from death. The greater part of the *juste milieu* and *haute finance* has fled and is now living in its country houses. The true representatives of wealth, however, the von Rothschilds, have calmly stayed in Paris and have thus demonstrated that their greatness and boldness are not confined to their financial dealings.[9]

In this passage Heine subtly undermines the image of Jewish timidity by seeming at first to confirm it with his scathing caricature of Alexandre Aguado, a banker of Sephardic origin, and then triumphantly subverting it with his compliment to the French Rothschilds. As a group, it would seem, the Jews are neither more nor less brave than others—they have their Aguados, and they have their Rothschilds. Heine also reports truthfully, that he himself braved the cholera when his 'best friend' (in actual fact his cousin, Carl Heine) fell ill and could not be moved from Paris.

There are other ways in which *Conditions in France* uses stereotyped prejudices about Jews in order to counteract them. In *The Baths of Lucca*, as we have seen, he experimented with the speech rhythms and speech habits of German Jews; he now uses such rhythms and turns of phrase when reporting the alleged sayings of patently non-Jewish contemporaries. Louis Philippe, for instance, is made to say to Talleyrand:

'Herr von Talleyrand, was man Ihnen auch bieten mag, ich gebe Ihnen immer das Doppelte.'

[M. de Talleyrand—whatever any one else offers you, I'll always double the offer.']^[10]

Then again—Jews were often thought shamelessly importunate, 'pushy', by the aristocracy and the bourgeois establishment. Heine once again turns his around:

Princes should be educated by the best citizens chosen by popular suffrage. Whoever is of ill repute or has the slightest stain of suspicion on his character should be prevented by law from approaching a young prince. If such a person should nevertheless elbow his way to the prince with that shameless pushfulness which the aristocracy habitually exhibits in such cases, then he should be flogged in public.[11]

Drängt er sich dennoch hinzu mit jener unverschämten Zudringlichkeit, die dem Adel in solchen Fällen eigen ist—Heine is clearly delighted to throw such charges in the teeth of the very men who most often bring them against others.

For the rest, the Jews supply an occasional simile in *Conditions in France* ('As the Jews would never pronounce the name of their God in an everyday context, so Napoleon is seldom called by his name—he is always termed "the Man", *l'homme*'); there is, as ever, some biblical parody (Louis Philippe is made to say: 'Talleyrand gave, and Talleyrand hath taken away; blessed be the name of Talleyrand'); and the great democrat Jesus Christ ('who died for the equality and fraternity of men') is played out against Luther's alignment with tyrannous authority at the time of the Peasant Wars.[12] And there is one passage in the work which has a close if unacknowledged connection with the history of Jewish emancipation as well as the history of Heine's own family. In this particularly eloquent passage he contrasts the funeral of Casimir Périer, at which he could detect no sign of genuine national mourning, with that of the Bishop of Blois, the Abbé Henri Grégoire, where there was no such official pomp as accompanied Périer to his grave. At Grégoire's funeral, however,

the people wept, grief showed on every face; although the rain poured down in bucketfuls heads stayed uncovered, and the people harnessed themselves to the hearse and drew it to Montparnasse cemetery with thier own hands. Grégoire, a true priest, fought throughout his life for the liberty and equality of all men, whatever their nation and whatever their creed. He was always hated and persecuted by the enemies of the people, and the people loved him and wept when he died.[13]

The best-known document of Grégoire's fight for liberty and equality was, of course, his plea for the civil emancipation of French Jews which he published in 1787 and which was to be heeded by the French Revolutionary Assembly a few years later—a document which he is said to have composed with some help from Heine's great-uncle Simon van Geldern.

Conditions in France is relevant to our present concerns in two further ways. The first of these is suggested by Heine's eloquent proclamation, in his Preface to the work, of the function he now wants to perform as a German writer living in Paris.

> If we can bring it about that the great mass of mankind understands the present age, then the people of different nations will no longer allow themselves to be incited to hatred and war by the hired scribblers of the aristocracy. The great united league of peoples, the Holy Alliance of nations, will become a reality . . . and we shall gain peace and prosperity and liberty. This is the task to which my life will be dedicated; this is the office I shall perform.[14]

That conveys Heine's self-image with admirable clarity, and suggests the wide context in which his dealings with Jews and Judaism must now be seen. Lest this imply too much solemnity, however, we must also remind ourselves that the very first article of *Conditions in France* deals with the subject of *caricature*. It tells, with obvious glee, the story of Charles Philipon's defence against the charge of *lèse majesté* brought against him: a defence in the course of which he drew further caricatures of Louis Philippe before the very court that was trying him; and it describes with gusto how Philipon's journal, *La Caricature*, defiantly continued to published *poires*—heads of Louis Philippe in the likeness of a pear—even after its editor had been found guilty.[15] Here Heine might indeed find encouragement to exercise without fear, if not always without favour, his own exceptional talent for verbal cartoons.

(ii)

In December 1833 Heine republished his essays on French painting in book form; he added some poems and a picaresque mini-novel and named the whole collection after that annual exhibition of contemporary painting in the main hall of the

Louvre which is known as *le Salon*. *Salon I (Der Salon. Erster Band)* was published by Hoffmann und Campe in Hamburg and bore the date 1834. The preface of this volume evokes the memory of Rahel Varnhagen; she is not named, however, but appears simply as a patriotic German lady, without any reference to her Jewish ancestry.

In a book I have at hand at the moment, a book containing the letters of a dear departed friend, I was deeply moved yesterday by a passage in which she describes herself living in a strange land and seeing her countrymen at war . . . I will here set down her loving words.

'The whole morning I have been weeping, again and again, bitter tears of compassion and vexation. I never realized just how much I loved my country! Like one whose knowledge of physiology is not enough to teach him the value of blood—if he were deprived of his blood, he would collapse just the same.'[16]

'That's it', Heine adds, aligning his own patriotism with Rahel Varnhagen's; 'we ourselves *are* Germany.' Never had he felt more fully German than in these early years in France.

Among the poems contained in *Salon I* is the cycle *Angelique* in which the poet, tiring of a mistress, wearily promises to take her to hear the most popular opera then playing in Paris—if he can get tickets. That opera, of course, is once again *Robert le Diable*; it is full of magic, the poet explains, full of diabolic enjoyment and love; its music is by Meyerbeer and its text—a rotten one!—is by Eugène Scribe.

> Es ist ein großes Zauberstück
> Voll Teufelslust und Liebe;
> Von Meyerbeer ist die Musik,
> Der schlechte Text von Scribe.[17]

The unadorned mentioned of Meyerbeer's music, the association between his magic opera and a love-affair whose magic has gone, and the contemptuous dismissal of the opera's text, strongly suggests that this work, for all its appeal to the Parisian public, did not command Heine's own unalloyed enthusiasm.

Salon I concludes with the fragment of a picaresque novel entitled *Leaves from the Memoirs of Herr von Schnabelewopski (Aus den Memoiren des Herren von Schnabelewopski)*; and the account this gives of the adventures of its central protagonist affords us more glimpses of Jewish figures than any other work of Heine's early years in Paris. Although there is nothing in this fragment to suggest that the eponymous hero himself should be thought to have Jewish origins, the portrait Heine paints of that hero's parents has so many close verbal parallels with the portrait he paints of his own parents in the post-humously published fragment of his *Memoirs* that the auto-biographical relevance can hardly be missed. A chapter on Schnabelewopski's stay in Hamburg discourses on the cult of good food which characterizes a city which presented itself to Heine at times as the very essence and concentration of a commercial, materialist spirit. The Jews in particular like their food—and it makes no difference whether they are traditional-ists or adherent of 'Temple' reform:

Among the Jews in Hamburg there may be a party that says grace in German while another chants it in Hebrew; but both parties eat, and eat well.[18]

The author of a projected book on notable Hamburgers 'had hardly got from Aaron to Abendroth' when he gave up.[19] Schnabelewopski buys cloth to be made into dresses for some lights of love from a draper called Seligmann. It costs 4 Marks and 3 shillings per ell, and Herr Seligmann guarantees that even when washed the pink stripes won't lose their colour. Years later the hero returns to Hamburg; the dresses have been discarded, the material has probably lost its colour by then, and so has Herr Seligmann, for his firm is now managed by 'Seligmanns selige Witwe'—a tangle of puns and meanings that depends in part on German ways of speaking respectfully of the dead, Jewish clumsiness in handling German, and the suggestion that Madame Seligmann is less than inconsolable at her widowhood.[20] Hamburg, Schnabelewopski sums up, is probably identical with the ancient city of Tharshish whence King Solomon 'received whole shiploads full of gold, silver, ivory, apes, and peacocks.'[21] 'Salomon', Schnabelewopski comments, using the German form of the biblical name, 'al-ways had a predilection for gold and monkeys,' and to make sure that those of his readers who knew Hamburg would not miss the allusion to its most prominent Jewish citizen, Heine's millionaire uncle Salomon, he makes Schnabelewopski add: 'I mean the King of Judah and Israel, of course.' 'Gold' refers, no doubt, to Uncle Salomon's vast fortune, 'monkeys' to his hangers-on and sons-in-law whom Heine bitterly resented and whose enmity he had cause to fear. He liked, occasionally, to insert such barbs into his work in order to remind his family that he too had weapons at his command. In the case of *Schnabelewopski* the esoteric reference would be all the more discernible by those for whom it was meant because they would already have recognized the autobiographical substratum in the hero's account of his parents.

Schnabelewopski has become famous chiefly for its version of the Flying Dutchman story—a version Wagner obviously knew and drew on. For the hero of Heine's mini-novel that story is merely the variant of the legend of the Wandering Jew. The Dutchman is therefore explicitly called 'The Wandering Jew of the Sea'.[22]

The fragmentary tale culminates in the portrait of little Samson, *der kleine Simson*, which plays on the symbolic contrast between the mighty biblical hero and the puny modern Jew that bears his name and which serves, at the same time, to introduce reflections on the nature and fortunes of the Jewish God. 'God', Schnabelewopski tells us, 'never came to the aid of little Samson, although the latter constantly championed His cause'.

Despite such divine indifference and almost human ingratitude little Samson remained a constant champion of Theism, out of what I believe to have been an inborn inclination. For his ancestors belonged to God's Chosen People, a people that God once protected with especial fondness and that has therefore retained a measure of loyalty and affection for the good Lord right up to the present hour. Jews are always the most obedient of Theists, especially those born, like little Samson, in the free city of Frankfurt. In political matters these can be as republican as anyone, they can even roll in the mud like any old *sansculotte*—but when religious ideas come into play they remain humble servants of their Jehovah, that old fetish who wants nothing more to do with the entire crowd and has had Himself newly baptized as pure divine Spirit.

This pure divine Spirit, I think, this parvenu of the heavens who is now so moral, so cosmopolitan, so universally cultured, bears a secret ill will towards the poor Jews, who knew Him in His first crude form and who, in their synagogues, remind him every day of

His obscure national origins. Perhaps the Old Gentleman no longer wants to know that He stemmed from Palestine, that He was once the God of Abraham, Isaac, and Jacob, and that in those days His name was Jehovah.[23]

References to little Samson's nativity in Frankfurt, to his physical weakness joined with ardour of spirit, and to his staunch republicanism which does not preclude religious leanings, suggests that Heine conceived him partly with Ludwig Börne in mind; and little Samson also has something of the temperament and physique of Ludwig Marcus. What stands out in the passage just quoted, however, is Heine's satirical refashioning of the Jewish God in the image of modern descendants of his ancient worshippers. These are less faithful to Jehovah than little Samson: many are parvenus who have changed their names, who seek their philosophy and rule of life in Hegel rather than in the Talmud, and who have no desire to be reminded of their Jewish origins. On all these counts Heine was vulnerable himself—as so often, his satire glances at tendencies in his own life and mind as much as at the foibles or villainies of others.

Little Samson derives his inspiration and spiritual sustenance from the Old Testament—a much-loved book, he calls it, adding that

'my ancestors carried it about with them all over the world; they endured much grief, misfortune, disgrace, and hatred on its behalf, some even endured death itself. Every page it contains has cost tears and blood; it is the written fatherland of the children of God; it is our sacred inheritance from Jehovah.'[24]

The memorable phrase 'the written fatherland', *das aufgeschriebene Vaterland*, is one of Heine's happiest comments on the role of the Bible in post-exilic Jewish life. But it is not only Jews who live at once in the prosaic world of nineteenth-century Holland and in Old Testament Palestine. There is also the interesting case of Schnabelewopski's Dutch landlord, 'by trade a maker of trusses and by religion an Anabaptist', who

read the Bible so assiduously that it passed into his nightly dreams, and while his eyes twitched and twinkled he would tell his wife over their morning coffee how he had again been honoured by converse with the highest dignitaries, how he had even met that most exalted of

all sovereigns, His Majesty King Jehovah, and how all the ladies of
the Old Testament treated him in the friendliest and tenderest man-
ner.

It is this last point which particularly sticks in his wife's gullet:
she resents his nocturnal drinking bouts with Lot's daughters
and encounters with Judith and the Queen of Sheba; she loses
patience altogether, not surprisingly, when her husband tells
her, one morning, how he helped the half-clad Queen Esther at
her toilet.

Then she beat the poor man with his own trusses, threw hot coffee in
his face, and would certainly have made away with him if he had not
sworn, in the most solemn manner, to avoid all relations with Old
Testament women and keep company in future with no one but
patriarchs and male prophets.

The result of this ill-treatment was that from that time onwards
Mynheer took good care to say nothing of his nocturnal happiness;
he became a thoroughgoing religious roué; he confessed to me that he
now even had the courage to make the most improper propositions
to the naked Susanna; in the end he had the impudence to dream
himself into King Solomon's harem and to take tea with his thousand
wives.[25]

This characteristic *jeu d'esprit* provides a humorous context for
little Samson's more serious relationship to the figures of the
Old Testament, and illustrates the way in which these figures
have become part of the life of Christians as well as Jews.

Heine's affectionate fun with the less respectable episodes of
the Old Testament has yet another serious context: it is embed-
ded in speculations about the place of dreams in human life.
These again involve the Jewish people along with the European
Christians in whose lands they lived out the time of their
Diaspora.

True dreaming began with the Jews, the People of the Spirit, and
reached its apogee among the Christians, the spectral people. Our
descendants will shudder when they come to read what a ghostly life
we led, how our humanity was cleft in two and only one half had a
real life. Our epoch—that which begins with Christ's crucifixion—
will be regarded as a great period of sickness in the course of man's
existence.

And yet—how sweet our dreams could be! Our healthy descen-
dants will hardly be able to understand that. All the splendours of the

world fell away from us, and we found them again in our innermost soul . . .[26]

Little Samson is a dreamer too; for him too the figures of the Old Testament come alive; but the form this takes in his case is that of seeing himself called upon to shoulder, in the modern world, the task God had imposed on his great namesake in the Bible. He champions Theism against the unbelieving and blasphemous Philistines of a latter day; and as he does so, he is made to translate the Jewish concept of God into what can be recognized as the imagery of Heine's own *Book of Songs*, the *Buch der Lieder*.

'What the sun is for flowers, God is for mankind. When the rays of that heavenly body touch the flowers, they grow happily upwards and open their chalices and unfold their most varied colours. At night, when the sun is far away, they stand there sadly, their chalices closed up, they sleep, or they dream of the way the golden rays kissed them in the time that has been. Flowers that always stand in the shade lose their colour and their power to grow, become crippled and pale, and wilt away . . . Flowers that grow entirely in the dark, in old castle vaults, under ruined monasteries—they become ugly and poisonous, they creep along the ground like snakes, their very odour brings disaster, benumbs, presages death . . .'

Little Samson's atheist opponent, a latter-day Philistine, sees very well where this parable is tending:

'You, little Samson, see yourself as a pious blossom which, in the sunshine of God, sucks up the sacred rays of virtue and love with such intoxicated delight that your soul flowers into all the colours of the rainbow while you see our soul, turned away from the Godhead, fading away in colourless ugliness even if it does not, as it well may, spread pestilential odours.'[27]

What the atheist does not comment on is the anti-aristocratic and anti-clerical slant little Samson introduces into his comparison by mentioning the 'old castle walls' and 'ruined monasteries' beloved of Romantic writers in Germany and all over Europe.

Little Samson caps his parable of the flowers with another, a parable which plays a homely Jewish variation on one of the great metaphors of the Enlightenment: the Leibnizian or Newtonian world clock. 'At Frankfurt', he tells his atheist opponent, 'I once saw a watch that did not believe in the existence of a watchmaker. It was pinchbeck and went very badly.'[28] This remark leads to a duel in which little Samson fights 'for the existence of God, the ancient Jehovah, the King of Kings'; but the Jewish God fails to come to his champion's aid. Stabbed through the lungs, then bandaged and brought to bed, the little man has the story of his biblical namesake read to him. His comments show that in the manner of many unsophisticated Jews he applied the stories of the Old Testament to his own life in an almost literal way. What he says of the Philistines, for instance, points unmistakably to the indignities to which Jews were subjected in many parts of Germany and brilliantly suggests how in the consciousness of Jewish traditionalists the contemporary scene and the biblical event could merge:

Oh these Philistines! they have enslaved and mocked us, they made us pay toll like pigs, they made me ride the rail and threw me out of a dance-hall, they kicked me at Bockenheim . . .[29]

As the biblical narrative is read to him, little Samson interposes reminiscences of similar humiliations at various points—how they tried to have him arrested and taken to a police cell, how he was attacked in the Eschenheimer Gasse—until in the end he tries to emulate the original Samson's heroic death.

At this little Samson opened his eyes uncannily wide, raised himself convulsively, grasped the two pillars at the foot of his bed and shook them, stammering angrily: 'Let my soul die with the Philistines.' But the strong pillars of his bed remained immovable; exhausted, the little man fell back on his pillows with a melancholy smile, and from his wound, whose bandage had become displaced, a red stream of blood oozed out.[30]

Little Samson has traits taken from several of Heine's acquaintances, but ultimately it is futile to see in him a portrait of Ludwig Marcus, say, or of Ludwig Börne. He is, rather, a symbolic creation, suggesting the physical weakness of ghetto Jews while also showing us how brave a spirit may dwell in a feeble body, how religious Jews may be more admirable than the God they serve, and how for all the valiant efforts of its champion, theism was—Heine was coming to believe—

doomed in nineteenth-century Europe. Whatever the reader may forget about *Schnabelewopski*, he will surely carry with him for ever that final melancholy smile of the dying little Jew, who had done his best but had not found himself able to emulate, in a modern, unheroic world, the feats of his biblical namesake. While we cannot but feel such pathos, however, we must recognize absurdity too: an absurdity inherent in Heine's description of little Samson's philistine life-style (his obsessive tidiness for instance) and of a spiritualist feebleness which is thrown into relief when we hold it against the sensual vigour of the original Samson, conqueror of Philistines, lover and victim of the fair Delilah. And let us not forget one other fact: the poet who exercised great care in naming his characters gave to this figure a variant of the name borne by his own father.

(iii)

The doom of Theism, and in particular the death of the Judaeo-Christian God, is one of the principal themes of a series of articles which Heine wrote for the *Revue des deux mondes* in the course of 1834. Like the subtitle of Heine's essays on German literature in *L'Europe littéraire* ('De l'Allemagne depuis Mme. de Staël'), the title of this new series, *De l'Allemagne depuis Luther*, was meant to recall Germaine de Staël's celebrated work, a work Heine intended at once to continue and to correct. Heine wrote in German and looked over the French translation by another hand; he then edited the German text and published it, together with a cycle of poems, in the second volume of his *Salon* (January 1835). It now bore the title: *Towards a History of Religion and Philosophy in Germany* (*Zur Geschichte der Religion und Philosophie in Deutschland*).

The history of *religion* in Germany is naturally seen as bound up with that of the ancient Hebrews. Heine professes no love for the 'thundering tyrant' Jehovah, nor can he sympathize with a devaluation of the body (which he quite wrongly attributes to the Hebrews) whereby the body is seen as 'nothing but the poor sheath of the *ruakh hakodesh*, the holy breath, the spirit'. There is respect, however, in his depiction of Judaism as a religion that encourages the faculty of dreaming, and of the Jews as

in a true sense the people of the spirit, chaste, abstemious, serious, abstract, stiff-necked, fitted for martyrdom. Their most sublime flower is Jesus Christ. He is truly Spirit incarnate, and the beautiful legend that he came into the world by means of an immaculate Virgin, engendered by pure Spirit, is deeply significant.[31]

The Jewishness of Jesus is once again emphasized: 'The poor Rabbi of Nazareth', Heine terms him, and he recalls with gratification how this poor rabbi,

over whose dying head the Roman pagan wrote the mocking words: 'King of the Jews'—even this despised king of the Jews, crowned with thorns and adorned with ironic purple, became in the end the god of the Romans, and they had to kneel to him.[32]

This triumph of Christ did not bring with it the prosperity of the Jews—on the contrary, these lived a ghostlike existence in the ghettos of Europe. They were found, however, to be guardians of a treasure. Heine is here speaking of German Jewry in the fifteenth and sixteenth centuries, when Christian Europe had to read the Old Testament in the distorting medium of Latin and Greek translations. Heine's handwritten draft of this passage shows that he intended at one time to stress the persecution of the Jews even more. He contemplated saying that they were 'pursued through every country with sword and derision', and that they were 'treacherously murdered and mocked', but decided, in the end, to omit these phrases.[34] From this despised and persecuted people Luther derived much of his knowledge of the Hebrew Bible, and he repaid the debt, in some measure, by bringing Christianity back to something nearer its Judaic origins: 'the Indian, Gnostic element disappears and we see, once again, the Jewish-theistic element rising within it.'[35] In a later passage Heine speaks of Luther's restoration of 'the true religion, the Judaic-theistic gospel' after years of idolatry; the draft of this passage has the telling variant 'Judaic cosmopolitan gospel', but that is abandoned for reasons about which we can only speculate.[36] Luther's notorious outbursts against the Jews remain unmentioned.

The Jewish books whose persecution Heine chronicles include the great gathering of laws, rabbinical discussions, and exempla, which is known as the Talmud. Heine could not speak of this with the unqualified enthusiasm he showed for the Bible, but his description bears witness to a profound respect.

Knowledge of Hebrew was quite extinguished in the Christian world. Only the Jews, hidden here and there in some corner of that world, preserved the traditions of the Hebrew language. Like a ghost guarding a treasure that had been entrusted to him while he was still among the living, this murdered people, this ghost of a people, sat in its dark ghettos and there preserved the Hebrew Bible; into those ill-famed recesses German savants secretly descended in order ot raise the treasure, in order to acquire a knowledge of the Hebrew language. When the Catholic clergy noticed the danger threatening it from that side, noticed that the people might, by means of this bypath, reach the true word of God and uncover the Roman forgeries—then it would dearly have liked to suppress the Jewish tradition. An intention took shape to destroy all Hebrew books, and in the Rhineland there began that persecution of books against which our splendid Doctor Reuchlin fought so gloriously.[36]

The Talmud is indeed the Catholicism of the Jews. It is a Gothic cathedral, overladen, it is true, with childish ornamentation, but yet astonishing in its bold aspirations toward heaven and its gigantic proportions. It is a hierarchy of religious ordinances which often deal with the most curious, ridiculous subtleties. These are so ingeniously ordered, however, so support one another, and work together with such terrifying consistency, that they form a frighteningly defiant, colossal whole.[37]

The Talmud, Heine concludes, served the Jews as a bulwark against the Romans and enabled them to withstand the threats and the blandishments of Christian as well as pagan Rome.

Unlike the Bible, however, the Talmud is said, in *Towards a History of Religion and Philosophy in Germany*, to have had its day; and the orthodox who swear by the Talmud are presented in an unlovely light when Heine comes to draw the portrait of the man who may be regarded, along with Luther, Lessing, and Kant, as the hero of this book: Benedict Spinoza.

Heine begins his intellectual portrait of Spinoza with a reference to Descartes, from whom Spinoza is said to have learnt his mathematical form and method, and whose philosophy is said to have given an impetus to Spinoza's own philosophizing.[38] Spinoza's way of thinking, Heine believes, looks beyond the philosophies of his own day and adumbrates the future; but there is also to be traced within it the heritage of Spinoza's Jewish ancestry and the influence of Spinoza's Dutch environment.

Spinoza's writings are pervaded by an atmosphere that cannot be explained. It is as though the winds of the future were playing about us. Perhaps the spirit of the Jewish prophets still rested on their late descendant. His seriousness, his pride in his own worth, his *grandezza* of thought, would also appear to have been inherited; for Spinoza belonged to the families of martyrs driven out from Spain by Their Most Catholic Majesties. To this must be added the patience characteristic of Dutchmen, which shows itself unfailingly in Spinoza's life as well as in his writings. It has been shown beyond doubt that Spinoza's way of life was as free from reproach, as pure and unspotted as the life of his divine kinsman Jesus Christ. Like him he suffered for his teaching, like him he wore the crown of thorns. Wherever a great spirit gives voice to his thoughts, there is Golgotha.[39]

Spinoza's Jewishness—a matter of 'spirit' and family descent—is thus stressed without devaluation of his wider environment: without, that is, any playing down of the influence exerted on him and his ancestors by the non-Jewish societies in which they lived. At the same time the life of Jesus Christ, on whose Jewishness Heine also insists once again, is seen as a paradigm of the life of all great men whose message ordinary humanity is not yet ready to accept.

Spinoza's Golgotha, like that of his 'great kinsman', was preceded by a clash with Jewish orthodoxy, and it took the form of a solemn expulsion from the Jewish community.

Dear reader, if you ever go to Amsterdam let the verger show you the Spanish Synagogue. This is a beautiful building, its roof is supported by four gigantic pillars, and at its centre you can still see the platform from which the anathema was once pronounced on the despiser of the Mosaic law, the hidalgo Don Benedict de Spinoza. A ram's horn called the *Shofar* was sounded on this occasion . . . The blowing of this horn accompanied Spinoza's excommunication; he was solemnly expelled from the community of Israel and declared henceforth unworthy to bear the title of 'Jew'. His Christian enemies were magnanimous enough to leave him in the enjoyment of that title. The

Jews, however, that Swiss Guard of Theism, were inexorable, and visitors are still shown the square before the Amsterdam synagogue where they once stabbed at him with their long daggers.[40]

We might note in passing that the synagogue Heine here describes is not, in fact, the somewhat less grand one that saw the ban, the *kherem*, pronounced against Spinoza. There is also evidence that Heine intended, at one time, to let the philosopher's rabbinical enemies down rather more lightly that he did in the end; a draft passage places Spinoza's antagonist Voltaire next to the rabbi of the Amsterdam synagogue and adds the gloss that of these two it was not the rabbi who seemed the more ridiculous.[41] That gloss he deleted, however, in order to distance himself more effectively from representatives of an orthodox Judaism that sought to cast out a philosopher whom Heine clearly regarded, like most of his fellow members of the now defunct Society for the Culture and Science of the Jews, as a Jew of whose achievements and personal qualities the Jewish people had every right to be proud.

Just as Spinoza learned about religion, Heine tells us, by a bitter experience connected with daggers, so he learnt about politics by a no less bitter experience connected with a rope; for just as Spinoza had collided with the Jewish religious establishment, so the father of his betrothed collided with the Dutch political establishment and was hanged—badly and painfully—for that offence. That last experience, Heine concludes, lay behind his *Tractatus theologico-politicus*; a work whose critique of biblical religion the poet clearly knew and bent to his purposes.

In the passage just quoted, an implied parallel is drawn between the behaviour of Spinoza's Christian enemies (who continued to abuse him as a Jew when the Jewish community had taken away his right to that appellation) and the behaviour of Heine's own enemies, particularly in Germany, who did not cease regarding him as a Jew even after his baptism. He also projects into this passage—when talking about the *Shofar* and the part it plays in the expulsion ceremony—a scene from a later time than that of Spinoza: a scene, that is, from the life of the philosopher Salomon Maimon, who died in 1800 and whose autobiography still remains one of the most valuable sources of our knowledge of Jewish life in eighteenth-century Germany.

There must be something terrible about this horn. I read in the life of Salomon Maimon that the rabbi of Altona once sought to lead this disciple of Kant back to the old faith; when Maimon obstinately insisted on his philosophic heresies, the rabbi resorted to threats and showed him the *Shofar*, saying in gloomy tones: 'Do you know what this is?' When the disciple of Kant calmly answered: 'It is the horn of a ram', the rabbi was so horrified that he fell over backwards.[42]

The name of Kant resounds through this passage, anticipating the point Heine is soon to make: that Kant more than any other hastened what Heine regarded, in these his early years in France, as the imminent demise of the Judaeo-Christian God. From Heine's handwritten notes it appears that he envisaged joining Kant's name with that of a contemporary littérateur whose career he had sought to further in earlier years: 'In a Novelle by one of our best writers of narrative fiction, A. Lewald, I recently read a description of Kant's way of life . . .'[43] In the finished version of *Towards a History of Religion and Philosophy in Germany*, however, August Lewald's name does not figure. Was it too anticlimactic in this context? Had Heine conceived doubts that Lewald was in fact 'one of our best writers of narrative fiction'?

It cannot be stressed strongly enough, in defiance of biographers and critics who speak of Heine's 'atheistic period', that even in the 1830s the poet never adopts a stance that might truthfully be called atheistic. He is careful, therefore, to exculpate Spinoza too from charges of atheism that might be brought against him.

'God', termed the 'One Substance' by Spinoza and the 'Absolute' by German philosophers, 'is everything that there is.' He is matter as well as spirit; both are equally divine, and whoever abuses sacred matter is just as sinful as the man who sins against the Holy Spirit.[44]

Here Spinoza merges with Heine himself; for the words 'God is everything there is' come from a poem Heine had first published in *Salon I*.

Auf diesem Felsen bauen wir
Die Kirche von dem dritten,
Dem dritten neuen Testament;
Das Leid ist ausgelitten.

Vernichtet ist das Zweierlei,
Das uns so lang betöret;
Die dumme Leiberquälerei
Hat endlich aufgehöret.

Hörst du den Gott im finstern Meer?
Mit tausend Stimmen spricht er.
Und siehst du über unserem Haupt
Die tausend Gotteslichter?

Der heil'ge Gott, der ist im Licht
Wie in den Finsternissen;
Und Gott ist alles, was da ist;
Er ist in unsern Küssen.

[On this rock we build
the Church of the Third
New Testament;
suffering is now at an end.

The duality which so long fooled us
is annihilated;
the stupid mortification of the body
has ceased at last.

Do you hear God's voice in the dark ocean?
He speaks with a thousand voices,
And do you see above our heads
the thousand lights of God?

God's Holiness resides in the light
and also in darkness;
God is everything there is;
He is in our kisses too.][45]

Spinoza and Heine's own earlier self are here made to proclaim
the same message: matter and spirit are both informed by the
divine; the tyranny of the spirit over the flesh will come to an

end, and from afar a new age of harmony can be discerned. In the perspective of *Towards a History of Religion and Philosophy in Germany*, Spinoza and Heine become joint prophets of a more human religion than that proclaimed by their orthodox opponents: a religion which promises to still the greatest longing of the time, to resolve its dissonances and heal its self-division.

Two passages may serve to illustrate another important aspect of Heine's portrayal of Spinoza.

The pantheism of Goethe is quite different from pagan pantheism. To put it in a nutshell: Goethe was the Spinoza of poetry. That Goethe was wholly devoted to the teachings of Spinoza cannot be doubted. He occupied himself with them throughout his life; he has himself freely confessed this at the beginning of his autobiography and again, recently, in the latest volume to appear. I no longer remember where I read that Herder, annoyed by this constant preoccupation with Spinoza, once exclaimed: 'If only Goethe would just once take up another Latin book, instead of always reading Spinoza!' But this is true not only of Goethe . . .

And again:

However much Herr Schelling protests that his philosophy should be distinguished from Spinozism, that it represents a more 'living interpenetration of the ideal and the real', that it differs from Spinozism 'as fully moulded Greek statues differ from rigid Egyptian originals', I must nevertheless declare categorically that in his earlier period, when he still *was* a philosopher, Herr Schelling did not differ from Spinoza in the least. He only reached that philosophy by another route, as I will demonstrate later when I narrate how Kant found a new path, Fichte followed him, Herr Schelling in his turn trod in Fichte's footsteps and, straying through the dark forest of the Philosophy of Nature, at last stood face to face with the great statue of Spinoza.[46]

Heine ever emphasizes that German-Jewish intellectual and literary relations were not all one way; that Germans had learnt from Jewish teachers and traditions, just as he, Heine, had profited from the cultural heritage of the land in which he was born and educated.

Even this, however, is not quite the end. The history of philosophy Heine sketches in the work under discussion reserves a key position for Spinoza: his brand of pantheism or panentheism presents a viable alternative to the empiricism of Locke and the idealism of Leibniz, while at the same time enabling those who build on it to avoid the pitfalls of materialist atheism. This helps to explain the fascination Spinoza exerted on Goethe—a fascination which ensured that Spinoza became a vital force, not only in philosophy, but also in poetry. 'Spinoza's doctrine', Heine tells his readers, 'has emerged from its mathematical chrysalis and now flutters about us as Goethe's lyric poetry. That accounts for some of the anger with which Goethe's poems were greeted by some of the orthodox and the pietists of our day.'[47] Since Heine sees himself as Goethe's heir in the realm of lyric poetry, he is here forging another link between the writings of Spinoza and his own art.

Last but not least: Spinoza's panentheism leads Heine to speculate on the idea, familiar to German thinkers from Herder to Hegel, that each people has a particular cultural 'mission'.

Each people has, perhaps, the mission to recognize some part of this cosmos permeated by God; to make visible a particular set of ideas and to hand down the result to later peoples that have a similar mission. God is therefore the hero of world history . . . and of all humanity one may, justifiably, assert that it is an incarnation of God.[48]

The Jews, clearly, are one of these world-historical peoples; and Heine's dealings with Jewish thinkers who appeared long after the original proclamation of ethical monotheism strongly suggests that—in despite of Lessing, in despite of Hegel, and in despite of Schleiermacher—the Jewish 'mission' has not yet come to an end.

The second of the great Jewish historical figures of modern Europe which Heine draws into the portrait gallery of *Towards a History of Religion and Philosophy in Germany* is Moses Mendelssohn. Mendelssohn first appears at the head of Heine's list of eighteenth-century German moralists, representatives, as he puts it, of a *juste milieu* between philosophy and *belles-lettres*, ethically motivated, lacking the urge to build elaborate systems and the strict methodology of the great philosophers, inclined towards rationalism in religion and cosmopolitanism in politics, leading virtuous lives, passing strict judgement on themselves but lenient in their judgement of others. Among these moralists, Heine tells us, Mendelssohn has several peers; but in social importance he transcends them all, for in the history of German Jewry he figures as the great reformer, the man who founded a 'pure Mosaic religion' based on the Bible instead of the Talmud.

Throughout this work Heine had sought to show the political significance of placing a German translation of the Bible into the hands of German-speaking worshippers. The ultimate effect of Luther's ministrations, he had asserted, would be to give a voice to German revolutionaries: 'Liberty will be able to speak everywhere, and its language will be biblical.'[49] Mendelssohn, who translated the Pentateuch into German against rabbinical protest, but who nevertheless remained an orthodox Jew bound by Talmudic precepts, is therefore presented, with scant historical justification, as the Luther of German Jewry. This is not, it should be remembered, Heine's own invention: the Protestant preacher Daniel Jenisch, in a biographical sketch prefixed to a collection of Moses Mendelssohn's writings in 1789, had called him 'the Luther of the Jews (for what else was Mendelssohn for that nation but the torch-bearer of the Enlightenment) . . .'[50] Here, then, is Heine's elaboration of that topos:

In the same way as Luther overcame the sway of the Papacy, Mendelssohn overcame that of the Talmud: he rejected tradition, declared the Bible the source of religion, and translated its most important parts. Thereby he destroyed Jewish Catholicism just as Luther had destroyed Christian Catholicism. For truly, the Talmud is the Catholicism of the Jews . . . After the downfall of Christian Catholicism Jewish Catholicism too, that is, the Talmud, had to fall . . . Mendelssohn therefore deserves great praise for overthrowing Jewish Catholicism, at least in Germany. For what is superfluous is harmful.[51]

Mendelssohn was by no means the iconoclast whom Heine here presents, and had nothing like the negative attitude to the Talmud that Heine attributes to him; but Heine has described truly what many contemporaries *felt* Mendelssohn to be doing, and has clearly seen the effect his writings and activities had on many of the 'enlightened' Jews of Germany (including

Mendelssohn's own family). He has also seen the other side of the coin; he notes specifically that unlike so many of his 'enlightened' contemporaries Mendelssohn prided himself on his strict observance of Jewish ceremonial laws.

Rejecting tradition, he yet sought to preserve the obligation to keep the ceremonial laws of the Jewish faith. Was this cowardice or wisdom? Was it a melancholy attachment to the past which prevented him from laying violent hands on matters that were sacrosanct to his forefathers and for which the blood and the tears of martyrs had so copiously flowed? I do not think so. Like the kings of the material world the kings of the spirit must ruthlessly extirpate family feelings; on the throne of thought too one must not abandon oneself to comfortable softness. I therefore incline to the opinion that Moses Mendelssohn saw in the pure Mosaic religion an institution that could serve—so to speak—as a last bulwark of Theism. For that Theism was founded on *truth* he believed with his innermost soul, with deepest conviction. When his friend Lessing died and was accused of being a follower of Spinoza, Mendelssohn defended him against this suspicion with the most anxious zeal and he fretted himself literally to death over this affair.[52]

Moses Mendelssohn is thus presented, in *Towards a History of Religion and Philosophy*, as a king of the spirit, a worthy adversary of that other Jewish king of the spirit, Spinoza, whose opinions he could not share. This intellectual and spiritual 'royalty' was not reflected, however, in Mendelssohn's physical appearance and the circumstances of his youth.

This man, whom his compatriots called the German Socrates and whom they admired so reverently because of the nobility of his soul and the force of his intellect, was the son of a poor beadle in the synagogue of Dessau. Not content with inflicting this congenital malady on him, Providence burdened him further by giving him a humped back—as if to teach the vulgar in the most drastic way that a man should be judged, not by his outer appearance, but by his inner worth. Or did Providence make him a hunchback with the benevolent intention of allowing him to ascribe many of the insults and injuries heaped on him by the vulgar to an affliction about which a wise man can soon comfort himself?[53]

Here we have Heine's most striking evocation so far of the feeling shared by many cultivated Jews of his time: the feeling that they were being mocked and insulted on account of the

Jewishness with which they were born and which they could no more help than they could some congenital illness or malformation. We have to remember this feeling when we hear Heine speak—as we soon shall—as if Judaism itself were an inherited malady.

These things are never simple or one-way, however, in Heine's writings; and true to form he interrupts his portrait of Mendelssohn to sketch a very different type of Jew, and with it a very different kind of feeling. He had earlier cast a brief glance at the 'court Jews' of pre-nineteenth-century Europe and seen them as 'lackeys' (*Kammerknechte*) of whoever happened to be in power; and in his description of the Talmud he had presented that elaborate compilation as a defence first against pagan and then against Christian Rome. Both these things are recalled as Heine introduces his sketch of a man who contrasts as much with the courteous and scholarly Mendelssohn as he does with the subservient court Jews of former ages whose natural successor he would seem to be.

Like pagan Rome [conquered, Heine had told us, by the religion of 'the poor rabbi of Nazareth'] Christian Rome too was overcome and even obliged to pay tribute. If, dear reader, you will go to the rue Lafitte in Paris in the first days of the law term, and will stop by no. 15, you will see a lumbering coach draw up before a lofty front door and a portly man descend from that vehicle. He will go up a stair to a little room where a fair-haired young man is sitting who is somewhat older than he looks and whose aristocratic, grand-seigneurial nonchalance has something so solid, so positive, so absolute about it that you might be inclined to think that he had in his pocket all the money of this world. And indeed—he does have all the money of this world in his pocket; his name is James de Rothschild, the portly gentleman is Signor Grimbaldi, emissary from his Holiness the Pope, and what he is bringing in the Pope's name is the interest on the Roman Loan, the tribute of Rome. What further need, then, of the Talmud?[54]

In times in which power relations have so drastically altered, Heine asks his readers to believe, the traditional Jewish fence around the law has become unnecessary, even though Moses Mendelssohn himself refused to breach it.

It will have been noticed that the description of James de Rothschild as a fair-haired, youthful-looking man of aristocratic bearing goes counter to that stereotype of a Jewish banker's

appearance and behaviour which Heine had recalled and ex-
aggerated in his portrait of Gumpelino. And indeed, the
'triumph' of Rothschild, as he here presents it, is as much a
triumph of Germany as of the Jews.

Strange! *We Germans* are the strongest and most intelligent of
peoples. The scions of our princes sit on all the thrones of Europe,
our Rothschilds rule over the stock exchanges of the whole world, our
learned men reign supreme in all the sciences, we have invented
gunpowder and printing—and yet if, at home, one of us shoots off a
pistol, he has to pay a fine of 3 thaler, and if we want to announce in a
Hamburg newspaper: 'My dear wife has given birth to a daughter as
fair as Liberty' then Dr Hoffmann the censor will grab his red pencil
and strike out the word 'Liberty' . . . [my italics][55]

What has here happened to the stereotype of the Jew also
happens to that of the Jewish God. As a child, Heine tells us, he
had seen God as an aged man with a pious face and a little
Jewish beard; schooled by Hegel and his predecessors, he
could then go on to trace the whole series of transformations
which the image of that God had undergone in the minds of
successive worshippers. Now, however, these transformations
are coming to an end; and some of the most unforgettable
passages in Heine's survey of religion and philosophy deal
with the coming death of the Jewish God.

Our heart is full of a terrible pity. It is old Jehovah himself who is
preparing for his death. We have known him so well from his cradle
onwards, in Egypt, where he was brought up among divine calves,
crocodiles, sacred onions, ibises, and cats. We saw him say farewell to
the playfellows of his childhood and to the obelisks and sphinxes of
his native Nile valley in order to become a little god-king in Palestine
to a tribe of poor shepherds, where he lived in a temple-palace of his
own. We saw him later coming into contact with the Assyrian and
Babylonian civilizations and putting off his all too human passions,
no longer fulminating wrath and revenge right and left, or at least not
sending down thunderbolts for every trifle.
  We watched him emigrate to Rome, where he renounced all his
national prejudices and proclaimed the celestial equality of all
peoples, and where he organized an opposition against Jupiter with
such fine phrases, and went on intriguing for so long, that at last he
came into power and reigned from the Capitol over the city and
world, *urbem et orbem*. We watched him becoming yet more spir-

itualized; whimpering tenderly, he became a loving Father, a friend of humanity, a universal benefactor, a philanthropist—but nothing could save him.

Do you hear the passing bell? Kneel down—they are bringing the sacrament to a dying god.[56]

Jew and Gentile alike will have to learn to live in a world bereft of the personalized God in Whom they had once believed.

What this would mean Heine spells out in the justly famous concluding paragraphs of *Towards a History of Religion and Philosophy in Germany*. Here he foresees a Germany liberated from the shackles of its Judaeo-Christian heritage following up its philosophical revolution with a political sequel that would make the French Revolution of 1789 appear a harmless idyll. Heine's prophecy was not fulfilled in all its aspects; but his image of the terrors which a paganized Germany would one day unleash has proved only too applicable. 'Christianity', he wrote, '—and that is its highest achievement—has to some degree assuaged the Germanic peoples' brutal love of fighting, but it could not extirpate it altogether; and when, one day, the talisman which held it in check is broken, the savagery of the ancient warriors will burst forth once more, with that berserk rage of which Nordic tales and Nordic songs are so full.'[57] Heine addresses his warning, above all, to the French; but the Jews of Europe, alas, have had all too much cause to apply it to themselves.

In the early 1840s Heine seems to have considered elaborating the notion, expressed in *Towards a History of Religion and Philosophy in Germany*, that the Jews were the appointed guardians of one of humanity's greatest treasures, the Bible. The fragment which suggests this elaboration sounds a Messianic theme that might have provided a useful counterpoint to the terrifying passage which has just been discussed. Not surprisingly, however, the Messianism that appears in this unpublished fragment is thoroughly modernized and secularized. The new wordly Messiah, Heine writes, *der weltliche Heiland*, will make his entry by railway rather than on a donkey's back. 'Roses will be strewn on iron' as men and women celebrate a saviour who comes to bring them the blessings of 'industry, work, and joy'.[58]

(iv)

Towards the end of 1832 Heine had begun a series of articles in which he sought to correct the picture of German literature which Frenchmen derived from Mme de Staël's *De l'Alle-magne*. He had written them in German and had then gone over a translation into French by François-Adolphe Loève-Veimars. This French version appeared in *L'Europe littéraire. Journal de la littérature nationale et étrangère* between 1 March and 24 May 1833. The editors of that journal had added a note to the second article (8 March 1833) describing Heine as an *écrivain protestant* who had set himself the task of explaining German literature to Catholic France from a Protestant standpoint. When the first volume of the first German edition appeared, a few weeks later, under the imprint of Hoffmann and Campe, Heine referred to this note and to the objections he had made, vainly, to the French editors.

It was no use objecting, as I did, that there was no such thing as a Catholic France; that I did not write for a Catholic France; that it was enough if I myself mentioned that in Germany I belonged to the Protestant Church. This observation, which merely records the fact that I have the pleasure of figuring in a Lutheran church register as an evangelical Christian, still permits me to proclaim, in scholarly matters, any opinion I please, even if it should be contrary to Protestant dogma; while a note stating that I wrote my essays from a Protestant standpoint would confine me in dogmatic shackles.—It was in vain; the editors of *L'Europe littéraire* left such Teutonic subtleties unheeded.[59]

Heine goes on to explain that in order to make himself understood by the French, he occasionally used the vocabulary of Saint-Simonism; and he warns his enemies not to mistake him for an atheist or out-and-out materialist. 'Let them call me a Jew', he adds, 'or, for that matter, a Saint-Simonist': he, Heine, would not, be deflected from his determination to speak the truth, as he sees it, about 'the most important question humanity has to face: the nature of God'. 'I do not belong to the materialists who see spirit as body: I reinfuse spirit into material bodies. I respiritualize them, I hallow them. I do not belong to the atheists who negate; I affirm . . . that God is the beginning and end of all things.'

'Let them call me a Jew', we have heard Heine say; but if someone did just that—as happened, for instance, in the *Journal des Débats* of 22 September 1835, where Heine found himself described as an *israélite*—Heine was usually quick to react. 'Je n'appartiens pas à la religion israélite',[60] he wrote, quite truthfully, on this occasion—on other occasions he would deny, with less candour, that he had ever set foot in a synagogue, and he would show extreme anger if someone proposed to include his name in a reference book listing famous Jews. He increasingly looked on himself, in this period of his life, as a German explaining his own country to the French and working for the political and social amelioration of his fatherland in a way that would entitle him to be called a German patriot with greater justification than the nationalists, Francophobes, and anti-Semites who all too often usurped that title. He left unpublished, however, a passage in which he sought to describe to French readers the standpoint he had consciously chosen to adopt.

You know that I am not an adherent of Catholicism; I saw in Protestantism not just a religion but also a mission, and for fourteen years now I have been defending Protestant interests against the machinations of our German Jesuits. Later, however, my zeal for dogma cooled, and a few years ago I declared openly in my writings that my Protestantism reduced itself to the fact that my name figures in a church register of the Lutheran community. But our hearts always retain a secret affection for the cause in which we have fought and suffered; and my religious convictions are still animated by the spirit of Protestantism.[61]

Heine may have come to feel that this statement was excessively open to misrepresentation and decided to allow his Protestant persona to appear more obliquely in the tone and tenor of his work.

In November 1835 appeared the fullest version yet of the thoughts on German literature and society which Heine had first expressed in his articles for *L'Europe littéraire* two years before. The piece now bore the title *The Romantic School* (*Die romantische Schule*) and it was dated 1836 by its publishers, the firm of Hoffmann and Campe. This was the work in which Heine stated unequivocally his belief that the most important relations conditioning human experience and behaviour were political and religious: 'die zwei wichtigsten Verhältnisse des Menschen, das politische und das religiöse'.[62] Unlike its companion piece, *Towards a History of Religion and Philosophy in Germany*, this new book and the articles it embodied contained no full-length portraits of Jewish figures; but it nevertheless illustrates the theme we have already isolated in the Spinoza passage of *Towards a History of Religion and Philosophy*: the interpenetration of European and especially German, cultural life with elements brought to it by men and women of Jewish origin.

The first of the gifts which the Jewish people bequeathed to the culture described in *The Romantic School* are its history and the records of that history. Heine stresses this heritage in various ways: unobtrusively, as when he compares Lessing's activities as polemicist and dramatist to that of 'pious Jews who, frequently disturbed by enemies when they were building the Second Temple, fought against such enemies with one hand while continuing with the other to build the house of God';[63] more explicitly, as when he claims that the non-secular poets of the Christian Middle Ages celebrated 'nothing but the Jewish people, which alone was thought sacred, and its history, which alone was called sacred history, the heroes of the Old and New Testaments.[64] A fragment not included in the published versions of *The Romantic School* envisages a new and original way of presenting Israel as the 'suffering servant' of the European world.

As an excuse for persecuting the Jews, they were accused of having crucified Christ. It was vain for these poor long-bearded fellows to protest their innocence. A Jean Calas among the nations, the Jewish people suffered an execution drawn out over a thousand years, because of the accusation that it had murdered the Son . . .[65]

Jean Calas, of course, was the Protestant martyr of an unjust judiciary in whose defence Voltaire had shown so much of the human concern absent from most of his remarks about Jews. Indeed, Voltaire's *Traité sur la tolérance à l'occasion de la mort de Jean Calas* had included some notably hostile remarks on

Jews ancient and modern—a failure of tolerance in its self-styled apostle which Heine shows up by making Calas the symbol of the persecuted Jewish people.

The second gift of the Jewish people of which *The Romantic School* speaks is, of course, Christianity itself. This was of doubtful value to the Romans, as Heine had learnt from d'Holbach, Gibbon, and others; and in the spirit of their eighteenth century he now finds occasion to use the image he had deleted from *Pictures of Travel*: the image of Christianity as the shirt of Nessus bequeathed to the Herculean Romans by the Judaea they had helped to destroy. What may have been poison to the cultured Romans, however, was healthful medicine for the barbarians of the North, whose 'all too full-blooded bodies' were spiritualized by the teachings of Christ and his disciples.[66] But in the modern world, a new creed is being born—a creed proclaimed in a programmatic passage which Heine thought wiser, in the end, to omit from published versions of his book.

We believe in God, who is at once Father and Mother of all men; we believe in a Creator-God, in God's creation, in God the Holy Body; we believe in ourselves, our sanctity, our perfectibility, and our right to happiness. We do not seek agony, darkness, solitude—we seek joy, light, society. We do not withdraw and retreat into ourselves; we step out of the bounds of our narrow egos ... We love and we hate; for hatred too partakes of the divine if the hater is prepared to sacrifice himself. A Christ of hatred dies as divinely as a Christ of love. The sword is as sacred as the plough, but only the sword which is drawn in a divine cause ...[67]

This Saint-Simonian passage, intended for the version of *The Romantic School* published in *L'Europe Littéraire*, culminates in a paean to the *new* Germany about to be born: a free and regenerated fatherland permeated by a religious spirit that transcends all Christian and Jewish orthodoxies.

The third set of gifts the Jewish people brought to the Germans were certain philosophical ideas and ways of looking at the world. Here Heine once again adduces Spinoza, subtly reminding his readers, by his closing image, of the philosopher's humble profession as a grinder of optical lenses.

Nothing is more ridiculous than to claim exclusive property rights in the realm of ideas ... Herr Schelling has borrowed more from

Spinoza than Hegel ever borrowed from Schelling. When the day comes that sees Spinoza released from the rigid, old-Cartesian, mathematical form in which his works are cast, and when his works have thereby become accessible to the general reader, it will perhaps be seen that he has more right than anyone else to complain that his ideas have been 'stolen' by others. All our present-day philosophers—without knowing it, perhaps—look through spectacles that Baruch Spinoza has ground.[68]

'Baruch' Spinoza, Heine writes, not 'Benedict' as in *Towards a History of Religion and Philosophy*. The very form of the name reminds the reader of the philosopher's links with the Jewish people.

In the fourth place the German people owes to the Jews a fund of visions, images, symbols, and legends which have a moral as well as a poetic dimension. Here once again it is, of course, the Bible that first springs to mind; and Heine finds eloquent words in praise of the unknown poet who gave the world the Book of Job. 'Who', he asks, 'has written this book that has brought comfort to so many generations of suffering men? Mankind is only too apt to forget the name of its benefactors.'[69] But there are other, later additions to Germany's stock of poetic and moral imagery—the legend of the Golem, for instance, the man of clay animated by the Holy Name, which Heine discusses, without specific reference to its Jewish sources, in the work of Achim von Arnim.[70]

Lastly: a number of biblical figures (like Noah and his son Ham) are introduced to illuminate modern happenings; and as usual, a number of men and women of Jewish ancestry flit through Heine's pages in various culture-bearing or culture-furthering capacities. There is the author of the novel *Florentin*, for instance, 'a daughter', Heine informs us, 'of the famous Moses Mendelssohn, whom Friedrich Schlegel abducted from her first husband and who converted to Roman Catholicism along with him'. Heine adds to this a note on the gentlemanly conduct of Dorothea Schlegel's first husband, the banker Simon Veit, who forgave Schlegel the abuse of his hospitality and supported him and Dorothea financially for years after. Then there is Julius Eduard Hitzig, the biographer of E. T. A. Hoffman and of Zacharias Werner. 'A conscientious piece of work' Heine calls the later biography, 'which is as interesting for the psychologists as it is for the historian of literature'. We also meet, in Heine's pages, the translator Loève-Veimars, who had worked for Heine and whose translations of the works of E. T. A. Hoffman 'had presented that author in so splendid a guise and had thereby helped him to achieve a great reputation in France'; and later, in a French edition, Moritz Gottlob Saphir, 'le spirituel bonmotiste de Vienne'.[71] Neither Hitzig, however, nor Loève-Veimars, nor Saphir, is reminded of his Jewish connections and antecedents in the pages of *The Romantic School*.

Heine's eagerness, in these early 1830s, to diminish the Jewish dimension of his work may also be gauged from the French edition of his *Pictures of Travel*, published under the imprint of Renduel in 1834. This omits a number of allusions to, and jokes about, Jewish matters: remarks on Moser, for instance, on 'Israel Löwe', and on a friend in the Sephardic community, fall victim to what would seem to be a deliberate act of self-censorship, A glance at the Preface dated 20 May 1834, which Heine wrote for his *Tableaux de Voyages I* suggests a reason for this: for here we find Heine presenting himself to his French audience as a 'sauvage allemand' who penetrates the Parisian salons 'avec toute son originalité d'Outre-Rhin, fantastiquement colorié de germanismes et surchargé d'ornement par trop romantiques'. In translating his *Pictures of Travel* into French, he explains, he thought it right to tone down what he once again terms his 'Protestant zeal':

En Allemagne, un tel zèle n'était nullement déplacé; car, en ma qualité de protestant, je pouvais porter aux obscurantistes et aux tartuffes en général, aux pharisiens qu'aux sadducéens allemands, des coups beaucoup mieux assurés que si j'eusse parlé en philosophe . . .[72]

Heine may well have thought that too much emphasis on Jewish matters and too many allusions showing a keen and sympathic interest in Jewish personalities could only have weakened the German-Protestant–Romantic persona he was here attempting to project.

(v)

What must have become clear by now is the resolute historicity of Heine's mode of thinking. This has been brought out with admirable clarity by Nigel Reeves, whose book *Heinrich Heine. Poetry and Politics* usefully sketches the evolution of his historical thought.

In the early years he embraced the cultural critique of the Romantics, which was itself derived from Herder, and his experiments with the folk-song and later his undeterred enthusiasm for folklore and legend should be seen in the light of this philosophy. The transition to a political interpretation of Hegel's thought was almost a natural development from such beginnings, while the Saint-Simonian theory of history and avowed intention to bring about the Golden Age also belong to the tradition. The surprising continuity of Heine's ideals is, then, the result of his adherence to the historical philosophy. It is a philosophy which sees in human history the key to the understanding of mankind. It claims that history follows a meaningful and recognizable pattern of progression and rests its argument on the metaphysical assumption that God has either preordained this pattern or constitutes the pattern itself.[73]

Such faith in meaningful, providential pattern is an essential part of the Jewish tradition of historical thinking. What Heine learnt from Hegel and the Saint-Simonians secularized what he could already have learnt from the Old Testament. But in a posthumously published essay of the early 1830s to which its earliest editor gave the title: *Different Ways of Looking at History* (*Verschiedenartige Geschichtsauffassung*), Heine opposes to this view another which he found deeply abhorrent but which nevertheless haunted him all his life. Let us listen to Nigel Reeves once again:

The vision of history as a dreary and unending cycle, which he here associates with the Historical School, was in fact one of his own deepest fears and is an almost constant foil to his Utopianism.[74]

What has not been sufficiently noted is that here too Heine finds a sanction in the Jewish tradition: for the motto which he assigns to all those who hold this view comes from the Hebrew Bible, where it is attributed to Solomon the Preacher: 'There is nothing new under the sun.'[75] As for the third view, to which Heine gives his own vote in the 1830s—that is one which resolutely asserts the claims of the present against optimistic Utopians and pessimistic preachers of eternal sameness alike. For this he takes his motto, not from the Scriptures, but from those annals of the French Revolution which at this period of his life he so often likened to them: ' "Le pain est le droit du peuple," said Saint-Just—and that is the greatest sentence spoken in the whole course of the Revolution.'[76] The sense of social justice which attracted him to this saying by Saint-Just he was to recognize, in later years, as an important feature of the code of laws enshrined in the Pentateuch.

CHAPTER 5
Imperfect Sympathies

(i)

On 1 March 1836, after a night which had begun with the première of Meyerbeer's *Les Huguenots* and continued with a ball given by the Rothschilds in their newly refurbished house in the Rue Lafitte, Heine sat down to write out his impressions of both events for the readers of the *Augsburg Gazette*. He gladly seized on his tiredness and the multiplicity of impressions he had received to give only the vaguest details of the music of *Les Huguenots*; what he did say, however, was so complimentary that some suspected an element of parody. 'The whole beauty of this masterpiece', he says of *Robert le Diable*, 'can only be appreciated by those who have heard it a dozen times,' and the same must be true of *Les Huguenots* which experts have declared even more perfectly formed and even more inventive [*geistreich*]. In Meyerbeer Heine claims to see the greatest living master of counterpoint, the greatest contemporary musician; the forms he created are wholly new, and so are the melodies, which are declared extraordinary in themselves and also extraordinarily well placed. Other composers of genius, he asserts, know how to invent melodies, but not how to marshal them; they are carried away by the stream of their own melodiousness and are commanded by the music instead of commanding it. In Meyerbeer Heine finds no such 'anarchy'; he places his melodies when and where he wills, in whatever place it is 'right' for them to be. Heine therefore agrees with those who, he alleges, in conversations held in the foyer of the Opéra during the première of *Les Huguenots*, compared Meyerbeer's art with that of Goethe.[1]

But—and now Heine turns from the work to the composer himself—'our great Maëstro', unlike Goethe, cannot distance himself: his love for his art, for music, is so passionate that his admirers are often worried that he may do himself a mischief.

For him the oriental image of the candle which consumes itself is indeed most apt. He hates all unmusical sounds—especially those made by cats; just having a cat in the same room can drive him out or even send him into a swoon. Meyerbeer would die for a musical phrase [*einen musikalischen Satz*] as others die for an article of faith [*Glaubenssatz*]. If, Heine elaborates, an angel blew his trumpet badly at the Last Judgement, Meyerbeer would be capable of remaining in his grave and refusing to participate in the general resurrection.

There is (and here the little knife up Heine's sleeve does seem to be showing for a moment in the midst of his paeans of praise) a party of opposition to Meyerbeer; this was called into being by the unprecedented success of *Robert le Diable* and small though it is, it has had ample time to rally and marshal its forces. It will, Heine feels sure, make all sorts of slanderous noises during the new opera's triumphant procession into public favour. Do not therefore be surprised, the poet tells his German readers, if you hear some discordant notes among the universal shouts of acclamation. The head of this opposition is a publisher who has not had the good fortune to acquire the rights to *Les Huguenots*; but Meyerbeer's enthusiasm for the cause of music, his personal modesty and noble, benevolent personality, are bound to win through.

And then Heine turns away from the composer to his audience—an audience which treated its visit to the première of *Les Huguenots* almost as though it were an attendance at High Mass. 'It was a marvellous sight . . . to see the most elegant audience in Paris assembled in the great opera house, festively attired, trembling with expectation, with solemn reverence, almost with religious devotion . . .'

Are Heine's readers supposed to swallow all that? Are they not supposed to suspect irony somewhere? By reiterating and exaggerating the kind of praise which Meyerbeer received from a large section of the French press Heine seems to be rendering Meyerbeer (with whom he was on good terms at this time) a friendly service; but some readers might well perceive a knowing wink here and there. 'You and I', Heine would seem to be saying to them, 'realize what's behind all this; but let us not rob the public of its pleasant illusions.'

And after Meyerbeer's opera, the Rothschild's ball.

Since I only left it at four o'clock this morning and have not yet had any sleep, I am too tired to report on the setting in which this festivity took place, the new palace built in Renaissance style; nor can I adequately report on the audience which, full of amazement, strolled about there. This audience consisted, as at all Rothschild soirées, of a strictly selected set of aristocratic illustrations, able to make an impression by reason of great name or high rank or (in the case of the ladies) beauty and finery. As for the palace and its decoration—here everything comes together which the spirit of the sixteenth century could invent and the money of the nineteenth century could pay for; here the genius of the visual arts competes with the genius of Rothschild. The palace and its decorations have been continuously work-ed on for two years, and the sums expended on them are said to be enormous. M. de Rothschild smiles when someone questions him about this. It is the Versailles of the absolute reign of money. One must, however, admire the flair with which everything has been done, as much as the costliness. M. Duponchel has directed the decoration and ornamentation, and everything bespeaks his good taste. In the whole and in detail one can also recognize the fine artistic sense of the lady of the house, who is not only one of the best-looking women in Paris but who is also distinguished in intellect and know-ledge and has had some practice in one of the arts—that of painting.[2]

Es ist das Versailles der absoluten Geldherrschaft—that de-scription of the Rothschilds' new home strikes the keynote of everything Heine will have to say about them in the years to come. The ironies are more patent here than in the Meyerbeer passage: the aristocratic guests seem to be part of the decora-tion, and all the guests are an 'audience' invited to admire the Rothschild splendour rather than friends and fellow citizens invited for their conversation. Yet there is a note of respect here which is respect less for money than for the way in which it is spent: on objects which are not tasteless even if they are ostentatious. And if it is true that nineteenth-century money can find nothing better to spend itself on than the products of a *past* era, then the choice of that era is, to Heine's way of thinking, a respectable one.

The Renaissance, as the age of François the First is called, has now become the rage in Paris. Everything is being furnished and cos-tumed in the taste of that period; with some this has even become a mania. What is the meaning of this sudden passion for the epoch of newly-awakened art, newly-awakened gaiety and delight in life, newly-awakened love of the witty and the ingenious in beautiful form? Perhaps there are some tendencies in our time which are declaring and defining themselves by means of such sympathies.³

Given the acquisitive rage of the nineteenth century, Heine would seem to be saying, given the worship of wealth to which Parisian society has devoted itself in the era of Louis Philippe, there are worse uses that could be made of money than the tasteful ostentation of the Rothschilds.

(ii)

On 8 March 1836, the very day on which this apparent puff for two of the most prominent Jewish figures in Paris appeared, anonymously, in the *Augsburg Gazette*, Heine sent to his publisher Julius Campe the manuscript of a new volume of his *Salon*. He had had a great deal of trouble with German censorship of late—not least because of the denunciation of his writings and of the 'Young Germany' movement by the influential literary critic and historian Wolfgang Menzel. Heine therefore tried to keep everything too censurable out of his new volume; he even suggested that Campe might call it *The Quiet Book* or *Nursery Tales* (*Märchen*).⁴ Being Heine, however, he could not keep his resentments to himself; they flooded into a long Preface written for this third volume of *Salon* but ultimately published as a separate pamphlet under the title *The Informer* (*Über den Denunzianten*). The two volumes appeared together in mid-July 1837.

The Informer contains a pointed reminder that Heine was nominally a Protestant (he speaks of '*our* Lord and Saviour Jesus Christ') and a public renunciation of the Jewish religion. Wolfgang Menzel, it must be remembered, had seen the 'Young German' movement as a subversive Jewish plot against the purity of German life and culture. Heine counters this as follows:

The public must be shown the true nature of this boastful champion of national integrity, this guardian of Germanness who constantly rails against the French and declares us poor Young Germans to be nothing but Frenchmen and Jews. To classify us as 'Jews' does little harm: we do not seek the allegiance of the common mob, and *the better educated surely realize that men who are accused of being enemies of Deism could harbour no sympathies for the synagogue. One does not address oneself to the faded charms of the mother when one grows tired of her ageing daughter.* But to make us out to be enemies of Germany, men who betray the Fatherland to France— that was a piece of villainy as cowardly as it is perfidious. (my italics)[5]

Against Menzel's attacks on the Jews as an alient irritant in the German body politic Heine asserts his Germanness and his love for his 'more immediate compatriots, the Westphalians'— though he does humorously lament the difficulties he has had with the case-endings of the German language. But that, as every German reader would know, is no reflection on the 'impure' German spoken in the Jewish home in which his childhood was spent; Gentile Berliners notoriously had the same difficulty.

In a later polemic work, however, the *Mirror for Swabians* (*Schwabenspiegel*, 1838) in which Menzel once again figures prominently, Heine does mock specifically Jewish 'distortions' of German speech. Recalling the time in which Menzel was still in favour of the emancipation of Jews, he imagines a scene in which Menzel is surrounded by grateful admirers who call him *die Memme des Vaterlandes*.[6] *Memme* here represents a variant of Yiddish *Mamme*, mother; but it is also the German word for a coward. Heine thus uses a caricature of Jewish speech to call the anti-Semite Menzel 'an unmanly coward'.

Salon III contains just two works: *Florentine Nights* (*Florentinische Nächte*) and *Elemental Spirits* (*Elementargeister*). The former once again presents Meyerbeer as an unequivocally 'German' or 'Northern' artist (this was, indeed, customary in French musical criticism of the time), but now the narrator also makes his music spiritually akin to that of Italy.

Here in Italy music is not represented by individuals; it reveals itself in the whole population, music has become incarnated in the people. With us Northerners things are different; there music incarnates itself in individual human beings, Mozart or Meyerbeer by name. But one other thing must be remembered: if one examines, with minute care, the best works of such Northern composers, one will find

Italian sunshine there, and the scent of Italian orange-blossoms. They belong to fair Italy, the true home of music, much more than to Germany.[7]

When *Florentine Nights* appeared again, in a posthumously published French edition whose text Heine himself had still had time to revise, the name 'Meyerbeer' was found to have been deleted.

The most celebrated passage in this work is Heine's evocation of the personality and art of the great violinist Niccolo Paganini. A carefully fostered legend had it that in return for the gift of virtuoso musicianship Paganini had sold his soul to the devil; and since he was usually accompanied on his German tours by his manager and factotum Georg Harrys, nothing would seem more obvious than to connect that apparently subservient figure with Old Nick himself. A sardonic friend informs the narrator of *Florentine Nights*:

'The ignorant populace . . . thinks that this companion is a Hanoverian writer of comedies and anecdotes called Georg Harrys, whom Paganini takes with him on his concert tours to look after his financial arrangements. The vulgar do not know that Georg Harrys's outward form has been borrowed by the devil and that the poor man's soul must, in the meantime, stay at Hanover, locked in a box along with other rubbish, until the devil restores its carnal envelope and accompanies Maestro Paganini through the world in the more dignified shape of a black poodle.[8]

Heine's caricature of a subservient and serviceable agent and manager contains, it is worth noting, not so much as a hint at Harrys's Jewish ancestry. We shall find him less reticent when he comes to talk, in the 1850s, of Parisian impresarios.

As for *Elemental Spirits*—this essay on Germanic folklore presented for most of its length no temptation to introduce portraits of Jews, or discussions of Jewish affairs. Right at the end, however, after quoting the ballad *Der Tannhäuser* in the form in which Arnim and Brentano had printed it in their collection of doctored folk-songs entitled *The Boy's Magic Horn (Des Knaben Wunderhorn)*, Heine adds a bonus: a personal variation or *Kontrafaktur* of the old Tannhäuser ballad in which, once again, he finds occasion to glance at the Jews he had known in Germany. Passing through Germany, the modern Tannhäuser stops over in Frankfurt on the Jewish sabbath and—characteristically—wedges praise of the Jewish religion between two allusions to items greatly favoured in Jewish cookery.

> Zu Frankfurt kam ich am Schabbes an,
> Und aß dort Schalet und Klöße;
> Ihr habt die beste Religion,
> Auch lieb ich das Gänsegekröse.

> [In Frankfurt I arrived on the sabbath,
> and ate *shalet* (*tsholent*) there, and dumplings.
> Your religion is the best there is:
> I like goose-giblets too.][9]

This is the first of many public allusions Heine makes to the sabbath dish he knows as *Schalet*—his juxtapositions here suggest that the best evidence one can adduce for the excellence of the Jewish religion is the excellent cookery of its orthodox adherents.

The pleasant tickling of Tannhäuser's palate during his stay in the Jewish quarter of Frankfurt is followed by a less pleasant aural experience at Potsdam: Eduard Gans's voice is so penetrating that his lectures at Berlin university can be heard sixteen miles away (see the *Prologue*, above). And last of all, Tannhäuser passes through Hamburg, a city of which Heine had many bitter memories:

> Zu Hamburg frug ich: warum so sehr
> Die Straßen stinken täten?
> Doch Juden und Christen versicherten mir,
> Das käme von den Fleeten.

> [In Hamburg I asked why
> there was such a stench in the streets.
> Jews and Christians, however, assured me
> that it came from the canals.]

Heine clearly suggests that when it comes to assaults on the sense of smell there is nothing to choose between the Jewish and the Gentile quarters of Hamburg; and the *Doch*, the 'however', in the last-quoted stanza slyly insinuates his Tannhäuser's suspicion that the source of the offence is not the canals, but the people who live alongside them. Like the adventures of his palate at Frankfurt and those of his ears at Berlin, the adventures of his nose at Hamburg have a moral and symbolic as well as a physical significance. No wonder that this modern Tannhäuser decides to shake the dust of Hamburg from his feet and to return to his Parisian Venusberg.

(iii)

The year that saw the appearance of *Salon III*, with its parting thrust at the Jews and Christians of Hamburg, also witnessed a new edition of the *Book of Songs*, that phenomenally successful collection of Heine's lyric poems first published in 1827. Various 'Dedications' which had graced that first edition were omitted in 1837; but in a new preface Heine paid tribute to two of the dedicatees, his uncle Salomon Heine and Rahel Varnhagen.

'Lyrical Intermezzo' is taken from a book that appeared in 1823 under the title *Tragedies (Tragödien)* and was dedicated to my uncle Solomon Heine. By means of that dedication I wanted to demonstrate the great respect due to that impressive man, and the gratitude I owe him for all the love he has shown me. 'Homecoming', which first appeared in *Pictures of Travel*, is dedicated to the late Friederike Varnhagen von Ense, and I can boast to have been the first of those who paid public homage to that great lady. August Varnhagen performed a noble deed when he put all petty considerations aside and published the letters in which Rahel reveals her total personality. This book came at the right time, when it could best do its work of strengthening and consoling. It came at a time that had need of such consolation. It is as though Rahel knew what her posthumous mission would be. She thought, it is true, that things would get better, and she waited; but when there proved to be no end to her waiting, she shook her head impatiently, looked at Varnhagen, and quickly died—only to rise again the more speedily. She reminds me of the legend of that other Rahel, who rose from her grave and stood by the wayside and wept, as her children went into captivity.

I cannot think of her without melancholy, that loving friend who always, untiringly, took an interest in me and often showed herself afraid for me, in those days of my youthful high spirits, in those days

when the flame of truth gave me more heat than illumination . . .
That time is past! I now have more light than heat . . .[10]

Whatever private resentments Heine may have felt towards his
uncle (and they were many, as his letters attest) he did always
feel that there was something impressive, something *großartig*,
about him. His public tribute to Uncle Salomon should there-
fore not be written off as a product of sycophantic expediency.
Nevertheless his words about the uncle have nothing of the real
warmth that can be felt in those about Rahel Varnhagen.
'Friederike Varnhagen von Ense' he calls her at first, as though
to remind readers of the status she had assumed in German
society after her baptism; but as he recalls her originality and
her kindness, Heine reverts to the name 'Rahel' which she had
been given at birth and by which she was called by most of
those who knew and who loved her. The Jewish atmosphere of
the passage becomes palpable as the biblical Rachel is recalled
and made into a prefiguration of her later namesake in a passage
so phrased that the political and social ills of Germany are
suggested along with the religious consolation and promise
associated with the risen Christ. It is probably no accident that
the biblical passage to which Heine refers in this tribute to a
woman known both as 'Rahel' and as Friederike is one that
occurs in almost the same form in the Old Testament and in the
New: in Jeremiah (31: 15) and in the Gospel according to St.
Matthew (2: 18). The 'children' that Rahel comforts are not
only the children of Israel.

(iv)

The third volume of August Lewald's *Theatre Review*
(*Allgemeine Theater–Revue*, 1838) contains a series of essays,
couched in the form of letters to Lewald, which Heine had
written during a brief stay in the country in May 1837. In these
'letters', entitled *On the French Stage* (*Über die französische
Bühne*), Heine describes and discusses what he had seen on
various French stages in the last few years and relates this to a
social scene in which the 'absolute reign of money', the *abso-*

lute Geldherrschaft he had diagnosed in his essay on Meyer-
beer and Rothschild, was everywhere open to view. He also
glances at another, more time-hallowed absolutism: that of
German monarchs who administered their countries as though
they were still living in the era of Frederick the Great. But,
Heine declares, there is comfort to be drawn from the history
of Israel.

The Lord will see to it that everything turns out for the best. He,
without Whose providence no sparrow falls from the roof and Coun-
cillor Streckfuß does not write a single line of verse, will surely not
allow whole nations to become the victims of miserable, short-
sighted, arbitrary government. I know for certain that He Who once
led the children of Israel out of the land of Egypt, the land of rigid
castes and deified oxen, will likewise show His signs and His won-
ders to the Pharaohs of modern times.[11]

'From time to time', Heine continues, with a glance at the
German middle classes, 'He will drive the presumptuous Phi-
listines back to their own territories, as He did long ago, when
Judges ruled over Israel.'

    The history of Israel, then, as recorded in the Bible, provides
parallels and paradigms for that of modern nations—and it also
contains prefigurations of those who, like Heine himself, seek
to predict and to warn. In his own times, he believed, the will
of the Lord, or the drive of history, can be perceived in the air
like the silent mysteries of the telegraph; but those who can
hear such messages resemble the prophets of old in that they
too are derided by the populace. Sometimes, indeed, they
suffer other pains and indignities recorded of the biblical
prophets:

Sometimes . . . those whom the prophet warns are angry at his
doom-laden message and stone him. Sometimes the prophet is cast
into a dungeon until his prophecy comes true—and his sojourn there
may be very long. The Lord always performs what seems best to Him
and what He has determined; but He takes his time over it.
    O Lord! I know You are Wisdom and Justice itself, and all You do
will be just and wise. But, I pray You: whatever it is You mean to
perform, do it a little more quickly! You are eternal and have time
enough; You can afford to wait. But I am mortal and I shall die.[12]

Having cast himself in the role of a modern equivalent of the

Hebrew prophets, Heine holds with the Lord one of those familiar colloquies, addressing to the Lord one of those respectful reproaches, which have provided a characteristic ingredient of the Jewish religious tradition from the time of Moses to that of the Chassidic rabbis and Tevye the Dairyman.

The 'letters' to Lewald published in *Theatre Review* also contain some reminiscences of events in the London theatres which Heine witnessed during his brief stay there some ten years earlier. Chief among these are his memories of Edmund Kean in the part of Shylock.

The Jew of Venice [Heine writes] was the first heroic role I saw him assume. I say 'heroic role' deliberately; for Kean did not play Shylock as a broken old man, as the kind of Sheva of hatred which Ludwig Devrient gave us, but rather as a hero. Thus he still lives in my memory: dressed in his sleeveless gaberdine of black silk which extended only to his knees so that the blood-red garment he wore beneath it, which reached down to his feet, stood out, by contrast, all the more. A hat of black felt with a broad rim turned up at both sides, its high crown enveloped by a blood-red band, covered a head whose long black hair and beard hung down in tangles, framing a healthily red face out of which two bright, keen eyeballs peered weirdly and frighteningly. His right hand clasps a staff [one notices the change of tense as recollection grows more vivid] that seems a weapon rather than a support. Only the elbow of his left arm leans upon it; the left hand sustains his dark head full of darker thoughts in an attitude at once treacherous and pensive, while he explains to Bassanio how the expression 'a good man' is to be understood. When he tells the story of Jacob and Laban's sheep, he cocoons himself, as it were, in his own words, suddenly breaking off: 'Ay, he was the third'; during a long pause he seems to mull over what he wants to say, you can see the story gradually rounding itself in his head; and when he suddenly continues, as though he had found the thread of his tale again: 'No, not take interest; not, as you would say,/Directly interest . . .', you think you are hearing, not a role learnt by heart, but a speech made up, thought out with effort, then and there. At the end of his tale his smiles, like an author happy with his own invention. Then he begins again slowly:

> Signor Antonio, many a time and oft . . .

> until he comes to the word 'dog', which he ejaculates with some violence. His anger rises:

> You call me misbeliever, cut-throat dog,

> And spit upon my Jewish gaberdine,
> And all for use of that which is mine own.

Then he steps nearer, erect and proud, saying with derision and bitterness:

> Well then, it now appears you need my help:
> Go to, then; you come to me, and you say,
> Shylock, we would have moneys:—you say so;
> You, that did void your rheum upon my beard,
> And foot me as you spurn a stranger cur
> Over your threshold: moneys is your suit.
> What should I say to you? Should I not say,
> 'Hath a dog money? is it possible
> A cur can lend three thousand ducats?'

But then, suddenly, he bows his neck, and with submissive gestures he says:

> or
> Shall I bend low, and in a bondman's key,
> With bated breath and whispering humbleness,
> Say this:
> 'Fair sir, you spit on me on Wednesday last;
> You spurned me such a day; another time
> You call'd me dog; and for these courtesies
> I'll lend you thus much moneys?'

Yes, his voice too is submissive at that instant, only faintly one hears in it his sullen rancour; but his eyes cannot dissemble, incessantly they shoot forth their poisoned arrows, and this struggle of outward humility and inner rage ends at the last word, the word 'moneys', with an eerily prolonged laugh which suddenly breaks off, while the face, convulsively distorted into submission, remains for some time mask-like, unmoving, while the evil eye stares out of it, threatening and deadly.

But all this is vain. The best description cannot bring the essential Edmund Kean before you. His manner of declamation, his broken utterance, has been successfully imitated many times; the parrot can mimic the voice of the eagle, king of the air. But the eagle's eye, the fiery piercing glance that can gaze into the sun to which it is kin—Kean's eye, a magic lightning-flash, a fiery flame—no common theatrical bird has ever been able to imitate that. Only in the eye of Frédéric Lemaître, when he acted the part of Kean [in Dumas's play of that name], I detected something that closely resembled the real Kean's glance.[13]

That last paragraph is no empty rhetoric. Heine evidently did feel disatisfied with what will seem to later readers a valuable record of Kean's way with Shakespeare's Jew, and he deleted the passage just quoted when he edited *On the French Stage* for inclusion in *Salon IV*. Kean's conception of Shylock was, however, to prove a powerful influence on his own portrait of that character when he came to draw it in *Shakespeare's Girls and Women*.

No consideration of the French stage would have been complete, in the late 1830s, without renewed discussion of the phenomenal success of Meyerbeer's *Robert le Diable* and *Les Huguenots*. Such a discussion in fact provides the climax, the real high point, of Heine's 'letters' to Lewald.

Heine begins by recalling the constant disputes which had gone on ever since the appearance of *Robert le Diable* between the champions of Meyerbeer and those of Rossini. Heine pretends, at first, to have remained neutral in this contest, but it soon appears that his instinctive preference is for Rossini. Searching for the psychological motive of this preference gives Heine the cue for one of his periodic self-presentations: he is being forced into all sorts of political and social battles while remaining by temperament a hedonist; and the sensuous melodies of Rossini will always appeal to such a temperament. Meyerbeer's works, on the other hand, subordinate melody to counterpoint and harmonic development, thus mirroring the mental divisions, the battles of will, of modern times, along with the passion and enthusiasm with which these are fought out. Where Rossini's operas are a musical equivalent of the Restoration, Meyerbeer's reflect the rage, the jubilation, and also the lamentations of those who have lived through the July Revolution—and that is the ultimate cause of their popular success. This somewhat dubious analysis leads Heine to a reflection on the problems that success such as Meyerbeer's brings with it.

He is the man of his age; and the age, which always knows how to choose its representatives, has raised him on its shield with tumultuous acclamation. It proclaims his rule and celebrates in him its joyous entrance. Being borne in triumph in this way is not, however, very comfortable; the misfortune or clumsiness of a single bearer can make the one who is being carried wobble precariously, or even do him serious damage. The garlands of flowers that are thrown at his head can, on occasion, cause injury instead of delight; if they issue from dirty hands, they can soil him. The excessive load of laurel with which he is garlanded can make him break out in a sweat of anxiety . . .[14]

Gradually, almost imperceptibly, the glorified portrait of Meyerbeer in the midst of his admirers is turning to caricature. But what of the man underneath all that laurel? Well—there certainly is a contrast.

In his external appearance and in his enjoyments Meyerbeer is modesty itself. Only when he has invited friends will you find a good table at his home. When I wanted to take pot luck with him one day, I found that his whole dinner consisted of a miserable dish of dried cod; I pretended, of course, that I had already dined.

As so often in these portraits, Heine portrays himself along with his models and victims; here, once again, we find him exhibiting that hedonist and *bon vivant* persona which he so often adopted in these years as a rebuff to those who wanted to make him into a full-time freedom fighter. Meyerbeer's austerity is emphasized and underlined by this feature of the poet's self-portrait.

Some readers (including, no doubt, Meyerbeer himself) would by now begin to suspect that what looked at first like a sympathetic and admiring portrait, a veritable advertisement for Maestro Giacomo, in fact concealed quite different feelings and intentions. Heine therefore hastens to assure us that personal austerity is not the same as miserliness—that in his relation with others, and especially in his financial dealings with needy German compatriots, Meyerbeer is generosity itself. This gives Heine his cue for bringing another member of the Meyerbeer family on to his stage.

Charity is a family virtue of the Meyerbeers, especially marked in his mother to whom I am in the habit of sending all those in need of help—never without success. This lady is the happiest mother on this earth. Everywhere she hears her son's praises sung; wherever she goes fragments of his music flap about her ears; everywhere she is bathed in the light of his fame—and at the opera, where the whole public expresses its enthusiasm for Giacomo in the most thunderous applause, his mother's heart trembles with delights we can hardly guess at. In the whole history of the world I know of only one mother to whom she might be compared: and that is the mother of St. Borromaeus, who saw her son canonized in her own life-time and who could kneel down and worship him in church along with thousands of the faithful.[15]

This wry presentation of the ultimate in proud Jewish mothers achieves an element of high ironic comedy through its excursion into the history of the Catholic church.

Concern with Meyerbeer's mother turns Heine's thoughts back to Meyerbeer's beginnings and his own first encounters with him. These took place in Berlin, he tells Lewald and his readers, 'between the university and the military barracks', where Meyerbeer was often to be found in the company of the music critic Adolf Bernhard Marx.

Dr Marx . . . belonged at that time to a certain dominant clique which, while waiting for the coming of age of a certain young genius who was regarded as legitimate heir to the throne of Mozart, paid continual homage to Sebastian Bach. Enthusiasm for Sebastian Bach was not only meant to fill that interregnum, but also to destroy the reputation of Rossini whom the governing clique of that musical Regency most feared and (therefore) most hated. Meyerbeer, at that time, was thought of as an imitator of Rossini, and Dr Marx treated him with a certain condescension, an affable kind of hauteur, which now amuses me greatly. 'Rossinism' was then accounted Meyerbeer's great crime; he had a long way to go before being accorded the honour of incurring hostility on his own account.[16]

Heine does not name the 'young genius' who was considered the white hope of a specifically German, a definitely non-Italian, non-Rossiniesque music; but there can be no doubt that he is referring once again to Felix Mendelssohn-Bartholdy.

From Berlin in the throes of the Bach revival, Meyerbeer escaped to Italy, where, as Heine tells us,

he enjoyed his life, surrendered to his private feelings, and composed those delicious operas in which Rossinism is heightened with the sweetest exaggeration: here gold is gilded over again, flowers are perfumed with additional, even stronger scents. That was Meyerbeer's happiest time; he wrote in pleasurable intoxication, stimulated by the sensual delights of Italy, and in life as in art he plucked the lightest flowers.[17]

'Gilding refined gold', as readers of *The Merchant of Venice* know, is hardly the most commendable of activities—and despite its apparently approving adjectives this passage can hardly be said to constitute high praise of the music Meyerbeer wrote in his 'Italian' period. And indeed, Heine tells us, Meyerbeer was too good a German to go on like this for any length of time.

This kind of thing could not, in the long run, satisfy a German temperament [*eine deutsche Natur*] . . . A fresh reaction took place, Signor Giacomo suddenly became a German again and threw in his lot with that of Germany: not the Germany of narrow-chested and narrow-hearted philistinism, old, decayed, and at its last gasp, but rather a young Germany, generous and open to the world, the Germany of a new generation which has made all the problems of humanity its own and inscribed them, not always on its banner, perhaps, but always (colourfully) on its heart.[18]

Ostensibly praising the new-found 'Germanness' of the Jewish maestro, Heine is in reality seizing an opportunity of slipping into the German press a paean to that 'Young Germany' movement with which he had himself been publicly associated and on which the full brunt of reactionary censorship had, of late, been brought to bear. As for the music which resulted from Meyerbeer's 'conversion'—this can only have been *Robert le Diable*, whose 'wretched libretto' (*der schlechte Text*) Heine had already censured in the poem–cycle *Angelique*. Now, in the guise of praising its representative nature, he also expresses doubts about the value of the music.

With its hero who does not know exactly what he wants, who is constantly at war with himself, *Robert le Diable* represents a true image of the moral vacillation of the age, an age which oscillated with such painful restlessness between virtue and vice, exhausting itself with aspirations and running against obstacles, and not always possessing the strength needed to resist the promptings of Satan. I do not love this opera, this masterpiece of faintheartedness—faintheartedness in respect not only of theme but also of execution. The composer did not yet trust his genius, he did not dare surrender himself to its inspiration, he timidly served the crowd instead of commanding it without fear.[19]

Heine would therefore agree with those who, as he avers, have called Meyerbeer 'a timid genius', *ein ängstliches Genie*; and that gives him the cue for broaching a subject which will henceforth loom large in his public comment on Meyerbeer, just as it had loomed large in his private—not always wholly reputable—dealings with Meyerbeer and on Meyerbeer's behalf. This is the maestro's eagerness to hear himself praised and his fear of adverse criticism. The passage which deals with this weakness relates it, unobtrusively, by means of the phrase *poignées de main*, to Louis Philippe's attempts to court popularity by shaking hands with all and sundry.

He lacked a victorious belief in himself . . . The slightest adverse criticism would frighten him, and so he flattered all his public's whims, eagerly offering *poignées de main* right and left, as though in music too he had come to recognize the principle that the people is sovereign and were now founding his reign on a majority vote—quite unlike Rossini, who ruled in the realm of music as an absolute king by the grace of God. Such timidity still marks Meyerbeer's life; he remains anxiously concerned with public opinion; but the success of *Robert le Diable* happily caused him to abandon such fears while in the act of composition. He writes with greater sureness now, and allows the great will of his soul to appear in her creations.

In other words: while Meyerbeer remains as anxious as ever to influence his public's judgement once his operas have been heard, he will not now allow such considerations to trim the sails of his music to every prevailing wind. With *Les Huguenots*, Heine concludes, Meyerbeer has won an eternal right of citizenship in 'the heavenly Jerusalem of art'.

There are no immediately apparent ironies in the praise of *Les Huguenots* which follows this passage; here, Heine asks his readers to believe, enthusiasm and artistic perfection, the integrity of a committed human being, and the shaping power of the true artist, are for once combined. The composer now appears as a man of genuine conviction in an age in which convictions have been replaced by opinions.

Meyerbeer, on whom the princes of this world have showered every conceivable honour, greatly appreciates distinctions of this kind, yet bears in his breast a heart that warms to the most sacred interests of mankind. He plainly confesses his reverence for the heroes of the revolution. It is fortunate for him that many Northern authorities do not understand music, for otherwise they would see in *Les*

Huguenots more than just a struggle between a Protestant and a Catholic party. Yet his convictions are not really political—even less are they religious. Meyerbeer's religion is that of Mozart, Gluck, and Beethoven: it is the religion of music. Music is what he believes in, only in that faith does he find felicity . . . I would go so far as to call him the apostle of this religion.

High praise, one might think; praise of a man who can walk with princes yet keep the common touch, a man of progressive views on political and social questions who nevertheless remains an artist first and foremost, a veritable apostle of music. Heine is piling it on; but very soon we find the image of the apostle giving way to a considerably less exalted, more domestic image, an image of which Heine will one day make the most hilarious use in his feud with Meyerbeer: the maestro is suddenly compared to a woman at her lying-in.

While other artists are content when they have created something beautiful, and even lose all interest in the work as soon as it has been completed, Meyerbeer finds that his worst labour pains begin after delivery. He cannot rest content

(and here, we notice, Heine modulates back into the 'religious' key)

until the creation of his spirit reveals itself to the rest of the people in its full glory, until the whole of the public is edified by his work, until his opera has poured into every heart the feelings he wishes to preach to all the world . . . As an apostle reckons neither effort nor pain when he tries to save a lost soul, so Meyerbeer will, should he hear that someone is denying his music, wrestle with him untiringly until he has converted him to himself; he rejoices more in the saving of a single lamb—even if it should be the insignificant soul of a single newspaper scribbler—than in the whole world of the faithful that worships him with orthodox steadfastness.

The mock-heroic and mock-religious tone forms a deliberate contrast with the pettiness of the concerns which are here described. This is the very stuff of comedy; and Heine makes that element explicit when he tells his readers that Meyerbeer's anxieties, his *Ängstlichkeiten und Bekümmernisse*, are apt to raise a smile.

When he is getting up a new opera, he becomes the tormentor of all musicians and singers, whom he tortures with incessant rehearsals. He can never rest content; a single false note in the orchestra is to him a dagger-blow that will cause his death. This disquiet pursues him long after the operas have been performed and been received with storms of applause. He remains as anxious as ever, and I think he will not be happy until a few thousand people that have heard his opera are safely dead and buried; these, at least, will not become apostates; of their souls he is sure. God can never do the right thing by him on days on which his operas are being performed. If it rains and the air is cold, he fears Mlle Falcon will catch a chill; if the evening is bright and warm, he fears that the lovely weather will tempt people into the open air and that the theatre will therefore be empty. Nothing exceeds the punctiliousness with which Meyerbeer reads his proofs once his music reaches the printing stage; his indefatigable mania for proof-correction has become proverbial among the artists of Paris. One must consider, however, that all this is due to the transcendent value he places on music, which he considers more, even, than his own life. When the cholera began to rage in Paris, I implored Meyerbeer to leave as quickly as possible; but he had to stay in Paris for several days yet, for he had business there that he could not put off: he had to collaborate with an Italian writer on the Italian version of *Robert le Diable*.[20]

As we can see, Heine is modulating, once again, towards the laudatory; and he does, indeed, go on to shower what seems unstinting praise on *Les Huguenots*, comparing it with the work of Mozart, Shakespeare, and Tasso. Since he displays no technical knowledge of music, Heine's praise is not backed up by analysis or demonstration; instead, he uses Meyerbeer's creation as an excuse for an excursus on the psychology of artists. The maestro's opera shows that a work may be bold when its creator is timid. *Les Huguenots* also raises, however, in Heine's mind at least, still wider questions.

How comes it that an artist who has, from his cradle onwards, had all the blood-sucking flies of care chased away from his head, who was born in the very lap of wealth and pampered by a family that readily, enthusiastically even, favoured all his inclinations, who found himself predestined to happiness beyond any mortal artist that has ever been—how comes it that such a man was able to feel the immense, the prodigious sorrows whose sighs and groans we hear in his music? For no musician could express so powerfully, so affectingly, what he does not feel himself. It seems strange that the artist whose material wants are wholly satisfied is beset all the more powerfully by moral afflictions. This is fortunate, however, for the public, which owes much of its ideal joys to the artist's sorrows. The artist is that child of whom the nursery tale tells—the child all whose tears are pearls. The world, alas, that evil stepmother, beats the child all the more unmercifully in order to ensure that it will weep as many genuine tears as possible.[21]

In Heine's references to Meyerbeer's wealthy relatives there is no hint that any of them showed the hostility towards artistic aspiration which he had experienced among some of the rich members of his own family—and there can be little doubt that he was painfully aware of this contrast.

We heard earlier in this Epistle on Meyerbeer that the maestro's work was not without its critics and detractors. Heine now turns to these, and addresses himself first to the charge that *Les Huguenots*, and (to a lesser extent) *Robert le Diable*, was short on melody. Not at all, he replies; the melodies *are* there, but instead of being allowed to obtrude themselves 'egoistically' on the hearers' undivided attention, they are combined into harmonic configurations which reflect a complicated modern society and its multiplicity of simultaneous human concerns. There is another charge against Meyerbeer's work, however, that Heine does not feel able to rebut—and it is his desire to introduce, and concur with, this charge that now brings one more important element into his portrait of Meyerbeer.

Great wealth was expended on his education, and his mind was receptive. He was initiated into all the realms of learning, and in this respect he differs from most musicians . . . What he learnt became second nature to him; the school of the world then developed him to his highest potential; and he now belongs to that small company of Germans whom even the French have recognized as models of urbanity.[22]

Such *Bildung*, such heights of cultivation, Heine continues, were perhaps necessary to create *Les Huguenots*, to give it form with a proper sense of what today's society needs. But has not what is gained in comprehensiveness and perspicuity entailed losses elsewhere? Heine thinks it has. An artist as highly cultivated as Meyerbeer is said to be loses the capacity for sharp accentuation, the ability to paint in effectively stark colours, the originality of thought, the immediacy of feeling, which can be admired in rougher, more limited, less cultivated natures (*bei rohbegrenzten, ungebildeten Naturen*).

Meyerbeer, then, appears as the very type of the hyper-cultivated, cerebral artist whose education, made possible by family wealth sympathetically deployed, has sapped his originality and immediacy. Heine softens the blow of this judgement by his apparent denigration of ruder creators; and he gives it a humorous, apparently inoffensive turn by allowing the maestro's little daughter, Blanka, to have the last word on the subject of the *Bildung*, the education and cultivation, with which her father was so anxious to endow her as well as himself.

'How unlucky it is for me to have educated parents! From morning till evening I have to learn every conceivable thing by heart, to sit still and behave myself, while the uneducated children down there can happily run about all day and amuse themselves!'[23]

The Meyerbeer family, as Heine here presented it, practised in its modern, emancipated way two of the virtues traditionally enjoined on Jews: that of charity, and that of supporting learning. Learning, however, education and cultivation as it was understood in Meyerbeer's day, may exact a price. It may atrophy the natural man and may dry up the springs of spontaneous creation.

The portrait of Meyerbeer which Heine presents to his readers in *On the French stage* is that of a complex, contradictory individual artist; but it also seeks at every point to relate the work of that artist to more general questions: the relationship between music and politics; the different factions which competed for the public ear in Parisian musical life, and in the musical life of Europe; and last but by no means least, the meaning of popularity in art. By 1837 Heine had come to have grave doubts about the value of such popularity—doubts that appear clearly in his strictures of those aspects of Meyerbeer's work which show him 'timidly serving the crowd instead of commanding it without fear'.[24]

(v)

I know a good Christian of Hamburg who could never reconcile himself to the idea that our Lord and Saviour was a Jew. He grew thoroughly cross whenever he had to admit to himself that the pattern of perfection, the man worthy of highest veneration, was related to those unblown long noses whom he saw hawking their wares about the streets, and whom he found even harder to bear when, like himself, they engaged in the wholesale trade, selling spices and dyestuffs and thus prejudicing his own interests.

What this Hammonian worthy feels about Jesus Christ I feel about William Shakespeare. I grow queasy when I think that he is, when all is said and done, an Englishman . . .[25]

So begins the text Heine was commissioned to write as an accompaniment to a series of engravings depicting Shakespeare's female characters. It illuminates two kinds of anti-Semitism. The first is that of contempt: through the eyes of the Hamburg merchant we look at the wretched pedlars and hawkers—many of them immigrants from Eastern Europe—who fail to conform to German patterns of beauty, who do not use their handkerchiefs in the refined German way, and who scratch a living in a way a German tradesman would disdain. But then comes the second kind: suddenly we see, again through the Hamburg merchant's eyes, how these Jewish itinerants begin to enter the same trades as well-settled German Christians, and making a good job of it. They now become serious competitors; and that brings with it the anti-Semitism of jealousy and fear.

Fear and contempt are distorting agents; but—Heine implies—is not all our apprehension of national and individual character bound to be distorted to some degree? Is there not an affinity between the mechanism at work in his own portrayal of the English and that which makes the good Christian of Hamburg dislike Jews? And finally: is not the Hamburg merchant *right* in his perception of the vast gulf between the mass of the people and the world-historical individuals that spring from it? Heine's own dealings with Shakespeare suggest that in this one respect at least he may well *be* right; but our recognition of this fact hardly serves to increase our respect for the motives, or the discernment, of the 'good Christian of Hamburg'.

The persona Heine chooses to adopt in *Shakespeare's Girls and Women* turns out to be, once again, a close relative of the cicerone who had spoken in *Letters from Berlin*. It is that of a guide who shows us round a picture-gallery, rattling his keys to command attention, interrupting the spectator's contemplation of the exhibits with his explanatory patter, obtruding his own reminiscences and reflections. The gallery contains only one Jewish character, Jessica from *The Merchant of Venice*; and for her the guide shows little liking. She robbed and betrayed the father who loved her, made common cause with his enemies, joined with these enemies in speaking ill of her father . . . She is a shallow thing whose main concern is adventure, escape from her father's dull house.

Did Shakespeare want to depict a Jewess here? Surely not! What he depicts is a daughter of Eve, one of those beautiful birds who flutter out of the paternal nest as soon as they have learnt to fly, in order to join some beloved male. So Desdemona followed the Moor, and Imogen Posthumus. That is woman's way. What is distinctive about Jessica, however, is the shamefaced hesitation she cannot overcome when asked to dress up as a boy. In this one trait, perhaps, it is possible to recognize the peculiar chastity of the Jews which lends their girls such wondrous charm.[26]

This leads our guide to speculate about the historical reasons for such chaste hesitations—he sees it as a 'spiritualistic' reaction against the 'sensualism' of surrounding peoples like the Egyptians, the Phoenicians, the Assyrians, and the Babylonians; and that, in its turn, gives him his cue for speculations about the moral affinity between Jews and Germans.

The Jews are a chaste, a continent, I might almost say an abstract people, and in the purity of their morals they approximate most clearly to the Germanic tribes . . . It is indeed striking to note how intimately akin are the two moral peoples, the Jews and the Germans. This kinship did not emerge historically because the great family chronicle of the Jews, the Bible, served the whole Germanic world as a textbook, or because the Jews and the Germanic peoples were from early on the most inexorable foes of the Romans and therefore natural allies. There is a deeper cause: both peoples were from the beginning so similar in nature that the Palestine of yore might be regarded as an oriental Germany, just as present-day Germany should be considered the home of the sacred word, the mother-soil of prophecy, the stronghold of pure spirituality . . . But not only Germany bears the physiognomy of Palestine; the rest of Europe too is raising itself up to the Jews. I say 'raising itself up', for from the start the Jews carried within themselves the modern principle, which is only today becoming visibly manifest among the nations of Europe . . . The Jews adhered only to the law, to the abstract idea, like our more recent cosmopolitan republicans, who respect as their highest good not the land of their birth or the person of their prince, but only the law. Cosmopolitanism, it might truly be said, sprang from the soil of Judaea; and Christ who (*pace* the Hamburg spice merchant mentioned earlier) was truly a Jew, founded what may well be called a propaganda of world-citizenship [*eine Propaganda des Weltbürgertums*].[27]

William Rose, whose translation I have just adapted, points out that the idea of an affinity between Germans and Jews remains constant with Heine from now on, and rightly stresses how significant it is that the word he employed to describe such affinity should be *Wahlverwandtschaft*—the chemical term Goethe had used as the title of a novel which depicts the involuntary, mutual attraction towards one another experienced by people with kindred natures.

In the late 1830s Heine's imperfect sympathies with Jessica found expression in a poem, too, in which *The Merchant of Venice* forms the background to an abortive love-affair and provides an emotional commentary on it.

> Als ich dich zum ersten Male
> In der Welt von Pappe sah,
> Spieltest du in Gold und Seide
> Shylocks Tochter: Jessica.
>
> Klar und kalt war deine Stimme,
> Kalt und klar war deine Stirne,
> Und du glichst, o Donna Clara,
> Einer schönen Gletscherfirne.

Und der Jud verlor die Tochter,
Und der Christ nahm dich zum Weibe;
Armer Shylock, ärmrer Lorenz!
Und mir fror das Herz im Leibe.

Als ich dich zum andren Male
In vertrauter Nähe sah,
War ich dir der Don Lorenzo
Und du warst mir Jessica.

[When I saw you first
in the cardboard world
You were dressed in gold and satin, and you played
Shylock's daughter: Jessica.

Cold and clear was your voice,
cold and clear was your brow—
you resembled, Donna Clara,
a beautiful snow-capped glacier.

And the Jew lost his daughter,
and the Christian took you to wife.
Poor Shylock! Poorer Lorenzo!
My heart froze in my body.

When I saw you again,
in familiar proximity,
I was your Lorenzo,
and you were my Jessica.][28]

The end is foreseeable: the actress and her lover turn out to be ill-matched, love dries up, freezes to death: 'Jessica turns her back on me.' The poem in which all this happens is aptly entitled *Cold Hearts [Kalte Herzen]*.

Lorenzo, the poet's *alter ego* in this poem, does not emerge as a sympathetic character from Heine's account of *The Merchant of Venice*, any more than the other Christian males who appear in that play. The opportunity to bait a Jew brings out the worst in them; and that gives Heine his cue, in *Shakespeare's Girls and Women*, to reflect on anti-Jewish feelings in his own time. Quoting, ostensibly, from a private letter he had received from Frankfurt, Heine maintains that the popular instinct which is directed against the Jews is aroused by resentments that have a basis in real life, but is mistaken in its object. Hatred of the Jews was always essentially hatred of the rich—of men who had the means to make life more joyous and pleasurable than was possible to the hewers of wood and drawers of water.

What the common people hated in the Jew was always the man who possessed money; it was always the heaped-up metal which drew down upon the Jews the lightning of popular wrath. From the spirit of each age that hatred then drew its changing slogans. In the Middle Ages the slogan was draped in the sombre colours of the Catholic Church; the Jews were killed and their houses sacked 'because they slew Christ'. The logic was the same as that used by black Christians who ran about during the massacre of St. Domingo brandishing the image of the crucified Saviour and shouting fanatically: "Les blancs l'ont tué, tuons tous les blancs!"[29]

But these black Christians, Heine makes his correspondent continue, also had some justice on their side. The whites, after all, were living in luxury while blacks had to work, 'receiving no wages but a little rice flour and many lashes of the whip'. In the same way the common people of the Middle Ages had reason to resent the rich—a resentment which the powers that enjoined them to practice self-denial, stay within their station, and obey duly constituted authority, channelled in the direction of the Jews.

We no longer live in the Middle Ages. The common people is becoming more enlightened, it no longer massacres the Jews *en masse*, and no longer decks its hatred with the fair mantle of religion. Our age has lost the naïve fervour of faith, traditional resentments are clothed in modern terms of speech, and the mob that assembles in beer cellars or Chambers of Deputies declaims against the Jews with mercantile, industrial, scientific, and even philosophic arguments. In our present time only incorrigible hypocrites will give their hatred a religious colouring and persecute the Jews for Christ's sake; the larger crowd confesses freely that material interests are at stake here, and uses any means in its power to make it more difficult for Jews to deploy their industrial skills. Here in Frankfurt, for instance, only twenty-four persons who profess the Mosaic faith are allowed to marry in any one year—a measure designed to prevent an increase in number and the severe competition this would bring in its train for

Christian traders. Here the true reason for hatred of Jews shows its face, a face that now bears no dark, fanatic monkish mien, but shows, rather, the slack features of an 'enlightened' huckster afraid that the Israelites' business sense will outstrip his own capacity for higgling and haggling.

But is it the Jews' fault that their business sense has become so hypertrophied? No—it is the fault, rather, of that medieval madness which failed to understand the importance of industry, which looked on trade and especially on money transactions as something shameful, and which therefore pushed the most profitable portions of this branch of industry into the hands of the Jews. Excluded from other trades, the Jews had of necessity to become the keenest merchants and bankers. They were forced to become wealthy and were then hated because of their wealth; and although Christendom has now abandoned its prejudices against industry and the Christians have become just as rascally and just as rich as the Jews in industry and in trade—yet the people's traditional hatred has clung to the Jews who are still regarded and still hated as the representatives of money ownership. You see, in world history both sides are right: the side of the hammer and that of the anvil.[30]

Though this passage purports to come from a letter written by someone else, it bears many of the hallmarks of Heine's own style: the metaphor of heaped-up metal that attracts lightning, the symbolic St. Domingo anecdote, the mingling of Hegelian and Saint-Simonian arguments—all these point strongly to his authorship. In the economy of *Shakespeare's Girls and Women* it represents his answer to the Hamburg merchant with whose prejudices the work had opened, and his attempt to explain the standpoint of Shylock's enemies as well as that of Shylock himself.

But if these formulations are indeed Heine's, he had good reason for distancing them in the way he does. He was always powerfully aware of economic factors in anti-Judaism as in everything else; but he could never take economic analyses for the sole truth. He knew how much of Christian hostility, from St. John Chrysostom to Luther, was in fact religious; he knew the meaning of the Christian legend of the Wandering Jew, knew of the Christian sense of the 'mystery of Israel', and the way Israel's fate was thought to bear witness to God's will. He knew also, as we have seen, that the Jewish people was to some degree protected by the Christian dispensation, and that it had more to fear from a new paganism than from Christianity itself. And even within the economic sphere he was far removed from simplistic class analysis: he may present Shylock as a primitive capitalist, but he also sees his financial power nullified by oppression, by his position—as K. J. Höltgen has said—as a barely tolerated alien.

It will, by now, have become apparent that the poet's real interest focuses, not on Jessica, but on her father. His commentary on Shylock, which should, by rights, have figured only peripherally in a book devoted to Shakespeare's *female* characters, turns out to be more elaborate than any other. It is conceived, not only as a personal reading of *The Merchant of Venice* in the light of Jewish history and the experience of oppression, but also as a counterblast to the most influential discussion of that play in Heine's own time: August Wilhelm Schlegel's in *Lectures on Dramatic Art and Literature* (*Vorlesungen über dramatische Kunst und Literatur*, 1809 ff.). Schlegel would have us see in Shylock only the 'selfish cruelty of the usurer' and in his adversaries 'a royal merchant with a retinue of noble friends'. What Heine thought of that 'retinue of noble friends', we have already seen; let us now look at his dealings with Shylock.

His commentary begins with another reminiscence of Edmund Kean's performance, as he had witnessed it in 1827. What he shows us this time, however, is not what went on on the stage, but what effect Kean's assumption of the role had on the audience. The description of a British lady which begins the commentary differs so sharply from Heine's usual descriptions of English men and women that one may suspect her to be, in fact, Jewish—a nobler specimen of Jewish womanhood than Jessica.

When I saw this piece played in Drury Lane there stood behind me in the box a pale British beauty who, at the end of the fourth Act, wept passionately, and many times cried out, 'The poor man is wronged!' It was a countenance of noblest Grecian cut, and its eyes were large and black. I have never been able to forget them, those great black eyes which wept for Shylock!

When I think of those tears, I must include *The Merchant of Venice* among the tragedies, although the framework of the play is ornamented with laughing masks and sunny faces, satyr forms and putti, and though the poet himself meant to make it a comedy. Originally, perhaps, Shakespeare wanted to please the mob by representing a werewolf at bay, a hated creature of fable that craves blood, pays for that yearning with daughter and ducats, and is then laughed to scorn for his pains. But the genius of the poet, the world spirit informing and controlling him, is stronger, always, than his own will; and so it came to pass that in Shylock he presented—despite glaring elements of caricature—the justification of an unfortunate sect which Providence, from inscrutable motives, loaded with the hatred of the lower and the higher mob, and which was not invariably inclined to requite this hatred with love . . .[31]

That may be seen as a characteristically Hegelian version of intentionalist criticism. Shakespeare intended presenting Shylock in the medieval way—but since he was a world-historical individual, the spirit of world history spoke through him, shouldered out his original intention, and made him present Shylock as something quite different. In that presentation Shylock looks much more respectable than any of his adversaries, with the sole exception of Portia! Our guide maintains, and demonstrates in detail that may have been borrowed by Heine from Eduard Gans's essay on Shylock and the Law, that if Christendom held no characters except those here shown as Shylock's enemies, *The Merchant of Venice* would constitute as savage a satire on Christianity as had ever been penned.

But, the guide concludes, Shakespeare and the world spirit that spoke through him did not really make *The Merchant of Venice* a satire on Christianity. What he has ultimately represented is not the difference between Judaism and Christianity at all, but rather the psychology of the oppressed. In Shylock he depicted in exemplary fashion the mingled madness, joy, and pain that seizes the oppressed when they see a chance to get their own back on those who have demeaned and tortured them—when they can pay their oppressors back, with interest, in their own coin.

Shakespeare's portrait of a Jew, then, is not part of a contrast between Judaism and Christianity; but it does embody a world-historical contrast none the less. The contrast between Shylock and Portia, Heine maintains with Anna Jameson, expresses itself in the nature of the language these two characters are made to speak and that of the houses they inhabit: it is the confrontation of a child of misfortune and one of good luck, Nazarene and Hellene, of rigid serious-mindedness hostile to art and gay, artistic Renaissance humanism. Shylock and Portia are fully individualized; but they are also embodiments of forces which have shaped, and are shaping, the modern world.

After his reminiscence of theatre-going in England and of a raven-haired spectator who felt that Shylock had been wronged, Heine causes his narrator to introduce another reminiscence—of Italy, this time, where the two forces represented by Shylock and Portia may be felt to have had their most fateful world-historical encounters. On the Rialto in Venice, the guide says, he searched for Shylock with his Jewish gaberdine, his suspicious face, his ill-sounding voice croaking 'Three thousand ducats—well . . .' He was anxious, he tells us in Heine's own best vein, to give him a piece of good news: his cousin, M. de Shylock of Paris (James de Rothschild is clearly meant) has become the most powerful baron in Christendom and has been decorated by His Most Catholic Majesty of Spain with the Order of Isabella, founded to celebrate the expulsion from Spain of the Jews and the Moors. Not finding Shylock on the Rialto, however, our guide went to look for him in that Venetian synagogue where in Shakespeare's play he arranged to meet his friend Tubal.

The Jews happened just then to be celebrating their sacred Day of Atonement and stood wrapped in their white prayer shawls with uncanny noddings of their heads, looking like an assembly of ghosts. There they stood, these poor Jews, fasting and praying, since early morning; they had tasted neither food nor drink since the evening before, and had also begged the forgiveness of all their acquaintances for any evil things they might have said of them during the past year so that God might pardon them too—a beautiful custom, which exists, strangely enough, among people who have, we are told, remained strangers to the teachings of Christ.

But while, looking around for old Shylock, I passed all these pale, suffering Jewish faces in review, I made a discovery which—alas!—I cannot suppress. I had visited the madhouse of San Carlo that same day, and now it occurred to me, in the synagogue, that in the glances of the Jews there flickered the same dreadful, half-staring and half-unsteady, half-crafty and half-stupid expression which I had seen shortly before in the eyes of the lunatics in San Carlo. This indescribable, puzzling look indicated not so much absence of mind as the supremacy of a fixed idea. Has faith in that extra-mundane thunder-God whom Moses preached perhaps become the fixed idea of a whole people, so that, though they have for two thousand years suffered in straitjackets and shower-baths, they just will not give it up—like that lunatic lawyer whom I saw in San Carlo, who would not be dissuaded from the thought that the sun was an English cheese, the rays of which were long red maggots, and that one of these maggot-rays was gnawing away at his brain?

It is not that I want to dispute the value of that fixed idea. All I want to say is that those who have it are too weak to control it, and that it therefore makes them depressed and incurable. How great a martyrdom they have already endured on its account! What greater martyrdom awaits them in the future! I shudder at the thought, and an infinite pity ripples through my heart. Throughout the whole Middle Ages, right up to the present day, the predominant world view did not stand in direct contradiction to the idea which Moses had laid upon the Jews as their own special burden, which he had tied onto them with sacred leather thongs, which he had cut into their flesh. They did not differ from Christians and Mohammedans in essentials, were not opposed to them by some antagonistic synthesis of beliefs—it was only exegesis and shibboleths that differentiated them. But if one day Satan, or sinful pantheism (from which all the saints of the Old and New Testaments and of the Koran may preserve us!), should conquer, there will gather over the heads of the poor Jews a tempest of persecution that will far surpass all they have had endure before.[33]

This passage conveys something of the mingled attraction and repulsion Heine felt when contemplating observant Jews. On the one hand he stresses the humane spirit of the Day of Atonement, and the irony that it should be the Jews who sounded to the depths the 'Christian' principles of atonement and forgiveness. On the other hand the passage conveys unmistakably Heine's feeling that full commitment to this ancient religion, literal adherence to its multitudinous commandments and prohibitions, partook of the nature of an *idée fixe*, that it was even akin to lunacy. We now understand better why an earlier passage in *Shakespeare's Girls and Women* had called the Jews an unfortunate *sect*; but at the same time we cannot but be impressed by the symbolism of the Jewish religion as Heine here presents it: the wearing of prayer shawls, the Yom

Kippur fasting and prayer, the phylacteries on head and arm, and the circumcision enjoined by Moses. The religion to which such symbolism attached the Jews does not, in Heine's eyes, differ in essentials from other great world religions, from Christianity and Mohammedanism—it is when the hold of these religions weaken that the worst persecutions will come upon the Jews. The dire prophecy contained in the last sentence of the passage just quoted supplements the final paragraphs of *Towards a History of Religion and Philosophy in Germany* in ways which show once again how correctly Heine could read the signs of his times.

Into the Yom Kippur setting, so essential to Heine's purposes, thoughts of Shylock now intrude for the last time.

Though I looked all around in the synagogue of Venice, I could not see the face of Shylock anywhere. And yet it seemed to me that he must be there, hidden under one of those white robes, praying more fervently than any of his fellow believers, with stormy wildness, even with madness, to the throne of Jehovah, the stern divine monarch. I did not see him. Towards evening, however, when, as the Jews believe, the gates of heaven are closed and no further prayer can enter, I heard a voice in which tears flowed that were never wept from human eyes. . . . It was a sobbing that might have moved a stone to pity . . . These were sounds of agony that could come only from a heart that held locked within it all the martyrdom which a tormented people had endured for eighteen centuries . . . And it seemed to me that I knew this voice well; I felt as though I had heard it long ago, when it lamented, with the same tone of despair: 'Jessica, my child!'[34]

This visionary recreation of Shylock in a nineteenth-century synagogue scene may well be thought Heine's most successful attempt to express that 'great Jewish sorrow', *der große Judenschmerz*, which it had been his ambition to shape into art ever since his work with Gans and with Zunz, with Moser and with Marcus, during his fateful stay in Berlin. His sympathies with Shylock and his more modern progeny may have been imperfect—but they *were* sympathies just the same.

CHAPTER 6
Martyrs, Artists, and Plutocrats

(i)

The opening chapter of *The Rabbi of Bacherach*, written in the 1820s, acquired a new and terrible relevance in 1840—for that year saw a revival of the blood-libel, the accusation of ritual murder, which had furnished the excuse for so many massacres in the Middle Ages. This time the accusation was made in Damascus, whose Jewish community was charged with murdering a Capuchin monk and using his blood for ritual purposes. Torture was used to extract 'confessions'; and the French government, which had political interests in Syria, did not protest with anything like the vigour one would expect from a civilized and liberal nation. Indeed, the French consul in Damascus, Count Ratti-Menton, aided and abetted the Syrian authorities in their action against the Jews; and Adolphe Thiers, the President of the Council of Ministers, whom Heine admired as a historian if not always as a statesman, did not dissociate himself from the consul or refuse unequivocally to give credence to the accusation. To make the irony complete it turned out to be the consul of Austria—reactionary Austria!—who showed the greatest zeal in exposing the falsehood of the accusations and seeking the release of the tortured Jews.

More than most of his 'assimilated' contemporaries, Heine felt that all this was his business, that what was happening in Damascus concerned him immediately. He saw to it that influential journals were supplied with documents detailing the inhuman ways in which 'confessions' had been extracted from the unfortunate Jewish suspects, offering to subsidize the publication of such documents out of his own pocket; and what is more important, he deployed every weapon in his writer's armoury to discredit the blood-libel. On 7 May 1840 he despatched an article to the *Augsburg Gazette* in which he denounced what was happening in Damascus as a return to the darkest Middle Ages.

While we in Europe use such medieval tales as material for literature and take delight in such naïve horror stories as used to inspire great fear in our ancestors, while we use stories of witches, werewolves, and Jews that need the blood of pious Christian children for their Satan worship as literary material for poems and novels, while we laugh and forget, the Orient is beginning to recall old superstition in a more sinister way and to pull very serious faces that speak of dark rage and pain and despair and death. The executioner wields his instruments of torture, and on the rack the Jew 'confesses' that as Passover approached he needed some Christian blood to moisten his dry cakes of unleavened bread and that he therefore butchered some old Capuchin monk.[1]

Heine then proceeds to warn his readers that what is being done to Syrian Jews today may be done to Christians tomorrow, somewhere in the dying Turkish empire. They had better look out, and nip such atavistic cruelties in the bud.

An article dated 14 May 1840 returns to the attack with redoubled vigour, denouncing Ratti-Menton and the ultramontane faction that controlled the French journal *L'Univers*, where torturers and libellers were given support and comfort. Here Heine sought to analyse the political considerations that prevented Thiers from condemning outright those of his countrymen who maintained in the teeth of justice and reason that Jews were in the habit of eating aged Capuchins; and he proclaimed with earnestness and vigour his conviction that in championing the cause of the Damascene Jews he was championing the interests of all mankind. If Western nations encouraged reversions to medieval barbarism in the Middle East, they were harming the cause of freedom and justice in the whole world.[2] A later article, dated 25 July 1840, seeks to leave no doubt that the correspondent is not being carried away by undue affection for, or feelings of special kinship with, the Jews of Damascus.

What is at stake here is not Ratti-Menon's reputation for impeccable virtue or the character of the Damascene Jews. Perhaps there is not much to choose between them, perhaps the latter are as unworthy of our love as the former is too low for our hatred. That, however, is not the point. The Orient must be made an example to show once and for all that we will no longer sanction the use of torture.[3]

The Austrian and British consuls in Syria had seen this point of principle, and had asked for a fair trial at which no evidence extracted by torture would be admissible; but the French were taking the part of the torturers and resisting such calls for justice.

Heine's articles for the *Augsburg Gazette*, we must remember, were published anonymously, like all such contributions. In the 1972 edition of the *Encyclopaedia Judaica*, however, Gershom Scholem has lent the authority of his name to the legend that from 1840 Heine 'signed his correspondence from Paris' in the *Augsburg Gazette* 'with a *magen David* instead of his name', and that this should be regarded as 'a remarkable indication of his Jewish identification in spite of his conversion' (Vol. XI, col. 696). There is no evidence which would lead us to suppose that Heine *chose* the hexagram as his 'signature'—it was a device assigned to him by the editors of the journal in question. Nor is there any evidence that either he, or the editors, or the majority of his readers, realized that this hexagram had occasionally been called *magen David* since the fourteenth century, and that it was to become, under that name, the most widely recognized symbol of Judaism and the Jewish people in our own time. We have no reason to assume that when he speaks of 'the shield of David', he would have us see it in the shape of a six-pointed star.

What can not be doubted, however, is that despite the anonymity of his contributions many readers of the *Augsburg Gazette* recognized Heine's style and manner. He therefore felt vulnerable to a charge that was making the rounds at the time: the charge of excessive Jewish influence on what was being written in the press. His article of 27 May 1840 begins by facing this head on. It attacks a German correspondent who had suggested that vast sums of 'Jewish' money were being expended to exaggerate the Damascus affair in European eyes, and that the French press in particular was in the hands of rich Jews eager to advance the cause of their co-religionists, at the expense, if need be, of the political interests of France. In a skilful counter-manœuvre Heine insinuates that the boot is on the other foot; that it is the correspondent making these charges who is involved in a conspiracy designed to lead German opinion astray in the interests of French Middle-Eastern politics. Then he goes on to delimit his field. 'We shall leave the personality and the motives of this correspondent unexamined [*unbeleuchtet* is the term Heine actually uses, suggesting the murky darkness within which his adversary has been operating], and shall also refrain from any examination of what actually happened in Damascus [for that, we must remember, Heine had done his best to ensure that authentic documents reached German journals]—all we offer is a few remarks to correct what has been said about the connection between the Damascus affair, French Jews, and the French press.' He is only interested in the truth, Heine protests: 'and with regard to the Jews here in France it is possible that our testimony will go against them rather than speak in their favour.' For alas: the German correspondent who speaks of vast sums being expended by French Jews on behalf of their Syrian co-religionists is wretchedly misinformed. Heine would praise the French Jews rather than blame them if they showed such financial zeal 'to save the honour of their maligned religion'.

The Jews in France have been emancipated too long for the tribal bonds not to have loosened and slackened. All of them have become submerged or—to use a better expression—been dissolved in the nationality of the French. They are Frenchmen just like the rest, they too have fits of enthusiasm that last for twenty-four hours, or even three days when the sun is hot; and that refers to the better ones among them.[4]

Here, at the beginning of his group-portrait of French Jews, we see the poet quietly inverting yet another anti-Semitic argument. It is not the Jews who are corrupting the French in order to bring about *une France juive*—it is the French who are assimilating the Jews to such an extent that they come to share such alleged national failings as Gallic fickleness. What, then, becomes of the Jewishness of these Frenchmen professing the Mosaic faith? Heine offers the following answer:

Many of them still observe the ceremonies of Jewish worship, as an external cult, in a mechanical way, without knowing why, out of old habit; there is no trace of inner faith, for in the Synagogue as in the

Christian Church the witty acid of Voltairean criticism has done its destructive work.

Again we witness the inversion of a stereotype: instead of seeing Jewish assimilation harming Christianity, we are invited to watch Gentile scepticism eroding the religion of the Jews. Only then, after these important caveats, do we come to the statement which is so often quoted out of context: 'Among the French Jews, as among the other Frenchmen, gold is the god of the time, and industry is the predominant religion.' The real force and drift of Heine's argument can best be seen, as so often, by contrasting it with that of Marx. The religion of money, Heine tells us, is not to be equated with Judaism, as Marx was to assert soon afterwards. On the contrary: Jews have been swept along by a current of materialism and commercialism in the non-Jewish society that has accepted them; and their history has ensured that they proved strong swimmers in these muddy waters. The ability to turn propositions 'standing on their head' into counter-propositions 'standing on their feet', for which Marx is so often given credit, belongs much more surely to Heine.

But Heine is a poet, master of metaphor and metonymy, and with a witty conceit he now elaborates the (to him clearly abominable) identification of God with gold, and of industry with religion, that has affected the Jews along with the rest of Europe.

In this respect the Jews here in France might be divided into two sects: the sect of the *rive droite* and the sect of the *rive gauche*. These names refer to the two railway lines which run to Versailles, one along the right bank of the Seine, the other along the left bank, and which are managed [wait for it!] by two celebrated rabbis of finance [*zwei berühmten Finanzrabbinen*] who quarrel and clash with one another in just the same way as Rabbi Shammai and Rabbi Hillel once did in the older city of Babylon.

The last adjective in this witty passage reminds us that Paris is the *new* Babylon, whoring after gods abhorrent to a pristine, pre-exilic Israel. It may well be that Heine's transference of the Hillel-Shammai debates from Jerusalem, where they took place just before the birth of Christ, is not an error, but artistic licence deliberately employed for just this effect. The elder Hillel was, after all, *born* in Babylon.

Within his unconventional variation of the stereoscopic view that brings together religion and high finance Heine has now focused his readers' gaze on two prominent individuals. General traits are now personalized, given the names of actual people—names prepared for by his previous portrayal of assimilated French Jewry and given a wider context by the contrasting evocation of the two great Jewish teachers of an earlier age. The two famous *Finanzrabbinen* into whose presence Heine conjures us are, of course, Baron James, head of the house of Rothschild in Paris, and the banker-politican Benoît Fould. But just as Shammai and Hillel were two wholly different personalities, so, Heine tells us, were their modern financial successors—and here he leads us firmly back to the question of the Syrian Jews and their French co-religionists.

We must, in justice, admit that the great rabbi of the *rive droite*, Baron Rothschild, showed a nobler sympathy for the house of Israel than his scripturally learned antagonist, the great rabbi of the *rive gauche*, M. Benoît Fould, who—while his co-religionists were being tortured and strangled in Syria at the instigation of a French consul— made, with the calmness of soul so characteristic of Hillel, some beautiful speeches in the French Chamber of Deputies about the conversion of annuities and the discount rate of the Bank.

Heine's unsympathetic sketch of Fould is made even more unsympathetic by seeing him as the 'Hillel' of the team. Hillel's 'unerschütterliche Seelenruhe', he bids us recall, was due to a steadfast morality and trust in God which contrast strikingly with his modern counterpart as Heine portrayed him. In a later gloss that *may* have been written in 1840 but did not surface publicly until 1854, the poet declared himself obliged to offer an *amende honorable* to Benoît Fould, who did speak out in the French Chamber of Deputies against the French atrocities, and used, on that occasion, a phrase that gained him a rare moment of sympathy from Heine: 'la religion à laquelle j'ai l'honneur d'appartenir.'[5] In his eagerness to present typical attitudes in personalized form Heine was often unfair to individuals—but that, surely, is a danger run by every caricaturist and satirist. How fair was Aristophanes to Socrates? How fair was Daumier to Guizot?

Rothschild fares better than Fould, as always in Heine's pages—for whatever he might think of him as high priest of the Golden Calf or as a revolutionary *à l'insu*, Heine believed that James Rothschild and his family had managed to preserve, in their personal lives, the virtues of pity and charity along with the Jewish religion which enjoined them. The Rothschilds fare better, too, than the Jewish Consistory of France, of which Baron James was a prominent member; its deliberations, Heine tells us, resulted in no more than a resolution to publish a few documents about the Damascus affair. When Heine speaks of the Rothschilds and other bankers in the same breath, the former invariably come off better. Discussing the connection between property-owning and conservatism, the poet quotes an anecdote about an 'enlightened banker' who claimed that if he put his hand into the pocket of his trousers in which he kept money, he favoured the monarchy; but if he put his hand into the pocket that he kept empty, he favoured a republic. 'The enlightened banker who told me this', Heine adds,

was neither the great Baron de Rothschild nor the little Herr Königs-wärter. I need hardly spell this out: for everyone knows that the former has so much money that *both* his pockets are full of it and that the latter has too little intelligence to explain why he veers from royalism to republicanism and back again twenty times a day.[6]

James de Rothschild, this passage suggests, is not only richer but also more sympathetic and intelligent than his would-be rivals.

Rothschild is outshone, however in these *Augsburg Gazette* essays, by the lawyer Adolphe Crémieux whose portrait the poet now begins to draw with evident admiration.

M. Crémieux, the celebrated advocate, who devoted his high-souled oratory to helping, not only the Jews, but the oppressed of any creed or doctrinal persuasion, undertook the task of publishing the documents indicated by the Consistory. With the exception of a beautiful lady

(here Heine is paying another, more oblique compliment to the

French branch of the Rothschild family, for the lady referred to is without a doubt Baroness Betty Rothschild)

and a few young scholars, M. Crémieux must be the only person in Paris who actually did something for the Israelite cause. Generously disregarding his personal interests, disdainful of all treacherous trickery, he resolutely and constantly refuted lying insinuations dictated by hatred, and even offered to travel to Egypt if the Jews of Damascus were brought to trial before Pasha Mehemet Ali.[7]

Again we cannot but note the deliberate subversion of anti-Semitic stereotypes: the common charge that Jews, if they help at all, help only their own kind, that they are cowardly and underhand; and in the passage that follows, Heine makes short work too of contemporary insinuations that Crémieux was backed by vast Jewish finances. As he does so, he reveals the deep personal hurt of the poor poet in a rich Jewish family and the even deeper hurt of a man who had submitted to baptism for the sake of a career that never took off the ground. His article is full of caricatures of rich men who refuse to open their money-bags to further the good cause so generously and selflessly taken up by Adolphe Crémieux. In this case as in others Gustav Kolb, the editor of the *Augsburg Gazette* who had *carte blanche* to alter or curtail Heine's anonymously published articles, would not let the names of his correspondent's Jewish butts appear in full—Worms de Romilly, for instance, the president of the *Consistoire Central des Israélites*, appeared as 'Hr. W. de R . . .'; but such lacunae were not difficult to fill by those in the know, while others could see easily enough what *types* were being satirized. Here is the characteristic example already referred to:

One of the most highly prized members of the French Consistory—he is prized, or estimated, at some thirty million francs—M. W. de [Romilly], would not, perhaps, give as much as a hundred francs if he were asked to contribute to a fund for rescuing his entire tribe [*seines ganzen Stammes*];

and full of even more malevolent caricatures of those who abandoned their Jewish names and the religion of their fathers without economic necessity, for reasons of social snobbery:

A former Prussian contractor who, with an allusion to his Hebrew name Moses (which means 'pulled out of the water' in German, *del mare* in Italian) took his cue from this last rendering and called himself by the resounding name Baron [Delmar] . . .

Another such Baron pulled out of the water, who poses as a *gentilhomme catholique* and a great writer in the Faubourg Saint-Germain . . .[8]

The best such snobs can hope for is that the nobility they court and ape will not ridicule them aloud and to their face. Here the Rothschilds, as Heine said more than once, again provided a salutary counter-example: they remained Jews, they never changed their family name, however high they rose in Gentile society. Heine's most withering scorn, however, is reserved for a type that he encountered all too frequently in his historical studies as well as among his contemporaries, a type he ranges among 'baptized Jews'. A most significant locution! It acknowledges beyond peradventure that in Heine's view baptism was not, and could never be, an automatic way of escaping one's Jewishness.

Among the baptized Jews there are many who, out of cowardly hypocrisy, abuse Israel more vilely than its born foes do. And in the same fashion certain writers, in order not to draw attention to their origin, either speak very ill of the Jews, or ignore them altogether. This familiar spectacle is as ridiculous as it is sad.

It is therefore absurd, Heine tells his German readers, to suspect French Jews of using their financial power to present a distorted, one-sided case for their Damascene fellow Jews in plain contradiction of French political interests. It is more than ridiculous, in fact, it is sinister—for the tactics here employed are the same as those recently employed against the movement known as *Young Germany*. What German reactionaries had then not just insinuated but loudly proclaimed, in plain contradiction of the facts, was that *Young Germany* should really have been called *Young Palestine*, that its critique of German society and German culture was part of a Jewish plot, masterminded by Börne and Heine, to subvert German national traditions and national pride along with the Christian religion. The same people who saw only Jewish money behind the agitation on behalf of the Syrian martyrs saw only Jewish machinations behind the attempt to liberalize German society and German culture—and in fighting the one lie, Heine thought, he was also nailing the other.

Heine had not yet done with the Damascus affair—he returned to it, with varying degrees of emphasis, in articles dated 11 June, 25 July, and 30 July 1840, and on 1 February 1841. On 11 June 1840 we find him, in an article the *Augsburg Gazette* did not choose to print, surveying the stand various French newspapers and journals had taken in the controversy. At ministerial behest, he tells his readers,

Le Constitutionnel, Le Siècle, Le Temps, Le Messager, Le Charivari, who but a few months ago would have championed with fiery zeal the cause of those poor Jews tortured with the most refined cruelty at the behest of a French consul,[9]

had insinuated that there was no smoke without a fire, that the Jews of Damascus might indeed be in the habit of drinking blood. They had done so in phrases that betrayed, to any ears sensitive to stylistic nuance, how much the writers hated the task that had been imposed on them by ministerial and editorial policy. Their spinelessness contrasted with the decent behaviour of the *Journal des Débats* and the *Courrier Français,* which vindicated the honour of the French press by speaking out against superstition, slander, and torture. These courageous correspondents said openly what the others knew in their heart of hearts to be true—even those of *La Quotidienne,* whose habitual anti-Jewish policy was mitigated on this occasion by sympathy with the innocent victims of blood-libel. Only *L'Univers* had no editorial doubts about the Oriental Jews' habit of drinking blood; and in his article of 30 July Heine expresses his deep consternation at finding how widely its absurd suggestions were, in fact, believed.

It cannot be denied: a great many Frenchmen are not averse to the belief that Oriental Jews drink human blood at their Passover celebrations. That they don't impute such a thing to Jews in the Occident is due to sheer politeness.[10]

Can this be the France of Voltaire, the home of enlightenment? But perhaps it is just because enlightened Frenchmen think religion capable of inspiring every kind of infamy that they believe adherents of the Jewish faith to be avid for the flesh and blood of aged Capuchin monks. Be that as it may, Heine concludes: there is certainly a good deal of credulity mixed up with French scepticism.

That no such obtuse opinions about the happenings in Damascus could gain ground in Germany is only a sign of our greater learning. The German people is so steeped in historical knowledge that even the most savage resentment dare not use these ancient bloody fables to achieve its dire purposes.[11]

Here Heine's gift of prophecy for once deserted him. The blood-libel found only too ready credence in Germany when Hitler's minions found it politic to revive it for their own murderous purposes.

Heine's articles for the *Augsburg Gazette* usually ended with some sign that what he had described was only what appeared to a particular observer at a particular time, and that the future might bring illuminations as well as changes. One of the most hopeful signs that the Damascus incident was a temporary aberration, and that its horrors would usher in a new enlightenment, was to be found in the activities of the lawyer Adolphe Crémieux, to whose celebration Heine devoted articles dated 25 July 1840 and 1 February 1841.

Heine's paean to his new-found hero begins with another look at the wider implications of the Damascus affair.

The old system of exterminating whole peoples is being slowly driven out of the Orient by European influence. The individual's rights of existence are also gaining greater recognition there; and the cruelties of torture in particular will give way to milder procedures in criminal investigation. It is the Damascus blood-libel affair which will produce this last-named result; and in this respect M. Crémieux's journey to Alexandria will be entered as an important event in the annals of humanity. This famous legal scholar, one of the most celebrated men in the whole of France . . . has already begun his providential pilgrimage, accompanied by his wife who wanted to share the dangers with which he was threatened. Let us hope that these dangers, which were perhaps only intended to scare him away from his noble attempt, will turn out to be as slight as the people who place them in his path. For indeed: this advocate of the Jews is pleading the cause of all mankind . . .[12]

The article of 1 February 1841 (later redated '31 January' in *Lutezia*) elaborates the same theme.

When M. Crémieux tackled Mehemet Ali about the gross abuses of justice perpetrated in Damascus he found him inclined to the most beneficial reforms—and if political events had not so tempestuously intervened, the celebrated advocate would have persuaded the pasha to introduce into his dominions European methods of conducting criminal investigations and trials.[13]

This Franco-Jewish lawyer, Heine thus tells us, in intervening on behalf of persecuted Jews, is advancing the cause, not just of Jews, but of Mehemet Ali's other subjects too—is helping to induce the rulers of the Middle East to accept principles of justice which will save non-Jews from the fate of his tortured co-religionists. Crémieux, he has heard, is preparing for publication the diary he kept during his journeys to Syria and Egypt; and that leads him to speculate on the interesting parallel such a diary might offer to the famous *De Legatione ad Gaium* of Philo Judaeus. 'There is in fact', Heine comments, 'a strong resemblance between these two missions; and Adolphe Crémieux, like the learned Alexandrine, has immortalized his name in the annals of the unhappy people that cannot die.'[14] Once again Heine is covertly using the folk image of *der ewige Jude*, the 'Eternal' rather than the 'Wandering' Jew, to characterize the Jewish people and suggests, by this analogy, that its extinction (in the sense, no doubt, of complete assimilation) might be a blessing. This strikes a note we shall hear again in his writings of the 1840s—but we may well think that there is a contradiction between this idea on the one hand, and Heine's praise of Philo Judaeus and Adolphe Crémieux on the other. Is not the continued production of such characters sufficient justification for the continued existence of Israel?

Heine's portrait is rounded out by a passage in which the Jewish advocate, whose work benefited, not only his co-religionists, but all mankind, is presented as a true champion of the ideals of universal justice, of liberty, fraternity, and equality proclaimed by the French Revolution; and by another which appears expressly designed to remove from Crémieux' picture any taint of Robespierrean dourness and austerity.

Crémieux is one of the noblest knights of humanity; the best of his contemporaries have attested this. The story of his life, fully told in the *Biographie des contemporains célèbres*, is the story of continual championship of the persecuted, whatever creed they might profess. Whoever suffered innocently found in him the most willing advocate . . .; it made no difference whether the accused was a Catholic or a Jew, a peer of France or a common labourer. Some of our Pharisees may nurse a grudge against him, for he loves music, especially that of the Italian school, he loves beautiful horses, he loves the tragedies of Racine—and he was the protector of a tragédienne by the name of Mlle Rachel. But these surly zealots would do well to forgive his love of life and his pagan tastes—were it only because of the energy with which he championed their beards and their limbs against the torturers of Damascus.[15]

Here Heine strikes up the theme he so emphatically sounds in *Ludwig Börne. A Memorial*: the necessity to cut across divisions into 'Jews' and 'Christian', or 'Jews' and 'Gentiles', or 'Jews' and 'Germans', 'Frenchmen' etc., by means of other, more significant distinctions, notably that between the ascetic human type and the type that enjoyed the pleasures of this world without pangs of conscience. In *that* dichotomy Crémieux would be found on the side of Jan Steen, or Mirabeau, or Goethe, while the other side would bring together the racially proud German Wolfgang Menzel and the Christian theologian Hengstenberg with many a bearded Jew. It might be said in passing that Heine never did anything like full justice to the joyous, life-affirming side of the Jewish religion—despite his warmly affectionate appreciation of its intimate culture, its family celebrations of the sabbath, of Passover, and of Chanukah.

All this cannot, however, obscure the fact that here, for the first time, Heine presents a Jewish hero of his own time: a man who selflessly serves all the world as well as his own people, who champions the oppressed wherever he finds them; who rejects Nazarene asceticism without losing his moral fervour; who combines deep feelings with the cool head and persuasive tongue that enable him to marshall his arguments in a persuasive way; who partakes fully of the cultural delights offered by European civilization without ever denying his Jewishness. In later articles Heine will show us his culture hero when the Damascus affair is not in question. That of 5 May 1843, for instance, which brings in Crémieux as legal adviser to the Rothschilds, calls him 'the great jurist with the noblest of hearts'; while that of 22 March 1848 (not printed by the *Augsburg Gazette*) lists Crémieux among the heroes of the day and proudly shows him as spokesman of the revolution—as the deputy to whose lot it fell to read out to a jubilant crowd the names of those who would head the provisional government of the new republic.[16] It comes as something of a shock to read Armand Marrast's account of this same event, as reported in the *Souvenirs* of Alexis de Tocqueville:

I cannot resist repeating a story I heard some months later from M. Marrast . . . It gives a wonderful picture of two men who at that moment played important parts, and points the difference, if not between their feelings, then at least between their education and mores. 'A list of candidates for the Provisional Government', Marrast told me, 'had been hastily prepared; the question was how to announce it to the people. I gave it to Lamartine, asking him to read it aloud from the top of the steps.

"I can't do that",' Lamartine answered when he read it; "my name is there."

I passed it to Crémieux to read, and when he had done so, he said: "You are laughing at me, asking me to read to the people a list from which my name is absent."

De Tocqueville also describes, however, how Crémieux 'announced the establishment of a provisional government to the silent disapproval of the deputies and the cheers of the people', and how he later explained that event in a multitude of speeches, 'always eloquent, always heated, always cheered'. 'I don't think', de Tocqueville adds, 'anyone has ever met, or perhaps even conceived of, a man so ugly and so eloquent.'[17] How significant it is that Heine, always so eager to see the relation between outer appearance and inner reality, never even hints that Crémieux might have been considered ugly! What matters in this case is the nobility of spirit he perceived in him.

(ii)

In Heine's reports from the Paris of the 1840s the musical and artistic life of the French capital loomed large: partly because the editors of the *Augsburg Gazette* specifically requested this, partly because reports on the arts enabled their author to disguise social and political comment sufficiently to deceive a censor, but mostly because the poet himself was fascinated by the way in which the artistic life and the entertainments of a great capital reflected or refracted the social forces that were shaping nineteenth-century Europe. The Parisian concert scene enabled him to observe and describe forces of mechanization, specialization, entertainment industry, publicity, and press-corruption in which he himself, as a journalist, became to some degree involved. His early essays had already helped the career of Ferdinand Hiller and spread even further the fame of Giacomo Meyerbeer—and in the 1840s he could hardly talk about musical life in France without once again reverting to the composer of *Robert le Diable* and *Les Huguenots*.

An article of 20 April 1840 makes clear to its readers that Heine still believed Meyerbeer to be a great composer. There is no dectable irony in the phrase 'Mozart, Meyerbeer, and Beethoven' which frames him, as it were, between two men of whose musical genius there could be no doubt at all. Meyerbeer, we are told, is a worthy representative of the German spirit in Paris; his music introduces the French public to a world identical with that of German poetry; and if—now comes the characteristic little sting—there is rather a lot of advertising going on, if Meyerbeer's name is bandied around rather freely when matters such as the engagement or non-engagement of certain singers and musicians come into question, then this must surely be against the maestro's own wishes and intentions. There can be no doubt, Heine reports, of 'the extraordinary popularity of the great master who created *Robert le Diable* and *Les Huguenots* and whose third [*sic*] opera, *Le Prophète*, is being awaited with a feverish, palpitating impatience of which no one who has not experienced it can have any idea.'[18] Meyerbeer's international success, Heine declared, is an earnest of a new European art, an art transcending national divisions, an art that would testify to the great brotherhood of nations and peoples which was the true goal of the age: *der großen Völkerverbrüderung, der eigentlichen Aufgabe unsere Zeitalters.* Such cosmopolitanism, Heine adds, in a passage that proved too much for the editors of the *Augsburg Gazette*, who promptly deleted it, is becoming a more and more prominent feature of the genius of the German people; and with a glance, no doubt, at the concept of 'world literature' which Goethe had advanced in the last years of his life, Heine pronounces Meyerbeer to have an elective affinity, a *Wahlverwandtschaft*, with Germany's greatest poet.[19] An anonymous Frenchman is made to say to Heine that

it was Meyerbeer's operas which initiated him into Goethe's poetry, opened the doors of Goethe's writings to him.

This saying, Heine comments,

has a deep significance. It leads me to think that German music may be destined, here in France, to be the prelude or overture which will lead to a real understanding of German literature.[20]

His insistent desire that Meyerbeer should set some of his poems to music—a frustrated desire which helped to precipitate his later break with him—may be explained by this passage. The poet is already repelled by some of the puffing that went on around Meyerbeer's work, past, present, and to come; but he is ready to concede, on 20 April 1841, that his 'well-informed sources' may be right when they suggested 'that Meyerbeer may not be to blame for the delay in the performance of his new opera, and that the authority of his name is occasionally exploited to further other people's interests.'[21] An article dated 7 February 1842 makes this last point even more emphatically: 'Music at Parisian soirées consists, nowadays, of hackneyed motifs from the works of Rossini and Meyerbeer, two silent maestros who have been talked about more than ever this winter—not, to be sure, in the interests of art, but in those of MM Troupenas and Schlesinger.'[22]

(iii)

The tone in which Heine speaks about Meyerbeer in his reports from Paris becomes perceptibly sharper after the composer had accepted the post of *Generalmusikdirektor* in Berlin which King Frederick William IV of Prussia offered him in 1842. Attacking Meyerbeer now meant attacking the Prussian establishment—a task Heine was ever eager to perform. When the *Generalmusikdirektor*'s long-heralded new opera failed to make its appearance in 1843, Heine decided to blow his first really icy blast in the direction of a man whom he could no longer regard as an ally.

Le Prophète is still being awaited with an impatience which, stretched beyond endurance, might in the end turn into downright annoyance. Even now a perceptible reaction may be felt against Meyerbeer on the part of the Parisian public, which is not inclined to pardon the gracious attentions he is receiving in Berlin. Parisians are unjust enough to make him the scapegoat of their political displeasure. It is much easier to pardon the servility of needy men of talent than to overlook that of the great maestro, who was born with a silver spoon in his mouth, inheriting the kind of riches that amount almost to genius. He has thus exposed himself to dangerous misunderstandings; we shall, perhaps, find an opportunity in the near future to return to this subject.[23]

What Heine clearly finds unendurable is that Meyerbeer should have renounced his independence voluntarily; that he should have compromised his status as a supranational composer by becoming the King of Prussia's musical court Jew. Even now, however, he refrains from attacking the composer in his own name (though the final sentence just quoted suggests that he may do so at the next opportunity); he adopts, instead, the tone of a seemingly dispassionate reporter of what is being said about Meyerbeer by others. That same method serves him particularly well in the article he dated 1 May 1844; a report on the operatic scene in Paris which caricatures Meyerbeer's rival Gasparo Spontini but manages in the process to place in Spontini's mouth the whole range of Heine's own complaints about his quondam friend and ally, from acceptance of a 'servile post at [the Prussian] court' to his failure to deliver some compositions of Heine's poems which he had promised. He also complains again about the non-appearance of *Le Prophète* and speaks of the vile singing to be heard in performances of other Meyerbeer operas; but he does pay tribute to the continuing popularity of *Les Huguenots* and *Robert le Diable*, calls them 'masterpieces' without having his tongue visibly in his cheek, and prophesies that their hold on the Parisian operatic stage will long endure.[24] The wind of criticism is still being tempered to the shorn lamb.

In Paris, meanwhile, Meyerbeer's predominance was being challenged by another operatic composer whose very name announced his Jewishness: Jacques Halévy. Heine speaks respectfully of him as a man whose modest natural talents had been conscientiously and painstakingly cultivated; but he opines that like his librettist Casimir Delavigne, with whom he had collaborated on *Charles VI*, Halévy lacked the spark of genius, that he owed more to a thorough schooling than to a true creative urge. 'Both, therefore,' Heine wrote on 20 March 1843, 'will never produce anything really bad, as occasionally happens to men of genius and originality; their work will always have something pleasant, good-looking, respectable, academic, classical about it.' Such men, he adds, are upright and decent—they are current silver, not to be sneezed at when gold is scarce.[25] When Halévy's next opera, *Il Lazzarone*, appeared, Heine's tone sharpened, however; we shall hear him castigate the new work in his best mock-heroic vein when he comes to talk about its composer's association with his publisher Maurice Schlesinger.[26]

Jacques Halévy, then, would never be a serious rival for Meyerbeer. But what of the composer whose career Heine had watched ever since he first appeared before the public as an infant prodigy? What of Felix Mendelssohn-Bartholdy? The portrait he paints of him in the early 1840s is one of the most interesting in the whole canon, and deserves our closest attention.

In an article published in the *Augsburg Gazette* and dated mid-April 1842, Heine takes Rossini's *Stabat Mater* as an occasion for formulating anew his perception of the relationship between Christianity and art. Here is his key sentence:

The truly Christian element in art is not indicated by outward dryness and pallor, but rather by a certain inner exuberance which, in painting as in music, cannot be acquired by baptism or study.[27]

Die weder angetauft noch anstudiert werden kann—the familiar charge of German nationalists against Heine himself, that despite his German schooling and his Christian baptism he had always remained a Jew, is here taken up by the poet himself and applied to an analysis of Mendelssohn's art that culminates in the finding that Rossini's *Stabat Mater* is 'more truly Christian' than *St. Paul (Paulus)*, 'the oratorio by Felix Mendelssohn-Bartholdy which is being lauded by the opponents of Rossini as a veritable model of Christianness'.

Muster der Christentümlichkeit: can we not hear, in the very formulation, the voice of Heine the parodist superseding that of the sober analyst and chronicler? If we miss it here we can hardly miss it in what follows, as we listen to Heine adopting a pious phraseology which deliberately conflicts with his attitude and tone elsewhere. 'May heaven preserve me', he writes, 'from wishing to use this as a reproach against the meritorious master who composed *St. Paul* . . .' and having made this disclaimer, he brings out what must have made anti-Semites rejoice at the contrast he has drawn between Mendelssohn's expression of the Christian spirit, and Rossini's: '. . . least of all would the writer of these lines dream of cavilling at the Christianity of the oratorio in question because Felix Mendelssohn-Bartholdy was born a Jew.' This statement contains a deliberate and characteristic ambiguity. When the article in question was first published, anonymously like all such contributions to the *Augsburg Gazette*, readers would take it to mean that to reject *St. Paul* because its composer was Jewish would be the last thing any truly civilized man—and that includes the author of the article—would think of doing. Better-informed readers, however, and those who recognized Heine's style, would catch an allusion to Heine's own history: the writer of these lines, they would understand him to say, would be the last person to condemn *St. Paul* on such grounds because he too had submitted to baptism, he too arrogated to himself the right to speak for a community other than the Jewish one to which so many of his enemies sought to confine him. As so often, Heine is speaking *pro domo*—he is investigating a problem that concerned him deeply, probing a wound of his own, putting his own portrait alongside that of his sitter. 'But I cannot refrain', he therefore continues with self-torturing insistence, 'from pointing out that at the age at which Mendelssohn started his Christianity in Berlin (he was not baptized until his thirteenth year) Rossini had already left it and had plunged wholeheartedly into the worldliness of operatic music.' The implications are clear: the Jewish-born artist accepts Christianity at the very moment in which the Christian-born one leaves it *for the good of his art*. What, then, becomes of the vaunted Christian spirit of Rossini's *Stabat Mater*? Heine has his answer ready, an answer once again of the greatest interest in view of his own development, in view of his own relationship to Judaism in the tragic last years of his life. 'Now', he says of Rossini, 'when he left this worldliness and dreamt himself back to his Catholic youth, to the days in which he sang or assisted at mass as a choral scholar in the cathedral of Pesaro; when the old organ tones surged again in his memory and he seized his pen in order to write a *Stabat Mater*—then he did not need to reconstruct the spirit of Christianity in a scholarly way, and he needed even less to copy Handel or Bach slavishly; all he had to do was to summon up from the deep recesses of his sensibility the sounds he had heard in earliest childhood . . .' That's what Christianity could be to the modern artist, and what Heine was later to find in Judaism too: a return to childhood, to a ceremonial from which the grown man has become estranged but which he can see, in his later years, to have had a profound relation to his experiences as a man.

It will not have escaped the attentive reader that even while ostensibly concentrating on one pole of his comparison, on Rossini, Heine keeps the other pole, Mendelssohn, unobtrusively in view. When he tells us that Rossini had no need to construct the spirit of Christianity artifically, that he needed even less to copy Handel or Bach in order to write music breathing a Christian spirit, he is clearly alluding to Mendelssohn's activities as a rediscoverer of Baroque music, and more particularly as rehabilitator, re-editor and re-performer of the sacred music of Johann Sebastian Bach. That contrast must be in our mind as we turn to Heine's account of the reception of Mendelssohn's music by the Parisian public. Rossini's *Stabat Mater*, he tells us, was received with rapture, both in the concert-hall of the Italian Opera and in the concerts arranged by the editors of *La France musicale*; and when Mendelssohn's *St. Paul* turned up in the same season and the same *France musicale* series, the public was bound to feel invited to measure the one against the other.

This comparison did not work to our young compatriot's advantage with the Parisian public; it was rather like comparing the Italian Apennines with the Templower Berg near Berlin. But this does not mean that the Templower Berg has no merits—the very fact that it bears a cross on its summit ensures the respect of the crowd. *In hoc signo vinces*! Not in France, though—in this land of unbelief Herr Mendelssohn has always proved a fiasco. In the present season he was the lamb that was sacrificed while Rossini was the musical lion whose sweet roar continues to sound in our ears.

With their multiple ironies these lines widen our perspective. The Jewish component, they tell us, cannot be eliminated from an artist who was born a Jew—our childhood impressions inevitably form an essential part of our mature personality; but that does not make 'our young compatriot' Mendelssohn any the less a German. He has been affected by everything the Templower Berg represents in this passage, so that the French public, when it rejects Mendelssohn, is rejecting much that Prussia stood for in the age of Frederick William IV. The Emperor Constantine may have been rightly told, in the fourth century, that he would conquer under the sign of the Cross; all King Frederick William and the artist under his Most Christian protection could do was to parody that feat rather than re-enact it. Mendelssohn-Bartholdy might carry with him the *große Menge* that furnished his auditors in Berlin; the *großes Publikum* of Paris, capital of the land of unbelief, was bound to reject an art that smacked of Prusso-Christian revivalism. And so the Christian imagery returns, with new ironic resonances, as Mendelssohn is termed *das geopferte Lamm der Saison* and Rossini opposed to him (with biblical as well as hagiographic echoes) as the lion who, in this season, bears off the victory.

Wittingly or unwittingly, Heine here exaggerates Mendelssohn's 'failure' with French audiences; Michael Mann has pertinently pointed out that at the first performance of the oratorio *St. Paul* the applause was such that one chorus had to be repeated.[28] But even this climactic distortion or exaggeration is not the end of Heine's dealings with Moses Mendelssohn's grandson; for he adds no less than two codas to his article. The first begins with the news that Mendelssohn-Bartholdy plans to visit Paris in person in the near future. There is no certainty about this; but, Heine tells the readers of the *Augsburg Gazette*, he has another piece of information to which more unqualified credence may be given.

So much is certain: M. Léon Pillet has been induced, by the influence of exalted persons and various diplomatic *démarches*, to commission a libretto from M. Scribe which Herr Mendelssohn is to set to music as a grand opera. Will fortune smile on our young compatriot as he undertakes this business?

Here the signals are coming in thick and fast to tell us that Mendelssohn is being manœuvred in the same direction as Meyerbeer, whose *Robert le Diable* had a text by Scribe of which Heine had a notoriously low opinion. The word *Geschäft*, in which the passage just quoted culminates, is charged with meaning: art, Heine tells us, is becoming a business in the modern world; it is increasingly a matter of diplomacy, of enlisting the help of the powers that be, and it needs the kind of management talents which Meyerbeer, in Heine's view, had been able to deploy with the aid of a great deal of money, a venal press, and the advertising genius of Maurice Schlesinger. Will this younger German composer, 'our young compatriot' as Heine now calls Mendelssohn-Bartholdy for the second time, be able to emulate Meyerbeer in this respect? 'I do not know,' he says, and launches into his second coda, in which an important theme of the essay is restated for the last time and given a significant extension.

He is gifted with great artistic talent—but it has considerable limits and lacunae. In this respect there is a striking resemblance between Felix Mendelssohn and the tragic actress Rachel Félix. They both exhibit an undeviating serious-mindedness, a tendency to lean on classical models with an importunity that verges on intrusion, ingenious calculation of effects, sharpness of intellect and, finally, a complete lack of any kind of naïvety. But can there be any original artistic genius which has not something naïve about it? Up to the present there has never been any instance of this.

In the first coda the parallel between Mendelssohn and the most famous Jewish composer of his day, Meyerbeer, had been implied rather than made explicit; in the second the parallel between him and a Franco-Jewish artist in a different sphere, the tragedienne Rachel, is overtly drawn and elaborated. And the charges Heine brings against Mendelssohn and Rachel are the very charges that were so often brought against Heine himself and have, since his day, been heard again and again when artists of Jewish extraction are being discussed: that with all their intellectual penetration, their diligence in studying the best models, their industry, their skill, their seriousness, they lacked some essential ingredient, an ingredient common to 'real genius' however defined. One only has to listen to Heine's keywords to recognize features of the portrait drawn of European Jews from the era of emancipation to our own day by their cultural opponents: *ein ... beinahe zudringliches Anlehnen; geistreichste Berechnung; Verstandesschärfe; Mangel an Naivetät.* This is something Heine often does: he brings stereotypes out into the open, in order to see how they work in his own context; he never thought, as so many others did, that if one ignored them they would just go away. The trouble with this procedure, of course, is that it can easily merge into another: that of internalizing the standards of the enemy. Heine's discussion of Mendelssohn's music has a disturbing, and surely not fortuitous, affinity with Richard Wagner's later discussion of the same phenomenon in *Judaism in Music (Das Judentum in der Musik).*

But Heine is not Wagner, and the differences are at least as instructive as the resemblances. Again it pays to listen carefully to what Heine actually says. His answer to the question whether it is possible to have great art without *Naivetät* turns out to be that this has never happened—as yet. 'Bis jetzt ... noch nicht.' Mendelssohn, Rachel Félix, and (dare we add?) Heine himself are different from the great geniuses of the past; they do lack an element which has hitherto been deemed an essential part of genius—but may they not, by virtue of this very fact, be the harbingers of a new art, an art of the future, an art more consonant with the modern world than that which formed the horizon of expectation of their nineteenth-century public? In the creation of this new art, we may surmise, artists of Jewish origin may have an important part to play.

In the modern world artists need agents, and Heine has a good deal of fun at the expense of Jewish promoters of German art in Paris—notably that same Maurice Schlesinger who played such a fateful role in the life of Gustave Flaubert. But there are amateur promoters too; when no professional concert-agent, Heine tells us, showed himself eager to bring Mendelssohn's music to Paris, a private concert was arranged:

The banker Leo, I am told, who has been for years an agent of the house of Mendelssohn in Paris and who is a very genteel man with aspirations towards culture, has had these compositions performed in his house.[29]

Leo is branching out into culture, another kind of 'agency', while continuing to promote the Mendelssohns' business interest; we are to surmise, I suppose, that the methods used will be similar. But, Heine continues, this attempt at artistic promotion failed to achieved the effect it was designed to have.

It was not favourable for Mendelssohn that the audience invited to hear him consisted for the most part of people who professed the Mosaic faith; for some of those present thought that they detected, here and there, passages plagiarized from the *kinnot*, the songs of lamentation for the destruction of Jerusalem. How far this reproach may be justified we cannot judge—but we can note that it is not new in the history of music, where it has already been levelled at Marcello, whose settings of the psalms (it has been said) closely resembled the old chants of the Synagogue.

It is possible, therefore, that Mendelssohn, Marcello's learned imitator, thought he was borrowing something from that admired model when in reality he unwittingly robbed his own house.

Here, once again, we see Heine making the point about the derivativeness and ultimate lack of effectiveness which he thought characteristic of Mendelssohn's music—but from a wholly different perspective. Let us once more contrast him with Wagner, who saw in Felix Mendelssohn-Bartholdy the tragic result of an endeavour by the Jews, a people (as Wagner thought) without a native musical tradition, to write in the idiom of an artistically more gifted people: the Germans. 'The Jew', Wagner tells his readers in *Judaism in Music*, 'never had an art of his own'; his synagogue music is a caricature, 'a concatenation of gargling, yodelling, and babbling sounds that no deliberate parody could distort into more revolting forms than those which it naïvely and earnestly presents to the listener.'[30] Heine, on the contrary, believed that synagogue music was good enough to inspire Christian composers such as Benedetto Marcello, composers from whom Mendelssohn-Bartholdy derived at second hand what should have been his own birthright.

This gives the poet his cue for speaking about the deepest considerations which Mendelssohn's art and its fate in the new world of advertising and promotion suggested to him. The occasion he seizes, in an article dated 25 April 1844, is the performance of Mendelssohn's 'Scottish' Symphony in a concert season whose main attraction was Berlioz's *Symphonie fantastique*. After discussing what he calls the 'Assyrian-Babylonian-Egyptian architecture' of Berlioz's work, Heine continues:

What a proper modern man our celebrated compatriot Felix Mendelssohn-Bartholdy is by comparison! We mention him today because his symphony was performed in the concert-hall of the Conservatoire. We owe this pleasure to the active zeal of Mendelssohn's friends and well-wishers here in Paris. Although the work was received with regrettable coolness, its merits deserve to be recognized by all who truly understand art.

Some technical details follow, culled from French reviews— the poet's own competence in musical theory was *nil*; and then Heine asks why it is that Mendelssohn never had, and never would, become popular in Paris. He relates the answer to a fundamental question of aesthetics.

What is the difference between art and mere labour? We admire this master's formal capacity, his talent for appropriating the most extraordinary effects, his charmingly beautiful elaborations, his fine lizard-like ear, his sensitive feelers, and his earnest, I am almost tempted to say passionate, indifference.[31]

The parallels with Wagner's notorious estimate of Mendelssohn become even more striking if one looks at the version of this passage in *Lutezia*, where Heine speaks of the difference between 'art and falsehood' (*Lüge*) instead of 'art and mere labour' (*Arbeit*). *Lüge* probably represents what Heine had originally written—*Arbeit* is the deliberately weakened substitute supplied by the editors of the *Augsburg Gazette*.[32] But even here the difference between Heine and Wagner outweighs their resemblance.

If we look for an analogous phenomenon in another artistic sphere, we can find it in poetry this time, where its name is Ludwig Tieck. This master too always knew how to reproduce the choicest effects, he could even manufacture the naïve—yet he never created anything that captivated the multitudes and kepts its place in their hearts. Both have the keenest desire for achievement in the field of drama; but Mendelssohn too will become old and crotchety, perhaps, without contributing anything truly great to the stage. He will try—but he must fail, for here the first requirements are truth and passion . . .[33]

What ails Mendelssohn, Heine tells us, is not what ails the Jews; it is rather what ails so many modern artists, including those very Romantics whom German anti-Semitic nationalists venerated as true begetters of their own ideology and as indigenous geniuses that had nothing in common with Jewish outsiders and other such marginal men. But in Mendelssohn's case, of course, the problem was exacerbated because it linked itself with the problem of Jewish assimilation, the denial of Jewishness in favour of 'Germanness' or Christianity.

As so often, Heine is here pointing to dangers that beset his own art—dangers all the greater because of his social position, because of his need to make a living by gaining as many readers as possible. This leads to a special animus which appears most clearly in a letter to Ferdinand Lassalle, dated 11 February 1846. Here he felt he could spell out clearly what he would not, for obvious reasons, say in public. This passage, with its bitter attack on Christianizing ex-Jews, will be quoted in the Third Intermezzo. What needs to be noted here is once again the difference from Wagner rather than the likeness: the veneration of German-Jewish traditions deriving from Moses Mendelssohn, the Jew who scorned baptism yet conquered the respect of the non-Jewish world; and the scabrously expressed belief that in trying to please an ostensibly Christian society in Christian garb Felix Mendelssohn was making unworthy use of his talents. In a way Heine had said it all in those few lines of *Germany. A Winter's Tale* in which the Emperor Frederick Barbarossa is made to show an incongruous and anachronistic interest in Moses Mendelssohn by asking questions that elicit from the poem's narrator the following characteristic reply:

'O Kaiser', rief ich, 'wie bist du zurück!
Der Moses ist längst gestorben,
Nebst seiner Rebekka, auch Abraham,
Der Sohn ist gestorben, verdorben.

Der Abraham hatte mit Lea erzeugt
Ein Bübchen, Felix heißt er,
Der brachte es weit im Christentum,
Ist schon Kapellenmeister.'

['O Emperor', I cried, 'you are so out of date!
That Moses died a long time ago,
and so did his Rebecca; Abraham too,
their son, is dead and gone.

Abraham had begotten upon Leah
a little boy, whose name is Felix;
He went a long way in Christendom:
He's an orchestral conductor already!']34

Several of Heine's Parisian reports for the *Augsburg Gazette* concern themselves with virtuoso performers, especially on the piano. Among these there were several artists of Jewish origin who fare no better and no worse than their Gentile colleagues when they come under this correspondent's gaze. Eduard Wolf is briefly praised as composer as well as performer: one essay tells us that he is 'full of verve and originality', while another speeds him on his matrimonial way:

A few days ago we learnt that our excellent Eduard Wolf is about to marry, that he is venturing out into high seas of matrimony for which no compass has yet been invented. May the wind be gentle to you, bold mariner!

(25 April 1844)35

Usually, however, Heine's comments are more vitriolic. Here is what he has to say about Alexander Dreyschock:

I have to report, faithfully, that public opinion has proclaimed him one of the greatest of all piano virtuosos, the equal of the most celebrated among them. He makes an infernal noise.

(20 March 1843)[36]

And here is Heine's old friend and host Ignaz Moscheles:

Poor Ignaz Moscheles suffered the saddest of fates when he came over from London a year ago to freshen up a fame that commercial exploitation had caused to fade. He played in one of Schlesinger's concerts and fell miserably flat . . .

(20 April 1841)

The older Pharaos are being outplayed every day and sink into discouragement and darkness. Henri Herz is approaching mummification; and Moscheles, the Amenophis or Amasis of the piano, visited us again last autumn and played another touching variation on his disappearance in the Red Sea of oblivion.

(25 April 1844—manuscript variant)[37]

As we read this parody of Exodus tricked out with popular Egyptology we cannot but reflect on the wisdom Moscheles' wife had shown in 1827, when she requested Heine never to speak about her husband in any of his works.

Heine's portraits of virtuosos should not, however, be mistaken for mere exercises in humorous appreciation or disdain. They are an essential part of his picture of Parisian society and its tastes, and a no less essential illustration of his views on true art and its enemies. What he fought against above all was the principle that admiration should be lavished on mere technical accomplishment, according to the principle of 'difficulties overcome'. Such admiration, he believed, could only encourage soulless displays of technique—a mechanization of art which Heine deplored in the same way in which E. T. A. Hoffmann had deplored soulless virtuosity among singers. The continuities between Heine's views on art and those of the German Romantics remain as marked as ever.

A special place among these sketches of piano virtuosos is reserved for Henri Herz, who not only played the instrument himself but who also encouraged others to do so. Herz's *salon* is presented on 3 July 1840, as a feeding-ground for what has become, in Heine's eyes, a 'plague' of piano-players—the plague of parliamentarians, he adds, is no better. Thank God that the political and the musical virtuosi are silent at the height of summer! On 6 January 1841 we find Heine referring to Herz and the non-Jewish piano-manufacturer Sébastian Érard as rival 'artists in wood' [*Holzkünstler*]. 'Like Kalkbrenner and Pixis', he tells his readers on 20 March 1843, 'M. Herz belongs with the mummies; his one claim to distinction is his beautiful concert-hall. He died a long time ago and has recently married.' Heine had intended to go further still—but the *Augsburg Gazette* did not, in the end, print what he had intended as his parting shot:

These wooden whirrings without natural diminuendo, these heartless tones of a man who bears the heart in his very name [*diese herzlosen Töne des Herrn Herz*], this effervescent thumping, is destructive of all thought and feeling. Such fortepiano-bashing will be the death of us all![38]

The impresario Maurice Schlesinger, whose name we have just heard again in connection with that of Ignaz Moscheles, was a German-born Jew who had become one of the most important music publishers in France. Contact with him brought Heine important insights into the way reputations were stage-managed in nineteenth-century France. He saw virtuosos and their agents besieging the offices of Schlesinger's *Gazette musicale* in quest of good notices—notices for which they were ready to pay in various coin, including that of lending lustre, by their presence and co-operation, to his concerts.

The celebrated Döhler has returned to Paris and given several recitals; he has also appeared at one of Schlesinger's *Gazette musicale* concerts and been liberally rewarded with laurel-wreaths . . . But how can one classify this famous man? Some say he is the best of the second-rate pianists, others that he is the greatest of the third-raters . . . He leaves an impression of dainty feebleness, elegant impotence, interesting pallor.[39]

Döhler was not of Jewish origin; and Heine is careful to show (i) that Schlesinger did not confine his puffs to Jews; (ii) that the power of the puff, of *réclame*, could be studied as easily in the Escudiers' *France musicale*, which was neither owned nor

edited by men of Jewish descent, as in the *Gazette musicale*;
and (iii) that Schlesinger's puffs, as the case of Moscheles
shows, were frequently unsuccessful. There is, after all, a limit
to the power of advertising—though not, apparently, to the
length virtuosos would go to in order to obtain a favourable
notice. On 20 March 1843 Heine looks back on his dealings
with Schlesinger:

When I was still in the good books of the managing director of the
Gazette musicale (alas—I have forfeited his favour through youthful
indiscretions) I saw with my own eyes how the famous lay humbly at
his feet and crawled and wagged their tails in order to earn themselves
a little praise in his journal. One might well say of our most cele-
brated virtuosos, who have been fêted like royalty in all the capitals
of Europe, that their laurel-crowns still bear the dust of Maurice
Schlesinger's boots.[40]

If Schlesinger had done well out of Meyerbeer, whose melodies
were being endlessly ground out, along with those of Rossini,
at countless soirées which benefited the music publishers more
than they benefited art, he was considerably less fortunate—in
Heine's opinion—when he championed the early operas of
Jacques Fromental Halévy. The fate of one of Halévy's operas
is reported in the mock-heroic, mock-mythological manner
which Heine so often adopted in face of the 'heroes' of his
time.

The *Lazzarone* of Halévy has suffered a terrible fate. Halévy here
met his Waterloo without ever having been a Napoleon. What made
the débâcle worse for him, however, was the defection of Maurice
Schlesinger. The latter had always been his Pylades; and even if
Orestes-Halévy wrote a disastrously bad opera and fell flat on his
face before the public in the most pitiful way, his friend calmly defied
death on his behalf and went on to print his opus just the same. In our
egoistic, self-seeking age this always provided a most gratifying and
refreshing spectacle: the self-sacrifice of one friend for another.
Now, however, Pylades maintains that his friend's madness has
increased to such an extent that he can no longer publish his works—
unless he too were to go mad.[41]

Despite all the leg-pulling we can see Heine's recognition of
the risks entrepreneurs such as Schlesinger took, and the useful
function they performed in the cultural life of Europe by their

willingness to shoulder such risks. That Schlesinger in fact never did 'desert' Halévy is part of Heine's joke.

One other point must not be overlooked in Heine's presentation of Schlesinger and the Escudier brothers: his charge that Jewish and Gentile impresarios alike often praised artists, and induced others to praise them, for extraneous, non-aesthetic reasons. Schlesinger puffed Döhler because he had agreed to act as his agent; the Escudiers puffed Döhler and other pianists because they were feuding with Franz Liszt and wanted to belittle him by exalting his rivals.[42]

Heine's discussion of Mendelssohn-Bartholdy, it will have been noticed, brought in a host of other figures of Jewish origin: Moses Mendelssohn, the Jew who worked for the amelioration of his co-religionists and became a *praeceptor Germaniae* without ceasing to be a Jew; his son Abraham, who had his own son baptized in his thirteenth year, the year in which by Jewish law he came of age; Meyerbeer, the commercial manager of his ever-increasing musical fame; August Leo, the Hamburg banker settled in Paris who attempted to mediate, with what Heine clearly considered inadequate cultural resources, between German celebrities and the French public; Maurice Schlesinger, the editor and impresario; and Rachel Félix, the interpreter of a literary classicism for which the poet could never work up any real enthusiasm. 'Mlle Rachel', he tells readers of the *Augsburg Gazette* on 20 March 1843, 'serves up [to the new bourgeois masters of French society] the mouldering dregs of the old classical sleeping-draughts.'[43] As a cultural phenomenon Rachel clearly fascinated Heine; she turns up in his conversations as well as in his writings in a series of rapid sketches which suggest different aspects of the significance she had for him. One of these was that of the 'respect revolution' he saw taking place all around him: an upsetting of establishing hierarchies in which the acceptance of Jews into European society played, in the poet's eyes, an important part. How this works can best be shown in his own words. The passage to be quoted appeared in the *Augsburg Gazette* under the date 22 May 1841.

At the moment all is quiet here in Paris. People have tired of discussing the forgery of letters purporting to come from the king, but have found an amusing diversion in the abduction of the Infanta of Spain by Ignaz Gurowsky . . . Last summer friend Ignaz was in love with Mlle Rachel; but since her father, who is descended from a good Jewish family, refused him his daughter's hand, he made up to the Princess Isabella Fernanda of Spain. All the ladies-in-waiting of both the Castiles—and those of the whole universe—will hold up their hands in horror. Now, at last, they understand that the old world, the world of traditional respect, has come to an end![44]

Louis Philippe, Heine adds, realized this perfectly, and therefore sought to secure his power by appeals, not to traditional feelings of respect for royalty, but to people's real needs, to naked necessity—*reelle Bedürfnisse und nackte Notwendigkeit*.[45] Jewish emancipation is thus seen as an index of the same revolutionizing potential which made Heine number the Rothschilds, those props of the establishment execrated by the left wing, among the 'greatest revolutionaries' of Europe.

(iv)

James de Rothschild and his family play a modest but significant part in Heine's reports from Paris in the early 1840s. Heine had with them the same kind of tangled relationship that he had with Meyerbeer and the Beer family of Berlin; and the facts brought to light by an analysis of these relations are not always conducive to a belief in the impartiality of the poet's judgements. This study need not, however, concern itself with Heine's manœuvring for money, or for musical compositions of his works, or for free opera tickets to be used by Mathilde and her friends, or for railway shares, or for interventions in his favour at the court of Uncle Salomon—its subject are the portraits and caricatures in Heine's writings that were influenced by a multitude of factors and considerations among which those just mentioned formed only one tiny part. We must, however, occasionally remind ourselves that Heine's characterizations of his contemporaries are not dispassionate and disinterested; that they are affected not only by his desire to catch the very physiognomy and the very accents of the age, to lay bare the roots of social existence, and to indulge his artist's delight in literary portraiture and caricature, but also by a mundane striving for personal advantage and by the urge to avenge actual or imagined slights.

In the *Augsburg Gazette* articles of the 1840s the Rothschilds appear, on the whole, to advantage—though as always Heine cannot resist a pinprick or two. Such power as they have, he seems to believe, they use benevolently, wisely, for the public good. Their power is, indeed, one more check on the arbitrary rule of princes; unlike the court Jews of earlier times, they are not simply instruments in the hands of any monarch that employs them. There is an unmistakable touch of *schadenfreude* in Heine's description of a royal indigence which makes European kings dependent on Rothschild loans:

To this financial plight Rothschild owes the great attentions paid to him at court; a few hundred years earlier the king of France would simply have had his teeth pulled out to make him agree to a loan. But the naïve manners and customs of the Middle Ages have sunk beneath the stream of revolution, and M. de Rothschild, Baron and Knight of the Order of Isabella, can walk about the Tuileries unmolested, without risking so much as a stump if he shows the king his teeth.

(4 February 1840)[46]

On 27 February 1840 we find Heine at pains to deny the authorship of some malicious quips against James de Rothschild which had been attributed to him in the columns of *La Quotidienne*.[47] In the *Augsburg Gazette* he redresses the balance by speaking of the Rothschild charities; his report on the great fire of Hamburg, for instance, dated 20 May 1842, tells us that among Germans who distinguished themselves by their zeal in helping the victims James de Rothschild deserves special mention, adding the comment that 'the name of this house [of Rothschild] is ever prominent when philanthropy is called upon to do its work.'[48]

The virtues of James de Rothschild appear particularly luminous in Heine's pages when he is contrasted with such lesser luminaries of the Jewish banking world as Maximilian Königswärter,[49] or with the Fould family.

It is generally rumoured that M. Benoît Fould will . . . be raised to the peerage, and it is indeed more than likely that we shall shortly see this

at once ridiculous and distressing spectacle. That's all that was
needed for the poor French peerage to draw down the world's full
power of mockery. And that's all *we* needed too, this dazzling
victory of the driest and hardest materialism. Raise James Rothschild
as high as you like—he is a man and has a human heart. But this M.
Benoît Fould! *Le National* tells us today that the only man to shake
the hand of Public Prosecutor Hébert at the opening session of
parliament was Banker Fould. 'M. Fould', the paper adds, 'ressemble
beaucoup à un discours d'accusateur public.'[50]

In later times Heine found it convenient to deny the authorship
of the anonymous article dated 28 December 1841 in which
this passage occurs; but no competent editor now doubts that
it has come from his envenomed pen. It would seem, however,
that even in the early 1840s Heine was aware of the need for
some self-censorship in such matters: as when he excised from
his *Augsburg Gazette* article of 20 June 1842 a snide reference
to Achille Fould's successful candidature as member of parlia-
ment for the Hautes Pyrénées district. He presented the elec-
tion in which Fould was one of the candidates as a *horse-race*
and noted that among the listed runners were 'almost a dozen
of Arabian race'. 'Among these', he added, 'we find Achille
Fould—as though having Benoît were not enough for us!'[51] It
may well be that Heine deleted the phrase just quoted not for
reasons of prudence (or fairness), but because he learnt that
Benoît Fould had not in fact been re-elected in 1842.

  The image of horses belonging to the 'Arabian race' is worth
noting. Like Voltaire and so many others Heine occasionally
spoke of 'Arabs' when he meant 'Jews': there is an amusing
later example in the French version of the *Augsburg Gazette*
article of 27 May 1840, where we read:

Les israélites de la nouvelle génération sont encore plus chiches que
leurs pères; je suis porté à croire que parmi la jeunesse doré d'Israël, il
se trouve plus d'un millionnaire qui hésiterait peut-être de donner six
francs, s'il peut à ce prix sauver de la bastonnade toute *une tribu de
bedouins coréligionnaires.*' (my italics)

The German word translated as 'tribu' in this passage is
Stamm, which elsewhere in this French version of the article is
rendered by the French word *race* (when *die Stammesbande*
becomes *les liens de race*).[52] We have already glanced at Heine's

use of the word *Stamm* in his *Augsburg Gazette* articles. It occurs, in fact, in several contexts in which contemporaries would have used the word *race*; and it is notable that in one place in which this happens Heine goes out of his way to set himself apart from all who believed in racial purity by stressing, with Michelet, the beneficial effects of a genetic mingling of the *celtischer Stamm* with the *germanischer Stamm*: 'the fusion of . . . Germanic and Celtic elements will always bring something excellent into the world.'[53]

The Rothschilds move into the centre of Heine's panorama of modern life when he talks about the development of the railways, which he rightly sees not only as a most powerful agent of social transformation in France, but also as a turning-point in world history.

All eyes are now turned to the House of Rothschild which represents the society formed to construct the Northern French railway system in a way that is financially as sound as it is socially praiseworthy. The House of Rothschild, which in former times directed its talents and resources exclusively to the needs of governments, now places itself at the head of great national undertakings, devoting its enormous capital and its immeasurable credit to the advancement of industry and the prosperity of the people.[54]

This is indeed a change from the Börnean image of the Rothschilds as modern court Jews, as the prop of tyrants and tyranny! Heine's flirtation with Saint-Simonism had served to alert him to the benefits of the industrial transformation as whose agents he here presents the great bankers of kings. They are seen as powers in their own right, whose dynastic relationship recall those of European royalty and whose family gatherings are described in terms that suggest the congresses at which the fate of Europe was so often decided in the nineteenth century.

The majority of the members of this house—or rather, this family—is at present assembled in Paris; but the secrets of such a Congress are too well guarded for us to be able to report on them. These Rothschilds harmonize with one another in the most remarkable fashion. Strangely enough, they even choose marriage partners from among themselves, and the strands of relationship between them form complicated knots which future historians will find difficult to unravel. The head, or rather the brain, of this family is Baron James, a remarkable man whose unique ability manifests itself solely in financial affairs . . .

A back-handed compliment, one might think! What follows, however, seems designed to show, through its comparison of Baron James with the French Sun King, that the Rothschilds, like other royalty, developed talents that compensated in some measure for their limitations. And if Baron James is then compared with other Parisian bankers, it will be seen that he outshone his rivals as effectively in cultural as in financial dealings.

. . . he has the capacity of finding (if not always of judging) the leading practitioners in every other sphere of activity. Because of this gift he has been compared with Louis XIV; and it is true that in contrast with his colleagues here in Paris, who like to surround themselves with mediocrities, M. James de Rothschild always appears in association with the notabilities of every branch of the arts and sciences. Even when he knew nothing of a subject, he always knew who most excelled in it. He does not, perhaps, understand a single note of music; but Rossini was always a friend of the family. Ary Scheffer is his court painter; Carême was his cook.

Some pinpricks will have been felt here. Rothschild's cultural innocence is being prodded; there is something suspect about joining painter and cook in the same sentence, as though their services were being judged as equal contributions to the civilized life; and Ary Scheffer is hardly a name to launch a thousand ships. Heine modulates into a more genuinely complimentary vein, however, when he passes from Rachel Félix to Adolphe Crémieux: two names that always come readily to his mind when he surveys the French intellectul and cultural scene in the early 1840s.

M. de Rothschild knows as little Greek, surely, as Mlle Rachel; but the scholar he favours most is J.-A. Letronne. His personal physician was the great Dr Dupuytren, with whom he formed a brotherly friendship. Rothschild came to appreciate very early the worth of Crémieux, the great jurist with the noblest of hearts, and found in him a faithful advocate. In the same way

and here we come to a climax, as Heine inverts the traditional relationship between European monarchs and the court Jews they chose for their 'usefulness'—

[Rothschild] appreciated the political capacities of Louis Philippe from the first, and he has always stayed on an intimate footing with that grand master of politics.

The man who could thus appreciate the merits of that devalued commodity, a nineteenth-century monarch, also had little difficulty in discovering the usefulness of Saint-Simonists such as Emile Péreire, who, Heine tells us, became 'the pontifex maximus of the railways' after Rothschild had 'made him his chief engineer and used him to found the railways from Paris to Versailles, on the right bank of the Seine, where no accident ever happens'. Having allowed us this glimpse of another figure of Jewish origin in the social and financial panorama of Paris, Heine gives at last the answer to a question that will have been on the minds of all readers who responded to his parallel between Rothschild and Louis XIV. Where are the poets who give lustre to the court of this new-style monarch? Where is his Corneille, his Racine, his Molière?

Poetry, whether French or German, stands alone in having no eminent living representative in M. de Rothschild's favour. He loves only Shakespeare, Racine, Goethe, all taken from this earth, all transfigured, purified spirits removed from the financial needs attending life here below.[55]

Heine, it may well be thought, is here throwing his own hat into the ring as a living poet worthy of the Rothschilds' patronage; and in the revised version of this passage, which he included in *Lutezia*, he alludes clearly to his habit of asking for (and receiving!) railways shares at par on which he could realize an immediate profit.[56]

The pointed reference, in the passage on Rothschild and Péreire, to the fact that there had been no accidents on the *right* bank of the Seine, alludes obliquely to a terrible train crash which occurred on the *left* bank on Sunday, 8 May 1842. Some 350 people lost their lives, mainly by fire, in what still remains one of the worst railway disasters in world history. Drawing an ironic parallel between the Sunday crowd which lost its life, and the 'sabbath' company which lost part of its anticipated profits, Heine once again homes in on some of his favourite Jewish targets—including Benoît Fould, whom he had once called the Chief Rabbi of the Left Bank but whom, on this occasion, he forbears to name.

In this vile and shameful year mankind has suffered much, and even the bankers have incurred some losses. What a dreadful disaster, for instance, was the fire on the Versailles railway! I am not referring, now, to the Sunday crowd roasted or parboiled on this occasion; I refer, rather, to the surviving sabbath company, whose stock tumbled by so many per cent, and which now awaits, with fear and trembling, the outcome of the lawsuits brought against it after this catastrophe. Will the promoters or founders of the company be made to disgorge some money to compensate the orphaned or maimed victims of their avid pursuit of profit? How terrible that would be! These millionaires are much to be pitied, for they have already lost so much, and the profits from their other enterprises may hardly cover their loss this year.

All this leads once again to a more general satire on Jewish financiers whose antics contrast with the comparative dignity of James de Rothschild.

There are enough other unpleasant things to drive one mad; on the Stock Exchange it was rumoured yesterday that * * * no longer believed in Moses and the prophets and was preparing to have himself baptized. Others are better off; even if the whole of the *rive gauche* should go to the dogs, we could console ourselves with the thought that the *rive droite* flourishes all the more. The Southern French railways are also doing well, as are all those networks which have recently been granted their charter; and the entrepreneur who yesterday was no more than a poor tattered scamp is a wealthy scamp today. Scrawny Mr * * * assures us that he has good 'weasons' ['er habe "Gründ"'] to be satisfied with Providence. Yes, while the rest of us are wasting our time with philosophical speculations this skinny spectre confined its speculations to railway shares; and one of its patrons in high places and lofty banks said to me the other day: 'Just look at this little fellow: he came from nothing, and now he has made money and will make even more money—and he has never had any dealings with philosophy in all his days!'[57]

In the later *Lutezia* version of this passage, the names of the dramatis personae are filled in. The speculator who no longer believed in Moses and the prophets is called Läusedorf, while the thin man who made a killing in railway stock turns out to be S. J. Stern, often portrayed, in Heine's writings, under the sobriquet 'Nasenstern'.[58] Once again, however, the poet is careful to make the point that he is scourging rich parvenus generally, and not just *Jewish* parvenus in particular.

How these mushrooms resemble one another in all places and at all times! They have always looked down with especial disdain on writers who devote themselves, unselfishly, to the studies we subsume under the name 'philosophy'. Petronius tells us of a Roman parvenu who, eighteen hundred years ago, had the following epitaph engraved on his tomb: "Here lies Straberius; he started with nothing, and left three hundred million sesterces behind him at his death, although in his entire life he never paid heed to philosophy. Follow his example, and you will do well!"[59]

It is hard to believe that when he penned these words Heine was not casting covert glances in the direction of his uncle Salomon. And when we then come to read, in an article of the *Augsburg Gazette* which is dated 11 June 1843 and whose theme is expressly stated to be the moral bankruptcy of the social order the communists sought to overthrow:

A poet once said that the first king was a successful soldier; in respect of those who founded our present financial dynasties we might, perhaps, venture the more prosaic observation that the first banker was a successful rogue[60]

we must surely feel that not only the Heines and the Foulds but the Rothschilds too might well have taken the poet's quip as a slur on the honour of their house. The Rothschilds seem to have had a well-developed sense of humour and proportion, however, and therefore bore the poet no grudge. Whether Uncle Salomon took note of this passage, and recalled his nephew's quip that Salomon became a banker because his mother during her pregnancy had read a biography of the robber-chief Cartouche, must remain a matter for speculation. He certainly took steps to see that after his death financial subventions to his ever-needy Harry would be made conditional on curbing his pen—at least in respect of his relatives in Hamburg.

(v)

What Heine shows us of Jewish life in his own times must always be seen in a multiplicity of contexts. Some of these involve historic contrasts, as when he speaks, in an article dated 20 November 1840 which the *Augsburg Gazette* did not choose to print, of the dignity of different kinds of 'service': loyal service to a liege-lord among the Germans, to nation and soil among the Romans, to a supra-sensual God among the Hebrews.[61] Other contexts that need to be kept in mind are Heine's changing views on human nature throughout the ages, and his views on the virtues and vices of the period in which he himself lived, where so much remained to be done towards emancipating Jews along with other groups that suffered civic discrimination.

Let us hope that the great conflagration [which had devastated Hamburg in 1842] has also brought a little illumination to inferior intelligences, and that the whole population of Hamburg has now come to realize that the spirit of the time, which brought it succour in its time of need, must not later be offended by a mean huckster's spirit. Now, surely, Hamburg will not be able to put off yet again the granting of full civil equality to adherents of the different religions.[62]

Above all we must not lose sight of the poet's estimate of the sufferings, the deformations, and the cultural achievements of the Jewish people from biblical times onwards. Very early on in the contributions he sent to the *Augsburg Gazette* in the 1840s, in the article dated 1 October 1840, he has the great Lafontaine run through the streets of Paris asking his acquaintances whether they had read the Book of Baruch—one of the apocryphal books of the Old Testament whose beauty and profundity Lafontaine had just discovered for himself. 'One of the best books ever written', he is made to say of this work;[63] and Heine's anecdote is no doubt intended to send his readers in quest of a product of the Jewish genius of which they might never have heard.

In a memorable passage of the article of 5 May 1834 the poet takes Horace Vernet's painting of Judah and Tamar as his occasion for speaking of the different ways in which writers and artists not noted for their religiosity had used the sacred Scriptures of the Hebrews.

The painter has dipped his brush neither in the searing malice of Voltaire's satire nor in the filthy paintpots favoured by Parny and his like. He is moved by no polemical or immoral intentions; in his eyes the Bible is just another book, he no longer has a prejudice against it, he even finds it winsome and amusing, and he does not disdain it as a source of subjects. That's how he painted Judith, Rebecca at the well, Abraham and Hagar—and that's how he painted Judah and Tamar too, as a fitting altar-piece for Notre Dame de Lorette.[64]

Heine too, of course, could set aside reverence when dealing with biblical motifs—but for all his worldliness and scepticism he has a respect for the human and literary values of the Bible which give him the right to scorn the attitudes he has here ascribed to Voltaire, Parny, and Horace Vernet. One of the most interesting ways in which he introduces biblical motifs into his newspaper articles of the 1840s varies a time-honoured mode of exegesis: as prefigurations of modern events, as symbols applicable in all ages, as models or standards against which modern phenomena can be measured.

Even champagne seems to have losts its power; it only clouds the senses, but leaves the heart stone sober; at many a merry banquet the guests turn pale, a joke dies on their lips, they look at one another with terror—for they see the writing on the wall: *Mene, Mene, Tekel Upharsin*!

(6 January 1841)

The French too dance around the Golden Calf; but their dancing conveys derision, persiflage, self-mockery—it is a kind of cancan . . .

(15 June 1843)

The dance is accursed, a pious Breton folksong asserts, ever since Herodias's daughter danced before the evil Tetrarch who had John the Baptist killed to please her . . .

(7 February 1842)

The principle of atonement which we find in Hegel is the same as that enunciated by Moses—except that Moses bore deep in his heart the

ancient sense of fate, while Hegel is permeated with the modern idea
of freedom . . .

(July 1843)[65]

The early disciples of Jesus exercised an influence on world
history which was quite disproportionate to their numbers and
social position; in this respect Heine compares the communists
of his own day with these disciples. Jesus himself appears in
these writings as 'the son of the carpenter', the man from the
labouring classes who sought to sweep away a rotten world of
privilege. One can hardly call this 'prefiguration': it is rather a
reflection of modern times and conditions backwards into
biblical history.

Communism is favoured by the circumstance that the enemy it fights
lacks moral stability and hold. The established society of our time
defends itself only out of an instinct of self-preservation; it has no
belief in its own justification, no self-respect. In this it resembles that
former society whose rotten timbers gave way when the carpenter's
son appeared.

(15 June 1843)[66]

Paris therefore takes on the likeness, not only of Babylon, but
also of Jerusalem.

'France is finished'—with these words many a German correspon-
dent runs about the streets prophesying the destruction of the Jeru-
salem of our own day . . .

(13 February 1841)

I am convinced that if ever Paris were to be destroyed its inhabitants,
like the Jews of old, would disperse throughout the world and in this
dispersion spread the seed of social transformation even more effec-
tively than before.

(ibid.)[67]

This last quotation tell us as much about Heine's views of the
Jews' function in history as it tells us about his view of modern
Parisians.

We also find significant attempts, in these articles of the
1840s, to assert his spiritual kinship with Jewish figures of the
past whose images, Heine came to feel, were being distorted by
artists and scholars alike. These figures range from Jesus of

Nazareth to Spinoza. In the salon of 1843, he tells the readers of the *Augsburg Gazette*, he had seen

a painting of the scourging of Christ in which the central figure, with his suffering face, resembled the chairman of a failed joint stock company who now stood before his shareholders and had to render his account. The shareholders appear in this picture too—they take the shape of executioners and Pharisees who are very angry—they seem to have lost a good deal of money when their shares took a tumble . . .[68]

No clue is given to the identity of the painter in this *Augsburg Gazette* version. In later years, however, when Heine reworked this article for the French edition of his *Lutezia*, he gave his readers a broad hint: 'It is said', he writes in *Lutèce*, 'that in the principal figure the painter has portrayed his uncle Léo.'[69] So now we know who the 'chairman' of the failed company is: August Leo, whose unfortunate business ventures are unsympathetically glossed elsewhere in *Lutezia*—and we can also supply the name of the painter. It can only be Heinrich Lehmann (1814–82), for whose pictures Heine could never work up any enthusiasm.[70]

Heine tried, as we have just seen, to project an alternative picture of Jesus, a Jesus for the mid-nineteenth century, as the carpenter's son who enlisted his small band of disciples in the cause of overthrowing a rotten society. Some time after May 1844 he added that one of the important consequences of Jesus's life and death was the mitigation of the *ius talionis* which Moses had still proclaimed in its uncompromising form: a life for a life, a tooth for a tooth.

With the martyr's death of the great atoner this idea of expiation also came to an end; one can say that here as elsewhere the gentle Christ satisfied the ancient law so far as his own person was concerned, while abolishing and sublating it for the rest of mankind. It is strange that in this respect religion progressed while philosophy remained stationary. Despite all differences of dialectical expression the theory of law to be found in our philosophers from Kant to Hegel remains tied to the old *ius talionis*.[71]

As for Spinoza—he had recently been introduced to the French public by Victor Cousin, whose popularizations always tempted Heine to irony and caricature. Cousin had shown himself far too eager, Heine complained, to defuse the possibly explosive effects of Spinoza's anti-establishment opinions. For his own part, therefore, the poet projects an image of Spinoza that brings out the latter's hostility to established religion, his subversion of orthodox Catholicism as well as orthodox Judaism. Spinoza was clearly one of the world-historical figures in whom Heine saw prefigurations of himself—a God-seeker outside synagogue and church alike; a proudly independent thinker; a man born within the Jewish fold who kept his ethnic identity even though he rejected the Jewish religion, and even though the Jewish community of his day had sought to cast him out.

CHAPTER 7
A Fellow Exile and his World

(i)

In February 1837 there died in Paris the man whose name had been constantly coupled with Heine's in denunciations of 'Young Germany' and of the role that Jews were beginning to play in German literature: the great liberal patriot Ludwig Börne, who had abandoned his original name Louis Baruch at his baptism in 1818. Heine and Börne had once been on friendly terms; but Heine's writings and political attitudes displeased Börne more and more, and by the time he died a mutual dislike had grown up between them. After Börne's death Heine began to think of setting down his memories and impressions of his fellow exile and at the same time to defend himself against the charges, levelled against him by Börne and his friends, that he lacked firmness of principle and dignity of character, and that this lack showed in his writings. Some time in 1837 or 1838 he drafted the beginning of a memoir of his fellow writer and fellow exile, in which he said that he had never pardoned an insult, but that he would make an exception for Ludwig Börne.

I forgive the slanders he has attached to my name and spread about all the world by direct and indirect means. Not a single spiteful syllable will I utter against him; I shall confine myself to searching my memory in order to set down faithfully into what contacts we have been brought in person and in spirit. The public will then see how these contacts necessarily rendered the opinion he had of me more and more gloomy and bitter. Our contacts were never close, they were always accidental, and they never brought about—never could have brought about—true friendship between us. This last point especially I could never have discussed while he was still alive, for fear that he would take it as a personal slight.[1]

This draft of an opening chapter, never published in Heine's lifetime, gives another reason why he had felt it advisable to keep his counsel.

I would have had to expose the intrigues of some of the Jewish shield-bearers of this great agitator; and that might have led me to air reflections which would have been subject to even uglier misunderstandings. Strange! When they wanted to affront me most grievously they declared me one of themselves.[2]

The spectacle of one Jew insulting another by reminding him of his Jewish origins is a touch we must not miss in Heine's sad Jewish Comedy.

In the event Heine did not begin the book in the way he had planned—he started again, opening this time with an account of a first meeting with Börne, and had his manuscript ready for the printer early in 1840. The first title he thought of seems to have been *The Life of Ludwig Börne* (*Leben Ludwig Börnes*); but he soon altered that to *Ludwig Börne. A Memorial by H. Heine* (*Ludwig Börne. Eine Denkschrift von H. Heine*). When the book came out, however, it bore a title supplied by the publisher, Julius Campe:

Heinrich Heine
über
Ludwig Börne

This could be interpreted as meaning a book by Heine about Börne; but because of the multiple connotations of the preposition *über*, and the arrangement of the text on the title-page, it seemed to suggest that Heine was ranking himself above Börne. Both these interpretations were in fact supported by the book itself; but that made Heine all the more furious at Campe's highhanded action in giving the book a title its author had never authorized.

The poet's anger at his publisher was as nothing, however, compared to the anger with which the German public received his book. Börne was a revered father-figure for many German liberals, who felt that Heine had besmirched his memory. Those who had been close to Börne were particularly incensed by the personal insults directed at his associates and friends, and unleashed a press campaign designed to discredit Heine in his turn. The poet was even forced to fight a duel with the husband of Börne's friend Jeanette Wohl, whom he had made the target of some unsavoury and gratuitous insults. Not since *The Baths of Lucca* had a work of Heine's provoked such universal indignation. Now that passions have cooled, however, the book can be seen, despite some lapses of taste, as one of Heine's most accomplished and characteristic performances.

The Jewish portraits in this memoir or 'memorial' must be seen, first of all, in the context of the poet's endeavour to construct a human typology that would transcend the usual distinctions between 'Jews' and 'Christians'. He proposes making these two terms synonymous and opposes to them the terms 'Greek' or 'Hellene'. 'Jewish' (or 'Hebrew') and 'Christian' (or 'Nazarene') would then stand for a spiritualistic, ascetic mentality, 'Greek' (or 'Hellenic') for a sensualistic, realistic one. Judaic spiritualism would be opposed to Hellenic glorying in life. The two character types might even be linked with different physical constitutions, the 'Jewish' learning towards the thin, the 'Greek' leaning towards the well-fleshed; and the task of European civilization might be seen as an ultimate synthesis and reconciliation of the two types. Such a synthesis was prefigured in Shakespeare, whom Heine saw as Jew and Greek at the same time.[3] In the meantime it gave the poet a malicious pleasure to apply his categories to his more puritanical enemies, and especially to Christian Jew-haters, by speaking of 'the Jew Menzel' or 'the Jew Hengstenberg', in the certain knowledge that they would not relish this taste of their own medicine.

'In our sense there may be no great difference between Jews and Christians; but such a difference is very sharply etched into the consciousness of Frankfurt philistines.'[4] Here we have another context into which the poet places his portrait of Börne: the history of Judaeophobia throughout the ages. Heine shows in detail how traditional *religious* hostilities were being shouldered out, or supplemented, by the more openly *economic* hostility of those who saw Jews as dangerous business rivals or held them responsible for the evils of nascent capitalism; by the *social* hostility of those who saw them as pushful interlopers; and by a *philosophical* hostility which was beginning to draw on dubious racial theories and was fuelled by various nationalisms as well as by fear of subtle Jewish revenges for centuries of oppression. Heine documents very interestingly how much talk of 'race' there was towards the end of the 1830s, particularly after Cotta's *German Quarterly*

(*Deutsche Vierteljahrsschrift*) had published Hermann Hauff's essay on 'Human Races' (*Die Menschenracen*):

In North Germany Teutomania . . . was more of an affectation, if not a deliberate lie: especially in Prussia, where the champions of German nationality tried in vain to deny their Slav descent. My own dear Swabians deserve more credit in this respect—they treat it all much more seriously, and they have a greater right to insist on the purity of the Germanic race. Cotta's *Quarterly*, which is at present their chief organ of publication, is animated by such racial pride; its editor, the diplomat [C. F. K. von] Kölle (an intelligent man but the greatest tattle-tale on this earth—he never, I am sure, kept any state secret to himself!) is the most inveterate smeller-out of racial characteristics; every third word he speaks concerns the Germanic, Romanic, and Semitic races . . . His greatest sorrow is that the champion of *Germanentum*, his darling Wolfgang Menzel, has a face that bears every sign of Mongolian descent.[5]

And when, in a later passage, we find Heine recalling once again an experience to which he had already alluded in *Towards a History of Religion and Philosophy in Germany*:

In the Göttingen beer cellar I once admired the thoroughness with which my Teutonic friends compiled proscription lists for the day on which they would come to power. Anyone descended (even unto the seventh generation) from a Frenchman, a Jew, or a Slav, was condemned to exile . . .

then we cannot but agree with Ruth L. Jacobi that Heine has here conveyed something of the spirit of the Nuremberg Laws nearly a hundred years before Hitler enacted them.[6]

The passage just quoted from *Towards a History of Religion and Philosophy in Germany* prompts two further observations. The first of these is that it requires no uncanny powers of prophecy to convey the spirit of the Nuremberg laws in the first half of the nineteenth century: Heine had read such works as J. F. Fries's *On the Danger Posed to the Welfare and Character of the German People by the Jews* (1816), which advocated suppression of Jewish educational institutions, encouragement of Jewish emigration from Germany, coupled with the prohibition of Jewish immigration into Germany, forbidding Christians to accept employment as domestic servants in Jewish households, making it mandatory for Jews to wear distinctive marks on their clothing, together with other measures designed to prevent Jews from 'contaminating' German purity. Other pamphleteers—Hartwig Hundt-Radowsky, for instance—went even further in the direction of the Final Solution. Such writers looked for sanction of their anti-Jewish stance not only to modern philosophers like Fichte, but also to Luther's intemperate pamphlets against the stiff-necked people that resisted conversion to Protestantism.

The second observation draws attention to a typical piece of Heinesque irony. His Jew-haters are made to proclaim their decree with the help of a phrase clearly derived from Luther's translation of the Old Testament: the phrase *im siebenten Glied*, 'unto the seventh generation', based on Exodus 20: 5. Enemies of the Jews are forced to take their very weapons from what is ultimately a Jewish source.

Despite his attempt to use the concept 'Jewish' in new ways, Heine shows himself fully aware, in *Ludwig Börne*, of the actuality of a Jewish people shaped by and shaping its own history. He sought to recreate the Jewish cultural atmosphere even more precisely than the book now makes it appear; before publication Heine deleted a number of references that non-Jews might find difficult to understand. He contemplated, for instance, a reference to the *afikoman*, a piece of unleavened bread that plays a part in the Passover ceremony. In another passage, also later amended, he alluded to the *Tz'enah u-re'enah*, a Bible paraphrase in the Yiddish language which first came out in the seventeenth century and which soon established itself as a household work for Jewish women whose Hebrew was not up to reading the Bible in the original.[7]

The Jewish sense of history, of the living actuality of the past within the present, is constantly suggested. Talk of the fall of Warsaw immediately brings to mind the fall of Jerusalem that led to the Diaspora—the destruction of Jerusalem is, in fact, mentioned no less than five times in this short work. Heine's sojourn in Paris is linked with the Babylonian exile; and a walk through the Jewish quarter in Frankfurt reveals that there the very stones can be made to recall dark stories of Jewish persecution and oppression in the Middle Ages. The people that is shown to have emerged from this often terrible history contains knaves and fools enough; but it also contains men and women of the highest ideals, capable of noble self-sacrifice.

In truth, the Jews are of the stuff of which gods are made; trodden underfoot today, they are tomorrow worshipped and kneeled to. While some of them wallow in the filthiest mire of huckstering, others ascend the highest peaks of humanity, and Golgotha is not the only height on which a Jewish god shed his blood for the world's salvation. The Jews are the people of the spirit, and whenever they return to that principle, they are great and glorious—then they can shame and conquer their clumsy oppressors. The profound philosopher Karl Rosenkranz compared them to the giant Antaeus; but while that giant was strengthened whenever he touched the earth, the Jews gain new strength whenever they touch heaven. What a strange phenomenon, what glaring contrasts! While you find among these people every possible caricature of vulgarity, you also find the purest ideals of humanity among them; and as they once led the world into new paths of progress, the world may, perhaps, expect them to open up others yet unknown . . .

'Nature', Hegel once said to me, 'is very strange. She employs the self-same tools for her highest and her lowest purposes. The very member, for instance, which is entrusted with the highest mission, the propagation of mankind, also serves . . .' Those who complain of Hegel's obscurity will understand his meaning here; and even though he did not have Israel in mind when he made that remark, it can be applied to it.

However that may be, the mission of this tribe or ethnic group [*Stamm*] is possibly not yet wholly fulfilled, particularly with regard to Germany. Germany too awaits a redeemer, an earthly Messiah—with a heavenly one the Jews have blessed us already—a King of the Earth, a saviour with sceptre and sword; and this German redeemer is perhaps the same as the one for whom Israel is waiting . . .[8]

The ordained function of the Jews, then, did not end with the Dispersion, and a sense of their historic mission is alive even in those who, like Heine himself and like Börne, consciously transcended their specifically Jewish allegiances to work for the emancipation of all mankind. The writings of Benjamin Disraeli, who was of course baptized even earlier in life than Heine and Börne, bear witness to a similar sense of Hebraic mission and destiny; but we will search Disraeli's works in vain for anything like the irreverent application we have just heard

Heine make of Hegel's observation on dual physiological functions.

The book in which Heine perceives the moral and poetic genius of the Jews most clearly at work is, of course, the Old Testament; and like most of his works, *Ludwig Börne* too is therefore shot through with references to biblical characters and incidents. A typical passage has Börne reflect on anti-Jewish feelings in his own day and remind those who find it expedient to whip up such feelings of the fate suffered by earlier enemies of Israel. He cites the Emperor Titus first, as he appears in Jewish history and tradition rather than in Corneille and Mozart, and accurately recalls Talmudic legends about his painful last days. Then he turns to the Old Testament.

'It is remarkable that all Israel's enemies have come to a bad end of this kind. What happened to Nebuchadnezzar you know: you remember how he became an ox in his latter days and had to eat grass. And look at that Persian minister of state, that Haman—was he not hanged in the end, in Susa, the capital? And Antiochus, King of Syria, did he not rot while he was still alive, eaten up by lice? Those latter-day villains, our present-day Jew-haters, had better beware! But what's the use, they are not frightened off by such terrible examples, and a few days ago I read yet another pamphlet against the Jews by a professor of philosophy, no less, one who calls himself *magis amica*. He'll eat grass one of these days, you'll see; an ox he is already by nature, and perhaps he'll be hanged some time for insulting the Sultana, the favourite of the Duke of Flachsenfingen; already, I'm sure, he is as lousy as Antiochus!'[9]

What Heine here puts into Börne's mouth, effectively caricaturing Börne's speech rhythms, is very much his own witty application of Old Testament stories.

The Bible appears in more serious context in Book II of *Ludwig Börne. A Memorial.* This evokes, in letter or diary form, a holiday Heine had spent on the island of Heligoland in 1830, just before and during the July revolution in France. Heligoland was, at that time, under British rule, and therefore observed the old-fashioned British Sunday.

Since it was Sunday yesterday and a cloud of leaden boredom weighed down the whole island and almost crushed my skull, I took up the Bible in sheer despair . . .

Having once started to read Heine discovered, he tells us, that despite his intellectual Hellenism he found in this product of the Hebraic genius not only splendid entertainment but also spiritual nourishment.

What a book it is! As great and wide as the whole world, rooted deep in the abysses of creation and reaching far upward into the blue mysteries of heaven ... Dawn and dusk, promise and fulfilment, birth and death, the whole drama of mankind—this book contains them all, this book of books, Biblia ... The Jews can take comfort—they lost Jerusalem, it is true, and the Temple, and the Ark of the Covenant, and the golden vessels and trinkets of Solomon, but all that is of little weight when compared with the Bible, the indestructible treasure which they saved.

In an original attempt to define the 'nationhood' of the Jews Heine now presents the Hebrew Bible as their 'portable fatherland':

It was Mahomet, if I am not mistaken, who called the Jews 'the people of the book'; a name they have retained in the Orient right up to the present day. .... A book is their fatherland, their property, their ruler, their good and evil fortune. Within the boundaries of this book they live; here they exercise an inalienable right of citizenship, here they cannot be expelled or despised, here they are strong and admirable. Engrossed in this book they noticed little of the changes that took place in the real world around them; nations rose and fell, states flourished and disappeared, revolutions swept the earth—but they, the Jews, sat hunched over their book and noticed nothing of the Wild Hunt of time which passed over their heads.

If Mahomet, the prophet of the East, called the Jews 'the people of the book',[10] Heine continues, Hegel, the prophet of the West, saw in them the people of the spirit, of *Geist*. This gives the poet his cue for putting forward a view he claims to have held in 1830—a view of Judaism as an abstract, spiritual, dialectical religion which contrasted vividly with the religious art and symbols of the peoples of the Near East among whom it was conceived. This, he tells us, explains the life and activity of Moses, who

erected ramparts of the spirit, as it were, against the aggressive throng of neighbouring nations; around the field in which he had sown

Spirit he planted a protective hedge of thorns made up of a strict ceremonial law and an egoistic nationalism.

In using this image of the 'protective hedge of thorns' to describe what Moses was doing Heine translates into his own terms, or rather into terms familiar to his readers from European fairy-tales, an image from the Talmud: the rabbis' image of the 'fence around the law', made up of marginal precepts designed to protect the inner centre. It is an image that Kafka would later transport into world literature in his own deeply disturbing way. In these Heligoland chapters of *Ludwig Börne* Moses is not yet, however, what he was to become for Heine some ten years afterwards: *mein liebster Heros*, my favourite hero. Moses, the lawgiver of his people, needs to be complemented, once his work is done and 'Spirit' ineradicably implanted, by Jesus of Nazareth who called all the peoples of the earth to share in the Kingdom of God that had once been the exclusive domain of the one chosen people. He gave the right of Jewish citizenship to the whole of humanity. *Er gab der ganzen Menschheit das jüdische Bürgerrecht.* Heine's very choice of vocabulary here recalls a later age, an age in which Jews petitioned for equal rights of citizenship in Germany. The question of citizenship was seen as a question of emancipation; and here again Heine could point to the still relevant message of the Christian Gospels.

There indeed was a great 'emancipation' question, and one which was solved in a far more generous way than is the case in Saxony and Hanover today . . . But the redeemer, it must be admitted, who liberated his brethren from the ceremonial law and the constraints of nationality, who inaugurated cosmopolitanism, became a victim of his humanity: the city magistrates of Jerusalem had him crucified, and the mob reviled him.[11]

It was only Christ's body, however, Heine concludes these reflections attributed to his own younger self, which was reviled and crucified; his spiritual religion conquered the world, and must now be overcome by a counter-movement, in politics and in art, in which the rights of the material world are vindicated alongside those of the spiritual, Hellenic principles asserted alongside Hebraic ones. The task of European civilization may well be the kind of harmonious mingling of these two principles which Heine thought he had found in the art of Shakespeare.

The overview of the Bible which Heine introduces into Book II of *Ludwig Börne* is supplemented by a more detailed look at some of its figures. A rereading of Genesis gives birth to a vision in which the poet feels his kinship with the characters there depicted so intensely that he begins to speak as one of their number. Laban, Rachel, Leah, Jacob, and Reuben pass before us; there are tongue-in-cheek speculations on the nature of *dudaim*, the flowers with which Leah bribed her way into Jacob's bed (could they have been Swabian wallflowers?); and the poet dwells at length on the story of Dinah and Sichem, which he sees as cruel and primitive in appearance only—beneath that appearance, he tries to show, it speaks of a true morality, a morality independent of dogma and legislation, a morality whose inalienable dwelling is the human heart. Once again, however, the New Testament is summoned up to supplement this image of the Old, and once again even Moses loses some of his lustre when seen against Jesus.

What a great drama the Passion is! . . . And what an attractive figure this divine man, *dieser Gottmensch*! How limited the hero of the Old Testament appears when compared with him! Moses loves his people with an affecting fervour; he cares like a mother for this people's future. Christ loves humanity—he was a sun that irradiated the whole earth with the warming rays of its love. What a soothing balm for the world's wounds his words provide! What a fountain of healing for all that grieve was the blood which flowed on Golgotha!—The white marble gods of the Greeks were splashed with this blood, they sickened with an inward horror and could nevermore recover . . .[12]

Once again we see the pale Galilean conquer a world already sickening from within, we hear of the death of the Great God Pan, and we are made to feel that however necessary and salutary the Judaeo-Christian religion was, and however admirable its Jewish founders, what the modern world really needs is a new synthesis in which Judaism and Hellenism would at last be merged.

The most memorable words of the New Testament are, for me, those of the sixteenth chapter of St. John, verses 12 and 13: "I have yet many things to say unto you, but ye cannot bear them now. Howbeit when he, the Spirit of truth is come, he will guide you into all truth: for he shall not speak of himself: . . . and he will show you things to come." The last word, then, has not yet been spoken; here, perhaps, is the ring on to which may be linked a new revelation.[13]

In that new revelation the legacies of Goethe and Napoleon, the poetic and the political, will have a part to play; and one of its prophets, surely, is Lessing, whom Heine does not mention here, but whose *Education of Mankind* had prefigured a good deal of his thought.

The Sermon on the Mount, it may be noted, often served Heine as an image for noble oratory in a good cause; but when he uses it in *Ludwig Börne* to commend the teachings of French liberalism as proclaimed to Germany at the Hambach festival of 1832, he merges the 'Nazarene' with the 'Hellenic' by adding a suggestion of Dionysian intoxication: 'Auf Hambach hielt der französische Liberalismus seine trunkensten Bergpredigten.'[14] Who but Heine would have thought of an 'intoxicated' Sermon on the Mount?

There seems to be nothing consciously humorous about the merging of the Nazarene with the Hellene in the passage just examined; but Heine would not be Heine if he contemplated all biblical characters with a straight face. In more parodistic mood the Heligoland section of *Ludwig Börne* introduces yet another such figure when Heine describes a choppy sea voyage; and that figure, of course, just had to be Jonah. Made more than a little queasy by the motion of his ship, the poet imagines himself to be, not Jonah himself, but the whale that had swallowed him and that now feels him churning up its stomach. As befits a prophet, Jonah is indefatigable in making speeches, even in the whale's belly, and he won't give over until he is finally spewed out. Before this ejection, however, Jonah is allowed to give to the world, or to that portion of it which reads Heine, a version of his denunciation of Nineveh which turns out to be a scarcely-veiled attack on the status quo in Europe just before that July revolution in France with which the Heligoland section of *Ludwig Börne* ends. And if we read that denunciation in the context, not only of Book II, but of *Ludwig Börne* as a whole, we soon realize that its scourging of a corrupt and servile clergy, a tyrannous bureaucracy in the service of kings, and a society of philistines and boors, has lost little of its timeliness even in 1840, ten years after the revolution which should have swept all such cobwebs away. Heine's disappointment with the results of the July revolution of 1830 is as patent, in *Ludwig Börne. A Memorial*, as his suspicion of the new breed of revolutionaries which he encountered in Börne's entourage.

(ii)

The very opening of *Ludwig Börne* warns us not to expect conventional historical accuracy in our walk around Heine's more modern portrait gallery. What he describes as his first recollection of Börne cannot correspond completely to the facts of their brief encounter—in 1815 no one could have said 'That is Dr Börne who writes against actors' for the simple reason that the name 'Börne' did not then exist (the person in question was still called 'Louis Baruch') and that Baruch-Börne did not start writing dramatic criticism until several years afterwards. When Heine tells us, in a later passage, that he walked with Börne through the Frankfurt Jewish quarter while Chanukkah was being celebrated, we look at the calendar and find that the poet had left Frankfurt before that festival had begun; when he says that he met Börne for the last time after certain conversations, we look at Börne's letters and find there unimpeachable evidence of subsequent meetings; when he tells us that Börne said such and such a thing on such and such an occasion, we find that he has clearly elaborated hints from Börne's published writings, or has put into Börne's mouth words that are demonstrably and unquestionably Heine's own.[15] The portraits and caricatures he draws for us are composites, like portraits in fiction, rather than straightforward biography; he brings out essentials by combining, foreshortening, heightening, or toning down; and he puts his figures into settings of time and place which are symbolically appropriate to what he shows them doing and saying. Comparison of what Heine tells us with historical records also shows him concerned, at times, to gloss over embarrassing features of his own involvement—no one would guess from his account of a meeting of German emigrés, which he describes as an ironic (and faintly disgusted) witness, that not only Börne but he himself too had been elected to the committee of the 'Patriotic Union' that staged this meeting![16]

Ludwig Börne. A Memorial begins with a glimpse of a Jewish merchant visiting the Frankfurt trade fair 'in the year 1815 after the birth of Christ'.[17] The phrase *nach Christi Geburt* in this opening sentence is not simply a convenient way of dating; it serves to suggest immediately the Christian world with which Heine's Jewish characters have to come to terms in various ways. Indeed, Christ himself, as we have already seen, becomes a prominent character on Heine's world stage. The merchant, Heine's own father of blessed memory (*mein seliger Vater*, as he calls him with unironic piety and affection), has brought his son with him on this occasion in order to introduce him to the mercantile world in which he is to live and work, in order—as we are specifically told—to further his son's education. That son, now grown up and become a poet, ironically recalls the *Bildungsreise* he took with his father some twenty-five years before. The journey took him, he relates, to some large warehouses or stores (*Magazine*), Christian as well as Jewish, where one could buy goods at 10 per cent below factory price and still be cheated. The Christian stores, it will be noticed, come first in the sequence, in order to counteract the tendency, documented in *The Hartz Journey*, where a variant of this joke first appeared, of attributing to Jews sharper business practices than are thought characteristic of non-Jewish merchants. Heine goes on to chronicle other sights and sounds, including the hall where one could once buy Holy Roman Emperors at 10 per cent below factory price, until that article was discontinued; and he then returns to his father whom he shows in the reading-room of a Freemason's Lodge 'where he frequently took his supper, drank coffee, played cards, and performed other masonic labours of this kind.' The Lodge in question is clearly the *Loge à l'Aurore naissante*, the first one in Germany to admit Jewish members on a footing of equality, which Börne had in fact joined in 1808. A little later we catch another glimpse of Heine *père* when we hear him tell his son of the oxen that used to be allowed to live out their lives in the Frankfurt Jewish cemetery. This custom, he tells his son, has now been abandoned; but he himself still remembered how, in his own youth, he heard cattle lowing among the graves.[18] In this way the father serves as a living link between his son and the earlier history and customs of German Jewry.

The scene of young Harry Heine walking the streets of Frankfurt with his father is paralleled a few pages later in a story Börne is made to tell of his own childhood. That story shows young Louis Baruch walking with his father through the Jewish quarter of Frankfurt on the eve of the sabbath and encountering old Mayer Amschel Rothschild, the founder of the Rothschild dynasty, who had just come from the synagogue. The two men exchange sabbath greetings, and after saying a few kindly words to the boy too, old Rothschild lays his hand on little Louis's head in order to bless him. 'I am firmly convinced', Börne is made to say after telling his story of patriarchal customs in the Frankfurt ghetto, 'that I owe it to this blessing by Rothschild that later on, although I became a German writer, I never failed to have at least some ready money in my pocket.[19]

The fathers of Heine, Börne and Baron James Rothschild, and the owners of Jewish stores in Frankfurt, are not the only Jewish merchants and financiers to be glimpsed in the pages of this 'memorial'. There is a whole scale of others, beginning at the bottom with the Jewish door-to-door pedlar, the *Hausier-jude*, introduced in the course of a simile as praising his tawdry wares beyond their desert. This principle, Heine tells us, can be applied in the literary and cultural life too, by Jews and non-Jews alike: Salomon Strauß hawks Börne's fame around in much the same way, and Wolfgang Menzel his German patriotism.[20] The strategy is clear: don't feel superior to the poor Jewish pedlar trying to scratch a living, the poet says to German patriot and Jewish intellectual alike; look at yourself in my mirror and consider whether your own activities are more respectable than those of the little man trying to earn a few pence.

A little higher up the social scale is an earlier creation of Heine's, introduced into the Börne memoir through a reference to one of his humorously self-depreciating sayings: Hirsch-Hyazinth, that Jewish lottery agent, corn-cutter, and general factotum whose portrait, imaginary but based on actual denizens of Hamburg, the poet had painted *con amore* in *The Baths of Lucca*.[21] In referring to his *Pictures of Travel* within the world of the Börne memoir Heine suggests the essential unity and continuity of his works, and the necessity of looking beyond the confines of any individual book if we wish to see the full social panorama that his writings present to us.

Hirsch-Hyazinth's counterpart, within the Börne memoir, is the anonymous figure of a little spectacle-seller whom Heine's younger self asks the way to Börne's house in Frankfurt and who responds with a characteristic sly wagging of the head. The spoken answer which supplements this expressive gesture is enigmatic, roundabout, in a way many of us will recognize as typical of a people notoriously prone to answering one question with another. 'Where Doctor Börne lives', the little man is made to say, as he wags his head, 'I don't know; but Madame Wohl lives on the Wollgraben.'[22] This, of course, suggests that there is some not quite patent relationship between Börne and Madame Wohl—a theme which Heine will take up later.

Heine's portrayal of the Jewish community of his time would not be complete without at least a glimpse of a group that made up an important stratum of it: the *Viehhändler* or cattle-dealers. It is, once again, Börne who is made to introduce such cattle-dealers in one of the historical disquisitions with which he regales Heine as they walk through Frankfurt. Heine's main source of information, it would seem, besides his own father's reminiscences, was J. J. Schudt, whose *Jewish Curiosities* (*Jüdische Merkwürdigkeiten*, 1714–17) he first read during his preparations for writing *The Rabbi of Bacherach*.

'It was a custom here, in the old days, that Jewish cattle-dealers followed the biblical injunction to dedicate the first male offspring of their cows to the good Lord. In order to do this they brought the young animals here, to Frankfurt, from all over Germany. The oxen were put out to graze in the Jewish cemetery, where they lived out the rest of their lives and often made the most infernal din with their bellowing. But the old oxen are now dead, the horned brutes of today lack the true faith, and their firstborn stay quietly at home where some of them even go over to Christianity. The old oxen are dead.'[23]

This characteristic passage, which speaks of men and beasts in order, in the end, to confound them with one another, clearly has more of Heine than of Börne. It is an application of that method of caricature and characterization which we know so well from Grandville.

On another rung of the social scale we find the stockjobbers of the Frankfurt Exchange; but here again, as in the case of warehouseowners and those who peddle national feelings instead of needles and brushes, Heine's satirical glance embraces Christians as much as Jews. The former, he tells us, haggle just as much as the latter; and what is more surprising, and more deliberately deviating from the usual stereotype, they also speak the same dialect, although the contemptuous name usually given to that dialect, *mauscheln*, would seem to confine it to Jews. *Mauscheln*, Heine avers, is simply the lingua franca of Frankfurt tradesmen and speculators, whatever religion they profess, and it is usually abandoned by those who no longer engage in huckstering. When, however, a little later in *Ludwig Börne. A Memorial*, Heine actually gives us a specimen of such *Mauscheln*, he places it in the mouth of a Jewish figure we shall meet again in *The Rabbi of Bacherach*: that distant relative of the Rothschilds known, by a conflation of his surname with his most prominent feature, as *der Nasenstern*. Cringing and squirming, the timorous Nasenstern informs Heine of his awkward position (*eine delikate Posiziaun*) as relative alike of the Rothschilds and of Jeanette Wohl, and he begs him not to reveal to Rothschild that he pays visits to the dangerous revolutionary Börne, whose attacks on the great financiers were notorious. 'Ich hab Grind', he keeps repeating, wishing to indicate that he had good reasons, *Gründe*, for such a request; but through his distortion of the word *Gründe* into *Grind* he unconsciously ascribes to himself an unpleasant eczema of the scalp which is often caused by lack of personal hygiene.[24] It is characteristic of Heine's compositional principles that the phrase Stern here distorts is one which the poet himself habitually used as a formula for valid reasons he found impolitic or painful to spell out ('Ich kann's nicht ertragen, ich hab meine Gründe'); and that the word Stern distorts becomes, in that distorted form, a keyword in Heine's rejection of Börne's recipes for social betterment.[25] The 'cure' of society's ills advocated by German radicals, Heine maintains, will remove the social eczema, the *Grind*, of the old order, but will leave untouched the inner rottenness that is the cause of such symptoms.

The introduction of Nasenstern into the Börne memorial gives Heine an opportunity to cast an amused, peripheral glance at yet another Jewish merchant. Nasenstern (Siegmund Jakob Stern) had a father who had made a comfortable living as a wine merchant; and this enabled the poet to quip that his favourite butt 'was the son of old ✻, wine merchant of Frankfurt-am-Main, who must—however—have been in a very sober state when he engendered his offspring.'[26] What is more important, however, is to notice how the introduction of Nasenstern into the book on Börne and his times demonstrates once again that method of 'recurring characters' which Heine shares with Balzac. Readers might already have met Nasenstern—or his all but identical ancestor—in *The Rabbi of Bacherach*, and could look forward to meeting him again in those reports from Paris to which Heine gave the name *Lutezia*.

More fully in Börne's orbit than Nasenstern is another Frankfurt businessman, Salomon Strauß, whom the poet treats with a withering and (it would seem) ill-deserved contempt. He presents him as a mean-souled huckster with intellectual longings, who married Jeanette Wohl (in whom Heine sees Börne's mistress in every sense of that word) in order to attach himself to Börne, and who then condoned a *ménage à trois* while allowing himself to be used as Börne's errand-boy. In his most savage vein Heine therefore compares Strauß to a donkey with horns, and relates with mock solemnity that he found a reference to such horned asses in Ktesias's *De rebus indicis*. While other donkeys, Ktesias is reported to have said, have hardly any gall, these horned ones have such an abundance of it that their flesh tastes bitter all the way through. Needless to say, the reference to 'bitter flesh' is elaborated into a sexual metaphor with which, happily, we need not concern ourselves in this context.[27]

The caricature of Jeanette Wohl is even more violent than that of Strauß: it includes indirect references to her Jewishness which operate by such mechanisms as comparing her pockmarked face to an old *Matzekuchen*, a pitted piece of unleavened bread used during the Feast of Passover[28] The poet himself later regretted these passages and intended to remove them from any subsequent edition of *Ludwig Börne. A Memorial*—an intention his death prevented him from every carrying out.[29]

But savage as the caricatures of Stern and Strauß and Jeanette Wohl are, they nevertheless serve to show the respect in which the intellectual life is held by Jews who are not themselves intellectuals either by nature or by training. The very fact that such men and women seek Börne's company and are ready to make sacrifices in order to enter his orbit tells us something about their aspirations which is not discreditable—something which bears a direct relation, surely, to those descriptions of the Jews as 'the people of the Spirit' or 'the people of the Book' which we have already examined in the Heligoland chapters which form Book II of this Börne 'memorial'.

The most striking association of financier and poet, businessman and intellectual, to be found in the book is, of course, the celebrated account of Heine's own association with the head of the Rothschild family in Paris. Baron James Rothschild was still very much alive when the book was published; yet Heine could depict himself without fear of contradiction as strolling through the streets of Paris with the man who was then regarded—along with his brother Nathan in London—as the most powerful financier in the world. *Ganz famillionär* he calls their relationship, 'as familiar as one can be with a millionaire', thus taking over the portmanteau phrase Hirsch-Hyazinth had used in *The Baths of Lucca* and vindicating in advance Freud's contention that in this respect as in many others Hirsch-Hyazinth spoke for his creator.[30] The mingled resentment, admiration, and feeling of kinship which characterize that phrase animate everything Heine tells us in the paragraphs of his 'memorial' devoted to the Rothschild family. Like Toussenel and other purveyors of the myth of Jewish power, Heine constantly speaks of the Rothschilds in terms of royalty: they are said to constitute a 'dynasty' that receives homage from Christian and Jewish sycophants alike, and Baron James Rothschild is described as a 'Nero of finance, who has built his golden palace in the rue Lafitte and there reigns as absolute emperor over the stock exchanges of the world.'[31] This pillar of the establishment, however, whose loans were said to have enabled the monarchs and ministers of Europe to maintain the status quo, is depicted by Heine as an essentially revolutionary force. 'Like his predecessor, the Roman Nero, he is ultimately', Heine tells us, 'a powerful destroyer of patrician privilege, and the founder of a new democracy.' The Rothschilds' transference of power, privilege, and influence from the landed gentry to owners of stocks and shares who may be here today and gone tomorrow, is said to have completed a social upheaval begun in France by Richelieu and carried on there by Robespierre. 'Richelieu, Robespierre, and Rothschild', the poet therefore declares, alliteratively and aphoristically, 'are the three most terrible levellers of Europe.'[32]

Heine's portrait of James Rothschild is remarkable, like his portrait of Börne himself, for its multiple perspectives—for Rothschild is here presented from three converging points of view. The first of these is Rothschild's alleged self-estimate, as a man who has advanced civilization by allowing his stockholders to leave their estates and provincial posts to concentrate in large cities, and thus to provide a nucleus of energies which can transform the world for good.[33] James de Rothschild, as I have said, was still alive when this was printed and could have protested if he had thought that Heine's report seriously distorted his own thoughts and his own words. The second perspective on the great banker is that of the poet himself, who regards him, as we have seen, as a great leveller, as a man whose activities furthered social revolution Europe while seeming to prop up the establishment. The third perspective, of course, is that of Börne who (as Heine rightly reports) hated in the Rothschilds the incarnation of money and the pillars of the Holy Alliance, yet could not refuse them his respect. 'These people', he makes Börne say in 1827, 'have chosen the surest means of avoiding the ridicule that attaches to so many baronized millionaire families of the Old Testament: they have declined the holy water of Christianity. Baptism is now the order of the day among rich Jews, and the gospel that was preached in vain to the poor of Judaea now flourishes among the wealthy.' But since, Heine makes Börne continue, 'the acceptance of this gospel is self-deception where it is not a downright lie, and since their hypocritically professed Christianity occasionally stands in glaring contrast to the expression of their old Adam, such people expose themselves in the most questionable way to the attacks of wit and ridicule.' Börne is allowed to continue in this vein for another half-page or so, until Heine interrupts him with the reminder that since both speaker and listener, both Börne and Heine, are baptized Jews, he is treading on rather delicate ground.[34]

James de Rothschild is destined to become one of Heine's stock company of recurring characters, and the poet duly promises, in his Börne memorial, to discuss the Rothschilds' personal qualities at greater length elsewhere. In the meantime he completes his sketch of Baron James by adding one tiny individualizing touch: when he is in a good mood, the Baron is apt to break into doggerel.[35] But this too, like every other feature Heine notes in this world-historical figure, has its general or symbolic application. Did not Richelieu and Robespierre, those other 'levellers', show similar signs of an 'unnatural love for poetry'? Might not the reader connect this 'unnatural love', in Rothschild's case, with his *famillionär* treatment of Heine, and use it as a starting-point for reflections on the relationship of finance to the cultural life? We shall certainly see Heine introduce such reflections into his later works.

(iii)

Besides Mayer Amschel and Baron James, there is one other member of the Rothschild family who plays a thematically important part in *Ludwig Börne. A Memorial*; and that is Gudel Rothschild, Mayer Amschel's widow and James's mother. In their walk through the Jewish quarter of Frankfurt in 1827, Börne and Heine pass the modest house in which old Madame Rothschild has continued to live. Heine sets this walk at Chanukkah time, when candles are lit in the Rothschild home as elsewhere to commemorate the victory of the Maccabees over a would-be oppressor of the Jews towards the end of the second century BC. Börne, Heine reports, compared that victory to the victory of the Prussians over Napoleon at the battle of Leipzig, and went on:

'The Germans should take lessons in patriotism from old Madame Rothschild. Look, there she lives, in that little house, the Laetitia who has borne so many financial Bonapartes, the great mother of all loans, and has no wish, despite the world-wide sovereignty exercised by her royal sons, to leave her hereditary little castle in the Jewish quarter, whose windows she has today adorned with white curtains in celebration of the great feast of joy. How gaily the candles sparkle—those candles which she has lit with her own hands in order to celebrate the day of victory on which Judas Maccabeus and his brothers liberated their fatherland as heroically as did in our own day King Frederick William, the Emperor Alexander, and the Emperor Francis II! When the good lady looks at these little lights, her eyes fill with tears, and she remembers with melancholy joy her younger days when Mayer Amschel Rothschild, of blessed memory, still celebrated the Feast of Lights with her, and when her sons were still little boys who placed candles on the floor and leapt over them with childlike pleasure, as is the custom in Israel.'[36]

Börne's sketch of old Gudel Rothschild and her family, as recollected, elaborated, and rearranged (or, indeed, invented!) by Heine, thus turns—despite its ironic touches in the sentence about the three 'liberating' monarchs of early nineteenth-century Europe—into one of those celebrations of the 'intimate culture' of Judaism, of Jewish domestic and synagogue ceremonial, which may be found throughout his writings. Such ceremonial is depicted as significant for the cohesion of the Jewish community scattered among the nations—hence the praise of Madame Rothschild's Jewish 'patriotism' as poetic and beautiful in itself, and as having a symbolic or exemplary import which far transcends its purely Jewish interest.

The Börne 'memorial' contains sabbath reminiscences too: the scene already described, in which Mayer Amschel Rothschild blesses the boy Börne after attending the sabbath eve service in the synagogue, is supplemented a few pages later by a scene in which Heine himself professes a nostalgic longing for the Judaism he has left behind—or *tried* to leave behind!—when he tastes again the sabbath dish he knew, and often celebrated, under the name *Schalet*. In his half-mocking, half-melancholy vein Heine then goes on to describe his own and Börne's reaction to the pleasing sight of Jewish girls taking their postprandial sabbath walk in Bornheim near Frankfurt: 'They were beautiful girls, and they exuded a most charming odour of *Schalet*.'[37]

Heine identifies the benefactor who treated him to the sabbath meal in question as 'Dr St . . .'—an abbreviation behind which all those familiar with the Frankfurt community would recognize a well-known physician, Dr S. F. Stiebel. The painter Moritz Oppenheim, however, claims in his memoirs that it was he and not Dr Stiebel who delighted the poet's palate in the way he describes, and adds: 'I am sure Heine remembered perfectly well he was not given this sabbath treat in the house of the person he names; but he counted, maliciously no doubt, on the annoyance that would be felt by the newly baptized Jew on having such Old Testamentarian cookery attributed to him. When I spoke to Dr Stiebel about this I was able to convince myself that Heine's pinprick had not failed in its effect.'[38] Oppenheim seems to have confused the Frankfurt visit Heine describes in *Ludwig Börne*—a visit which took place in 1827—with another one paid in 1831; but we may nevertheless be sure that the wicked urge to needle and annoy has affected more than one of the portraits which are the subject of the present book.

Dr Stiebel is not the only physician of Jewish origin to flit through the pages of *Ludwig Börne*. A later passage pays a delicate compliment to a man whom Heine had himself consulted to good effect during his early years in Paris, and whom he thought capable of saving Börne's life if the latter had not been too obstinate—so, at least, Heine asserts—to consult him during his final illness. This was Dr Jules Sichel, at whose wedding Börne and Heine had both acted as witnesses and whom Heine now terms, with a characteristic side-swipe at other fashionable doctors, 'a physician not only celebrated but also extremely conscientious'.[39] Heine's presentation of nineteenth-century Jewish types in his Börne memorial would hardly have been complete without the Jewish-born doctor! He himself, I suppose, as *doctor utriusque iuris*, could represent the legally trained Jew who found it impossible to gain a professional footing in Germany even after baptism, while poor Ludwig Wihl, poet and scholar *manqué*, flits anonymously past us in this book in the guise of a rogue who is said to have mulcted the poet of 200 francs and then written insulting journalistic nonsense about him.

The Chanukkah and sabbath scenes in the Frankfurt Jewish quarter which Heine describes in *Ludwig Börne. A Memorial* appear the more joyous and pleasant because of the sombre first impression Heine gives us of the narrow streets through which he walked in Börne's company. Heine knew as well as Balzac or Dickens how important it is to present his characters within the physical setting in which they live, which they have helped to shape, and which has helped to shape them. The black houses of the Jewish quarter, he tells us, seemed to cast dark shadows into Börne's mind and induced him to reflect on the more sombre side of those Middle Ages which the German Romantics—'mad poets and madder historians', he calls them, 'fools and knaves'—were even then trying to present in the brightest possible light. 'Yes indeed', Heine agrees; 'the houses in that street looked as if they wanted to tell me distressing tales, tales one knows well but would rather not know, would rather forget . . . 'And then he zooms in on to one particular house,

a high-gabled dwelling whose blackness struck the eye more forcefully because a row of chalk-white tallow-candles hung beneath its windows; its entrance, half occluded by rusty iron railings, led into a dark cave, where the damp seemed to trickle down the walls; and from within there issued a most strange nasal singing. The broken voice seemed that of an old man, the melody rocked into a most gentle plaint which gradually swelled into terrible sounds of rage.

The figure Heine here presents to us remains unseen; he can be guessed at only by the sound of his voice issuing from the dismal, cave-like house. Börne, however, can supply further information. The voice, he is made to tell Heine's own younger self, is that of one Rabbi Khayim [Chaim]; and the song he is singing is a lyrical masterpiece transcending any to be found in the keepsakes of the day, the *Musenalmanache*. What he is intoning turns out to be Psalm 137, the psalm which recalls the Israelites' sorrow at their Babylonian exile, whose Hebrew version Moses Moser used to recite to Heine when they both lived in Berlin, and whose German words—in Luther's translation—resound through the poet's work ever after. Rabbi

Chaim's voice, Börne continues, may not rival that of the celebrated prima donna Henriette Sontag in euphony; but Sontag—to whom the historical Börne had devoted one of his most amusing essays—could not have sung this particular song with such powerful feeling and expression.

'For the old man still hates the Babylonians, still weeps every day at the fall of Jerusalem brought about by Nebuchadnezzar ... This misfortune he cannot forget, although so many new things have happened since then, although only the other day the Second Temple was destroyed by that evil-doer Titus Vespasianus.'

And Börne goes on to contrast the Mozartian view of Titus as the noblest of men with the Jewish view of him as the archetypal enemy of the just; and entering half humorously into Rabbi Chaim's spirit, he goes on to cite, in ways already examined, biblical and Talmudic examples of punishments that were visited on such traditional *Roshoim* (Jew-haters) as Haman, Nebuchadnezzar, and Titus, and to think out grotesque punishments that might fittingly be inflicted on the Jew-baiting ideologues of nineteenth-century Germany.[40]

In presenting his voice-print of Rabbi Chaim, Heine has personalized an attitude to history inculcated by orthodox rabbis such as Johanan Eibeschütz of Metz, who, in the mid-eighteenth century, had reprimanded his congregation for idle talk about the wars of their present day—all that, he said, should be left to 'rulers and their underlings' whose business it was to deal with it. What Jews should do is to mourn the destruction of Jerusalem and the calamities brought on the Jewish people by Nebuchadnezzar and Titus. It was indeed common in the ghettos or *shtetl* to find minute acquaintance with the events of long ago, as chronicled in the Torah and the Talmud, coupled with relative indifference to great forces transforming the world outside. Time shrinks in such a perspective—it was 'only the other day' that Titus sacked Jerusalem! But one essential element is still lacking in this presentation of the ghetto attitude to history, and to remedy this the voice-print of Rabbi Chaim in Book I is supplemented in Book IV of *Ludwig Börne* by the portrait-sketch of another orthodox Jew steeped in traditional lore. This new character Heine calls Manasse ben Naphtali; he claims to have met him in

Cracow, a place the poet never visited; and he uses him to proclaim the Messianic hopes that accompany the ghetto's confident expectation that God will punish those who wrong the Jewish people.

I listened with a joyously open heart whenever he spoke of the Messiah . . . I no longer know in which book of the Talmud the details the great rabbi faithfully communicated to me may be found, and altogether I remember only the basic, essential features of his description of the Messiah. 'The Messiah', he said to me, 'was born on the day on which Jerusalem was destroyed by the wicked Titus Vespasianus; and since that day he dwells in the fairest palace of heaven, surrounded by brightness and joy, and wearing a crown on his head, just like a king . . . but his hands are fettered with golden chains.' 'What', I asked with astonishment, 'is the meaning of these golden chains?' 'They are necessary', the great rabbi replied, with a sly glance and a deep sigh; 'for without such fetters the Messiah would—when, as sometimes happens, he loses patience—suddenly rush down to earth and undertake the task of salvation before the time is ripe. He is far from being a placid sleeper. He is a good-looking, slender yet immensely strong man, with the bloom of youth still upon him. The life he leads is very monotonous. The greater part of the morning he spends with his servants, who are angels in livery, sing very prettily, and blow the flute. Then he has his long hair combed, he is anointed with nard and attired in princely robes of purple. The whole afternoon he spends studying the Cabbalah. Towards evening he calls for his aged chancellor (who is another dressed-up angel, as are also the four mighty councillors who accompany him). The chancellor then has the duty of reading to his master from a great book that chronicles the events of each day . . . This book contains all sorts of stories which cause the Messiah to smile gaily or to shake his head with ill humour . . . But when he hears how down below on earth his people are being maltreated, he falls into the most terrible rage and roars so that all the heavens tremble . . . Then the four mighty councillors must hold the enraged Messiah back lest he rush on to the earth; and they would probably not be able to overpower him if his hands were not fettered by those golden chains . . . They quieten him with gentle words, telling him that the time is not yet ripe, the hour of salvation not yet come; and in the end he sinks down on his couch, covers his face, and weeps . . .'

'That or something near it', Heine concludes, 'is what Manasse ben Naphtali told me in Cracow, affirming the truthfulness of his narrative with references to the Talmud. I have often had to think of these tales, especially in the most recent times, those which followed the July Revolution. Yes, on bad days I sometimes seem to hear with my own ears a clinking as of golden chains, followed by a sob of despair . . . O do not lose heart, fair Messiah, who wants to save, not just Israel, as the superstitious Jews believe, but all suffering humanity! O do not break, you golden chains! Hold him fettered a little while longer, let him not come too early, the king who will save the world!'[41]

That, needless to say, gives us more of Heine than of any orthodox rabbi—the passing allusion to the saviour of German legend, the 'placid sleeper' Barbarossa, the ironic sidelights on the Messiah's occupations and attendants in heaven, the concluding authorial comment on 'superstitious' Jews, and the pervasive ambivalences of thought and expression, are obvious distancing devices. But the composite portrait of a rabbi who answers questions 'with a sly glance and a deep sigh' ('mit einem schlauen Blick und einem tiefen Seufzer') is respectful and affectionate, and Heine's original variation on Jewish folktales and Talmudic legends[42] suggests a sincere appreciation of the imaginative power that brought such tales into being. It is true that he is not altogether just to his 'superstitious' Jews— for the *Alenu* prayer with which Jewish religious services end does indeed look forward to day on which '*all* the children of flesh' will call on the Lord's name and thus have equal share in the work of salvation; but if one compares what Heine has to say about Jewish Messianism with Lazarus Bendavid's denial, in the days of the Berlin Society for the Culture and Science of the Jews, that it had any significant part to play in the future life of Israel in the European Diaspora, one can only admire the superior insight the poet had acquired through independent reading, observation, and reflections.

It is curious to remember that 1840, the year in which *Ludwig Börne* appeared in print, was in fact widely rumoured—among the Jews of Eastern Europe—to be a Messianic year, a turning-point in world history, the advent of salvation. When the year passed without any obvious Messianic irruption, Rabbi Judah Alkalai speculated that the rescue of the Jewish community of Damascus by means of the intervention of their Western co-religionists—ranging from Sir Moses Montefiore to Heine himself—constituted a new model of salvation: a more gradual Messianic procedure than any previously envisaged. It may be that Heine had heard rumours of such expectations; but that is not what is important. What matters here is the way in which he announced the relevance of Jewish Messianism to the rest of the world. Shut up in their ghettos, poring over their sacred books to the virtual exclusion of all others, living in the Jewish past rather than the European present, the rabbis guard treasures of poetry, wisdom, and—as Heine shows so eloquently in Book II of *Ludwig Börne*—morality, which can claim the admiration of all who are not blind to the riches of the human mind and the human spirit.

It is against this background that we must see the ferocious portrait Heine paints, in *Ludwig Börne* as elsewhere, of baptized Jews. He puts the main attack into the mouth of Börne: but Börne's speeches on this subject have all the hallmarks of Heine's own most uncompromising polemic style. 'Do you think', he makes his Börne ask, 'that one can turn lice into fleas by pouring water on them?' 'I do not believe it', Heine's younger self meekly replies, for all the world like one of those complaisant interlocutors who take on Socrates in a Platonic dialogue. 'Nor do I,' Heine's Börne continues; 'and I find it a sight as melancholy as it is ridiculous when the old lice that originate in Egypt, in one of the plagues that visited Pharaoh, suddenly imagine they have become fleas and start to jump about in Christian fashion. In the streets of Berlin I have seen aged daughters of Israel who wore long crosses about their necks, crosses even longer than their noses, reaching down to their very navel; they held evangelical prayer books in their hands and enthused about the excellent sermon they had just heard in the Church of the Holy Trinity. One of them asked the other where she had taken Holy Communion—and all the while both of them emitted clouds of bad breath. What disgusted me even more, however,' Börne is made to continue, in what is easily recognized as Heine's own least endearing manner, 'was the spectacle of grimy-bearded Jews newly come from their Polish dunghills to be recruited for heaven by the Berlin Society for the Conversion of the Jews, and now preaching Christianity in their halitosis-infected dialect while giving off a dreadful stench.' 'It would be a good thing' this speech concludes with Heinesque savagery, 'if that lousy

Polish crew were baptized, not with common or garden water, but with eau de cologne.'[43]

Nothing in Börne's writings suggests that Heine is here reporting him verbatim; the most that can be said is that Börne may have made some hostile comments along these lines which Heine then elaborated in his own unmistakable manner. He could, in this way, vent his own more extreme opinions without committing himself to them—instead of agreeing wholeheartedly, in fact, he appears in his own person to dampen them down. 'In the house of the hanged man', his younger self is made to say to Börne, alluding to the fact they were both, after all, baptized Jews themselves, 'one should not speak of the rope'; and he pretends to be trying to divert the course of the conversation by asking Börne what had happened to the oxen that used to graze in the Jewish cemetery. But Heine's partner in this conversation, as we saw in a passage quoted earlier, is not so easily deflected from his exercise in self-hatred: even the oxen, he speculates, may have 'gone over' to Christianity!

In the context of Heine's polemic there is an additional bonus to be had from making Börne speak in the way we just observed. One of the themes of the 'Memorial' is the arrogant nationalism, the 'Teutomania', Heine had first encountered among the student corporations of Göttingen, whose chief targets were Frenchmen, Jews, and Slavs. When in a later passage he accuses Börne of having more than his share of 'patriotic gall',[44] we are no doubt meant to recall what he is alleged to have said about baptized Polish Jews, and ask ourselves whether he had not been affected by the Teutomania of his political associates. But one cannot read far in Heine without appreciating a conviction he shared with Börne: that the spectacle of baptized Jews aping Christian manners had something undignified and ridiculous about it. This helps to explain one tiny but significant change in the passage just quoted. Börne, Heine complains, 'spoiled the best dishes for me with his patriotic gall, which he prattled over my food, as it were, like a bitter sauce. My favourite dish at that time was *pieds de cochon à la Mennehout* . . .'[45] Remembering the old Berlin restaurant joke—'You don't have to yell for pork at the top of your voice—people can see you're a Jew without that!'—Heine thought it more dignified to transform his favourite dish from the pig's trotters forbidden by the Mosaic law to the more innocuous 'calf's feet *à la Maître d'Hôtel*'.

The hostile caricature of the baptized Jewish women of Berlin is relativized in two significant ways. The first of these is the introduction, into the Börne memoir, of a wholly sympathetic character sketch of the most eminent of the converted Jewesses whom Heine had met in Berlin: Rahel Varnhagen née Levin. Rahel is described in terms which suggest that she managed to strike the perfect balance between reason and a sense of mystery, between sadness and gaiety, between a strong individuality and the ability to appreciate other points of view and other temperaments. She appears as a hostess of taste and intelligence who not only stimulated the appreciation of existing works of literature—notably those of Goethe—but who also, through her keen understanding and stimulating (if occasionally cryptic) criticism played an essential part in the creation of new modes of writing. Having commended 'the smile that hovered about . . . Rahel's lips, her well-known, mysteriously melancholy, rationally mystical smile', Heine demonstrates her awareness, through her many friendships and contacts, of details of Börne's life which were as yet unknown to the public at large, and then goes on to give his readers a brief impression of her manner of criticism and her beneficent influence.

Rahel also commented on [Börne's] style, using words that will be totally misunderstood by those who are not familiar with her critical idiom. What she said was: 'Börne can't write, just as little as I can, or Jean Paul.' By 'writing' she meant that calm marshalling or 'editing' of thought, that logical building up of oratorical sequences, that art of constructing periodic sentences, which she admired in Goethe's writings and those of her husband. We used to debate such questions almost every day. Our present-day prose, I might say in parenthesis, has not been called into being without a great deal of trial and error, of consulting together, of contradiction and of effort. Rahel loved Börne all the more, perhaps, because they both belonged to that company of authors which needs to be in a state of intellectual stimulation or spiritual intoxication: they were bacchantes of thought who followed their god in a sacred ecstasy. She preferred natures that resembled her in this; but she also admired in the highest degree those calm sculptors of words who can detach their feelings, their thoughts, their observations, from the soul that gave them birth and can treat them as so much given material, *Stoff*, that has to be moulded into a work of plastic art . . .[46]

Rahel is thus shown to have made a vital contribution to the evolution of German culture: just how vital can only be appreciated by those who realize what enormous importance Heine attached to prose style. He saw in good German prose not only an object for aesthetic contemplation, but also a weapon in the fight for the emancipation of mankind. And in order to heighten our sense of Rahel's critical insight and fairness, Heine brings us back to the main subject of his 'memorial', to Ludwig Börne himself:

Unlike that great lady, Rahel, Börne disliked this kind of literary presentation; imprisoned in his subjectivity he was not able to appreciate the objective freedom that characterized Goethe's way with words. He resembled nothing so much as a child that has no inkling of the passionate meaning of a Greek statue, fingers its marble forms, and complains that they are cold.

Börne's own prose, Heine then reveals, bore traces of such insensitivity—and he presents himself as one of the few contemporaries who could hear the hidden cacophony, the *geheimer Mißlaut*, which characterized it.

In making her contribution to German culture Rahel is not alone; pointedly and humorously Heine juxtaposes with hers, in a speech given to Börne, such diverse other contributions as the history of the convert August Neander and the manual of arithmetic compiled by the presumably unbaptized Meyer Hirsch.[47] There is also just a glimpse, for those in the know, of another celebrated German-Jewish hostess, Henriette Herz, when Heine refers, in the early pages of his book to letters Börne addressed to someone he loved (*eine geliebte Person*) before the reign of Jeanette Wohl.

Madame Wohl, it must now be said, offers Heine another way of throwing his remarks on baptized daughters of Israel into perspective; for his notorious caricature of that lady shows beyond doubt that a Jewish woman need not formally abjure her faith to draw down the full vials of his wrath. He knew very well that his savage caricature, introduced at a late stage of composition, would make him enemies; but he consoled himself with the recollection of moribund scorpions imported into Paris along with the great obelisk of Luxor. When the Obelisk was erected on its new site, he tell us, timid spirits feared the harm the scorpions might do—but in fact the monument went up without any ill effects to anybody. The obelisk and the scorpions, Heine pointedly relates, both stemmed from Egypt, *aus dem alten Mizraim*; but while the little poisonous beasts soon died and were forgotten, the great monument remains sublime and indestructible.[48] He leaves it to his readers to work out the full implications of his parable; but the reader who missed the point of using the *Hebrew* term for Egypt would have to be very dull indeed.

(iv)

Heine's image of the *obelisk* can be linked with that of the *portrait-statue (ein ikonisches Standbild)* which he claims to be erecting, in his memoir, to his erstwhile friend, rival, and later enemy Ludwig Börne. This may, however, be felt to be too static an image for what the poet actually achieves; for he evokes a changing, an evolving Börne, seen from different distances and in different perspectives by an observer who also changes and evolves. And, as the editor of the great Düsseldorf edition of Heine's works rightly points out, though the poet often merges his own reflections with Börne's, or puts into the latter's mouth speeches that unmistakably derive from Heine, he does in many cases report Börne's opinions accurately: the attacks attributed to him on the Rothschilds or on Christianizing Jewesses, his reflections on the necessity of reconciling the Christian and the pagan, and those on the sleepiness of German would-be revolutionaries, can all be paralleled in Börne's writings.

We first glimpse the eponymous hero of the book, ostensibly with the eyes of the eighteen-year-old Heine, in a Freemasons' reading-room in Frankfurt. He is presented as already the feared and admired dramatic critic he was to become after 1818 ('that's Börne over there', someone is said to have whispered, 'who writes against actors'); but his appearance seems to betray the revolutionary, titanic discontent of a man who feels himself cut out—as did so many Jews when their disabilities were restored after the fall of Napoleon—for more important work then he is actually allowed to do. He uses his attacks on the Frankfurt actors, Heine surmises, as a proving-ground for later attacks on politically and socially more important figures. Heine describes his clothes in a way that characterizes him as a man of independent means who buys the best, wears the cleanest and newest, but who is not at all interested in presenting an elegant appearance. The whole description suggests a man whose full potential still has to be brought out:

He seemed neither tall nor short, neither thin nor fat, his face was neither ruddy nor pale, but showed a reddish pallor or pallid redness; and it expressed at that time a certain dignified distancing, a certain disdain, such as we find in men who feel themselves superior to the station they occupy in life but who doubt that people recognize their true worth.[49]

Ten years later Rahel Varnhagen and her husband, always alive to what is significant and new on the cultural scene, draw Heine's attention to Börne's transformation of German journalism; and when in 1827 Heine passes through Frankfurt on his way to Munich, where he too is to become a political journalist, he not unnaturally decides to look up a man whom he had only glimpsed, and with whom he had not held converse, in that brief encounter of 1815. Börne's appearance has now significantly changed.

No trace remained of his former distinguished discontent and gloomy pride. I now saw a contented little man, very thin but not at all sickly, a little head with smooth little black hairs, with even a patch of red on his cheeks; his light-brown eyes sparkled merrily, a cosy good temper spoke from every glance, from every movement, and from the very tone of his utterances. He wore a little waistcoat knitted from grey wool which fitted him snugly like a coat of chain-mail and gave him an amusingly fantastic appearance.[50]

Under the influence of Jeanette Wohl, we are to surmise, with whom Börne had by now struck up a celebrated liaison, the philistine component of his character had come to the fore.

This impression of philistinism is counteracted, however, by much of Börne's conversation. During the days the two men spent together, Heine reports, they spoke of Napoleon (whose crime against liberty on the eighteenth Brumaire Börne finds it impossible to forgive); of the tendency of property to make men conservative (a tendency Börne hopes to be able to over-come); of the various Jewish matters already discussed in this chapter; and of the political and social state of Germany. Though Börne is constantly shown to be sympathetic to the aspirations of the Jewish people from whom he sprang and with whom he still feels kinship, he is depicted, above all, as 'a great patriot' whose whole love went out to the [German] fatherland.[51] We are also shown that despite his financial suf-ficiency he is wholly opposed, for idealistic reasons, to the capitalism, the money orientation, whose spirit he sees incar-nated in the Rothschilds. In most political and social matters Heine sees eye to eye with him at this stage; and his own aspirations towards 'creating for the liberal press organs that might exert a wholesome influence on the future' harmonize well with those attributed to Börne.[52] The atmosphere is cor-dial throughout; but Heine presents himself as already totally opposed, in termperament, to Börne, and as unable to recon-cile, even at that early stage of their acquaintance, their respec-tive views on philosophy, art, and nature. 'We were complete opposites', Heine reports, 'in the very depth of our being—not only in our moral but perhaps also in our physical constitu-tions.' Where Börne is by temperament, a Nazarene or Heb-rew, Heine thinks of himself as a 'secret Hellene'; where Börne, despite his temporary contentment, belongs among the thin, like Cassius with his lean and hungry look, Heine sees himself as belonging to the plumper party—like Hamlet, as he humorously adds, whom Queen Gertrude declares to be 'fat and scant of breath'.[53]

In this early part of his book Heine experiments significantly with characterization through speech rhythm. He renders the effect Börne's conversation made on him by giving him a series of short-breathed phrases to speak. There is nothing gramma-tically wrong with the German here; there are no Yiddish words of expressions; but the sentence to be quoted has just the kind of emphatic rhythm which is often found in the speech of excitable German Jews.

Der Menzel, der hat Mut, der ist ein ehrlicher Mann, und ein Gelehr-
ter; den müssen Sie kennen lernen, an dem werden wir noch viel
Freude erleben; der hat viel Courage, der ist ein grundehrlicher
Mann, und ein großer Gelehrter!

[That Menzel now, he has spunk, he is an honest man, and a scholar;
him you must get to know, from him we'll have a lot of pleasure yet;
he has lots of courage, that one, he's a thoroughly honest man, and a
great scholar!][54]

Later on Heine will criticize Börne's *written* German for just
the sort of staccato quality which he here caricatures in his
speech. The passage gains an especially sharp satiric edge, of
course, from the reader's knowledge that Börne would soon
have to eat his words: that he was, in fact, thoroughly mistaken
in the man whose praises he here sings with such emphasis.

The last words we hear Börne speak in this section, as Heine
leaves to take up the editorship of a political journal in Munich,
is a warning against antagonizing the clergy there; and with
these words sounding in our ears Heine makes us look forward
to the time, soon to come, in which Börne will have left the safe
philistine haven he had temporarily found in Frankfurt, a time
of shipwreck in which Börne, cast adrift, stretches out his hand
towards Heine who cannot stop to grasp it: for Heine's ship,
he tells us, with characteristic hubris, bore the gods of the
future.[55]

If Heine's account of the impression Börne's appearance
made on him in 1827 is marked by a sense of diminution—what
had appeared potentially 'titanic' in 1815 has dwindled to the
littleness indicated by diminutives like *Männchen*, *Köpfchen*,
Härchen, and *Kamisölchen*—the first meeting in Paris is de-
scribed in a passage dominated by an expressive animal
image: the image of a tortoise peering suspiciously from its
shell.

It was in the autumn of 1831, a year after the July Revolution, that I
saw Börne once again, this time in Paris. I visited him in the Hôtel de
Castille and was not a little astonished at the change that expressed
itself in his whole being. The little flesh I had noticed on his body in
earlier years had now completely vanished—perhaps it had melted
away under the rays of that July sun which had also, alas, affected his
brain. His eyes had a dangerous gleam. He sat, or rather he dwelt, in a

large dressing-gown of coloured silk, like a tortoise in its shell; and I could not suppress an uncanny shudder when, on occasions, he suspiciously stretched forth his thin little head. But pity was my predominant feeling when his poor emaciated hand reached from his sleeve in order to greet me or offer a friendly handshake. His voice already trembled with some kind of sickness, and the red gleam of consumption already grinned from his cheek. The penetrating distrust that peered from every feature and every movement was perhaps the consequence of that hardness of hearing which had afflicted him since earlier days, but which now increased and did much to diminish my taste for his conversation.[56]

The tortoise image at the centre of this description is reanimated later in the book—notably in the passage in which Heine recounts how Börne would 'creep' after him into restaurants and eating-houses.[57]

After this passage no one need be surprised to find that the last three books of *Ludwig Börne. A Memorial* turn out to be, in the main, an account of the widening rift between the two German expatriates who met again in the Paris of Louis Philippe. Heine depicts Börne as drifting further and further towards political radicalism and egalitarianism; he descants at length on the distaste he felt at Börne's entourage, which included not just Jeanette Wohl and Salomon Strauß but also a motley crew (described once again with significant animal imagery) of uncouth and frequently unwashed revolutionary artisans and agitators. These later books of the memoir do much to substantiate Heine's contention in a letter to Campe, dated 24 July 1840, that his book dealt less with Börne than with his time and the circles in which he moved: 'über den Zeitkreis worin er sich zunächst bewegte.' He dwells particularly on the later Börne's sympathies with the radical priest Lamennais, whose chief work Börne had translated into excellent German. When evoking the dangers he saw in 'the union of two fanaticisms, the religious and the political', Heine describes for the first time what one might call (with a glance at Thomas Mann's *The Magic Mountain*) the 'Naphta syndrome': the confluence of the three Js, Jew, Jacobin, and Jesuit. No wonder that *Ludwig Börne. A Memorial* was Thomas Mann's favourite among all Heine's works, and that his Naphta has at least as much of Börne in him as of Georg Lukács.[58]

Heine depicts himself as increasingly worried by the threat that the kind of egalitarian revolution with which Börne sympathized in his later years would pose to cultural values—values he declares sacred to himself but incomprehensible to Börne. But however much he might deplore Börne's cultural blind spots, as well as the company he kept in his private and in his public life, his dangerous revolutionary rhetoric, and his frequently staccato prose style, he ensured that his readers would not lose sight of his adversary's essential dignity: the dignity of a true German patriot who never, despite his baptism, denied his Jewish origins, who even drew attention to them when he humorously called himself a 'cousin' of Jesus Christ; who never ceased fighting for the rights of his Jewish brethren, and who (on the other hand) never refrained from attacking abuses just because Jews participated in them. 'Yes, this man Börne was a great patriot, perhaps the greatest that ever drew the most ardent life and bitter death from Germania's stepmotherly breast.' 'He was not only a good writer, but a great patriot too.'[59] What Börne showed, once and for all, was that championship of the cause of the Jews was wholly consistent with loyalty to Germany.

Of course, Heine is notoriously far from being Börne's champion in these later portions of his work. He compares him to Robespierre at his most 'Nazarene', full of suspicion and with a deadly mixture of sentimentality and rationalism: 'lurking mistrust in his face, bloodthirsty sentimentality in his heart, and his head full of dry concepts.'[60] He compares him, too, to a police inspector who goes mad and sets out to teach the street urchins how *really* to cause mischievous damage.[61] (There is a sly reference here, of course, to Börne's early career in the city police department of Frankfurt-am-Main.) Yet at the same time he is allowed to utter some of Heine's own best witticisms and—what is more important—to present his case in his own words. Heine quotes at length Börne's dignified reply to anti-Semitic insinuations against him, and cites at even greater length the unfavourable opinion he expressed of Heine's own alleged flightiness and lack of character.[62] These charges the poet shows himself concerned to rebuff by defining the word 'character' in what he thinks of as a fuller, truer way than any that Börne could understand;[63] and as he does so, he launches into a programmatic statement which is of the utmost importance for an understanding of the portraits he paints of his contemporaries.

> I am drawing [Börne's] likeness while giving exact data about the place and the time he sat for it; and I do not conceal the favourable or unfavourable mood in which I found myself during each of these sittings. By these means I supply the yardstick which best indicates how much credit may be given to what I say.
>
> Such constant exhibition of my own personality is the most suitable means for allowing the reader to form his own judgement; but in the present book I have, I believe, a particular duty to place my own person in the foreground: for a confluence of the most hetero-geneous circumstances ensured that neither Börne's enemies nor his friends ever failed, when they discussed him, to drag in more or less benevolent or malevolent reflections on my writing and thinking.[64]

The portrait of Börne is not complete without that of Heine himself. When he puts his own words and ideas into Börne's mouth, when, in his own person, he interrupts one of Börne's non-Heinean tirades with the unmistakably German-Jewish question: 'Sind Sie Gemeindeversorger?' ('Who has asked you to mind everyone else's business?'), when he descants on diffe-rent types of temperament or on differing views about the connection between genius, talent and character, when he dramatizes his own activities as a publicist by saying that he 'bore aboard [his] ship the gods of the future', or describes his visions of the decline and death of older gods and spirits—then we are being deliberately kept conscious of personae Heine wishes to project, aspects of his own nature that he chooses to present to his readers. This is particularly obvious in Book II, where Heine reworks notes—or perhaps a diary dating back to 1830—into a section purporting to contain letters he had writ-ten on Heligoland just before and just after the news of the French July Revolution reached him. Here he presents himself as a seismograph: as a poet who can sense the approach of great events, as a man who feels the depression and excitement that precedes them, and reacts to their actual occurrence, more deeply, more sensitively, than his fellow countrymen.

Nigel Reeves has drawn welcome attention to the way in

which *Ludwig Börne* marks a nodal point in Heine's sense of
world history. The poet sees this history

> dominated by the conflict between two antagonistic modes of civi-
> lization. The first, which is his ideal, welcomes man's physical ex-
> istence and believes that life is worth living for its own sake. Its
> principal value is beauty. The second, which stems from Judaism and
> incorporates Christianity, sees man's true reality in his soul; this has
> constantly to fight against and rise above his animal nature, which is a
> temporary, earthly obstacle to the attainment of spiritual fulfilment
> in life after death.

In *Ludwig Börne*, however, these social and historical phe-
nomena, Sensualism and Spiritualism, are seen to be 'rooted in
the very temperament and physical constitution of the indi-
vidual':

> This essay documents the clash between two such antithetical na-
> tures, men whom one would have expected to be kindred spirits,
> co-operating to promote political freedom in Germany. Both were
> emancipated Jews, both lived in exile yet were passionately involved
> in the fate of their homeland, both were articulate exponents of
> liberal thinking, and yet from the moment of Heine's arrival in Paris a
> vehement sense of antipathy and hostility developed between them.
> This was an experience in direct contradiction to Heine's view of the
> two attitudes as the expression of particular cultures and the product
> of particular historical constellations.[65]

Heine would never recapture the optimism of *Towards a His-
tory of Religion and Philosophy in Germany*. But *Ludwig
Börne*, as we have seen, introduces into Heine's work a Mes-
sianism which—for all the poet's irony at the expense of
'superstitious' Jews—is firmly rooted in the Jewish tradition: a
Messianism which unlike the Christian variety can conceive of
redemption only as a catastrophic event on the public stage of
history, in this our world, and not as spiritual process in the
individual soul. Such Messianism, joining a 'restorative' with a
'Utopian' component, is encapsulated in the notion of *tik-
kun*—at once restoration, reparation, and reform.[66] The com-
ing of the Messiah will be the greatest upheaval the world has
ever seen; therefore 'love must not be awakened too soon', as
the Talmud says, and the advent of a better age is something to
be feared as well as desired. 'O do not break, you golden

chains! Hold him fettered a little while longer, let him not come too early, the king who will save the world!'

Surprisingly, Heine makes little of a widely-reported event replete with symbolism that served Gutzkow and other biographers as a starting-point for historico-social reflections: the fact that a storm toppled the cross that had been set on Börne's grave. He chooses instead to fill the final pages of *Ludwig Börne. A Memorial* with an unforgettable series of dream-visions. In one of these dreams the poet sees himself sitting at a corner of the rue Lafitte—a street associated with Börne no less than James de Rothschild—and watches with impotent horror how the carriages of stockjobbers and parvenus that roll by splash mud all over his clown's tricot and his poet's laurels. He tells us explicitly that one of the carriages held the financier Alexandre Aguado. Another dream has the poet encountering the wood-nymphs of ancient Greece, who are wanly dying in a chilly Northern forest while in the distance rough proletarian voices bellow incomprehensible slogans ('Long live the Republic, perhaps, or 'Long live Lamennais') and a tinkling bell summons the faithful to mass.[67] Such dreams of humiliation and death belie the consciously projected self-image of earlier pages, in which Heine had sought to present himself to his readers as a gay pantheist ('einen Pantheisten von der heitersten Observanz'),[68] as a Hellene whose enjoyment of the good things of this earth contrasts with Nazarene fanaticism and self-denial. And when we read, in Hannah Spencer's intelligent book, of the deep psychological insights that characterize Heine's portrayal of Börne—ranging from a Nietzschean perception of the motivating power of envy to a pathology of art worthy of Thomas Mann[69]—then we cannot but conjecture that such insight owes at least as much to the poet's self-analysis as to his anatomizing of a fellow exile whose Jewish experience and residual Jewish identity matched his own.

CHAPTER 8
The Shadow of the Ghetto

(i)

B: If I belonged to the people from which Our Saviour sprang, I would boast of the fact—not be ashamed of it.

A: Alas! So would I, if the Saviour were the only scion of that people; but since His time so much riff-raff has also sprung from this stock that one has to think twice before acknowledging such kindred.[1]

The riff-raff (*Lumpengesindel*) of which Heine speaks in this undated fragment plays a prominent and unenviable part in *Ludwig Börne. A Memorial*, and it surfaces too in a series of newspaper articles of the late 1830s usually grouped under the title Heine gave to one of them: *Tribulations of a Writer* (*Schriftstellernöten*). It there takes the form of the honest and decent though intolerably maladroit scholar, poet, and journalist Ludwig Wihl, who had published an ill-informed piece about Heine in a journal that bore the imprint of Hoffmann and Campe, the poet's own publishers. Heine did not even have to chastise Wihl in his own words: he could cite their publisher Julius Campe himself, who was horrified (as well he might!) to find publicly quoted a highly unflattering characterization of Wihl which he had been incautious enough to include in a private letter to Heine. Hardly had Campe issued his justifiable protest, however, when the poet returned to the attack with a hilarious parody of a public statement by Wihl himself—a parody that took the form of a dignified declaration by Campe's dog Hector. Hector finds his honour besmirched by that half-forgotten poet Heine, along with the honour of Karl Gutzkow and Ludwig Wihl, but he bears these trials with the dignity and fortitude befitting a noble canine: 'I for my part could let that stain on my honour—which Heine has besmirched along with such celebrated names as Platen, Tieck, Schelling' (which is true—Heine did say uncomplimentary things about all three of these), 'Hegel' (quite untrue—Heine admired that philosopher, and before 1848 he always spoke of him with respect), 'and Ludwig Wihl' (a glorious anti-climax! But let Hector continue now without further interruption).

I could let the stain be, with silent contempt, if only I could exhibit before the world anything like the great deeds associated with the names I have mentioned. I may not even put myself on the same level as Ludwig Wihl; for I am only a dog in the *literal* sense . . .[2]

When it came to elegant abuse, Heine could hold his own with the best; and Jews who crossed him came to feel this as powerfully as others.

The Christian Saviour, whom the fragment at the head of the present section opposes to the riff-raff that could claim kinship with him, also appears again in Heine's poetry. This happens in a cycle entitled *Katharina*, whose seventh section takes a form Heine had adopted before and would soon adopt again: an ironic view of the afterlife promised to religious believers. In *Katharina 7* we find the poet dreaming that he is walking with his love (for without her heaven would not *be* heaven!) in what turns out to be an interdenominational abode of bliss; among the Fathers of the Church, the apostles, the hermits and the capuchin monks he espies a party of Jews who look and behave much like the others:

> Lange heilige Gesichter,
> Breite Glatzen, graue Bärte,
> (Drunter auch verschiedne Juden),—
> Gingen streng an uns vorüber,
>
> Warfen keinen Blick nach dir,
> Ob du gleich, mein schönes Liebchen,
> Tändelnd mir am Arme hingest,
> Tändelnd, lächelnd, kokettierend . . .
>
> [Long, saintly faces,
> broad bald heads, grey beards
> —some Jews were among them—
> went sternly by,

Casting no glance at you,
although, my fair love,
you held my arm playfully,
dallying, smiling, flirting . . .][3]

One figure, however, stands out in this saintly company:

Nur ein Einzger sah dich an,
Und es war der einzge schöne,
Schöne Mann in dieser Schar;
Wunderherrlich war sein Antlitz.

Menschengüte um die Lippen.
Götterruhe in den Augen,
Wie auf Magdalenen einst
Schaute jener auf dich nieder.

Ach! ich weiß er meint es gut—
Keiner ist so rein und edel—

[Only one looked at you—
and that was the only handsome man
in this whole crowd.
His face was gloriously beautiful.

Human goodness played about his lips,
his eyes showed divine calm,
and as once he had looked on Mary Magdalene
so he now looked down to you.

I know, alas, that he means it kindly;
no one is as pure and as noble as he . . .]

The end of the poem shows the poet feeling a very human jealousy—jealousy of Jesus Christ himself.

Katharina 7 has given a good deal of offence to believing Christians, and not without cause. It does, however, add an essential element to Heine's developing a portrait of Jesus whom he had always seen as one of the greatest figures ever produced by the Jewish people. After the world-encompassing, peace-promising Christ of *The North Sea*, the blood-bespattered Nazarene who broke up the gay banquet of the Greek and Roman gods in the sixth chapter of

the *Town of Lucca*, and the precursor of cosmopolitan re-
publicanism in *Shakespeare's Girls and Women*, the char-
ismatically handsome Jesus of *Katharina 7* adds a sensualist
nuance that we cannot afford to miss in our investigation of
Heine's Jewish portraits. We must not forget to notice, in our
context, that in every respect the Jesus of *Katharina* contrasts
favourably with the Jews as well as the Christians who inhabit
the ecumenical heaven of the poet's dream.

To the same period as *Katharina 7* belongs a little poem
Heine thought it wiser not to publish—a poem that purports to
contain the poet's last will and testament and is therefore
usually entitled *Testament*. It contains the following stanza:

> Wem geb ich meine Religion,
> Den Glauben an Vater, Geist und Sohn?
> Der Kaiser von China, der Rabbi von Posen,
> Sie sollen beide darum losen.
>
> [To whom will I leave my religion,
> My faith in the Father, the Holy Ghost, and the Son?
> Let the emperor of China and the rabbi of Posen
> draw lots for it!][4]

One wonders what the good pastor of Heiligenstadt, who had
baptized Heine in the firm belief that he had convinced him of
the truths of the Christian religion, would have made of *that*.

(ii)

In Chapter 1 we looked in some detail at the opening of *The
Rabbi of Bacherach*—a historical novel which was to have
painted a sympathetic portrait of late medieval Jewry to match
that of historic England and Scotland in the novels of Sir
Walter Scott. Heine had laid the fragment aside when he
became absorbed in the new genre of 'Travel Pictures' but had
never abandoned the idea that he might one day complete it. By
1840 it must have become obvious to him that he was unlikely
to achieve this—especially since some of his notes seem to have
been lost in a fire at his mother's house in Hamburg. Suddenly,

however, in February 1840, the ritual murder accusation against the Jews of Damascus gave his opening chapter an unexpected topicality; Heine therefore decided to publish his fictional account of how such monstrous libels had worked in medieval Germany. We do not know how much of Chapter 2 was already written—it is clearly based on research Heine had done in Berlin and Göttingen; but whatever he already had, the poet worked over thoroughly, in a spirit rather different from that which had dictated the sombre opening. Adding a fragmentary third chapter, he then included the incomplete novel in the last volume of his *Salon*, where it appeared, in the company of some poems (which included the *Katharina* cycle), and a revised, abbreviated version of his essays on the French stage, in November 1840.

Heine's attitude to the Jewish people was now more detached than it had been in 1824–5, and his narrator, therefore, no longer stands as unequivocally on the Jewish side as he had done in earlier years. Where in the first chapter such irony as there was seemed for the most part directed against the Christian world, the later chapters direct their irony against Jews and Christians alike. It soon becomes clear that the rabbi's earlier confidence in the survival of his community had been mistaken or merely assumed. Sarah is shown to feel this in her heart even before she hears her husband intoning the prayer for the dead on behalf of relatives and friends he now knows to have been massacred. In the light of such knowledge the gaiety and serenity the rabbi is made to exhibit, and Sarah's delight in the finery and trumpery she sees for sale, are difficult to understand. We find no hint, either in the novel itself or in the letters in which Heine refers to it, that his presentation of the rabbi and his wife in these later chapters is intended as a cynical revelation of human thoughtlessness and moral bluntness. What it exhibits, rather, is the ill effect of trying to complete or further the tale at a time when he no longer felt as warmly towards his Jewish characters as he had done in the days of the Society for the Culture and Science of the Jews; his inability to construct a novelistic action in such a way that it not only has structural and thematic unity but that it also reveals, reflects, and sets in motion the consistent development of complex characters; his discomfort with a mode of writing that compelled him to third-person narration instead of the allusive and digressive first-person form which he had found so congenial in *Pictures of Travel*. It also shows, I believe, the poet's—hardly conscious—need to return to the subject of Jewish renegades in the way one probes an aching tooth.

The continuation of *The Rabbi of Bacherach* after fifteen years or so is not, then, wholly successful, and leaves important ethical questions tantalizingly unresolved. Nevertheless the later portions of the novel cannot be simply written off. They explore further the Passover themes of bondage, oppression, and the quest for freedom, of exile and the search for a homeland, of Jewish identity and the relation between past and present. They contain, in particular, many incidents which convey in effective, symbolic form Heine's apprehension of the nature and fate of the Diasporean Jew.

In Chapter 2, which is unmistakably based on material collected in the course of reading Heine had imposed on himself in preparation for writing his novel in the 1820s, we watch the Rabbi and his wife walk through a vividly evoked fifteenth-century Frankfurt towards the ghetto which is their destination. In the course of this walk they are made to encounter various representatives of the Hellene and Nazarene temperaments, whose clash occupied the later Heine so deeply; and ever again Sarah is bidden by her husband to close her eyes to profane sights, sights not fit for religious Jews shut out from the common life of Christian Europe. For these Jewish characters even the world outside the ghetto holds constant Jewish associations. The green hills and gay houses of Sachsenhausen, for instance, glimpsed in the sunlight across the river Main, reminds the rabbi of 'lame Gumpertz' who limps his way there every year to collect plants used during the feast of Tabernacles. In the same way the bridge across the Main brings to mind tales told by 'Cousin Täubchen' of a baptized Jew who has a house there from which he pays everyone who brings him a dead rat the sum of six heller on behalf of the Jewish community—for that community is obliged by law to deliver to the town council the tails of five thousand rats each year.[5] In such passages as these Heine makes good use of picturesque details he had collected from J. J. Schudt's *Jewish Memorabilia* and other works studied and excerpted in the 1820s. Such details are not merely picturesque, however; Sarah's laughing reference to the war the Jewish community is obliged to wage against rats has a symbolic charge which may be constantly felt in the incidents and descriptions of these later chapters. It is still part of the narrator's function to use historical details to paint a colourful picture of the world in which the characters live or through which they pass; but his narrative style is now less periodic and leisurely, more dynamic and nervous, more like Heine than Walter Scott, and his attitude to the Jewish people, as I have said, is more ironic. All this becomes clear as he allows us to watch the rabbi and his wife approach the Frankfurt ghetto; he tells us the history of that ghetto, the tale its stones could tell of murder and persecution, before showing us the often far from admirable effect its protective and limiting walls have had on the community inside. One other important item of continuity with Chapter 1 should be noticed: the narrator carries on his custom of making Sarah, at intervals, the centre of apprehending consciousness—of letting us see various scenes from her point of view without abandoning third-person narration.

The ghetto scenes of *The Rabbi of Bacherach* are of great importance in our present context because of the many portrait-sketches of individual Jews to which they give rise. Most of these are consciously conceived as grotesques; and though we meet them in a fifteenth-century Frankfurt evoked with as much local and historical colouring as Heine could muster, many of them are deliberately endowed with names still current among the Jews Heine knew in his own day. This is only one of many pointers to the fact that they are based on observations Heine had made among his contemporary acquaintances. It comes as no surprise, therefore, to find frequent references to modern Frankfurt—the Frankfurt he had visited in his father's company in 1815 and in Börne's in 1827—in Heine's evocation of the Jewish quarter of an earlier period.

The first of the Jewish grotesques appear in a scene by the entrance gate to the medieval ghetto, a scene whose symbolic import the Rabbi himself is made to underline. 'Look', he says to his wife, 'how badly protected Israel is! False friends guard its gates from without, and from within and it is guarded by folly and fear.'[6] In the rabbi's mouth the phrase *und drinnen sind seine Hüter Narrheit und Furcht* acquires a specially powerful resonance if we remember that the phrase 'guardian of Israel' (*shomer Yisrael*) refers, in the Jewish liturgy, to God Himself. The 'false friends' of whom the rabbi speaks are represented by a drummer called Hans who sings anti-Jewish songs as he fulfils his appointed task of guarding the ghetto gate on the Gentile side, while on the Jewish side of the same gate 'folly' is represented by a Jewish jester, *Jäkel der Narr*, and 'fear' by a character who will henceforth belong to Heine's stock company of Jewish butts: 'Stern of the Long Nose', *der Nasenstern*.

This medieval Nasenstern we must suppose to be an ancestor of a man Heine had met in person in his own day—a point Heine allows Jäkel the Jester to make in a speech on Stern's lady-love, Schnapper-Elle, which also makes ingenious use of an image from the *Song of Songs*.

'He is dangerous only to Schnapper-Elle. She has fallen in love with his nose, but that organ really deserves such love. It is fair as the tower that looks towards Damascus and lofty as the cedars of Lebanon. It shines without, like fool's gold and syrup, and it is full of music and loveliness within. It blossoms in the summer and freezes in the winter, and Schnapper-Elle's white hands fondle it tenderly in both these seasons. Yes, Schnapper-Elle is head over heels in love with him. She looks after him, she feeds him, and as soon as he is fat enough, she will marry him; she is young enough for her age, and visitors to Frankfurt three hundred years hence won't be able to see the sky, for there will be nothing but *Nasensterne!*'[7]

That last sentence, with its pun on the literal meaning of *Stern* (= star), makes Heine's point clear enough: he has dressed up a contemporary butt in fifteenth-century costume. Jäkel the Jester is a squat, bowlegged fellow, with a laughing red face and huge hands; Stern emerges from behind him, 'a long, thin figure whose scraggy neck was feathered with a white ruff of fine cambric and whose slender pale face was wondrously adorned by a nose of almost incredible length which moved to and fro with anxious curiosity.' The speech of this Jewish bird-man is characterized by a hasty, nervous flow of words, whose short-breathed rhythmic phrases, tumbling one over the other, Heine mimics with an artist's joy. 'Hans', he calls out to the drummer on the other side of the gate, who is baiting him by singing a song with which flagellants had accompanied a massacre of Jews, 'Hans, there's only one of me here, it's a dangerous song you're singing, I don't like to hear it, I have my reasons, and if you like me you'll find something else to sing, and tomorrow we'll have a drink together . . .' Two of the phrases Heine makes Stern use here, 'there's only one of me' (*ich bin ein einzelner Mensch*) and 'I have my reasons' (*ich hab meine Gründe*), become the man's catch-phrases, repeated over and over again; the second of these, 'I have my reasons' pronounced with a Frankfurt accent, we have already met in a similar context in *Ludwig Börne. A Memorial*. In the *Angelique* cycle of poems Heine adapts the same phrase to the uses of his lyric I.[8]

When Jäkel the Jester admonishes Stern to show some courage and thus rise above the status of a hare (an animal which has become, in German, a byword for timidity), Stern is made to defend his lack of courage in a speech that at once characterizes him and brings in, from his own perspective, three further figures bearing names still current in nineteenth-century Frankfurt. He begins by reminding Jäkel that Jewish dietary laws forbid the eating of hares.

'A hare you call me! "Hare" is a bad comparison; a hare is an unclean beast. And "courage" you say! I haven't been put by the gate here to show courage, I've been put here by way of precaution. When too many come along, I am to sing out—but I can't hold them back by myself. My arm is weak, I'm not all that well, and there's just one of me. If they shoot me, I'll be dead. Then rich Mendel Reiss can sit at his table on the sabbath, wipe the raisin sauce from his gob, stroke his belly and say: "That lanky *Nasensternchen* was a good little fellow, if it hadn't been for him they would have battered the gates down, he got himself shot dead for our sake, he was a good little fellow, it's a pity he's dead . . ." His voice gradually became soft and tearful in the course of this speech, but then changed to a rapid, almost bitter tone: '"Courage", he says! So that Mendel Reiss should wipe off the raisin sauce, stroke his belly and call me a good little fellow, I should get myself shot dead? Courage, he says. Brave I should be! Little Strauß, he had courage! And they beat him on his blue coat until his back was also blue and didn't look like a human back at all. Courage I should have! Leizer the hunchback, he had courage, and he called our rogue of a mayor a rogue. They strung him up by his feet, between two dogs, while Hans beat the drum. There's courage for you! I should not be a hare? When a hare goes among the hounds, that's the end of him. There's just one of me, and I *am* afraid . . . It's in my blood, I've inherited it from my mother, may her memory be blessed . . .'⁹

This transposition of Falstaff's speech on honour into a Frankfurt setting not only characterizes a certain type of timidity, but also manages to convey some social resentments along with some of the truly terrifying facts of Jewish life in Christian Europe. Unlike Marx, Heine was never blind to class conflicts *within* the Jewish community. Unlike Marx, he never mistook the spirit of Judaism for the spirit of capitalism *tout court*.

Nasenstern depicts the Jew whose natural timidity has been reinforced and increased by persecution. Jäkel the Jester deplores such timidity—he caps Stern's excuse that he has inherited his fears from his mother by saying that she, no doubt, had it from her father, who had it from *his* father: 'and all your ancestors had it from one another, right up to the founder of your family who marched against the Philistines under King Saul and was the first to run away.' But Jäkel knows that the ghetto would stand little chance if it marched against the fifteenth-century equivalent of the Philistines. All he can do is sing, with crazy grimaces, a Passover version of the *Jockellied* in which dog bites cat and stick beats dog and fire burns stick, and so on right up to the Lord himself Who slays the angel of death (an obvious image of inevitable retribution),¹⁰ and—most characteristically—vent his bitterness in jokes.

Besides being the archetypal teller of Jewish jokes, Jäkel the Jester is also avid for news, keen to hear others tell of their experiences—a trait which Heine glosses as 'that nervous curiosity which *even in those days* marked out the Frankfurt Jews'¹¹ (my italics). Once again, we see, Heine's evocation of Frankfurt past shades into a satiric image of Frankfurt present.

Guarding the ghetto gate along with Stern and Jäkel is a third figure, one on whom Heine bestows the name of the Frankfurt banker Rindskopf in whose counting-house he had once worked. This fifteenth-century Rindskopf of Heine's invention is a taciturn, pious man, of small stature and with a sour yet good-natured face; he has charge of the keys, but is deaf to all appeals to open the gate while he is saying the traditional Jewish morning prayers. When at last he unlocks the gate to let the rabbi and Sarah in, he does so dreamily, like one who does not wish his thoughts to be disturbed, and after re-securing the lock he retreats to a corner to begin a further set of prayers. Here we have another kind of reaction to a hostile world: unlike his banker descendant this medieval Rindskopf is the Jew who becomes wholly absorbed in prayer and ritual; who looks on the demands of the outer world as something to be fulfilled, and fulfilled conscientiously, but of no lasting importance when compared with the demands of the ritual law.[12]

The rabbi seems scarcely to notice the self-effacing Rindskopf; but the other figures, Hans the drummer on the Gentile side and Stern and Jäkel on the ghetto side, elicit the observation aside already quoted which leaves the reader in no doubt of the symbolic meaning of Heine's caricatures. 'Look, fair Sarah, how ill Israel is protected! False friends guards its gates from without, and within its guardians are folly and fear!' We may well suspect that Heine had more recent times in mind when he put these words into the rabbi's mouth—especially when the passage that follows insists on the continuity between the medieval ghetto and the Jewish quarter of modern Frankfurt:

Slowly the two visitors wandered through the long, empty street, where only here and there the head of a girl in the bloom of her youth looked out of the window while the sun mirrored itself, with festive gaiety, in the sparkling panes. For in those days the houses of the Jewish quarter were still new and pretty; they were lower, too, than they are now, since it was only later that the Jews of Frankfurt, when they increased and multiplied but were not allowed to extend the district assigned to them, built up their houses storey upon storey and squashed into them so tightly that they became crippled in body and soul. The part of the old Jewish quarter which remained standing after the great fire—the *Alte Gasse* with its high blackened houses in which a grimy, damp tribe higgles and haggles—is a horrifying memorial to the Middle Ages. The old synagogue no longer exists; it was less roomy than the present one, which was built later, after the Jews driven out of Nuremberg had been received into the Frankfurt community. The rabbi did not need to ask where it was: he could hear the confused chanting of very loud voices from quite a distance away . . .[13]

Heine's evocation of the medieval ghetto, the fruit of a good deal of reading and research, is no mere antiquarian exercise; Jewish life in his own day, as he had himself experienced it in his early years in Germany, is never far from his thoughts. The Frankfurt *Judengasse* becomes a sort of shorthand for medieval survivals into the nineteenth century, and the ghetto gate a threshold on which Christian and Jewish worlds confront one another with suspicion and fear.

The description of the customs and institutions of the synagogue which follows the passage just quoted may be incorrect when it comes to such details as the passage from the *Torah* ordained for Passover reading, but it does suggest firsthand acquaintance with the customary arrangement and furnishing of the women's gallery as well as the main body of the synagogue, with the order of prayers, and with the way in which Jews tend to behave during various sections of the service. Heine's description includes warm tributes to synagogue melodies ('Those ancient, solemn chants which Sarah knew so well and which now blossomed out in a loveliness she had never suspected') and to the *Torah* (again seen through Sarah's eyes as 'the book . . . which God wrote with His own sacred hand and for whose preservation the Jews endured so much misery and hatred, so much disgrace and death, in a martyrdom that had lasted a thousand years').[14] It also includes—and this, of course, makes it important in our present context—another memorable group of Jewish portraits.

The first we hear of the Jews assembled for worship in the Frankfurt synagogue is their excessively loud voices—the rabbi and Sarah need not ask their way, they simply follow the sound. We then accompany Sarah up into the women's gallery, watch the assembled ladies pray and gossip, and look down with them into the main body of the synagogue at the men 'in their black mantles, their pointed beards stretching downwards over their white ruffs, their skull-cap-covered heads more or less hidden by their prayer-shawls.'[15] Heine's knowledge of the history of costume is not extensive; he feels this himself, and therefore describes the women's dress as 'a mixture of the fashions of several different ages'—which hardly explains why in some details the clothes he describes seem to belong to a *later* age than that in which his story is set. But this matters as little as the clock which ticks away on the wall of a medieval room at the opening of Novalis's *Heinrich von Ofterdingen*, or the 'football player' whom Kent offers to trip up in the ancient Britain of *King Lear*.

Looking through Sarah's eyes the reader first detaches, from the throng in the main hall of the house of prayer below, the figure of the synagogue cantor. We learn that he has a splendid tenor voice and that he does full justice to the traditional melodies in which he is accompanied by a rumbling bass and a trilling descant singer. His excellence makes Sarah remember, by contrast, the cantor of the synagogue in Bacharach, a man named David Levi:

When this aged jittery man tried to wrest from his crumbling, bleating voice trills like those of a young girl, straining so hard that the arm which hung down by his side shook as if he had a fever, he provoked laughter rather than religious devotion.

Sarah follows the Frankfurt cantor with her eyes as he takes the sacred scroll out of the ark and then steps back from the grille that hides the women's gallery from the men's gaze. This is Heine's cue for introducing the reader to the congregants in the women's gallery. The women he singles out bear names still current in the Frankfurt of Heine's day; they are probably modelled on Jewish ladies he had known.[16]

The most elaborate of these portraits is that of Ella Schnapper, a character we had already met as the beloved of Nasenstern. The Rothschild dynasty, we must remember, was descended from the female line of the Schnapper family! In *The Rabbi of Bacherach*, 'Schnapper-Elle' figures as the owner of a small kosher restaurant; she has little learning, has run to fat, but though well past the first flush of youth she still takes pride in her appearance—especially her still beautiful hands. She appears decked out in flashy ornaments, among which a brooch on which the city of Amsterdam is painted plays a thematically important part; she speaks affectedly and gossips freely, while the synagogue service is going on, about her own widowhood, her unforgettable stay in Amsterdam, and about the cantor—who, we now learn, is giving a trial performance on this Passover sabbath before being invited to come to Frankfurt permanently at a salary better than that paid by his present congregation. Despite her weaknesses, however, and her unprepossessing appearance, Schnapper-Elle is a good soul, and is presented more sympathatically than the other women Heine picks out for his readers' scrutiny. The first of these is a *Vorklatscherin*—a grotesque verbal coinage meaning 'leader in gossip' modelled on *Vorsagerin*, 'leader in prayer'. Her name, 'Hündchen Reiss', is no less grotesque; she is described as 'a flat, greenish woman with a fine nose for other people's misfortunes, always eager to relate the latest scandal'. The sharpness of her tongue is felt particularly by Schnapper-Elle, whose tender relations with Nasenstern have not escaped Dame Reiss's prying eyes. Schnapper-Elle is let off the hook, however, when Hündchen Reiss catches sight of two ladies who (she knows) have cause to dislike each other, and who yet greet one another with apparent amiability. She lets go of her victim and glides towards these others 'like an animal that lies in wait'.

'On feast-days, especially in the synagogue,' Heine now interposes, drawing, one suspects, on observations he had himself made, 'the women seek to outdo one another in conspicuous finery—partly in order to excite envy, and partly also to demonstrate the wealth and credit standing of their husbands.' It is this display of finery which causes the conflict whose propsect had drawn Hündchen Reiss away from Schnapper-Elle. One of the two women, whose name is Fläsch, has a special grievance against the other, Süschen Flörsheim. Daniel Fläsch had borrowed money from Süschen's husband and had left his wife's necklace as a pledge—and here she sees Dame Flörsheim appearing in the synagogue with Dame Fläsch's favourite ornament sparkling on her neck! A conversation about the difficulty of baking the unleavened bread used in the Passover ritual soon takes on bitter overtones and would have led to an open quarrel, to Hündchen Reiss's delight, had not Sarah suddenly collapsed in a dead faint. This brings the women to her side—they are now joined by one Vögele Ochs, whose name (compounded of 'bird' and 'ox') demonstrates once again the amusement Heine found in combining the many animal names that are still to be found among Jews. As Sarah recovers and the 'Eighteen Benedictions', the *Shemoneh Esreh*, bring the congregation to its feet, the reader learns that Sarah's swoon was caused by her hearing her husband recite a prayer for the dead. She now has good cause to believe that her relatives and friends have been slaughtered in the wake of the hideous blood libel brought against the Jewish community of Bacharach.[17]

This dreadful occurrence, however, is not mentioned again in the rest of Heine's fragmentary tale; indeed, in the course of the third chapter which now begins, the rabbi exhibits a serenity and gaiety which would be revolting if Heine were aiming at psychological consistency and depth. Nor does the lovely Sarah ever again mention the congregation she and her husband have abandoned while saving their own skins. They are both caught up in a festive throng, significantly introduced by insect images: black-bearded men swarming like ants, ornamented women glittering like golden beetles, boys in new suits carrying prayer books, girls inclining their curly heads to receive the traditional parental blessing—all of them wending their way towards excellent dinners whose alluring smell wafts from pots (marked with chalk to indicate ownership) which have just been fetched from the communal kitchen by laughing maids. And from this throng there now emerges another figure—one which, as the poem *Donna Clara* would seem to indicate, Heine had envisaged when he first started to write *The Rabbi of Bacherach* in the 1820s, although the chapter in which he now makes his appearance was not written until some fifteen years later.

In this bustling crowd there stood out the figure of a Spanish cavalier whose youthful features bore that alluring pallor which women generally attribute to an unhappy love-affair and men to a happy one. His gait, though careless, had a somewhat affected, dainty grace; the feathers on his hat were agitated more by the aristocratic toss of his head than by the wind; his golden spurs and sword belt seemed to jangle more than strictly necessary . . . the jewelled hilt of his sword flashed from the white cavalier's cloak which enveloped his slender limbs with an apparent carelessness that yet betrayed, in the fall of its folds, the most careful arrangement. Now and then he approached the women who walked by partly with curiosity, partly with the air of a connoisseur; steadily and calmly he looked into their faces, lingering over his scrutiny when the faces were worth the trouble, sometimes paying a quick compliment to a passing girl but continuing on his way without waiting to observe its effect. He had circled the lovely Sarah more than once, and found himself repulsed on each occasion by her imperious glance or by her husband's enigmatic smile. At last, however, he put diffidence proudly aside, boldly intercepted them both, and delivered the following address with foppish confidence and in the dulcet tones of gallantry: 'I swear, Señora! Listen to me, Señora, I swear by the roses of both kingdoms of Castile, by the hyacinths of Aragon and the granate-blossoms of Andalusia—by the sun which illuminates all of Spain, with all its flowers, onions, pea soups, forests, mountains, mules, he-goats and Old Christians; by the canopy of heaven on which the sun is nothing but a gold tassel; and by the God Who sits on this heavenly canopy and meditates day and night on the creation of lovely women in ever-new forms—I swear, Señora, that you are the loveliest lady I have seen in all the realm of Germany; and if you are willing to take me into your service I pray for the grace and favour of being allowed to call myself your knight and, henceforth, to bear your colours in jest as in earnest.'[18]

There are features in this portrait of a man trying, half ironically, to play Don Juan or Casanova, which recall Heine and his self-image. The studied carelessness (concealing meticulous art and artifice) of the fellow's dress and bearing suggest Heine's way with his poems, just as the diction of his address to Sarah suggests the world of Heine's love poetry and that of *Pictures of Travel*. Sarah, one is glad to see, shows a properly indignant sense of the inappropriateness of such speech and behaviour in a medieval ghetto; but the rabbi regards it all with indulgent humour, for he has met the man before and loves him. He appreciates, perhaps, that this new character is a fundamentally serious man who has adopted a humorous persona as a sort of camouflage, and whose whole demeanour is the result of deliberate stylization laced with self-mockery.

The cavalier, it turns out, is a renegade Jew, nephew of a far-famed Spanish rabbi; Rabbi Abraham of Bacharach had come to know him during his years of study in Spain and had once saved him from a watery death in the manner beloved by writers of fiction the whole world over. When the rabbi reveals that he knows the cavalier to be a scion of the Abarbanel family and teases him about this provenance from an intellectual rather than a wordly aristocracy, the young man fails to recognize his erstwhile friend and reacts with ranting anger.

The chain of the sword rattled under the Spaniard's cloak, his cheeks turned from red to the most pallid whiteness, his upper lip twitched as if scorn were struggling with sorrow, death-dealing glances of anger shot from his eyes, and in an utterly changed, ice-cold, sharp tone he said: "Señor Rabbi! You know me then. That means you also know what I am. And once the fox knows that I belong to the brood of the lion, he will beware, will he not, and will not endanger his foxy beard by arousing my anger! How can the fox judge the lion? Only he who feels like a lion can understand his weaknesses . . ."

The curl of the lip, that famous twitch which so many visitors noted in Heine, again indicates that this portrait of a Jewish cavalier owes something to Heine's conception of himself. And he puts into the rabbi's mouth an answer which carries on the cavalier's Aesopian imagery and, in so doing, touches on that problem of baptism and its effects which Heine had so often pondered since his own nominal change of religion.

"Oh, I understand very well", replied the rabbi, and a mournful seriousness clouded his brow. "I understand very well that the lion, for sheer pride, casts off his royal fur and masks himself in the scintillating, scaly armour of the crocodile—just because it is the fashion to be a whining, sly, voracious crocodile! What can you expect of the lesser beasts when the very lion denies his nature! But beware, Don Isaac, you were not made for the crocodile's element. Water—you know what I am talking about—water is your evil fortune, and you will go under. Your kingdom is not of the water; the weakest trout can live in that element better than the king of the forest . . ."

And the rabbi goes on to remind the cavalier, whom we now know to be Don Isaac Abarbanel, how he once saved him from drowning in the Tagus—a reminder which brings about an anagnorisis, making Don Isaac fall about the rabbi's neck and at last adopt what Heine describes as 'his natural tone of gay sincerity'.

All is now sweetness and joy—no thoughts of the massacre of Bacharach intrude to disturb the 'gay serenity' of the rabbi's face, as he presses his friend's hand over and over again, saying 'I am *so* glad.' And for readers not nauseated by such serenity in face of what happened at Bacharach, Heine adds a new detail to his characterization of Rabbi Abraham: through contacts with Sephardic culture during his years of study in Spain the rabbi had acquired a social grace and polish unusual among his

German co-religionists—he had become a love poet, putting his thoughts of Sarah into verse and accompanying himself on the guitar![19] Heine's portrait of medieval German Jewry is clearly acquiring some *very* odd patches as he tries to continue in Paris what he had begun in Berlin so many years before.

From these exalted heights of poetry, however, the reader's thoughts, like those of the characters of *The Rabbi of Bacherach*, descend to a subject which held perennial fascination for Heine: the subject of Jewish food. More and more Don Isaac Abarbanel comes to speak with the very voice of his creator. 'Well then', Heine makes him exclaim, 'let me take you to one of the best little restaurants in Israel, to the house of my friend Schnapper-Elle, who lives quite near here. I can already smell the lovely fragrance of her kitchen! This it is which lures me so often to the tents of Jacob while I sojourn in this city. Intimacy with God's own people is not generally one of my weaknesses—in truth, I visit the Jewish quarter in order to eat, not in order to pray . . . I love your cookery better than that creed of yours which lacks the right sauce. My digestion never did manage to cope with *you*! Even when you had your best times, in the reign of my ancestor King David who ruled over Judah and Israel, I could not have stood living amongst you; I am sure that early one morning I would have escaped from the citadel of Zion and would have emigrated to Phoenicia or Babylon, where the joys of life foamed in the temple of the gods . . .'[20] The parallel with Heine's own 'escape' from Judaism, and his emigration to Paris, where he set up as a German 'Hellene', is patent enough; and when the rabbi accuses Don Isaac of being 'worse than a Christian—a pagan, a worshipper of idols', the latter is made to seize the opportunity thus offered to proclaim the 'sensualist', anti-Nazarene creed which Heine had recently adopted:

'Yes, I *am* a pagan; the gloomy self-tormenting Nazarenes are as little to my taste as the dry, joyless Hebrews. May Our Blessed Lady of Sidon, sacred Astarte, forgive me for kneeling in prayer before the sorrowful mother of the Crucified . . . Only my knee and my tongue worship death; my heart has remained faithful to life!'[21]

The rabbi, not unnaturally, is hardly pleased with this speech, which not only reminds him of Don Isaac's apostasy from what he is professionally bound to consider the one true faith, but which also ascribes to Jews a joylessness that no one who has ever celebrated Chanukkah, or Purim, or Passover, or the Rejoicing at the Law, could accept for a moment. Heine's own description of the *Seder*, in the first chapter of this very work, is enough to give the lie to *that* legend.

Don Isaac therefore deflects the conversation from the contentious topic it had reached back to the delicious smells of food that pervade the ghetto at that festive lunch-time. 'My nose', he declares characteristically, 'has not become a renegade.'

'When chance led me one day to this street at dinner time, and my nose encountered the familiar savoury odours that arise from Jewish kitchens, I was seized by the yearning which our fathers felt when they recalled the flesh-pots of Egypt. Tasty memories of youth rose up in me; in spirit I saw again the carp in brown raisin sauce which my aunt prepared so edifyingly on Friday evenings; I saw again that stewed mutton with garlic and horse-radish which might tempt the dead back to life, and the soup in which dumplings swam about so dreamily ... and my soul melted like the notes of an enamoured nightingale—and since that moment I take my meals in the restaurant run by my friend Schnapper-Elle.'[22]

The super-imposition of three world pictures in this passage— that of the gourmet, that of devout religion, and that of conventional love poetry—makes for the kind of *jeu d'esprit* in which Heine delighted in this period of his creative life. Once again we hear the accents of his voice speaking, unmistakably, through the mouth of Don Isaac Abarbanel.

Heine's fragmentary novel ends with a scene before Schnapper-Elle's restaurant, in which the latter has a chance to exhibit at once her affectation and the true goodness of her heart. Don Isaac, on the other hand, is once again credited with a tirade that does as little honour to his heart as it does to his taste. He compliments Schnapper-Elle on her 'beauty'.

"Señora! your eyes rival the light of the sun! But as eggs become harder the longer one boils them so my heart, by contrast, grows softer the longer it is cooked in the flames of your fiery eyes. From the yolk of my heart the winged god Amor flies up to seek a cosy nest in your bosom. And oh, Señora, with what shall I compare that bosom? There is not, in all the world, a flower or fruit that could serve for comparison. This plant is of its own kind alone. Though the storm wind tears leaves from the tenderest rose, your bosom is a winter rose that defies all storms. Though the sour lemon becomes yellower and more wrinkled the older it grows, your bosom rivals the sweetest pineapple in colour and softness. Oh Señora, even if the city of Amsterdam were really as beautiful as you told me yesterday, and the day before, and every day before that, yet the bosom on which its image rests is fairer still."

The cavalier spoke these last words with an affectation of diffidence, and squinted as if yearning at the great picture which hung from Schnapper-Elle's neck. Nasenstern look down with inquisitive eyes, and the much-lauded bosom began heaving so violently that the whole city of Amsterdam rocked from side to side.

"Ah!" sighed Schnapper-Elle, "virtue is worth more than beauty. What use is my beauty to me? My youth is passing away, and since Schnapper is gone—anyhow, he had lovely hands—what avails beauty?"

With that she sighed again, and like an all but inaudible echo Nasenstern sighed behind her.

"Of what avail is your beauty?" cried Don Isaac. "Oh, Donna Schnapper-Elle, do not sin against the goodness of creative Nature! Do not scorn her most gracious gifts. She might take a dreadful revenge. These enchanting eyes would become glassy and stupid, these lovely lips grow flat and insipid, this chaste inviting body would be changed into a clumsy barrel of tallow, the city of Amsterdam on that brooch of yours would come to rest on a fusty morass . . ."

And so he went on describing, item by item, the actual appearance of Schnapper-Elle, so that the poor woman felt strangely bewildered and sought to escape the uncanny compliments of the cavalier.[23]

This cruel and showy tirade mocks the pathos of an ageing body in ways that were not foreign to Heine himself—his book on Ludwig Börne, indeed, written at about the same time, exhibits a parallel to Don Isaac's address to Schnapper-Elle in some descriptions of Jeanette Wohl. The tirade is interrupted, none too soon, by a last Jewish vignette. One of Schnapper-Elle's customers, Squiffy Aaron Hirschkuh from Hamburg an der Lahn, comes out with a white serviette held in his teeth (*im Maule*—this squint-eyed grotesque not only has an animal name but his features are given appellations applied more to animals than to men). He breaks up the conference of the rabbi, his wife, Schnapper-Elle, and Don Isaac by complaining that while the soup has been served and the guests are all seated, the hostess has not yet deigned to take her place and do the honours.[24]

There is much to admire in *The Rabbi of Bacherach* as we now have it. Structurally its three chapters are well integrated; they progress logically from a first chapter dealing with exodus and flight under threat of persecution to a second centring on the deformation caused by a ghetto existence and a third which overtly introduces the problem of the renegade or apostate. As for individual passages—who could ever forget its affectionate and poetic evocation of Passover in the home and the synagogue; the moment of terror in which a blood libel prepares for a pogrom; symbolically significant scenes like that by the ghetto gate; vivid evocations of Jewish life and folklore; the mingling of the historic and the contemporary, the antiquarian and the satiric; its incidental portraits, landscapes, and townscapes; and that dream-vision of Sarah's which anticipates one of Heine's most haunting later poems, *Nocturnal Journey* (*Nächtliche Fahrt*)?[25] Its central protagonist, however, becomes so intolerable when the sombre first chapter is succeeded by chapters in which grotesque humour, parody, and gaiety determine the prevailing tone, when the poet's desire to chronicle ancient Jewish sorrows with due seriousness yields to more satiric intentions, that most readers will feel relief when the story breaks off. The rabbi's joking and leg-pulling after he has learnt that the congregation he has abandoned in its moment of peril has been massacred, the cavalier's cruel and self-dramatizing tirades, set the teeth on edge—even if we reflect, as is now fashionable, that Rabbi Abraham is a narrative device and not a real human being. Those of us who cannot abstract narrative function from character in this way must surely feel that neither the pious nor the renegade Jew comes off at all well in Heine's continuation; and this conflicts so radically with what we know of the poet's original conception that it may well have been a determining factor in his decision not to complete the work. 'The conclusion and the chapters which follow', he had caused Campe to print under the fragment when it appeared in *Salon IV*, 'are lost, through no fault of the author's'.[26] No evidence has been found that more chapters than those we now have of *The Rabbi of Bacherach* ever existed—though it may well be true that some notes and fragments were lost when the house of Heine's mother burnt down in 1833, and though the poet almost certainly used notes and excerpts made in 1823 when he revised Chaper 2 and added Chapter 3 in later years.

The shock of the Damascus blood libel, which set Parisians joking about the 'Father Thomas cutlets' they might be offered at Rothschild's banquets, and which made Adolphe Thiers talk as though the Jews' favourite dish were Capuchin friars' meat (he politely made an exception, it seems, in favour of the more civilized Jews of Paris)—that shock had sent Heine back to the tale he had once abandoned, a tale which started with just such a dastardly accusation of ritual murder. But alas: its ghetto setting had grown too strange and remote to him, and the world of a medieval German rabbi, however broadminded, however tempered by Hispano-Jewish culture, could not be a home for his own soul. He was therefore glad to break off his tale and publish it as a fragment, in the knowledge that he would, eventually, have to find other ways of expressing the Jewish component which would always be part of his complex personality. The solution proposed by his admired patroness and friend Rahel Varnhagen—'The Jew in us must be rooted out; that is a sacred truth, even if life itself is sacrificed in the process'—he found neither possible nor desirable. He might wear masks, assume personae, play games of hide-and-seek with his readers; but in the end the whole of him insisted on coming through, acknowledging wryly, or resignedly, or regretfully, or with proud affirmation, that bonds of history, kinship, and fate tied him to the Jewish people.

SECOND INTERMEZZO
Lions and Bedbugs

(i)

I had a choice: to lay down my arms altogether, or to go on fighting for the whole of my life. I chose to fight on—but it was not, decidedly not, a choice I made lightly. As for taking up arms in the first place: that was due to the scorn others poured upon me, to the insolent pride they took in what they considered their superior origin. The route along which I was destined to march throughout my life was mapped out in my cradle.

So wrote Heine to Varnhagen on 16 July 1833, two years after his emigration to Paris. The strategy he adopted in the battle to which he saw himself thus committed involved, as we have seen, some playing down of his Jewish origins. He wanted to be regarded as a mediator between Germany, the country of his birth, the country whose culture he had absorbed in earliest youth, the country whose language he continued to speak and continued to write in, and France, the country he had chosen as his place of residence and in which he was to live to the end of his days. He had formally abjured the Jewish religion when he submitted to baptism into the Protestant faith, and he now wanted to be seen as a Protestant, not in a narrowly doctrinal sense, but in the sense, rather, of 'protesting' against entrenched authority and privilege in the name of the individual conscience. He told Philarète Chasles in an autobiographical sketch dated 15 January 1835 that some of his enemies 'favoured' him with the title of 'Jew' (*d'autres me gratifient de judaïsme*) but that for his own part he saw himself as a champion of Protestantism, understood

not just as a liberal religion, but also as the beginning of the German revolution. I belong to the Lutheran religion, not just by virtue of having gone through the ceremony of baptism, but also by virtue of an embattled enthusiasm which led me to join in the struggles of this

militant Church. While defending the social interests of Protestant-
ism, I have never made a secret of my sympathies with pantheism . . .

Sympathies with pantheism, needless to say, brought him as
much into the vicinity of Spinoza as it distanced him from
Luther, whose views on duly constituted authority, *Obrigkeit*,
he signally failed to share. He was furious, however, to find
himself included, in 1835, in a *Portrait Gallery of the Most
Distinguished Israelites of All Times*, co-edited by his old
friend Eugen Breza; and when the editor of the *Journal des
Débats* printed an article that described him as as 'israélite' he
was moved to write, on 26 September 1835: 'I do not belong to
the Israelite religion' (true enough, since he was baptized); 'I
have never set foot in a synagogue' (plainly untrue, as his letters
reveal); 'I am an adherent of the Augsburg Confession and do
not intend abdicating a title which, in some German states, not
only confers spiritual beatitudes but also gives one greater
temporal and material rights . . .' To Heinrich Laube Heine
explained, on 23 November 1835, that the Protestantism he
championed meant 'freedom of thought and judgement', and
that he scorned the machinations of enemies 'who would like
to banish me to the synagogue—me, the born antagonist of
Jewish-Mohammedan-Christian theism'. So much for Heine's
belief in Luther's God. One of his many complaints against
Gutzkow was that the latter had publicly referred to his
Jewishness—but when he heard news of riots against the Jews,
Judenkrawalle, in 1835, his sense of solidarity at once
reawakened and he anxiously sought news and information
about them. A year later he defended himself, in a last letter to
Moses Moser, against the charge that he had not stood up for
his Jewish brethren.

Christians and Jews alike malign and slander me; the latter are angry
because I haven't drawn my sword to fight for their emancipation in
Baden, Nassau, or other such obscure Gothams. How shortsighted
they are! Only before the gates of Rome can Carthage be defended!
Could it be that you too have failed to understand me?

(8 November 1836)

His ability to 'fight before the gates of Rome' was, Heine felt,
weakened by those who vaunted their own impeccable origins
by 'direct[ing] their shafts against the cradle I left a long time

ago' (to Laube, 7 January 1839). Laube, in fact, saw in Heine's origin, his birth among a persecuted people, one of the reasons why he always 'had something of an animal that is constantly on its guard'. When Laube remonstrated with him about his pathological suspiciousness, Heine is said to have answered:

How can I jump out of a skin that derives from Palestine and has been tanned by Christians these 1800 years? Baptismal water . . . altered none of this; and the expression 'eternal Jew', *ewiger Jude*, has a thousand meanings.[1]

It is not surprising, therefore, to find Heine anxious to prevent the publication of early letters in which he had expressed himself freely, to Jewish or ex-Jewish correspondents, on the subject of Judaism and Christianity. The papers left by Moser and Gans after their early death worried him particularly. On 5 February 1850 we find him asking Varnhagen most earnestly to try every means of having his letters to such correspondents either destroyed or sent back to him. The letters he wrote from Paris are made more circumspect by fears of indiscretion. Constantly, however, his delight in the Old Testament, and his feeling that the writings it contained had applications to his own life, come out very clearly. In a letter to August Lewald, for instance, which he wrote on 11 April 1835, he referred to his affair with the young Frenchwoman whom he renamed 'Mathilde' (a name current in his own family, and one hallowed by Novalis's *Heinrich von Ofterdingen*) and whom he later married, in the following terms:

Have you read King Solomon's Song of Songs? You have? Then read it once more, and you will find in it everything I could possibly say to you today.

And again, a few lines later in this same letter:

Read King Solomon's Song of Songs! I commend its author to your most serious attention.

(ii)

In November 1837 Count Anton Alexander von Auersberg, who wrote under the pen-name 'Anastasius Grün', visited Heine in Paris. He took a good deal of pleasure in the poet's company, he wrote to his friend Eduard von Bauernfeld on 4 December 1837; but there was one big snag:

His dark side, and his misfortune, is his entourage: a dreadful mixture of political refugees, poetasters, unemployed commercial travellers and clerks, loafers and adventurers of every kind. Most of these are Jews, and I am always embarrassed when I want to ask one of them whether another is a Jew—for it is more than likely that the man I ask will himself turn out to be Jewish.[2]

This quotation from a writer reasonably sympathetic to Heine himself shows two things clearly: that the frequency with which Jewish figures turn up in Heine's later writings had some basis in the company he kept; and that non-Jews with whom he associated were acutely conscious of differences between themselves and the Jews they encountered. Frenchmen as well as Germans showed such curiosity about ethnic provenance and affiliation—and Heine's ability to appear as a champion of Protestantism and the German spirit had therefore very severe limits. This is no less true of those who shared Heine's Jewish ancestry; Börne in particular, who complained that those he dealt with could never for a moment forget that he had once been called Baruch, had a powerful nose for smelling out what he thought 'Jewish' traits in Heine. After Börne's death his Jewish friends, insulted by Heine, saw to it that French and German journals were supplied with items of information that would make the poet's claim to a Protestant mission look doubtful indeed.

Though absent from his family in body, Heine was never long absent from them in thought, as loving and dutiful letters to his mother, and affectionate references to her, to the poet's late father, to brother Max, and even to 'gossippy' sister Charlotte (*Plapperlotte*) who annoyed him by some indiscretions, may serve to show. But all these pale beside his constant recurrence to the true head of the family, Uncle Salomon, on whom he was financially as dependent as ever—the uncle at whose head he had once flung a sentence Salomon Heine would never forget: 'The best thing about you is that you bear my name!' (*HSA* XXI, 162).

I will write to Uncle Salomon, the lion of our menagerie. Don't be frightened every time he roars. He has a good and noble heart. He is always very tame at feeding-time.

(to Rudolf Christiani, 15 July 1833)

With my uncle, the millionaire, I have had a most bitter quarrel recently; I could no longer bear his contemptuous way of treating me.

(to Moser, 8 November 1836)

My mother informs me that I am about to publish a book containing the most grievous insults to my uncle Salomon. Who is it that invents such lies? My relations with my uncle are bad enough as it is; I am up to my neck in pressing debts, and he just lets me flounder—but I am not the man to take revenge for such miserable causes with a single line. When I wrote my memoirs, in which I often had reason to talk about him, our relationship was still excellent, thank God, and I portrayed him *con amore*.

(to Campe, 20 December 1836)

My relations with Uncle Salomon are very bad; he insulted me dreadfully last year, in a way that is harder to bear at a mature age than in one's easy-going youth. It is bad enough if a man who, as I hear, founds institutions to help hucksters that have seen better days, leaves his own nephew, along with his wife and child [*sic!*], to founder in miseries he has not brought upon himself.

(to Campe, 10 May 1937)

Heine repeats this last accusation to his brother Max, and adds that he wrote his uncle a letter which should have moved him to pity but which, instead, drew further wrath down upon him. This letter to Max, dated 5 August 1837, is full of aposiopeses, sudden breakings-off, to suggest that the writer could say much more but is restraining himself, if only with difficulty:

The few thousand francs I cost him are hardly a cause for lament on his part; he is, after all, the greatest millionaire in Hamburg, whose generosity—but enough of this!

You know that I always loved this man as though he were my father; and now I must—but enough of this.

Some of Heine's rhetorical protestations are part of his *Informationspolitik*; he expected some of his letters to be shown to his uncle, some of his arguments to be repeated to his uncle, and worded them accordingly—but the characteristic dual note of respect and admiration for Salomon Heine's good qualities of head and heart, and of resentment at his despotic ways (*le grand despote*, he called him, 'before whom everyone trembles'), can be heard throughout, and is surely genuine.

The letter to Maximilian Heine of 5 August 1837 which has just been quoted contains a bitter complaint about the hostile atmosphere at Uncle Salomon's court, which anticipates the late poem *Castle Contumely (Affrontenburg)* and may serve as a commentary or 'key' to that poem.

I hope you will turn a deaf ear to the scandalous rumours you will hear about me in our uncle's house. That place has always been pervaded by an *aria cattiva* that is poisonous to my reputation. The serpents that sought to destroy my good name for their own advantage have always been royally received there. But I have taken good care to see that the temple of my fame will not be erected on the Jungfernstieg in Hamburg, or in Ottensen [where Salomon Heine had a country house]; nor will I place my fame in the keeping of Uncle Heine's toadies and protegés. Even what Salomon himself or Cousin Carl (who has also sinned against me) tell you with regard to myself you must take with a pinch of salt . . .

Among the 'sins' against him of which Heine suspected his cousin Carl was that of suppressing his letters, hiding them from Uncle Salomon, and discouraging that uncle in other ways from showing his nephew the generosity and nobility for which he was renowned (to Maximilian Heine, 15 August 1837). Yet another letter to brother Max complains of a 'miserable worm with a university degree' who insulted Heine by referring, in some not specified way, to the circumstances of his birth and who was nevertheless entertained by Salomon at his own table; and to another of his enemies, 'that old maid

Speckter' whose trousseau uncle Salomon provided when she finally managed to hook herself a husband.

I have never needed my family's help in making my reputation in the world at large; but that the family should never have felt the need to further that reputation in even the slightest way I find quite inexplicable . . .

(to Maximilian Heine, 29 August 1837)

To this letter Heine added a conciliatory note addressed to Uncle Salomon himself, in which he apologized for harsh words he might have used in the heat of some moment—did not the uncle too allow his temper free rein occasionally?—and asks him and Carl not to listen to malicious gossip. But along with expressions of affection and submission, and pleas for financial support, he includes a passage the family must surely have felt as a threat, even if it did ostensibly refer only to the battles the poet had to fight in Paris.

Day in day out I have to struggle against unheard-of persecutions, just to retain the ground under my feet—you can have no idea of the crawling intrigues that succeed the open battle of party against party, by which all the sources that sustain my life are poisoned. What keeps me from going under is pride in my innate intellectual and spiritual superiority, and the knowledge that no one in the world could revenge himself more powerfully than I, with just a few strokes of the pen, for all the injuries that are being inflicted on me openly or secretly.

(to Salomon Heine, 1 September 1837)

Passages like these must have strengthened the family's resolve to muzzle Heine, to keep him on a financial leash sufficiently tight to prevent any publication that might (in their own judgement) insult or injure them. Heine's gestures of submission counted for little by the side of his threats, threats Heine repeated, in milder form, in a letter to Meyerbeer, dated 24 March 1838, which he accompanied with a note urging Meyerbeer to show that letter to his uncle, to whom he attributes deep feeling, correct intuition, an 'intelligent heart', and for whom he protests his love. This letter is particularly interesting in our context because it appeals to Jewish traditions of helping men of learning, of honouring the scholar more highly than the wealthy ignoramus:

His soul is high and noble, and he respects the poor and needy scholar far more than rich huckstering Jews.

This new appeal to Uncle Salomon, in which Heine deliberately presents himself as a scholar or savant (*Gelehrte[r]*) rather than a poet, seems to have done the trick, at least for a time; on 18 September 1838 Heine reports to Campe that he is reconciled with his uncle, from whom he is expecting a visit. The visit took place, and we find Heine writing to Cécile Furtado in March 1840, after a characteristic side-swipe at the *juifs inodores* of Hamburg: 'Tell my uncle that I am angry with him for showing himself so amiable in Paris. That's a refinement of malice: he wants to make me miss him now that he has returned home!'

If Heine was conscious, as many of his utterances show, of some affinity of temper between himself and his millionaire uncle, he also felt an increasing likeness to that uncle's much less successful brother, his own father. The poet's health was giving rise to some anxiety, he was gaining weight, and—as he wrote to brother Max on 5 August 1837—'Sometimes, when I look at myself in the mirror, I am startled: I look exactly as my late father did, when he stopped being handsome.' His father frequently came into his mind now; he startled a visitor called Seliger by playing on that visitor's name with an (untranslatable) pun made possible by the Judaeo-German expression *mein Vater seliger*, 'my late father of blessed memory': 'Sie heißen wie mein Vater Seliger'.[3]

(iii)

Reminiscences of German-Jewish men and women outside his own family occur frequently in the letters Heine wrote during his early years in Paris. In a letter to Moses Moser, dated 27 June 1831, he cast a distanced look at the man who had, for a time, been his chief confidant:

I was never touchy about your estimate of my worth as a poet; and though I was not indifferent whether you praised or blamed some action I performed as a human being, your judgements never hurt or

insulted me. My failure to write to you before now is not, therefore, a
silent reproach. But I do blame the gods for deluding me, for such a
long time, about the kind of understanding of my life and endeavours
that I might expect from you. You have never understood these—and
it is my consciousness of this which now causes me such distress. You
are still failing to understand them, you have never grasped what my
life and my striving were all about. Our friendship, therefore, has not
come to an end—it has, alas, never existed.

The last sentence of this letter nevertheless assures Moser of
Heine's respect and love; and it was, I suppose, a kind of
compliment that over five years after writing this obituary of a
friendship that never was he should once again turn to Moser
with a request for money (8 November 1836).

   Other figures from earlier days that turn up in Heine's
letters from Paris include the painter Moritz Oppenheim, for
whom he had sat in Frankfurt (to Ferdinand Hiller, 24 October
1832), as well as various members of the Beer family in Berlin:

Our friend [Michael] Beer I shall talk about when I see you—if such
insignificant beings are worth talking about at all.
                              (to Karl Immermann, 9 December 1832)

Though he may have thought Michael and Amalie Beer insig-
nificant, he could not dismiss Giacomo Meyerbeer so easily—
especially since he was constantly thrown into association with
him in Paris. We shall look in some detail at references to
Meyerbeer in Heine's letters; suffice it to say that for all their
ostensible praise, they are nothing like as affectionate and
genuinely respectful as his references to Rahel Varnhagen,
whom he was never to see again. 'I need your sympathy', he
wrote to her husband in May 1832, 'and that of Frau v. Varn-
hagen, as much as I ever did at the beginning of my career; for
I am as alone now as I was then. The only difference is that I
now have more enemies—which is some comfort, though
hardly an adequate one.' 'You need tell Frau v. Varnhagen
nothing on my behalf', he concludes: 'She knows what I feel,
that is to say, what I suffer. Farewell, and keep a place in your
heart for me.' Then, in March 1833, came the news of Rahel's
death, and Heine conveyed his condolences to her bereaved
husband by applying to his late friend the 'good soldier'
metaphor which he so often used when talking of himself:

Alas, dear Varnhagen, now I know the meaning of the Roman saying 'to live is to wage war'. I stand in the breach and see my friends going down all about me. Our friend [Rahel] has fought bravely and earnt a laurel wreath. My tears prevent me from writing more.

(28 March 1833)

Varnhagen asked him for copies of any letters Rahel might have written to him; but these, Heine reported, had been lost in a fire which had burnt down his mother's house. To Campe, however, he confesses on 3 May 1837 that he still possessed some of Rahel's letters:

I still have some letters she wrote to me after I had gone to Paris in which she speaks of Saint-Simonianism. These are the most memorable lines ever to flow from her pen. I am planning to make use of them in my memoirs, which will include a fully rounded representation of that remarkable woman.

However much Heine might fulminate against the use others might make of his own letters and unpublished writings without specific authorization he clearly had no scruples about unauthorized introduction of letters *he* had received when it suited his publication plans.

On 31 March 1838 he informs Varnhagen that some twenty letters from Rahel had been lost in the fire, says nothing about any letters he still had, and adds:

It is strange that the time has not yet come, and will not come in the near future, in which I could permit myself to say without prevarication all that Rahel confessed when, in hours charged with emotion, she bared her soul to me.

On 5 February 1840 Heine writes another letter of condolence to Varnhagen, and again speaks of Rahel. 'The new generation', he tells his friend, 'knows neither what we wanted to do nor what we suffered.'

And how could they have known us? We never spoke our innermost secret, and we shall descend into our graves with our lips still sealed. We understood one another with the merest glance, we looked at one another and knew what went on within us—this language of the eyes will soon be lost, and the writings we have left, Rahel's letters, for instance, will seem but indecipherable hieroglyphs to those that come after us.

Heine never saw Rahel again after he left Germany in 1831; the writer Berthold Auerbach he never met at all, though he read some of his works, praising his *Spinoza* with some reservations:

> Volume One I like uncommonly well; Volume Two rather less. The author has some intelligence, a good deal of narrative talent, but no poetry.
>
> (to August Lewald, 4 December 1837)

and of Ludwig Börne he saw, if anything, too much. 'This otherwise intelligent man', he complains to Baron J. F. von Cotta on 20 January 1832, had become the dupe of would-be Jacobins like F. G. Franckh; but he adds that he felt it to be impolitic to spread this opinion abroad. A year later, the breach has become irreparable; Heine speaks to Varnhagen of 'villains like Börne and those he consorts with' and contracts a habit of referring to Börne and his friends as 'Falstaff and his crew'.[4] 'What have I to do with Börne', he once said to Ferdinand Hiller; '*I* am a poet!'[5] He had come a long way since the days in which he had thought Börne the ideal reviewer of his *Book of Songs*, that principal pillar of his fame as a writer of lyric verse. Börne's death did little to mellow his feelings—*de mortuis nil nisi bene* was not a principle that commended itself to Heine. 'Börne', he wrote, resentfully, to J. H. Detmold, 'seems about to be canonized by the Germans. This honest man has gone into his grave spreading slanders about me.' (29 July 1837.) He determined to set the record straight by writing about Börne: 'not a biography', he assures Campe on 12 April 1839, 'but a depiction of our personal contacts in times of storm and stress. In will, in fact, amount to a depiction of this whole Storm and Stress period.' What became of this has already been seen in Chapter 7.

Many German-Jewish visitors looked Heine up in Paris during his early years there—members of his family, notably Carl Heine and uncle Salomon, as well as literati of modest fame, like O.L. B. Wolff and August Lewald, whom Heine thought respectable writers and decent men. There were also, of course, visitors of whom fame has nothing to say, like that 'Herr Rosenstein from Berlin' whose knowledge of modern languages and virtuous way of life Heine commended to

Meyerbeer on 29 March 1834. Sometimes a rapid sketch of some such obscure contemporary will preserve his image for posterity—like those moustachioed Jews which afforded the poet such amusement in the early 1830s.

> The German booktrade is not without its representatives here in Paris. We even have some with moustaches: the son of the great Maurice Schlesinger, and the noble Franckh.
>
> (to J. F. von Cotta, 31 October 1831)

> Give my regards to Carl; I could tell him the most alluring things, for instance that I saw [Benno] Goldschmidt here: he now wears an enormous moustache, so that anyone who did not know him might take him for a bandit from Calabria, for the most furious swaggerer. But he hasn't really changed at all, and when he sees the shadow of his own moustache on a wall he is frightened by it.
>
> (to Maximilian Heine, 21 April 1834)

This is just the kind of caricature-sketch which Heine was to perfect in *Lutezia*. His memory, he told Cécile Heine-Furtado early in 1840, now teemed with material for verbal cartoons:

> Everything remains engraved on my memory, the most disagreeable things along with the best, the most absurd Hamburg caricatures along with the pictures by Raffael which I saw in Florence—only it gives me greater pleasure to think of the Madonna della Sedia than of Sir Gumpelino whose golden wedding you are celebrating [in Hamburg] at this moment.

In Paris he even tried to find illustrators who would translate his verbal caricatures into terms of their own art. He asks Charles Duveyrier, in a letter dated 6 July 1834, to tell him 'si vous pouvez traduire sur ces planches le gros Gumpelino'. 'N'oubliez pas cette idée!' he adds, urgently. He must have reckoned with the possibility that Cécile Heine-Furtado would tell the Hamburg branch of the family of Heine's scarcely veiled suggestion that other public caricatures of Hamburg figures would follow those already published in *The Baths of Lucca*; and he knew for certain that his notoriously talkative brother Max would spread the glad tidings conveyed in his letter of 5 October 1837 with its characteristic slip into Hebrew:

> My memoirs are my most important work. They won't appear in the

near future, though, and what I would like best is that they did not appear at all until after I am dead. But I need the money! And it is this need for money which makes it necessary for me to treat the world to a great scandal. I have pricked many people with little knives, and some I have treated to a *khalaf*, a guillotine blade . . .

(iv)

One acquaintance that Heine was glad to renew in Paris was that of August Lewald, whom he now commended to Cotta as an efficient and conscientious editor and journalist. 'I recommend Herr Lewald all the more gladly because he combines a modest and peaceable disposition with his praiseworthy talents' (to J. F. von Cotta, 11 April 1832). Lewald showed that he deserved this compliment by never quarrelling with Heine, despite their many literary contacts, and despite the confidences Heine saw fit to make him about his love-life and his political temporizing. 'What happiness it is', the poet tells Lewald on 1 March 1838:

to have a friend to whom one can reveal one's most material interests without having to fear that this will blind him to the spiritual, idealistic concerns which underly them! And what a comfort it is to know that with you I need not spell everything out . . . that when it comes to essentials we understand one another without words.

The poet could use Lewald to feed back to Germany information about him that might help to shape his image in the way he wanted it to be shaped. When he was tired of being seen as the self-divided man, *der Zerrissene, par excellence*, he could say to Lewald: 'Tell the people in Germany who call me torn and self-divided that I am perhaps the most unified, the most whole, of you all.'[6] Not that the relationship was altogether without its ups and downs. In a letter in which he likens his powers of literary satire to 'a ton of arsenic' when compared with the miserable 'half ounce of verdigris' which is all his opponents can muster, Heine refers to one grievance he had against his new friend:

It is not that I ever doubted your friendship; but, to be honest, I had

to shrug my shoulders more than once of late, when I considered
how weakly you allied yourself—for reasons of expediency—with
people who gnaw away like rats at every friendship, who try to
poison such friendships; people who always hated me, secretly,
because I was your friend. How could you, who know me so well,
form alliances with the likes of Karl Gutzkow, that envious worm
who resented you from the first because it was said that you posses-
sed a few silver spoons?

(to Lewald, 16 November 1839)

Lewald turned out to be one of the few friends who recognized
the essential goodheartedness which was so frequently
obscured by Heine's quick temper and unruly tongue.[7]

The poet's contacts with another German-Jewish journalist,
Ludwig Wihl, proved—as we have already had occasion to
see—much less pleasing and profitable than his contacts with
August Lewald. He was astonished to learn, one day, that he
was said to be co-editing a Keepsake (*Musenalmanach*) with
the obscure Wihl, and asked Lewald to deny this rumour
wherever it appeared—but to do this in such a way that Wihl
would not notice the ultimate source of the disclaimer. 'I don't
like to make enemies of young people of this kind. He has
visited me a few times, but I have had little real contact with
him' (18 October 1837). Less than a year later we find him
actually recommending Wihl to Campe's attention; he sees in
him 'merits among which a talent for writing poetry is the
brightest and most noteworthy', and he asks Campe most
earnestly to be of service to his protégé (16 June 1838). When
Campe obliged and employed Wihl in his publishing house, he
received a characteristic note which showed that Heine now
expected Wihl to come across with some useful publicity, but
also that he had conceived some doubts about his fitness for the
task. 'I truly did not know', the poet writes on 7 July 1838,
'that Herr Wihl was planning to write a major essay devoted to
me.' (Campe will have taken that with a large pinch of salt—
later readers will do likewise.) 'He is a good and honest man,
and I pardon in advance that he is going to compromise me—as
he surely will do, since he is deficient in understanding of men
and has more than his share of the kind of vanity to which
poets are subject.' When the essay in question appeared in
Campe's journal *The German Telegraph* (*Der Telegraph für*

Deutschland), Heine found his worst suspicions confirmed. Wihl, Heine complains on 18 August 1838, is seeking to make him 'the pedestal of his own desire to play the great man': 'He means well, but the devil rides him into the most detestable urges to satisfy his vanity . . .' Never, the poet now insists, should Campe tell Wihl anything at all about Heine's literary plans and activities! Indignation gave way, at times, under the pressure of Heine's sense of humour: 'I cannot think of Wihl without laughing', he had told Campe on 18 September 1838, and several visitors attest that he liked to exercise his wit on the unfortunate younger man. Wihl is also, in all probability, the unnamed visitor of whom the poet said in later years: 'You will find me stupid today; I had a visitor, and we exchanged ideas.'[8] He was anything but delighted, however, when a bank draft he had cashed for Wihl failed to be honoured.

It is distasteful to me to drag names like that of Wihl from their shabby obscurity; but it is he who constantly supplied Stuttgart with gossip about me and has reconciled Gutzkow with the Swabians (perhaps even with Menzel) at my expense.

(to Campe 23 January 1839)

Wihl is never again to be allowed to claim friendly relations with Heine himself, as he has been doing in newspaper items all over Germany:

I aided him, as I did so many compatriots, because he was a poor devil. In Hamburg he even had the impertinence to go to my mother and pretend that he was privy to my most delicate personal relationships. How revolting it all is!

(to Campe 7 April 1839)

The disgust indicated by this last exclamation overwhelms the poet's sense of humour again in his letter of 12 April 1839. He now speaks of 'the poisonous stupidity of that wretch Wihl, who is capable, when his vanity as a poet comes into play, of the basest actions . . .' Show Wihl the door, he warns Campe, or ask Gutzkow to call him to heel; and above all, make sure that Wihl is never again given the opportunity to present Heine publicly in his own garrulous image, *wie einen klatschsüchtigen Wihl*. In this letter of 12 April Wihl is 'a swinish fellow'; in a letter to G. F. Kühne, dated 19 May, he has become a 'poor insect', a 'bedbug I cannot touch with my finger without dirtying myself in the most revolting way'; in a published skit already discussed Wihl appears as fit companion and equal to Campe's dog. The letter to Kühne enjoins that editor to discredit Wihl, whom the poet now regards as an enemy, in as many German journals as he can without revealing that this campaign was inspired by Heine himself. Wihl has been publicly threatened with cuffs to the ear, he says, and has cheated him, Heine, out of 200 francs. He lays the matter to rest, at last, in a letter to Campe dated 30 September 1839, in which Wihl is branded as a fool and a liar whose miserable activities are beneath his notice.

For the task of discrediting Wihl in German eyes, which Heine wanted to entrust to the unwilling Kühne, he found a more ready agent in another littérateur whom he admitted to his home: the Alsatian Jew Alexandre Weill. It was, in fact, Kühne himself who had recommended Weill to Heine; on the strength of that recommendation the poet wrote to Weill on 17 March 1839 and asked him to call. 'It will', he added, 'be a pleasure, I am sure, to get to know you personally.' The interview seems to have been a success—Weill himself has left an exuberant account of it, in which he tells us that he tested Heine's knowledge of Hebrew and Jewish traditions and vocabulary[9]—with the result that the poet commended Weill to the editor of the *Augsburg Gazette* in the very letter in which he complains of having to drag such names as that of Ludwig Wihl from their shabby obscurity. 'He seems to be a good-natured man,' Heine writes to G. F. Kühne on 19 May 1839, 'and his essay on Rachel [Félix], which I have recently read, shows some talent.' Weill, for his part, obliged by sending Heine-inspired items such as the following to German newspapers.

Heine has characterized Herr W[ihl] in his own inimitable way. We were laughing, in company with others, at the mystifying effects Herr W's self-image as a poet has had on his conduct and writings. None of this was new to me, for I had heard many stories about him from my Frankfurt contacts. At last Heine said: 'W is insane, really; but he does have lucid moments in which he is only a fool.' No one could sum him up more precisely and truly than that.[10]

Heine made use of Weill's talents as a journalist not only to discredit Wihl, but also to correct the image of Heine himself which Wihl and others had helped to fashion among German readers. He also set Weill the task of drawing attention to references to Heine's life and work in various journals; he used him as an occasional translator, and he showed himself ready to admit him to his private as well as his public world. 'You were the only German to whom my house stood open,' he writes to Weill on 26 August 1841, towards the end of a whole series of friendly notes—and though he steadfastly refused to lend the ever impecunious Weill money, he did induce Meyerbeer to come across with some financial assistance and wrote a preface to one of Weill's books in order to make it sell better. A later chapter will show how this relation also turned sour.

Heine's contacts with Wihl and Weill, and partly with August Lewald too, can best be understood in the light of what Michael Werner has called his *Imagepflege*: his attempt to control the way in which the public's growing curiosity about his life and circumstances was satisfied.[11] Wihl proved too clumsy for this task, and what he wrote about Heine did more harm that good—Weill showed himself much more adroit and adept at propagating what Heine wanted people to think. In return for services of this kind, Heine was prepared to smooth the path of the man who rendered them by means of introductions and recommendations. In the same way he rewarded François-Adolphe Loève-Veimars, to whom he looked for help with translations that would spread his fame in France, by recommending him warmly to Cotta. 'One of the best pens in France', he called him, crediting him with useful connections that made it highly desirable to enlist his services as correspondent of the *Augsburg Gazette* (to J. F. v. Cotta, 11 January 1833). Privately he showed himself greatly amused by Loève-Veimars' dandified appearance and surroundings. Several of his *bon mots* on this subject circulated in Paris—notably his alleged remark to the man himself: 'Monsieur Loève-Veimars, vous êtes logé comme une femme entretenue . . .'[12]

(v)

The Paris of Heine's day had a considerable population of German émigrés and temporary residents: these included artisans, journalists, political commentators, and adventurers whom Jacques Grandjonc has characterized as 'a mixture of confidence-trickster, secret agent, journalist, and language teacher'.[13] Heine soon learnt to keep away from these as much as he could—but he found himself constantly compelled, nevertheless, to sweeten fellow exiles with loans or praise or services, *ne noceant*. 'That old she-bear Germania', he wrote on 6 June 1835, 'has shaken out her fleas all over Paris, and I, poor man, more than anyone, am constantly being bitten by them.' The recipient of this complaint was Giacomo Meyerbeer, with whom Heine now formed what is perhaps the strangest of all his relationships. There can be no doubt that he helped Meyerbeer, in various ways, to manipulate the composer's public image; and the negotiations in which this involved him left him with a deep suspicion of the whole publishing world, and in particular of the press. He seems also to have envied Meyerbeer's lavish financial resources, and to have drawn on them without too many pangs of conscience. His letters to Meyerbeer during the 1830s are amiable in tone; they do not spare ostensible praise and admiration, but not infrequently one detects something that suspiciously resembles blackmail.

The first reference to Meyerbeer in Heine's letters from Paris sets the composer in the circle of his family. A simile shows Amalie Beer, that worthy matron and archetype of all proud Jewish mothers, eagerly awaiting her son's next great opus. Heine is writing to J.–F. von Cotta on 20 January 1832:

Wouldn't it be terrible if I had come to Paris to describe great events only to find that such events no longer occurred there! But I refuse to give up—even if I had to wait as long as old Madame Beer waited for the appearance of *Robert le Diable*. That her son has been awarded the cross of the Legion of Honour you will no doubt have read in the papers the day before yesterday . . .

Well before this, however, on 25 June 1831, Meyerbeer had himself written a letter to Heine which he must have had many occasions to regret in later years.

My dear master and friend,
I hear you have composed many new Spring songs which still lie buried in your desk, unmarvelled at by the public—Madame Valentin told me that you had given several to Herr Hiller, but that others are still musically unwed. Might my coy muse ask for the hands of these charming maidens? I shall enquire of your decision at Madame Valentin's.

Your Admirer
Meyerbeer.

Ever afterwards the poet felt aggrieved that Meyerbeer never did set to music such poems as he sent him, from time to time, in reply to his request. His letters often advert to this grievance while also making other demands on the busy composer: free tickets to the Opera, intervention with the Hamburg Heines in the poet's favour, patronage for a German-Jewish language teacher—and, ever again, money to sweeten various journalists or scandal-mongers who might otherwise attack Meyerbeer, or Heine, or both. One particularly important letter, dated 6 April 1835, reminds Meyerbeer of their common ancestry by carefully placed references to Jewish history and equally carefully placed Hebraic-Yiddish words like *Roshe* (evil-doer, anti-Semite) and *nebbish* (an expression of mock regret). In comparison with the letters of Heine's German period those he wrote in Paris between 1831 and 1845 use words of Yiddish or Hebrew provenance more rarely—a fact which makes such words stand out more prominently when he *does* introduce them.[14] One other linguistic point is worth noting in this connection: the word *Jude* with its analogues and composites takes a back place, in these letters, while terms like 'Israelit(e)' and 'professing the Mosaic creed' (*mosaischer Konfession*) move into the foreground. It is difficult, at this distance of time, to estimate the exact degree of irony and self-persiflage with which such alternative terms are employed.

I often show myself in an unfavourable light. I indulge in persiflage and mystification with most people. I do not often act like a Marquis Posa or a Titus (I mean the Titus described by the Romans and set to music by Mozart—the *real* Titus, as you know, was a *Roshe*). As I was saying, I am no Posa, no Titus Vespasianus, no Nathan the Wise; I am even the very opposite of all these, there is much about me that is questionable . . . But one thing is sure: deep down in my heart there is sympathy for everything that is glorious and tragic, for my fellow martyrs in poetry and art, for genius that is akin to mine. Perhaps I am made up of two different people. One of these, the better one, is writing to you today; writing, not to the workaday Meyerbeer, who is usually dressed in a brown coat and constantly plagued by . . . bad singers, enlightened Israelites, unprejudiced Christians, worthy dilettantes, possessors of autograph albums (this is the Meyerbeer to whom I addressed a recommendation, a few days ago, which will be presented to him by a young language teacher professing the Mosaic creed who probably plays the violin too)—I am writing today to the second Meyerbeer, the *maestro divino*, the creator, the triumphant hero with the laurel wreath, the prince in the realm of the spirit, who, like myself, will long be remembered by mankind. I even nourish the hope that the name of this Meyerbeer will not infrequently be mentioned alongside my own when the two of us, *nebbish*, have long been mouldering in our graves.

The rest of this letter lets the workaday Heine talk to the workaday Meyerbeer; it deals with the machinations of refugee journalists who have to be kept quiet, or favourably disposed, by contributions from the composer's purse.

In November 1836 Heine left the French capital and stayed for a while in Lyons, where he found himself dreadfully bored. To alleviate this boredom he patronized the local theatre, where he had an opportunity (or so at least, he tells the composer Ferdinand Hiller on 19 November) to learn how a less sophisticated public regarded the Meyerbeer who revealed himself in his operas.

Last night *Robert le Diable* was performed. The man in the seat next to mine said to me: 'This Meyerbeer is not a composer—he is a god.' I told him that I knew Meyerbeer personally; whereupon he invited me to lunch with him today. Now you see how useful it is when my friends compose great operas, and become great musicians or even gods . . .

But while he was helping this 'god' to maintain his reputation ('What you say about Meyerbeer must be favourable' he writes to J. H. Detmold on 14 June 1837), and while he sent him and his wife copies of his work with respectful dedications, resentments were building up. These discharged themselves, in private, by means of jokes about the whole Beer family. Börne has described in a letter to Jeanette Wohl, dated 24 October 1831, how Heine used to tease Meyerbeer's brother Michael Beer whenever he ran into him at some Parisian social gathering.

He will ask Beer, for instance: 'Why do you write when you can afford not to?' Behind his back Heine says: 'I wonder what would happen if I presented a bill to the Beer family for all the jokes I have already expended on them?' Or again: 'When I come to quarrel with the Beers, I'll become a rich man.' Michael Beer feels in his bones that Heine will, one day, really set about him in public; and however intimate they are, he treats him with the utmost circumspection, as a little dog will treat a lion.[15]

Fear of Heine's malicious tongue and pen animated Meyerbeer too, who hoped that he might keep his dangerous friend from criticizing and ridiculing him in public by treating him with the generosity and consideration to which his nature inclined him in any case.

In a long letter to Meyerbeer in which Heine asks the composer to intervene on his behalf with his uncle Salomon (24 March 1834), he also speaks of one of Meyerbeer's rivals for the favours of the opera-going public, Jacques Fromental Élie Halévy.

Halévy's *Guido* is bad, and it is doubtful whether it will remain in the repertoire. Except for the third act all is utter tedium. And yet this opera has something that makes me respect Halévy. If only I knew what it was! There is about his work something tedious but solid, in the German fashion—perhaps it will appeal to our compatriots. He does not strain after effect, he goes about his work with such plodding methodicalness, that people like us feel like jumping out of our skins (or at least out of our box at the opera). He is an artist, but one who has not a single spark of genius.

In a passage clearly designed to flatter Meyerbeer himself Heine adds:

I know a master who is all fire and artistry at the same time!—I recently talked about that master with Henri Blaze, and put Blaze to shame because of his earlier shortsightedness. What triumphs you have been granted over your enemies!

Heine also maintains in this letter, written after Meyerbeer had left for Berlin, that he missed the composer's company dreadfully: for in him he had found the only man with whom he could talk freely of the most secret afflictions and discomforts (*die geheimsten Mißlichkeiten*) of the artist's life in nineteenth-century Paris.

(vi)

Along with Meyerbeer and Halévy the music publisher Maurice Schlesinger inevitably invades Heine's letters. Schlesinger, Heine tells Meyerbeer on 6 April 1835, rather overdid the puffing when Halévy's *La Juive* made her first appearance.

The whole of Paris speaks with but one voice about the excellence of this opera—and that voice belongs to M. Maurice Schlesinger. The latter is piqued because the public does not believe his assurances that the opera is excellent. He and Véron must be grieved because neither their lavish production nor their trumpetings have deceived the public—for these two gentlemen had already come to believe that it was they who made reputations. His obstinacy is likely to cost Schlesinger a good deal of money . . .

Heine himself had business dealings with Schlesinger (as a somewhat huffy letter of 20 May 1837 may serve to show) and was glad to listen to his informed gossip about music, musicians, and journalists—for he could turn such gossip to good account in his reports for the *Augsburg Gazette*. What he really thought of Schlesinger's activities, however, comes out drastically in a letter to Franz Liszt: 'The tree of music is in full bloom, although Herr Schlesinger pisses on it every week.' (12 October 1836.)

(vii)

Besides journalists, musicians, and publishers Heine's acquaintances in Paris included Jewish doctors and financiers of various kind. Among the medical men was David Ferdinand

Koreff, that friend of E. T. A. Hoffmann whom we have already encountered in *Letters from Berlin*. He was living in Paris where Heine met him soon after his arrival there; on 20 January 1832 he reported to Cotta that Koreff had joined him in ridiculing the vanity of August Wilhelm Schlegel, who had just been awarded the Cross of the Legion of Honour. Koreff treated Heine for the paralysis of one of his hands (to Varnhagen, 28 March 1833); and though Heine did not consult him any more when his condition became more serious, he thought highly enough of Koreff as a literary figure to ask J. H. Detmold, on 14 June 1837, to refrain from criticizing Koreff's work in public: 'for I know', he adds, 'that you have a low opinion of him.'

Another doctor of Jewish extraction whom Heine consulted during the early days of his stay in Paris was the oculist Julius Sichel, who successfully treated Heine's sudden, frightening onset of near-blindness in 1837. Heine's contact with Sichel during his very first year in Paris is described in a letter from Börne to Jeanette Wohl, dated 25 October 1831, which is to be cited in the Conclusion of the present book. Dr Sichel's skill as an oculist was such that Heine sought an apartment in his proximity when his eyes began to give serious trouble (to Meyerbeer, 24 March 1838); and he also relied on Sichel, as a letter to Ferdinand Hiller shows, for news of the German musical world (7 October 1839).

Dependent as he continued to be on remittances from Germany, Heine perforce came into contact with Parisian banking houses that had German connections. Among these were the firms of Jules (or Julius) Cohn, August Leo, Fould, Fould & Oppenheimer, and, of course, Rothschild. With the heads of all these houses Heine had some private contact too: Jules Cohn was a distant relative; the Leos he had met in Hamburg; the Foulds he met not only in their bank but also in the home of their brother-in-law Elie Furtado, whose daughter Cécile later married Carl Heine ('I made that match', Heine was to say later, after his private opinion of Cécile had been urgently solicited by her future husband.) From Heine's letters of the late 1830s Cécile Furtado emerges as a real little charmer, with a genuine affection, and genuine admiration, for the famous poet to whom she was distantly related. To Rose Furtado,

Céciles mother, Heine writes with unwonted warmth on 8 July 1839:

Tout ce qu'elle m'écrit est embaumé d'affection et de cette bonté enfantine qui lui va si bien; on croit voir les grands yeux qui disent tout son âme:—on croit l'entendre parler, disant les choses les plus aimables d'un ton brusque et saccadé: singulier mélange de vivacité et de douceur!

Alas—this relationship too, as we shall see, was to be poisoned by suspicion and family feuds, and the bright image of Cécile, like so many others in Heine's life and art, was to become irremediably tarnished.

The Parisian Rothschilds invited Heine to their house because of their business connections with his uncle Salomon, because he was a literary lion, and also, perhaps, because they feared his wicked tongue and pen. This last motive was certainly in Grillparzer's mind when he encountered the poet in the Rothschilds' house.

Much as I liked Heine when I met him privately, he displeased me when we both lunched at Rothschild's house a few days later. It was apparent that the hosts feared Heine; he misused that fear in order to ridicule them at every opportunity . . .[16]

Heine's letter to Detmold asking Detmold to rough out an article on Parisian-German personalities which he, Heine, could work up, asks that journalist to go easy on Meyerbeer and Koreff: but as for James de Rothschild, 'there you can say what you want, be as malicious as you like.' (14 June 1837.) There is no lack of anecdotes claiming to embody Heine's own jokes at Rothschild's expense.

'Dr Heine', James de Rothschild once called over to him while they were sitting at table, 'could you tell me why this wine is called "Lacrymae Christi"?' 'All you have to do is translate,' Heine answered. 'Christ weeps when rich Jews can afford such good wines while so many poor folk go hungry and thirsty.'

When Rothschild is said to have asked visitors to his splendid palace in the rue Lafitte: 'Comment trouvez-vouz mon chénil?' Heine is said to have commented: 'Don't you know that *chénil* means "dog-kennel"? If you have so low an opinion of yourself, at least don't trumpet it abroad!' When Rothschild is

said to have intervened in a discussion on the filthy state of the
Seine with the information that he had visited that river at its
source and found it clear and pure there, Heine is reported to
have riposted: 'Yes, M. le baron; and I hear that your late father
was a most honest man.'[17] When someone showed himself
eager to meet the great James Rothschild, Heine is credited
with the comment: 'He only wants to get to know him because
he does not know him.' (One has to think about that one a bit.)
Yet though he complained about a boring German entertainer
whose visit Baron James had wished on him (to Maximilian
Heine, 21 April 1834), Heine's letters contain no jokes at the
expense of the Rothschilds. He sent his books to Baroness
Betty Rothschild with expressions of veneration and compli-
ments on her beauty as well as her generosity; 'my earliest
patroness in Paris' he called her in a letter to Pauline Bosse of
7 July 1835. On 1 June 1840 he sent Baroness Betty galley proofs
of the earlier books of his *Ludwig Börne*, along with the
Passover chapter from *The Rabbi of Bacherach*, and added a
note of apology for 'harsh passages on the House of Roth-
schild'.

You now hold in your hands the *corpus delicti* that gives me some
anxiety. May I still appear before you? I beg you . . .
    Perhaps you will forgive me with a merry smile. For my part, I
cannot reproach myself enough for having spoken, not with ill
intent, but in an unbecoming manner, of a family that conceals so
much nobility of feeling and so much good will. 'Conceals' is the
right word; for I discovered the other day, by chance, that the
beautiful lady whom I took to be only intelligent and virtuous also
possesses a great soul. Baron James is indeed the richest of men—but
not because of his money. Of the generation that is now growing up I
also have a high opinion: Charlotte shows splendid promise, and I
hope your boys will flourish and prosper.
    Please believe, Mme la baronne, that the interest I take in your
house is of no common sort; and accept my assurance of complete
devotion for the rest of my days.

Whatever Heine may have said, in public or in private, about
the House of Rothschild and the head of its Parisian branch, he
never showed anything but admiration and affection for Baro-
ness Betty.
    The Jewish figures exhibited in this chapter from Heine's

point of view are, for the most part, men and women reasonably well known in their time, so that their reflection in the writings of others can be studied alongside those in Heine's. It must not be forgotten, however, that obscurer contemporaries also appear and disappear again in the mirror of his correspondence—from Aaron Hirsch, Uncle Salomon's trusted factotum, to someone Heine dismisses as 'that rogue Ascher' (not Saul Ascher, of course, who had died many years before Heine went to Paris), a man the poet charges with shady bookselling and publishing practices in letters to Campe dated 18 August and 18 September 1838. One might say, adopting Heine's own favoured imagery, that his menagerie could boast a flea circus as well as a pride of lions.

PART III
Roads from Damascus

CHAPTER 9
Kith and Kin

(i)

In his essays on the Jewish Question the young Karl Marx, baptized as a child and thus taken out of the Jewish sphere by his father, sought to put his own Jewishness firmly behind him; and one tiny lapse apart, he henceforth wrote and acted as though he had no part in the Jewish community of kinship and history. Heine had been forced by the circumstances of his life to make for himself the choice Karl Marx's father had made for his son; and the Damascus affair brought home to him with renewed force what he had felt from the first—that for all his Protestantism, or Saint-Simonism, or anti-Nazarene Hellensim, he could not and would not deny his own origins. This did not mean acceptance or even approval of the Jewish religion, nor did it mean abandonment of his belief that true Jewish emancipation could only be achieved in the context of a wider emancipation, a fight for human rights and civic equality extended to all. We must therefore expect to see Heine avoiding, even after Damascus, specifically and narrowly Jewish personae and perspectives. In this one regard the third person narration of *The Rabbi of Bacherach*, so uncongenial to Heine in other respects, served as a welcome distancing medium between himself and the protagonists of his tale.

One of the aims Heine pursued when writing his *Rabbi* was, as we have seen, that of giving literary expression to specifically Jewish pains and sorrows—*den großen Judenschmerz,*[1] as Heine called it, varying Börne's *ungeheuren Judenschmerz.*[2] This meant, in the first instance, the sorrows inflicted on Jews by the Gentile world; but it also took in the feeling once expressed by Moritz Saphir when he called his Judaism a birth defect corrected by his baptism. Jews were only too prone to internalize the scorn of others and thus to see Jewishness as a defect or a sickness. This sensation Heine expressed in his own

distinctive way by means of a poem composed shortly after his
Uncle Salomon had endowed a Jewish hospital in 1842.

Das neue Israelitische Hospital zu Hamburg

Ein Hospital für arme, kranke Juden,
Für Menschenkinder, welche dreifach elend,
Behaftet mit den bösen drei Gebresten,
Mit Armut, Köperschmerz und Judentume!

Das schlimmste von den dreien ist das letzte,
Das tausendjährige Familienübel,
Die aus dem Niltal mitgeschleppte Plage,
Der altägyptisch ungesunde Glauben.

Unheilbar tiefes Leid! Dagegen helfen
Nicht Dampfbad, Dusche, nicht die Apparate
Der Chirurgie, noch all die Arzeneien,
Die dieses Haus den siechen Gästen bietet.

Wird einst die Zeit, die ew'ge Göttin, tilgen
Das dunkle Weh, das sich vererbt vom Vater
Herunter auf den Sohn—wird einst der Enkel
Genesen und vernünftig sein und glücklich?

Ich weiß es nicht! Doch mittlerweile wollen
Wir preisen jenes Herz, das klug und liebreich
Zu lindern suchte, was der Lindrung fähig,
Zeitlichen Balsam träufelnd in die Wunden.

Der teure Mann! Er baute hier ein Obdach
Für Leiden, welche heilbar durch die Künste
Des Arztes (oder auch des Todes!), sorgte
Für Polster, Labetrank, Wartung und Pflege—

Ein Mann der Tat, tat er was eben tunlich;
Für gute Werke gab er hin den Taglohn
Am Abend seines Lebens, menschenfreundlich,
Durch Wohltun sich erholend von der Arbeit.

Er gab mit reicher Hand—doch reichre Spende
Entrollte manchmal seinem Aug, die Träne,
Die kostbar schöne Träne, die er weinte
Ob der unheilbar großen Brüderkrankheit.

[The New Jewish Hospital in Hamburg

A hospital for poor, sick Jews,
for people afflicted with threefold misery,
with three evil maladies:
poverty, physical pain, and Jewishness.

The last-named is the worst of all the three:
that thousand-year-old family complaint,
the plague they dragged with them from the Nile valley,
the unhealthy faith from ancient Egypt.

Incurable, profound suffering! No help can be looked for
from steam-baths, shower-baths, or all the implements
of surgery, or all the medicines
which this house offers its sick inmates.

Will Time, the eternal goddess, one day annihilate
the sombre woe which passes from the father
to the son; will the grandson, one day,
recover, will *he* be rational and happy?

I do not know; but meanwhile let us
praise the heart which, wise and loving,
sought to alleviate what can be alleviated,
soothing wounds with temporal balm .

That good and well-loved man! He built a dwelling
for healing such wounds as *can* be healed—
by doctors or by death. He provided
soft pillows, soothing draughts, and careful nursing.

As a man of action, he acted where acting was of use.
In the evening of his life he sacrificed, for others' benefit,
what he had earned in his life's day.
A true philanthropist, he rested by doing good.

His hand was never slow to give; but a richer tribute
dropped sometimes from his eye: a tear,
that fair and precious tear he wept
for the great, incurable sickness of his kin.]³

Judaism, then, and Jewishness, is felt as a survival from a dark
past, an Egyptian relic in modern times. It is felt as an irrational

obstacle to happiness in times moving towards greater rationality. It is felt above all—through the central metaphor of the poem—as a 'sickness' for which, as yet, no cure had been found (baptism, we may be certain, was no cure!). We may therefore agree with Max Brod when he spoke of this poem as the nadir of Heine's relation to Judaism.[4] It gives expression to sentiments entertained, as we know, by other emancipated Jews of Heine's day—Rahel Varnhagen is the obvious but by no means the only instance.[5] But in a pioneer work which has lost nothing of its value in well over thirty intervening years, Israel Tabak has pointed to a dual feeling inherent in this poem: the combination of Heine's occasional longing for a day in which Jews would lose their identity, and disappear as a people, with praise of the Jew who casts in his lot with his Jewish kinfolk, who identifies himself with them in the hour of their distress and helps them to the best of his ability.[6] While branding Judaism as a 'sickness', he also shows up the virtues that such 'sickness' may engender in those who are themselves 'afflicted' with it. For it is not only the *inmates* of the hospital who are subject to this *unheilbar große Brüderkrankheit*; the *founder* of the hospital belongs to the same family and is subject to the same fate. Dare we add that the same is true of the writer of the poem—and that the 'sickness' which activated the beauty of the founder's benevolence also animates the beauty of the writer's compassionate poetry? Health, though desirable, is not always the *supreme* good. There may be beauties of mind and action which blossom from what is felt as sickness, or what the world terms so.[7]

In the light of the bitter family quarrels of later years it is worth recalling that the feelings of tenderness and admiration so memorably expressed in *The New Jewish Hospital* were directed towards Uncle Salomon; just as it is worth remembering that Heine's poems of the 1840s are full of loving references to his mother—one need think only of *Night Thoughts* (*Nachtgedanken*) or *Farewell to Paris* (*Abschied von Paris*) or the Hamburg section of *Germany. A Winter's Tale*. For the rest, his references, overt or veiled, to Jews and Judaism in the shorter poems of the early 1840s add little to the portrait he had already painted of the Jews of his time. We are on familiar ground when the poem which ends the 1844 version of *New*

Spring (*Neuer Frühling*) introduces the good citizens of Hamburg by first mentioning those *long noses* which cartoonists have for so long attributed to the children of Israel:

> Lange Nasen, noch langweilig
> Werden sie wie sonst geschneuzet,
> Und das duckt sich noch scheinheilig
> Oder bläht sich, stolz gespreizet.

> [Long noses are still being tediously
> blown, as of yore;
> this lot still sneaks along hypocritically
> or puffs itself up with pride and affection.]

We are on familiar ground still when King Frederick William IV is credited with drunken visions of grandeur and achievement in which he sees himself as the Emperor of China:

> Die große Pagode, Symbol und Hort
> Des Glaubens, ist fertig geworden;
> Die letzten Juden taufen sich dort
> Und kriegen den Drachenorden.

> [The Great Pagoda, symbol and shield
> of faith, has been completed;
> the last Jews are baptized there
> and receive the Order of the Dragon.][9]

For 'Great Pagoda' read Cologne Cathedral, which was still unfinished when Heine wrote this; for 'Order of the Dragon' read 'Order of the Swan' (*Schwanenorden*) or—more likely—'Order of the Eagle', the Prussian *Adlerorden* with its hierarchical division into four classes. The later French version of this poem, which Heine supervised, strongly suggests that *Adlerorden* is meant as it spells out that the 'reward' the Jews receive for zealously having themselves baptized to the last man, is anything but splendid: 'Les derniers juifs viennent se faire baptiser dans cette pagode romantique, et pour récompenser leur zèle religieux, je les gratifie tous de la décoration du dragon noir, *de quatrième classe.*'[10] (My italics.) The mess of potage for which Esau sold his birthright, we may well reflect, was worth more than this lowest of Prusso-Chinese decorations.

Not that Heine had much feeling for the Jewish *religion* in the early 1840s. One of the most revealing poems of this period is *Adam the First (Adam der Erste)*, where the poet assumes the voice of Adam after he had eaten the fruit of the forbidden tree. He casts defiance at the God who decrees his expulsion from paradise in terms which suggest, not only Jehovah, but also modern kings and heads of universities, ending with the lines

> Vermissen werde ich nimmermehr
> Die paradiesischen Räume;
> Das war kein wahres Paradies—
> Es gab dort verbotene Bäume.
>
> Ich will mein volles Freiheitsrecht!
> Find' ich die g'ringste Beschränknis,
> Verwandelt sich mir das Paradies
> In Hölle und Gefängnis.
>
> [I shall never miss
> the realms of paradise.
> That was no true paradise—
> it contained forbidden trees.
>
> I want the full liberty that is my due!
> If I find it circumscribed in any way
> paradise changes, for me,
> into a hell or a prison.][11]

This rejects the rules and proscription of Old Testamentarian religion as emphatically as the decrees of undemocratic or unconstitutional governments of the nineteenth century.

(ii)

In 1843 Heine published, in consecutive issues of a journal edited by his friend Heinrich Laube, an early version of *Atta Troll. A Midsummer Night's Dream*—a delightful mock epic which reappeared in book form, with some additions, deletions, and rearrangements, in 1847. Its eponymous hero is a dancing bear; dance and dancing, which always fascinated Heine, therefore figure quite naturally among its central images, and Jews too are swept into its gay round. Many of these Jewish or proto-Jewish dancers come from the Bible: we meet Deborah dancing in triumph and beating upon the cymbals, King David dancing before the Ark of the Covenant, and Herodias (who here has traits that later sufferers from the Romantic Agony would lend to Salome) demanding the head of John the Baptist in return for her dance before King Herod. But whatever he may think of the prowess of the Jews of old, Atta the Democratic Bear looks with a jaundiced eye on the efforts of their modern descendants to emulate them. Egalitarian though he is, he stops short of letting Jews freely practise the art which circumstances had made his own. Before he turns to them in earnest, however, he has a disquisition on dogs in which contemporaries could easily recognize a parody of the arguments usually put forward by advocates of Jewish emancipation when they encountered objections based on alleged defects in the Jewish national character.

'Was den Hund betrifft, so ist er
Freilich ein serviler Köter,
Weil Jahrtausende hindurch
Ihn der Mensch wie 'n Hund behandelt;

Doch in unserm Freistaat geben
Wir ihm wieder seine alten
Unveräußerlichen Rechte,
Und er wird sich bald veredeln.

Ja, sogar die Juden sollen
Volles Bürgerrecht genießen,
Und gesetzlich gleichgestellt sein
Allen andern Säugetieren.

Nur das Tanzen auf den Märkten
Sei den Juden nicht gestattet;
Dies Amendement, ich mach es
Im Intresse meiner Kunst.

Denn der Sinn für Stil, für strenge
Plastik der Bewegung, fehlt
Jener Rasse, sie verdürben
Den Geschmack des Publikums.'

[As for the dog—it is undeniable
that he is a servile cur
because for thousands of years
mankind treated him like a dog.

But in our free state we shall
restore to him his ancient
inalienable rights,
and he will soon acquire a nobler character.

Yes—even the Jews shall
enjoy full civic rights
and be equal before the law
to all other mammals.

Only dancing in the market-place
will not be permitted to Jews;
I make this amendment
in the interest of my art.

For a sense of style, of strict
plasticity of movement, is absent
in that race—they would corrupt
the public's taste.']¹²

What Heine caricatures here, in the first instance, is a certain
type of unselfconscious anti-Semitism among professed liber-
als—Heine once told Fanny Lewald that he derived Atta's
remarks from memories of a liberal apothecary who was all in
favour of complete emancipation of the Jews, except that he
would not allow them to become apothecaries.¹³ Philanthropic
or humanitarian convictions tend to make a halt where
professional and financial interests begin. But there is more to
it than that: if one looks at this passage in the context of
Heine's developing portrait of Jews and Judaism one cannot
help feeling that he is expecting us to have some sympathy with
Atta's view—that those who are treated like dogs for long
enough *will* develop cur-like qualities, and that there *is* some-

thing which strikes a Gentile as clumsy and ungainly about the movement of some Jews, from the kind of pedlar Heine describes in *The God Apollo* to Eduard Gans as described in *The Town of Lucca*. The fact that these criticisms are made by Atta Troll, whose own movements many human dancers would feel to be clumsy and ungainly, lends this brilliant passage an additional ironic dimension.

One other thing is noteworthy in our context. Like the 'horse-traders' of *Ludwig Marcus* (see Chapter 10 below), Atta Troll speaks of the Jews not as a religious community or a people or a nation or an ethnic family or a kinship group but as a *race*. This was clearly becoming more common in mid-nineteenth-century Europe; and it meant, of course, that neither baptism nor unconditional loyalty to the country of one's birth could henceforth be regarded as a possible device for ridding oneself of one's Jewishness. Heine himself used the word sparingly and (when speaking in his own voice) in a value-free way: a late letter, for instance, refers to the history of the Jews as 'l'histoire de notre race'. He also talks, at times, of blood-continuities—as when he presents himself as having in his veins some of the same blood as that which flowed in those of Jesus of Nazareth. The vocabulary of race and blood was to be heard in more and more sinister contexts later; but though Heine did not live long enough to see these developments he was, from the first, fully aware of the dangers they would pose to men of Jewish origin who also claimed—as he did—that they were Germans.

The altered and rearranged form in which *Atta Troll* appeared in 1847 still failed to satisfy Heine—he hoped to revise the work further and reissue it with additional 'Trolliaden' at some later date. His notes for some of these additions and revisions have been preserved; and they show clearly that the poet intended strengthening and underlining the reference to Jews in the chapter on which our attention has been focused so far. Winfried Woesler, who has studied these texts intensively, goes so far as to say that Heine makes the German liberals' relationship to the Jews a touchstone of their ability to change society for the better.[14] But as we have seen so often, these things are never simple, never single-edged, in this poet's writings. The irony of Atta's own naïve intolerance revealed at the end of Caput VI was to be strengthened by his promise to abolish Jewish 'intolerance' in the just animal kingdom of the future:

> Kein intoleranter Ausschluß
> (altmosaisch abergläubisch)
> Treffe mehr das arme Schwein
> Das im tiefen Erdenschlamm sich wälzet—
>
> [Let there be no further intolerant exclusion
> (by ancient Mosaic superstition)
> of the poor swine
> that wallows in the deep mire of this earth—][15]

Atta's remarks about the servility of dogs and its causes, which have already been quoted, were in this later version to be made more clearly applicable to unemancipated Jewry:

> Ja, er ward zu sehr gedrückt
> Durch barbarische Gesetze—
> Selbst im aufgeklärten Preußen
> Zahlt er Leibzoll, Hundesteuer!
>
> Ist er ganz entsittlicht? Nein!
> In dem Hund blieb eine Tugend,
> Drob die Menschen manchmal zittern—
> Er, der Hund kann rasend werden.
>
> Deßhalb wird er sich veredeln
> Wenn wir ihm in unserm Freistaat
> Wiedergeben seine uralt
> Unveräußerlichen Rechte . . .
>
> [Yes, the dog has been too much oppressed
> by barbaric laws—
> even in enlightened Prussia
> he has to pay travel toll, dog tax.
>
> Is he totally demoralized? No!
> One virtue remained with the dog
> which sometimes causes man to tremble:
> he, the dog, can fall into a mad rage.

Therefore he will become more noble
when in our free state
we restore to him his ancient
inalienable rights . . .][16]

The *Leibzoll* which Jews had to pay when entering Prussia
even in the days of the 'enlightened' monarch Frederick the
Great was rightly resented by them as degrading, as putting
men on the same level as taxable animals. By the time *Atta Troll*
was written it had long been abolished; but the memory of the
indignities and inconveniences caused by such *péage corporel*
long outlasted its abolition. As for the democratic bear's re-
ference to the 'mad rages' to which the dogs were subject—
the application of *that* to Jewish history becomes clearer if
we look again at the end of Heine's poem *To Edom*. It is char-
acteristic of Atta Troll that it should be precisely this ability to
fall into a rage which convinces him of the dog's innate
morality!

The Jews' implacable enemies, whose blood-thirsty raging
To Edom had sought to describe, also take on a sharper profile
in the additions Heine envisaged for the revised version of *Atta
Troll* which he did not live to complete. Atta's youngest son
was to be given a speech that sharpened his father's significant
reference to the new *racial* theories advanced by German
nationalists.

Nicht weltbürgerlich wie du
Bin ich liberal, mein Vater,
Und ich schwärme nicht ins Blaue
Für das Glück der ganzen Thierheit.

Ich bin Bär vor allen Dingen.
Meine Nazionalität
Zu behaupten, sie zu schützen
Vor dem Einfluß fremder Raçen

Zu bewahren meine alte
Bärenhaut wie [sie] gewesen
Zu der Zeit des Tacitus
Das ist meine Lebenssendung.

[Unlike you, my father,
I am no liberal citizen of the world.
I do not indulge in cloudy fantasies
about the happiness of all animal kind.

Above all else I am a bear.
To preserve my national identity
and to protect it
against the influence of alien races

To keep my ancient
bearskin in that pristine state
which it had in the days of Tacitus—
that is my mission in life.]

And if that reference to an ursine (read: German) mission is not sufficiently chilling in the light of later history, we need only read on to find even more sinister anticipations:

Dann auch bin ich Panursine
Und ich will daß die getrennten
Bärenstämme sich verein'gen
Und die Weltherrschaft erobern.

[I am Panursine too
and want to see the disunited
bear tribes come together
to conquer and dominate the world.][17]

Like Grandville in his famous caricatures, Heine designs his animal world in such a way that it clearly mirrors contemporary society.[18]

And just as human beings, according to Feuerbach and Marx, project their concerns, their virtues, their longings, into other-worldly religions, so Atta Troll paints for himself and his admiring audience a picture of heaven ruled over by a colossal Polar Bear enthroned in monotheistic majesty.[19] That is in line with a good deal of *Aufklärung* satire on religion; but since it is Atta Troll who projects these particular images, heaven has to be full of dancers and dancing. We have already seen Heine ransacking the Bible for allusions to the dance and coming up, amongst others, with King David dancing before the Ark of the Covenant. Whenever Heine speaks of King

David, we feel a degree of distance—his references to David's son Solomon, on the other hand, though often humorous, are much more obviously tinged with affection. In the later *Romanzero*, which presents King David as an archetypal despot, King Solomon, lover and sage, will become something like a culture-hero. In *Atta Troll* Solomon appears in conjunction with that Queen of Sheba who had set little Marcus's mind spinning in the direction of Abyssinia. The 1843 version shows Solomon and the Queen exchanging riddles by messenger, from afar, until the Queen decides to annihilate the distance between them:

> Rätselmüde zog die Kön'gin
> Endlich nach Jeruscholajim,
> Und sie stürzte mit Erröten
> In die Arme Salomonis.
>
> Dieser drückte sie ans Herz
> Und er sprach:, Das größte Rätsel,
> Süßes Kind, das ist die Liebe—
> Doch wir wollen es nicht lösen!"
>
> [Weary of riddles, the Queen
> went at last to Yerushalayim,
> and blushing she fell
> into Solomon's arms.
>
> He pressed her to his heart
> and said: 'The greatest riddle of all,
> my sweet child, is love—
> but let us not find a solution to that!']20

What is remarkable about this (later deleted) passage is its use of the *Hebrew* version of the name 'Jerusalem', in the pronunciation of German and Polish Jews, of the 'Ashkenazim' of central and Eastern Europe. A whole world of nostalgia, of longing for a lost homeland, adheres to its full vowels and soft consonants; and this nostalgia Heine summons up most powerfully in the central chapters of *Atta Troll*, the 'Wild Hunt' chapters, which in both versions repeat the word *Jeruscholajim* three times and actually come to rest on that word.21

Aber du, Herodias,
Sag, wo bist du?—Ach, ich weiß es
Du bist tot und liegst begraben
Bei der Stadt Jeruscholajim!

Starren Leichenschlaf am Tage
Schläfst du in dem Marmorsarge;
Doch um Mitternacht erweckt dich
Peitschenknall, Hallo und Hussa!

Und du folgst dem wilden Heerzug
Mit Dianen und Abunden,
Mit den heitern Jagdgenossen,
Denen Kreuz und Qual verhaßt ist!

Welche köstliche Gesellschaft!
Könnt ich nächtlich mit euch jagen,
Durch die Wälder! Dir zur Seite
Ritt ich stets, Herodias!

Denn ich liebe dich am meisten!
Mehr als jene Griechengöttin,
Mehr als jene Fee des Nordens,
Lieb ich dich, du tote Jüdin!

[But you, Herodias,
Tell me, where are you?—Alas, I know,
you are dead and lie buried
in the city Yerushalayim.

By day you sleep the rigid sleep of death
in your marble sarcophagus;
but at midnight you are awakened
by cracking whips, hallooing, and jubilations.

And then you follow the wild ghostly crew
along with Diana and Abunde,
with all your happy hunting companions
who detest the cross and all agonies.

What a delightful company!
If only I could hunt with you at night
through the forests! By your side
I would always ride, Herodias!

For you I love most!
More than that Greek goddess,
more than that fairy of the North,
do I love you, dead Jewess.][22]

Du tote Jüdin—here the poet brings into the open a nostalgia for a *Jewish* love-object, together with a Romantic longing to reanimate the past, a feeling for the close affinity of love and death, love and cruelty, which no one acquainted with his biography and mental set will find surprising. The appreciation of all this does not, however, depend in any way on knowing biographical facts about Heine.

The Wild Hunt, supernatural beings and ghosts of the departed traversing the sky, is part and parcel of Germanic folklore and the subject of many an eerie German tale. Heine uses it, as he had used the legend of Tannhäuser and Venus, for his own modern and idiosyncratic purposes; he introduces into it, in *Atta Troll*, not only the poets he admired—notably Shakespeare and Goethe—but also three female figures who symbolize (amongst many other things) the three worlds that meet in his poetry. The goddess Diana represents the Hellenic world, the fairy Abunde that of Germanic and Celtic legend, and the princess Herodias the world of biblical and post-biblical Judaism. In Heine's poem Herodias loved John the Baptist and *therefore* demanded his death; and the vision of her death-dealing beauty will not leave the 'I' that speaks in *Atta Troll* once she has nodded to him as she sweeps by with her wild companions. He therefore calls out to this figure to cast away the head of John the Baptist, and he offers himself as fitter companion; for he feels akin to those that hate the Cross and hate suffering (*denen Kreuz und Qual verhaßt ist*). Here at last he had found a Jewish figure who is not Nazarene, who does not scorn sensual enjoyment. But of course—supreme irony and ultimate frisson!—she is dead.

Bin so recht der rechte Ritter
Den du brauchst—Mich kümmert's wenig
Daß du tot und gar verdammt bist—
Habe keine Vorurteile–

Hapert's doch mit meiner eignen
Seligkeit, und ob ich selber
Noch dem Leben angehöre
Daran zweifle ich zuweilen!

Nimm mich an als deinen Ritter,
Deinen Cavalier-servente;
Werde deinen Mantel tragen
Und auch alle deine Launen.

Jede Nacht an deiner Seite
Reit ich mit dem Wilden Heere,
Und wir kosen, und wir lachen
Über meine tollen Reden.

Werde dir die Zeit verkürzen
In der Nacht.—Jedoch am Tage
Schwindet jede Lust, und weinend
Sitz ich dann auf deinem Grabe.

Ja, am Tage sitz ich weinend
Auf dem Schutt der Königsgrüfte,
Auf dem Grabe der Geliebten,
Bei der Stadt Jeruscholajim.

Alte Juden, die vorbeigehn,
Glauben dann gewiß, ich traure
Ob dem Untergang des Tempels
Und der Stadt Jeruscholajim.

[I am exactly the kind of knight
you need—I care but little
that you are dead and even damned—
I have no prejudices—

There's some difficulty about my own
salvation, and whether I myself
still belong to the living
I sometimes doubt!

Accept me as you knight.
your *cavaliere servente*,
I shall bear your cloak
and all your whims.

Every night, by your side,
I ride with the ghostly crew,
and we flirt, and we laugh
at my wild, mad speeches.

I shall beguile your time
at night—but by day
all delight will vanish, weeping
will I sit upon your grave.

Yes, by day I shall sit weeping
on the ruined tombs of kings,
on the grave of the beloved,
by the city Yerushalayim.

Old Jews that pass by
will surely think, then, that my lament
is for the destruction of the temple
and the city of Yerushalayim.][23]

The poet's scorn for Nazarene denial of the senses mingled with doubts about his own place in this world or the next; his Romantic nostalgia for the vanished age of the *cavaliere servente*, distanced and modernized by the humorous zeugma that joins the bearing of a lady's cloak with the bearing of her whims; his Baudelairean nostalgia for an exotic beauty that hurts and kills—these here merge with the yearning of aged Jews for their lost ancestral homeland. A manuscript variant makes the connection even clearer by incorporating a textual allusion to the psalm whose melancholy cadences had made an indelible impression on Heine:

Ihre Flammenblicke trafen
Mich wie Blitze der Erinnrung:
Sind das nicht dieselben Augen
Die vor achtzehnhundert Jahren

In mein junges Herz geleuchtet
Als ich Mundschenk war am Hofe
Unsres großen Viertelsfürsten,
In der Stadt Jeruscholajim?

Heilge Stadt Jeruscholajim!
Wenn ich deiner je vergesse
So verwelke meine Rechte
So vertrockne meine Zunge!

[Her burning glances flashed upon me
like lightnings of remembrance—
are not these the self-same eyes
Which, eighteen hundred years ago,

Shone into my young heart
When I was cupbearer at the court
of our great Tetrarch
in the city Yerushalayim?

Sacred city Yerushalayim!
If ever I forget thee
let my right hand forget her cunning
and let my tongue cleave to the roof of my mouth!]²⁴

Psalm 137, that great song of the Babylonian exile, is becoming a leitmotiv of Heine's work. Just as a *too* insistent dwelling on 'Yerushalayim' nostalgia, however, identified the poet of *Atta Troll* too crassly with the Jewish people, and therefore had to be toned down, so the notion of a metempsychosis, of a previous existence at the Jewish court of King Herod, seemed too direct for the poet's oblique purposes and had to be sacrificed. The place of such passages is taken by more subtle hints of the protagonist's feeling of kinship with a persecuted and despised people—as when he has his hunter hero look on a downtrodden Cagot as his 'brother'.²⁵ Characteristically, the I that tells the story cannot suppress a shudder of revulsion at kissing the Cagot's baby which resembles a sick spider as it greedily clutches at its mother's breast. The poor and underprivileged, it would seem, are not always easy to love.

The old Jews who mistake the object of the bear-hunter's longing at the end of the Herodias section of *Atta Troll* have an important function in the poem's narrative economy: that of introducing a point of view which differs from that of the narrator. But even where Heine does not bring in additional characters to relativize the point of view of his epic I, he introduces enough distancing devices—enough parody, irony, and humour—to make the reader wary of seeing the world exclusively through the bear-hunter's spectacles. Winfried Woesler has shown in interesting detail how Heine's *Salonton*, his urbanity and irony, prevents any unreflecting indulgence of masochistic fantasies even in those portions of the 'Wild Hunt' chapters which most deserve a place in Mario Praz's catalogue of Romantic agonies.[26]

Chapter XXI of *Atta Troll* once again plays on the stereotype of the Jewish nose: what do these stuffed birds' beaks remind me of, the hunter persona asks, where have I seen something like them? Was it in Hamburg? Was it in the 'Lane' at Frankfurt? The French version spells the answer out more directly when it speaks of *le quartier des Juifs* as the source of the protagonist's memory image.[27]

How pervasive Heine's Jewish references are in *Atta Troll* may be seen again by a brief look at the passage in which the dancing bear proclaims his pride at being a bear in the defiant accents of Jaromir, the robber hero of Grillparzer's play *The Ghost of the Ancestress (Die Ahnfrau)*. Here is an early version:

'Bin die Zielscheib eures Witzes,
Bin das Ungetüm, womit
Ihr die Kinder schreckt des Abends,
Die unart'gen Menschenkinder.

Bin das rohe Spottgebilde
Eurer Ammenmärchen, bin es,
Und ich ruf es laut hinunter
In die schnöde Menschenwelt.

Hört es, hört ich bin ein Bär,
Nimmer schäm ich mich des Ursprungs
Und bin stolz darauf, als stammt ich
Ab von König Salomon!'

[I am the target of your witticisms,
I am the bugbear with which
you frighten your children in the evening,
your ill-bred human children.

I am the phantom you mock, coarsely,
in your nursery tales; yes, I am all that—
down these mountains I proclaim it
loudly to iniquitous mankind.

Listen, listen: I am a bear,
and I am not ashamed of my descent;
nay, I am as proud of it as though I were descended
from King Solomon himself.]

In the printed versions, however, the last of the lines just quoted will be found to read:

als stammt ich
Ab von Moses Mendelssohn.

[as though I were descended
from Moses Mendelssohn.]28

This shift from the biblical to the modern German world does two things: it pays yet another compliment to Lessing's friend Mendelssohn, whom Heine respected throughout his life as one of the noblest scions of German Jewry; and it casts a cold eye on members of Mendelssohn's family, in particular Felix Mendelssohn-Bartholdy, whose 'Christianizing' (*Christeln*) Heine regarded as a betrayal of grandfather Moses's memory.

Meyerbeer, Felix Mendelssohn's great rival in the esteem of his German public, appears only obliquely in *Atta Troll*: his music for the ballet of the dead nuns, in *Robert le Diable*, accompanies a thematically important scene in Chapter XXI which has no bearing on our present theme.

More relevant, however, is the glimpse Heine allows us of a Spanish statesman of his own day whose alleged Marrano descent is held against him by some ravens (read: ultramontane Catholic reactionaries) who croak imprecations against him:

Sie verwünschten ganz besonders
Jenen Juden Mendizabel,
Der die Klöster aufgehoben,
Ihre lieben alten Nester.

[They cursed with especial fervour
that Jew, Mendizábal,
who dissolved the monasteries,
their beloved old nests.]29

Juan Alvárez Mendizábal (1790–1853), who tried, unsuccessfully, to ease the fiscal problems of Spain by means of a series of bills designed to drive out religious orders and sell off their property, seems to be Jewish only by courtesy of Heine's ultramontane ravens. The chapter that refers to him was deleted from the 1847 version of *Atta Troll*, and we have no indication whether the poet intended to reintroduce it into the expanded version he did not live to complete.

One last allusion to specific contemporary Jews, present in both printed versions of *Atta Troll*, could be fully understood only by those who knew something of Heine's private affairs. His hunter persona is spending the night in a wretched Spanish inn and is sadly plagued by bedbugs.

> Ach! die Wanzen
> Sind des Menschen schlimmste Feinde.
>
> Schlimmer als der Zorn von tausend
> Elefanten is die Feindschaft
> Einer einz'gen kleinen Wanze,
> Die auf deinem Lager kriecht.
>
> Mußt dich ruhig beißen lassen—
> Das ist schlimm—Noch schlimmer ist es,
> Wenn du sie zerdrückst: der Mißduft
> Quält dich dann die ganze Nacht.
>
> Ja, das Schrecklichste auf Erden
> Ist der Kampf mit Ungeziefer,
> Dem Gestank als Waffe dient—
> Das Duell mit einer Wanze!
>
> [bedbugs, alas,
> are mankind's worst enemies.
>
> Worse than the rage of a thousand
> elephants is the enmity
> of a single little bedbug
> that crawls on your couch.
>
> You have to lie still and let them bite—
> that's bad enough—but worse ensues
> if you crush it; the stench
> tortures you the whole night through.

Yes, the worst thing on earth
is a fight with vermin
that uses stench as its weapon:
a duel with a bedbug!][30]

That last line gives the game away: after a period of newspaper
charges and counter-charges arising out of Heine's treatment
of Börne's Jewish entourage in *Ludwig Börne. A Memorial* and
the physical revenge Salomon Strauß claimed to have taken,
Heine had fought a *duel* with Strauß in which the poet had
been slightly wounded. The bedbug, therefore, is in the first
instance Salomon Strauß, in the second instance any enemy
who used scandalous publicity to soil the poet's reputation.
Ever since his journey to Poland there had been a distressing
association, in Heine's mind, between Jews whose exterior or
whose behaviour revolted him, and bedbugs. Before we draw
any unwarrantable conclusions from this fact it behoves us to
remember, however, that he treated his non-Jewish enemies to
similar dehumanizing comparisons. Gutzkow, for instance, is
numbered among the crab-lice (*Filzläuse*) in a letter to Campe
dated 25 September 1840.

(iii)

Between the first and the second version of *Atta Troll* Heine
composed another, a more politically aggressive, mock epic:
Germany. A Winter's Tale (Deutschland. Ein Wintermärchen).
Its very Preface, written in January 1844, introduces Jewish
and Gentile readers with a cartoonist's shorthand when it
speaks of 'young ladies from the educated classes' by the banks
of the Spree or those of the Alster—in Berlin and Hamburg, in
other words—who 'will turn up their more or less curved little
noses' (*die mehr oder minder gebogenen Näschen*) at Heine's
occasional Aristophanic disregard of the bourgeois
proprieties.[31]
   Some of his improprieties concern biblical figures and inci-
dents—as when the narrator applies to Hammonia, that female

distillation or condensation of the spirit of Hamburg, the method of swearing an oath which Abraham commends to his eldest servant in Genesis 24:2.[32] A venerable ceremony is thus suffused with scatological suggestions. But images from the early history of the Jewish people recorded in the Old Testament are also reinterpreted and reapplied in a more serious spirit. In Exodus 12:7, for instance, we read of Moses's injunction to the Israelites to anoint the doorposts of their houses with the blood of a lamb so that the inhabitants of these houses should not be harmed when the Angel of Death stalks the land. Caput VII of *Germany. A Winter's Tale* deliberately recalls this passage when the narrator recounts a dream in which he anoints houses with his own blood while a bell announcing death, *ein Sterbeglöckchen*, rings out every time he does so. What averted doom in the biblical narrative attracts it in Heine's new context.

The most prominent biblical figure introduced into *Germany. A Winter's Tale* is that of Jesus Christ, who is here called the narrator's 'cousin' not only because of an ethnic connection but also because of the radical social policies he is said to have espoused. The Jesus here presented attacked the 'establishment' of his day and suffered at the hands of those who failed to appreciate his benevolence towards mankind.[33] Heine's own poem, the poem into which he introduces his martyred 'cousin' Jesus, is also directed against the establishment—one which is specifically said to include Jewish rabbis as well as Christian clergymen, *Rabbiner und Pastöre*.[34]

Germany. A Winter's Tale is full of symbols that convey different aspects of the struggle between conservative and revolutionary forces; and among these the cathedral of Cologne, which was thought to house the bones of the Three Wise Men, plays a prominent part. King Frederick William IV of Prussia was among those who supported the completion of this cathedral, left unfinished by its medieval builders—and when it came to collecting money for this cause, religious affiliations suddenly ceased to be important. 'They beg even from Jews and heretics', Caput IV tells us. But, the narrator warns, the *viri obscuri* of Cologne have their modern counterparts; the old hatreds live on in modern guise.

Der Cancan des Mittelalters ward hier
Getanzt von Nonnen und Mönchen;
Hier schrieb Hochstraaten, der Menzel von Köln,
Die gift'gen Denunziatiönchen.

Die Flamme des Scheiterhaufens hat hier
Bücher und Menschen verschlungen;
Die Glocken wurden geläutet dabei
Und Kyrie Eleison gesungen.

Dummheit und Bosheit buhlten hier
gleich Hunden auf freier Gasse;
Die Enkelbrut erkannt man noch heut
An ihrem Judenhasse.

[Here in Cologne monks and nuns
danced the cancan of the Middle Ages;
here Hochstraaten, Cologne's equivalent of Wolfgang Menzel
wrote his poisonous little denunciations.

Here flames around the stake consumed
books and men alike;
they rang the bells the while
and sang *Kyrie eleison*.

Stupidity and malice here coupled
like dogs in the open street;
the pack they engendered can still be recognized today
by its hatred of Jews.][35]

When Heine showed these lines, before publication, to the
liberal journalist François Wille, the latter objected. 'What
business do you still have with Jews? Your sympathies are
neither with their nationality nor with their religion. And why
must you, in the very work in which you ridicule one kind of
nationalism, exhibit weakness for another?'[36] Heine saw the
force of this argument; in this most radical of all his works so
far, he would weaken his case if he spoke through a Jewish
rather than a German persona, or if he played the Jewish
question too much into the centre field. He therefore changed
Judenhaß, 'hatred of Jews', to *Glaubenshaß*, 'sectarian intoler-
ance'.

Another of the prominent symbols of *Germany. A Winter's*

Tale is the medieval Emperor Frederick Barbarossa, whom posthumous legend had transformed into a sleeper in Mount Kiffhäuser, biding his time to emerge as Germany's saviour. Heine allows his narrator to dream of penetrating the mountain to find Barbarossa in one of his rare moments of wakefulness. The emperor asks to be informed about recent European history—the last information he has, it transpires, antedates the French Revolution. One of the question he asks concerns Moses Mendelssohn—and this elicits an answer which has already been quoted in Chapter 6.[37] The anachronistic fun of making a medieval emperor enquire after the fortunes of an eighteenth-century Jewish sage is obvious enough; it is given additional spice, however, by our recollection that the historical Barbarossa was in fact favourably inclined towards the Jews that came under his jurisdiction. Nor is this the only instance of such playful bending of historical fact to the requirements of the humorous imagination. Moses Mendelssohn's wife was in fact called 'Fromet', as Heine well knew; by calling her 'Rebecca' he completes a sequence in which all the early Mendelssohns bear Old Testament names. That sequence is then meaningfully broken by the first name of Moses's grandson, the baptized conductor of the Leipzig Gewandhaus and composer of Christian oratorios. Following 'Moses', 'Rebecca', 'Abraham', and 'Leah', '*Felix*' shows by his very name how the family had grown away from its Judaism to assume the classical Christian heritage of Europe.

One thing that requires further comment is the phrase 'gestorben, verdorben' applied to Abraham Mendelssohn. This is a folk-song formula, indicating an obscure death in misfortune—not unlike 'he's dead and rotten' in *King Lear* V.iii. 'Verdorben', however, can also have the sense of 'spoilt' or 'corrupted'. Might there, perhaps, be an ironic allusion here to the kind of departure from the ways of his father Moses Mendelssohn which is illustrated by Abraham's now famous letter to his son Felix, upbraiding him for retaining the great Moses's very name? This letter, written in 1829, is so characteristic of the early days of German-Jewish emancipation that I cannot forbear quoting its conclusion.

You cannot, you must not, carry the name Mendelssohn. Felix

Mendelssohn-Bartholdy is too long; it is unsuited for daily use. You must go by the name of Felix Bartholdy. A name is like a garment; it has to be appropriate to the time, the use, and the rank, if it is not to become a hindrance and a laughing stock. . . . There can no more be a Christian Mendelssohn than there can be a Jewish Confucius. If Mendelssohn is your name, you are ipso facto a Jew. And this, if for no other reason than because it is contrary to fact, can be of no benefit to you.

Dear Felix, take this to heart and act accordingly.'[38]

Had Heine known this letter, he might well have given Felix Mendelssohn-Bartholdy, who kept his grandfather's name and thus proclaimed the family's Jewish origins against the wishes of his own father, more credit for uprightness and courage than he actually did.

One of the remoter members of the Mendelssohn clan had penetrated so far into the Christian camp that few readers of *Germany. A Winter's Tale* will have had any inkling of that family connection. The celebrated Caput XI, in which the narrator speculates on what would have become of Germany if the Romans and not Arminius had won the battle of the Teutoburg forest unites in one stanza two Protestant theologians who did not see eye to eye; indeed, their views diverged to such an extent that the one whom Heine names in second place publicly repudiated the one whom Heine names first. If Germany had become Roman, Heine tells us, then 'Hengstenberg would be a *haruspex* pondering over the bowels of oxen', while 'Neander would be an *augur* and look up to swarms of birds.'[39] A simple opposition of an earthy and worldly to an airy, speculative theologian, one might have thought. But August Neander, the disciple of Schleiermacher, the inventor of 'pectoral theology' (*pectus est, quod facit theologum*), was in fact a relative of Moses Mendelssohn's wife who had—as we have already had occasion to see—borne the name David Mendel before he found his way to Christ. Of this origin Heine makes no mention whatever: Neander appears, in *Germany. A Winter's Tale*, as just another Christian theologian.

More overtly than in any other work so far Heine speaks, in *Germany. A Winter's Tale*, of his own family and its history. We hear of family origins in Bückeburg and Hamburg; an affectionate chapter depicts the relationship between the poet-narrator's mother (tender solicitude accompanied by lots of good food) and the poet-narrator himself (evasive answers so as not to distress the old lady); a deleted section even named the desire to see his mother again as one of the principal forces impelling him to revisit his native land:

> Auch nach der Mutter sehne ich mich,
> Ich will es offen gestehen,
> Seit dreizehn Jahren hab' ich nicht
> Die alte Frau gesehen.

> [I long for my mother too—
> openly I confess it;
> I have not seen the old woman
> for thirteen years now.][40]

The mention of thirteen years (1831–44) makes the autobiographical relevance unmistakable. The relative whom Heine disliked so cordially, Therese Heine's husband Adolf Halle, appears anonymously in a stanza which makes rather heartless fun of his recent mental breakdown; but Uncle Salomon, who is also not named directly, finds himself treated more gently, as befits a benefactor from whom further benefits may be expected. A projected stanza speaks of him as 'a certain old grumbler' (*einem gewissen Griesgram*) who scolded the narrator in a way the latter actually came to like; but this was later changed to something more patently complimentary. The final version of *Germany. A Winter's Tale* refers to

> jenem edlen alten Herrn
> Der immer mich ausgescholten
> Und immer großmütig beschützt . . .

> [that noble old gentleman
> who always scolded me,
> and always generously protected me . . .][41]

None of these figures are specifically described as Jewish. The same is true of the impresario Georg Harrys, who turns up again, posthumously, with Niccolo Paganini:

> Den Paganini begleitete stets
> Ein Spiritus familiaris,
> Manchmal als Hund, manchmal in Gestalt
> Des seligen Georg Harris.

[Paganini was always accompanied
by a familiar spirit
which sometimes took the form of a dog and
    at other times
that of the late Georg Harrys.][42]

The Rothschilds are simply an emblem of untold wealth; Hammonia, the patron deity of Hamburg, says of her commode:

> Die Mutter hinterließ ihn mir,
> Ein Möbel von scheinlosem Äußern,
> Doch böte mir Rothschild all sein Geld,
> Ich würde ihn nicht veräußern.

> [My mother left it to me—
> its outside promises little;
> but even if Rothschild offered me all his money,
> I would not part with it.][43]

Many of the Hamburg acquaintances summoned up in the final chapters might be either Christian or Jewish—indeed, this is precisely Heine's point, that social and occupational characteristics had come to count more than religious and ethnic ones. Nevertheless, about the ethnic affiliations of some old acquaintances there can be very little doubt. We remember, for instance, Hirsch-Hyazinth's fat lady love from the Hamburg Jewish quarter, *die dicke Gudel vom Dreckwall*—here she turns up again, fifteen or more years on:

> Die alte Gudel fand ich geschminkt
> Und geputzt wie eine Sirene;
> Hat schwarze Locken sich angeschafft
> Und blendend weiße Zähne.

> [Old Gudel I found heavily made up
> and got up like a Siren.
> She has acquired black curls
> and teeth of dazzling white.][44]

But alas—the original of the Marchese Gumpelino was no more:

Der Edle hatte ausgehaucht
Die große Seele soeben
Und wird als verklärter Seraph jetzt
Am Throne Jehovahs schweben.

[That noble man had just
rendered up his great soul;
he will be a transfigured seraph now
and hover about Jehovah's throne.][45]

The mention of Jehovah underlines Gumpelino's Jewishness—
but it is characteristic of Heine's method in this work that the
mock-heroic *Jewish* reference in this caricature of rich Gumpel
is immediately followed by an equally mock-heroic classical
Greek reference in a complementary sketch of a poor street-
vendor, who is also—again like Gumpelino, and perhaps for
the same reason—no longer to be seen.

Vergehens suchte ich überall
Den *krummen Adonis*, der Tassen
Und Nachtgeschirr von Porzellan
Feilbot in Hamburgs Gassen.

[In vain I sought, everywhere,
that *crooked Adonis*, who used to sell
cups and china chamberpots
in the Hamburg streets.]

(my italics)

But who would suspect that the friend evoked in the following
stanza was in fact Jewish?

Am besten hat sich konserviert
Mein Freund, der Papierverkäufer;
Sein Haar ward gelb und umwallt sein Haupt,
Sieht aus wie Johannes der Täufer.

[The best preserved of all
was my friend the paper merchant;
his hair has turned yellow and waves about his head—
he looks just like John the Baptist.]

Comparing Eduard Michaelis to John the Baptist was a private
joke only Heine's Hamburg friends and relatives could really
share.

Heine follows up his sketches of individual Jews with a series of group-portraits in which we first see Jews and Christians together and then look more closely at the two often feuding groups into which the former were divided. The Jewish community of Hamburg, it will be remembered, had split into a 'Temple Society' and a group that continued to conduct traditional acts of worship in a 'synagogue'.

> Die Population des Hamburger Staats
> Besteht, seit Menschengedenken,
> Aus Juden und Christen; es pflegen auch
> Die letztren nicht viel zu verschenken.
>
> Die Christen sind alle ziemlich gut,
> Auch essen sie gut zu Mittag,
> Und ihre Wechsel bezahlen sie prompt,
> Noch vor dem letzten Respittag.
>
> Die Juden teilen sich wieder ein
> In zwei verschiedne Parteien;
> Die Alten gehn in die Synagog
> Und in den Tempel die Neuen.
>
> Die Neuen essen Schweinefleisch,
> Zeigen sich widersetzig,
> Sind Demokraten; die Alten sind
> Vielmehr aristokrätzig.
>
> Ich liebe die Alten, ich liebe die Neu'n—
> Doch schwör ich, beim ewigen Gotte,
> Ich liebe gewisse Fischchen noch mehr,
> Man heißt sie geräucherte Sprotte.
>
> [The population of the state of Hamburg
> has consisted, for as long as anyone can remember,
> of Jews and Christians; the latter too
> are not in the habit of giving much away for nothing.
>
> The Christians are quite a good lot,
> they eat a good dinner too,
> and they honour their bills of exchange
> before the last extension runs out.

The Jews, for their part, divide
into two different parties;
the old ones go to the *synagogue*,
the new ones attend the *temple*.

The 'new' ones eat pork
and show themselves refractory;
they are democrats; the 'old', on the other hand
are more aristo-scratchy.

I love the old and I love the new—
but I swear by God the eternal
that I love certain little fishes even more:
the ones that are called 'smoked sprats'.][46]

This is Heine's characteristic way of crying a plague on both houses. He begins with the usual Jew stereotypes: the charge that Jewish businessmen are tight-fisted (the Christians don't give much away either), that they love their food excessively (so do the Christians), that they manipulate bills of exchange (so do the Christians), that they pay as late as ever they can (so do the Christians). Having devalued these alleged distinctive features and asserted, in effect, that between the typical Jewish bourgeois of Hamburg and his Gentile counterpart there is little to choose, he looks more closely at the Jews by themselves. Yes, there are some differences: one can distinguish 'Temple' Jews with democratic-progressive and 'synagogue' Jews with aristocratic-conservative tendencies. The latter are accused, by means of a typical portmanteau-word, of combining their 'aristocratic' sentiments with abrasiveness (they scratch!) and with insanitary habits that lead to psoriasis (*Krätze*). The French translation, made in Heine's lifetime and with his help, removes some of the sting of this passage by eliminating the pun along with the socio-political division into 'democrats' and 'aristocrats':

Les néo-juifs sont très éclarés et mangent du porc, les anciens sont superstitieux, ils ne croient pas au Saint-Esprit et détestent le cochon.[47]

In the end the narrator dismisses old and new alike by asserting that he loves them both—but that he prefers to either of them a dish in which no one could see more than one of the humblest of culinary delights. The French translation increases the distance between the narrator and the feuding Jewish factions by making him swear, not 'beim ewigen Gotte' but 'par les dieux éternels de l'Olympe'.[48] But by continuing to dismiss Jews modern and Jews ancient in the manner we have just seen, Heine's narrator ranges himself alongside them, and alongside their Christian fellow townsmen, in at least one significant respect: the orientation towards food, towards the joys of the table, which Heine celebrated so volubly and which he so often presented as his own strongest link with Judaism. Once we have grasped that, we will also be more inclined to look into our own hearts and consciences (how much do *we* give away?, how prompt are *we* with out payments?); and we shall then begin to realize that the Jewish and Gentile Hamburg businessmen are here simply variants of *l'homme moyen sensuel* in the bourgeois society of modern Europe.

Germany. A Winter's Tale and the shorter satirical poems of the mid-1840s show Heine as close as he ever was to the social and political standpoint of the young Karl Marx. 'Marx did not provide Heine with new ideas and certainly not with a system. He confirmed and refreshed what originally stemmed from Heine himself.'[49] Nigel Reeves, from whose perceptive essay on 'Heine and the Young Marx' I have just quoted, has also drawn attention to the fragment of a Preface with which Heine intended, at one time, to introduce his *New Poems* (*Neue Gedichte*, 1844) to their audience. This fragment not only provides useful material for those who seek affinities between Heine and Marx, but also furnishes an excellent example of the way in which Heine annexed characters and incidents from the Old Testament and made them serve his literary, social, and political concerns.

Our lyric poetry is entering a new phase. The somnambulist period of the *Lied*, that silent flower of the soul, has come to an end . . . Sunny interpreters of dreams, pious chaste Josephs, were just the thing for the period of dreaming Pharaos—it was right and proper, at that time, to give them our affection and respect. Our present day, however, calls for prophets made of sterner stuff. We are now concerned, not with dreams of the future, but with the harsh reality of forced labour in the present. Instead of grazing our lambs peacefully, as we used to do, we must now tread mortar and fire bricks; work on the fortifications of Pithom and Rameses is proceeding apace, and sluggish workmen are being set upon with some quite solid rods by their taskmasters. Such 'cultural concerns', as Laube would say, call for a lyric poetry that can get results—a poetry that does not meander along making pretty tunes, but one that trumpets harsher tones towards the *Mitzri* [Hebrew for 'Egyptian'], one that performs practical miracles like turning water to blood, or conjuring up frogs, lice, and so on. Let us, by all means, anoint the spokesmen of the past with every perfumed praise at our disposal, and let us build the costliest mausoleums to house these mummies whose day has passed. But throw . . .[50]

It is significant that the biblical passages Heine adapts to his purposes in this fragment are all connected with the institution of Passover: that Jewish festival of liberation which so often inspired Heine's poetry as well as his prose; a festival whose *contemporary* meaning the *Seder* service constantly stresses. And it is, surely, precisely this *Seder* atmosphere which the one Hebrew word so ostentatiously introduced into this German passage seeks to evoke for readers who have experienced it directly, or who knew it more indirectly from the opening chapter of *The Rabbi of Bacherach*.

(iv)

In looking at the portrait sketches of the Heine family in *Germany. A Winters Tale* we noticed how few specifically Jewish traits they exhibit—even the 'Eat, eat' syndrome, so often ascribed to Jewish mothers, appears in Chapter XX as no more than the touching solicitude of *any* mother for the physical as well as spiritual welfare of her child. The same is true of a poem of the early 1840s which portrays, explicitly, the daughter of his lost love Amalie, and by this means recalls Amalie's image too:

> Das ist der Jugend Frühlingstraum—
> Ich seh dich an und glaub es kaum!
> Das sind die Züge der teuren Sirene,
> Das sind die Blicke, das sind die Töne—

Sie hat ein süßkrötiges Stimmelein,
Bezaubernd die Herzen groß und klein—
Die Schmeicheläuglein spielen ins Grüne,
Meerwunderlich mahnend an Delphine—
Ein bißchen spärlich die Augenbraun,
Doch hochgewölbt und anzuschaun
Wie anmutstolze Siegesbogen—
Auch Grübchenringe, lieblich gezogen,
Dicht unter dem Aug, in den rosigen Wänglein—
Doch leider weder Menschen noch Englein
Sind ganz vollkommen—Das herrlichste Wesen
Hat seine Fehler, wie wir lesen
In alten Märchen. Herr Lusignan,
Der einst die schönste Meerfee gewann,
Hat doch an ihr, in manchen Stunden,
Den heimlichen Schlangenschwanz gefunden.

[That is the springtime dream of youth!
I look at you, and can hardly believe it:
these are the very features of that beloved siren,
these are her very glances, these the sounds she made—
she has a sweet, croaky little voice,
which enchants all hearts, be they big or small—
her cajoling little eyes have a greenish tinge
suggesting wonders of the sea, recalling dolphins—
the eyebrows are a trifle sparse,
but boldly arched, resembling
triumphal arches, at once graceful and haughty;
and charmingly shaped dimples
closely beneath the eyes, in the rosy little cheeks—][51]

How far all this is from any Jewish stereotype! How unlike the Herodias of *Atta Troll*! Yet both are dangerous. The mention of sirens, of wonders of the sea, even of triumphal arches project suggestions of danger into this highly individual portrait of a little charmer. The sense of danger is at first conveyed in Greek, classical images (the combination of sirens and sea, with the saving dolphins too, point in that general direction)—and it is then, in the poem's concluding lines, translated into terms of French and German legend by means of allusions to the *Histoire de Lusignan*, the tale of Melusine the mermaid, with which the poem ends.

But alas: neither men nor angels
are ever perfect—the most glorious being
has—so old tales tell us—
its faults. Sir Lusignan,
who wooed the fair mermaid in days of old,
found out, in secret hour's of amorous play,
the serpent's hidden tail.

Elisabeth Friedländer, for whose album these verses were composed, and her mother, Heine's once beloved cousin Amalie, are here transported into the two non-Jewish worlds of the 'Wild Hunt' vision in *Atta Troll*—the worlds of Diana and Abunde, of classical and Celtic-Germanic lore. Parodoxically enough, there is no suggestion here of the world of Herodias, into which Heine had infused so powerful a spirit of Jewish nostalgia. Did he, perhaps, recall François Wille's question: 'What business do you still have with Jews?' It was a question he would one day have to answer in other ways than that of deleting references to Jewish matters from his works. He would have to explain, one day, why he still felt kinship with a people whose religious covenant—the covenant which had kept it alive in darker times than his own—he had solemnly and ceremoniously renounced.

CHAPTER 10
Figures in the Gathering Gloom

(i)

'To prepare yourself for reading this obituary address', Heine wrote to Campe on 19 March 1854, 'ask your wife to hand you a cushion so that you can kneel down: you won't have a chance to adore such a stylistic wonder every day. Stylistically, I was delighted to find, almost the whole second part is worthy of adoration.' The *Denkrede* of which Heine speaks with such deliberately exaggerated yet none the less genuine satisfaction was never spoken at a grave-side or a memorial service. Its inception goes back to 1843, when the death of a fellow *émigré* who had also been a fellow member of the Society for the Science and Culture of the Jews, Ludwig Marcus, induced the poet to cast a backward look at the endeavours of that Society and at the men it had brought, for a short time, into association. In the context of the present book the essay *Ludwig Marcus*, written in April 1844 and published in the *Augsburg Gazette* a month later, is of twofold importance: it centers on a group of German Jews; and it employs the word *Karikatur* to describe the physical aspect of its eponymous hero. It is this early version that is now to be considered; the revisions with which Heine sent it to Campe in 1854 belong to a later stage of our story.

Why, the essay asks at the outset, have the shadows of insanity closed in on so many of the most honourable, clean-living, industrious German intellectuals who emigrated to France? Is it perhaps that Paris acts as a hothouse that develops with especial rapidity seeds of madness imported from Germany? Or is the very fact that Germans leave their fatherland to 'climb the hard stairs of exile'—one of Heine's favourite quotations from Dante—already a sign of incipient madness? It would be quite wrong, however, to think of such *émigrés* as eccentric Storm and Stress figures, idlers, or whore-masters.

On the contrary, those who succumbed were for the most part honourable, industrious, and abstemious in the highest degree. Witness 'our poor compatriot Ludwig Marcus', a 'German scholar as distinguished by the breadth of his knowledge as by his exalted moral sense'.[1]

In the introductory section of the essay, which I have just summarized, the poet has accomplished two important tasks. He has tacitly placed himself, the best-known German *émigré* in Paris, alongside the sitter whose portrait he is to draw; and he has given full weight to the *German* setting without which the unmistakably Jewish figure to be discussed cannot be understood. Only after that can he look at Marcus's more immediate origins in a poor family of Dessau 'which worshipped according to the rites of God-fearing Jews.' This environment Marcus transcended, without denying the heritage with which it had endowed him or betraying its values, when he came to Berlin as a medical student and found himself drawn from medicine—that traditional pursuit of German Jews eager to enter the professions—into the orbit of Hegel and German *Wissenschaft*. Heine himself, he now tells us, first met Marcus at Hegel's lectures, where the little man wrote down assiduously everything the master said. The year is 1821.

He was twenty-two years old at the time, but his appearance was anything but youthful. A tiny, thin body, like that of an eight-year-old boy, was surmounted by a wizened face of the kind that usually goes with a deformed spine. No such deformation, however, was to be seen on him, and one could not help wondering at its absence. Those who had been personally acquainted with the late Moses Mendelssohn remarked with astonishment how closely Marcus's features resembled those of this famous sage—whose birthplace, strangely enough, was Dessau, like that of Marcus. If chronology and virtue had not all too definitely exonerated the venerable Moses, Marcus's origins might have become the subject of some frivolous speculations.[2]

As so often in his portraits, Heine selects some one striking physical peculiarity which he proceeds to link at once with some quality of mind or soul; and as so often, he joins the portrait of his principal sitter with that of another person whom he resembles or with whom he can be contrasted. Accordingly we are at once told that the likeness between

Marcus and 'the great reformer of the German Jews', Moses Mendelssohn, was not just a matter of facial features—it extended to qualities of mind and soul such as lofty altruism, patient endurance of suffering, modesty coupled with a sense of fairness and justice, a smiling contempt for everything base, and an inflexible love for his oppressed co-religionists.

For Marcus as for Moses [Mendelssohn] the fate of the Jews was the painfully throbbing, ardent centre of all thought, the heart of his life.[3]

In its original German, the opening phrase of this sentence— *Für Marcus wie für jenen Moses*—brings into view, not only Marcus and Mendelssohn, but also the Moses of the Bible, to whom Heine's thoughts so often recurred. Marcus and his unassuming virtues are thus being unobtrusively placed within the whole span of Jewish history. He was, we are told, a polyhistor; specializing in geography, he worked his way through entire libraries of books, acquiring in the process a knowledge of many languages, living and dead—

but from all his mental excursions he always returned home, as it were, to the history of Israel's sufferings, to the Calvary or Golgotha of Jerusalem, to the little paternal dialect of Palestine for whose sake, perhaps, he had a special partiality for the study of Semitic languages.[4]

It was, Heine comments, precisely this devotion to Judaism, this constant striving in the cause of those to whom he felt most immediately linked by his origins, that made Marcus worthy of commemoration: 'for what gives us the right to honour and recognition after our death is not only our achievement, but our endeavour too'—especially if that endeavour had an unhappy outcome, if 'we failed in what we generously sought to do'.

   Heine's own distance, at the time at which he is writing, from Marcus's whole cast of mind and life, is becoming more and more obvious. He now confesses that he could never see much value in the knowledge Marcus had accumulated:

What he knew had no living, organic connection—it was all dead history. The whole of nature fossilized at his touch; at bottom he was acquainted only with fossils and mummies. He also lacked the power to give his work artistic form; it was pitiful to see him vainly striving, whenever he committed anything to paper, to find even the scantiest form for what he wanted to depict. The articles and, especially, the books he wrote were therefore unpalatable, indigestible, abstruse.[5]

Heine then goes on to characterize the geographical and anthropological works Marcus had composed, either by himself, or in collaboration with the Orientalist Professor F. Duisberg, and to dwell particularly on those of his writings which dealt with the culture of Abyssinia. Here Marcus had on one occasion been able to provide useful grist for the poet's mill.

I once made him happy by asking him to excerpt for me, from Arabic and Talmudic sources, everything that pertained to the Queen of Sheba. To the resulting compilation, which may, perhaps, still be found among my papers, I owe the knowledge why the kings of Abyssinia boast of being descended from King David: they derive their descent from a visit their ancestress paid to the wise King Solomon in Jerusalem. That lady, I learnt from Marcus, must have been as beautiful as Helen of Troy. Be that as it may—she suffered a fate similar to Helen's after her death; for there are amorous rabbis who know how to summon her from her grave by means of cabbalistic spells. They are not always, however, well served by the fair spectre they have conjured up; for she has the grave fault of outstaying her welcome once she has sat down somewhere . . .[6]

In this way the little man provided his friend the poet with analogies between Hebrew and German legends which the latter could then link with the myths of ancient Greece and use as material for grave or gay, incantatory or satiric poetry. Marcus himself, however, could do little that was worth while with even the most poetic material, and his clumsy mode of expressing himself sometimes moved his acquaintances to the same kind of involuntary laughter as was provoked by his appearance. At this point Heine introduces Eduard Gans, laughing, as we have already seen in the opening chapter of the present book, at a passage which can bear a scabrous interpretation Marcus certainly never envisaged, and inviting Heine to share his amusement.

This gives the poet his clue for the introduction of another series of portraits: those of the principal members of the Society for the Culture and Science of the Jews which met in Berlin in the 1920s and to which he now gives the name by which it was usually known later: Society for the Culture and Science of Judaism (*des Judentums*, not *der Juden*). Looking back on the aims of this group twenty years later, from his vantage point of 1844, Heine pronounces them 'a great idea that could not be carried through':

Men with great gifts of mind and spirit and with generous hearts here sought to save a cause that had long since been lost. The most they managed to do was to turn up the bones of some older fighters in the same cause on the battlefields of the past. The total yield of that Society's endeavours consists of a few historical writings, of researches into history among which Dr Zunz's monographs on the Spanish Jews in the Middle Ages belong to the most remarkable achievements of higher criticism.[7]

The cause the Society had championed seemed to have been lost on many fronts. It had failed to bridge the gap between highly educated, 'assimilated' Jews steeped in Hegelian philosophy, and their more traditionally minded brethren. It had failed to alter what was felt to be imbalances in the occupational structure of European Jewry—its endeavours, in fact, were to lead to new 'imbalances', new differences from the occupational structure of the surrounding society. It had failed, above all, to develop a rationale sufficiently strong to induce 'assimilated' Jews to remain Jews in name even at the expense of their careers in a nominally Christian society. But the cause of applying scholarly methods evolved in Western Europe to the history—especially the cultural history—of the Jewish people: that had emphatically *not* been lost, thanks largely to the influence of one man who now becomes, after Marcus, Gans, and Heine himself, the cynosure of the reader's attention. His name, of course, is Leopold Zunz.

'This excellent, eminent man', *dieser vortreffliche Zunz*, is characterized by Heine, who never wavered in his admiration for this great pioneering scholar, as one

who stood firm, constantly and unshakeably, in a period of transition, hesitation, and vacillation; and who, despite the sharpness of his intellect, his scepticism, and his learning, remained faithful to the promise he had made himself, to the generous caprice of his soul. A man of words *and* a man of action, he worked unceasingly, he did what needed doing, at a time when others lost themselves in dreams and sank to the ground, bereft of courage.[8]

Judaism, here, is not something to be simply accepted, but something to be freely chosen. Zunz, clearly, could see all the arguments that led others to accept baptism—indeed, we know that at one time he contemplated taking this step himself; but he made an existential choice, took a leap, not into faith, but into loyalty, loyalty to his origins, to his own early endeavours. And having taken this leap, having made what from one point of view might seem a capricious decision, Zunz found that there was much to be done, much to be achieved, in applying to Jewish literary and cultural documents the methods of philological enquiry pioneered in nineteenth-century Germany.

Heine's essay does not, however, want to convey the impression that the generation of Zunz, Gans, Marcus, and Heine, who were all born in the 1790s, was the first that attempted to combine European learning with Jewish loyalties. Moses Mendelssohn has already been mentioned in passing; and now Heine is ready to introduce a member of the Society for the Culture and Science of the Jews who was some thirty years older than most of the others, and who could therefore be seen as a living link with Mendelssohn's generation. In earlier years he had not always spoken kindly of Lazarus Bendavid, whose views on the 'outdated' nature of traditional Jewish beliefs in the Messiah he had never been able to share. But here, for once, distance lends enchantment even to Heine's view, and he turns an altogether affectionate eye on 'my dear Bendavid', *meinen lieben Bendavid*, reformer of the curriculum of Jewish schools and as faithful a disciple of Kant as the later generation was to be of Hegel.

With his intellect and strength of character he combined a generous and urbane culture; and although he was far advanced in years, he still participated in the Society's most youthfully erratic notions.[9]

Constantly, we see, Heine is concerned, even in his most respectful and affectionate tributes, to keep before us his reservations about the Society, the *Verein*, which united all these men. But he continues:

Bendavid was a sage of antique cut. The sunlight of Greek serenity played about him, who stood as a monument of true virtue, hardened like the marble of his master Kant's categorical imperative. Throughout his life Bendavid had been the most zealous disciple of Kant's philosophy and had suffered, in his youth, the most extreme persecutions on its account . . .

Here Heine has added a new touch to his essay: he alludes, for the first time, to Jewish resistance to European learning and the changes it brings in its train. The persecutions Bendavid had to endure were at the hands, clearly, not of German Christians, but of orthodox Jews. Yet for all that Bendavid

never wanted to divorce himself from the ancient community professing the Mosaic faith, he never wished to change the external badge of religion. The mere semblance of such a denial filled him with repugnance and loathing.[10]

Heine is twisting the knife in his own wound here, and, at the same time, preparing for the characterization of Eduard Gans, the leader who became an apostate, which is in an important sense the centre-piece of the whole Jewish portrait gallery contained in the essay on Ludwig Marcus.

He has not quite finished, however, with his characterization of Lazarus Bendavid. For this aged man, in Heine's view, not only shared the erroneous notions of the young men he associated with, but also compounded them with errors of his own. 'When we spoke of Hegel's philosophy, he shook his bald head and declared that it was all superstition.' Bendavid could never, it seems, see beyond the limits of the Kantian system for whose sake he had endured so much, and this made him look out of place in the largely Hegelian world of the Society for the Culture and Science of the Jews. Nevertheless his honesty, his critical faculty, and his ability to write and speak decent idiomatic German are commended—among German Jews of Bendavid's generation this combination of faculties was sufficiently rare to earn him posthumous notice and praise.

From Bendavid Heine passes to the remarkable man who had been his best and most trusted friend in Berlin, but from whom he had become sadly estranged in later years. Moses Moser, though employed in a bank, had shown himself the very opposite of those money-obsessed hucksters and speculators whom Heine had so often found among the Jewish bankers he dealt with, in Hamburg as in Paris. His portrait of Moser

is therefore a deliberate subversion of a stereotype found else-
where in his writings. Moser is described as 'the most active
member of the Society, and in every sense its soul':

In his earliest youth he already possessed the most thorough store of
knowledge; he capped this with a glowing compassion for humanity
and with an ardent desire to actualize knowledge by converting it
into good deeds. He took an untiring part in philanthropic en-
deavours, he was of a most practical turn of mind, and he performed
charitable works in an unassuming silence. The public at large never
learnt of his activities; he fought and bled incognito; his name re-
mained unrecorded in the directory of daily self-sacrifice. Our world
is not as poor as people think; it has brought forth an astonishing
number of such anonymous martyrs.[11]

No note of criticism intrudes into this tribute to a deceased
friend—a tribute which leads over, by laws of contrast, to the
portrait of Eduard Gans, the lost leader who was noted for
anything but unassuming silence and readiness for anonymous
martyrdom. That portrait, already examined in our first chap-
ter, contains self-reproach and self-exoneration in equal mea-
sure: for though Heine had succumbed, like Gans himself, to
the lure of a cultural world which seemed to demand baptism
as a price of entry and full participation, at least he was not a
leader in Israel, at least he was not—as Gans, President of the
Society for the Culture and Science of the Jews would appear
to have been—the captain who left a sinking ship in advance of
most of the passengers for whom he had assumed responsibil-
ity.

Before Heine can return to the starting-point and ostensible
subject of his essay, the characterization of Ludwig Marcus, he
has to say something more of the 'lost cause' which was so dear
to Marcus's heart—'the strivings and illusions of that Society
to which he dedicated himself in what must have seemed to him
the sunniest blossoming time of his whole pitiable life'.[12] He
could not possibly, Heine tells us, within the limitations of
space and speech imposed by the *Augsburg Gazette*, explain
the endeavours of the Society for the Culture and Science of the
Jews as thoroughly as their significance warranted; for that
would involve, not only a disquisition on the religious and civil
situation of the Jews, but also reflections on all 'deistic sects' in

the world. The distance implied by Heine's classification of Judaism in the Diaspora as a 'deistic' (or 'theistic') 'sect' is worth noting here; but so, surely, is his praise of those who, like Zunz and Marcus, remained unshakeably loyal to the 'sect' into which they had been born. One important point he felt impelled, however, to make explicitly about the Society, the *Verein*, whose members he has been characterizing. Its 'esoteric purpose', he now tells his readers, was 'the mediation between historic Judaism and a modern science of which it was assumed that it would, in the course of time, control the whole world'. Nor was this the first time such a mediation had been attempted: 'In the days of Philo Judaeus, when Greek philosophy declared war on all ancient dogmas, a similar attempt was made in Alexandria'—*mit mehr oder minderem Mißgeschick*, Heine adds, suggesting that the mediation had not been more successful in Philo's time than in Heine's own. But this does not devalue the endeavour itself, which had nothing to do with the promotion of schisms and with ramming shallow notions of 'enlightenment' down people's throats. Nor, he adds, must the endeavours of the Society be confused with the usual sort of tongue-wagging about emancipation:

that emancipation about which such revoltingly vapid stuff is being talked and written nowadays that one is in dire peril of losing all interest in it. Some of the Israelite emancipation-fanciers have succeeded especially well in gathering a grey and watery cloud of tedium around the whole question. These do more harm than the most venomously stupid among their opponents. Here one may find cosy pharisees who go so far as to boast that they lack the talent to write well, and who nevertheless take up the pen, in defiance of Apollo. Let us hope that the German governments will soon pity the aesthetically abused public and put an end to all this dreadful prattle by hastening emancipation.[13]

The passage just quoted shows clearly why Heine so frequently censured worthy men (including Ludwig Marcus) for their stylistic incompetence. Such censure had nothing to do, as Börne had mistakenly thought, with an effete aestheticism; it arose, rather, from genuine concern for a cause that could only be harmed by inept champions. Style is an important weapon; and in the paragraph that follows, Heine endeavours to show his contemporaries how it can be placed in the service of sociological analysis and the battle for social justice.

Emancipation will be granted, sooner or later: out of a feeling for justice, out of prudent wisdom, out of sheer necessity. Antipathy against the Jews is no longer rooted in religion among the upper classes, and among the lower classes it is being increasingly transformed, day by day, into *social* resentment. As for governments: these have come to know that the state is an organism, a body politic, and that such a body cannot attain perfect health as long as a single member—even its smallest toe—has to bear some affliction. Let the state raise its head ever so boldly, let it defy all tempests with the broadest chest: the heart in its bosom and even its proud head cannot but feel their share of pain when the little toe suffers from corns. Restrictions on the rights of Jews are corns on the feet of the German states.[14]

This humorous yet fundamentally serious paragraph was geared to what the German censors were likely to allow to appear in print; there are some manuscript notes for *Ludwig Marcus*, which are to be considered in a moment, where Heine elaborates his themes more boldly.

His panorama of Jewish striving towards self-definition, self-education, and civil emancipation has led the poet away, apparently at least, from his immediate subject. But this, he assures his readers, is not a matter for remonstrance or regret. How can we understand Marcus as a person if we do not have some degree of understanding of the historical, social, and moral ambience within which he lived out his formative years? How can we understand his individuality if we cannot compare and contrast him with his contemporaries, if we cannot appreciate what was typical about his person and endeavours, and what was genuinely and unmistakably his own? Marcus, in fact, Heine now tells us explicitly, deserves our interest more because of the moral and intellectual situation he exemplified than because of his individual significance and contribution. In any case, he had lost touch with Marcus after their brief contact in Berlin. Heine had heard that antiquated medieval laws (by which we are to understand, no doubt, those disabilities of the Jews which German states reintroduced after the fall of Napoleon) had prevented his finding adequate employment in his German fatherland—*im Vaterlande*—notwithstanding his extraordinary knowledge and unimpeachable character. He had therefore emigrated to France, after renouncing his small patrimony in favour of his brothers and sisters. Then, one day, fifteen years after their last meeting, Heine encountered Marcus again: in Paris, the city to which Marcus had come after giving up an academic teaching post in Dijon because of some administrative disagreement. The libraries of Paris were now to help him with material for his life's work on the confluence of African and Jewish history. It is at this point that Heine introduces into his essay one of his most characteristic and significant touches. He is talking about Marcus's decision to give up his teaching post.

As I heard from other people, a bit of obstinacy came into play here: the ministry was even said to have proposed that he follow a custom well established in France and delegate his duties to some junior deputy who would draw a much smaller salary; this would have enabled Marcus to continue drawing the major portion of what he had been paid in full-time employment. But the little man's great soul found this repugnant; he did not want to exploit the labour of others, and he left his successor in enjoyment of his full salary. His selfless conduct is the more remarkable because he himself lived, at that time, in the greatest poverty, the most touching indigence. He was in a very bad way, and without the angelic aid of a beautiful lady he would surely have succumbed to misery and want. Yes, it was a very beautiful and great lady of Paris, one of the brightest apparitions of the *grand monde*, who, when she heard of this quaint character, descended into the darkness of his pathetic life and induced him, with charm and delicacy of feeling, to accept a considerable yearly subvention. I believe that his pride was tamed, on this occasion, by the thought that his patroness, the wife of the richest banker on this earth, would later on have his great work printed at her expense. For, he reflected, a lady so celebrated for her intellect and culture could not fail to be anxious to see that a thoroughly researched history of Abyssinia be written at long last; and he found it only natural that she would seek to compensate the author of such a history for the great effort it cost him by making him an annual allowance.[15]

This portrayal of a quaint unworldly scholar, *ein wunderlicher Kauz*, has clearly a strong element of caricature—but it is a caricature wholly without malice. And what is perhaps most interesting of all, in the context of Heine's Jewish portraits, is to find that here, in 1844, when he was closer to Marx than at any other time of his life, he decisively contradicts Marx's mischievous equation of Judaism with money-grubbing capitalism. He does this by showing how a poor Jewish scholar refuses to accept the ethic of exploiting other people's labour (*er wollte nicht fremde Arbeit ausbeuten*) even when this would benefit his scholarly life's work, even when the practice he objects to is suggested to him by the French government; and how such a man is then enabled to carry on his selfless and commercially 'unproductive' work with the help of a member of a Jewish family which for Marx as for the whole of Europe personified capitalism. There can be no doubt that the lady Heine describes in such glowing terms is once again Baroness Betty de Rothschild; and in his most delicate compliment to her, he operates with terms of metaphoric opposition later made famous by Brecht:

. . . eine der glänzendsten Erscheinungen des hiesigen Weltlebens, die . . . in die Dunkelheit seines kümmerlichen Lebens hinabstieg . . .

Denn die einen sind im Dunkeln
Und die anderen sind im Licht . . .[16]

Heine sees the two worlds brought together by an act of meaningful patronage, an act that can be unequivocally situated in one of the best and most constant Jewish traditions: willing support of selfless and materially 'unprofitable' scholarship by wealthy business people with a genuine respect for learning.

One essential element is still missing from our account of Heine's Jewish portraits in the 1840s; and the final section of *Ludwig Marcus* will serve to introduce it. In the earlier part of the essay the poet had referred in a general way to 'the little man's external appearance which not infrequently tempted one to laughter'; and now, towards the end, he returns at greater length to Marcus's physical appearance.

The fifteen years or so during which I had not seen dear, good Marcus had not served to beautify his exterior. His appearance had always been droll; but now it had become a veritable caricature—but a pleasant, charming, I would almost say refreshing, caricature [*eine angenehme, liebliche, ich möchte fast sagen erquickende Karikatur*].

His old man's face, furrowed by suffering, in which jet-black little eyes sparkled in a merry, lively way, gave him a humorously sad look. And then there was his incredible hair! This had once been pitch-black and close to his skull; now it had grown grey and stood out around his disproportionately large head in an abundance of bristling curls. This gave him some resemblance to those broad-bodied figures with thin bodies and short little legs which we see on the glass panes of a Chinese shadow show. My heart, always susceptible to humour, rejoiced particularly when I encountered this dwarfish figure on one of the Boulevards in company with his collaborator, the enormously tall and generously proportioned Professor Duisberg. . . .[17]

This is an excellent example of the physical side of Heine's portraits: his ability to evoke the impression made by a man's outward appearance through foregrounding certain features in the manner of a caricaturist (the disproportion between Marcus's head and body, his shining eyes, his fantastic halo of hair); through bringing out other features by means of an analogy (here with Chinese shadow figures) and heightening yet others by means of contrasting juxtaposition (little Marcus and huge Duisberg). It is all summed up by a series of oxymora of which 'humorously sad', *spaßhaft wehmütig*, is the central one—oxymora leading over to the passage which follows that just quoted.

When one of my acquaintances asked me who the little man was, I answered: 'the king of Abyssinia'; and that nickname stuck to him for the rest of his life. Were you angry with me because of this, my dear, good Marcus? The Creator could surely have provided a better envelope for your beautiful soul. But the good Lord has too much to do; sometimes, when he is just about to give a noble pearl an appropriate setting of finely worked gold, he is suddenly disturbed, and in his hurry he wraps the jewel in the first piece of blotting-paper or the first rag that comes to hand. I can't explain the anomaly in any other way.[18]

This gives us an unusually tender instance of another means of characterization Heine adopts when he portrays his friends or his foes: the invented myth, parodying the myths of Greece, or Germany, or Palestine, and transforming static feature into dynamic story.

After this Heinesque exercise in popular theology we are

rapidly told of Marcus's final years. At first there is a short time of happiness and wise contentment of soul (*im weisesten Seelenfrieden*); Marcus has his own little apartment filled with his own furniture and situated near one of the libraries he frequents. But then the essay, already full of grotesque touches, modulates fully into the grotesque with a description of sudden insanity. A new character is introduced, a nephew of Marcus, who visits his uncle one evening and finds to his astonishment

that Uncle Marcus suddenly sits down on the floor and begins to sing the most repulsively vulgar songs (*die scheußlichsten Gassenlieder*) in a wild, defiant voice. This from the man who never sang and who was always modesty itself in word and sound! But this spectacle became even more horrifyingly strange when Uncle Marcus jumped up with rage, flung open the window, and threw down into the road first his watch, then his manuscripts, inkwell, pens, and purse. When the nephew saw that his uncle was throwing money out of the window, he could no longer doubt that he was mad. The unhappy man was taken to Dr Pinel's sanatorium at Chaillot, where after a fortnight of terrible suffering he rendered up his spirit. He died on 15 July and was buried in Montmartre cemetery on the 17th. I am sorry to say that I heard of his death too late to be able to pay him my last respects. In dedicating these pages to his memory today I wanted to make good this omission and, as it were, attend his funeral-procession in spirit.[19]

Every detail in this passage has been most carefully selected. First we are shown the nemesis of the Nazarene character: chastity exacts a price—the price of repression; and when the constantly watchful super-ego is suddenly relieved of its censorial duty, the repressed will break out in startling fashion. The first outbreak is sexual-scatological, while the second shows Marcus's fearful awareness, deep down, that the work for which he lived, with which he employed his time, for which he had accepted financial support, might not, after all, have been worth his while: hence the discarding of his time-piece, his writing-materials, his purse. In this way the portrait of Marcus gains an added dimension—we gain insight into some of his unconscious desires and fears as Heine interpreted them. As we gain this insight, we are led to reflect on two of the themes constantly raised by Heine's dealings with Jews and

Judaism: the problems of Nazarene spirituality, and the doubts that have to be conquered by those who devote themselves to the Jewish cause in the modern world.

The spectacle of Marcus's madness is not witnessed by the poet, and is therefore mediated by an observer. This mediation has a decidedly humorous effect: the nephew, we are shown, is quite unlike his uncle, he would seem to be a worshipper of the Golden Calf, like so many others in Heine's Jewish Comedy, for he only becomes convinced that his uncle is indeed insane when he sees him throw *money* out of the window. Then the nephew disappears from the scene, and some deliberately factual statements about Marcus's death and interment lead over to the reappearance of the poet himself in his role of observer. We see him at a particular moment—his tribute to Marcus, the tribute we are reading, has been penned and is now being offered to its hero and to the public at large as a substitute for attendance at the little man's funeral. And then, in the final paragraph, this offering up of a posthumous tribute becomes an imaginary attendance at Marcus's wake, and a delicate conciliatory gesture:

and now open the coffin once more, so that I can follow the old custom of asking the dead man's pardon for any offence I may have given him in his lifetime. How calm Marcus looks! He seems to be smiling at my failure to appreciate his scholarly writings at their true worth. This will be of little moment to him, though, for in these matters I am not as competent a judge as—for instance—his friend Salomon Munk, the Orientalist, who is said to be writing a comprehensive biography of the deceased and preparing an edition of his posthumous work.[20]

Marcus's serenity and his smile indicate to the reader that he has passed through his dark night of the soul, beyond the dreaded doubts and desires released by madness, and has regained his faith in the rightness of what he was doing. It is now for the poet to express doubts in his own competence to judge Marcus's work—and so he directs our eyes away from the moment depicted, and the moment at which readers of the *Augsburg Gazette* responded to the depiction, into the future; he directs them away from himself, as narrator and as mourner by the side of Marcus's coffin, to Salomon Munk, who had briefly come under the aegis of the Berlin Society for the Culture and Science of the Jews and who had since then, as a scholar and an archivist in Paris, dedicated his life to researches that had a direct bearing on the culture and history of the Jewish people. This eminent Orientalist might yet—who knows?—lead the world to a fuller and juster appreciation of what Marcus was and what he achieved than Heine himself had felt able to do.

What the poet has given us, in *Ludwig Marcus*, is the portrait of something like a grotesque Jewish saint; and for all the uncertainty of the final sentences he has not kept from us his conviction that admirable traits of character do not always yield the most beneficial results. As a human being, as a character, Eduard Gans appears decidely inferior, not only to Marcus, but also to the other members of the Society for the Culture and Science of the Jews depicted in this essay; and yet, as we saw in Chapter 1, Heine portrays Gans as a much more effective fighter against the enemies of Jewish emancipation and integration, and a more beneficial force in the society of his time, than any of the others. The question of the relation of talent to character, of genius to virtue, of unbending integrity to useful social action, is thus once again raised and shown to be far less straightforward than Heine's old adversary Börne could ever have believed.

(ii)

The textual history of *Ludwig Marcus* is somewhat complicated. The version discussed so far was published in the *Augsburg Gazette* in 1844; a slightly expanded version, to be considered in Chapter 13 below, appeared in Heine's *Miscellaneous Writings* (*Vermischte Schriften*) of 1854 under the title *Ludwig Marcus. Words in his Memory* (*Ludwig Marcus. Denkworte*). We also, however, have some manuscript passages belonging to the first period of composition which were never published in Heine's lifetime.[21] The first of these sets the quiet, scholarly life of the *émigré* Marcus against the mode of existence characteristic of more discontented political exiles

from the various German states whom Heine had met in the
1840s. Their anger, he tells us, would sooner or later break out
'in revolutionary rage, or even in communistic madness'. Yet
why, Heine asks, with heavy irony, should they be so enraged?
Many have died in poverty and distress in the free air of France,
but no one starved to death in a German prison. As for comp-
laints about religious intolerance—how could these be justified
when

the construction of Cologne Cathedral is finally being completed and
every German, regardless of his creed—Christian or Jew, Catholic or
Protestant—is being allowed to contribute his mite?[22]

Where the passage just quoted casts a brief glance at religious
prejudices against the Jews which do not extend to refusing
their money when it comes to cathedral building, another of
the manuscript passages looks at national and racial prejudices.
Complete emancipation of the Jews, Heine suggests, might
mean that they would ultimately merge completely with the
German people—and it is precisely this prospect which appals
German nationalists, because of the harmful effect they envis-
age on the German national character. Heine's reply to those
who think in this way is preceded by a threat which he could
hardly have expected the *Augsburg Gazette* to publish in the
teeth of censorship and official surveillance.

Our nationalists or so-called patriots, whose heads are filled with
nothing but 'race' and 'purity of blood' and other such horse-traders'
ideas—this rear-guard of the Middle Ages will soon have to face
opponents who could quickly bring to a terrible end their dreams of
pure distillations of the national character, the *Volkstümlichkeit*, of
German, Latin, or Slav. Then they would have little leisure to cavil at
the imperfect Germanness of the Jews. I am speaking, above all, of
the brotherhood of workers in every country, the savage army of the
proletariat [*von jener Verbrüderung der Arbeiter in allen Ländern,
von dem wilden Heer des Proletariats*], which sets out to do away
with all insistence on nationality in order to pursue a common
purpose all over Europe: the realization of true democracy.[23]

The tone and vocabulary of this passage reminds us once again
that Heine came very close to the tone and vocabulary of Karl
Marx in the years in which he collaborated with the radical
editors of the journal *Forwards!* (*Vorwärts*). He goes on,

however, to meet the nationalists on their own ground. He does not deny that there is such a thing as the 'German' or the 'Jewish' national character at a given time—what he does deny is that the one is necessarily inimical to the other.

Is there really so great a national difference between the German Jews, who have been settled in Germany for one and a half thousand years, and their Christian compatriots? Truly the answer must be no. Strangely enough the Jews and the Germans may be seen as linked even in the most distant past by a most powerful elective affinity [*Wahlverwandtschaft*]; and in comparison with its neighbouring peoples ancient Judaea always seemed to me a kind of Germany. I am almost tempted to call it the Mark Brandenburg of the Orient.[24]

Having stated his belief in the natural affinity of Jews and Germans, Heine now goes on to draw an ethnic portrait of both, dwelling on the characteristics he believes them to have in common: 'the most courageous detestation of Rome, a feeling for the freedom of the individual [*persönliches Freiheits-gefühl*], a strict moral code.'

It was the Germans, too, who most thoroughly absorbed Jewish spiritualism. The historical documents of the Jews, the Bible, became the national book of the Germanic North, became flesh of its flesh and blood of its blood, and gave the inner and outer life of the Germanic peoples its special stamp—and the very people who speak about the traces of the Oriental among the Jews fail to notice the Old-Testament, genuinely Jewish, physiognomy of the Germanic North in Europe and America.[25]

It will have been noticed that the national characteristics of which Heine speaks are not ahistorical, atemporal entities. Whatever original affinity there may have been among the Jews and the Germans has been strengthened and extended by the Jews' long residence in Germanic lands and by the Germans' absorption of the Old Testament.

The last passage which failed to surface in either of the versions of *Ludwig Marcus* published in Heine's lifetime, suggests yet another perspective in which the self-effacing, self-sacrificing life of the *émigré* scholar may be seen. The poet retells an episode from the history of the Jews of Metz, which he had recently read in the *Archives israélites*, edited by Samuel Cahen, 'the meritorious translator of the Bible into French'.

The Jewish community of Metz, he tells us, had been falsely and maliciously accused of desecrating the sacred wafers used in Catholic worship and had been asked, by the civic authorities, to hand over the 'culprits' for execution. If they failed to do this, the whole community would be slaughtered by the enraged populace. At this moment of peril two strangers appeared and offered themselves up as voluntary sacrifices; they died in torment, but the community was saved. To commemorate this event a lamp dedicated to the unknown martyrs has burnt in the synagogue of Metz ever since. With a covert allusion to Act I, scene 2 of Lessing's *Nathan the Wise* Heine offers the following comment on this extract from the blood-stained pages of Jewish history in Europe.

Most Jews are foolish enough to believe that these saviours were angels. No—they were men, human beings in whose breast there beat a truly human heart; nor were they the last anonymous martyrs who sacrificed their lives to the delusions of the populace for the good of their community. How many of this pale company have I seen succumbing to torture in these last few years![26]

The majority of Jews may be as foolish as the masses everywhere (even in his most radical period Heine never had that deep trust in the virtues of the common people which could have made him a communist); but the Jews have also produced their share, and more than their share, of self-sacrificing heroes whose martyrdom, whether under the physical torture of the Middle Ages or the mental torture of more modern times, bears witness to man's potential goodness and greatness. Here was indeed a reason to be proud of one's Jewishness, and to choose to remain Jewish, as Marcus had done, and Zunz, and Salomon Munk.

(iii)

To remain Jewish implied, in Heine's eyes, remaining part of a people that had given the world the saviour acknowledged by Christians as the Son of God. We need not therefore be surprised to find another of Heine's many rebuttals of anti-Jewish charges culminating in a proclamation of kinship with Jesus of Nazareth. The passage in question comes from some fragmentary *Letters on Germany* (*Briefe über Deutschland*) in which Heine tried out some ideas and sketched in some portraits which were to find their place in later works. He is looking back, once again, on Wolfgang Menzel's denunciation of the 'Young Germany' movement of the 1830s.

In his philippics against Young Germany he called down on our accursed heads all the flames at heaven's command—or, at the very least, in their absence, all the lightning at the disposal of the police authorities in the states that made up the German Confederation. He maintained that we were all Jews, although there was not a single Young German who adhered to the religion of Moses [*sich zum Kultus Mosis bekannte*] and although with the exception of your obedient servant none had in his veins a single drop of the glorious blood from which our Lord and Saviour sprang.[27]

The distinction Heine here draws is worth noting. He denies altogether that he is a Jew if that means adhering to the Jewish religion—he has, after all, been admitted into the Lutheran church and is therefore entitled to speak to a largely Gentile audience of '*our* Lord and Saviour'. He does not, however, deny—indeed, he proudly affirms—that he is a Jew 'by blood', by biological descent; that he belongs to an ethnic or kinship group which included, as we have heard him say earlier, as much riff-raff as any other, but which could also claim as its own Jesus of Nazareth, Spinoza, Crémieux, and the selfless scholars whom he praised so highly in his essay on Ludwig Marcus.

(iv)

The reports on French affairs which Heine sent to the *Augsburg Gazette* in 1840 had included, as we have seen, some fierce references to the Fould family: a wealthy clan allied not only to the banking branch of Heine's own family, but also to the Péreire brothers, whose financial power had greatly increased since their Saint-Simonian days because of their wise investment in industrial and railway development.[28] For some six years after these early reports the Fould family had escaped Heine's satiric lash—at least in public. In 1846, however, the poet returned to the fray. His victim this time was not Benoît Fould, whom he had once so unjustly accused of ignoring the plight of his tortured brethren in Damascus, but Benoît's more famous brother Achille.

The newspapers have given sufficient space to reports that M. Achilles Fould won the election at Tarbes and that he will therefore again represent the Hautes Pyrénées constituency in the next session of the Chamber of Deputies. Heaven forbid that I should here enter into particularities about the conduct of the election or the personality of the successful candidate . . .[29]

Mock-pious phrases (*Der Himmel bewahre mich* . . .) are always a signal, in Heine's writings, to look for impious insinuations. He clearly suggests that the 'particularities' he is withholding would not redound to the credit of electors or elected. But don't think, he continues, that the new deputy is an outstanding villain or even an outstanding fool.

The man is no better and no worse than a hundred others who will sit with him on the green benches of the Palais Bourbon and will vote along with him in a solid majority. . . .

After glancing at Fould's political colouring (he is a conservative supporting Molé rather than a 'Ministerial' supporting Guizot), Heine now springs his surprise. He has never, we know, been noted for excessive sympathies with mediocrities of conservative—or, indeed, any other—political complexion; but in the case of Achille Fould, he tells us, 'his elevation to the rank of Deputy affords me genuine pleasure . . .' After thus startling the reader to attention, the sentence continues blandly on its way by stating what Heine calls, tongue firmly in cheek, an 'utterly simple reason':

for the utterly simple reason that by means of this elevation the principle of equal civic rights for Israelites has been sanctioned even to its utmost consequences. True, here in France the law and public opinion have long recognized the principle that Jews who distinguish themselves through talent or nobility of character should be eligible for all appointments in the state, without a single exception . . .[30]

That, no doubt, is one in the eye for German readers whose

governments have not seen fit, in the year of grace 1846, to apply that principle of natural justice to their Jewish subjects, and who for their own part, as constituent elements of public opinion, have not accepted it wholeheartedly even as an ideal. Heine is once again speaking *pro domo* here, for it was precisely this failure of Prussian law and Prussian public opinion which had driven him first to baptism and then to emigration. But after his sober statement of the very different, much more humane assumptions of the French he goes on, in his wittiest manner, to complain of their insufficiency.

However tolerant this may sound, I still find in it a sour after-taste of obsolete prejudice. As long as Jews are not admitted to such offices of state even if they *lack* talent and nobility of character, just like thousands of Christians who can neither think nor feel but who can do their sums—as long as *this* kind of discrimination exists, prejudice has not been wholly uprooted and the old oppression continues. Even the remotest trace of medieval intolerance vanishes, however, as soon as Jews can emulate their Christian brethren by becoming members of the House of Deputies—the most honorific office that there is in France—without any other merit than that of having money. In this respect the election of M. Achille Fould constitutes a definitive victory of the principle which grants complete equality of rights to all citizens.[31]

The passage on Achille Fould's election at Tarbes shows once again the serious foundation of Heine's wit. It pillories the values of a society bent on enriching itself; ridicules the notion that Jews scrambling for money and honours were doing anything their Gentile neighbours were not doing with the same avidity and in greater numbers; and directs attention to the *Leistungsdruck* under which Jews stood in European society, the necessity to prove over and over again that they were not just equal to, but better and worthier than, their non-Jewish competitors—a pressure bound to produce reaction phenomena that would retard rather than advance the cause of their civic integration and social acceptance.

Heine has not yet finished with this subject, however. He now goes on to draw his readers' attention to a paradox they might have missed: that his witty demonstration of the workings of civic *equality* was triggered off by the election of a Jewish *millionaire* to the lower house of the French parliament.

Achille Fould was not the only rich Jew to be so elected—and this leads Heine to propose, humorously, a treatise on the national wealth of the Jews from the times of the patriarch Abraham onwards. 'Two further men who subscribe to the Mosaic faith and whose names have the good sound ring of money . . .' (*deren Namen einen guten Geldklang hat*—a typical Heinesque elaboration of the idiom *sein Name hat einen guten Klang*, 'his name is in good repute', 'he is held in high esteem')

have been elected to the Chamber of Deputies this summer. How far do they advance the democratic principle of equal rights for all? They too are millionaire bankers, and in my historical researches on the national wealth of Jews from Abraham to the present day I shall find opportunity to speak of M. Benoît Fould and M. de Eichthal. Honni soit qui mal y pense.[32]

Here, as so often, Heine keeps this victims in suspense, threatens further revelations at a later time. But having once conceived the idea of a work 'on the national wealth of the Jews from Abraham to the present day', he cannot forbear to elaborate it further in his own satiric way. Will its implications not be anti-Semitic? Not at all, Heine replies.

I would like to remark in advance, in order to obviate misinterpretations, that the result of my investigations into the national wealth of the Jews redounds wholly to their credit and, indeed, does them the highest honour. Israel, it will appear, owes its wealth simply and solely to that sublime faith in God to which it has clung for centuries. The Jews worshipped a highest being that reigned, invisibly, in heaven, while the heathens, incapable of rising to the purely spiritual, made themselves all sorts of golden and silver gods which they adored here on earth.

The paradox had been announced: a paradox, be it noted, based once again on a principle exactly the opposite of that advanced by Karl Marx who adopted the vulgar equation of Judaism and the worship of money. Not at all, says Heine; the spirituality of the ancient Jewish religion, the purity of its ethical monotheism, contrasted with that of the peoples all around who worshipped silver and gold, *kesev vezahav*. How then, we are to ask outselves, could an *erhabener Gottes-*

glaube', a 'sublime faith in God' of the kind described, become the cause of national wealth? Here is Heine's answer.

> If these blind heathens had converted into cash all the gold and silver they wasted on such wretched idolatry, and if they had then invested such cash at a decent rate of interest, they would also have become as rich as the Jews, who could place their gold and their silver at greater advantage: they went, perhaps, into Assyrian-Babylonian gilt-edgeds, or into Nebuchadnezzarean securities, or into Egyptian canal shares, or into five per cent Sidonians, or assembled other classical portfolios which the Lord blessed in the same way that he is wont to bless modern ones.[33]

This is surely an excellent *jeu d'esprit*, in which modern financial concepts, practices, and institutions are superimposed on the biblical world in such a way that the ancient is either an incongruous, distorted mirror image of the modern (as in 'Egyptian canal shares') or stands in an equally incongruous contrast to it (as in 'five per cent Sidonians'). But this sustained joke, heightened by the use of biblical phraseology, has once again a serious undertone which we miss at our peril. Is there not, Heine suggests to his readers, some real relation between a spiritual, ethically strict religion and capitalism—the sort of relation, in fact, to which Max Weber and R. H. Tawney were to point many decades later? But beyond that Heine's deliberately absurd demonstration enshrines a parodistic reversal of Jewish interpretations of recent history in terms of the biblical past, together with ridicule of those who regard Jews as an ahistorical entity, as a group whose characteristics have remained fundamentally unchanged from Abraham's day to the present.[34]

Achille Fould, as it happened, aroused Heine's admiration in later years—in the very years in which he became one of the chief targets of Marx's attack because of his collaboration with Napoleon III. His satiric portrait therefore disappeared from the German and French versions of the *Augsburg Gazette* articles which Heine published in the 1850s under the titles *Lutezia* and *Lutèce*.

(v)

Heine's attacks on the Foulds take on, increasingly, the taint of a family feud. Long-time business associates of Salomon Heine, they had become even more closely linked with the autocratic head of the Heine clan when their niece, Cecile Furtado, married Uncle Salomon's son and heir, Carl. The enmity of the Foulds, Heine believed, had been partly responsible for Uncle Salomon's posthumous attempt to muzzle him. When Carl made it clear that the financial hold he now had on the poet would be used to impose a new censorship on him, designed to protect the good name of the family, Heine's first reaction was an attempt to outwit this new censorship in the same way in which he had so often outwitted that of the various German states. He placed, or tried to place, a number of notes and 'news items' in various journals and newspapers during 1845 and 1846, designed to put pressure on the family in various ways. Some of these purported to come from would-be *defenders* of the poet's relatives in Hamburg—yet from these too there emerges a frightening picture of heartless plutocrats and their sycophants.[35]

It was not only his own family, however, which felt the sting of the poet's resentment in the second half of the 1840s. Relations with Giacomo Meyerbeer had soured, as we have already seen, from the very moment the maestro became Master of the King's Music at the hated Prussian court. To this were added rankling resentments at some personal slights or omissions which would seem to have been mostly unintentional; indeed, Meyerbeer was very much aware that it was dangerous to have Heine for an enemy, and tried to placate him in various ways. He attempted to make peace between the poet and his cousin Carl (a mission which failed to have any effect) and he was not niggardly with opera tickets and pecuniary favours. It was not easy, however, to placate Heine once his back was up—particularly since he had come to feel that in earlier publications he had sometimes exaggerated the importance and intrinsic merit of Meyerbeer's music for diplomatic reasons. He tried to make up for this in an article entitled *Verdi and Meyerbeer*, published in the *Augsburg Gazette* under the date 1 February 1847.

Verdi is the man of the day in the musical world now that Bellini is dead, Rossini and Donizetti have died to art while their body still shows traces of life, and Meyerbeer too bears the dreaded Hippocratic signs in his countenance. As far as the favour of the Parisian public is concerned, Meyerbeer might as well be dead. Much as we would like to conceal this

(Heine is always at his most dangerous when he pretends to be reluctant to impart a piece of information)

we must confess, at last, that Meyerbeer's fame—all that artfully constructed expensive machinery—no longer operates as efficiently as it used to. Has some screw or some little bolt worked loose in its delicate mechanism?[36]

Having thus spoken of Meyebeer's *fame* as mechanical rather than organically grown—a matter of paid puffs, promotion, and claques—the poet now applies the same metaphor to his actual *work*.

What Parisians felt for the great maestro never amounted to true, self-forgetful enthusiasm. All he knew was how to *entertain* his public. The public ceased being entertained, however, once continuous routine performances of *Robert le Diable* and *Les Huguenots* showed that Meyerbeer's operas were not organic growths but were put together from small bits; that the effects were all *calculated*, and that what peeped out from beneath the splendid cloak was meagrely prosaic. The public has now had a good look into Meyerbeer's mental workshop—and he will find it difficult, in future, to surprise his audiences as he did before. We cannot, therefore, prophesy that his *Prophet* [the opera *Le Prophète*, long announced but not yet performed] will be greeted with triumphant Hosannahs when, at long last, he comes riding in.[37]

So much for Meyerbeer's *fame* and Mayerbeer's *work*; now for his character as a man.

Many of his personal friends are turning away from Meyerbeer. One hears strange talk among them about the kind of egoism which is interested in human beings only insofar as they are exploitable; an egoism whose first and last thought, whenever a human being swims into its ken, is simply this: 'How can I use you to puff my fame?' We hear that after collecting his laurel crowns in Germany, Meyerbeer now intends travelling to the British metropolis too, and thence to the United States.

Having launched his most unmistakable attack yet, Heine seems to draw back:

Even if a good deal of the charge against Meyerbeer should turn out to be exaggerated

(do we detect some hedging of bets?)

Meyerbeer is now regarded by Parisians as a charade that has yielded up its secret, and it is very sensible of him that he should seek ovations in places where his riddle has not yet been solved.[38]

The spotlight falls on the Parisian public at large—but German readers would be in little doubt that the correspondent endorsed the judgement that the maestro's riddle had indeed been solved, and that this solution—which involved, as will have been noticed, the application of the 'organic'–'mechanical' dichotomy dear to an earlier aesthetic—invalidated most of the praise that had been showered on his operas.

The editors of the *Augsburg Gazette* in fact deleted some of Heine's most aggressive sentences about Meyerbeer before publication. Heinz Becker, to whom we owe a thorough investigation of the uneasy relationship between this poet and composer, quotes the following sentence cut from Heine's essay on the Swedish singer Jenny Lind:

We understand very well why Meyerbeer runs after this singer with such enthusiastic devotion. It is vampirically uncanny and truly comic at the same time to see how he clings to her, how he sucks the sweet blood of her singing voice in order to sustain his present semblance of life . . .[39]

This image of Meyerbeer the vampire, a true grotesque, at once horrible and comic, is a notable addition to Heine's gallery of caricatures. Neither here, however, nor in any other attacks of this period, does he suggest that Meyerbeer's deficiencies are specifically Jewish. They are the vices of a musical virtuoso and manager of fame in the 'new Babylon' of the nineteenth century.

In this connection it must once again be stressed that Heine shows himself ever eager, after the Damascus affair, to redistribute the stereotype: to show that what Judaeophobes regard as specifically Jewish failings can be found in equal or superior measure elsewhere. Here is a typical instance, from a piece Heine sent to the *Augsburg Gazette* from Barèges in the Pyrenees.

What cupidity one finds among these mountain people, who usually attract praise as children of nature of a sort, as remnants of a race of innocence! They worship money with a fervour which almost amounts to fanaticism—that is their real national cult. But then—is not money, in fact, the god of the whole world nowadays?[40]

Heine may say harsh things about his Jewish contemporaries; but he never allows us to forget that they cannot be understood, or truly distinguished from their non-Jewish neighbours, by those who know only the stereotypes by whose means their enemies sought to characterize and to ostracise them. Even while most incensed against Jews he regarded as his enemies, and most concerned to avoid the impression of being obsessed with inner-Jewish problems, Heine never forgot his self-imposed task of defending Semitic Carthage at the gates of Gentile Rome.

(vi)

In April 1847, just before his health broke down irretrievably, Heine sat down after a night of wakeful sickness to write a Preface that would help to launch a book of Alsatian village stories by his useful acolyte Alexandre Weill.[41] Among all his associates in Paris Weill was the one who most insisted on his own Jewishness, and who most often reminded the poet of his Jewish roots. There is thus a special piquancy in Heine's *dating* of this Preface to Weill's work: 'Written in Paris on Good Friday 1847'. *Ludwig Börne. A Memorial* had shown in its very opening sentence how fond the poet was of marking the time through which his Jewish characters move in a way that refers specifically to the institution of Christianity. In the context of the Preface to Weill's stories, however, the explicitly Christian date contrasts, not with the Jewishness of the author discussed—for unlike the essay on Ludwig Marcus, with which the present chapter began, that on Alexandre Weill never refers to its subject's Jewish provenance and loyalties—as with the vision of a new, pointedly non-Christian or even anti-Christian order in which the Preface culminates.

Heine begins with a rare declaration of non-competence. Friends have assured him that Weill has written the first and best village Novellen in the German language, a claim Heine is prepared to accept (without looking at those of Berthold Auerbach, be it noted!) because he has not of late had much opportunity to read the 'masterpieces written for the present day', *Meisterwerke der Tagesschriftstellerei,* produced on the German side of the Rhine. A *caresse perfide* indeed: *Tagesschriftstellerei* means journalism, quick scribblings, important today but forgotten tomorrow—is Weill's work to be classed only with this? What follows suggests that the answer is 'yes'; for Heine goes on to devalue the whole genre of the village Novelle to which Weill is here making his contribution. 'We would not wish', Heine tells his readers 'to assign to this genre . . . an important place in literature, nor do we overestimate the merit of *priority* in literary composition.' What matters, Heine adds, is that the work before us, Weill's collection of what the poet calls 'Alsatian idylls', 'is good and successful of its kind'; and in this respect at least he is willing to give it 'sincerest praise and kindest recognition'.

Well, now Weill has, at last, a little praise to show; his work may not be important, but it's good of its kind. Even this, however, needs qualification—and Heine therefore goes on to tell us what Weill is decidedly *not.*

Herr Weill is, admittedly, not one of those poets who are able to use a native gift for creation in the round to bring forth quietly thoughful, harmonious, artistic figurations.

He is not, in other words, the kind of artist whose ideal image had emerged from the writings of Weimar Classicism, from Winckelmann onwards. But that period of art, the *Kunstperiode*, Heine had often enough declared to be at an end. What, then, of the new art, the art exemplified in a minor genre by a minor writer like Weill? Heine begins by listing what he thought were Weill's positive qualities.

He possesses instead, in exuberant profusion, a rare originality of feeling and thinking, an easily excited, enthusiastic disposition, as well as a liveliness of mind which stands him in excellent stead when he comes to narrate and describe, and which lends his literary work the character of a product of nature.

So far, so good—here, at last, is something Weill's publishers might use as a blurb; but those who know their Heine will suspect that the phrase about the 'product of nature' at the end is not to be taken as unadulterated praise. It implies, rather, that Weill lacks the shaping power characteristic of true artists. What follows serves only to confirm that suspicion.

He catches the momentary expressions of life, seizes life in the act, as it were, and is himself what one might call an 'impassioned daguer-reotype' which mirrors the world of appearances more or less happi-ly and sometimes—if the caprice of chance wills it so—poetically.

There we have it in black and white: Weill's art is that of the snapshot. He is not *just* a camera, of course, he is too passionate for that; but he cannot penetrate to essences, and his art becomes poetic—that is to say, literary in the full sense—only by accident. His disposition, his *Naturell*, enables him to catch the superficies of life: this is true of village stories, his book on the Peasant Wars (*La Guerre des paysans*, 1847), and a number of 'very interesting, piquant, tumultuous essays' which take up, in praiseworthy fashion, what Heine calls 'the great cause of our time'. Heine forbears to name this cause; but we know him well enough by now to know that it is the cause of 'emancipation' in the widest sense.

Here our author reveals himself with all his social virtues and aesthe-tic deficiences; here we observe him in all the glory and all the incompleteness of his agitatorial talents.

Is it possible to say more clearly that Heine thinks Weill a good journalist rather than a writer posterity ought to remember?

These writings show him up as he is: the self-divided son of the great movement of our time, weary of Europe, no longer able to put up with the discomforts and disgusts of the present world order, there-fore galloping off into the future on the back of a great idea . . .
    Such men are not bearers of an idea—they are borne along by it, forced to ride it without a saddle and without reins; they are, as it

were, tied naked to the idea, like Mazeppa to his wild steed in Horace Vernet's well-known pictures . . .

Since such men, *zerrissen, europamüde*, are never in control, no one knows where they will end up: among the Cossacks of the Don, perhaps, like Vernet's Mazeppa, or at the golden gates of those gardens of felicity in which the gods like to walk . . .

Heine has had enough of his author by now; Weill is a good journalist, he has a good feel for what is in the air, but he is no more than a plaything of his times. The reader is therefore invited to turn away from Weill and his village stories to the 'gardens of felicity' that may be awaiting mankind—and to the 'I' that is writing the Preface, to Heine himself. Ignoring the possibility that his times may be moving towards the Russian or 'Cossack' alternative, he fixes his gaze steadily on the dreamt of gardens of felicity and the gods that will walk in them. 'I do not know the name of these gods', Heine tells us, 'but the great poets and sages of all the centuries have proclaimed them.' Weill, clearly, does not belong to this company; but Heine himself has been allowed, on occasions, to lift the veil that hides the sanctuary of the future. Yet he cannot speak of what he has seen, because he knows that he himself is 'a child of the past, not yet healed of the slavish abjection, the grinding self-contempt, which mankind has sucked in for a century and a half with its superstitious mother's milk'. This necessarily inhibits his tongue. But though he belongs irrevocably to an age of sickness, he can see a healthier future ahead:

Our healthier descendants will contemplate, confess, and proclaim their own divinity in happiest repose. They will hardly be able to believe how sick their fathers were. They will think that they are being told a fairy-tale when they hear how men refused the enjoyments this life has to offer, how they mortified their bodies and dulled their minds, how they cut down the flowers of maidenhood and the pride of young men, how they went on lying and whining and putting up with the most insipid miseries—I need not say for *whose* advantage!

And as if this rejection of asceticism and other-worldliness were not explicit enough, Heine goes on to give it a sharply anti-Christian edge by picturing a future race of god-like men, seated in their temple-like palaces in joyful celebration of their own share in divinity, listening to the stories their old men have to tell of what life was like in less happy times.

Then, perhaps, one of the old men will tell their beautiful grandchildren that there was once an age in which a dead man was adored as a god and celebrated by a gruesome funeral repast in the course of which men imagined that the bread they were eating was his flesh and the wine they were drinking was his blood. At this tale the women's cheeks will grow pale and the chaplets of flowers will tremble on their beautiful locks. The men, however, will strew fresh incense on the hearth that serves them as an altar, in order to chase away the dark, uncanny reminiscences with such sweet odours.

Written in Paris on Good Friday 1847.

Heinrich Heine.

Weill and his village stories have been left far behind as the poet, about to enter for ever the realm of the incurably sick, rejects Jesus as a living presence and summons up once more his favourite vision of mankind living in godlike enjoyment, without any sense of original sin, in a world whose divine element resides wholly in man and in nature. The anti-Christian stance of *Almansor*, the annunciation of a realm of universal cakes and ale, of unfettered spiritual and sensual enjoyment, proclaimed in *De l'Allemagne* and *Germany. A Winter's Tale*, are recalled, for the last time, by a sick poet on a Good Friday devoted to the uncongenial task of recommending to the reading public the work of a not very distinguished contemporary. Never again would he offer his readers so optimistic a view of a possible future here on earth, in the land of the living rather than the Utopia of death proclaimed in the poem *Bimini*. Never again would he be able to erect an altar to the divine element that resides in mankind without any thought of a God that transcends our world: the God Whose features he had learnt to discern in early childhood and Whose presence he would conjure up—with what reservations we shall see—in the course of many pain-racked nights and days spent on those mattresses laid on the floor which prompted him to speak of his *Matratzengruft*, his 'mattress-crypt' or 'mattress grave'. The shades of the prison house were about to close in on him with a vengeance.

THIRD INTERMEZZO
New Companions and Old Butts

(i)

The concerns raised in Heine's mind by the Damascus affair also agitate his letters. In April and May 1840 he writes to Gustav Kolb, editor of the *Augsburg Gazette*, urging him to publish documents exonerating the Syrian Jews and to expose the machinations of those who sought to discredit them in German newspapers. With a happy pun linking journalistic and military campaigning Heine tells Kolb on 15 May 1840: 'I count on the *columns* ['die Kolonnen'] of the Augsburg Gazette when the Syrian persecution of the Jews is dragged before the tribunal of Mehemet Ali in Alexandria . . .' (My italics.) The respect he gained for the lawyer Crémieux during the Syrian affair also spilt over into his correspondence; 'vous êtes, mon cher Crémieux', he writes to the man himself on 24 May 1842, 'du petit nombre de gens que j'aime et qui méritent d'être aimés.' What he said about other French Jews in his *Augsburg Gazette* articles involved him, however, in further hostilities—first with Baron Delmar, and then with the Fould family, whom he had to regard, from then onwards, as among his most determined and implacable enemies. In the foreground of Heine's letters of the early 1840s, however, is another set of squabbles caused by his public portraiture and caricature: those set in motion by his portrayal of Börne, and more particularly of Börne's friends Jeanette Wohl and Salomon Strauß. The attacks launched against Heine by these aggrieved champions of their own and Börne's honour, of which the pistol duel he ultimately fought with Strauß did the least damage, occupy Heine continually from 1841 onwards. When Strauß boasted of having boxed his ears in the street, Heine finds himself compelled to give his own version of the incident:

All it boils down to is that the individual in question approached me, trembling with nervousness, and stuttered a few words; I laughed and gave him my address . . .

(to Gustav Kolb, 3 July 1841)

Strauß is dubbed a liar, a coward, a good-for-nothing: 'What is confronting me here is the flower of the Frankfurt ghetto and a vengeful female' (ibid.). Heine's public declarations, rebutting Strauß's charges, contain no such references to the ghetto— instead, we have ironic allusions to Germanic legend and Spanish anti-romance. Strauß there appears as 'that hero, *der gehörnte Siegfried*'. This alludes to Strauß's alleged cuckoldry by punning on an adjective which normally refers to the hardened skin the archetypal Germanic hero acquired after bathing in the blood of the dragon he had slain; in Heine's context *gehörnt* clearly means, not 'hard as horn', but 'wearing the horns of the cuckold'. Strauß also appears as 'a poor devil, *a knight of the sorriest countenance* . . . in the service of a cunning woman' (the phrase I have italicized makes the *Don Quixote* parody plain). A letter to Strauß himself, proposing a duel, is full of insults designed to make him accept a challenge to a duel; and letters Heine wrote to others are not sparing with phrases like 'that cunning slut Wohl, Börne's ex-mistress, with her horned donkey' (to Campe, 7 July 1841), *Schmutzlappen, niedrigster Auswurf der Frankfurter Judengasse*, and so on (to Alexandre Weill, 30 June and to Heinrich Brockhaus, 7 July 1841). Very soon, however, a different note enters the correspondence:

Strauß is a poor devil. It was wrong of me to insult his wife; and therefore I am hardly angry with him—but all the more angry with other people.

(to Alexandre Weill, 19 August 1841)

Two days after his duel with Strauß, on 7 September 1841, Heine tells Campe that the latter showed 'more courage than I supposed him capable of'; and in 1845 he even wrote an *amende honorable* for Jeanette Wohl, attesting that he had done her wrong, though with some provocation, and proposing to delete the insulting passages from further editions of his works (to L. Wertheim, 22 December 1845). Since no new edition was called for in the poet's lifetime, he never had a chance to carry out the intention he here expressed.

Ludwig Börne. A Memorial, Heine told Laube on 6 October 1840, 'united Jews and patriots against me'; and again and again he referred to hostile press campaigns and private intrigues as 'a revenge such as can only be hatched in the Frankfurt Jewish quarter' (to Weill, 4 September 1841), or to a 'Frankfurt clique' (ibid.) determined to hound him:

The amount of intrigue and malice loosed upon me from that quarter surpasses belief. Truly, Damascus is not just a fairy-tale!

(to August Lewald, 13 October 1841)

That last, incredible, sentence Heine could only write to a man of similar origins to his own without fear of being misunderstood—but it is typical of the way he could enlist even the wost anti-Semitic stereotypes in his efforts to characterize his Jewish enemies. Neither he nor Lewald believed the accusation levelled against the Damascene Jews to be anything but the grossest and most dangerous libel; but it could be made to *symbolize* a type of vengefulness which he described to G. F. Kühne, on 6 January 1842, as that of a 'clique out to murder my honour in an unprecedented way'. He also used a character created by Schiller, and felt by many to be the portrait of a Jew, when he characterized the Frankfurt clique that intrigued against him as 'those Spiegelberger we know so well' (to Heinrich Laube, 19 October 1846. Spiegelberg is one of the dramatis personae of Schiller's play *The Robbers*).

What Heine felt to be particularly sinister about the activities of his Frankfurt enemies was the way in which they managed to use financial muscle to get items hurtful to the poet's interests into journals and newspapers. In Paris, Heine tells Heinrich Laube on 19 October 1846, Strauß and his faction were credited with having spent more than 4000 francs for this purpose. Even Heine's favourite forum, the *Augsburg Gazette*, was liable to be suborned. This paper, Heine complains to the editor, Gustav Kolb, on 27 December 1844,

is being used to support the most infamous insinuations against me. The public over here is gullible, and cannot see the absurdity of such attacks, or the miserable motives behind them. They emanate from the old clique of Frankfurt Jews who feed and misuse a few would-be saviours of the German fatherland that have fallen on evil days.

Exactly the same thing happened three years ago. The ringleaders are
M. Strauß and the miserable banker Königswärter.

The enemies *Ludwig Börne. A Memorial* had made for him in
Frankfurt were also, Heine felt, stirring up older enemies in
Hamburg; and there they found a most dangerous ally. That
ally was none other than Gabriel Riesser, a Hamburg lawyer
who was soon to become one of the best-known and most
respected Jews in Germany when he distinguished himself in
the Frankfurt parliament of 1848 as an eloquent advocate of the
rights and liberties of German Gentiles and Jews alike. Riesser
showed himself ready to believe lying testimony against Heine
without applying any of the tests his legal training should have
suggested to him; and he threw the weight of his authority
against the poet, both publicly and privately, by ranging him-
self unequivocally among the supporters of Salomon Strauß.
At first Heine was inclined to dismiss Riesser as a meddling
fool.

What you say about that dolt Riesser is true. What presumption, to
appear as the champion of others in affairs that don't concern him!
He is a super-fool—he has got Venedey to tell me that he is willing to
travel to Paris in order to fight a duel with me on Strauß's behalf.
Such folly deserves chastisement. I commend him to your pen, and
that of your friends . . .

(to Weill, 19 August 1841)

When one has disposed of the comet itself there is no need to do
battle with its tail. Herr Riesser is merely the tail in this affair . . .

(to Jakob Venedey, 19 August 1841)

The comic role in this story is played by your unfortunate fellow
citizen M. Gabriel Riesser, who interfered without any call to do so,
and who did all he could to get himself talked about in Paris. This last
goal he seems to have attained, but with little profit. Is it Quixotism
that drove him to act as he did, or is it an overblown sense of his own
importance? . . .

(to Campe, 23 August 1841)

Heine is extremely anxious, he tells Jakob Venedey, not to
pander to Riesser's Quixotism or vanity by accepting his chal-
lenge and appear in public as a 'fellow fool' (24 August 1841).
He changed his tune, however, when he found that Riesser had
become one of his uncle Salomon Heine's most trusted advis-

ers, and an executor of Salomon's will. In a letter to J. H. Detmold (23 January 1845) he now denounces 'that infamous Dr Rieser [*sic*], who concocted the basest plots against me on the occasion of the Strauß affair'; and when Campe confirmed Riesser's continuing animosity, Heine replied:

> I am not at all surprised by what you say about M. Rießer [*sic*]. That he had a hand in misrepresentations injurious to my dignity is, however, remarkable and strange. Is this Shylock still not content? Did he not have his desire and cut a pound of flesh from beneath my heart in the affair of my uncle's will?—O how I thank heaven that I am not like my enemies! . . .
>
> (2 March 1846)

Just as he had used the Damascus accusations as a metaphor to describe the malice of Salomon Strauß's Frankfurt friends, so he now uses the Shylock story as a metaphor for the conduct of a Jewish enemy in Hamburg. It is noteworthy that this new Shylock, unlike Shakespeare's, *does* get his pound of flesh. As for the final sentence: Campe cannot have failed to appreciate Heine's wry self-caricature as the Pharisee of the New Testament!

(ii)

The poet's relations with his uncle Salomon were founded on four suppositions: the first of these was Jewish family loyalty and cohesion; the second was the charitable Jewish precept that the rich had an absolute obligation to help those less well off; the third was the traditional Jewish belief that the rich man, whatever his own degree of education and culture, had a duty to support learning—though 'learning' in this context usually meant Talmudic scholarship, Heine tried to widen the concept to fit his own case; the fourth was Heine's belief that by his work he was bringing honour and renown to the family name, and that the head of that family therefore had the duty to smooth his path. Uncle Salomon shared the first of these suppositions, and he had indeed helped his brother's children to obtain an education that would enable them to stand on their own feet. The other three he did not think applicable to his nephew's case—the kind of renown which he respected was not that brought by works like *The Baths of Lucca*, which attacked an aristocracy whose ranks members of the Heine family were preparing to join. Relations with Uncle Salomon had therefore always been uneasy; and Michael Werner[1] has rightly pointed to the psychic damage made apparent by such a sentence as the following, written after his uncle's death by a poet of world renown who was forty-seven years old:

> He said many harsh things to me, and last summer, in his excitement, he even hit me with his stick—O Lord! How gladly I would be hit again!
>
> (to Charlotte Embden, 29 December 1844)

The memory of the humiliations he had endured made it all the more imperative that he should not be cheated out of what he now believed to be his due: financial independence secured for him by a substantial share in his late uncle's estate.

It turned out otherwise. The capital legacy Uncle Salomon bequeathed him was insultingly small; and it was left to the principal legatee, Salomon's son Carl, to pay out such annual subventions as he saw fit. Carl lost no time in making it clear to Heine that supplies would be cut off immediately if he published anything deemed insulting or detrimental to the family. Hurt and indignant, Heine decided to commence what he dubbed 'the battle of genius against money-bags' (to Ferdinand Lassalle, 27 February 1846), a battle he fought with a bitterness which fatally undermined his already precarious health. Cousin Carl, once the friend he had nursed during the cholera epidemic in Paris, had now become an enemy to be combated by any means in his power: by enlisting the press ('Public opinion is easily won over to the poet—against millionaires' he wrote to J. H. Detmold on 9 January 1845); or by vexatious legal proceedings.

> What people say leaves Carl Heine cold. He has only three passions: women, cigars, and a quiet life. If I could stir up a revolt of the Hamburg *filles de joie* against him, he would soon show the white flag. I can't take his cigars away from him—but I can disturb his quiet life. Here is the chink in his armour which I will use . . .
>
> (to Campe, 4 February 1845)

Legal proceedings soon proved impractical, for Uncle Salomon's will left no loopholes; Heine therefore had to fall back on needlings in the press, and on enlisting eminent men (including Prince Pückler-Muskau, Meyerbeer, and Baron James Rothschild) to appeal to Carl Heine on his behalf. That too proved useless. Carl, he told Campe, 'has grievously sinned against me and hasn't even an inkling of the gravity of his offence' (21 July 1845).

I listened to my tenderer feelings, while cold reason and experience constantly hissed in my ear that in this world little can be wrested from the hard men of money by tearful appeals—one has to use one's sword. My pen is my sword, and this can, in the end, hold its own against the silver, and the advocate's tricks, which are at the command of my cousin. Constant debate between my feelings and my reason has made me miserable and hesitant for a whole year, and only now, when I have seen that in Carl's breast there beats no human heart, after I have begged for my rights instead of fighting for them so as to avoid having to draw my sword against the brotherly friend of my youth, now I can do nothing but—yes, I have been engaged in the composition of a terrible pamphlet these past few days, after Carl Heine's insolence finally brought my cup to overflowing . . .

(to Campe, 6 February 1846)

Accommodation with Carl was finally reached, and Heine was not, in the end, financially worse off than he had been in his uncle's lifetime. We shall see below how, for the sake of his wife, he acknowledged Carl's financial generosity towards him; but the hatred into which his former affection had turned was never to be uprooted from his offended heart. *Meinem beleidigten Herzen*—that term which expressed his feelings more perfectly than any other—he had learnt, as he told Ferdinand Lassalle on 13 February 1846, from Rahel Varnhagen.

'The fight of genius against money-bags' was not only waged against Carl. In 1838 Carl had married into a Parisian family which had tried, at first, to cultivate friendly relations with Heine, but whose members he had then mortally offended: the Foulds. Rose Fould was the wife of Élie Furtado, and Carl Heine married their daughter Cécile, whose relations with Heine had, as we have already seen, been cordial and even affectionate. When Cécile had moved to Hamburg, Heine wrote to her there, asking her to intercede for him with Uncle Salomon, reminding her of an innocently tender scene in a garden at Roquencourt, and warning her against spiritual infections in the air she now breathed in Hamburg.

Je suis triste. Je vous charge aujourd'hui d'une commission épineuse, vous à qui je ne voudrais avoir à présenter que des roses! ... A propos de roses, vous souvient il de ce jour brumeux ou vous courriez avec moi dans le jardin de Roquencourt et cherchiez en vain sur tous ces rosiers une rose assez belle pour me l'offrir? Il-y-a deux ans au mois d'Août. Vous étiez alors une enfant, une jeune étoile enveloppée d'une mantille de soie noire doublée de cerise, et dont vous avez bien voulu affubler le poète aveugle.

Heine's portrait of the young charmer is heightened by the contrast with his own beginning sickness, affecting his eyes, and by the charming combination of romantic extravagance ('une jeune étoile'!) with the exact description of Cécile's coat. But the portrait here sketched refers to the past.

Mon Dieu, combien depuis le monde doit s'être changé pour la petite Cécile Furtado! Bien des choses ont dû vous paraître à présent sous une face moins brillante, moins gaie, d'autres se révéleront plus tard d'une manière plus affligeante encore ... et un jour vous comprendrez que tout esprit supérieur, tout cœur passioné, est condamné ici-bas à la souffrance sinon à la misère, que pour nous cette terre est l'enfer, tandis qu'elle est le paradis pour les sots, les *Fresser* et les brutes, qui vivent bien et prospèrent, comme vous le voyez dans la bonne ville de Hambourg.

(24 March 1840)

Regretfully, Heine soon came to believe that Cécile had indeed taken the infection. 'She is a rotten piece of work', he writes to Charlotte Embden on 23 January 1844. 'She has been completely spoilt here in Paris, and poor Carl will have to see how he can get along with her.' It was Paris, then, and not Hamburg, where the infection finally took hold; but in Heine's eyes Cécile had now joined the party of 'fools, guzzlers, and brutes' against which he had sought to warn her. When Carl's attitude towards him hardened, Heine suspected her influence along with that of her mother. In a letter to Campe dated 8 January 1845 he points an accusing finger at 'Carl Heine's wife and mother-in-law, whose interests I have crossed'; and in a letter to J. H. Detmold, written on the following day, he elaborates this accusation:

My enemies here in Paris, the Foulds, are inciting Carl against me; I once loved his wife (*ich war einst der Liebhaber seiner ·Frau*) and made the match between them. It is a mystical story . . .

What precisely Heine meant, in the letter just quoted, by the phrase 'ich war einst der Liebhaber seiner Frau' is something this book, happily, need not set itself to investigate. The 'maze of fact and fantasy' into which it leads has been admirably charted by Harry Steinhauer,[2] who comes to the conclusion that though Heine here caddishly suggest an actual love-affair, the relations between the famous poet and the young girl who admired him were in fact quite innocent. What alone concerns us in the present context is the sad and irreversible alteration in the image of Cécile that confronts us in Heine's letters. In later years, she will appear in his family correspondence as *Madame Schofelly*—a nickname denoting a shabbiness, meanness, paltriness, that could never have been guessed at in the gardens at Roquencourt.

The letter to Cécile dated 24 March 1840, from which I have just quoted, calls Uncle Salomon 'le grand despote'; and after that uncle's death Heine calls him, in a letter to Campe, 'the terrible tyrant before whom I trembled' (4 February 1845). Yet when he wrote to Mathilde, on 2 December 1844, that he was 'well thought of at court', he really did think he had made his peace with the tyrant; and there can be no doubt the provisions of his uncle's will came as a complete surprise and struck him quite genuinely as the infraction of a firm promise his uncle had made to him. He felt betrayed where he should have been able to put his trust: 'in the bosom of my family, where I was unarmed and trustful' (to Varnhagen, 3 January 1846). He turned his affection more and more towards his mother and his sister and, for a short time, his two brothers, while directing hatred towards the rest. First in line of fire stood Therese's husband, Adolf Halle. He composed a venomous character sketch calculated to undermine Halle's candidature for high office in the Hamburg judiciary; but this stratagem, like all the others, failed, and Heine never did gain the financial independence which would have allowed him to publish his memoirs

without interference from his family. All right then, he wrote
to Campe:

What I write I will never submit to censorship from my family; but I
will gladly swallow my private rage and not write about the rascally
crew at all. Let them enjoy their obscure existence in peace; they'll be
sure, now, of being ignominiously forgotten after my death . . . I
have, after all, better people to depict than my late uncle's sons-in-
law.

(4 February 1845)

The caricature sketch, in this very letter to Campe, of one of
these relatives, C. M. Oppenheimer, as 'an old bedbug smiling
out of a thick cravat' shows what he might have done if he had
not been gagged. How he nevertheless vented his rage and told
his griefs, in poems that named no names, will be shown in a
later chapter. There is every reason to believe, however, that
Uncle Salomon himself would not have come out of Heine's
uncensored accounts at all badly; Heine was surely sincere
when he wrote to his sister after their uncle's death, before the
terms of his will were known:

This man played a powerful part in the story of my life, and I shall
portray him unforgettably. What a heart he had! And what a head!

(29 December 1844)

Even the fact that Uncle Salomon had struck him with his stick
when they had met again in 1844 did not extinguish Heine's
admiration and affection—sentiments which made the feeling
of betrayal, when it came, all the more bitter. There would
seem to be just a grain of truth in the fulsome paragraph the
poet appended to his will on 26 February 1847, after Carl had
promised to pay Mathilde half of Heine's pension after her
husband's death:

Here [Carl Heine] showed his noble soul, and as he gave me his hand
in pledge of this solemn promise I pressed it to my lips, because I was
so deeply moved and because he so much resembled, at this moment,
his late father, my poor uncle, whose hand I had so often kissed like a
child when he conferred a benefit upon me. Alas, with my uncle the
star of my good fortune was extinguished.

One cannot help remembering, however, as one reads these
fawning lines, what Heine once said about having to kiss the

hand one cannot hack off, as well as many a harsh remark revealing his true feelings about his miserable kith and kin, *meine miserable Sippschaft* (to Campe, 20 June 1847).

We have already noticed, in earlier chapters, Heine's tendency to seek biblical parallels for his own concerns. Just as his love for Mathilde could best be expressed in terms of the Song of Songs, so his poverty and—later—his physical afflictions brough inevitable reminiscences of Job (to Campe, 10 June 1840). It is not surprising, therefore, to find the battle of genius with money-bags also taking on Old Testament guise. Here he is, writing to Ferdinand Lassalle in February 1846.

Tell Varnhagen: the hearts of the Pharaohs of Money are so hardenened that the mere *threat* of the plagues is not enough—although they know very well the magic power of an author who has wrought many a serpentine miracle before their very eyes. No, these people have to *feel* the plagues before they will believe in them and abandon their self-willed, stubborn ways. They have to be afflicted by blood, frogs, lice, wild beasts, the hail of plebeian insult [*Jan Hagel*—an untranslatable pun!]and only when the tenth item on the list hits them, when their beloved first-born is slain, will they give in, fearing an even greater evil: their own death. Truly, if Moses had gone in for kind words, half-threats, and reasonable argument, the children of Israel would be stuck fast in Egypt until this very day!

Heine's parodistic self-identification with Moses, in this passage based on Chapters 7–13 of Exodus, prepares the way for the prominent place this supreme hero of the Old Testament will occupy in his later writings.

When Heine met the dramatist Friedrich Hebbel in the autumn of 1843, he became sufficiently interested in the man to want to read his work; especially since the play Hebbel could show him dealt with a biblical heroine on whom Heine had himself reflected deeply in his early years in Paris. When he had read the play, *Judith*, he met its author again and praised it highly—especially its depiction of a period and a people, and its impressively sparse method of portraiture. 'A single trait', he said to Hebbel, in words that throw a good deal of light on the aspect of Heine's own art which the present book is seeking to examine, 'often gives us the whole picture.' Above all Heine was impressed by a contrast which he himself had so often attempted to explore and present: between the 'sensualist' heathens and the 'spiritualist' Jews, between those who deified themselves, deified man, and those who sought their God in the Wholly Other.

Heine thought my Holofernes, with his self-deification, very profoundly conceived. I might, he said, have made him enjoy life more boldly so as to set him off more effectively against pale Judaic spiritualism.

(Friedrich Hebbel's diary, 14 October 1843)

Heine is said to have added that Holofernes's personality did not come through in all its fullness, its unbroken totality, in Hebbel's play; the masses would never understand what the dramatist was trying to do.

(iii)

On 5 February 1840 Heine wrote to his friend Varnhagen von Ense that he, his late wife Rahel, and Heine himself, belonged to an older generation whose ways of thinking and feeling were being superseded. But Heine was not the man to let himself be ousted without a struggle; he tried to make contact with the new generation, to board the same ship as they. The poem *Life's Journey* (*Lebensfahrt*) uses this time-honoured metaphor and indicates that the voyage with these new companions was not, for the man of a different generation, smooth and happy.

> Ich hab ein neues Schiff bestiegen,
> Mit neuen Genossen; es wogen und wiegen
> Die fremden Fluten mich hin und her—
> Wie fern die Heimat! mein Herz wie schwer!
>
> Und das ist wieder ein Singen und Lachen—
> Es pfeift der Wind, die Planken krachen—
> Am Himmel erlischt der letzte Stern—
> Wie schwer mein Herz! die Heimat wie fern!
>
> [I have boarded a new ship,
> with new companions; the foreign waves
> rock and cradle me to and fro—
> how far from home! how heavy my heart!

And there is singing and laughter once more
the wind whistles, the planks groan and crack
the last star in the sky is extinguished—
how heavy my heart! how far from home!]³

Who were these 'new companions', then, whose high spirits
contrast so strikingly with the poet's nostalgia and heavy-
heartedness? A letter to Heinrich Laube, dated 7 November
1842, may help to point us in the right direction. Having called
himself, with scant justification, 'perhaps the most resolute of
all revolutionaries', Heine told Laube:

Dearest friend! This is not a time for playing the Prussian doctrinaire:
we must harmonize with the *Halle Yearbooks* and the *Rhenish
Gazette* . . .

The guiding spirit of the *Hallesche Jahrbücher* was the Left
Hegelian Arnold Ruge; the editor-in-chief of the *Rheinische
Zeitung* was the young Karl Marx.

Shortly afterwards Marx moved to Paris; and between the
end of 1843, when he first met him, and the beginning of 1845,
when Marx was expelled from Paris, Heine had many contacts
with the man who was to become a prophet for half the globe.
It is now clear that whatever influence there was went from
Heine to Marx at least as much as from Marx to Heine.⁴ Both
men had reached a crisis-point in their intellectual develop-
ment. They shared common enemies, too; but Heine was never
able to follow Marx into the detailed economic and social
analyses which led the latter to propound his celebrated
panaceas. What can not be in doubt is that the two men came to
like and to respect one another. Heine felt himself understood
by Marx ('We need but few signs in order to understand each
other', he wrote to him on 21 September 1844); he collaborated
with him on some short-lived journals, submitted chapters of
Germany. A Winter's Tale to his scrutiny before publication,
and declared himself enraged when Marx was forced to leave
Paris (to Campe, 4? February 1845). In his later years, as we
shall see, he spoke of Marx with some irony; but this too
remained tinged with unmistakable respect. It is true to say,
however, that even when his own views harmonized most
closely with those of the young Marx, he never found for the

latter such words of praise and approval as he lavished on the young Ferdinand Lassalle.

When Heine met the twenty-year-old Lassalle towards the end of 1845 he felt drawn to him as to a potential friend and ally, as to a man who personified a generation other than his own, the new generation which *Germany. A Winter's Tale* (1844) had hailed with greater enthusiasm than any shown in *Life's Journey*.

> Es wächst heran ein neues Geschlecht,
> Ganz ohne Schminke und Sünden,
> Mit freien Gedanken, mit freier Lust—
> Dem werde ich alles verkünden.

> [A new generation is growing up,
> without cosmetic disguise, without sin,
> with free thoughts, and unfettered pleasures—
> to that generation I shall proclaim my whole message.][5]

There is a doubtful tradition, going back to Gustav Karpeles and Lothar Bucher, which tells us that in a letter no longer extant Heine called the young Lassalle 'the Messiah of the century';[6] what remains undisputed, however, is that he characterized him with quite extraordinary enthusiasm in a letter to Varnhagen dated 3 January 1846.

A young man with the most splendid intellectual gifts; with the most thorough learning, the most extensive knowledge, the most penetrating mind, I have ever encountered; his superb talent for exposition goes with an ability to act decisively which has astonished me. If his sympathy for me is not extinguished I can expect the most active assistance from him . . .

What Heine here expects from Lassalle is not so much a furthering of radical political and social ideals as help in his squabbles with his family over Uncle Salomon's will. But however that may be, he concludes the letter to Varnhagen from which I have just quoted: 'This combination of knowledge with ability to act, of talent with character, is a phenomenon that has delighted me.'

Here a seasoned reader of Heine will surely prick up his ears. *Vereinigung von . . . Talent und Charakter*—is this not precisely the ideal Heine himself was always said to miss? The ideal had been proclaimed by Börne, with an edge against Heine, and it underlay much of the satire of *Atta Troll*. And having reminded Varnhagen of *Atta Troll*, Heine now recalls *Germany. A Winter's Tale* as he continues his epistolary eulogy of Lassalle, praising the very qualities that set Marx's teeth so much on edge when *he* had dealings with Lassalle in later years.

Herr Lassalle, it must be said, is in every particular the child of a new era that wants no truck with the kind of renunciation and humility with which we hungered and spun our fantasies in our time.

Now comes the transition so characteristic of Heine's portraits, where the individual is again and again made symbolic of his time, where the 'signature' of the time can be read in an individual's physical make-up and mental set.

This new generation wants to enjoy itself and to make its mark in the visible world; we, the old generation, humbly bowed down before the invisible, chased after shadowy kisses and the scent of blue flowers, renounced, and wept, and we were happier, perhaps, than the hardy gladiators of the new era who go so proudly to meet their death in combat. The thousand-year empire of Romanticism is at an end, and I myself was but its last mythical emperor—the one who gave up his throne. Had I not torn the crown from my head and thrown it away, had I not donned a plebeian smock, they would have cut my head off.

Having thus placed himself between the old and the new, having portrayed himself as an adherent of the old order who joins the new in fear of his very life, Heine turns to Varnhagen, the 'brother in arms' to whom he professes himself drawn by an 'elective affinity':

Like me you have helped to bury the old era and served as midwife to the new. Yes, we helped it to see the light of day, and now it terrifies us. Our fate is like that of the poor hen who hatched ducks' eggs and who now sees, with horror, how her brood throws itself into the water and swims about delightedly.

The image of the hen at the shore watching the little ducks she has hatched swim in the water complements the central image of *Life's Journey*, which had shown the poet unwilling to stay on shore when a new generation set out to sea. We see once again how Heine's portraits make us conscious of portrayer and portrayed at once, and how his metaphors convey events and states of affairs together with his attitude to them.

Heine's enthusiasm for Lassalle lasted a while longer. He finds him gratifyingly sympathetic and willing to help; he recalls his 'fine passionate lips' and addresses him as *mein teuerster Lassalle*:

Never has anybody done so much for me. Nor have I ever found anyone who united so much passion with so clear an understanding and brought both to bear on his actions. You have a right to be impudent—the rest of us only usurp that right, that heavenly privilege. Compared to you I am only a modest fly.

(10 February 1846)

'I love you very much', Heine ends this enthusiastic letter; 'you won't let one rest until one loves you!' On 11 February Heine again assures Lassalle of his 'inexpressible love' and adds that he never placed so much confidence in anyone else; and a few days later he apostrophizes him as 'my dearest brother in arms'. To others too he speaks of him as 'one of my dearest friends . . . who has my complete confidence' (to J. F. Dieffenbach, 10 February 1846) and as a 'splendid fellow' (*Prachtkerl*). On 16 February we find Heine telling Varnhagen that he has been unwell but that Lassalle cheered him up: 'His high spirits [*Übermut*] at least gave me some courage [*Mut*]; and that makes it easier for me to bear the most dreadful things.' By 27 February, however, a note of caution has crept into his letters to his young friend: 'I long to hear how you are. Knowing your character I am not without the most philistine worry on your account.' This worry increased tenfold when Lassalle sought to draw him into his championship of Countess Hatzfeld—another family affair with social implications, like that of Heine and his rich relatives, but one with which the poet would have no truck. The Hatzfeld affair and Lassalle's involvement in it, Heine writes to his young friend, 'belongs more to the sphere of Sue's novels than among my concerns', and he adds:

I often think of you and your future with profoundest worry . . . How many buffets you will still have to endure before you have gained *my* experience! But then you will be tired and old, as

I am now, and all your experience will be of no use to you. That's how life is—I am sick of it all.

(7 March 1846)

The letter is signed 'Your friend H. Heine'; but the tokens of cooling friendship are now too obvious to be missed.

The Lassalle Heine knew was not yet the charismatic leader of a socialist workers' movement: he did not found the Allgemeiner Deutscher Arbeiterverein until seven years after the poet's death. Nor were the new acquaintances that entered Heine's world along with him at all prominent in politics. There were three of them. The first was Ferdinand's father, Heymann Lassal [*sic*], of whom we hear little except that he had a reputation for honesty; the second was Ferdinand's sister, Friederike, who made a strong impression on the poet. Even before he met her, he speculated on whether she too had the 'passionate lips' that distinguished her brother (to Ferdinand Lassalle, 10 February 1849), and he was not disappointed—though it appears that what most attracted his attention was the splendid bosom and shoulders revealed by her *décolletage*. 'I am often in your sister's company', he writes to Lassalle on 27 February 1846, 'and we talk about you for hours together. She has extraordinary intelligence and she resembles you delightfully. I am giving a great dinner-party at my house, to which I am inviting Royer, Balzac, Gautier, Gozlan, etc.—if only you could join us!' By inviting her to meet such distinguished guests at that dinner-party Heine honoured Lassalle's sister in a way he did not honour many acquaintances; and he paid her a further unusual compliment by inaugurating her autograph album with an unpublished poem—the very poem which was, eight years later, to serve as motto for the *Hebrew Melodies* section of *Romanzero*.

The letter Heine wrote to Ferdinand Lassalle on 10 February 1846 precedes its speculation about possible physical resemblances between Lassalle and his sister with the following passage.

I have started playing the Stock Exchange again . . . But now for some great news which you may already have heard: Calmonius is coming here with your sister! I had a letter from him yesterday. He seems to be still mulling over the zinc project, the idea for which he owes to me. I look forward eagerly to seeing him and your sister.

'Calmonius' is a distortion of the name 'Kalonymus' borne by a family of prominent medieval Jews. Heine used it as a cypher for serviceable Jews in the Berlin of Frederick the Great (figures like Veitel Ephraim and Daniel Itzig) and finally appropriated it to designate the man whom he regarded as a kind of private court Jew of his own: Friederike Lassalle's husband, a financial speculator named Ferdinand Friedland. Heine had met Friedland as early as June or July 1838 and had been fascinated—as was Meyerbeer!—by this *Luftmensch* of a type that appears frequently in the annals of Jewish history in Europe. 'I have spoken of you to M. Meyerbeer several times since we met', the poet had written to Friedland in July 1838; 'he is full of your praise, and I am glad to see that he is able to appreciate your qualities.' He employs Friedland, as he does so many others, as a newsgatherer—but he sees in him, above all, someone who might help him to some share of the wealth he saw being made all around him by speculators in industrial stocks and shares. The zinc project mentioned in the letter of 10 February 1846 is soon dropped; but on 27 February Heine is able to report to Ferdinand Lassalle: 'I talk business with your brother-in-law; his affairs are going well, he is indeed a genius!' But he soon begins to worry, not without cause, about his investment, and to question Friedland's veracity. The letters to Lassalle show this clearly. 'Calmonius and your sister are living well and happily here in Paris; the former is the happiest of men! He believes everything and everybody, he even believes himself!' (7 March 1846.) To Friedland himself Heine writes on 14 September 1846: 'Business is bad, Calmonius! Come back soon. I want to hear you lie again before I die.' The 'lies' of which he accuses his court Jew, whose get-rich-quick schemes he had been so eager to join, concerned the prospects of *Iris*, a gas-light company in Prague, in which Friedland was heavily engaged and in which the poet had invested most of the lump sum Uncle Salomon had left him.

I beg you most earnestly, see that this matter is settled in such a way that I don't lose my money, at least not yet. It is, alas, only too likely that later on I shall indeed lose it, for it now appears that the doubts about the *Iris* company which you dismissed were only too justified. The millionaire who wanted to join in the scheme existed only in your imagination. In short: there was more hot air than cash.

When I say all this I don't, my dear Calmonius, accuse you of knowingly leading me astray. You have the strange talent of believing everything you want to believe, and such belief is contagious. I only blame myself for heeding you more than I heeded the warnings of experienced people and my own good sense. You wanted to make my fortune—well now I beg you to do all you can, at least, not to make me more unfortunate than I am already . . .

(14 September 1846)

Friedland and the *Iris* affair will occupy us again when we look at the letters Heine wrote after 1848. Even now, however, it is striking how much sympathy Heine still has for this Jewish *Luftmensch* who believed his own tall tales, and how he showed this sympathy at the very time when his importunate eagerness to join Friedland's get-rich-quick schemes threatened to cause him a financial loss he could ill afford. He pointed out to Alfred Meissner what an interesting phenomenon Friedland was—did he not have all the qualities necessary to the court Jew: a quick and penetrating intelligence, versatility, inexhaustible inventiveness when it came to choosing his means, together with an ultimately pessimistic outlook on life?[7] And though he blamed Friedland, often unjustly, when the schemes went wrong, he continued to like him far better than solidly established bankers like 'the miserable Königswärter' (to Campe, 12 November 1846), or Baron Delmar, or the Foulds, or his once so dear cousin Carl Heine.

The most prominent of the financiers that appear in Heine's letters of the 1840s is, once again, Baron James de Rothschild. Having had Baroness Betty's assurance that his published comments on the Rothschilds had not been taken amiss, he made himself the mediator between Campe and the baron in a ticklish affair. What was in question was nothing less than the suppression of a book, or possibly even two books, written against the Rothschilds. Money would be required to do this, and we find Heine writing to Campe on 29 December 1843:

I confess that I would like nothing better than to be able to recompense, as much as I honestly can, the kind and gentle services Rothschild has rendered me over the last twelve years; but what intimidates me, makes me almost cowardly, is the thought that Rothschild might think I am trying to take advantage of him . . . You will make it easier for me to satisfy the friendly zeal with which I would like to serve him if you send me the hostile manuscript in question.

Rothschild's good will would be particularly useful, he told Campe when he sent him some satires on King Ludwig I of Bavaria, because of the new virulence of his satiric poetry:

The influence of these people on the German chancelleries is very great, and it is possible that I shall have need of it if I write any more poems like those I enclose—which I have no intention of doing, however.

(20 February 1844)

On 10 February 1846 Heine tells his new confidant Lassalle that his relations with Baron James were 'very strained', but that this served his present projects rather well. He then informed Baroness Betty, in a letter dated 7 April 1846, that a new wave of German attacks was about to break on the Rothschilds' head. The cause, he explained, was their desire to become privileged landowners in Prussia. 'Prussian aristocrats', he said, 'would like to use the paw of the plebeian to stir up public opinion against the "exceptional family"—for that term, *die exceptionelle Familie*, is the one constantly used to describe the house of Rothschild in proceedings regarding the right of patronage over Schillersdorf and Ulschin.' Baron James showed his gratitude by attempting—in vain—to induce Carl Heine to make generous and unconditional provisions for his famous cousin; while the 'Fould dynasty', as Heine now called a family that was becoming as prominent in French politics as it had been in French banking (to Carl Heine, early December 1842), ranged itself implacably on the side of Heine's enemies. They never could and never would forgive what the poet had said about them in the *Augsburg Gazette*.

(iv)

'Literary Jews', Heine wrote to Campe on 7 July 1841, in the swirl of the dust thrown up by the Börne–Wohl–Strauß polemic, 'are stupid enough to show themselves hostile to me.' Such hostility Heine heartily returned. In M. G. Saphir he can now see only 'an old monkey who has been thoroughly thrashed' (to Campe, 1 December 1841). Berthold Auerbach, whose *Spinoza* had seemed a curate's egg to him in 1837, is now but a figure of fun, the inaugurator of a risible tradition, even though he had received the accolade of an appreciation from the pen of Saint-René Taillandier in the *Revue des Deux Mondes*.

My physical condition continues uncharged. My head is as weak as if I were the author of an Auerbachian village story—my stomach feels as hangoverishly sentimental and religiously-morally tepid as the contents of such a story . . .

(to Laube, 5 April, 1847)

One Jewish author of village stories entered Heine's orbit more closely than Berthold Auerbach; and that, of course, was Alexandre Weill. Weill assisted the poet in the Strauß affair by keeping him supplied with news and helping his side of the case to a hearing in various newspapers and journals. Heine was beginning to distrust him, however. A letter to Laube calls Weill 'the creature of that arch-intriguer [Gutzkow] who maliciously exploited the anarchy of our daily press to work against us' (7 November 1842). In another letter to Laube he shows himself amused by the notion that Weill was to have essays published in a 'Journal for the World of Elegance' (*Zeitung für die elegante Welt*)—the nervous, talkative little Jew and the world of elegance seemed poles apart to him. 'Sweep this Weill rubbish our of your journal!' is the advice he gave to Laube (19 December 1842). During his absence in Germany, where he received letters from Weill asking for a loan (he was *always* asking for loans!), the poet wrote to his wife:

Be careful that you don't meet this man anywhere and that he does not get to know you are back in Paris. His tactlessness, his connections, and his pushy impudence make him more dangerous than any enemy.

(2 September 1844)

In another letter to Mathilde he called Weill 'le digne représentant' of the German press—'cette presse cancanière' (19 September 1844). The quarrel over Uncle Salomon's will drew him closer to Weill, however, when Weill showed himself sympathetic and ready to help; the services of a 'presse cancanière' were precisely what the poet needed at that moment. He still refused to lend his acolyte money; but he did the next best thing, in 1847, by writing a preface to his Village Stories, and thus increasing their sale. When, in March 1848, Weill stood as a candidate for the Chamber of Deputies Heine showed himself as incredulously amused as when he had heard of his connections with something intended for the 'World of Elegance'. 'Weill has gained 16,000 votes,' he writes to Alfred Meissner on 12 April 1848. 'Il a l'air de député des talons jusqu'aux sourcils.'

Among other Jewish literati the poet encountered in Paris during the 1840s was Dr J. Karpeles, whom he commended to the attention of Baron J. G. von Cotta in unusually warm terms.

As correspondent [on Parisian affairs] I can ... recommend Herr Karpeles, who has for some years now been acting as correspondent for various German journals—notably those published in Hanover and Breslau—and who has all the qualities the *Augsburg Gazette* needs: understanding, conscientiousness, a capacity for taking pains, and a knowledge of men and affairs in politics. I think the *Gazette* will find in him precisely the man it requires. I can vouch for his character ...

(20 November 1841)

He also met Dr Felix Bamberg, whom he recommended to Franz Dingelstedt and entertained to dinner in 1846, but whose voluble devotion to Friedrich Hebbel soon got on his nerves. Later on he was to have more serious cause to shy away from Dr Bamberg. And then there was Baron Ferdinand von Eckstein, the baptized and ennobled uncle of his old acquaintance in Munich days, Wit von Dörring. Eckstein's career as Catholic authority on Eastern religions amused the poet greatly; he sent many a shaft of wit in his direction, particularly when yet another article on Eckstein's pet subject appeared in the *Augsburg Gazette*. Alfred Meissner records in his autobiography that Heine liked to pretend that the author of these articles had departed this life many years ago:

'Eckstein is really dead, you know. But what he has done is to leave a prescription with the editorial pharmacist of the *Augsburg Gazette*; and this is used, from time to time, to prepare the complicated

mixture as before. The complete formula is now listed in the Augs-
burg pharmacopoeia and is guaranteed to cause plentiful perspira-
tion.'[8]

Heine was equally caustic about Dr Karl Löwenthal, who was
beginning a distinguished publishing career (as co-founder of
the firm Rütten und Loening) and who had achieved notoriety
as a purveyor of what the Prussian and Austrian authorities
considered the dangerously subversive literature of Young
Germany (*Das junge Deutschland*). 'Several times now', Heine
reports to Heinrich Laube on 24 January 1843, 'I have seen
Löwenthal here, our Young Germany's bookseller. He wants a
great deal, but he has no idea what it *is* he wants.' The activities
of Heine and Löwenthal, it should be remembered, had caused
many a misguided patriot to believe that 'Young Germany'
was really 'Young Palestine', part of some sinister Jewish plot
to subvert German values.

Composers of Jewish origin once again join the literati as
subjects of Heine's concern and targets of his wit. About
Jacques Halévy he quipped in 1839 that Meyerbeer had had
him bribed to compose as much as he did—for the more of his
works appeared, the more people would see their ultimate
nullity.[9] On 16 February 1846 he wrote to Lassalle: 'All's quiet
here in Paris. For some eight days there has been no talk of
anything but Halévy's *Mousquetaires*. My wife is very enthu-
siastic about it.' Mathilde's enthusiasm speaks volumes about
the probable artistic emptiness of the work she admired—
Heine loved her very much, but hardly considered her a sound
judge of art. But the composer most constantly in the poet's
field of vision is, once again, Meyerbeer. In a particularly
revealing letter to the maestro himself, dated 12 May 1841,
Heine tries to turn him against his faithful publisher Maurice
Schlesinger. 'I can hardly tell you', he writes, 'how totally
Schlesinger has succeeded in compromising you'; and he goes
on to devalue in advance anything Schlesinger might say
against him, Heine, by attributing his hostility to the publicity
Heine had given to the failure of Schlesinger's latest German
import, the singer Johanna Löwe, with the Parisian public.

You can rest assured Mlle Löwe displeased all Frenchmen who heard
her; mainly, perhaps, because she appeared under Schlesinger's aegis,

but also because she *would* keep on singing Beethoven's *Adelaide* at every opportunity . . .

After seeking, by these means, to drive a wedge between Meyerbeer and Schlesinger for the benefit, perhaps, of a rival firm of music publishers, Heine goes on to speak of something Meyerbeer understood all too well: the need to arrest the malicious pens and tongues of fellow *émigrés* by giving them money. On 24 May 1842, he tells him:

Truly, the whole history of music has been revolving around your name for some ten years; and if one discusses any musician nowadays, the question of his relation to Meyerbeer's music will inevitably arise. In the future, when you will have fought your third victorious battle [over *Le Prophète*, presumably], this will be even more the case. I look forward to that!

The letter just quoted goes on to send regards to Meyerbeer's wife and 'your good mother, that kindly dowager of whom I often think. How I long to see her again! We always got on so well together. The only kinds of people with whom I could never live at peace are affected liars.' Heine ends his letter with professions of respect and love for Maestro Giacomo himself. On 17 October 1842 we then find the poet writing to Lewald about attacks launched against Meyerbeer by German newspapers—'he is so good and upright', he comments; he therefore does not deserve such treatment. A letter of 2 November 1842 is addressed to the composer's mother, Amalie Beer:

You are living, honoured and loved, in the midst of a flourishing family, about whose future you need have no worries; and you are the mother of Meyerbeer, whose good fortune and whose fame assume almost fabulous proportions.

Heine assured himself a portion of that good fortune by continuing to ask favours of Meyerbeer: loans of money (along with contributions to keep the composer's potential enemies and detractors at bay), free tickets, compositions of Heine's poems . . . When Meyerbeer did not send some compositions he had promised, a sour note entered the correspondence, though the poet still calls himself the composer's 'admirer'; and on 10 June 1844 we find him trying to explain away his digs at Meyerbeer in the *Augsburg Gazette* by saying that they were all part of his attempts to forestall Spontini's intrigues. How much credence Meyerbeer could give to such assurances, or to protestations of love and respect in this same letter, must remain in doubt; what is certain is that his fear of Heine grew, and that he sought to placate him wherever possible. He must certainly have been aware that Heine was fond of exercising his wit on the Meyerbeer family in private conversation, as when he revenged himself for the composer's refusal to meet Mathilde socially by saying that Meyerbeer's own wife was only tolerable because her daughters had managed to give her a veneer of education: 'Ihre Töchter haben sie leidlich erzogen.'[10]

In the battle over Uncle Salomon's last will and testament Meyerbeer supported the poet to the best of his ability; but he was no more successful in his appeals to Carl Heine's generosity of spirit than others had been. Heine in the mean time, annoyed by the non-arrival of promised compositions, was again showing his claws. On 24 December 1845 he formally declares their friendship at an end, though he protests his continued admiration of the composer's musical genius. 'You have no idea', he adds, 'how useful it was, for you and others, that for fifteen years I kept my sentry-post here in Paris, despite all the sacrifices of money and health this expensive and hectic place exacted.' He encourages his new-found abettor Lassalle to keep 'the shaggy bear' up to the mark: 'apply thumb-screws to the bear; spare no device that will make him dance to our tune.' (27 February 1846.) On 7 March 1846, in another letter to Lassalle, the bear has turned into a fox: 'Meyerbeer is a cunning old fox, but I shall pull his pelt over his ears just the same.' Vanity and avarice, he adds, somewhat ungratefully, are the composer's ruling passions: 'he cost me more than I cost him', for he had paid Germans in Paris to leave Meyerbeer and his reputation unscathed. 'Tell me exactly what he said to you', he adjures Lassalle, 'and I'll dress him down as has never been dressed down before.'

Before their quarrel Heine had written to Meyerbeer:

M. Mendelssohn and his clique have been very busy in Augsburg; he is a monarch on whom I am asked to go easy. He will not profit by this.

(13 May 1844)

Nor was it only the editorial staff of the *Augsburg Gazette* that felt disturbed by the hostile tone of Heine's remarks on Mendelssohn-Bartholdy. Lassalle too asked the poet to desist from attacks on him, and received a promise of compliance on 11 February 1846. To this promise Heine added a most instructive gloss:

I shall do everything you want. In respect of Felix Mendelssohn—though I don't see why you should attach importance to such an insignificant matter—I shall gladly comply with your request, and from now on not a malicious syllable shall be printed about him. What I resent in him is his Christianizing. I cannot forgive this man of independent means that he has seen fit to serve the pietists with his enormous talent. The more I appreciate the greatness of this talent, the more angry I am to see it so iniquitously misused. If I had the good fortune to be the grandson of Moses Mendelssohn, I would never employ my talents to set the urine of the Lamb [*die Pisse des Lämmleins*] to music. Between ourselves: the most immediate cause why I ventured to apply a few pinpricks to Mendelssohn was that I wanted to annoy some incorrigibly enthusiastic champions of his here in Paris; your compatriot Franckh, for instance, and Heller. These champions were ignoble enough to insinuate that I only attacked Mendelssohn in order to curry favour with Meyerbeer. I deliberately spell all this out for you so that you can get to know the reasons for my quarrel with Mendelssohn more perfectly than the mob, to whom they will be served up with the usual distortions. For the time being all that I have written here remains confidential between ourselves.

Here Heine speaks as a man who had undergone what he felt to be the trauma of baptism for the sake of making a living in a position worthy of his talents; a man who cannot, therefore, understand how rich and for that reason independent men of Jewish origin could voluntarily and freely pay homage to the Christian religion. Felix Mendelssohn-Bartholdy, he clearly felt, had betrayed his great ancestor, his grandfather Moses Mendelssohn, who had earned the respect of Germans not least by steadfastly choosing to remain within the Jewish fold.

Composers needed agents and publishers, and on 13 May 1844 Heine approached Meyerbeer with the direct proposition that he should allow the Escudier brothers rather than Schlesinger to bring out his future works.

The two Gascons [Léon Escudier and his brother] are so energetic, and have so much advertising talent, that your piece would be sure of the greatest possible success. For after all, Maestro, everything you write is good; all that is needed is that it should be properly introduced to the public for which it is destined. Schlesinger is no longer quite the man to do this effectively; he has grown tired, made too many enemies, become indifferent and lacking in confidence—he is not the pirate he once was! The Escudiers, by the way, pay as well as Schlesinger, if not better . . .

The Gascon and the Jewish entrepreneurs are engaged in the same game; they exhibit the same virtues and vices; they have the same talents which they employ for similar ends. In Heine's eyes the Gascons' commercial and advertising flair in the end outstrips that of their ageing Jewish competitor. One must, of course, reckon with the possibility that the Escudiers had found some means of inducing the poet to lure Meyerbeer away from Schlesinger . . .

(v)

Arnold Ruge, the Left Hegelian who later claimed, with some justice, that he and Marx had helped to sharpen the tone of Heine's satiric poetry in the 1840s, recorded some interesting conversations with the poet when they were both living in Paris. Here we may find Heine taking on, parodistically, the persona of Jesus himself—'if one is well and truly crucified', he is said to have remarked when confronted with adverse criticism, 'one can expect a proper resurrection too.'[11] Towards the end of 1844, Ruge found him cursing some Jews who had given him misleading information. 'Is it a family quarrel then?' Ruge asked, whereupon Heine is said to have replied: 'I am not a Jew, and have never been one.' If it is accurately reported, that reply would indicate the poet's anxiety not to be typecast as a Jew, and would sort well with annoyance at finding his name included with those of other 'Eminent Israelites'; and with the assurance he gave to a French enquirer that he had never set foot in a synagogue. He also showed, by his words and actions, that he saw the force of François Wille's warning that he should guard against giving an impression of Jewish nationalism at the very moment in which he was attacking the nationalist sentiments trumpeted by German hyper-patriots. In answer to an enquiry by his mother he said that the eponymous hero of his *Atta Troll* might have taken on a little colouring from Jews striving for emancipation, but that the main thrust of the satire was directed against a much wider target than the narrowly Jewish one (21 February 1843). The will Heine made in September 1846 stressed that he belonged, 'at least officially', to the Protestant community, but asked that for the sake of his wife his body should be allowed its last resting-place in a *Catholic* churchyard. In June 1848 we find Heine making another will which elaborated the reference to his 'official' protestantism.

By an act of baptism I belong to the Christian Evangelical Church, but my thoughts have never sympathized with any religion; having lived as a good pagan I also wish to die without having any sacred ceremonies performed at my funeral.

Neither of these two wills contains any reference to Judaism or Jewishness.[12] Most revealing of all is Heine's original use of the term *Rishess* (Jew-hatred) in a letter to Meyerbeer. Speaking of August Gathy, he plays a significant variation on a bitter joke he had made about Moses Mendelssohn's humped back in *Towards a History of Religion and Philosophy in Germany.*

Gaddy [*sic*], it is true, is not Jewish. He is greatly afraid of the press, however, he fears bodily *Rishess*, for he is a hunchback.

(10 June 1844)

Where Heine's poem on the Hamburg Jewish hospital had depicted Jewishness as a 'sickness', his letter to Meyerbeer makes it akin to a physical deformity that excites fear of mockery in the sufferer.

All this did not, however, prevent Heine from reading Jewish history with rapt attention, and even planning to contribute to Jewish historiography himself—a task for which, he believed, long submersion in the works of Herodotus would be an ideal preparation. Theodor Creizenach, who reports the conversation he had with Heine on this subject in the mid-1840s, adds that the poet asked him for help in finding records of the last forced debate between Christians and Jews about the merit and truth of their respective religions, and hazards a guess that Heine was already preparing, in his mind, the mock account of such a debate which was to end his *Romanzero*.[13]

There are other indications to suggest that even if Ruge were correctly attributing to Heine the remark 'I am not a Jew, and have never been one', it could only have represented a passing phase or mood or strategic consideration. Much of the charm of the affectionately bantering letters the wrote to his mother and sister in this period derives from indications that Heine was as aware of his Jewish past, and the Jewish component of his self, as ever. 'I shall never forget', he writes to his mother after a fire had burnt down her house, 'how heroically my dear sister behaved! Compared with her Wellington is a *Shabbes-goye*.' (23 May 1843.) *Shabbesgoye*, the Yiddish term for the Gentile woman who lights fires and performs other duties forbidden to Jews on the sabbath, is only one of a number of such terms designed to recreate the linguistic ambience of the poet's childhood home: *Verbrengerin, Beholes, zehkenen, chappen*, are others. He recalls unwitting distortions like *Nachtigohls*, indulges in deliberate, punning distortions for humorous effect (*Apollo und die neun Misen*), and remains fond of exhibiting his own faults and weaknesses by means of Jewish jokes. Heinrich Börnstein recalls in his memoirs that the poet glossed his own fondness for speculating in stocks and shares, and his consequent losses, in the following manner.

I can still see him before me, as he met me in the evening of that unhappy day [a crisis of confidence which sent the value of shares tumbling in 1847]. When I asked him whether he had lost some money, he answered: '*Some* money? A lot! But it serves me right. Rabbi ben Shloime in Prague knew what he was talking about.' 'What do you mean?' I asked, quite nonplussed. 'Well, you see', Heine answered, 'that's an old story which I heard when I was a boy, and which suddenly came to me again today. The rabbi is crossing the Moldau Bridge when an old Jewish woman rushes up to him and wails: "*Gott über die Welt! Gott über die Welt*: Help, *Rabbileben!* What a misfortune!" "What misfortune?" asks the rabbi. "My son, Itzig, has broken his leg!" "How come he has broken his leg?" "He climbed up a ladder and wanted . . ." "What?" the rabbi interrupts her. "He climbed up a ladder? It serves him right, then: what business has a Jew to climb up a ladder?" Now do you see', Heine concluded; 'that's exactly what happened to me. What business has a poet to play the Stock Exchange?'[14]

His continuing fondness for homely Jewish expressions, and for wry Jewish jokes, were ties that bound him to the Jewish community at least as strongly as the culinary Judaism, his fondness for *Schalet* and certain fish dishes which he so often praised in private and in public.

Philibert Audebrand, who met Heine in the late 1830s, soon noticed how much pleasure he took in writing about Jews; he thought it strange, however, that Heine, whose own Jewishness seemed to Audebrand never for a moment in doubt, said as many unfavourable things about Jews as favourable ones. When he was tackled about this, Audebrand reports, Heine would show himself full of admiration for the Jews and their ability to survive against all odds: what other important group had outlasted the destruction of the ancient world by two thousand years? But then, suddenly, he would fall into the satiric vein, and would quip that the Jews were a 'cursed brood that had conceived the idea of selling mankind spectacles through which it saw worse than before . . .'[15]

One other curious and significant fact deserves to be chronicled in our context. In the mid 1840s, in what seems to have been Heine's most socialist and 'godless' period, he became a Freemason, as his father had done before him. He advanced from the lowest rung of *louvton* in 1844 to the next rung of *compagnon* in 1847. Marcel Thomas, who has unearthed the relevant documents, has also asked the relevant questions:

Entre sa période socialiste et athée, et ce 'retour dans la région des croyances les plus banales', dont parlera Heine lui-même en janvier 1849, l'initiation maçonnique constitua-t-elle une nécessaire passerelle, ou ne fut-elle qu'un bref crochet, au cours de sa route? Convient-il d'y attacher de l'importance, ou ne faut-il y voir qu'une simple manifestation de curiosité, sinon même d'opportunisme?[16]

Such questions cannot be answered with authority unless further information comes to light. Nevertheless Heine's affiliation with Parisian Freemasons may serve to suggest his continuing identification with his father, even long after that father's death. It may also help to strengthen our conviction that Heine never had an atheistic, materialistic phase; that he sought for substitute religions long before his postulation of a personal God, a God akin to Jehovah, in his final years. We know that Saint-Simonism served him as such a substitute, as a secularized religion, for a short time—and we may well suspect that his involvement with Freemasonry is capable of explanation along similar lines. But Masonic ritual ceased to be of use to him when paralysis cast him into what he was to call his mattress crypt: when the *flâneur* was irrevocably confined to a single sick-room; when memories and fantasies had to take the place of experiences he had so eagerly sought in the streets, and the places of public resort, of Hamburg, or Berlin, or London, or Paris.

PART IV
View from a Mattress Crypt

CHAPTER 11
Faibisch Apollo

(i)

In 1848 Heine's health, long precarious, broke down irreversibly; half blind, paralysed, racked by cramps, he was from then on confined to his room for the rest of his life. The agony he suffered brought about an experimental return to a personal God, conceived in the likeness of the Jehovah of the Bible, to whom he could pray and complain, at whom he could rail, and of whom he could speak with humorous or witty irreverence. The postulation of such a God did not, in the poet's case, imply the acceptance of any given set of religious dogmas. It was accompanied by the adoption and projection of the new persona unveiled in the *Augsburg Gazette* in April 1849.

I am no longer a divine biped, nor am I 'the freest German after Goethe', as Ruge once called me in healthier days; nor am I the Great Pagan No. 2 who was likened to Dionysus wreathed in vine leaves while my colleague Goethe, the Great Pagan No. 1, was given the title 'Jupiter of the Grand Duchy of Weimar'; nor am I a well-fleshed Hellene who enjoys his life and smiles down on melancholy Nazarenes—all I am now is a poor Jew sick unto death, an emaciated image of wretchedness, an unhappy man.[1]

No reader of this book so far is likely to accept without heavy qualification the 'free', 'pagan', 'Hellenic' persona of the earlier Heine; nor is it possible to overlook the fact that this new identity is presented as a reduction, as a defeat. *Ich bin jetzt nur ein armer todkranker Jude* . . . The persona of the 'poor Jew sick unto death' obviously has an important relation to the poet's life, but our view of his art would be seriously impoverished if we allowed it to obscure the many other facets of the 'I' that appear in his last poetry and prose.

Not the least significant of these facets is that of *the German poet*, the representative of the German spirit in France; and as such Heine could clearly not contemplate going into his grave without having tried his hand at a version of the Faust legend. For a long time before his illness the image of the dance and the dancer had haunted his imagination.[2] The image took on a special ironic poignancy now that he was paralysed; and this not only animates his many incidental uses of it but also made him lend a favourable ear to suggestions from Benjamin Lumley, of the Covent Garden Opera House, that he should write a ballet scenario for the London stage. Had not *Giselle*, one of the most popular ballets of the day, been based on Heine's retelling of a Germanic legend?[3] Heine therefore cast his treatment of the Faust legend, *Der Doktor Faust*, in the form of a scenario accompanied by a long interpretative essay. Readers of his earlier writings will not have found it surprising that his Mephistopheles should turn out to be a Mephistophela, a female devil, and that the visions this diabolic temptress helps Faust conjure up should include Jews of modern times side by side with their biblical ancestors, among whom the dancing King David is understandably prominent.

The Ark of the Covenant stands on a cart drawn by Levites; King David dances before it, farcically gay and gaudily dressed, like the kings in a deck of cards. Behind the sacred ark the king's bodyguard jump and waddle along, dressed like Polish Jews in long kaftans, with high fur hats on their wagging heads adorned with pointed beards. After these caricatures have made their round, they vanish into the ground to loud applause.[4]

Amateurs of modern stage-dancing must dismiss from their minds the athletic, bearded, kaftaned and hatted chorus-line of *Fiddler on the Roof*. Heine's caricatures—his use of this word in the last sentence I have just cited will not have gone unnoticed—are grotesque, not only in appearance (the gaudy David, a playing-card sprung to life, and the modern Jews with their *pointed* beards) but also in movement. The stereotype of the 'ungraceful' Jew occurs so frequently in Heine's writings that most readers will suspect him of some sympathy with Atta Troll's views on the wisdom of preventing Jews from dancing in public. The biblical Bathsheba too, we remember, did not regard David's dancing as an edifying or dignified spectacle.

The elaborate commentary the poet added to his scenario contains a reference which many contemporaries must have thought puzzling, and which in fact contained a veiled threat directed at one of Heine's acquaintances. He tells us that he is engaged in composing a memoir of 'the excellent and honourable tape-worm-doctor Calmonius', of whom he speaks, later on, as 'Calmonius junior' in order to remind his readers of an earlier Calmonius. This latter worthy, he tells us,

lived in the middle of the last century, and he was also, probably, a great braggart and liar. He boasted, for instance, that he enjoyed the intimate friendship of Frederick the Great, and he often claimed that the king once marched past his house with his whole army and called up to him: 'Good-bye, Calmonius; I'm off to the Seven Years' War, and hope to see you, safe and sound, when I get back!'[5]

'Calmonius junior', as we know from Heine's letters, is Ferdinand Friedland, to whom the poet is giving public notice, in *Der Doktor Faust,* that he had better make good the losses the poet had sustained when the *Iris* gas company failed or face the possibility of being pilloried in his writings. Heine's family knew what it was about when it tried to use such financial hold as it had on the poet to prevent the appearance of unflattering portrayals in his works! Caricature, the satirical portrait-sketch, was a powerful weapon in Heine's hands, and the poet never hesitated to use the threat of such portraiture against those who had him financially at a disadvantage.

(ii)

In 1851 Heine gave to the world what he called 'the third pillar of [his] lyric fame'. The first, of course, had been *The Book of Songs,* first issued in 1827; the second was *New Poems,* 1844; and the third, which must occupy us for the rest of this chapter, bears the Spanish title *Romanzero.* It is divided into three books, entitled *Histories, Lamentations,* and *Hebrew Melodies* respectively; the third of these books, as its Byronic title indicates, is dominated by Jewish themes, but the earlier sections too have their share of overt or hidden references to Jews ancient and modern.

Many of these are, once again, biblical. In *The Golden Calf*
(*Das goldne Kalb*) the incident of backsliding recounted in
Chapter 32 of Exodus serves—as so often—as a symbol for the
modern worship of money. The mad round is dominated by
'Jacob's daughters', Israelites forgetful of the chaste modesty
Heine had so often praised as a characteristic virtue of Jewish
women:

> Hochgeschürzt bis zu den Lenden
> Und sich fassend an den Händen,
> Jungfraun edelster Geschlechter
> Kreisen wie ein Wirbelwind
> Um das Rind—
> Paukenschläge und Gelächter!

> [Their dress tucked up to their hips,
> holding one another by the hand,
> virgins of the noblest lineage
> circle like a whirlwind
> round the horned beast—
> the beat of kettledrums, the roar of laughter!]

The other dominant figure is Aaron the high priest:

> Und er selbst, der Glaubenswächter,
> Tanzt im Hohenpriesterrock,
> Wie ein Bock—

> [And he himself, the guardian of the faith,
> dances, in his high priest's robes,
> like a goat . . .][6]

It is quite obvious, however, that these are not meant to be, in
any specific sense, *Jewish* portraits: biblical figures are used to
illustrate general human propensities. In the same way the
eponymous hero of the poem *King David* (*König David*) is
seen with a jaundiced eye as an archetypal tyrant—as a despot
who is afraid to strike at the most powerful of his generals, but
who on his death-bed enjoins his son to carry out the murder
he himself could not afford to commit.[7] The view of history
that confronts us in this poem is bleak indeed: the names
change, the tyrants remain. There is every reason to believe
that at the back of Heine's mind is not only royal, political

succession, but also succession in his own family, where, he thought, Uncle Salomon had passed on to his son Carl the task of bringing the poet to book and to heel. Interestingly enough, the memoirs of Alexandre Weill contain a passage which suggests that Heine was prepared to retaliate in kind: since he did not have a *son* to whom to leave the deadly charge, he left it to his acolyte Weill, from whom he exacted a solemn promise that he would reveal to posterity the dastardly way in which (so the sick poet thought) his family had treated him.[8]

When, in *Romanzero*, King Solomon emerges from out of the shadow of his royal father, he appears as the favoured child of fortune which the poet had wanted to be but never was. The very angels guard this lover and sage, at once king and man of letters—and Heine introduces them in lines that carry half-remembered snatches of a Hebrew prayer he had learnt in childhood, as well as (appropriately enough) reminiscences of the Song of Songs:

> An Salomons Lager Wache halten
> Die schwertgegürteten Engelgestalten,
> Sechstausend zur Rechten, sechstausend zur Linken . . .
>
> [Angelic figures armed with swords
> keep watch by Solomon's couch:
> six thousand to the right, six thousand to the left . . .][9]

It is characteristic of the atmosphere of these late poems that even the monarch protected by angelic hosts should be troubled by dark dreams, horrors of the night, *das nächtliche Grauen*; and that the last words of the stanza which speaks of his love for Shulamith should suggest withering and dying:

> 'Doch liebst du mich nicht, so welk ich und sterbe.'
>
> ['But if you do not love me, I must wither and die.']

Even in a poem devoted to the most enviable figure of the Hebrew Bible, the final stress falls on decline and death. Vanity of vanities—all is vanity.

In other poems Belshazzar's feast appears again as an image of doom (*Spanish Atrides*) and Salome dances before Herod, King of the Jews (*vor dem Judenkönig Herodes*) with the same

intoxicating effect that Parisian dancers of Heine's own time
exerted on Parisian admirers before they ended, inevitably, in
the gutter or the hospital (*Pomare*).[10] Two biblical figures,
however, dominate *Romanzero*. The first of these is Lazarus,
Heine's favourite new persona, the man who personifies sick-
ness and poverty, but also the man who brings news from the
realm of the dead, and the man who will be posthumously
exalted over the Diveses of this world.[11] The other, of course, is
Moses. Though Heine anticipated Freud in seeing the Jewish
religion as based on Egyptian cults, he never shared Freud's
belief that Moses was not an Israelite at all, but a noble Egyp-
tian. He shows no Freudian doubts of the biblical account of
his hero's *Hebrew* parentage:

> Einer nur, ein einz'ger Held,
> Gab uns mehr und gab uns Beßres
> Als Kolumbus, das ist jener,
> Der uns einen Gott gegeben.
>
> Sein Herr Vater, der hieß Amram,
> Seine Mutter hieß Jochebeth,
> Und er selber, Moses heißt er,
> Und er ist mein bester Heros.
>
> [There is only one hero
> who gave us something more and something better
> than Columbus—and that is the man
> who gave us a God.
>
> His father's name was Amram,
> his mother's Jochebed,
> and his own name is *Moses*—
> and he is my favourite hero.][12]

Along with other hints in Heine's published work and in his
letters this passage strongly suggests that the God to Whom he
claimed to have 'returned' is, in essential respects, the God
proclaimed by Moses as the God of Israel—the God Who
bore, as Heine suggests in one important passage still to be
examined, such an uncanny resemblance to his Hebrew
prophet.[13]

Along with remembrances of the Old Testament we find

reminiscences of Jewish ritual even before we reach the *Hebrew Melodies*. We have just seen a Hebrew evening prayer half recalled in *Salomo*; the cabbalistic formulae which ring out in *Nocturnal Journey* (*Nächtliche Fahrt*)—'*Shaddai! Shaddai! Adonai!*'—are attributes of God which can be found in any synagogue prayer book; and the moving *Memorial Celebration* (*Gedächtnisfeier*) alludes in its title to the *Yiskor* memorial service and in the body of the text to the *Kaddish*, the Hebrew prayer for the dead.

> Keine Messe wird man singen,
> Keinen Kadosch wird man sagen,
> Nichts gesagt und nichts gesungen
> Wird an meinen Sterbetagen . . .
>
> [No mass will be sung,
> no Kaddish will be said—
> nothing will be said or sung
> on anniversaries of my death . . .][14]

When Heine's lyric I appears to speak as a Christian in these poems, it does so with patent irony. One need glance only at his vision of the Last Judgement in the poem *Resurrection* (*Auferstehung*) or his address to his 'Christian brothers' in *Retrospect* (*Rückschau*) to appreciate this point.[15] The poem *Legacies* (*Vermächtnis*) begins with what is specifically described as a 'Christian' resolution—

> Nun mein Leben geht zu End,
> Mach ich auch mein Testament;
> Christlich will ich drin bedenken
> Meine Feinde mit Geschenken . . .
>
> [Now that my life is reaching its end
> I will make my last will and testament;
> in Christian fashion I shall there bequeath
> gifts to my enemies][16]

but the nature of these gifts (colics, haemorrhoids, twitching limbs, diseases of the spinal marrow)—all beautiful gifts of God, *lauter schöne Gottesgaben*—soon make the irony of the opening lines jarringly obvious. The poem ends with what (as we shall see) Heine felt to be a particularly 'Jewish' curse: that the very names of his enemies should not be remembered in the annals and the memory of mankind.

Those who held the purse-strings in the Heine family had warned the poet of the dire financial consequences any public criticism of the late Salomon Heine and his entourage would immediately bring in its train; but the man who had so often outwitted the official censors appointed by the German governments was not likely to submit tamely to this new censorship of his work. Uncle Salomon *does* appear in *Romanzero*, though not under his own name. In *The Poet Firdusi* he has been transmogrified into the Persian monarch of whom Firdusi, the greatest poet in his kindgom, is made to say:

> 'Stattlich war er, würdevoll
> Von Gestalt und von Gebärden,
> Wen'ge glichen ihm auf Erden,
> War ein König jeder Zoll.
>
> Wie die Sonn am Himmelsbogen,
> Feuerblicks, sah er mich an,
> Er, der Wahrheit stolzer Mann—
> Und er hat mich doch belogen.'
>
> [He was good-looking, full of dignity
> in figure and deportment,
> few resembled him on earth—
> he was every inch a king.
>
> Like the sun in its celestial orbit,
> with fiery glance, he looked at me—
> he was proud, a man of truth—
> yet he fobbed me off with a lie][17]

In *Spanish Atrides* (*Spanische Atriden*) Uncle Salomon, again unnamed, appears in the guise of a more literally royal family tyrant. Indeed, this horror ballad, which speaks of crimes committed by an uncle (!) against his nephews, was at one time intended to bear the title *Family Story* (*Familiengeschichte*) and to have contained two stanzas that Heine later decided (for reasons of prudence, no doubt) to leave out.

Er erzählte mir zum Beispiel,
Wie der König dem Don Gaston,
Seinem leiblich eignen Vetter,
Abhaun ließ die beiden Hände—

Einzig und allein, weil dieser
Ein Poet war und der König
Einst geträumt, der Vetter schreibe
Gegen ihn ein Spottsirvente.

[He told me, for instance,
How the king had both the hands
of Don Gaston, his own cousin,
hacked off his body—

simply and solely because the latter
was a poet, and the king
had once dreamt that his cousin was writing
a mocking poem about him.][18]

The tyrant whose crime against his *nephews* forms the main body of the ballad is here credited with a crime against his *cousin* ('seinem leiblich eignen Vetter'); Uncle Salomon merges with Cousin Carl. Other members of Salomon Heine's immediate family have lent traits to unsympathetic figures in such poems as *Bad Dreams (Böses Geträume)*, *Ancient Rose (Alte Rose)*, *Meeting Again (Wiedersehen)*, and *Imperfection (Unvollkommenheit)*—but in none of these cases is there any overt reference at all to their Jewishness.

The Rothschilds turn up, in the opening section of *Romanzero*, in a particularly light-hearted skit, whose chief target seems to have been a fashionable beauty of the day. The poem is entitled *The White Elephant (Der weiße Elefant)*. The animal which gives its name to this poem is to be cured of its love-lorn melancholy by being sent to Paris, a journey for which its master, the King of Siam, is advised to make adequate preparations:

'Vor allem aber, o König, lasse
Ihm reichlich füllen die Reisekasse,
Und gib ihm einen Kreditbrief mit
Auf Rothschild frères in der rue Lafitte.

> Ja, einen Kreditbrief von einer Million
> Dukaten etwa;—der Herr Baron
> Von Rothschild sagt von ihm alsdann:
> Der Elefant is ein braver Mann!'

['Above all, o King, you must see to it
that he travels with plenty of money on him;
and give him a letter of credit
to Rothschild frères in the rue Lafitte.

The sum mentioned in that letter of credit should be
something like a million ducats; then Baron
de Rothschild will say of him:
"That elephant is a good man!"][19]

Light-hearted, yes; but such lines as these take on a more
sinister complexion when they are read together with such
poems as *The Golden Calf*, or *The Way of the World* (*Welt-lauf*), with their cruel paraphrase of Matthew 13:12, Luke 8:
18, and Luke 19: 26.

> Hat man viel, so wird man bald
> Noch viel mehr dazubekommen.
> Wer nur wenig hat, dem wird
> Auch das Wenige genommen.
>
> Wenn du aber gar nichts hast,
> Ach, so lasse dich begraben—
> Denn ein Recht zum Leben, Lump,
> Haben nur die etwas haben.

[If one has much, one will soon
receive much more in addition.
If one has little, that little too
will be taken away.

But if you have nothing at all,
well, let them bury you—
for, you miserable scamp, the right to live
is reserved for those who have something.][20]

In the light of these and other bitter poems it becomes clear that
the method of valuation attributed to Baron Rothschild in *The
White Elephant*—the blithe assumption that *ein braver Mann*

is a man who has a lot of money—is all too common in the poet's nineteenth-century world.

In our context the most revealing poem of these opening sections of *Romanzero* is without a doubt the one which Heine entitled *The God Apollo* (*Der Apollogott*). This begins high on a mountain-top, where a young nun looks out from her convent window to watch a boat sailing by on the Rhine. The boat bears a fair youth who sings and plays the lyre, while nine women, looking (from the distance) as beautiful as marble statues, recline about him. All are dressed after the fashion of the ancient Greeks and therefore suggest Apollo and the muses. These Hellenic sighs and sounds cast a spell on the young nun, vowed to a Nazarene life, and she makes the sign of the cross to exorcize this spell.

The second section of this tripartite poem lets us hear the song the young man sings. In accents of the modern fairground, with geographical references that merge the Greek Parnassus with the Parisian Montparnasse, he claims to be the ancient god of music who feels exiled in the modern Northern world and who therefore longs to return to his Castalian spring. Here Heine makes insistent—over-insistent!—use of vowel and consonant harmonies in order to let us hear the song that so enchanted the young nun. The section sounds, however, less like a Hellenic chant appropriate to Apollo than like a vaudeville song, a *couplet* or a *Schlager*; one can almost hear the Tin Pan Alley accents of a later age. While speaking of a true nostalgia, a true feeling of loss and self-division, Heine seems to be parodying all that appeared too easy and melodious in his own poetry—all that Karl Kraus would castigate in his work and its effect on its imitators. Is it naïve of the nun to be so affected by such a song? Or can she discern the genuine vision and the genuine longings conveyed in its over-jaunty accents?

The third section abandons rhyme and adopts a more conversational tone as it shows the nun descending from her poetic mountain-top to the prosaic world below. We watch her search everywhere for the sweet singer Apollo and his nine muses—no one seems to have any news of them until at last she meets a Jewish pedlar whose speech and movement are the very opposite of classical grace and dignity. Contrast this descrip-

tion with that of Firdusi's Sultan, the glorified image of Salo-
mon Heine!

> Doch des Wegs herangetrottelt
> Kommt ein schlottrig alter Mensch,
> Fingert in der Luft, wie rechnend,
> Näselnd singt er vor sich hin.
>
> Einen schlappen Quersack trägt er,
> Auch ein klein dreieckig Hütchen;
> Und mit schmunzelnd klugen Äuglein
> Hört er an den Spruch der Nonne:
>
> [But lollopping down the road
> comes a doddery old man,
> wagging his fingers in the air, as though he were doing
>   sums,
> singing through his nose as he trots along.
>
> He carries a limp bag
> and wears a little tricornered hat;
> with smirking, clever little eyes
> he listens to what the nun has to say.][21]

This amusing sketch of a Jewish pedlar who has done good
business (for so his empty scrip proclaims) gives only the
briefest details of apparel and facial features—but every detail
tells. We see him in action and movement: his singing and his
twinkling eyes proclaim contentment, and he is clearly reckon-
ing out costs and profits on his fingers as he trots along. The
nun then addresses to him the questions she has already
addressed—in vain—to many others:

> 'Habt ihr nicht gesehn Apollo?
> Einen roten Mantel trägt er,
> Lieblich singt er, spielt die Leier,
> Und er ist mein holder Abgott.'
>
> ['Have you not seen Apollo?
> He wears a red mantle,
> he sings beautifully, he plays the lyre,
> and I worship him as my idol.']

And yes—unlike the others the little man can answer the nun's

question, though hardly in the way she expected. The reply he
gives is accompanied by another set of gestures, and the fore-
grounding of yet another facial feature, which establish the
Jewish persona even more firmly.

> Jener aber gab zur Antwort
> Während er sein Köpfchen wiegte
> Hin und her, und gar possierlich
> Zupfte an dem spitzen Bärtchen:
>
> „Ob ich ihn gesehen habe?
> Ja, ich habe ihn gesehen
> Oft genug zu Amsterdam,
> In der deutschen Synagoge.
>
> Denn er war Vorsänger dorten,
> Und da hieß er Rabbi Faibisch,
> Was auf hochdeutsch heißt Apollo—
> Doch mein Abgott ist er nicht.
>
> [He, however, answered,
> wagging his little head
> to and fro, and pulling quaintly
> at his pointed little beard:
>
> 'Have I seen him?
> Sure I've seen him,
> often enough, in Amsterdam,
> in the German synagogue.
>
> He was the cantor there;
> his name was Rabbi Faibisch,
> and that's "Apollo" in High German—
> but I can't say that I worship him!'].

So there we have it: '*Phoebus* Apollo' is 'really' *Faibisch* the
cantor; and the pedlar now proceeds to tell us about his red
coat ('I know that coat—it's genuine scarlet cloth and cost four
florin per yard; it isn't all paid for yet!') and about Faibisch's
family:

> Seinen Vater Moses Jitscher
> Kenn ich gut. Vorhautabschneider
> Ist er bei den Portugiesen.
> Er beschnitt auch Souveräne.

Seine Mutter ist Kusíne
Meines Schwagers, und sie handelt
auf der Gracht mit sauern Gurken
und mit abgelebten Hosen.

Haben kein Pläsier am Sohne.
Dieser spielt sehr gut die Leier,
Aber leider noch viel besser
Spielt er oft Tarock und L'hombre.

Auch ein Freigeist ist er, aß
Schweinefleisch, verlor sein Amt,
Und er zog herum im Lande
Mit geschminkten Komödianten . . .'

[His father, Moishe the Mohel,
I know very well. He clipped off foreskins
For the Portuguese community;
He clipped sovereigns too.

His mother is a cousin
of my brother-in-law; she sells
sour gherkins in the market
as well as trousers that have had their day.

They had no pleasure from their son,
who played the lyre very well,
but unfortunately he played
Tarot and L'Hombre even better.

He's a free-thinker too; he ate
pork, lost his job,
and he went about the country
with painted actors . . .']

Into these four stanzas Heine concentrates a denser Jewish
atmosphere than any to be found in his earlier poems. They
show us the two communities, the Ashkenazis (*in der deut-
schen Synagoge*) served by Rabbi Faibisch, and the Sephardis
(*bei den Portugiesen*) served by Faibisch's father. We meet
important functionaries in the life of both communities: the
man who circumcizes male children, and the cantor who leads

the synagogue community in its prayers. The former was occasionally called in, or boasted that he had been called in, by non-Jewish parents in the highest reaches of society: that is one possible meaning of *er beschnitt auch Souveräne*. But if 'sovereigns' in this phrase is taken to refer to coins rather than top people, we are reminded that money-changing was an occupation followed by many Jews, and that the clipping of gold and silver coins was one way of making that occupation more profitable. Going still further down the social scale we meet the Jewish market woman trading in the humblest food-stuffs (sour gherkins) and also dealing—like so many of her co-religionists—in cast-off clothes. We are shown something of the intricate family relationships, the *mishpokhe* intercon-nections ('his mother is a cousin of my brother-in-law'), to which Jews like to refer. We hear demotic Jewish talk, not only in the pedlar's speech rhythms accompanied by expressive gestures of head and hand, but also in his vocabulary: *yitsher* [= Jewisher] is a popular Yiddish equivalent of the Hebrew *mohel*, the man who carries out the ritual circumcision deman-ded by Mosaic law. While all this is going on, we can also watch a process of change that leads to a conflict of generations: the pious father has seen his son move up one stage higher in the service of the Jewish community, only to find that son losing his faith, breaking the dietary laws, and therefore unable to serve the community any longer as prayer-leader. The passion for gambling, here imputed to Faibisch, is one that has often been described as a passion to which Jews were (and are) particularly prone. Faibisch's parents may thus be seen to lose that greatest of rewards looked for by Jewish parents: *nakhes fun kinder*, the pleasure to be derived from seeing one's chil-dren turn out well. Musical and theatrical talent was wide-spread among Jews, and its exploitation became one of the ways in which Jews might move into the Gentile community: Jewish actors and singers captured Gentile audiences with increasing frequency in the course of the nineteenth century. Part of their attraction may have been their air of the exotic and 'foreign'; and this is clearly something that Phoebus/Faibisch exploits in the fairground performances that utilize what he had once learnt as a cantor:

In den Buden, auf den Märkten,
Spielte er den Pickelhering,
Holofernes, König David,
Diesen mit dem besten Beifall.

Denn des Königs eigne Lieder
Sang er in des Königs eigner
Muttersprache, tremulierend
In des Nigens alter Weise . . .

[In booths, at fairs,
he played the Merry Andrew,
Holofernes, King David—
that last part earned him most applause.

For he sang the king's own songs
in the king's own
mother tongue, with the tremulous accents
of ancient synagogue melodies . . .]

Strange discordant synthesis of Heine's old antagonisms:
'Phoebus Apollo', who had sung his hyper- or sub-Romantic
song of exile and loss in the middle section of the poem, now
chants the sacred melodies of the Hebrews! The attraction of
this figure, a life-loving Hellene as well as a Romantic amalgam
of the ancient and modern, is real—the nun perceives an aspect
of his personality that the pedlar, for all his detailed knowledge
of the ex-cantor's background, is unable to appreciate; but
what we end up with, what the poem comes to rest on, is the
pedlar's vision, the perception of 'Faibisch's' humble Jewish
origins and later dissolute life. All this has a bearing on Heine's
feelings about himself and the kind of artist he was; and there
is surely something self-lacerating about the final stanzas
of this poem, which had begun on a high mountain-top over-
looking the Rhine and ends in the mire, with prostitute and
pig.

Aus dem Amsterdamer Spielhuis
Zog er jüngst etwelche Dirnen,
Und mit diesen Musen zieht er
Jetzt herum als ein Apollo.

Eine dicke is darunter,
Die vorzüglich quiekt und grünzelt;
Ob dem großen Lorbeerkopfputz
Nennt man sie die grüne Sau.

[From the Amsterdam cat-house
he enticed some whores recently,
and with these muses he now travels the world
in the guise of Apollo.

There is a fat one among these women
who is very good at squeaking and grunting;
because of the large laurel wreath on her head
she is generally known as the Green Sow.]

That Amsterdam has been chosen as the scene of Faibisch/
Phoebus's more prosaic activities is no accident, Holland al-
ways seemed to Heine pre-eminently the land of prose.[22]
In this uncomfortable variation on his old subject of the
classical gods in exile Heine strikes up themes we shall meet
again in those *Hebrew Melodies* which bring the *Romanzero*
to a close. Prominent among these themes is the tension be-
tween exaltation and degradation in Jewish life, treated expli-
citly in *Princess Sabbath*; and the view of the poet as at once
exalted and degraded, at once god and human being marked
out by undignified misfortune, which crystallizes in *Jehuda
ben Halevy*, where Apollo will be characterized as 'the divine
shlemihl'. All this is anticipated in *The God Apollo*, which
makes us look at a Jewish artist working in Germanic-
Christian Europe from three different but significantly related
perspectives. The first of these perspectives is that of a naïvely
receptive sensibility, an unworldly auditor who sees and hears
the poet's self-presentation and falls in love with what is seen
and heard. The mistake this auditor makes is to annihilate
artistic distance, to seek the artist in the world instead of in his
work. The second perspective is that of the artist himself, as
expressed in his work: a man who feels himself exiled and
self-divided, whose body inhabits one place and time while his
imagination or his 'heart' dwells in another, who expresses
over-sweetly, in proto-Tin Pan Alley accents, his longing for
the kind of harmony and wholeness which may be imagined in

Castalia, in an idyllic classical world belied by his very voca-bulary and versification. The third perspective is that of the Jewish pedlar, who appreciates and venerates the psalms of David and the traditional melodies to which their Hebrew text is sung in synagogues and in Jewish homes, but who has no understanding of the art which has so bewitched the young nun of the opening section, and which has spoken to us so directly in the middle section that followed. The pedlar, then, knows nothing of Faibisch/Phoebus's art—but he knows all about the price of the coat that has not yet been paid for, about family connections, about the renegade's vices and weaknes-ses, about struggles to make a living. All three perspectives are 'right', they all have their justification; but it is only when they are taken together that justice is done to that complex phe-nomenon which is the ultimate subject of The God Apollo: a modern artist of Jewish origin who feels the attraction of classical Greece and it mythology, and who makes his living in the Germanic-Christian world. By coming to rest, however, on the pedlar's perspective, the worm's-eye view, Heine warns his readers that it may not be salutary to search too zealously for origins and antecedents—that it may be better to seek the artist in his work than to seek him in a world that inevitably soils him.

This warning not to enquire too curiously into origins, suggested in a Jewish setting in *The God Apollo*, is reiterated within a setting of Germanic folklore in the Romantically titled poem *Forest Solitude* (*Waldeinsamkeit*) which opens the second section of *Romanzero*. The stanzas in question deal with the mandrake, which was believed to owe its existence to the involuntary seminal discharge of a hanged man.

> Die klügsten Waldgeister sind die Alräunchen,
> Langbärtige Männlein mit kurzen Beinchen,
> Ein fingerlanges Greisengeschlecht;
> Woher sie stammen, man weiß es nicht recht.
>
> Wenn sie im Mondschein kopfüber purzeln,
> Das mahnt bedenklich an Pissewurzeln;
> Doch da sie mir nur Gutes getan,
> So geht mich nichts ihr Ursprung an.

[The cleverest of these forest-sprites are the mandrakes—
little men with long beards and short legs—
a race of old men no bigger than a finger;
where they stem from, no one quite knows.

When they turn their somersaults in the moonlight
They remind one of pissenlit-roots in a way that gives one pause;
but since they have shown me nothing but kindness
I need not concern myself with their origins.][23]

Clever little men with long beards and short legs—is it fanciful to see here another allusion to the ghetto stereotype? However that may be, an anecdote with which the later Heine liked to illustrate the distance between an artist and his origins is once again firmly set in a Jewish milieu. It concerns a figure we have met several times before in these pages: the actress Rachel Félix. Here is the version recalled by Fanny Lewald in 1849.

Suddenly he began to laugh. 'I must tell you one of my funniest stories. When I was to make Rachel's personal acquaintance, some years ago, friends dragged me miles out into the country, where her family had taken summer quarters. I arrive at long last, I am invited to sit at a table, Papa Rachel appears, then Mama Rachel, la soeur Rachel, le frère Rachel. "Where is Rachel then?" I asked. "Elle est sortie", they answered; "mais voilà toute sa famille!" At that I began to laugh as though I had gone mad. For I then remembered the anecdote of the man who goes to see a monster which was said to have been produced by crossing a carp with a rabbit. When he arrives and asks "Where is the monster?" he is told: "We have sent it to the museum; but here are the carp and the rabbit—see for yourself!"—I shall never forget my insane laughter and the way it astonished the civilized Frenchmen around me.'[24]

Readers of *The God Apollo* will not have overlooked the point that the analogy Heine here chooses for his Jewish artist figure is that of a fairground freak.

The final section of *The God Apollo* mimics the pedlar's very voice and manner. This is something Heine had been prone to do from his earliest years; it is therefore not surprising to find, among the happy memories and wishes of the Lazarus figure who speaks in some of the most memorable poems of *Roman-zero*, the following address to a friend:

> Manche polnische Geschichte,
> Die dein Lachen immer weckte,
> Wollt ich wieder dir erzählen
> In Judäas Dialekte.

> [Many a Polish story
> which you always used to laugh at
> I would tell you once more
> in the dialect of the Jews.][25]

The mocking adoption of Polish-Jewish dialect, or of that more Germanic version which Heine called *mauscheln* and located principally in Frankfurt, appears to have been something to which he remained prone ever since he translated passages from the ancient classics into Judaeo-German for the delectation of fellow pupils at Vahrenkampf's commercial academy[26]—and we have already seen, and will see again, how often in his later letters he included words current in Western Yiddish for nostalgic reasons or in order to establish a community of experience with a Jewish correspondent. The happiness and gaiety, however, which his Lazarus persona remembers as the accompaniment of youthful sallies into Jewish speech patterns, has become an all too rare commodity in *Romanzero*:

> Goldne Wünsche! Seifenblasen!
> Sie zerrinnen wie mein Leben—
> Ach, ich liege jetzt am Boden,
> Kann mich nimmermehr erheben.

> Und Ade! sie sind zerronnen,
> Goldne Wünsche, süßes Hoffen!
> Ach, zu tödlich war der Faustschlag,
> Der mich just ins Herz getroffen.

> [Golden wishes! Soap-bubbles!
> They melt away like my very life—
> alas, I now lie on the ground
> and cannot ever rise again.

Farewell! They have melted away,
these golden wishes, these sweet hopes!
It was fatal, alas, that blow of the fist
which landed straight in my heart.][27]

Thus ends the poem *Vain Desires* (*Verlorene Wünsche*) in which Heine speaks of the delight he and his friends had once taken in mocking the speech of Jews incompletely assimilated to their Gentile environment. Whose fist delivered the blow which shattered that gaiety, and whether the hand thus clenched was human or divine, the poem leaves the reader to determine for himself.

CHAPTER 12
Hebrew Melodies

(i)

The final section of *Romanzero* announces its subject, and its central preoccupation, in the title *Hebräische Melodien*—a straight translation of the title of one of Byron's collections, *Hebrew Melodies*, which the young Heine had consulted to good effect when he played his own variation on the story of Belshazzar's Feast. It opens with a deliberately un-Byronic motto which implores the reader to catch whatever enjoyment he can in this world of fleeting fortune, to let others shoot to their heart's content if he himself is safe from shots, and to build his hut in the valleys rather than on the summits. The motto thus suggests a persona very different from those to which Heine has accustomed us—very different, certainly, from the famous 'good soldier in mankind's war of liberation'.[1] It is a *Biedermeier* persona, almost, one that seeks to make a corner of good living in the chaos of the world. We cannot but notice, however, that the poem works throughout with injunction and advice (*O laß nicht* . . . 'do not let . . .', *Auch rat ich dir* . . . 'and in addition I advise you . . .'); this leaves the reader free to infer that the poet whom he knows, by now, from so many other works, is the man least likely to heed injunctions or accept advice of this kind. Indeed this very collection, *Romanzero*, contained poems like *October 1849* (*Im Oktober 1849*) which left their readers in very little doubt of the contempt the poet felt for those who retired to safety and enjoyment while their friends, who had taken up arms in a cause they too believed in, were being persecuted and killed. One need only juxtapose two lines from the motto of *Hebrew Melodies*:

> Und bist du sicher vor dem Schuß,
> So laß sie nur schießen . . .

[And if you yourself are safely out of range,
let them fire away . . .]

with the ironic opening of *October 1849*, to see the poet's scorn
of those who abdicated their responsibilities, who retreated
into philistine contentment, who abandoned the struggle to
create a juster world without being forced to do so by a dread
disease that removed them, against their will, from most of the
activities of their fellow men:

> Gelegt hat sich der starke Wind,
> Und wieder stille wird's daheime;
> Germania, das große Kind,
> Erfreut sich wieder seiner Weihnachtsbäume.

> Wir treiben jetzt Familienglück—
> Was höher lockt, das is vom Übel—
> Die Friedensschwalbe kehrt zurück,
> Die einst genistet in des Hauses Giebel.

> Gemütlich ruhen Wald und Fluß,
> Von sanftem Mondlicht übergossen;
> Nur manchmal knallt's—Ist das ein Schuß?—
> Es ist vielleicht ein Freund, den man erschossen.

> Vielleicht mit Waffen in der Hand
> Hat man den Tollkopf angetroffen,
> (Nicht jeder hat so viel Verstand
> Wie Flaccus, der so kühn davongeloffen).

[The strong wind has died away,
and things are calming down at home;
Germany, that great big child,
can enjoy its Christmas trees again.

We are now cultivating family happiness—
what tempts us to reach higher must be evil.
The swallow of peace returns,
which once nested in the eaves of our house.

Forest and river are comfortably at rest,
bathed in gentle moonlight;
only sometimes one hears a bang . . . 'Is that a shot?'
Perhaps it was a friend they have shot down.

Perhaps they found him with weapons in his hand,
this mad-brained fellow,
(not everyone has as much good sense
as Horace, who so boldly ran away).][2]

The first of the *Hebrew Melodies* proper is entitled
Princess Sabbath (*Prinzessin Sabbat*). It begins with the
Arabian Nights legend of a prince changed by a spell into a
hirsute monster: at times he regains his human, regal shape,
but then the spell takes effect again and he is changed back into
a beast.

> Einen Prinzen solchen Schicksals
> Singt mein Lied. Er ist geheißen
> Israel. Ihn hat verwandelt
> Hexenspruch in einen Hund.
>
> Hund mit hündischen Gedanken,
> Kötert er die ganze Woche
> Durch des Lebens Kot und Kehricht,
> Gassenbuben zum Gespötte.
>
> Aber jeden Freitag abend,
> In der Dämmrungstunde, plötzlich
> Weicht der Zauber, und der Hund
> Wird aufs neu ein menschlich Wesen.
>
> Mensch mit menschlichen Gefühlen
> Mit erhobnem Haupt und Herzen,
> Festlich, reinlich schier gekleidet,
> Tritt er in des Vaters Halle.
>
> [A prince who suffered this fate
> is the subject of my song. His name is
> Israel. He has been changed,
> by an eldrich spell, into a dog.
>
> As a dog, thinking doggy thoughts,
> he curs it all week long
> through the filth and rubbish of this world,
> while street-urchins mock him.

But every Friday night,
as dusk falls, suddenly
the spell is lifted, and the dog
turns, once again, into a human being.

As a man, with a man's thoughts,
Head and heart proudly uplifted,
dressed festively, cleanly and neatly,
he enters his Father's house.][3]

The distinction 'Sabbath Jew'—'workaday Jew' is one we know all too well from Karl Marx;[4] but in Heine's poem it has quite a different meaning. Marx would discount the Sabbath Jew—he is irrelevant in the way 'musical banks' are irrelevant, in Samuel Butler's *Erewhon*, when compared with banks in which actual money transactions are carried on. For Heine, however, the Sabbath Jew is the true reality, and the workaday Jew only a humiliating disguise that a malign fate has compelled him to assume.

The portrait Heine has drawn of this workaday Jew is once again that of the pedlar, who carries his pack through the land, with Gentile urchins at his heels calling out insults. He depicts him as occupied only with thoughts of scratching a living until, on Friday night, he returns home for the sabbath. It is a portrait from the outside, an unassimilated Jew partially seen by a Europeanized observer: nothing is said, for instance, of those frequent daily prayers which bound such pedlars to their God, reminded them of other, higher values in the midst of the 'filth and rubbish of this world'. 'Dog with doggy thoughts' hardly covers that! There is a tiny but characteristic distancing touch, too, in the use of the adverb *schier*; this can mean 'purely' or 'neatly', but it can also mean 'almost', so that the line which tells us that on the sabbath the Jew is dressed 'cleanly and neatly' might be read as saying that his garb is *'almost* clean': reminding us of the insanitary appearance poor Jews would so often assume in the eyes of a fastidious Westernized poet. But Heine leaves us in no doubt that within an outside that inspires Christian urchins to cruel mockery, and well-scrubbed Europeans to a pernickety shying away, there lives a princely being which can feel numinous awe as it enters the synagogue and responds sensitively to the poetry of Hebrew prayer and the

enchantment of synagogue cantillation. Such awe is suggested
in one of Heine's most hauntingly melodious stanzas which
speaks at once of the familiar-domestic, the numinous, and the
uncanny aspect of the Jewish God. The scene is the synagogue.

> Durch das Haus geheimnisvoll
> Zieht ein Wispern und ein Weben,
> Und der unsichtbare Hausherr
> Atmet schaurig in der Stille.

> [Mysteriously through the house
> drifts a whispering and a murmuring,
> and the house's invisible master
> breathes eerily in the stillness.][5]

The stanzas that follow evoke, with minor inaccuracies as
usual, the ritual encounters which the Jewish 'prince', newly
released from his spell, has with 'Princess' Sabbath, the bringer
of peace and dignity. They introduce various figures who are
concerned with this ritual. First we are shown the *Shammes*
('der Seneschall/(Vulgo Synagogendiener')')—the synagogue
verger who lights the candles before the sabbath begins and
who rushes busily hither and thither ('Springt geschäftig hin
und her') to see that everything is in order. Our gaze then
travels, with that of the verger, across the synagogue, taking in
the *Almemor*, the central dais or prayer platform, and the Ark
of the Law: and as our gaze lights on a prayer stand beside that
ark, we perceive a second figure, a synagogue functionary who
had also played an important part in *The God Apollo*.

> Vor dem Schreine, der die Thora
> Aufbewahret, und verhängt ist
> Mit der kostbar seidnen Decke,
> Die von Edelsteinen funkelt—

> Dort an seinem Betpultständer
> Steht schon der Gemeindesänger;
> Schmuckes Männchen, das sein schwarzes
> Mäntelchen kokett geachselt.

> Um die weiße Hand zu zeigen,
> Haspelt er am Halse, seltsam
> An die Schläf den Zeigefinger
> An die Kehl den Daumen drückend.

Trällert vor sich hin ganz leise,
Bis er endlich lautaufjubelnd
Seine Stimm erhebt und singt:
Lecho Daudi Likras Kalle!

[Before the shrine in which the Torah
is housed and which is covered
with a curtain of precious silk
encrusted with jewels—

there, at his prayer-stand
the cantor is already in position;
a spruce little man who wears his black gown
coquettishly across his shoulder.

To show off his white hand
he fumbles at his neck, oddly
pressing an index finger to his temple
and a thumb to his throat.

Softly he hums to himself
until at last, in loud jubilation,
he raises his voice, singing:
'Come, beloved, to meet the bride!']

Here we have a vivid portrait of a vain little man who is nevertheless an artist in his way, and whose function is as worthy of respect as the manner in which he fulfils it. With an odd gesture of finger and thumb, suggested to Heine by a passage in Schudt's *Jewish Memorabilia*, and by means of a jubilantly rising voice, the cantor introduces the work of another and greater Jewish artist: the sabbath hymn *Lekha Dodi* by Solomon Halevi Alkabets, which Heine, here as elsewhere, attributes to the earlier and more distinguished poet Yehuda Halevi. The sabbath appears, in that poem, as a bride coming to meet her bridegroom Israel. 'The quiet princess', Heine calls her, *die stille Fürstin*, and he contrasts her favourably with that biblical Queen of Sheba to whom the later Heine so often returned in thought and who now finds herself dismissed as 'an Ethiopian bluestocking, constantly straining to cut a brilliant figure by means of her *esprit*, who becomes tiresome, in the end, with her clever riddles.' Princess Sabbath is wholly different—and as Heine tries to pinpoint that difference, he launches once again into one of his frequent tributes to the chastity and modesty of Jewish women from pious households; a chastity and modesty that increases an attractiveness which can most fittingly be suggested by means of images taken from the Song of Songs.

> Sittsam birgt die stille Fürstin
> In der Haube ihre Zöpfe;
> Blickt so sanft wie die Gazelle,
> Blüht so schlank wie eine Addas . . .

> [Modestly the quiet princess conceals
> her tresses under her cap;
> her glances are soft like those of a gazelle,
> she is slender, blooming, like a myrtle . . .][6]

To conceal her hair from all but her husband was, we remember, and is, a requirement of the *eshet khayil*, the orthodox Jewish wife. She leads over from the poetic and musical delights of the synagogue to the domestic pleasures the Jewish home offers on the sabbath: smoking is forbidden, but many other delights are allowed and provided. Among these delights Heine praises with particular fervour the culinary ones—notably his favourite dish, *Schalet*, which (the poem tells us) Schiller would surely have celebrated as a 'daughter of Elysium' if only he had been fortunate enough to know it. Eating this dish transports the Jewish 'prince' into the biblical, patriarchal world which was once that of his people.

> Speist der Prinz von solcher Speise,
> Glänzt sein Auge wie verkläret.
> Und er knöpfet auf die Weste,
> Und er spricht mit sel'gem Lächeln:

> 'Hör ich nicht den Jordan rauschen?
> Sind das nicht die Brüßelbrunnen
> In dem Palmental von Beth-El,
> Wo gelagert die Kamele?

> Hör ich nicht die Herdenglöckchen?
> Sind das nicht die fetten Hämmel,
> Die vom Gileathgebirge
> Abendlich der Hirt herabtreibt?'

[When the prince tastes such food
his eyes shine, as though he were transfigured;
he unbuttons his waistcoat
and says, with a happy smile:

'Do I not hear the murmuring waters of Jordan?
Are not these the wells
in the palmy valley of Beth El,
where camels take their rest?

Do I not hear the cow-bells?
Are not these the fat wethers
whom the shepherd, in the evening,
drives down from Mount Gilead?']⁷

Through his affectionately realistic portrait of a simple Jew
after his sabbath meal—the post-prandial unbuttoning of the
waistcoat is a characteristic touch—Heine conveys something
of the ability of orthodox Jews to live in divided and distin-
guished worlds: to enjoy the delights of the table in some corner
of modern Europe while transporting themselves, in imagina-
tion, to those lands of the Bible with whose ancient inhabitants
they felt themselves in immediate rapport. But such imagina-
tive flights to a happier, bucolic, pastoral existence had to be
followed by disenchantment—or rather, in Heine's Arabian
Nights metaphor, by the renewed effect of a malignant spell.
The ceremony with which Prince and Princess, Jewish hus-
band and Jewish wife, mark this moment of renewed meta-
morphosis into a dog, this *hündische Metamorphose*, is the
ceremony of *Habdalah*, the 'separation' of the holy day of rest
from the weekday world of tribulation and toil—a ceremony
in which, as Heine correctly shows, a cup of wine, a spice box,
and a candle play a ritually prescribed part.

> Doch der schöne Tag verflittert;
> Wie mit langen Schattenbeinen
> Kommt geschritten der Verwünschung
> Böse Stund—Es seufzt der Prinz.
>
> Ist ihm doch als griffen eiskalt
> Hexenfinger in sein Herze.
> Schon durchrieseln ihn die Schauer
> Hündischer Metamorphose.

Die Prinzessin reicht dem Prinzen
Ihre güldne Nardenbüchse.
Langsam riecht er—Will sich laben
Noch einmal an Wohlgerüchen.

Es kredenzet die Prinzessin
Auch den Abschiedstrunk dem Prinzen—
Hastig trinkt er, und im Becher
Bleiben wen'ge Tropfen nur.

Er besprengt damit den Tisch,
Nimmt alsdann ein kleines Wachslicht,
Und er tunkt es in die Nässe,
Daß es knistert und erlischt.

[But the beautiful day flutters to its end;
as with long shadowy legs
the hour of the evil spell
draws nigh—the prince sighs,

He feels as though the icy-cold fingers
of a witch seized his heart.
Already he senses the shudder
of his canine metamorphosis.

The princess hands the prince
her golden spice box.
He sniffs at it slowly—desiring, once more,
to gladden his heart with sweet scents.

The princess also presents
the cup of parting to her prince.
He drinks hurriedly and in the cup
only a few drops remain.

These drops he sprinkles on the table
and then he takes up a little wax candle
which he dips into the spilt wine
so that it splutters and goes out.][8]

With these lines, with the symbol of the spluttering and finally extinguished candle of which Heine had made powerful use earlier in *Romanzero*, ends one of Heine's most beautiful

portrayals of the Jewish world of his time. It exhibits to per-
fection his ability to be at once humorously detached and
tender; to fuse caricature, realistically observed detail, alle-
gory, and symbolism into a complex whole; to show how the
poetic and the prosaic, the religiously exalted and the domestic,
the numinous, the uncanny, and the sordid, exist together in
the same world, how the sabbath Jew and the everyday
Jew are distinguishable from one another and are yet one and
the same person. Behind the poem we sense the presence
of the Talmudic conception of the *neshama yeteira*, the
'second soul' a Jew acquires on the sabbath.[9] With the help
of this pious legend Heine has found a way of expressing, in
Princess Sabbath, his sense of the poetry of Judaism, of the
spiritual and imaginative qualities of the Jewish people, of
the delights of Jewish domestic life, along with his shudder-
ing horror at a *hündische Metamorphose*, at what centuries of
oppression, persecution, and poverty had made of so many
Jews.

(ii)

The medieval poet and philosopher Yehuda Halevi (*c.*1085–
*c.*1140) makes a brief appearance in *Princess Sabbath* and
then moves on to the centre of the stage in the second and
longest poem of *Hebrew Melodies*: the fragmentary *Jehuda
ben Halevy*.[10] That poem begins with an adaptation of
two verses from Heine's favourite Hebrew text, Psalm 137,
the song of Israelite exiles in Babylon which he clearly
felt to have some special application to his own world and
fate. It then launches into one of those hallucinatory dream-
visions which characterize so many of the poems Heine
wrote in years of sickness and of pain occasionally soothed by
opium.

> „Lechzend klebe mir die Zunge
> An dem Gaumen, und es welke
> Meine rechte Hand, vergäß ich
> Jemals dein, Jerusalem—"

Wort und Weise, unaufhörlich
Schwirren sie mir heut im Kopfe,
Und mir ist als hört ich Stimmen,
Psalmodierend, Männerstimmen—

Manchmal kommen auch zum Vorschein
Bärte, schattig lange Bärte—
Traumgestalten, wer von euch
Ist Jehuda ben Halevy?

Doch sie huschen rasch vorüber;
Die Gespenster scheuen furchtsam
Der Lebend'gen plumpen Zuspruch—
Aber ihn hab ich erkannt—

Ich erkannt ihn an der bleichen
Und gedankenstolzen Stirne,
An der Augen süßer Starrheit—
Sahn mich an so schmerzlich forschend—

Doch zumeist erkannt ich ihn
An dem rätselhaften Lächeln
Jener schön gereimten Lippen,
Die man nur bei Dichtern findet.

['Let my parched tongue cleave
to the roof of my mouth, and let
my right hand wither, if ever I
forget thee, O Jerusalem!'

These words and their melody, incessantly
buzz in my head today;
I seem to hear voices
singing psalms, men's voices . . .

sometimes there appear before me
beards, shadowy, long beards—
figures of my dream: which of you
is Yehuda Halevi?

But they flit swiftly by;
ghosts shy away from
the clumsy address of the living . . .
yet I recognized him—

I knew him by his pale
proud pensive forehead,
by the gentle, concentrated look of his eyes,
which looked at me with grief and questioning—

but most of all I knew him
by the mysterious smile
of those beautiful rhyming lips
which are only found in poets.][11]

Moses Moser had often sung the Hebrew version of Psalm 137
to Heine, using the traditional cantillation; and of late the poet
had had more opportunities to hear such 'Hebrew melodies'
from the lips of Alexandre Weill. The opening of *Jehuda ben
Halevy* which I have just quoted evokes—in stylized and
distanced form—one of the processes by which visions of the
Jewish past could come to the sick poet. It begins with sensa-
tions of the sick-room (parched tongue, withered limbs) which
blend with recollections of Psalm 137—words and tune
together, heard over and over again, with almost torturing
insistence. Sensations of taste and touch merge with auditory
sensations, and out of these arise the first visual sensations:
shadowy beards, the beards of orthodox Jews. But then, char-
acteristically, Hebrew poetry, specifically invoked in the
opening stanza, merges with recollections of Greek poetry: for
the timid shades challenged by a living man recall unmistakab-
ly the *Nekiya*, the descent into the underworld, of the *Odyssey*.
Like Odysseus, the lyric I of *Jehuda ben Halevy* summons one
hero from the midst of this shadowy throng—not a warrior,
however, but a poet, described in terms which suggest that the
medieval Spanish Jew who now moves into the centre of
attention is to be seen as exemplifying the poet *per se*. Yehuda
Halevi is to show, in a specific instance, what it means to be a
great poet in this our sublunary world. He is firmly presented
as a particular man from a specific historical period; but he
stands out from the throng because he bears the mark of the
poet upon him, and shares the fate of other poets in other ages.
    First, however, Heine focuses on the historical individual.
He not only tells us specifically where and when Yehuda was
born, but he also makes sure that his own historical distance
from his hero is fully recognized.

Jahre kommen und verfließen.
Seit Jehuda ben Halevy
Ward geboren, sind verflossen
Siebenhundert funfzig Jahre—

[Years come, years flow away.
Since Yehuda Halevi
was born, seven hundred and fifty years
have flowed down the stream of time . . .][12]

We are looking, then, at the period around 1100 from the
vantage-point of the 1850s; the Middle Ages we are about to
enter are those recreated in the imagination of a nineteenth-
century poet. And what he shows us in Yehuda Halevi's educa-
tion is something of enormous importance to Heine himself:
the confluence of Hebrew culture with the great culture of a
European Golden Age, the age of the troubadours and trou-
vères, in one particular European country, the country in
which this Jewish poet was born:

Hat zuerst das Licht erblickt
Zu Toledo in Kastilien,
Und es hat der goldne Tajo
Ihm sein Wiegenlied gelullet.

[He first saw the light of day
at Toledo, in Castille,
And the golden river Tagus
soothed him with its lullaby.]

Now Heine gives us his account of the future poet's Jewish
education; and the stanzas in which he does this turn out to be
a unique paean to the aesthetic as well as the intellectual and
moral satisfactions that can be gained from traditional Judaism.
Yehuda is taught the Pentateuch, the Torah, by his strict
father; and Heine specifically tells us that this was an education
of mind and spirit, *Entwicklung seines Geistes*—and that the
book which furthered this education was a *Gottesbuch*, a book
by and about God, a book, therefore, which trained the mind
to look not only at a present earthly existence, but also to
something beyond. But more than that: there was beauty here,
beauty which inhered not only in the text itself, but in the very

letters that composed it and the traditional cantillation in which Heine imagines it recited. Here is Yehuda's father introducing his son to the sacred text, the Torah.

Diese las er mit dem Sohne
In dem Urtext, dessen schöne,
Hieroglyphisch pittoreske,
Altchaldäische Quadratschrift

Herstammt aus dem Kindesalter
Unsrer Welt, und auch deswegen
Jedem kindlichen Gemüte
So vertraut entgegenlacht.

Diesen echten alten Text
Rezitierte auch der Knabe
In der uralt hergebrachten
Singsangweise, Tropp geheißen—

Und er gurgelte gar lieblich
Jene fetten Gutturalen,
Und er schlug dabei den Triller,
Den Schalscheleth, wie ein Vogel.

[He read it with his son
in the original text, whose lovely
picturesque hieroglyphs,
that ancient square Chaldean script

Stems from the childhood
of our world, and therefore
appeals to each childlike spirit
with such familiar joy.

This uncorrupted ancient text
the boy recited
in that pristine traditional
singsong fashion which is known as *Tropp*—

and he gurgled deliciously
those fat gutturals,
and when he came to the *Shalshelet*
He trilled it like a bird.][13]

The cantillation the poet here describes is that which gave Wagner such pain when he heard it in some synagogue or other; but for Heine the gurglings and gutturals, the singsong and the occasional trills, combine into a whole that has a beauty of its own. There is nothing fulsome about Heine's tribute: he shows us what must strike the modern non-Jewish European as odd and (at first blush) unappealing; but he tries with all the beauty of sound and rhythm at his command to convey the attraction such an ancient art may still exert. He also tries to find parallels between the ancient phenomena he is re-evoking and the experience of his modern readers—parallels which juxtapose two worlds in surprising and amusing ways.

> Auch den Targum Onkelos,
> Der geschrieben ist in jenem
> Plattjudäischen Idiom,
> Das wir Aramäisch nennen
>
> Und zur Sprache der Propheten
> Sich verhalten mag etwa
> Wie das Schwäbische zum Deutschen—
> Dieses Gelbveiglein-Hebräisch
>
> Lernte gleichfalls früh der Knabe,
> Und es kam ihm solche Kenntnis
> Bald darauf sehr gut zustatten
> Bei dem Studium des Talmuds.

> [Onkelos's paraphrase of the Pentateuch
> written in that
> Low Judaic idiom
> which we call Aramaic,
>
> whose relation to
> the language of the prophets is something like
> that of Swabian to Standard German—
> this Swabian-Violet-Hebrew
>
> the boy also learnt early on;
> and such knowledge
> soon came in very useful
> when he studied the Talmud.]

Heine has now reached a subject which for many assimilated Jews of his generation acted as a red rag to a bull. The Talmud, those vast compendia of rabbinical debate, had seemed to many of those who wanted to transport Jews from their ghetto civilization into that of the European nations among whom they lived as the chief obstacle to be got out of the way. Heine, however, had formed a different view, a view derived from Zunz, from Michael Sachs, and from a good deal of casual reading and conversation. He turns his attention first to the *Halakha*, the legal debates and wrangles which mingled matters of the highest moral importance with such questions as what was to be done with an egg that had been laid on the sabbath. That there may be something numbing about such discussions of apparent trivia, Heine's narrator readily admits; but the *Halakha* does offer a training of the mind and intellect which no poet can afford to despise.

> Ja, frühzeitig hat der Vater
> Ihn geleitet zu dem Talmud,
> Und da hat er ihm erschlossen
> Die Halacha, diese große
>
> Fechterschule, wo die besten
> Dialektischen Athleten
> Babylons und Pumpedithas
> Ihre Kämpferspiele trieben.
>
> Lernen konnte hier der Knabe
> Alle Künste der Polemik;
> Seine Meisterschaft bezeugte
> Späterhin das Buch Cosari.
>
> [Yes, very early on his father
> guided him to the Talmud;
> and he opened up to him
> the Halakha, that great
>
> fencing school, where the best
> dialectic athletes
> of Babylon and Pumpeditha
> fought out their tournaments.

Here the boy was able to learn
all the arts of polemic debate;
the mastery he attained in this was later
shown by his book *Kuzari*.][14]

Alle Künste der Polemik—as we read of this part of Yehuda's education we cannot but recall how important the polemic arts were to Heine's own time, what a vital role polemic poetry, the poetry of persuasion, rebuttal, and witty ridicule, played in the art of the *Zeitgedicht*, the poem treating burning questions of the day, of which Heine had made himself such a master. A great deal of the power of *Jehuda ben Halevy* lies in the way the nineteenth and the eleventh centuries are held in focus simultaneously.

If the Halakha is the light of the sun, the orb of the intellect, then the non-legal portion of the Talmud, the Aggada, is that of the moon, orb of the imagination and the soul. To give his readers some inkling of the delights offered by the legends and stories contained in the Talmud, Heine compares the Aggada to another Babylonian wonder, the hanging gardens of Semiramis—and he describes it as a welcome refuge from the dialectic exercises of the Halakha. Our gaze is still focused on the boy Yehuda.

> der Knabe
> Floh alsdann sich zu erfrischen
> In die blühende Hagada,
>
> Wo die schönen alten Sagen,
> Engelmärchen und Legenden,
> Stille Märtyrerhistorien,
> Festgesänge, Weisheitsprüche,
>
> Auch Hyperbeln, gar possierlich,
> Alles aber glaubenskräftig,
> Glaubensglühend—Oh, das glänzte,
> Quoll und sproß so überschwenglich—
>
> Und des Knaben edles Herze
> Ward ergriffen von der wilden,
> Abenteuerlichen Süße,
> Von der wundersamen Schmerzlust

Und den fabelhaften Schauern
Jener seligen Geheimwelt,
Jener großen Offenbarung,
Die wir nennen Poesie.

[The boy
Then fled, in order to refresh himself
to the flower-garden of the Aggada,

full of beautiful old tales,
stories of angels, legends,
the history of martyrs, quietly told,
festival songs, gnomic sayings,

amusing hyperboles too—
but everything suffused with the power of faith,
with the warm glow of faith—how everything shone
and welled up and blossomed in rich abundance!

And the boy's noble heart
was captivated by the wild
adventurous sweetness,
the wondrous mingling of pain and pleasure,

and by the fabulous awe
of that blissful secret world of the soul,
that great revelation
which we call poetry.][15]

What Heine tries to convey in these insistent lines is the emotional power poetry radiates to all, as well as the power with which it inspires those who are themselves destined to become poets. This is precisely what Yehuda found in that much-maligned Talmud from which unimaginative reformers of Judaism had tried to wrest nineteenth-century Jewry away! But Heine's Yehuda also knows that poetry is a matter of technique, a craft to be learnt and practised—and that it has an important intellectual dimension which not only the aggadic but also the halakhic part of the Talmud might help him to find. Because he knew this, because he had trained his intellectual and his imaginative faculties alike, he became a master, *der Dichtkunst Meister*. And that brings us to the lines towards which this whole long section has been moving: lines which describe the poet in ideal perfection *in relation to his people.* The people in this instance is the Jewish people, a people in exile, dwellings among Gentiles.

> Auch die Kunst der Poesie,
> Heitres Wissen, holdes Können,
> Welches wir die Dichtkunst heißen,
> Tat sich auf dem Sinn des Knaben.

> Und Jehuda ben Halevy
> Ward nicht bloß ein Schriftgelehrter,
> Sondern auch der Dichtkunst Meister,
> Sondern auch ein großer Dichter.

> Ja, er ward ein großer Dichter
> Stern und Fackel seiner Zeit,
> Seines Volkes Licht und Leuchte,
> Eine wunderbare, große

> Feuersäule des Gesanges,
> Die der Schmerzenskarawane
> Israels vorangezogen
> In der Wüste des Exils.

> [The craft of poetry too
> that gay science and those graceful skills
> which we call *ars poetica*
> opened its wonders to the boy's understanding.

> And Yehuda Halevi
> became more than just a scholar:
> he became a master of the art of poetry,
> he became a great poet.

> Yes, he became a great poet:
> the star and guiding torch of his time,
> the light, the illumination, of his people—
> a marvellous great

> fiery pillar of song
> which went before Israel's
> caravan of grief and pain
> in the desert of its exile.][16]

In these great lines Heine suggests, by means of vocabulary and imagery, what kind of a poet his Yehuda had become. *Heitres Wissen* is a German equivalent of *la gaya scienza*, a phrase applied to the troubadour poetry of medieval Europe; but the fiery pillar, the desert, and the caravan of exile come from the Hebrew Bible. Yehuda united both traditions—and it was this which made him the great guide of the Jewish people as Heine presents him. He could never have arrived there by himself; he needed the traditions which Heine has so eloquently evoked; but he needed something else too, something which Heine can only describe, in terms hallowed by theology as 'the kiss of God', the 'grace' of God which 'sanctifies'. And these theological terms, which invade the final stanzas of the first section of *Jehuda ben Halevy*, have a political resonance too: for kings have traditionally been looked upon as ruling 'by the grace of god'. All these echoes are to be heard in the stanzas in which the narrator of the poem, Heine's lyric or epic I, ranges himself alongside Yehuda and proudly proclaims that though a poet learns much from the traditions of his people, though in an important sense he represents his people, he is never that people's servant. Heine's Yehuda may be a Spanish Jew of the twelfth century, but he also has marks of genius that raise him far above the multitude of any age.

> Wie im Leben, so im Dichten
> Ist das höchste Gut die Gnade—
> Wer sie hat, der kann nicht sünd'gen,
> Nicht in Versen, nicht in Prosa.
>
> Solchen Dichter von der Gnade
> Gottes nennen wir Genie:
> Unverantwortlicher König
> Des Gedankenreiches ist er.
>
> Nur dem Gotte steht er Rede,
> Nicht dem Volke—In der Kunst,
> Wie im Leben kann das Volk
> Töten uns, doch niemals richten.
>
> [As in life, so in art:
> the highest possession is Grace;
> whoever has Grace cannot sin
> in verse or in prose.

A poet by the grace
of God we call a 'genius'—
he is absolute king
in the realm of thought.

He is answerable only to God
not to the people—in art
as in life the people can
kill us, but never judge us.][17]

'Töten *uns*'—suddenly the poet-narrator ranges himself along-
side his hero. Yehuda's experience, the experience of a Jewish
poet at a particular time of Spanish history, becomes general-
ized. As the narration passes from preterite to present tense it
soars well beyond the Spanish-Jewish context, a soaring which
had been prepared by the way Heine had used concepts of,
Calvinist theories of grace and election, and terms from the
political theory of absolutism in Europe, to describe the poet's
elevation above other mortals. And characteristically enough:
at the very moment in which Heine proclaims the poet's divine
exaltation, he also suggests his martyrdom. He controls the
verse rhythms of the last stanza just quoted, a stanza which
ends Section I of *Jehuda ben Halevy*, in such a way that they
crash down on the word *töten*, 'to kill'.

The opening of the second section takes us back to the
opening of the first as Heine once again recalls Psalm 137; but it
also latches on to the end of the second section by linking the
martyrdom of poets to the martyrdom of the Jewish people.
The 'we' of Section I (töten *uns*') now becomes the 'I' of
Section II—the 'I' of a poet who feels at one with suffering
Jews and suffering poets throughout the ages.

Bei den Wassern Babels saßen
Wir und weinten, unsre Harfen
Lehnten an den Trauerweiden—
Kennst du noch das alte Lied?

Kennst du noch die alte Weise,
Die im Anfang so elegisch
Greint und sumset, wie ein Kessel,
Welcher auf dem Herde kocht?

Lange schon, jahrtausendlange
Kocht's in mir. Ein dunkles Wehe!
und die Zeit leckt meine Wunde
Wie der Hund die Schwären Hiobs.

Dank dir, Hund, für deinen Speichel—
Doch das kann nur kühlend lindern—
Heilen kann mich nur der Tod,
Aber, ach, ich bin unsterblich!

Jahre kommen und vergehen—
In dem Webstuhl läuft geschäftig
Schnurrend hin und her die Spule—
Was er webt, das weiß kein Weber.

Jahre kommen und vergehen
Menschentränen träufeln, rinnen
Auf die Erde und die Erde
Saugt sie ein mit stiller Gier—

['By the waters of Babylon
we sat down and wept, our harps
leaned against the willows'—
can you still recall that ancient song?

Can you still recall the ancient melody
which begins with an elegiac
weeping and humming, like a kettle
boiling away on the stove?

For a long time, for thousands of years,
a dark woe has boiled within me,
and Time licks my wounds
as the dog licked Job's sores.

Thank you for your spittle, dog;
but that can only cool and soothe for a while.
Only death could bring complete cure,
but, alas, I am immortal.

Years come and years pass away—
the shuttle revolves busily on the loom,
with a whirring noise—
no weaver knows what he is weaving!

Years come and years go,
the tears of men drip, flow
upon the earth, and the earth
sucks them up with silent greed . . .][18]

The Lazarus of *Lamentations* is here joined by a new persona, that of Job, and he in his turn merges with that of the psalmist who sang the song of the Babylonian exile. There are many and varied images within this passage which speaks of thousands of years of suffering—the central image, for instance, of Heine's own poem of 1844, *The Silesian Weavers*; but the predominant suggestions are unmistakably Jewish. The martyrdom of the poet, the martyrdom of the sick man, the martyrdom of the Jewish people (for the figure that laments its immortality at the end of the fourth stanza is once again the Wandering Jew, *der ewige Jude*): all these merge as Heine forgets his twelfth-century poet for a moment and speaks of the situation in which he himself is writing his poem about Yehuda. This passage culminates in an outburst of rage against the corruptions of the contemporary world—but then the splenetic vision fades and the poet turns his Pegasus back towards his eponymous hero. In what follows he uses some poetic licence: the historical Yehuda Halevi, though a great master of form, did not employ the wide variety of metres which Heine pretends to find in his work.

Ja, er ward ein großer Dichter,
Absoluter Traumweltherrscher
Mit der Geisterkönigskrone,
Ein Poet von Gottes Gnade,

Der in heiligen Sirventen,
Madrigalen und Terzinen,
Kanzonetten und Ghaselen
Ausgegossen alle Flammen

Seiner gottgeküßten Seele!
Wahrlich, ebenbürtig war
Dieser Troubadour den besten
Lautenschlägern der Provence . . .

[Yes, he became a great poet,
absolute monarch of the world of dreams,
wearing the crown of the kings of the spirit world—
a poet by the grace of God.

who, in sacred sirventes,
madrigals and *terza rima*,
canzonets and ghazels
poured out all the flames

of his God-kissed soul.
Truly, he was the peer,
this troubadour, of the best
Provençal lute-players . . .][19]

Not only the sweet singers of Provence, but also those of
Poitou, Roussillon, and Guienne, are here summoned up to
yield a standard of comparison for Yehuda's mastery of the
medieval poet's art; but his principal beloved, Heine claims,
was not the lady of the troubadours, trouvères, and minnesin-
gers.

Jene, die der Rabbi liebte,
War ein traurig armes Liebchen,
Der Zerstörung Jammerbildnis,
Und sie hieß Jerusalem.

Schon in frühen Kindestagen
War sie seine ganze Liebe;
Seine Gemüte machte beben
Schon das Wort Jerusalem.

[The lady Rabbi Yehuda loved
was sad and poor,
a melancholy image of destruction:
and her name was Jerusalem.

In the earliest days of his childhood
he already loved her with all his heart;
his soul trembled
at the very word Jerusalem.]

With complete historical justification Heine uses his portrait of
Yehuda Halevi, the singer of many Jerusalem songs, to depict

once again the Jerusalem nostalgia of the Jews, their unquenchable longing for a lost homeland. And to deepen this nostalgia he now confronts his Yehuda with a pilgrim in whom we can once again recognize the Wandering Jew; a pilgrim who tells him of the ruined, neglected, sparsely inhabited state of Jerusalem and awakens in the poet a desire to do more than *write about* Jerusalem: to *see* it with his own eyes. The last glimpse we then have of Yehuda is in Jerusalem, where he sings his celebrated songs of Zion:

> die vielberühmte Klage,
> Die gesungen wird in allen
> Weltzerstreuten Zelten Jakobs
>
> An dem neunten Tag des Monats,
> Der geheißen Ab, dem Jahrstag
> Von Jerusalems Zerstörung
> Durch den Titus Vespasianus.
>
> Ja, das ist das Zionslied,
> Das Jehuda ben Halevy
> Sterbend auf den heil'gen Trümmern
> Von Jerusalem gesungen—
>
> Barfuß und im Büßerkittel
> Saß er dorten auf dem Bruchstück
> Einer umgestürzten Säule;—
> Bis zur Brust herunterfiel
>
> Wie ein greiser Wald sein Haupthaar,
> Abenteuerlich beschattend
> Das bekümmert bleiche Antlitz
> Mit den geisterhaften Augen—
>
> Also saß er und er sang,
> Wie ein Seher aus der Vorzeit
> Anzuschaun—dem Grab entstiegen
> Schien Jeremias, der Alte—
>
> [that celebrated lament
> which is sung in all the tents of Jacob,
> dispersed over the whole world,

on the ninth day of the month
which is named Ab, the anniversary
of the destruction of Jerusalem
at the hands of Titus Vespasianus.

Yes, that is the song of Zion
which Yehuda Halevi sang
as he lay dying on the sacred ruins
of Jerusalem.

He sat there, barefoot and in penitential garb
on the broken fragment
of a fallen pillar;
down upon his breast fell

his hair, like an overgrown forest,
throwing strange shadows upon
the troubled, sad countenance
with its ghostly eyes . . .

Thus he sat and sang,
looking like a seer of olden times,
as though Jeremiah the ancient
had risen from his grave.[20]

As Job prefigured the teller of the tale, so Jeremiah, the prophet of exile and return, prefigures Yehuda newly turned from *la gaya scienza* to songs of Jerusalem. The story now takes on more and more legendary elements. We see Yehuda killed by a passing Saracen—who may, however, have been an angel in disguise, a messenger from another, heavenly Jerusalem; and the traditional legends on which Heine has drawn so far are now capped by a charmingly conceived apotheosis that is all his own:

Droben, heißt es, harrte seiner
ein Empfang, der schmeichelhaft
ganz besonders für den Dichter,
eine himmlische Sürprise.

Festlich kam das Chor der Engel
Ihm entgegen mit Musik,
Und als Hymne grüßten ihn
Seine eignen Verse, jenes

Synagogen-Hochzeitcarmen,
Jene Sabbat-Hymenaen,
Mit den jauchzend wohlbekannten
Melodien—welche Töne!

Englein bliesen auf Oboen,
Englein spielten Violine,
Andre strichen auch die Bratsche
Oder schlugen Pauk und Zimbel.

Und das sang und klang so lieblich,
Und so lieblich in den weiten
Himmelsräumen widerhallt es:
"Lecho daudi likras kalle."

[The story goes that up above
he was given a reception that is flattering
especially for a poet:
a heavenly surprise.

The angelic choir met him
with festive music;
the hymn that greeted him was
his own verse, that

wedding song of the synagogue,
that sabbath epithalamion,
set to those jubilant melodies
he knew so well. What sounds these were!

Angels blew oboes,
angels played the violin
while others sounded violas
or struck kettledrums and cymbals.

It all sounded so beautiful,
and it all echoed so beautifully through the vast
halls of heaven:
'Lekha dodi likrat kallah.']21

Alas, since Heine was mistaken in believing Yehuda Halevi to
have been the author of *Lekha dodi*, the 'heavenly surprise'
must have lost just a little of its effect.

(iii)

Heine's partly factual, partly legendary, partly individualized, partly symbolic portrait of Yehuda Halevi is interspersed with glimpses of other Jewish figures, both ancient and modern. We have already met Jeremiah lamenting the fall of Jerusalem and Job having his sores licked by dogs, as well as the mourners by the waters of Babylon whose song opens two of the poem's three sections. Nor is Yehuda Halevi the only Spanish-Jewish poet to be portrayed in the poem that bears his name. Ironically, the poet asks his French wife to leave her pursuit of frivolities and to start learning Hebrew:

> Widme ein'ge Jahre solchem
> Studium, du kannst alsdann
> Im Originale lesen
> Iben Esra und Gabirol
>
> Und versteht sich den Halevy,
> Das Triumvirat der Dichtkunst,
> Das dem Saitenspiel Davidis
> Einst entlockt die schönsten Laute.
>
> Alcharisi—der, ich wette,
> Dir nicht minder unbekannt ist,
> Ob er gleich, französ'scher Witzbold,
> Den Hariri überwitzelt
>
> Im Gebiete der Makame,
> Und ein Voltairianer war
> Schon sechshundert Jahr vor Voltair'—
> Jener Alcharisi sagte:
>
> 'Durch Gedanken glänzt Gabirol
> Und gefällt zumeist dem Denker,
> Iben Esra glänzt durch Kunst
> Und behagt weit mehr dem Künstler—
>
> Aber beider Eigenschaften
> Hat Jehuda ben Halevy,
> Und er ist ein großer Dichter
> Und ein Liebling aller Menschen.'

[Devote a few years to this
study—you will then be able
to read in the original language
Ibn Ezra and Gabirol

and, of course, Halevi himself,
that triumvirate of poetry
which in former times conjured
the loveliest sounds from David's harp.

Al-Harizi—who, I am willing to wager,
is no less unknown to you than these others,
although, with French wit, he
made jokes better even than those of Hariri

in the 'maqama' form of Arabic poetry,
and who was a Voltairean
some six hundred years before Voltaire—
well, this Al-Harizi said:

'Gabirol's strength is brilliance of thought,
and it is the thinker whom he pleases most;
Ibn Ezra's strength is brilliant art,
and he pleases the artist far more—

but the qualities of both
unite in Yehuda Halevi;
he is a great poet
and is loved of all men.']²²

This characteristically conversational passage offers three important additions to Heine's portrait of a Spanish-Jewish poet. The first of these is the estimate of another authority—the narrator of *Jehuda ben Halevy* is not alone in believing the hero of that poem to have been a supremely great practitioner of the literary arts. The second is the demonstration that Yehuda did not have to rely solely on Jewish traditions and contemporary Gentile models: that his endeavours were shared, that there were other Spanish Jews who wrote valuable verse and brought about a general flowering, a *Blütezeit*, of Hispano-Jewish literature. The third is illumination by comparison: Al-Harizi can be better understood by modern readers if they remember their Voltaire, just as earlier they had been asked to place Yehuda Halevi alongside Jaufre Rudel, who died, according to legend, at the feet of his beloved Melisande with a last love-song on his lips.

> Wunderbare Ähnlichkeit
> In dem Schicksal beider Dichter!
> Nur daß jener erst im Alter
> Seine große Wallfahrt antrat.
>
> Auch Jehuda ben Halevy
> Starb zu Füßen seiner Liebsten,
> Und sein sterbend Haupt, es ruhte
> Auf den Knien Jerusalems.
>
> [What a wondrous resemblance there is
> in the fate of these two poets!
> Except that Yehuda was already old
> When he began his great pilgrimage.
>
> Yehuda Halevi too
> died at the feet of his beloved,
> and his dying head rested
> in the lap of Jerusalem.][23]

As always when Heine suggests comparisons, we must be at least as alive to differences as to likenesses—there is, after all, some distinction to be made between Jaufre's *amor de lonh* for his *princesse lointaine*, and Yehuda's love for the lost capital of what had once been, and might yet become again, the Jewish homeland.

Towards the end of *Jehuda ben Halevy* Heine paraphrases a passage from Yehuda's account of his voyages in order to introduce the second of his triumvirate of Spanish-Jewish poets. He does this in the conversational tone that is so well adapted to the unrhymed trochaic stanza form in which the poem is written—a form derived from Spain and therefore wholly approrpiate to Heine's subject.

> Iben Esra war ein Freund
> Und ich glaube auch ein Vetter
> Des Jehuda ben Halevy,
> Der in seinem Wanderbuche

Schmerzlich klagt, wie er vergebens
In Granada aufgesucht hat
Seinen Freund, und nur den Bruder
Dorten fand, den Medikus,

Rabbi Meyer, auch ein Dichter
Und der Vater jener Schönen,
Die mit hoffnungsloser Flamme
Iben Esras Herz entzunden—

Um das Mühmchen zu vergessen
Griff er nach dem Wanderstabe,
Wie so mancher der Kollegen;
Lebte unstet, heimatlos . . .

[Ibn Ezra was a friend
and—I think—a cousin too
of Yehuda Halevi,
who, in the journal of his journeys,

laments that he failed to find
his friend at home when he called on him
in Granada; he met only Ibn Ezra's brother,
the physician, whose name was

Rabbi Meyer—he was a poet too,
and he was the father of the beautiful girl
who inflamed Ibn Ezra's heart
with such hopeless passion.

In order to forget his little cousin
he wandered far from home,
like so many of his colleagues;
he lived a roving life, without a home . . .][24]

Wie so mancher der Kollegen—Ibn Ezra's love for his cousin, his life in self-imposed exile, are clearly parallels to Heine's own experiences. Such parallels are intended to keep the nineteenth-century perspective in view, and to make the fate of a medieval poet an exemplar of the fate of poets everywhere and always.

Ibn Ezra, the poet now relates, like Yehuda Halevi, made the pilgrimage to Jerusalem—and as fact gives way to legend once more, we hear how Ibn Ezra's master, moved by the melancholy beauty of the songs in which he lamented his exile and servitude, gave him his freedom and sent him home. This could not, however, deflect his fate, the fate of all sons of Apollo:

> Dichterschicksal! Böser Unstern,
> Der die Söhne des Apollo
> Tödlich nergelt . . .

> [The fate of poets—an evil star
> which fatally troubles
> Apollo's sons . . .][25]

Fate, symbolized by a spear thrown at a guilty man only to hit an innocent one, a *shlemihl* who just happened to be in the way, always seems to strike down the best and noblest of hearts—a sad reflection which leads over to a characterization of the third member of the poetic triumvirate, Salomon Gabirol. A Jewish son of Apollo, Gabirol unites what is best in the 'Hellenic' and 'Nazarene' temperaments—and he does this in an age in which the majority of his fellow Europeans were (so the poem would have us believe) lost in spiritual darkness.

> Und die besten Herzen trifft er—
> Wie Jehuda ben Halevy,
> Traf er Moses Iben Esra
> Und er traf auch den Gabirol—

> Den Gabirol, diesen treuen
> Gottgeweihten Minnesänger,
> Diese fromme Nachtigall
> Deren Rose Gott gewesen—

> Diese Nachtigall, die zärtlich
> Ihre Liebeslieder sang
> In der Dunkelheit der gotisch
> Mittelalterlichen Nacht!

> Unerschrocken, unbekümmert
> Ob den Fratzen und Gespenstern,
> Ob dem Wust von Tod und Wahnsinn,
> Die gespukt in jener Nacht—

Sie, die Nachtigall, sie dachte
Nur an ihren göttlich Liebsten,
Dem sie ihre Liebe schluchzte,
Den ihr Lobgesang verherrlicht!—

[And this spear pierces the best of hearts.
As it hit Yehuda Halevi
so it hit Moses ibn Ezra
and it hit Gabirol too—

Gabirol, this faithful
minnesinger consecrated by God,
this pious nightingale
whose rose was God—

this nightingale which sang
her tender love-songs
in the darkness of the Gothic
medieval night!

Undaunted, untroubled
by the grotesque apparitions, the ghosts,
and all the tangled throng of death and madness
which haunted that dark night—

this nightingale thought
only of her divine beloved,
towards whom she sobbed her love,
whom she glorified by her song of praise!][26]

Gabirol, we learn, lived only thirty years—he was murdered by a Moor, a fellow poet who envied Gabirol's superior poetic prowess and fame. The fragmentary poem ends with a plainly legendary account of the discovery of the Moor's crime, and its punishment on the gallows on the very day on which Gabirol's body is worthily reinterred amid the mourning of his brethren. These mourning brethren, we surmise, are his fellow poets, his fellow Jews, and his fellow Spaniards.

The ancient and the modern worlds, seen together in *Jehuda ben Halevy* in ways already analysed, are historically bridged by a *jeu d'esprit* in which Heine's narrator pretends to trace the fate of a jewel-case, a little golden treasure chest, which Alexander the Great is said to have taken from Darius after the battle of Arbela. In this fanciful saunter through history, in which not only Darius and Alexander, but also Aristotle, Thaïs, Cleopatra, sultans and Khalifs, Moors and Catholic kings play their part, it is hardly surprising that Jewish figures should appear among the handlers, and the temporary owners, of the treasure chest and the fabulous pearls it had once contained. We can watch these pearls pass from the Spanish finance minister, who had been called a Jew by the ultramontane ravens of *Atta Troll*, to 'Baroness Salomon'—probably the wife of Salomon Rothschild. Before we do so, however, Heine has made us witness the cruelties to which Jews were subjected by the very Spaniards whose culture the great poetic triumvirate had enriched.

> Nach dem Fall der Mohrenherrschaft
> Gingen zu den Christen über
> Auch die Perlen, und gerieten
> In den Kronschatz von Kastilien.
>
> Die kathol'schen Majestäten
> Span'scher Königinnen schmückten
> Sich damit bei Hoffestpielen,
> Stiergefechten, Prozessionen,
>
> Sowie auch Autodafés,
> Wo sie auf Balkonen sitzend
> Sich erquickten am Geruche
> Von gebratnen alten Juden.
>
> Späterhin gab Mendizabel,
> Satansenkel, diese Perlen
> In Versatz, um der Finanzen
> Defizit damit zu decken.
>
> An dem Hof der Tuilerien
> Kam die Schnur zuletzt zum Vorschein,
> Und sie schimmerte am Halse
> Der Baronin Salomon.
>
> [After the end of Moorish rule
> the pearls too went over to the Christians,
> and they landed
> in the treasury of Castilian kings.

Their Most Catholic Majesties
the Queens of Spain adorned themselves
with these pearls when they attended courtly festivals,
bullfights, processions,

and also *autos-da-fé*,
where they sat on balconies
and drank in the refreshing smell
of old Jews being fried.

Afterwards Mendizábal,
Satan's grandson, pawned
these pearls, in order to cover
a deficit in the state accounts.

In the end the necklace surfaced
at the court of the Tuileries;
it shone around the neck
of Baroness Salomon.][27]

An ironic contrast is intended between the cruel treatment of
Jews in the Middle Ages—here seen, with bitter humour, from
the perspective of the queens who sanctioned it and even
enjoyed the spectacle thus furnished—and what happens in
more modern times: a minister of allegedly Jewish ancestry
runs the financial affairs of their Most Catholic Majesties while
wealthy bankers' wives, wearing the world's riches around
their necks, are ennobled and received in the Tuileries! The
mock horror which calls the supposedly Jewish Mendizábal
'Satan's grandson' reminds us of the association, in many pious
minds, between the Jew and the Devil. There is, I suppose, an
element of poetic justice in seeing the stone the builders re-
jected become the corner-stone of modern courts and govern-
ments; but the poet of *Jehuda ben Halevy* clearly detects
something incongruous in the shift of power and influence
symbolized by the progress of pearls that once adorned

Alle Notabilitäten
Dieser mondumkreisten Erde,
Thais und Kleopatra,

Isispriester, Mohrenfürsten,
Auch Hispaniens Königinnen . . .

[all the notabilities
of this moon-encircled earth:
Thais and Cleopatra,

priests of Isis, Moorish kings,
the queens of Spain too . . .]

only to land, at last, around the neck of a (highly respectable
and respected!) Rothschild baroness:

> Und zuletzt die hochverehrte
> Frau Baronin Salomon.[28]

The nineteenth century is notoriously an unheroic age.

If the story of Darius's pearls represents a Heinesque canter
through history from ancient to modern times, the mock en-
quiry into the origin of the word *schlemihl* furnishes an excuse
for a number of fanciful leaps from the Middle Ages to ancient
Greek, thence to modern, thence to biblical, thence back to
modern, thence back to medieval times. In three of the ages
covered by these leaps Jews come clearly into focus. The fate of
the Spanish-Jewish triumvirate makes Heine speculate that
poets, beginning with their ancestor Apollo, are all *Schle-
mihle*—a contraction of the biblical name Shelumiel which had
become, by virute of some complicated rabbinical exegeses of
the first chapter of Numbers, a synonym for 'simpleton' or
'unlucky bungler'.[29] The word had recently been naturalized in
Germany by Chamisso's famous tale of the man who sold his
shadow, Peter Schlemihl. When the narrator asks Chamisso
about the origins of this word, the latter confesses that he does
not know; he had learnt it from his friend Julius Hitzig, who
might have further information. This gives Heine his cue for
another high-spirited sally into satiric caricature of Jewish
adaptation to Christian society. *Hitzig* was of course as we
have already seen, descended from the *Itzig* family, whose
fortunes had been founded by one of Frederick the Great's
tax-farmers and financial advisers. The narrator of *Jehuda ben
Halevy* therefore betakes himself to Berlin:

> Alsbald nahm ich
> Eine Droschke und ich rollte
> Zu dem Kriminalrat Hitzig,
> Welcher ehmals Itzig hieß—

Als er noch ein Itzig war,
Träumte ihm, er säh geschrieben
An dem Himmel seinen Namen
Und davor den Buchstab H.

Was bedeutet dieses H?
Frug er sich—etwa Herr Itzig
Oder heil'ger Itzig? Heil'ger
Ist ein schöner Titel—aber

In Berlin nicht passend—Endlich
Grübelnsmüd nannt er sich Hitzig,
Und nur die Getreuen wußten
In dem Hitzig steckt ein Heil'ger.

'Heil'ger Hitzig!' sprach ich also,
Als ich zu ihm kam, 'Sie sollen
Mir die Etymologie
Von dem Wort Schlemihl erklären.'

Viel Umschweife nahm der Heil'ge,
Konnte sich nicht recht erinnern,
Eine Ausflucht nach der andern,
Immer christlich—Bis mir endlich,

Endlich alle Knöpfe rissen
An der Hose der Geduld,
Und ich anfing so zu fluchen,
So gottlästerlich zu fluchen,

Daß der fromme Pietist,
Leichenblaß und beineschlotternd,
Unverzüglich mir willfahrte
Und mir Folgendes erzählte:

[Speedily I took
a cab and rolled off
to see Councillor Hitzig,
whose name, once upon a time, had been Itzig.

When he was still an Itzig
he dreamt that he saw, written
on the heavens, his own name,
and before it the letter 'H'.

'What can this H mean?',
he asked himself. '*Herr* Itzig', perhaps?
Or *Holy* Itzig? *Holy*
is a beautiful title, but it's

hardly the right thing for Berlin. At last,
tired of racking his brains, he called himself Hitzig,
and only a few faithful companions knew
that *Hitzig* contained a Holy Saint.

'Holy Hitzig!' I therefore addressed him,
when I arrived at his house; 'be kind enough
to explain to me the etymology
of the word *shlemihl*.

The holy man rambled in a roundabout way,
said he couldn't quite remember,
made one excuse after another,
Christian to the last—until, in the end,

All the buttons popped
on the trousers of my patience;
and I begun to curse
with such blasphemous oaths

That this pious pietist,
pale as a corpse and shaking all over,
did what I asked without further ado,
and told me the following tale . . .][30]

What Heine here satirizes is the kind of assimilation which not
only accepts, with meek conformity, the worship and values of
some particular Christian sect or community, but also seeks to
erase its past by denying even the *knowledge* of Jewish words,
Jewish legends, and Jewish affairs gleaned in the pre-baptismal
segment of its life. The tale the narrator of *Jehuda ben Halevy*
at last prises out of the reluctant Pietist Hitzig turns out to be
the fanciful exegesis of two passages in Numbers (7:36 and
25:6–15) which suggests that an innocent man was hit by a
spear intended for a guilty one and thus perished simply
because he happened to be in the way at the wrong moment.
The unfortunate innocent, Hitzig is made to claim, echoing
Numbers 7: 36, bore the name Schlemihl ben Zuri Schaddai. (It

should be said in passing that the interpretation here put into Hitzig's mouth is quite unwarranted; Shelumiel *was* the guilty party for whom the spear was intended.)

Dieser nun, Schlemihl I.,
Ist der Ahnherr des Geschlechtes
Derer von Schlemihl. Wir stammen
Von Schlemihl ben Zuri Schadday.

Freilich keine Heldentaten
Meldet man von ihm, wir kennen
Nur den Namen und wir wissen
Daß er ein Schlemihl gewesen.

Doch geschätzet wird ein Stammbaum
Nicht ob seinen guten Früchten,
Sondern nur ob seinem Alter—
Drei Jahrtausend zählt der unsre!

Jahre kommen und vergehen—
Drei Jahrtausende verflossen,
Seit gestorben unser Ahnherr,
Herr Schlemihl ben Zuri Schaddai.

Längst is auch der Pinhas tot—
Doch sein Speer hat sich erhalten,
Und wir hören ihn beständig
Über unsre Häupter schwirren.

[This man, Schlemihl the First,
is the ancestor of the family
von Schlemihl. We are descended
From Schlemihl ben Zuri Schadday.

It must be admitted that the records show no heroic feats
performed by him—all we know
is his name and the fact
that he was a *shlemihl*.

But a family tree is valued
not because of the goodness of its fruits
but only because of its age—
and ours goes back three thousand years!

Years come and years pass away—
Three thousand years have flowed down the stream of time
Since our ancestor died,
Sir Schlemihl ben Zuri Schaddai.

Pinhas, whose spear killed him, is also dead and gone—
But his spear has been preserved,
And we hear it constantly
Whirring above our heads . . .]³¹

The family of *shlemihls* that stretches from biblical times to the
present is the family of poets—but may it not also, in one sense
at least, the sense of the innocent unfortunate caught up in the
battles of others, be that of the Jews? What is certain is that at
the root of this family tree (the biblical story fancifully embroi-
dered), in its middle (the story of three Spanish-Jewish poets),
and at its topmost point (the confrontation of Eduard Hitzig
with the narrator of *Jehuda ben Halevy*), Jewish figures are
made to appear with conspicuous and deliberate prominence.

(iv)

When the curtain rises again, for the last time in this final
section of *Romanzero*, the reader once more finds himself in
medieval Spain. Before the king, the queen, and the assembled
nobles a strange duel is to be fought out: a *Disputation* (this
word forms, in fact, the title of the poem) between Franciscan
monks and Jews, led respectively by the Capuchin friar José
and Rabbi Judah of Navarre. The subject is the merit of the two
religions represented: that of the Hebrews, with its *starrer/
Großer Eingott* ('inflexible, great, one and indivisible God') or
that of the Catholic Christians which claims allegiance to a
dreifalt'ge[r] Liebegott (threefold God of Love). The penalty
for losing the contest is acceptance of the other's faith. Heine
knows, and his readers know, that this premise is absurd—no
Christian monarch of the Middle Ages, and no medieval
churchman, would have considered forcing Christians to con-
vert to Judaism! But that is all part of the fun, like dressing
medieval Spanish Jews not only in the ritual *Arbakanfot*

(Heine calls this fringed garment *Arbekanfeß*, using a German-Jewish pronunciation as usual), but also in the skull-cap (known disrespectfully as *Schabbesdeckel* or 'sabbath tile') of nineteenth-century Jews. Fun, some of it rather sour, is what Heine's broad caricature of religious zealots has most to offer. He presents the Christian party as mortally afraid of their opponents' intellectual agility and penetration—of their notorious Jewish 'cleverness'. Friar José therefore opens the proceedings with an act of exorcism directed against 'the cursed seed of Jacob':

> Denn bei solchen Kontroversen
> Sind oft Teufelchen verborgen
> In dem Juden, die mit Scharfsinn,
> Witz und Gründen ihn versorgen.

> [For in the case of such controversies
> little devils are often hidden
> inside the Jew, to furnish him with a sharp sagacity,
> with wit, and with arguments.][32]

Despite the absurd spectacle of the Jews sharpening their circumcision knives in anticipation of their victory, despite the aspersion slyly cast on their cleanliness by attributing their refusal to be baptized to *Wasserscheu* (an antipathy to water), the Jews appear intellectually and morally superior to their Christian opponents in the first part of Heine's poem. Friar José calls them every animal name under the sun and paints the afterlife they would enjoy if they submitted to baptism in crudely sybaritic colours. Heine seems to take a masochistic delight in entering into the spirit of anti-Semitic abuse:

> Judenvolk, ihr seid Hyänen,
> Wölfe, Schakals, die in Gräbern
> Wühlen, um der Toten Leichnam'
> Blutfraßgierig aufzustöbern.

> Juden, Juden, ihr seid Säue,
> Paviane, Nashorntiere,
> Die man nennt Rhinozerosse,
> Krokodile und Vampire.

Ihr seid Raben, Eulen, Uhus,
Fledermäuse, Wiedehöpfe,
Leichenhühner, Basilisken,
Galgenvögel, Nachtgeschöpfe.

Ihr seid Vipern und Blindschleichen,
Klapperschlangen, giftge Kröten,
Ottern, Nattern—Christus wird
Eur verfluchtes Haupt zertreten.'

['You pack of Jews there—you are hyenas,
wolves, jackals that rummage through
graves, greedy for bloody food, and
dig up again the bodies of the dead.

Jews, Jews, you are pigs,
baboons, beasts with horns on their noses
that are called rhinoceroses,
crocodiles, and vampires.

You are ravens, owls of various kinds,
bats, hoopoes,
churchyard chickens, basilisks,
gallows-birds, creatures of the night.

You are vipers and blindworms,
rattlesnakes, poisonous toads,
otters, adders—Christ will
crush your cursed head with His foot!']³³

Those who know the sorry catalogue of insults hurled at the
Jews by their Christian adversaries, from St. John Chrysostom
to Luther, will not think Heine's depiction at all exaggerated.

Rabbi Judah revenges himself for these 'chamber-pots full of
insults' emptied on his head by taking a rationalistic, Voltai-
rean (!) look at Christian doctrine. Attempting to answer insult
with argument, he rejects the doctrine of the Trinity by an
appeal to mathematics, the divinity of Christ by an appeal to
divine genealogy, and the charge that the Jews are responsible
for Christ's death by an appeal to the laws of evidence. He then
follows this up with the evocation of a stern, jealous, patriar-
chal, all-powerful Jehovah:

Unser Gott ist nicht die Liebe;
Schnäbeln ist nicht seine Sache,
Denn er ist ein Donnergott
Und er ist ein Gott der Rache.

Seines Zornes Blitze treffen
Unerbittlich jeden Sünder,
Und des Vaters Schulden büßen
Oft die späten Enkelkinder.

Unser Gott, der ist lebendig
Und in seiner Himmelshalle
Existieret er drauflos
Durch die Ewigkeiten alle.

Unser Gott, und der is auch
Ein gesunder Gott, kein Mythos
Bleich und dünne wie Oblaten
Oder Schatten am Kokytos.

Unser Gott ist stark. In Händen
Trägt er Sonne, Mond, Gestirne;
Throne brechen, Völker schwinden,
Wenn er runzelt seine Stirne.

Und er ist ein großer Gott.
David singt: Ermessen ließe
Sich die Größe nicht, die Erde
Sei der Schemel seiner Füße.

Unser Gott liebt die Musik,
Saitenspiel und Festgesänge;
Doch wie Ferkelgrunzen sind
Ihm zuwider Glockenklänge.

[Our God is not Love:
He does not indulge in sloppy kissing;
He is a God of thunder
and a God of vengeance.

The lightnings of His rage inexorably
find out each sinner,
and the sins of the fathers are often visited
on the grandchildren born long afterwards.

Our God is a living God—
in His heavenly hall
He exists, on and on,
through all eternity.

Our God is also
a healthy God; He is not a myth,
wafer-pale and wafer-thin;
nor is He a shade by the banks of Cocytus.

Our God is strong. In His hands
He bears the sun, the moon, the stars;
thrones break asunder, whole peoples vanish,
if He but knits His brow.

And He is a great God.
David sings: it cannot be measured,
this greatness of God: the whole earth
is but His footstool.

Our God loves music,
the sound of the lyre and of festive song;
but like the grunting of pigs He
abhors the clanging of bells . . .][34]

The picture of God here painted by the rabbi is not unlike that
which emerges from the letters Heine wrote to various friends
and relatives after he claimed to have 'returned' to belief in
Him: until, that is, the point about the clanging of bells. From
then on the rabbi is on his own, ironically watched by a
seemingly impartial narrator—though those who remember
Princess Sabbath may feel a sneaking sympathy when Rabbi
Judah counters Friar José's sybaritic image of afterlife in the
Christian heaven with praise of a Jewish heaven in which fish
will be prepared in the traditional way:

Teils mit weißer Knoblauchbrühe,
Teils auch braun in Wein gesotten,
Mit Gewürzen und Rosinen,
Ungefähr wie Matelotten.

In der weißen Knoblauchbrühe
Schwimmen kleine Schäbchen Rettich . . .

[Partly with white garlic sauce,
partly cooked in a brown sauce made with wine,
with spices and raisins—
rather like fish ragout.

In the white garlic sauce
swim thin little slices of radish . . .][35]

The fish so prepared is no ordinary carp or bream, however—it
is Leviathan, no less, served up to pious and just Jews in the
afterlife under the motto: God's Cookery Is Best! (*Was Gott
kocht, ist gut gekocht*). Despite these absurd enticements,
however, the monks refuse to have their foreskins scalped
away and counter with another volley of insults. The Jews bear
this patiently enough, and offer in return arguments based on
the Talmud and on quotations from the seventeenth-century
rabbinical commentary known as *Tosafot Yomtov*—which
becomes *Tausves-Jontof* in Heine's transcription of an Ashke-
nazic pronunciation.[36] A more recent Ashkenazic world breaks
into the medieval Sephardic world exalted in *Jehuda ben
Halevy*. The anachronism is deliberate, of course, and part of
the fun. When the monks contemptuously reject this text,
consigning it to the devil, the rabbi at last loses his temper. A
new shrillness enters the debate: the *Tosafot Yomtov*, written
by Rabbi Yomtov Lipmann Heller, is to the rabbi and his like
indistinguishable from the word of God Himself—God must
therefore now be called upon to avenge this insult offered to
His name as He did in the days of Korah, of Sodom and
Gomorrah, and of the exodus from Egypt. It is a constant
feature of Heine's portraits and caricatures of pious Jews that
he makes them look at their own concerns in the mirror of
Jewish history—makes them seek parallels in the past which
will yield clues to God's actions in the future. The Hebrew
word for Egypt, *Mizrayim*, and the Hebrew word for hand
(*Yad*, plural *Yadayim*), lend a touch of local colour to these
rabbinical expectorations, while the terms in which the rabbi is
made to describe the exodus from Egypt reveal once again the
presence of an ironic, amused, irreverent narrator.

Treffe, Herr, die Kapuziner,
Wie du Pharaon getroffen,
Der uns nachgesetzt, als wir
Wohlbepackt davongeloffen.

Hunderttausend Ritter folgten
Diesem König von Mizrajim,
Stahlbepanzert, blanke Schwerter
In den schrecklichen Jadajim.

Gott! da hast du ausgestreckt
Deine Jad, und samt dem Heere
Ward ertränkt, wie junge Katzen,
Pharao im Roten Meere.

Treffe, Herr, die Kapuziner,
Zeige den infamen Schuften,
Daß die Blitze deines Zorns
Nicht verrauchten und verpufften.

Deines Sieges Ruhm und Preis
Will ich singen dann und sagen,
Und dabei, wie Mirjam tat
Tanzen und die Pauke schlagen.'

['Smite these Capuchins, O Lord,
As you once smote Pharaoh
who pursued us when we
ran away with well-filled packs.

A hundred thousand knights followed
this king of Egypt,
clad in steel, bearing naked swords
in their terrible hands.

O God! Then You stretched forth
Your hand, and with his army
Pharaoh was drowned, like kittens,
in the Red Sea.

Smite these Capuchins, O Lord,
show these infamous blackguards
that the lightnings of your rage
do not waste themselves in puffs of smoke.

Then I shall praise the glory of your victory
in speech and song;
and I shall emulate Miriam the while,
dancing and beating the drum.']³⁷

And so it goes on, both champions now hurling abuse at one
another, yelling, shouting, and snorting, for hour after weari-
some hour. The audience grows sweaty and restive, and at last
the king turns to his queen, the beautiful Blanche de Bourbon
who had been transplanted to the Spanish court from Paris,
and asks her opinion. Her answer, alas, ends *Hebrew Melodies*
and the poems of *Romanzero*.

> 'Welcher recht hat, weiß ich nicht—
> Doch es will mich schier bedünken,
> Daß der Rabbi und der Mönch,
> Daß sie alle beide stinken.'
>
> ['Who is in the right I do not know—
> but it seems to me . . . I think . . .
> that the rabbi and the monk . . .
> that both of them stink.']³⁸

Heine could not keep on the exalted level of some of the
portions of *Jehuda ben Halevy*; he just could not, in all hones-
ty, conclude on a high note. The structure of *Hebrew Melodies*
as a whole, from the Arabian fairy-tale of its first line to the
stinking contestants of its last, mirrors the structure of *The
God Apollo*, which had also begun in high exalted regions and
ended in the mire. In *Hebrew Melodies*, however, the mire too
had been present at the outset, when the little workaday Jew
had to be rescued from *des Lebens Kot und Kehricht*, the filth
and rubbish of this our life. Poor Heine might have exclaimed,
with *King Lear*: 'Give me an ounce of civet, good apothecary,
to sweeten my imagination!' The disturbing, unsettling way in
which *The God Apollo* and *Hebrew Melodies* end is necessary
if Heine is to remain true to the pattern of his experience.

In an article as yet unpublished when this book went to
press, Sander L. Gilman has shown how with this shift from a
medieval Sephardic to a more recent Ashkenazic world, Heine
opposed disputatious ghetto Jews to Jews capable of a more
generally acceptable manner of discussion and analysis—the

unemancipated Jew to the emancipated, 'Western' Jew whom he admired in Moses Mendelssohn and whose avatars he sought in the world of Yehuda Halevi. Gilman then links the olfactory disgust expressed by the displaced Parisian princess at the end of *Disputation* with Heine's own shrinking from 'garlic breath' in the early essay *On Poland*. What is very important to notice here, however, is how carefully Heine distances himself, at the end of the *Hebrew Melodies*, from pernicious Gentile myths about some specifically Jewish odour, the *foetor judaicus*. The monk's smell is no less offensive to the princess than that of the rabbi. 'What stinks', Gilman rightly observes, 'is their rhetoric . . . the disputatious rhetoric of . . . aggressive disputants.'[39] The stench that ends *Disputation* is thus the olfactory equivalent of the cacophony at the end of the poem *I dreamt of a summer night (Für die Mouche)*: a cacophony compounded of the cries of Pan, Moses's anathemata, and the braying of an ass.

Despite the inevitable jokes and ironies, *Princess Sabbath* and *Jehuda ben Halevy* had both been paeans to the spirit of the Jewish faith and to its high or humble adherents. Heine had therefore to redress the balance if he was not to be written off as a deathbed convert—he had to show that his tender regard for a little Jewish pedlar and the great constellation of Spanish-Jewish poets, his admiration of the synagogue service and the poetry of the Talmud, did not imply that he now subscribed to orthodox Judaism. By ending his *Hebrew Melodies* in the way he did, Heine demonstrated at once the tartness of his unsweetened imagination and the refusal of his freely-ranging intellect to be fettered by orthodoxies of *any* kind.

(v)

The end of *Hebrew Melodies* is not yet the end of *Romanzero*. Heine adds an autobiographical 'Afterword' (*Nachwort*) which tells of his confinement to a 'mattress crypt' in Paris, his revulsion from atheism, and his 'return' to a living, personal, un-pantheistic God.[40] He speaks of having made his peace with his creator, even at the expense of sacrificing some of his poems: of having returned to God like the Prodigal Son, after keeping swine with the Hegelians. He assures us that what brought him to act in this way was not so much his misery as the logic of his thinking—as well as those longings for personal immortality which all men know even if, like Heine himself, they cannot help ridiculing them. He is far, however, from forgiving his enemies—they receive many a swipe in this very *Nachwort*; and he is so far from total and irrevocable commitment that he can speak of the belief to which he claims to have returned as a 'superstition':

. . . indem ich . . . zu dem alten Aberglauben, zu einem persönlichen Gotte, zurückkehrte . . .

[. . . in returning . . . to that ancient superstition, a personal God . . .][41]

This aside occurs in the course of a passage which speaks of his rejection of all orthodox theologies; and it is so worded as to leave the reader free to surmise that the poet has here adopted the idiom of the 'enlightened and well-meaning friends' (*mancher aufgeklärte und wohlmeinende Freund*) who have tried to discount his 'return' to God—or that he is keeping his own ultimate options open. What Heine spells out explicitly and unmistakably, however, is what the structure of *Hebrew Melodies* had already implicitly said: that his postulation of God's existence in no way implied acceptance of further religious dogmas or creeds.

In the course of his demonstration of a sovereignty of mind which could ridicule belief in an afterlife even while fervently desiring it, and in order to counteract any tendencies to tearful complaint natural in so sick a man as Heine then was, the poet indulges in a hilarious exercise in Swedenborgianism, which had recently been explained to him by Immanuel Hermann von Fichte. He transports himself and his readers into a Swedenborgian afterlife in which we encounter, once again, the heroes and heroines of the Old Testament, along with Christian saints. They are not quite as we remember them, however; they have developed in unexpected yet psychologically believable ways.

Chaste Susannah had been ignominiously tripped up by the haughty presumption that her morality could withstand any and every assault; she, who had once so gloriously resisted the old men, succumbed to the temptation put in her way by young Absalom, the son of David. Lot's daughters, on the other hand, had turned very virtuous in the course of time and come to be looked on, in that other world, as models of propriety. Their old man, alas, remained addicted to the bottle.[42]

These hilarious projections of Bible figures are supplemented by caricatures of more modern butts, including one of his characteristic vignettes of baptized ex-Jews: that of

the late Baron Eckstein, who had one and the same article printed over and over again in the *Augsburg Gazette* for some twenty years, in which he ruminated for ever the sour old Jesuit cud.[43]

Heine's humour, his gift for irreverent characterization, stayed with him to the end—in sickness as in health, in Nazarene dejection as in Hellenic self-confidence, in days when he felt the hand of the living God heavy upon him as in those in which he had thought that God to be dead or dying.

(vi)

One of the main endeavours of the Society for the Culture and Science of the Jews had been, in Eduard Gans's famous phrase, 'die jüdische Welt sich selbst vorstellig zu machen'—to give the Jewish world a clear idea of itself. It would be a mistake to see Heine's *Hebrew Melodies* as a fulfilment of that programme. True, it is full of partly accurate, partly deliberately distorted, occasionally erroneous details from Jewish history, religion, and folklore, drawn from a variety of sources that range from Michael Sachs to Victor Hugo. A sprinkling of Hebrew terms—of which, as textual variants show, Heine envisaged even more than were ultimately printed[44]—makes it seem, at times, as though Jews were the ideal audience to whom the poet here addressed himself. Such a supposition, however, is no more justified than the related claim that Heine had returned to the Jewish *religion* in his final years. In *Hebrew Melodies* Heine conveyed his own problems, the problems of a nineteenth-century poet, a German liberal of Jewish birth living in France, a life-loving man struck down by a crippling disease, to the same German and European readers to whom the rest of his work had endeavoured to speak. For most of these readers the Jewish colouring of *Hebrew Melodies* would fulfil some of the functions fulfilled by the Oriental colouring of Goethe's *West-Easterly Divan*—a work Heine had unreservedly praised in *The Romantic School*.[45] Through his evocation of the Hanging Gardens of Semiramis in *Jehuda ben Halevy* and of an Arabian Nights legend in *Princess Sabbath* he links his Jewish material with other writings felt by Western readers to be equally 'exotic' while at the same time reminding them of their own world by a host of allusions to it. Heine had a more intimate knowledge of the Jewish experience than his Gentile readers and a far greater emotional commitment to it. *Hebrew Melodies* is not, as some critics have claimed, just an exercise in Oriental local colour; at the same time, however, one can only agree with Jeffrey Sammons's finding that it does not represent an unequivocal affirmation of the poet's Jewish heritage.[46] Appreciating the poetry of the Jewish religion, feeling the spiritual benefits acceptance of its tenets might bring, and respecting some of those who found it possible to subscribe to the faith it inculcates and perform the many ritual actions it demands, Heine remains sufficiently detached to direct at Jewish beliefs and practices a volley of frivolities, irreverences, and mild blasphemies which bespeak anything but a humble 'return' to the God and the people of his fathers.

We have seen how *Romanzero*, like so many of Heine's works from 1826 onwards, is suffused with biblical imagery and allusions. Even after publicly proclaiming his 'return' to theistic beliefs, however, the poet is far from regarding the Bible as sacrosanct. On the contrary: he plays on the sanctity the Bible possessed for others in order to shock them into awareness and attention by the secular uses to which he puts allusions to its characters, narrated incidents, and gnomic sayings. The Bible remains for him, as Peter Guttenhöfer has so throughly demonstrated, a source of words, phrases, and stylistic figures which coalesce into a recognizable Bible tone; of immediately recognizable incidents and character types which can be used for humorous or serious games of variation;

and of ethical precepts which even those who have no deep commitment to Judaism or Christianity may respect. It also remains for him a collection of great writings—and it is therefore only logical that Heine should treat the biblical God and His servant Moses as fellow artists whose work can be appreciated or criticized in ways the final chapters of this book will seek to document and explore.

CHAPTER 13
Moses, Nebuchadnezzar, and Job

(i)

Romanzero was followed, in 1852, by new editions of the *Book of Songs* and *Salon II*, and to these last-named works Heine added material highly relevant to our present concerns. *New Poems* now contained a poem entitled *Hoffart*—a word signifying haughtiness, ostentation, and vanity which could also punningly refer to a journey to a royal court (*Hof-fahrt*), a journey, that is, to the highest reaches of society. The heroine of this tripartite poem bears the name Countess Gudel of Gudelfeld; a name behind which the reader rightly suspects a rather humbler name, 'fat Gudel of Dreckwall Street', *die dicke Gudel vom Dreckwall*, whom Hirsch-Hyazinth had adored in *The Baths of Lucca*. The metamorphosis, the translation from ghetto to court, has been wrought by money:

> O Gräfin Gudel von Gudelfeld,
> Dir huldigt die Menschheit, denn du hast Geld!

> [O Countess Gudel of Gudelfeld,
> mankind pays you homage, for you have money!][1]

With her financial wealth the new Countess can buy a coach and four, a gilded coach which will convey her to some German court or other where she will be presented to royalty and admitted to glittering festivities. The train of her gorgeous dress will sweep up the marble stairs as the lackeys announce, loudly: *Madame la comtesse de Gudelfeld*.

The second section of the poem describes the Countess's progress through the rooms of the palace, laden with diamonds, pearls, and genuine Brussels lace, her ample white bosom swelling with pride. All is smiles, gracious nods, curtseys; the Duchess of Pavia calls her *cara mia*, the Junkers and hangers-on all want to dance with her, and the heir to the crown, renowned for his 'wit', gives a specimen of it when he calls out, in admiration:

> 'Süperbe
> Schwingt sie den Steiß, die Gudelfeld!'

> ['Superb!
> Just look at the way she swings her butt, that Gudel-
> feld!']

All this has been done by the magic of money—the ghetto seems to have been left far, far behind. In the third section of the poem, however, we are asked to imagine what would happen if the Countess suddenly lost her wealth.

> Doch, Ärmste, hast du einst kein Geld,
> Dreht dir den Rücken die ganze Welt.
> Es werden die Lakaien
> Auf deine Schleppe speien.
> Statt Bückling und Scherwenzen
> Gibt's nur Impertinenzen.
> Die cara mia bekreuzt sich,
> Und der Kronprinz ruft und schneuzt sich:
> Nach Knoblauch riecht die Gudelfeld.

> [But, poor wretch, if one day you should find yourself
>   without money,
> The whole world will turn its back on you.
> The lackeys
> will spit on your train.
> Instead of bowing and scraping
> you'll meet nothing but insolence.
> La *cara mia* will cross herself,
> and the crown prince will shout as he blows his nose:
> 'She smells of garlic, that Gudelfeld!']²

What Heine shows in this poem is the impossibility of leaving the ghetto behind. Money will buy compliments and apparent acceptance; but traditional Gentile hostility to Jews (let's spit on them; they are in league with the devil, so let's cross ourselves; let's hold our noses—they stink of garlic!) is always there, always waiting for the opportunity to reappear.

The poem about Gudel at court has a companion-piece among Heine's works which he once sent to Campe for publication but which he then withdrew again—ostensibly because of the trouble it might cause him among relatives and acquaintance at Hamburg who might recognize their own likeness. This poem is entitled *What I Overheard* (*Erlauschtes*)[3] and purports to reproduce snatches of conversation between two Hamburg Jews on the Jungfernstieg in that city. The two speakers, whose speech rhythms have been beautifully caught, are clearly differentiated from one another: one of them is a successful speculator in railway shares but naïve in his social relations with the non-Jewish world, while the other is characterized as the Talleyrand of the Jewish quarter. What they are discussing is the cash price of Christian husbands for their daughters—they speak of these potential or actual husbands as though they were commodities that can be quoted on the Stock Exchange or bargained for over the counter. As they do so, their different characters and attitudes emerge clearly while other figures flash on to the screen of our attention for a moment: different types of Christians that will marry Jewish girls (some of them are not quite Christian enough—they have cousins in the ghetto!); the pernickety daughter who is in danger of being left on the shelf—*schon ein bißchen verrostet*, a little rusty already, says one of the speakers—and now has to be bought a husband with a large dowry; the humpbacked son of 'clever Jake' (*der kluge Jekef*) who is being groomed for high office in the city of his birth and who will one day lord it in Gentile society; the brother-in-law who may be a great rogue but who also has a gift for rapid assessment of human character. What this poem shows is where Gudel von Gudelfeld came from, the sort of ambitions that fuelled her rise, ambitions that were leading, in Heine's view, to an abandonment of the old Jewish dislike of intermarriage with Christians. Such intermarriage, as he could observe within his own family, was even being sought as a means of social advancement. Heine explained his decision not to publish *What I Overheard*, as we saw, with his apprehension that it might get him into hot water with Hamburg Jews; we may suspect, however, that he had at the back of his mind the fear that ill-disposed Gentiles might use it to fuel anti-Semitic suspicions of Jewish wire-pulling and lust for the power that money can buy. The ultimately murderous 'myth of the powerful Jew' had, after all, been propagated with enormous success in Heine's own Paris by Fourier's disciple Toussenel in *Les Juifs, rois de l'époque* (1844).

What I Overheard remains one of Heine's most disturbing works. It is no accident that he makes one of the speakers in the poem compare the other to Lessing's noble *Nathan the Wise*. 'Look here upon this picture and on this', the poet seems to be saying to his readers. Look at the contrast between the characters here portrayed—characters whose outlook has been shaped by nineteenth-century capitalism—and those envisaged by the early champions of Jewish emancipation, by the eighteenth-century propagators of humane, enlightened values to which all men of good will would happily subscribe.

(ii)

Salon II, of which a new edition had also become necessary in the 1850s, contained *Towards a History of Religion and Philosophy in Germany*, with its optimistic anticipation of a "Hellenic' enjoyment of life for men and women freed from the incubus of Nazarene spiritualism. Since his confinement to the 'mattress crypt', however, Heine's views on the perfectibility of human life had radically altered. Reading *Towards a History* again in the light of his latest experiences, he decided that it contained enough insights to warrant republication, that it was too much of one piece to be revised in the spirit of the 1850s, that the unaltered text of 1835 should therefore be reissued, but that this should be accompanied by a new Preface which would spell out the doubts the poet now harboured about some of its contentions and attitudes.

Heine begins this new Preface with a re-evocation of his 'Hellenic' period: the time when, intoxicated by Hegel and the Saint-Simonians, he had thought himself a god. He in fact plays down the Saint-Simonian experience now, preferring to recall, rather, the presumptuous conclusions he and others had drawn from the close connection Hegel had posited between progression in man's consciousness of God and the progression of human *self*-consciousness. To convey this hubristic spirit and its nemesis, Heine has recourse, as so often in these latter days, to a figure from the Hebrew Bible. 'I was as haughty, as presumptuous, as King Nebuchadnezzar before his fall.' That image introduces the great change Heine had already described in the Afterword of *Romanzero*—the change that had come over him after his health had finally broken down in 1848.

How often since those days have I thought of the story of this Babylonian king, who took himself for the Good Lord Himself but who fell miserably from the summit of his pride, crawled on the ground, and ate grass (it was salad, I presume).[4]

That last parenthesis confirms again how little Heine had lost his sense of humour, how far removed he was from any self-abasing reverence. This attitude only enhances, however, the respect he professes for the literary and moral qualities of 'the splendidly grandiose Book of Daniel' and the other books of the Hebrew Bible which he finds capable of the most varied allegorical and symbolic exegesis. He bids Hegelians like Ruge, Marx, Feuerbach, and Daumer, he bids orthodox theologians like Hengstenberg, ponder the story of Nebuchadnezzar. He bids all who are under the spell of German philosophy think of the implications of the Book of Genesis, where the serpent, 'that Bluestocking without feet', summed up the whole of Hegelian philosophy some 6,000 years before Hegel, while Eve exemplified feminine psychology in a way that is as applicable in modern Paris as it ever was in the Garden of Eden.[5] He was constantly being asked, Heine tells his readers, how the change of views he had announced in the *Romanzero* postscript had come about—whether as the result of a sudden illumination, like that of St. Paul on the road to Damascus, or as the result of persuasion, as when the ass turned round to speak to Baalam.

No, you credulous souls, I never journeyed to Damascus; all I know of Damascus is that the Jews there were recently accused of eating old Capuchin monks; and perhaps I would not even know the name of this city if I had not read the Song of Songs in which King Solomon likens the nose of his beloved to a tower that looks towards Damascus. Nor did I ever see an ass—a four-footed one, that is—who spoke like a man, though I have met a multitude of men who spoke like asses every time they opened their mouth.[6]

Having thus used the figures of the Bible in his own character-
istic way, and having in the process reminded his readers of the
cruelties, indignities, and injustices inflicted in the most recent
times on those whose ancestors produced the Bible, he goes on
to praise the book itself as simple, modest, natural, unpreten-
tious, and everyday, like the sun which warms and the breast
which nourishes us; as familiar, benevolent, and beloved as the
old grandmother who reverently reads it.

It is right that it should be called Holy Writ: if you have lost your
God, you can find Him again in this book, and if you have never
known Him His divine breath will breathe upon you as you peruse
its words.[7]

And now Heine turns from the book itself to those who not
only produced but who also preserved it throughout the cen-
turies; and he begins his praise of these preservers by summon-
ing up the stereotype of the Jew as one who knows the value of
gold, silver, and jewels. There are other, greater treasures,
Heine avers, and the Jews know the value of these too.

The Jews, who know about precious things, were fully aware of what
they were doing when, during the conflagration that destroyed the
second Temple, they abandoned the sacrificial vessels of gold and
silver, the candelabra and the lamps, even the high priest's breastplate
with its huge precious stones, and saved only the Bible. This was the
true treasure the Temple contained; and, God be thanked, it did not
fall victim to the flames or to Titus Vespasianus, the evildoer who
came to such a bad end, as the rabbis relate.

The Gentile reader, we see, who may be inclined to view Titus
through the eyes of Corneille, or Racine, or Thomas Otway, or
Mozart, is being asked to adopt the Jewish perspective for a
change, and this rabbinic-Jewish perspective Heine deliberate-
ly retains until the very end of his Preface by citing what he
now calls *Meshalim*—the Book of Joshua ben Sirah, Chapter
24, verse 32 ff., in praise of the Pentateuch. The quotation is
introduced by a characterization of Ecclesiasticus which con-
stitutes a prose equivalent of that celebration of the poetic and
moral genius of pious Jews which plays so large and so impor-
tant a part in the poem *Jehuda ben Halevy*.

A Jewish priest, who lived in Jerusalem two thousand years before the burning of the second Temple, during the most glorious period of Ptolemy Philadelphus, and who was named Joshua ben Sirah ben Eliezer, has given voice in *Meshalim*, a collection of gnomic sayings, to the esteem in which his generation held the Bible. I will here cite his beautiful words. They are festive, sacerdotal, yet fresh and inspiring as though they had sprung only yesterday from the heart of a living man.[8]

Here Joshua ben Sirah joins Heine's roll of honour: a gallery of Jewish masters which includes the authors of other books of the Old Testament, the tellers of tales whose work lives on in the Aggadah portions of the Talmud, Gabirol, Yehuda Halevi, and Baruch Spinoza.

The published version of the new Preface of *Towards a History of Religion and Philosophy in Germany* fails to find room for two passages the poet had sketched out in April or May 1852. The first of these draws, once again, a favourable contrast between medieval Jews and their European surroundings, and adds picturesque, accurate details about the way in which Jews, right up to the present day, deck out the Torah scrolls from which they read prescribed passages from the Pentateuch in their synagogues.

In the great bankruptcy of the Roman world, when the Germanic hordes, the Cossacks of those days, the Northern peoples in their bearskins, the crude drunken barbarians stormed through the land, the Jews again saved first and foremost their book, their Bible, and guarded it faithfully despite all the terror and the oppression that the public madness of those days inflicted on them. Mobs raged, drunkards roared out their tavern songs, the robber-knights' war-horses whinnied, the whole romantic music of the Middle Ages—the howls of flagellants, Kyrie Eleisons, the ringing of bells, blood-curdling yells—sounded all about them; but the Jews, unconcerned by the danger that awaited them outside, threatening to overwhelm them at each moment, sat sheltered in their synagogues, comforting themselves with the delight they took in the Bible, in those sacred parchment scrolls which they wrapped carefully in ribbons of silk as though they feared the sacred book might catch cold. Over these scrolls they drew, in addition, a precious little coat of brocade, embroidered with flowers and decked out with pearls and precious stones; and on the wooden handles by means of which the scrolls were unfurled they placed a silver head-dress adorned with little bells, over which they hung a shield of gold foil. The book was thus made to resemble a person richly dressed. All this was performed with especial fervour on the day known as the Rejoicing at the Law, on which a member of the congregation is chosen Bridgegroom of the Torah and then—as the representative of all Israel—symbolically married to the Torah.[9]

The passage reveals very close familiarity with what goes on in Jewish houses of worship; and the same can be said of a sentence eliminated at an earlier stage, in which Heine describes how orthodox Jews dance around the *Almemor*, the central prayer platform, cradling Torah scrolls in their arms, when they celebrate the Feast of the Rejoicing in the Law.[10] He clearly felt that the Preface was becoming too long and encroaching to much on the *Confessions* (*Geständnisse*) he was preparing to write; but he may also have refrained from publishing the details I have just cited because they seemed to refute his earlier contention that he had never set foot in a synagogue. The other upublished passage also exhibits knowledge of Jewish lore and institutions. Seeking to describe contacts between Jews and Germans from the fifteenth century onwards, Heine adopts a stance of some distance from the Jewish protagonists—but the keynote is still admiration and approval.

Throughout the Middle Ages the Bible was the exclusive possession of the Jews, for its Latin version, the Vulgate, was hidden away by the Church and even forbidden to laymen. As for its Greek version, the Septuagint—that did not need to be forbidden or concealed, for *graeca sunt non legatur*; and Holy Scripture in its original text did not exist for Christians because they were ignorant of the Hebrew language. Only in the ghetto was the tradition of understanding the Bible kept alive; and the lice in the beard of an old Jewish trader understood more Hebrew than all the doctors and masters of Christendom. It was not until the mid-fifteenth century that some German scholars succeeded in assuaging the religious jealousies or civic worries of the rabbis and obtained lessons in biblical scholarship. Such rabbis taught them the Hebrew language, including the Chaldaean dialect in which the most ancient paraphrases of Holy Scripture, the Targumim, are written. They taught them the Aramaic and Babylonian idiom—Babylonian in more than one respect!—used by annotators and commentaors, the so-called *lingua rabbinica*; they introduced them to masoretic textual criticism; they even unlocked for them the secret lore of the Cabbalists, that interpretation by *gematria* in which combinations of numbers associated with letters of the Hebrew alphabet play a part. Here German industriousness showed its mettle once again: the pupils soon equalled their teachers' knowledge of the Bible, though they never acquired that nasal chant with which the Chosen People reads Hebrew—an accomplishment for which it is perhaps necessary to have a Chosen Nose. These studies enabled such learned men to translate the Bible into various German dialects and thus make it accessible to the generality of their compatriots, who could now compare God's word with the ordinances of the Church . . . At last there appeared the splendid Bible translation by Martin Luther, that well-known Augustinian monk; and this became the battleaxe of the Reformation and was used to smash in the teeth of the ultramontane wolf, liberating Germany a second time from the Roman yoke. The Jews, great purveyors that they always were, had furnished the weapon which accomplished this liberation, just as they had supplied the German people with other fine articles of its creed—including even its God. They were ill rewarded for their services and continued to be held down and degraded by civic oppression; except that the treatment meted out to them was now informed, not by medieval *naïveté*, but by modern pedantry, philistinism, and mercenary pettiness. But Israel can take comfort; the people of the Book, as it is called in the Orient, did have the satisfaction, at least, of seeing its beloved tome attain the highest possible honour and glory.[11]

Here Heine plays, adroitly, with the Jews' traditional role of army purveyors: a role his own father had briefly filled. But for all the marks of distance in this passage—its playfulness, its humour, its shuddering away from the insanitary appearance of Jewish pedlars—it conveys unmistakably Heine's belief that the Hebrew Bible was one of the greatest treasures of the human spirit and an inestimable gift bestowed by the Jews on an ungrateful world.

If we look at Heine's drafts, we can see him defining the ingratitude of that world even more closely. A deleted passage seeks to draw a distinction between Protestant and Catholic persecutors of the Jewish people. 'Protestants', Heine had written, 'levelled their kicks at the Jews in a pedantic, philistine, prosaic fashion, while Catholic maltreatment always had a sombre, fanatical poetry. When [after the Reformation] Israel charged a few pennies too much for the cast-off trousers it peddled, an outcry went up in German lands as though the

Anti-Christ were at the gates.'[12] Heine clearly had second thoughts about speaking of the 'poetry' inherent in persecution; and he also held back for a while his somewhat left-handed commendation of the British and Foreign Bible Society, which had ensured that the treasured book of the Jews became the whole world's property. 'We must commend the zeal of [this] Society', he had written. 'Admittedly, it consists, in the main, of hucksters and snivellers; but nevertheless it is fulfilling with great success its mission of spreading the Bible in every tongue over all the countries of this earth.'[13] There are other omissions on whose motives one can speculate: that of a draft in which Heine voices some reservations about the 'sacerdotal pride and hyperbolic colouration' he detects in some passages of Ecclesiasticus; and that of a sentence of warm praise for a book on early Jewish poetry by the German scholar Franz Delitzsch, which he thought of calling 'a masterpiece of German scholarship and intellectual profundity'.[14]

(iii)

The year 1854 saw the appearance of Heine's last major publication—a set of three volumes under the general title *Miscellaneous Writings* (*Vermischte Schriften*). The first volume of this set contained an autobiographical piece entitled *Confessions* (*Geständnisse*); a section of poems (*Gedichte 1853 und 1854*); an essay on folklore, entitled *The Gods in Exile* (*Die Götter im Exil*); and an expanded version of the obituary of Ludwig Marcus, now entitled *Ludwig Marcus Words in his Memory* (*Ludwig Marcus. Denkworte*). Volumes 2 and 3 consisted of revised and amplified versions of articles on French affairs which Heine had contributed to the *Augsburg Gazette* and other journals in the course of the 1840s and which he now called, collectively: *Lutetia. Reports on Politics, Art, and Life among the Common People* (*Lutezia. Berichte über Politik, Kunst und Volksleben*). I shall always refer to this last work as *Lutezia*, using Heine's Germanized form of the Latin name for Paris.

The importance of *Confessions* (*Geständnisse*) in German-

Jewish intellectual history has recently been underlined by Julius Carlebach. Carlebach shows in impressive detail how Heine here 'combats the hostile and arrogant conceptions of Jewish history of both Bruno Bauer and Karl Marx':

He dismissed Bauer's argument that Jews were themselves responsible for their persecution and, like Max Weber, totally rejected the Marxian thesis that the Jew is a trader because he is a Jew. With consummate skill Heine wove his arguments into the Marxian concept of class-conflict, and, by linking the persecution of Jews with the 'interests' of both the ruling and the working classes, destroyed Marx's contention that the Jews were the eager creators and representatives of a capitalist bourgeoisie . . . While thus rejecting Bauer's and Marx's version of Jewish history, Heine did not, however, reject the Marxian view that religious conflict is often only a 'fantastic reflection' of underlying social tensions—'a protest against real suffering' . . .[15]

The perceptive analyses of Heine's writings by this professional sociologist show up with salutary clarity dimensions of the poet's work that literary critics are all too apt to ignore.

Confessions is preceded by a Preface in which Heine complains, not for the first and not for the last time, of the German-speaking rogues and rascals with whom he had come into contact in Paris.

Strange! Among all the rogues that I have come to know to my cost, there was only one Frenchman; and he was a rogue born in one of those German provinces which were once snatched from the German Empire and are now being demanded back by our German patriots.[16]

Readers of Heine's letters will have no difficulty in supplying the name of the 'rogue' the poet here had in mind and thus see its relevance to our context. He is thinking of Alexandre Weill, whose Alsatian village tales he had recently accompanied with a Preface as a less painful alternative to lending Weill money, and whom he had since come to dislike and distrust. There are other satiric sketches in the Preface of *Confessions*—sketches of individual acquaintances whom again he refuses to name.

Our industrial knights of the road are not content with being just egoists out to rob other people in order to feather their own nests. No, forsooth—they must be philanthropists as well, in the very act of relieving their victims of their cash. In their free time, the time not occupied by such business activities as directing a company to supply the Bohemian forests with gaslight illumination, they patronize pianists and journalists; and under their waistcoats, resplendent with all the rainbow colours of Iris, their soul is being gnawed by the tapeworm of *Weltschmerz*.[17]

That gives us another typical verbal cartoon, in which financiers and industrial entrepreneurs appear in the guise of highwaymen— a conceit Heine had first used some thirty years before in the Stock Exchange scenes of *Letters from Berlin*. The dragging in of the name *Iris*, however, and the mention of gaslight in Bohemia, leave no doubt that the poet is once again serving notice to Ferdinand Friedland that he had better see to it that the money Heine had invested in the Prague gaslight company did not go down the drain altogether; otherwise Friedland would be in for some very undesirable publicity, in which his name would *not* be tactfully omitted. In the case of Friedland, however, as in that of Weill, Heine makes no public reference to the fact they were both Jewish—a fact he clearly regarded as irrelevant to his charges and purposes.

Such reticence is abandoned in the text of the *Confessions* themselves, where Jewish themes are explicit and ubiquitous. We need only look at the way in which Heine brings the German journalist and literary critic Wolfgang Menzel once more into the centre of his stage. Menzel, we are reminded, had begun as a supporter of Jewish emancipation, and as a good European, but had later changed his mind. This later Menzel had been dubbed *der Franzosenfresser*, 'the Francophage', by Ludwig Börne, and Heine now adopts, and gleefully elaborates, Börne's pungent description of their common enemy.

When Menzel had eaten his daily ration of six Frenchmen, he used to gulp down a Jew as well, *pour se faire la bonne bouche*, as the French say.[18]

Having thus disposed of an anti-Semite, Heine takes us on a quick gallop through successive stages in the life of a an ex-Jewess, the daughter of his revered Moses Mendelssohn who had left her Jewish husband for Friedrich Schlegel and who had converted first to Protestantism and then to Roman Catholicism: he calls her 'Schlegel's courtly consort, Dorothea, née Mendelssohn, runaway Veit'. That malicious little sketch is succeeded by the fuller portrait of a figure which had already made a fleeting appearance in the *Romanzero* postscript, Baron Ferdinand von Eckstein:

He is a German baron whom the brothers Schlegel commended as a representative of German scholarship in Paris. He was born in Altona [near Hamburg], where he belonged to one of the most respected Israelite families. His family tree, which reached as high as Abraham the son of Terah and ancestor of David, King over Judah and Israel, offered sufficient justification for calling himself a nobleman; and since he said farewell, not only to the Synagogue, but, later on, to the Protestant Church as well (formally renouncing the latter and clinging to the bosom of the Catholic Church) he had an equally good right to the title of a Catholic nobleman. In this last capacity he represented feudal and ecclesiastical interests by founding a journal in Paris which bore the words *Le Catholique* in its title. Not only in the columns of this journal, but also in the salons of pious dowagers of the Faubourg Saint-Germain, the learned nobleman spoke of Buddha, and then again of Buddha, and he proved that the dogma of the Trinity was already to be found in the Indian Trimurti. He cited the *Ramayana*, the Mahabharata, the Upanishads, Sabala the cow and King Viswamitra, Snorri's *Edda* and God knows what other fossils and mammoth bones, with the kind of antediluvian dryness and tediousness which never fails to take a Frenchman in. Since his discourses constantly returned to the subject of Buddha, and since he (perhaps) pronounced that name rather oddly, the frivolous French finally took to calling him 'Baron Buddha'. Under this name I found him when I came to Paris in 1831; and when I heard him grind out his learning with a sacerdotal, not to say synagogic, gravity he reminded me of an odd fellow in Goldsmith's *The Vicar of Wakefield* whose name, I think, was Jenkinson and who, whenever he met someone he wanted to bamboozle, cited some gobbets of Manetho, Berosus, and Sanchuniaton. Sanscrit had not yet been invented in Mr Jenkinson's time.[19]

So this, Heine would seem to be saying, is what people desert Judaism for! This is what they do with their newly acquired Christianity! This is how they actually expend their energies and their time when they manage an entry into Gentile society! Heine's portrait presents Baron Eckstein as at once rogue and fool, at once bamboozler and dupe. In the course of doing this, he applies to his victim the very same joke which the Catholic theologian Ignaz Döllinger had once made about Heine himself a quarter of a century earlier. Did he, one wonders, know where he had found this mockery of the Jewish family tree? Or had he internalized Christian jokes at the expense of Jews to such an extent that he thought of them as his own?

To put the later Heine's attacks on assimilated German and French Jews into perspective, one should remember that he was liable to make no less acid comments about their less sophisticated Polish brothers. There is a characteristic aside in one of his attacks on autodidactic socialism which deserves quotation in this context.

These self-satisfied sciolists who mistake every bit of their autodidactically acquired knowledge for a wholly new discovery which will bring happiness to all the world remind me of the Polish-Jewish boy who discovered a secret vice by experimenting on his own body, and who then offered to travel from Posen to Berlin in order to patent his invention.[20]

Back now, however, to Heine's *Confessions* and his portrayal of Jews more sophisticated and assimilated than the poor Polish boy of this anecdote. Heine focuses once again on the Berlin Beers, the family whose most illustrious member was Maestro Giacomo Meyerbeer. The Maestro himself is dismissed briefly as an anticipation of modern television personalities, well known for being well known: he is said to be 'celebrated everywhere on account of his fame and praised by the most talented journalists'.[21] But even where he is not overtly named, Meyerbeer makes his presence felt in Heine's columns. Let us look at his portrait of Giacomo's brother, Heinrich Beer, in a passage which is remarkable, not only for its caricature of its ostensible victim, but also for its portrayal of Hegel and its newly sympathetic presentation of Felix Mendelssohn-Bartholdy.

This Heinrich Beer was of such severely limited intelligence that his family declared him an imbecile in the end and put him under tutelage. Instead of using his great wealth to make a name for himself in the arts and sciences

(a side-swipe, this, not only at Maestro Giacomo but also at Michael Beer, whose plays the young Heine had praised, insincerely, in his Munich days) this Heinrich Beer wasted his riches on all sorts of nonsense—such as spending six thousand thalers on walking sticks one day. This poor fellow, who had no ambition to be regarded as a great writer of tragedies, or a great star-gazer, or a laurel-crowned musical genius rivalling Mozart and Rossini,

(Giacomo Meyerbeer and Michael Beer again! They, clearly, are as much the cynosure of Heine's attention as their brother Heinrich, whom alone he here pretends to be portraying)

but preferred, instead, to spend his money on walking-sticks—this Beer, so totally unlike the rest of his family, was admitted to Hegel's intimate company. He became Hegel's Pylades, accompanying him everywhere as though he were his shadow. Felix Mendelssohn, whose wit rivalled his musical talent, once tried to explain this phenomenon by declaring that Hegel did not understand Heinrich Beer. I now believe, however, that the secret of this intimacy is to be sought in Hegel's conviction that Heinrich Beer understood nothing at all of the things he heard him say, and that in his company he could therefore give his thoughts and utterances free rein . . .[22]

The poet then goes on to claim that he once had a conversation with Hegel, in the course of which the latter followed the logic of his ideas into dangerous regions, regions in which it was not prudent to stray if one wanted to remain the favoured philosopher of the Prussian state. Having had his say, Heine tells us, Hegel 'looked anxiously about him; but he was visibly reassured when he saw that no one was around except Heinrich Beer, who had come to ask if he would care for a game of whist.[23] It is not, of course, likely that Hegel would have had conversations of this sort with a student who occasionally attended his lectures; Heine's anecdote, like so many others, has been invented to serve his polemic and satiric purposes.

It will have been noticed that Heine here adds another touch to his developing portrait of Felix Mendelssohn-Bartholdy, whose wit is set off by the dullness attributed to Heinrich Beer. This last-named member of a family that suffered a great deal from Heine's pen, fills an important place in the poet's Jewish portrait gallery: the caricature Heine draws of him is designed to show, amongst other things, that the Jewish community did not lack its quota of harmless fools. The ubiquitous myth of universal Jewish 'cleverness' is exploded by Heine's occasional caricatures of stupid Jews. The point comes across even more forcibly in the French version ('Aveux de l'auteur') included in *De l'Allemagne* in 1855.

C'est ainsi que nous ne pouvions comprendre la grande amitié qui existait entre le profond philosophe Hégel et l'idiot Henri Beer, frère défunt de M. Giacomo Meyerbeer, le grand homme que vous savez; ils étaient inséparables, et le spirituel Félix Mendelssohn expliquait ce phénomène par la malicieuse remarque que Hégel ne comprenait pas ce M. Henri Beer.[24]

Mendelssohn's malicious wit is wholly to Heine's taste: it not only characterizes Michael Beer, but also sets off, by contrast, that worthy's alleged stupidity. The irony at the expense of Beer's more famous brother is patent and needs no further gloss.

Heinrich Beer was incapable, in Heine's view, of understanding what Hegel was about; but *Confessions* also introduces more iettectually respectable contemporaries who drew conclusions from Hegel which were, in Heine's opinion, justified by Hegel's philosophy, but which the poet himself is now at pains to reject. He does this in a characteristically biblical context—a context in which he seeks once again to draw a lesson from the fate of Nebuchadnezzar. The passage is in fact identical with that already quoted from the new Preface Heine had provided for the second edition of *Towards a History of Religion and Philosophy in Germany*; but we shall follow it a little further this time.

How often since those days have I thought of the story of this Babylonian king, who took himself for the Good Lord but who fell miserably from the summit of his pride . . . This story may be found in the grandiose Book of Daniel, which I would like to commend, not only to dear old Ruge, but also to my much more obdurate friend Karl Marx.[25]

There is irony here, of course, but no suggestion that the word 'friend' is anything but sincere. Heine repudiated Babouvian communism, and he no longer subscribed to all the ideas he had once shared with Marx; but the respect Marx had inspired in him remains almost intact, along with some, at least, of his former affection.

In accusing Marx of persistent deification of man, Heine

pointed back to the Feuerbachian bases of Marxism, to Marx's critique of religion, with which he now had little sympathy. He never denied, however, that he shared Marx's dislike of the existing order, of political tyranny by bourgeois and aristocrat, and of gross economic inequalities; and though he could not look forward with joy to the victory of the proletariat, as Marx could and did, he believed, like Marx, that the overthrow of the unjust order was likely to be accomplished by the impoverished working class. In his revision of *Ludwig Marcus* he drafted a passage in which he talked of this threat to the bourgeois world in terms that have recalled Marx's formulations to many informed commentators.[26] German censorship never allowed him to publish the passage in question; but he spoke out loud and clear in his preface to the French edition of *Lutezia, Lutèce*, where he declared his sense of justice and logic (though not his aesthetic aspirations) satisfied by the prospect of a victorious communism that would sweep away the inequities of the bourgeois order.[27]

Weill and Friedland, Dorothea Schlegel, von Eckstein, the Beer family—they all appear in *Confessions* as less than admirable figures; but they do so in the context of a veritable paean to Judaism and its great liberator and lawgiver Moses. 'What a giant!', Heine exclaims:

I cannot imagine Moses out-topped even by Og, King of Bashan. How small Sinai appears when Moses stands on it! The mountain is only a pediment for the feet of the man whose head reaches high into the heavens as he speaks with his God. May the Lord forgive me this sin, but it sometimes seems to me as though this God were only a reflection of Moses's own refulgence—He so resembles Moses in anger as in love.[28]

Heine rejects this last idea quickly, for such anthropomorphism would lead him in a Feuerbachian direction he had explicitly renounced. Instead he now paints a glowing picture of Moses, whose greatness he had not been able to appreciate fully in his years of Hellenic pride because he had believed him to have been an out-and-out enemy of the arts. True, he admits, Moses was hostile to the making of graven images; but

what I failed to see was that Moses, for all his hostility to art, was himself a great artist and possessed the true artistic spirit. In his case, as in that of his Egyptian countrymen, this artistic spirit was directed solely towards the colossal and the indestructible. But unlike the Egyptians he did not fashion his works from baked bricks and granite. He built human pyramids, *Menschenpyramiden*; he carved out human obelisks; he took a poor shepherd tribe and from it he created a people that was also to defy the centuries—a great, immortal, holy people, a people of God, which could serve as a prototype for the whole of humanity. Moses created Israel! This artist, this son of Amram and of Jochebed the midwife, might have prided himself with greater justice than the Roman poet on having erected a monument which would outlast monuments of brass.[29]

Exegi monumentum aere perennius—Horace's boast, the proud claim of an heir to Hellenism, is here applied by Heine to a great liberator who was at once a 'countryman' or compatriot of the ancient Egyptians and the archetypal Judaic hero. He is spelling out what he had meant by his brief but fervent tribute to Moses in *Vitzliputzli*, the poem that ended the first section of his *Romanzero*.

Heine's positive characterization of Moses leads inevitably to an equally positive appraisal of the people from whom he sprang and whose character he indelibly affected. In his 'Hellenic' days, he had overestimated the Greeks and underestimated the Hebrews:

I see now that the Greeks were only beautiful youths, while the Jews were always men, powerful, unyielding men. This applies, not only to ancient times, but also to the present day, despite eighteen centuries of persecution and misery. I have learnt to appreciate them better; and if pride of birth were not a ridiculous contradiction in a champion of the [French]Revolution and its democratic principles, the writer of these pages would take pride in the knowledge that his ancestors belonged to the noble house of Israel; that he is descended from martyrs who have given the world a God and a morality and who have fought and suffered on all the battlefields of the spirit.[30]

This last phrase gives Heine his cue for the resuscitation of an image he had once applied to himself after his baptism: the image of the Knight of the Holy Spirit (*Ritter von dem heilgen Geist*). This image, wrested away from Christian theology and applied to those who fight for freedom and equality here below, is now applied to the people of Israel. There have been Jewish Knights of the Holy Spirit all through the Middle Ages and more recent times; they went unrecognized because they fought with their vizors closed.

The deeds of the Jews are as little known to the world as their true nature. Some think they know the Jews because they have seen their beards—but that's all that appeared of them. In the Middle Ages and in modern times too the Jews are a walking mystery. This mystery will be resolved, perhaps, and all will be revealed, on the day which the prophet has foretold: when there will be only one shepherd and one flock, and when the righteous who suffered for the salvation of mankind will receive recognition and glory.[31]

This new view of the mystery of Judaism Heine owes, he tells us, to his study of Jewish history, beginning with the historical portions of the Bible; and to the Bible he is also indebted, as he now reiterates, for the reawakening of religious feelings. But he adds once again that as a poet he does not need any positive religious dogma; the poet, he maintains, 'has Grace, the symbolism of heaven and earth discloses itself to his spirit. He has no need of the keys of any Church.'

This is the point of view from which Heine now looks back on his own baptism. He has not, after all, made the sort of unworthy use of this which he diagnosed in Baron Eckstein; he became a Protestant in order to protest, and he is proud of a Lutheran Protestantism which gave Germany its Book of Books, its Bible, as a heritage it could share with the Jewish people. But he tells us once again, it was only because the Jews guarded this treasure that Luther was able to transmit the Old Testament along with the New.

The Jews, who snatched their Bible from the great conflagration of the second Temple and dragged it about with them in exile as a portable fatherland throughout the whole of the Middle Ages—they kept this treasure well hidden in their ghetto, whither German scholars, those who preceded and those who began the Reformation, crept secretly in order to learn Hebrew and thus find the key which would unlock the shrine that held the treasure.[32]

That explains why obscurantists conceived a new and fiercer hatred of the Jews and tried to burn their Hebrew books, and why they fanned the already existing hatred of the Jews among the common people. Here Heine takes another opportunity to look at the Jews in the context of a history of anti-Semitism.

The poor common people, heirs of a primal curse of misery, already hated the Jews because of the treasures they had amassed; and what we call, today, the hatred proletarians bear towards the rich, used to be called hatred of the Jews. Indeed, the Jews, barred from all ownership of land, and from every trade by which they might have made a living, were thrown back on those activities and money-transactions which the Church forbade all true believers—thus the Jews were condemned by law to be cursed, to become rich, to be hated, and to be murdered.[33]

That, Heine tells us, is the economic reality. But in earlier times such realities could not be openly acknowledged; they had to be covered with a cloak of religion. The call therefore went out to kill those who had killed the Christian God.

How strange! The very people who had given the world a God, and whose whole life was inspired by devotion to God, were branded as deicides! We have seen the bloody parody of such madness when revolution broke out in St. Domingo, where a negro mob that broke into the plantations to murder and to burn was led by a black fanatic carrying a huge crucifix who shouted with bloodthirsty zeal: 'The whites have killed Christ; let us beat all the whites to death!'

This last apocryphal anecdote, which we have met before, is one of many parables Heine introduces into his work—parables designed to make strange what men take for granted, in order to force them to look afresh at attitudes and behaviour which have become so much second nature that they don't even notice their absurdity.

By means of the Bible, Heine now believes, the Jews still have a great providential mission to fulfil— a mission in which they are being aided by as unlikely an ally as the British and Foreign Bible Society. Part of that mission has already been accomplished, for the Bible has inevitably moulded the character of the nations that adopted it in the image of ancient Jewry. In some nations that image is more a caricature, or a black-and-grey daguerreotype, than a true copy:

But one day the caricature will vanish, the genuine, imperishable, true morality of ancient Judaism will flourish in these countries and exert the same divine attraction which it once exerted on the banks of the Jordan and the hills of Lebanon.[34]

Having thus distinguished original and distortion, Heine goes on to define the outlines of his collective portrait of the Jews in the way in which he so often defined his portraits of individuals: by means of contrast and comparison. The *contrast* is with the peoples that surrounded Israel in its formative years:

... with its spiritualist faith, with its strict, chaste, even ascetic manners and morals, this country and its people present the strangest possible contrast with neighbouring countries and peoples, who indulged in the most luxurious, colourful, and voluptuous nature cults and dissipated their existence in sensual Bacchanalian revels. Israel sat piously under its fig tree, sang the praises of an invisible God and practised virtue and justice, while in the temples of Nineveh, Sidon, and Tyre they celebrated those bloody and lascivious orgies whose mere description makes our hair stand on end even now! If one remembers these surroundings one cannot admire Israel's early greatness enough . . .

The *comparison*, on the other hand, is with the Germanic and Celtic peoples with which ancient Israel is once again said to have an 'elective affinity', a *Wahlverwandtschaft*. 'Judaea', the poet now declares, 'has always seemed to me a piece of the Occident lost in the midst of the Orient.[35]

One of the most constant and unchanging features which Heine, in this last period of his life, seeks and finds in Jewish history is love of freedom and independence. He details various features of the Mosaic laws that seem to show this—notably laws concerning the distribution of property and the limitation of slavery; and he exclaims, after a somewhat idiosyncratic (and historically hardly tenable) interpretation of the twenty-first chapter of Exodus:

O Moses our teacher! *Moshe rabbenu*! exalted fighter against servitude! Hand me hammer and nails so that I may nail our complacent slaves in red-white-and-gold livery to the Brandenburg gate by their long ears![38]

By his use of a Hebrew phrase to describe Moses as '*our* rabbi', followed by a passage in which he employs the German language to characterize contemporary Prussians as '*our* slaves', Heine deliberately presents himself as Jew and German at once. Elsewhere he assumes, with equal conviction, his favourite Protestant persona—I have italicized the keyword 'our' in the following instructive comparison between Moses and Jesus of Nazareth.

I will not speak of Israel's love of freedom at a time when slavery was being justified, and flourished, not only in Israel's immediate vicinity, but among all the peoples of antiquity, including even the philosophically-minded Greeks—I will not speak of this, for fear of giving the Bible a bad name among those who hold the reins of power at the present moment. There has never been a socialist more terroristic than *our* Lord and Saviour; and Moses too was a socialist of this kind, although Moses, as a practical man, sought to do no more than remodel existing customs, especially those that concern property. Instead of seeking to decree the abolition of property with obstinate rashness, Moses tried only to moralize it—to bring it into harmony with morality, with the true law of reason.[37]

In the process of bringing together the various facets of his historically fashioned personality—his Jewishness, his Germanness, his Protestant Christianity (a 'protesting Protestant' he calls himself in *Confessions*)[30] and his melioristic social beliefs—Heine extends his portraits of Moses and Jesus of Nazareth by insisting on the greater practicality, the greater readiness to accommodation with the status quo, which he thinks he discerns in the first-named, the man who had now become his favourite hero. The contrast is hardly justified by the words and actions of the biblical Jesus; but it serves to convey once again the poet's equivocal attitude to revolutionary socialism, compounded of sympathy with the social underdog and dislike of radical subversion, terrorism, and their likely cultural aftermath.

Towards the end of *Confessions* Heine looks once more towards the God in Whom he had earlier detected such a striking resemblance to Moses; and after describing some of the miseries of his mattress crypt he paints a picture of that God in the likeness of a fellow author—or more specifically, a fellow satirist.

Alas—God's mockery weighs heavily upon me. The great author of the universe, the Aristophanes of Heaven wanted to show the little earthling, who has been called the German Aristophanes, as crassly as possible that the latter's wittiest sarcasms were only feeble mockeries compared with His. How miserably I trail behind Him when it comes to humour, to jesting, on a *colossal* scale!

Yes, the caustic derision the lord is pouring down on me from on high is terrifying, and His jest is uncannily cruel. Humbly I acknowledge His superiority, and I bow in the dust before Him.[39]

Such self-abasement is not, however, Heine's natural posture—a colleague, a fellow satirist, however superior, must be able to take criticism.

Even though I lack that highest creative power [which belongs only to God] my spirit nevertheless has a spark of eternal Reason—and that allows me to submit even God's jesting to its forum and to subject it to respectful criticism. And here I would venture first of all, with due respect, to suggest that in my opinion at least the cruel jest which the Master is inflicting on his poor pupil is somewhat long drawn out; it has lasted six years already, and is beginning to be wearisome. And then I would also like to remark, with due deference, that the jest in question is not a new one; the great Aristophanes of Heaven has used it on an earlier occasion and has therefore plagiarized His exalted Self.[40]

Heine ends this confrontation with his God, and ends the *Confessions*, with the retelling of a medieval story about a poet afflicted with leprosy in whose case he sees a parallel with his own.

Peter Guttenhöfer has analysed very well how Heine used biblical words, phrases and rhythms, not as a signal of sanctity, but as yet another item in his repertoire of tones that could be adapted to a whole range of attitudes, from the reverential to the blasphemous. Long association with holiness has lent biblical language a greater 'specific gravity' than other language registers, and this can be used to lend special emphasis to a serious context, or shock audiences to attention in a parodistic or frivolous one.[41] The late Heine found in the Bible great ethical and aesthetic value, but no inviolable sanctity; he could draw on it as a repertoire of character types which could be subjected to ironic sidelights or used to illuminate analogous types in the modern world or presented as measuring rods to show up the unheroic stature of their most recent successors. As for the portrait of God which emerges from *Confessions* and other late texts: this must always, as Guttenhöfer rightly stresses, be seen in the context of Heine's self-presentation as an 'ex-God', one whom Hegel and his successors had induced to deify man and whom sickness now forced to become conscious of the humiliating frailty to which he, and all his fellow-men, were subject. The sick Heine had himself become a parody[42]—a parody of the Aristophanes of Heaven, the God to Whom he now assigned the directorship of the world theatre. But this revivification of the God he had once declared dead is presented as an act of reason, not of faith. Man needs a 'dose' of monotheism in order to make sense of the world. And since there has been no blinding religious illumination, the 'return' to God can be treated with irony, with a freedom of mind foreign to the faithful, and with a sense of humiliation that has nothing of the exaltation of the God-seeker who has been vouchsafed a glimpse of what he has sought.

Heine's revision of his theological views has to be understood, not only in the light of his personal need for a god, but in that of the intellectual and spiritual history of his time. This point has been powerfully made by Wilhelm Gößmann who has shown how far Heine was from any unequivocal 'return' to the Jewish God of his childhood, to what extent he retained a freedom of interpretation which was a legacy of the *Aufklär-ung*, and how demonstrably he stands in a tradition that can be traced to Lessing, Goethe, and Hegel, even after his apparent rejection of that tradition. For orthodox worship he substituted public confessions (*Aveux d'un poète* is one of the titles he authorized for the French version of his *Geständnisse*) tinged with irony.[43] The irony is an essential part of Heine's rhetoric: it belongs to what recent critics have called his *Appell-struktur*, the way in which his works activate the reader, invite the reader's alert co-operation in the production of meaning rather than his fascinated or drugged assent.

The French title of *Confessions* of which I have just spoken obscures an analogy the German title deliberately courts: Rousseau's celebrated essay in autobiography. Heine seeks to investigate and describe his own nature in order to understand all the better the forces that shape the modern world. But how could anyone *know* the truth about himself? How could anyone *present* that truth to others even if he did, for once, know it? How far is it possible to paint a true self-portrait in words?

To undertake a self-characterization is not only dangerous but downright impossible. I would be a vain fop if I crassly emphasized all the good I know of myself; and I would be a complete fool if I laid bare to the whole world the many failings of which I am no less conscious. And then: however willing one may be to be candid and frank, no man can speak the truth about himself. No one has as yet succeeded in doing this—neither St. Augustine, the pious bishop of Hippo, nor Jean-Jacques Rousseau from Geneva . . .[44]

Nevertheless, Heine explains, he did exhibit himself to his public as fully as he was able to do; and he did this by seeking and finding occasion to allow his own personality to move into the foreground of his picture—to a degree, in fact, that might seem questionable to some. He has constantly endeavoured, however, not to paint himself too white and his fellow man too black, and has ever tried to keep in mind the principle which he had already announced in *Ludwig Börne. A Memorial* and which he now restates: 'I will always faithfully show my own colour so that readers may know how far they may trust my judgement when I bring before them people of a different hue.' And *Confessions* should also bring to mind once more what the present book has so constantly tried to demonstrate: that one of the ways in which the poet sought to convey the truth about himself was to project his own problems and qualities on to others—to let the lineaments of his own face peep through his portraits of predecessors and contemporaries.

One other feature of *Confessions* should not be overlooked in our special context. In this work Heine once again introduces his mother, who had already featured prominently in early poems and in *Germany. A Winter's Tale.* What he attributes to her here, in this late work, is an effort to give her son an almost entirely *non-Jewish* education in the hope of seeing him obtain the highest distinctions which the Gentile world had to bestow. One of his Jesuit teachers, he tells us, asked Heine's mother to send her son to Rome to be trained for an exalted position in the Catholic church:

When my mother told me this, she regretted greatly that she had not followed the intelligent old gentleman's advice—for he had truly understood my nature and had gauged more correctly than others what climate would be most suitable and salutary for it. The old lady felt sorry that she had rejected so sensible a suggestion; but in that early period her dream was that I should attain high *worldly* dignities. As a pupil of Rousseau and a strict deist she did not, in any case, feel it to be right that her son should don the cassock which she saw being worn by German priests with such clumsy awkwardness . . .[45]

But if he disappointed his mother in one way, Heine tells us, he did her proud in another—for he became, as he now claims with unshakeable self-confidence, a great poet in a land of great poets; a poet whose name had rivalled, and always would rival, that of Goethe himself.[46]

The group of poems with which Heine supported this claim in his *Miscellaneous Writings* of 1854 opens with one entitled *Panting for Peace (Ruhelechzend)*—a celebration, rare in Heine, of night, death, non-being, which has to be read in the context of the whole group, a group of poems that in fact ends with an affirmation of life, *quand même*.[47] In our context *Panting for Peace* is a key poem not only because of its irony in speaking of 'the good Lord' in the midst of pain and tears, but also because of its unusually subtle presentation of the secret pleasures of grief (*'geheime Wollust schwelgt im Schmerz'*) and of the urge towards self-torture:

> Verwundet dich nicht fremde Hand,
> So musst du selber dich verletzen;
> Auch danke hübsch dem lieben Gott,
> Wenn Zähren deine Wangen netzen.

> [If a stranger's hand does not wound you,
> you have to hurt yourself;
> and give due thanks to the good Lord
> when tears bedew your cheeks.][48]

The poem praises night, death, and non-being for the release they bring from the noisy intrusion of a brash world:

> Hier wirst du nicht verfolgt, geplagt
> Vom eitlen Virtuosenpacke
> Und vom Genie Giacomos
> Und seiner Weltberühmtheitsclaque.

> [Here you are not pursued and tortured
> by a vain rabble of virtuosos,
> and by Giacomo Meyerbeer's genius,
> with paid hirelings applauding his world fame.]

Maestro Giacomo also makes a brief appearance in another poem, a dialogue between the body and the soul (*Leib und Seele*), in which the soul shudders away from the wearisome emptiness and sameness of eternity, only to be comforted by the body with the thought that perhaps the afterlife won't be as bad as all that:

> Nun lebe wohl und tröste dich!
> Vielleicht auch amüsiert man sich
> Im Himmel besser als du meinst.
> Siehst du den großen Bären einst
> (Nicht Meyer-Bär) im Sternensaal,
> Grüß ihn von mir vieltausendmal!

> [Now farewell, and take heart!
> Perhaps there is better amusement
> in heaven than you think.
> If, some day, you should see the Great Bear
> (Not Meyer-bear) in the hall of the stars,
> Greet him most warmly from me.][49]

Meyerbeer had become a symbol of all that was most distasteful to Heine in the culture industry of the day. He used his name, accordingly, as a kind of shorthand for a certain cultural type in the same way as that in which he had used the name of the nationalistic professor Hans Ferdinand Maßmann in earlier years.

In one of the more light-hearted poems of this distinctive group, *Ascent to Heaven* (*Himmelfahrt*), St. Peter, receiving a newcomer at heaven's gate, makes the Lord Himself appear as a kind of celestial Meyerbeer.

> Der Weltkapellenmeister hier oben,
> Er selbst sogar, hört gerne loben
> Gleichfalls seine Werke, er hört es gern
> Wenn man lobsinget Gott dem Herrn,
> Und seinem Preis und Ruhm ein Psalm
> Erklingt im dicksten Weihrauchqualm.

> [The conductor of the world orchestra up here,
> He Himself, also likes to hear
> His works lauded; He is pleased when He hears
> songs of praise to the Lord God,

when a psalm proclaims His glory and His fame
amidst thickest clouds of incense.][50]

What shows itself here, and elsewhere in Heine's later works, is
that Meyerbeer's wealth and organizing capacity enable him to
carry to extremes something all artists, good or bad, must
know: the quest for approbation, for public acclaim. Meyer-
beer too has something of Heine in his make-up.

If Meyerbeer's name could be freely used, without fear of
hurtful reprisals, there were other names on which Heine had
perforce to go easy in his later years. Cousin Carl, who now
controlled the purse-strings to which the sick poet continued
to be tied, had made it clear beyond any doubt that if he
published anything derogatory about Carl's immediate family
his allowance would be discontinued at once. Refusing to be
gagged altogether, Heine included in *Miscellaneous Writings*
one of his most sustained exercises in Aesopian language—a
poem which names no names yet alludes unmistakably to the
grievances he had been ordered to keep to himself. The poem is
entitled *Castle Contumely (Affrontenburg)*. The 'castle' of the
title may easily be recognized by those who know anything at
all of Heine's life history as a representation of Salomon
Heine's country house at Ottensen, where the guests—*blödes
Menschenvolk*, a stupid rabble, in the poet's eyes—looked up
to the weathervane, before opening their mouths, to see which
way the wind was blowing. The force that strikes terror into
them all is described as 'Boreas, growling and grumbling like a
bear', always ready to jump down people's throats—an amus-
ing representation, no doubt, of Uncle Salomon himself. The
poem then describes, with increasing bitterness, the way in
which any words spoken in the garden of Castle Contumely
were at once distorted by a malevolent echo; it tells of the
heartlessness and the insults which met the poet every-
where, and of the creepy-crawly company that infested the
grounds:

> Die Kröte, die im Gras gelauscht,
> Hat alles mitgeteilt der Ratte,
> Die ihrer Muhme Viper gleich
> Erzählt, was sie vernommen hatte.

Die hat's gesagt dem Schwager Frosch—
Und solcherweis erfahren konnte
Die ganze schmutz'ge Sippschaft stracks
Die mir erwiesenen Affronte.

[The toad that listened in the grass
retailed everything to the rat
who, in its turn, let Cousin Viper in
on everything it had heard.

Viper told brother-in-law Frog—
and in this way the whole unsavoury family
could straightaway learn
with what contumely I had been treated.][51]

The roses of that garden were beautiful (Heine is thinking of Amalie and her sisters) but they died early of some poison in the soil. The nightingale too, that traditional emblem of lover and poet, grew sick unto death . . . The poem ends as it began with a reference to the captivity in which the castle holds the speaker. What was done to him there will be with him for as long as there is life in his body and memory in his brain.

Castle Contumely introduces a development essential to our understanding of Heine's literary portraiture: like so many other caricaturists and satirists before him, he tends more and more to portray men in animal guise. Acquaintance with the caricatures of J. I. I. Grandville may have strengthened that tendency. One should not, however, make too much of this, for Grandville had a host of literary predecessors whose work Heine knew at least equally well.

Even the terrifying poem *The Slave Ship* (*Das Sklavenschiff*), which attacks man's profit-orientated inhumanity to man in the person of a Dutch slave-trader, may have a poisoned barb aimed at the Heine family—for if we can believe Friedrich Hirth, there was one branch of the Heine family which had grown rich from investment in such human cargo. But it cannot be sufficiently stressed that Heine's last poems do not ask to be read as autobiographical *poèmes à clef*, that they can stand on their own, as works of art, that their tenor can be understood even if we know and care nothing about long dead Uncle Salomon, his daughters, his son, and his sons-in-law, and all the sycophants that once gathered at Ottensen near Hamburg. Indeed, some of the poems in *Miscellaneous Writings* are actually diminished if one tries to undo their generalization by reading detailed autobiographical allusions into them. Number 8 of the *Lazarus* cycle (*Zum Lazarus*) is a case in point.[52]

Jewish figures flit across Heine's screen in quite a few poems of this late collection. Some of these come from the Bible: Lazarus, for instance, the poet's favourite *alter ego*, in the cycle that bears his name; or the precedents King Frederick William IV of Prussia is made to invoke and reject when preparing to receive the poet Herwegh at a once notorious audience:

> "Ich laß nicht die Kindlein, wie Pharao,
> Ersäufen im Nilstromwasser;
> Ich bin auch kein Herodestyrann,
> Kein Kinderabschlachtenlasser.
>
> Ich will, wie einst mein Heiland tat,
> Am Anblick der Kinder mich laben;
> Laß zu mir kommen die Kindlein, zumal
> Das große Kind aus Schwaben."

> ['I don't have little children drowned,
> as Pharaoh once did, in the Nile;
> nor am I a Herodian tyrant,
> a causer of infant massacres.
>
> I will, as my Saviour once did,
> refresh my sight with children;
> suffer little children to come unto me—especially
> that big babe Herwegh from Swabia.']53

In another poem Heine lets us hear the Prussian authorities appeal to their Jewish as to their Christian subjects for order and calm. The period evoked is unmistakably that after the 1848 revolutions—and Heine's readers would no doubt be aware that among those who had been elected to the short-lived Frankfurt parliament were several prominent Jews, notably Johann Jacobi from Königsberg and Heine's old enemy Gabriel Riesser from Hamburg.

'Der Obrigkeit gehorchen, ist
Die erste Pflicht für Jud und Christ.
Es schließe jeder seine Bude
Sobald es dunkelt, Christ und Jude!'

['To obey the duly constituted authorities is
the first duty of Jew and of Christian.
Everyone must put his shutters up
as soon as it grows dark, be he Christian or Jew.']⁵⁴

The poem from which this satirical appeal to traditional German submissiveness comes bears the title: *Days of Terror in Hicksville (Erinnerung an Krähwinkels Schreckenstage)*. Most significant of all, however, is yet another glimpse Heine allows us of the Jewish pedlar, a figure who seems to have inspired much affection in him in these his later days. It is, again, a memory poem and bears the title *A Memory of Hamburg (Erinnerung an Hammonia)*. It opens with a procession of children (processions play a great part in the visionary poems of Heine's latter years) from one of the Hamburg orphanages, walking, two by two, through the streets, exciting various emotions, stimulating various actions among the passers-by. Each stanza ends with the exclamation 'What pretty orphan children!'—'O die hübschen Waisenkinder!'

Schmulchen wirft verschämten Blicks
Einen Taler in die Büchs—
Denn er hat ein Herz—und heiter
Schleppt er seinen Zwerchsack weiter.
O die hübschen Waisenkinder!

[With a shy glance little Sammy
throws a thaler in the collecting-box—
For he has a heart—and gaily
goes on his way, loaded down with his pedlar's pack.
O what pretty orphan children!]⁵⁵

The obligation to practise charity, Heine bids us remember, applies to the Jewish poor as well as to the Jewish rich, and is not confined to charity towards fellow Jews. The pedlar's shy glance—the glance of unostentatious charity—and the strength his good action, prompted by a good heart, gives him to go on living his hard life, are beautifully observed. To

appreciate the tenderness of Heine's portrait to the full, one
need only compare it with the unsympathetic presentation of
similar figures in the works of Wilhelm Busch—Schmulchen
Schiewelbeiner in *Plisch und Plum*, for instance. Heine's little
Sammy, the refrain suggests, is also one of the world's
orphans—and in the end, in the final stanza of the poem, this
refrain extends its application to all who are poor and despised.
The whole world now becomes an orphanage, whose inmates
are by no means as well looked after, housed, and fed as the
children who called forth the little Jewish pedlar's timid char-
ity. Where, the reader may ask, does that leave the God to
Whom the poet had 'returned'? What does the image which
presents the world as one great orphanage make of the Father-
God?

In Heine's late poems, as in *Confessions*, God is treated as a
fellow author, fellow satirist, fellow artist, whose creations are
subject to criticism. In the *Poems of Creation* (*Schöpfungslied-
er*) which Heine wrote in the 1830s and 1840s, he had pro-
claimed the joys and the glories of creation by assuming God's
own voice; now, in an addition made in the 1850s, the same
divine voice is made to speak of *sickness* as the ultimate spur to
creation:

> Warum ich eigentlich erschuf
> Die Welt, ich will es gern bekennen:
> Ich fühlte in der Seele brennen
> Wie Flammenwahnsinn, den Beruf.
>
> Krankheit ist wohl der letzte Grund
> Des ganzen Schöpferdrangs gewesen;
> Erschaffend konnte ich genesen,
> Erschaffend wurde ich gesund.
>
> [Why I created the world
> I will gladly confess:
> I felt my calling burn within me,
> it flamed like madness in my heart.
>
> Sickness, I suppose, was the ultimate cause
> of this whole urge to create:
> creating, I was able to recover,
> creating I returned to health.][56]

Elsewhere in these late poems God becomes a kind of Super-
reader to whom Heine addresses his texts:

> O Herr! Ich glaub, es wär das Beste,
> Du ließest mich in dieser Welt;
> Heil nur zuvor mein Leibgebreste
> Und sorge auch für etwas Geld.
>
> Ich weiß, es ist voll Sünd und Laster
> Die Welt; jedoch ich bin einmal
> Gewöhnt, auf diesem Erdpechpflaster
> Zu schlendern durch das Jammertal.
>
> [O Lord! I think the best thing would be
> if you left me in this world;
> only heal my physical malady
> and see that I have a little money.
>
> I know, it's full of sin and vice,
> this world of ours; but it so happens
> that I am used to strolling along
> the, unhappy pavements of this vale of tears.][57]

The tone of this poetry ranges from mock-submissiveness to
impassioned apostrophe—but even when it uses the traditional
vocabulary of worship, praise, and invocation, it could never
be mistaken for the prayer of a humble believer in revealed
truth.

(iv)

In the folkloristic discussions which follow the group of poems
included in Heine's *Miscellaneous Writings* of 1854, there is
only one fleeting glimpse of a Jewish figure. This occurs in *The
Gods in Exile* (*Die Götter im Exil*), where Heine describes the
various masks and disguises the gods of Greece and Rome were
forced to assume when Christianity dethroned them. Hermes,
or Mercury, chooses to disguise himself as a Dutch merchant.

Perhaps it was not just caprice that made him light on this particular
disguise. Mercury was, as you know, the god of thieves as well as of

merchants. It was natural for him to take account of this antecedent and these talents when it came to choosing a mask behind which to hide and a trade by which to make a living. His talents had been well in evidence: he was the most inventive of all the gods of Olympus, he had invented the tortoise-shell lyre and had drawn gas from the sun, he had stolen from men and from Gods; as a child he had already shown himself a little Calmonius when he escaped from his cradle to do a bit of cattle-stealing. He had to choose between two ways of life which are not, when one comes down to it, all that different from each other: they both offer a solution to the problem of how to acquire other men's property as advantageously as possible. The intelligent god took into consideration, however, that the profession of thief was not as highly respected as that of merchant—that the former is proscribed by the police while the latter draws down the special favour of the law; that merchants can ascend the highest ladder of public esteem while the ladder thieves have to ascend occasionally offers a much less pleasant prospect; that thieves risk their life and their liberty while merchants, if it comes to the worst, lose nothing but their capital and that of their friends—and so the wiliest among the gods decided to become a merchant, and in order to be as complete a merchant as possible he even became a Dutchman.[58]

Here we have no *overt* reference to Jews at all. On the contrary: it is the Dutch rather than the Jews who fulfill the mercantile ideal most completely and exclusively. Yet behind it all there is a specific Jewish figure, for whose sake all those references to the manufacture of gas, to Calmonius, to the acquisition of other people's property, and to losing the capital of one's friends have been introduced. Beside the figure of Hermes-Mercury, beside that of the Dutch merchant, beside that of the historical family from whose name Heine has adapted the name Calmonius, we may once again discern that of Ferdinand Friedland, brother-in-law of Ferdinand Lassalle, agent of the Iris gas company, speculator, *Luftmensch*, and court Jew extraordinary.

The last text Heine included in Volume I of his *Miscellaneous Writings* is one that has already been discussed in detail: the Ludwig Marcus obituary which now bears the title *Ludwig Marcus. Words in his Memory* (*Ludwig Marcus. Denkworte*). This text had been subject to considerable self-censorship on Heine's part, and we have seen earlier that the version printed in the *Augsburg Gazette* in 1844 left out important passages which can still be read in manuscript. When he came to include *Ludwig Marcus* in *Miscellaneous Writings*, the poet pencilled some revisions into a copy of the *Augsburg Gazette* printing, and tacked a topical note on to the end. After he had done that, however, he came across his old unexpurgated manuscript, had it transcribed, and pencilled some extra notes into it, intending to use that rather than the printed version as copy for *Miscellaneous Writings*. Among the alterations he projected we find phrases that show clearly how even in his last years his thinking could run along lines drawn in the days of his collaboration with Karl Marx: he seeks to relate modern hatred of Jews to resentments created by 'the proliferating power of capital' and 'the exploitation of the poor by the rich' ('die überwuchernde Macht des Kapitals', 'die Ausbeutung der Armen durch die Reichen').[59] In the event, confusion in the printing works, or covert policy in Campe's publishing house, led to the publication, not of the revised manuscript text, but of the *Augsburg Gazette* copy with its minor alterations—a version which does, however, give Eduard Gans more explicit credit than before for his achievement in combating the reactionary school of law associated with Savigny.

That still leaves one major addition to the new printing of *Ludwig Marcus*: the 'later note' (*Spätere Note*) dated March 1854. This begins with reflections on a retrograde movement Heine discerns—necessarily from afar—in Germany after the 1848 revolution, a retrograde movement that would affect the question of Jewish emancipation along with every other tendency towards a more liberal and tolerant state. The poet thinks it timely, however, to reiterate a warning that had often been sounded before, from the time of Börne onwards: that German Jews must not take too narrow a view of emancipation; that they must remember the close connection between their fate and that of their non-Jewish fellow citizen.

It is time the Jews realized that they can be truly emancipated only when the emancipation of Christians has also been fought for and secured in full. Their cause is identical with that of the German people; they must not demand as Jews what has long been their due as Germans.[60]

Now the poet feels ready to take up the thread where he dropped it in 1844, when he had ended his obituary of Marcus with a glimpse of another German-Jewish Orientalist living in France, Salomon Munk. Munk had been presented to Heine's readers as the man who would edit Marcus's posthumous works and who might also be expected, in the fulness of time, to write a better informed and more sympathetic account of Marcus's scholarly labours than Heine had felt able to provide. But this had now become impossible, for in the interval between the first and second version of this obituary, Munk had become blind.

I have learnt this sad fact only recently; and now I remember that despite alarming symptoms this excellent man would never agree to husband his failing eyesight. The last time I had the privilege of seeing him in the Bibliothèque Royale, he sat buried in a pile of Arabic manuscripts—and it was painful to see how he strained sick, clouded eyes in his efforts to decipher their fantastically curlicued abracadabra. He was employed in this library as Keeper of Oriental Manuscripts—but he has now become incapable of performing his duties. The income he derived from his literary labours was the principal means by which he gained a livelihood for himself and his large family. Blindness is the harshest fate that can befall any scholar—and this time it has afflicted the best soul that one could hope to find anywhere. Munk is selfless to the point of arrogance, but despite his wealth of learning he is touchingly modest. He will bear his fate, I am sure, with stoic patience and with pious submission to the Lord's will.[61]

The portrait Heine has sketched here is that of a true scholar cruelly deprived of the chief instrument of his scholarship—it springs to life particularly in the psychologically acute remark about the 'arrogance' of selflessness which is the last infirmity of truly modest men. The final sentence just quoted ends with a stress on pious submission—the kind of submission that refuses to raise the questions which Heine now puts forward on his own behalf as well as that of Munk and Marcus. These are questions that the poet had most powerfully posed in one of the greatest of his later poems, the one that begins with the line 'Leave your sacred parables . . .' [Laß die heil'gen Parabolen . . .][62] Now, as he poses them again in the postscript of his Marcus obituary, he demonstrates that all such questions had already been familiar to the authors of the Hebrew Bible, where they are associated above all with the figure of Job.

Why must the righteous suffer so much on this earth? Why must talent and honesty come to grief while swaggering clowns that never clouded their eyes with Arabic manuscripts loll on Fortune's couch and well nigh stink with well-being? The Book of Job does not solve this horrible problem. On the contrary: the Book of Job is the Song of Songs of scepticism, and in it terrifying serpents hiss their eternal question: Why? How comes it that when Israel returned from Babylon the pious commission compiling the temple archives, whose president was Ezra, included this book in the canon of Holy Writ? I have often asked myself that question. My conjecture would be that divinely inspired men did not do this out of stupidity, but because in their exalted wisdom they knew very well that doubt is deeply fixed in man's nature and that it is justified. Therefore, they must have reasoned, it serves no purpose to suppress doubt with clumsy zeal; what one must do with doubt is cure it. They proceeded according to the homoeopathic principle which fights like with like; but instead of tiny homeopathic doses they increased the quantity inordinately. That is what we find in the Book of Job: an exceedingly strong dose of doubt. Such poison was an essential ingredient in the Bible, that great medicine cupboard of the human race. Just as men must weep their fill when they suffer, so they must doubt their fill when they find their expectations of finding happiness in this world cruelly thwarted. Like violent weeping, the highest degree of doubt, *Zweifel*, which the Germans rightly name 'despair', *Verzweiflung*, brings about a crisis leading to our moral recovery. But happy is the man who is sound and needs no medicine![63]

Even while asking his questions Heine conveys, through the portraits to which they give rise, one possible answer: suffering and the consciousness of suffering may sometimes reveal men's greatness, men's capacities, to a higher degree than a life of ease. The towering literary and spiritual achievement of the Book of Job, the decision of Ezra and his commission not to withhold from the world masterpieces that fail to accord with a narrow and unimaginative orthodoxy, the work which Heine himself wrested from his sickness and pain and frustration—all these represent human achievements whose most admirable qualities were called forth by the very suffering that might have led to the inactivity of despair. Suffering is not something to be glorified—'happy the man who is sound and needs no medicine'; but even as the reader agrees, he cannot but be conscious of something in this very text that the experience of suffering has called forth in its writer, something which in a happier and less troubled life might never have been given to the world. That is an insight which the great *tragic* writers have perennially conveyed to readers and spectators; here we find it, characteristically, lending depth and perspective to Heine's Jewish Comedy.

CHAPTER 14
Valkyries and Weather-Frogs

(i)

Volumes 2 and 3 of *Miscellaneous Writings* contain considerably revised versions of the reports Heine had contributed to the *Augsburg Gazette* and to the *World of Elegance* (*Zeitung für die elegante Welte*) in the era of Louis Philippe. He now introduces a characteristic reference to Jewish ritual into his account of the trial of Madame Lafarge, a *cause célèbre* of the early 1840s:

In their prayers Jewish men thank the Lord every day for not having made them come into the world as women. What a naïvely revealing prayer by people who were not born into the happiest of circumstances and who yet think that being created a woman is the most terrible misfortune of all! They are right—even in France, where women's misery is decked out with so many roses . . .[1]

Some of the more extravagant attacks on the Fould family now disappear; criticism of Mendelssohn-Bartholdy is occasionally toned down in expression though not in substance; passages in praise of Meyerbeer, or apparently in praise of Meyerbeer, are rewritten to redound to that composer's discredit; and a number of other portraits are either added or overpainted. Where the *Augsburg Gazette* version had been content to speak of the dinners which 'King Agrippa' gave every Saturday to the diplomatic corps of Rome in ancient times, the new version reads 'the *Judaic* king Agrippa' (my italics), in order to suggest more surely the parallel with modern Jews who entertain lavishly. The importance of such entertainments for the breaking down of social barriers is emphasized elsewhere; the 'soirées of tolerant Jewish bankers' ('des banquiers israélites les plus riches et les plus tolérants', the French version reads) are mentioned among the places in which actors are no longer regarded as social pariahs. Tiny touches are added to the

caricatures of minor dramatis personae to make them more
easily recognizable to those who have met them elsewhere in
the poet's work. What had read in the 1840s:

This Mr *** assures us he had reasons [*Gründ*] to be content with
Providence . . .

becomes in the 1850s

Thin and long-nosed Mr * [one star only!] assures us that he is
r-itchi-ly content [*er habe Grind*] . . .

Readers of *Ludwig Börne. A Memorial* and *The Rabbi of
Bacherach* will immediately recognize their old friend
Nasenstern. Names are added where none were mentioned
before; what read 'the Demi-banker ***' in the *Augsburg
Gazette* now reads 'the Demi-banker Läusedorf'[2]

Bankers, for obvious reasons, are prominent in the work
now entitled *Lutezia*,[3] whose subtitle promises reports on
'politics, art and the life of the people' in Louis Philippe's
Paris—a society whose motto was 'enrichissez-vous'. Among
these bankers the Rothschilds, as ever, rule supreme. All the
major passages dealing with Baron James and his family have
been revised and rewritten in *Lutezia*. The baron's very health
now becomes a political barometer:

M. de Rothschild, it is said, had the toothache yesterday; others say
he had a colic. What does this portend? The storm draws ever nearer.
The beating of the Valkyries' wings can be heard in the air.[4]

Heine's pronounced interest in symptoms of sickness—natu-
ral in a man who had of necessity to watch his own—are
impressed into the service of social diagnosis. The symptoms
of an individual portend sickness in society. Heine loves, in
those portraits, to yoke together the incongruous (Rothschild
and the Valkyries!) and the disproportionate (toothache or
colic as an index of the storm which threatens to sweep away a
whole social order). The French version, which Heine super-
vised as well as his health allowed and which appeared under
the title *Lutèce* in 1855, spells the implications out more thor-
oughly. *Lutèce* introduces an intermediary character, a
professional Rothschild-watcher or rather (in Heine's olfac-

tory image) Rothschild-*sniffer*, who can detect the great banker's colic at several paces' distance:

Je viens de parler à un agent de change dont l'odorat est très fin, et qui a eu l'honneur de pouvoir s'approcher un moment de M. de Rothschild; il m'assure que le baron est atteint d'une colique très prononcée, et que les rentes fléchiront davantage aussitôt que cette nouvelle sera connue à la Bourse. Mais qu'adviendra-t-il de toutes ces craintes et de ces espérances flottantes, de cette tourment sans relâche? L'orage approche de plus en plus. Dans les airs on entend déjà retenir les coups d'ailes et les boucliers d'airain des Walkyres, les déesses sorcières qui décident du sort des batailles.[5]

What this sketch of the fine-nosed stockbroker gives us is the febrile atmosphere of commercial speculation, the 'torment without end' of those whose whole existence depends on predicting accurately the fluctuating quotations of the Stock Exchange.

In other passages of *Lutèce* the French can clearly be expected to catch local allusions more easily than German readers. Where the German version tells us, in *Lutezia* as in the *Augsburg Gazette*, that the Chief Rabbi of the Right Bank is Rothschild and the Chief Rabbi of the Left Bank, Benoît Fould, the French version speaks only of 'grands rabbins' of the *rive droite* and the *rive gauche*, and leaves it to the reader to fill in the appropriate names.[6]

The idea of the Rothschilds as a political barometer, lightly introduced into the new version of the article dated 7 October 1840, is elaborated in the *Lutezia* version of that dated 31 March 1841.

M. de Rothschild, who seemed somewhat indisposed for a time, is now quite restored and looks sound and well. The augurs of the Stock Exchange, who are experts at interpreting the great Baron's physiognomy, assure us that the swallows of peace nestle in his smile, that every anxiety about the possibility of war has vanished from his countenance, that there are no electric sparks which forbode storms visible in his eyes, and that therefore the warlike stormy weather, the *Kanonendonnerwetter* which threatened the whole world, has been altogether dissipated. Even his sneezes, these augurs tell us, portend peace.[7]

Having given us this new glimpse of the world's greatest

banker through the eyes of the Rothschild-watchers of the Stock Exchange, presented in the incongruous guise of the augurs of the ancient world, Heine now introduces *himself* into the picture. He has recently had occasion, he tells us, to pay a respectful visit to Baron James, and can therefore testify that the augurs' observation is correct. The great banker was indeed in the best of health, able to regale his audience with the humorous speeches for which he was known—speeches that turn, occasionally, into impromptu rhyming. It was, Heine claims, in such a rhyming mood that he found Baron James; he was scratching his head in a vain endeavour to find a rhyme for 'Konstantinopel'. The visiting poet wickedly suggests that the word *Zobel* (sable, a *Russian* fur) might, in the circumstances, make a most suitable rhyme. This serves first of all to remind the reader of Balzac's caricature of Rothschild's speech in the *Comédie Humaine*, where the banker Nucingen constantly confounds the letters b and p; and it serves, secondly, to introduce the Eastern Question, the rivalry of Russia and England over the territorial possessions that were slipping from Turkey's grasp. Baron James's mind was clearly running on that question, whose effect on the Stock Exchange was constant and powerful, and he is shown bridling at the colloca-tion which the suggested rhyme would make. How could England allow such a conjunction of Turkey and Russia?

The rhyme I had suggested seemed to displease him greatly; England would never agree to it, he claimed, and it could therefore give rise to a European war which would cost the world a great deal of blood and tears and him a great deal of money.[8]

However incongruous such a notion might seem to conspiracy theorists, the interests of those who wanted peace in Europe coincided with the interests of those who wanted to prevent a diminution of their profit rate. The Rothschilds could there-fore be numbered among the peacemakers, among those who strove to the best of their ability to prevent unnecessary shed-ding of blood and tears.

Having now introduced himself into the picture, paying a respectful visit to the king of financiers and confirming from his own observation the contention that Baron James is 'the best political thermometer' ('I won't say "weather-frog"',

Heine adds, 'because the term is not sufficiently respectful'), the poet can turn back to other Rothschild-watchers. As he does so Jews once again come into view—though Heine is careful to point out explicitly, once again, that deference to money is far from being an exclusively Jewish trait in the society he is describing.

One must have respect for this man—if only because of the respect he inspires in others. I like best to visit him in the offices of his banking house, where I can philosophically observe how people—not only the Chosen People, but all the others too—bow and scrape before him. There you may watch a twisting and bending of backbones such as the most accomplished acrobat would find difficult. I have seen people who twitched convulsively when they drew near the great Baron as though they had touched a Voltaic battery. Even while approaching the door of his private office many experience a thrill of awe such as Moses once felt on Mount Horeb when he realized that he was standing on holy ground. And just as Moses then removed his shoes, so many a broker or commission agent, who dared to enter Rothschild's inner sanctum, would willingly remove his boots if he were not afraid that the odour of his feet might give the baron offence. That inner sanctum is a remarkable place indeed; it inspires sublime thoughts and feelings, like the sight of the ocean or the starry heavens. Here we may see the littleness of man and the greatness of God. For money is the god of our time, and Rothschild is his prophet.[9]

The language, not only of religion, but of classical German (especially Kantian) ethics and aesthetics are here employed to create in the reader a proper sense of the incongruity of money worship. At the same time the poet projects onto money worshippers the offence his own sick-chamber inevitably gave to his fastidious nose—an olfactory disgust that helped to inspire the characteristic symbolic anecdote which follows the passages just quoted.

Some years ago, when I was about to call on M. de Rothschild, a servant in livery crossed the corridor carrying the baron's chamber-pot—and a stock-exchange speculator who was passing at that very moment took off his hat before the mighty pot. That far—I say it with all due respect—some people carry their devotion. I took note of that respectful man's name, and I am sure he will, in time, become a millionaire.

The name the poet pretends to have noted is not vouchsafed to his readers; instead, they are taken to meet an old acquaintance yet once more.

When I told M. ٭ one day that I had taken my midday meal with Rothschild, *en famille*, in the inner apartments of his counting-house, he clapped his hands in amazement and declared that I had enjoyed an honour which had previously been vouchsafed only to Rothschilds of the blood or at most a few sovereign princes; he himself would give half of his nose to purchase such an honour. I will here remark that even diminished by half, M. ٭'s nose would be quite a respectable size.[10]

'Nasenstern' always affords Heine an occasion to introduce a verbal equivalent of, or variation on, the cartoonist's favourite play with the 'Jewish' nose.

The *Lutezia* version of the article dated 31 March 1841, from which I have been quoting, concludes with a rapid tour of James de Rothschild's banking establishment. The man and his activities are characterized by his physical surroundings.

M. de Rothschild's counting-house is very extensive; it is a labyrinth of halls, a barracks of wealth. The room in which the Baron works from morning till night—he has nothing else to do but work—has been greatly beautified of late. On the chimney-piece there stands, at present, a marble bust of the Emperor Francis of Austria, with whom the House of Rothschild has done the most business . . .[11]

The suggestion enshrined in the 'labyrinth' and 'barracks' images will not have been lost on the reader, any more than the reason why the Emperor Francis's bust appears on the Baron's mantelpiece—'at present'. This last detail now leads Heine to a characteristic elaboration which allows him to introduce, by way of comparison and contrast, one of his favourite non-Jewish butts.

The Baron intends, out of a deep regard, to commission busts of all the European monarchs who have contracted loans from his firm; and this collection of marble busts will form a Valhalla which promises to be far more magnificent than that of Regensburg. Whether M. Rothschild will celebrate his Valhalla companions in rhyme or in unrhymed lapidary royal Bavarian nonsense I do not know.

Rothschild—king of the age, as well as prophet of its god.

Parallels with a real reigning prince, with that of Ludwig I of Bavaria whose peculiar style and selective hall of fame (the 'Walhalla' at Regensburg) caused Heine so much amusement, may serve to suggest that the deference paid to the house of Rothschild is no more absurd than that paid to the house of Wittelsbach.

With a good deal of self-mockery Heine proceeds, in the *Lutezia* version of the article dated 5 May 1843, to join the Rothschild sycophants by comparing the banker to King Louis XIV—in respect of his ability to recognize and use other people's talents; and after likening him to a star at the height of its brilliancy he hastens (ironically) to magnify that not sufficiently extravagant compliment by comparing him to the very Sun which Louis XIV and so many other kings had adopted as their emblem.

In order to make quite sure of not causing offence I will today compare M. de Rothschild to the sun. I can do this, firstly, because it costs me nothing; and secondly, I can well justify it at a time like the present because now everyone pays homage to M. de Rothschild in the hope of being warmed by his golden rays.[12]

'If I may speak in confidence', Heine adds, *coram publico*, 'this frenzied veneration is no small affliction to the poor sun which gets no respite from its adorers—among whom there are some that are not worthy of having the sun shine on them; and it is precisely these Pharisees who are loudest in singing their psalms of praise.' And having pretended, mockingly, to join the sycophantic rabble, Heine continues by expressing pity for Rothschild because his money can be a plague:

I really believe that money is more a curse than a blessing to him; if he had a harder heart he would endure less discomfort . . . I counsel every man who is in dire need of money to go to M. de Rothschild; not in order to borrow from him (I doubt whether he would have much success in *that* endeavour!) but to comfort himself with the sight of the misery money can cause.[13]

With patent irony Heine declares Rothschild's money-misery to be more of a torture than the misery endured by the poor; here is a man, he tells his readers, who suffers agonies

because he has too much money, because all the money in the world has flowed into his gigantic cosmopolitan pocket, and because he has to carry such a burden around with him while all around the great rabble of starvelings and thieves stretch out their hands to him. And what terrible, what dangerous hands they are![145]

When he speaks of these 'terrible', 'dangerous' hands the poet alludes, as he so often does in *Lutezia*, to the communist have-nots that are threatening the plutocratic haves; and once again he links Babouvian egalitarianism with the teachings of Jesus, who is now termed, with scant historical justification, 'the divine Communist'.

'It is easier for a camel to pass through the eye of a needle than for a rich man to enter the kingdom of heaven'—this saying by the divine communist is a terrible anathema and bears witness to his bitter hatred of the Stock Exchange and the *haute finance* of Jerusalem.[15]

The superimposition effect is deliberate and characteristic: modern Paris and ancient Jerusalem mirror one another, and this mirror effect leads the poet to ruminate, with biting sarcasm, on 'the great camel question'—the question of what to do about the rich and their hard-heartedness. That last attribute, however, is not one he would willingly apply to Rothschild, from whom we take leave with another invented conversation.

'How are you!', a German poet once asked M. le baron. 'I am going mad', the latter replied. 'I won't believe that', said the poet, 'until you start throwing money out of the window'. The baron interrupted him with a sigh. 'That, precisely, *is* my madness: that I *don't* throw money out of the window occasionally!'[16]

The test once applied by a philistine nephew to the unworldly Ludwig Marcus is here applied to a great financier by a 'German poet' in whom many will surmise Heine himself. It is characteristic of him that he allows Rothschild to give a witty and reasonable reply.

The 'great camel question' leads away from the Rothschilds to other, lesser figures—and one particular butt is now thrust into the limelight the Rothschilds have vacated. This is August Leo, a Jewish banker from Hamburg who had settled in Paris and had sought to find greater respectability by converting to protestantism. But such conversions, as Heine knew from bitter personal experience, do not always have the desired effect. The lesson learnt by poor Gudel von Gudelfeld has to be learnt by Leo too:

I recently encountered poor August Leo and my heart bled at the sight of the man who had once been intimately linked with the chiefs of the Stock Exchange, with the aristocracy of speculators, and who had even been a bit of banker himself. But do tell me, you high and mighty gentlemen, what has poor Leo done to you that you expelled him so ignominiously from your congregation? I don't mean the Jewish one, I mean the congregation of financiers. Yes, this poor man has been loaded down with disfavour by his kind, and has been excluded like a leper from all meritorious—I mean profitable—enterprises.[17]

Leo is not allowed to float profitable loans, he has had to give up taking part in railway speculation, because his calculations went badly awry when he engaged his own and his clients' money in the *rive gauche* development of the Paris-Versailles railway. Leo's 'exclusion' gives Heine an opportunity to introduce other less than admirable financiers, beginning with the man whose name sounds like an invention of Heine's but may be genuine, the product of some German official's crude sense of humour when Jews were given Europeanized names:

No one wants to know Leo, everybody pushes him away, and even his only friend (who, by the way, never *could* stand him), even his Jonathan, the stockjobber Läusedorf, has left him. Läusedorf can now be seen perpetually pursuing Baron Meklenburg . . .

The last-named industrialist and speculator, Heine hastens to assure his readers, is not an Israelite and therefore not to be confused with Abraham Mecklenburg—it may be, he adds, that Baron Meklenburg is taken for a Jew

because he is always found among the mighty men of Israel, among the rag, tag, and bobtail of the Stock Exchange where they throng about him: for they love him greatly. These people,

Heine continues, rapidly sketching the Jewish *Krethi und Plethi*, the Cherethites and Pelethites, of the Paris Bourse,

are no religious fanatics . . . and their ill feeling towards poor Leo is therefore not at all due to confessional intolerance. They are not angry with him because of his apostasy from the beautiful Jewish religion, and they confined themselves to shrugging their shoulders, compassionately, at poor Leo's bad deal in the religious 'change business [*die schlechten Religionswechselgeschäfte des armen Leo*]. The poor man is now a churchwarden, a *marguiller* in a protestant chapel of the rue des Billettes—an important place of honour, no doubt, but a man like Leo would in time have risen to the highest honours in the synagogue too.

The thought of synagogue honours sets Heine's memory going; and he lists for the delectation of his Jewish and the instruction of his Christian readers some of the minor offices it is meritorious to perform at Jewish religious ceremonies.

Leo would, perhaps, have been entrusted with holding the child at the circumcision ceremony, or even the knife used at the same celebration, when the foreskin is removed; or he might have been showered with the costliest honours of the day at the reading of the Scroll of the Law or, since he is so musical and appreciates church music so much

(a reference, surely, to Leo's championship of Felix Mendelssohn's oratorios!)

he would perhaps have been charged with blowing the *shofar*, the sacred horn, at the New Year celebrations in the Jewish Church.

Having thus evoked some of the rituals of the religion which Leo, like himself, had formally abandoned, and having thus added further touches to his developing portrait of Judaism as well as Jews, Heine can turn once more to those who removed their favour from Leo—and to hammer home the point he so often made: that when it came to the commercial outlook on life, there was little to choose between Jew and Gentile, or Jew and Christian.

No, Leo is not the victim of religious or moral disapproval on the part of obstinate Pharisees. He is not being blamed for errors of the heart, poor man, but for errors of arithmetic. Even a Christian does not forgive lost millions. But,

Heine adds in mock-supplication,

have pity, at last, on this poor fallen man, pity his degraded greatness; take him once more into your grace and favour, let him share in some good piece of business, grant him just one little bit of profit—date obolum Belisario—give an obolus to this Belisarius who was not, admittedly, a great general, but who was, at least, blind, and who never in his life gave an obolus to a poor man.

This last savage sentence—particularly savage in its context, after the evocation of the rites of a religion which enjoins the dispensation of charity as one of the greatest of virtues—is toned down in the French version, which substitutes the words: 'un aveugle dont la cécité financière doit nous inspirer du respect et de la commisération'.[18]

We have not yet quite finished with Leo, however; Heine has still to deal with his attempt to propagate German music in Paris, and to keep open house for various celebrities. The poet therefore assumes the persona of a naïve German patriot who takes these cultural mediations seriously.

There are patriotic reasons, too, which make it desirable that poor Leo should be preserved from ruin. His wounded self-esteem and great losses are about to compel this once so well-to-do man to leave Paris, where life is very expensive, and to retire to the country where, like Cincinnatus, he can consume the cabbages he has himself raised or where he can graze on his own meadows as Nebuchadnezzar did in days of old.[19]

The comparisons with heroes of the past apply to Leo only at their least exalted point: with Belisarius he shares poverty and (metaphorical) blindness, with Cincinnatus the possibility of raising and eating cabbages, with Nebuchadnezzar that he resembles the ox rather than the lion. Nevertheless, Heine continues, Leo's departure from Paris would be felt, by some, as a great loss:

For all German travellers of the second or third class who came to Paris were hospitably received in Leo's house; and many of those who were put off by the frosty world of Parisian society could here find a refuge for their German hearts and could feel at home again in the company of like-minded souls. On cold winter evenings they could get a cup of tea here, somewhat homoeopathically prepared, but not quite without sugar. They saw Alexander von Humboldt here, that is to say his picture, hanging on the wall as a decoy. 'Nasenstern', however, they saw in natura. There was a real German countess too. The most illustrious diplomats from Hicksville and Hole-and-Cornertown put in an appearance, along with their Hicks-villian hole-and-corner wives. Sometimes one had the chance of listening, in this house, to some excellent pianists and violinists newly arrived in Paris and directed to the Leos by white slavers, vendors of souls who saw to it that they were musically exploited at these soirées. Germans here found themselves greeted by the well-loved sounds of their mother tongue, or even their grandmother tongue.[20]

The Jewish ambience, we see, is growing thicker: the distinction between mother tongue and grandmother-tongue, *mamme-loshen* and *booba-loshen*, is a distinction between different grades of Judaeo-German, as the reference to the Hamburg 'Dreckwall' in the next sentence strongly suggests.

Here the dialect of the Dreckwall was spoken in all its pristine purity, and whoever heard these classic sounds smelt again in his imagination the Mönkedamm canal.

Another olfactory image, another image suggesting an unpleasant smell! Then comes the modulation from the olfactory to the auditory, and from the Judaeo-German to the German at its most sentimental. Heine is not making fun of Beethoven's song, which is excellent of its arietta-like kind, but of the way it was received by nineteenth-century listeners.

But when it came to the singing of Beethoven's *Adelaide*—then flowed the most sentimental tears! Yes, that house was an oasis, a very oafish oasis, of German coziness in the midst of the sandy desert of French rationality; it was a tabernacle—

the word *Lauberhütte*, which Heine uses here, often served as equivalent of the Hebrew word *Sukkah*, the leafy structure erected by pious Jews during the Festival of Tabernacles; we are therefore unobtrusively having the Jewish superimposed over the German in Heine's evocation of the Leos' pathetic salon. Then a French element is blended in, when the salon is called 'a tabernacle of snug, gossipy *cancan*'; but that soon gives way to a reassertion of the German and the Jewish. 'Where they chattered as they do on the shores of the Main' (Heine means Frankfurt, of course, whose language he always associated with Judaeo-German *Mauscheln*):

where they chattered as they do on the shores of the Main, where they jabbered in the accents of the 'oly city of Cologne, where the gossip of the fatherland was occasionally accompanied by such refreshment as a small glass of beer has to offer. What more, O German soul, could you desire? It would be a great pity if this gossip shop were to be shut down for good.

Heine too, we must remember, was a baptized Jew who set up in Paris as a representative and apostle of German culture; he too was a relatively poor man associated with wealthy Jewish bankers. Perhaps his treatment of the Leo family was so particularly savage because it offered a caricature, a distorted mirror image, of some of his own endeavours and some of his own problems.

The attacks on the Foulds, which had been such a feature of the *Augsburg Gazette* articles, are toned down in *Lutezia*; Heine even goes so far as to deny his authorship of one virulent article which few modern editors would attribute to anyone but him.[21] As compensation he now prints, in *Lutezia*, a passage which—he tells us—the *Augsburg Gazette* had refused to print in the 1840s; as handsome an *amende honorable* as ever flowed from his pen.

A few days ago M. Fould also raised in the Chamber of Deputies a question about the conduct of the French consul at Damascus. I must therefore, first of all, withdraw the reproach which escaped me in one of my last reports. I never doubted M. Fould's intelligence, his intellectual powers; I think of him as one of the most capable members of the French Chamber of Deputies. What I doubted was his disposition or feeling. I am always glad to be put to shame when I have done people an injustice and when they confound my accusations by their deeds. M. Fould's interpellation manifested great shrewdness and dignity.[22]

It never entered his head, he now tells an 'enthusiastic friend' of Benoît Fould ('and what rich man cannot muster a swarm of such enthusiastic friends?') to cast aspersions on M. Fould's personal appearance; had he wished to do so, he adds, he would not have had to borrow his arrows from the quivers of the French press.[23] Achille Fould, for his part, the man he had so cruelly mocked in 1846, receives an even more unequivocal *amende*—and that in the very years in which Karl Marx poured the vessels of his scorn on Achille Fould's head because of the part he was playing in the government of Napoleon III. Heine pretends, in a note dated May 1854, to have been outraged by the ascription to himself of an anonymously published attack on the Foulds.

Since I never liked to suffer unjustly I conceived, in the end, the unhappy idea of actually committing the *lèse-majesté* of which I was [falsely] accused; and when I reported on the election at Tarbes, the Deputy of the Hautes-Pyrénées had to bear the brunt of my ill humour. Since in the end I confess everyone of my unjust actions, I will confess here and now, to my own shame, that the man of whom I said that he had no ability at all distinguished himself, soon afterwards, as a statesman of the highest importance. I rejoiced at this.[24]

The Deputy elected by the voters of the Hautes-Pyrénées district was, of course, none other than Achille Fould.

The longest and most elaborate of the additions Heine made to the articles from the *Augsburg Gazette* when he reworked them into *Lutezia* in 1853-4 was a piece entitled *Retrospective Explanation (Retrospektive Aufklärung)* in which he defended himself against the charge that the French government had bought his silence on certain matter by awarding him a government pension. Here he has, perforce, to speak of his reasons for accepting the pension—and among such reasons his need for money is the most obviously important. Having spoken of the way in which his literary income has been curtailed by censorship and proscription in Germany, he continues:

The indigent men whom I had liberally aided laughed at me when I said that in future I would not have enough for my own needs. Was I not related to all sorts of millionaires? Had not [Rothschild], the generalissimo of all millionaires, the millionairissimo, called me his friend? What I could never make my clients understand was that this great millionairissimo called me his friend only because I never asked him for money. Had I done so, our friendship would soon have been at an end. The days of David and Jonathan, of Orestes and Pylades, are past. The poor blockheads who wanted my help thought it was easy to obtain this commodity from the rich. They never saw, as I did, the terrible locks and bars with which their great money chests are secured . . .[25]

These are Heine's last words, in *Lutezia*, about his relations with the Rothschilds; and one does not have to read far in his letters to see that they are an equivocation. He may not have asked the Rothschilds for *cash*—but he did ask for *railway shares* which could be sold at an immediate profit and which the Rothschilds, in fact, bought straight back for a higher price, leaving the poet to pocket the easy profit. The very work which contains this equivocation, *Lutezia*, shows beyond any doubt that Heine knew exactly what charitable game the Rothschilds played with him on such occasions.

The House of Rothschild, which has made tenders for the concession of the Northern Railway line, and which will in all probability obtain this concession, is not a public company in the true sense of the word; every share which members of this house grants to individuals is really a great favour—speaking plainly I should say that it is in fact a present of money which M. de Rothschild makes his friends. The shares ultimately issued, bonds from the house of Rothschild, are from the beginning worth several hundred francs above par, and whoever asks Baron James de Rothschild for such shares at par, *begs* from him in the literal sense of the word. But then—the whole world is begging from him; he is inundated by begging letters, and where the greatest aristocrats have set such a noble example, begging can no longer be considered a disgrace.[26]

Even when Heine feels obliged to equivocate, he provides the clue that enables the perceptive reader to recognize the equivocation and to figure out the truth for himself. What is no equivocation, and no vain flattery, is the importance Heine attaches to the Rothschild phenomenon. 'I cannot, he tells us, 'judge his financial capacity; but if one goes by results it must be very great indeed'. What he can confidently assert, however, is that the Baron is a strange and remarkable person, *eine merkwürdige Person*; that thanks to his financial activities he has become the hero of the day, *der Held des Tages*, and that no one will ever be able to write the history of mid-nineteenth-century Europe without a close look at what he represents. Rothschild, Heine tells the readers of *Lutezia*, 'plays so important a part in the miserable state in which we find ourselves today, *in der Geschichte unserer heutigen Misère*, that I must speak of him often and with as great a seriousness as possible.'[27] That remark is dated 5 May 1843; but Heine clearly means it to apply to the 1850s too. And in our context it is worth noting the implications of the claim that he will speak of him seriously *as possible, so ernsthaft wie möglich*; for Heine was as alive as ever Balzac was to the comic possibilities of the good baron, though he seems to have exploited these more in his conversation than in his correspondence. The Rothschild family had been generous towards him in small ways and could be expected to do him further unobtrusive and unhurtful kindnesses—it would have been ungrateful as well as impolitic to hold them up to public ridicule. And Heine seems to have conceived a genuine (if not always unalloyed) respect for the French and Austrian branches of this most famous of banking families; a respect that made the task of suppressing the witticisms that would occasionally flow to his pen less burdensome than the same task would have been if the prospective victim had been Nasenstern or the Leo family or Giacomo Meyerbeer.

(ii)

In 1852, when he had introduced the story of Nebuchadnezzar into the Preface he supplied for the second edition of *Towards a History of Religion and Philosophy in Germany*, Heine had given his readers a glimpse of Karl Marx, with whom he had struck up a friendship in 1843. As we have seen, he twice commended the legend of Nebuchadnezzar to the attention, not only of Ruge, but also of 'my still more obdurate friend Marx, yes, and to Messrs Feuerbach, Daumer, Bruno Bauer, Hengstenberg [!!]and other such—to all these godless gods unto themselves . . .'[28] The inclusion of the pious Hengstenberg in this list is a joke, of course; but the other names mentioned are those of the Hegelian Left who had taken the road away from traditional beliefs in God to which the later Heine claimed to have returned. In some fragmentary *Letters on Germany*, which Heine wrote in 1844 but never published, Marx had in fact appeared in a very similar list of men described as belonging to 'the younger Hegelian school'.[29] Presenting him as the most 'obdurate' of these neo-Hegelians in 1852, Heine would have us look on Marx as one who had thought out his position thoroughly and was not likely to follow the poet along his theistic path. He deliberately calls him his friend, however, and thus suggests publicly that differences in outlook, in *Weltanschauung*, need not disturb their liking and respect for one another.

In the course of *Lutezia* Marx is cited as a character witness in Heine's 'Retrospective Explanation' of why and how had come to accept a pension from secret French government funds. The *Augsburg Gazette* had suggested, in 1848, when the fact that Heine had been drawing this modest pension was revealed, that he might have been paid for *not* writing certain things that could embarrass the French government. Heine indignantly rejects this accusation and adds:

> I remember that my compatriots, among them the most resolute and intelligent of them all [*der entschiedenste und geistreichste*], Dr Marx, came to me to express their indignation at the libellous article in the *Augsburg Gazette* and advised me not to answer in my own person since they had already expressed the opinion, in German journals, that I had only accepted the pension granted to me in order to support more effectively the poorer members of the party to which I belonged. This was said to me by the former editor of the *New Rhenish Gazette [Neue Rheinische Zeitung]* and by the friends who formed his general staff . . .[30]

Alas for historical truth! Marx *did* champion Heine publicly whenever opportunity arose, he took his side in the *Börne* affair, and never suggested that Heine had been bribed, or could be bribed, into silence—but he denied absolutely, in his letter to Engels of 17 January 1855, that the interview Heine described had ever taken place. It was impossible chronologically, he explained . . . but he only said such things in private, and always stood by Heine in his public utterances.[31] Heine did the same for him—the only serious criticism of Marx he ever made occurred in the course of a conversation with Moritz Carrière, who reported to Varnhagen on 11 October 1851:

> Marx is a very intelligent but rather abrupt man, who has a strong dictatorial streak and of whom Heine said: 'A man is very little, after all, if he is nothing but a razor.'[32]

Among the men of letters who make a fleeting appearance in the pages of *Lutezia* is once again Ferdinand Koreff, that friend of E. T. A. Hoffmann's who had settled in Paris, where he was well known as a doctor, writer, and wit. Heine, who had consulted him professionally for some of his ailments, enjoyed his *bons mots* and recorded one of them in *Lutezia*. After naming a German virtuoso who had come to Paris in search of fame and fortune, Heine adds:

Koreff could say of this man with as much wit as truth: 'He looks like a sticky sweet that has fallen into the mud.'[33]

A baptized and ennobled ex-Jew from Württemberg, Karl von Weil, whose name had appeared alongside Heine's own on the list of Germans who had received government pensions during the reign of Louis Philippe, did not fare as well as Koreff in the pages of *Lutezia*. Von Weil, he says, was

a submissive subject of the king of Württemberg, no great poet, no light of science, no astronomer, no famous statesman, no hero of art—he was no hero of any kind, he was, on the contrary, most unwarlike . . .[34]

Weil once refused a challenge to a duel, Heine wickedly adds with an allusion to his victim's mixed ancestry, 'for the sanitary reason that he found it impossible to digest balls of lead—his stomach could cope only with balls of baked *shalet* [*Schaletkugeln*] and Swabian dumplings.'[35]

(iii)

Koreff's witticism, quoted in the last paragraph, has already introduced a subject on which *Lutezia*, like the newspaper articles on which the whole work is based, has a good deal to say: the subjects of composers and executant musicians. In his book on Heine's music criticism, first published in 1971, Michael Mann has admirably described and analysed Heine's views on such matters. He has shown how the poet contracted temporary alliances with various factions; how he extracted from the writings of others technical information his own inadequate musical knowledge and training was unable to supply; how he tried to see the spirit of different nations expressed in their music and to trace connections between a given people's music and its political and social aspirations;

and how his growing distaste for methods of modern publicity, his belief that a concert-going public could be manipulated by press agents and venal journalists, and his increasing alienation from the cultural traffic of his time, gave an ever keener satiric edge to his discussions of composers and virtuosi. Foremost among these, as ever, is Meyerbeer, now irrevocably reduced, in Heine's eyes, from a composer who conveyed in terms proper to his art the spirit of emancipation in Europe to a fountain-head of modern musical eclecticism, a 'musical maître de plaisir of the aristocracy', and an unscrupulous manager of his own fame,[36] who fitly appears in *Lutezia* as 'the great Giacomo Machiavelli'.[37]

The much-maligned composer makes his bow in a long passage added to the *Augsburg Gazette* article of 12 June 1840, in which, it will be remembered, a verbal caricature of Gasparo Spontini played an important part. In the original article Heine had made M. Duponchel, the director of the Paris Opera, exclaim: 'Get this intriguing mummy [Spontini] off my back! I have enough intrigues by the *living* to put up with!' 'And yet', Heine had added, 'M. Schl.—for this was the good soul by whom Sir Gasparo had himself introduced to M. Duponchel—had summoned up all his eloquence to represent his protégé in the most favourable light possible.'[38] That last sentence becomes, in 1854:

And yet M. Moritz Schlesinger, the publisher of Meyerbeer's operas—for this was the good honest soul by whom Sir Gasparo had himself introduced to M. Duponchel—had summoned up all his credit-worthy eloquence, in order to represent his protégé in the best possible light.[39]

Heine has made three main alterations: (i) he has given Schlesinger's full name, so that he can be more easily recognized when, later on, he himself becomes the target of Heine's satire; (ii) he has added various laudatory epithets to his description of Schlesinger—'honest', 'credit-worthy'—which can be ironized later; (iii) he has directed the main thrust of the satire away from Spontini and on to Meyerbeer, whose name will resound through the rest of the passage with the persistence of a ground bass.

The alpha and omega of all Spontini's complaints is Meyerbeer.

When the noble knight [Spontini]did me the honour of visiting me here in Paris, he was a constant source of poisonous bitter stories. He cannot deny that the King of Prussia overwhelms our great Giacomo with honours and constantly thinks up high offices and dignities to load him with; but Spontini has ways of ascribing the basest motives to these signs of royal favour. In the end he comes to believe his own inventions . . .[40]

The 'inventions' that follow surely derive from Heine rather than Spontini. He makes the Italian suggest that the King of Prussia wants to keep Meyerbeer in Prussia so that his immense fortune should not be dissipated abroad; or that the King in fact hates music and wants to discredit it by exhibiting Meyerbeer in his capital—'a man', Spontini is made to say, 'who has no sense of truth or nobility but is solely concerned with flattering the mob'; or that Meyerbeer is a plagiarist, who has stolen tunes from Weber and others; or that he procures favourable notices by unethical means; or that he is a musical highwayman (*Cartouche der Musik*) whose vanity could lead him, even, to poisoning his rivals; or that his operas will not outlast his own lifetime. All this Spontini is made to say while Heine mimes indignation—*der welsche Neidhart*, he calls him, using a phrase for 'jealous Latin' that has all the ring of Teutomania, and therefore, in Heine's context, all the hallmarks of parody. And then, pretending to refute this *Neidhart*'s alleged contention that Meyerbeer's operas will die with their begetter, he goes even further than his Spontini in imputing to Maestro Giacomo a system of bribery and press corruption whose puff-effects will outlast him—at least for a while. He uses the method of sustained metaphor: Meyerbeer appears as a father seeing to it that his children, his operas, born and unborn, will have something to live on after his own death.

The great Giacomo has set up a trust fund, as it were, for his musical children, setting aside a capital sum for each of them. The interest from these capital sums is to be devoted to securing the future of these poor orphans. They will therefore be able to afford, even after their father's death, the expense necessary for the maintenance of their popularity—such things as gaudy advertisements, *claques*, praise by journalists and so on. Even the little *Prophet*, as yet unborn, is said to have been left the sum of 150,000 Prussian thalers by his affectionate progenitor. No prophet has ever come into this world with anything like such wealth; the carpenter's son of Bethlehem and the camel driver of Mecca had fewer riches. *Robert le Diable* and *Les Huguenots* are said to have been less generously endowed; I suppose they can live off their own fat for a while . . .[41]

And so it goes on, down the list of Meyerbeer's operas, until we come to *Emma di Resburgo*, which appears in the guise of an unmarriageable daughter who has somehow to be bought a husband by means of a weighty dowry and a fine trousseau—'for a parent's heart always beats most warmly for those of his children who turn out to be crooked changelings and freaks'. The ostensible subject of the satire is still Spontini—but there can be no doubt that its real target is Maestro Giacomo.

Heine returns to the charge that Meyerbeer has *bought* his fame in additions he makes to the article of 20 April 1841. He begins with some tasteless jokes about Meyerbeer's notorious digestion troubles, culminating in reminiscences of

the diarrhoea god of Tartar folklore, which tells in horribly droll fashion how this grim belly-aching *kakodaimon* one day bought six thousand pots for his own use and thus made the potter a rich man.[42]

He throws up his hands in mock despair as he envisages the possibility of the maestro's death:

What is to become of his fame when he himself, the most celebrated Maestro, should suddenly—God forbid!—be snatched by death from the scene of his triumphs? Will his family keep up this fame of which all Germany is so proud? That family will not be short of material capacity with which to achieve this—but intellectual capacity is another matter.

Another swipe, we see, at the Beer family, especially Michael and Heinrich. And now comes a dazzling passage in which Heine makes Meyerbeer's activity as conductor and director of music a metaphor to describe the management of his own fame.

Only the great Giacomo himself, who is not only Director General of all Royal Prussian musical academies and institutions, but also conductor-in-chief of Meyerbeer's fame—he alone is capable of directing *that* orchestra. He nods his head, and all the trombones of the great journals blare out *unisono*; he winks his eye, and all the violins of praise vie with one another in dulcet fiddling; he twitches his left nostril, and all the feuilleton-flageolets flute their most insinuating flatteries. There are antediluvian wind instruments too, Jericho trumpets, and some as yet undiscovered aeolian harps, stringed instruments of the future, whose deployment shows his extraordinary talent for orchestration at its very height . . .[43]

Heine here skilfully parodies the language used by music critics in the era of Liszt and Wagner when evaluating the work of a conductor and an orchestra. But even now he has not yet done with his sustained metaphor, whose fulcrum is a pun on the word 'instruments':

No composer has ever understood as fully as our Meyerbeer the art of using all sorts of men as instruments—the smallest along with the greatest—and conjuring up through their harmonization a consensus of opinion that is little short of fabulous . . . Heaven knows that he often uses the lowliest instruments; but perhaps that is why he can so powerfully impress the multitude which worships, honours, and even respects him . . . Laurel wreaths fly towards him from every side, he bears a whole forest of laurels on his head, he hardly knows what to do with them and pants under his green burden.

An excess of laurels: that image, as we shall see, provides the starting point of a satirical poem Heine composed on the subject of Meyerbeer. Here, in *Lutezia*, it leads away from the 'orchestra of fame' image to the sort of juxtaposition we have already seen in *Germany. A Winter's Tale*, where Paganini appeared attended by a spirit that could take the form either of a poodle or of his agent Georg Harrys. Paganini's poodle becomes Meyerbeer's donkey, the former's Harrys becomes the latter's Gouin.

He should get himself a little donkey which could trot behind him and carry the heavy load of laurel. But Gouin is jealous and will not allow anyone else to accompany him.[44]

(Alexandre Gouin was Meyerbeer's friend and one of his agents in Paris.) Heine ends his caricature of Meyerbeer as manager of his own fame with a *bon mot* he attributes to the same Ferdinand Hiller whom he had once presented as Meyerbeer's associate in worthily representing the spirit of German music in France. When someone asked Hiller what he thought of Meyerbeer's operas, Heine tells us, he is said to have replied: 'Let's not talk politics!' Hiller here becomes the poet's own mouthpiece even more obviously and directly than Spontini.[45]

In other places Meyerbeer is compared to a juggler and stage–
magician; he is said to out-intrigue even primadonnas; and he
is reminded of the inappropriateness of the line 'Money is only
a chimaera' in the text of *Robert le Diable*. He is also said to
avoid passing the statue of his great rival Rossini:

Whenever he went to the opera in the evening he carefully bypassed
that marble stumbling-block—he tried not to see it at all. In just the
same way the Jews of Rome always went a roundabout way when
they had to go out, even on the most urgent business errand: for they
did not want to pass that egregious triumphal Arch of Titus, erected
in memory of the destruction of Jerusalem.[46]

The comparison is carefully chosen, of course, to remind read-
ers of the Jewish origins of this prodigy of European music.

A similar reminder may be found in the later Heine's most
venomous caricature: that of the composer and impresario
Josef Dessauer. 'A nameless, crawling insect', Heine calls him,
incensed by a rumour that Dessauer had boasted of the sexual
conquest of George Sand; 'a self-vaunting bedbug'. This fellow
has to be distinguished, we are told with mock-solemnity,
from *der alte Dessauer*, one of Frederick the Great's generals,
after whom a famous march, *der Dessauer Marsch*, had been
named.

The Dessauer of whom we are here speaking has never won any
laurels; he has writen no famous marches; and no statues have been
erected in his honour and then fallen down. He is not the *alte
Dessauer* of Prussia; he only bears that name as *nom de guerre* or
perhaps as a nickname to indicate his elderly, cringing, crooked,
befogged appearance . . . He does not hail from Dessau—on the
contrary, he hails from Prague, where he possesses two large, reaso-
nably clean houses in the jewish quarter . . .[47]

Again, we see, the carefully placed clue. There is a great deal
more of this kind, until even Heine comes to feel that he may
be overdoing it:

Pardon me, dear reader, for entertaining you with such blowflies; but
their pushful buzzing can drive even the most patient man to take up
the fly-swatter. I also wanted to show in this place what kind of
dung-beetles our honest music publishers advertise as German night-
ingales, as successors, even as rivals, to Schubert.[48]

The dehumanizing images employed throughout, the bugs, blowflies, and dung-beetles which are used as analogues of Dessauer, show the depth of rage and contempt which this minor figure stirred up in Heine.

It will have been noticed that the indictment of Dessauer included an indictment of 'honest music publishers' who pushed his work and introduced him into society. To see one of these ranged alongside the hated 'blowfly', let us look at a passage which begins with a saying alleged to have been habitual with a woman whom Heine calls, with scant courtesy, *die alte Mosson*: 'if you have plenty of money, you don't *have* to compose!' *Die alte Mosson* was in fact Meyerbeer's mother-in-law; but the attitude implicit in her remark was one familiar to Heine from certain never-to-be-forgotten utterances of his own uncle Salomon. Having thus introduced Dessauer as a man who, in Mrs Mosson's sense, did not *have* to compose, he gives us a rapid sketch of his life's course from Prague to Vienna and thence to Paris. In Vienna we are told, he had little success:

No one knew what he was saying, and that was quite understandable: he spoke a confused jargon and had adopted a novel pronunciation of German which reminds one of rotten eggs. On the other hand— maybe people *did* understand what he was saying, and that is why no one wanted to know . . .[49]

After another distasteful sally into fun at the expense of a fellow-man's physical ailments Heine transports his Dessauer to Paris:

Here he won the favour of the celebrated Moritz Schlesinger, who published his song compositions and gave him a gold watch in lieu of an honorarium. When old Dessauer went to see his patron a little later on and complained that the watch did not go, the latter answered: 'Go? Did I say it would go? Do your compositions go? My experience with your compositions is the same as yours with my watch. They don't go!'[50]

There are two reasons why Heine's caricature of Schlesinger's speech has to be heard in the original. One of these is the triple sense of the word 'go', *gehen*, on which the poet plays: *gehen* as a watch does, that is to say 'work or function properly'; *gehen* as of a saleable commodity, in the sense of 'finding customers willing to buy it'; and *gehen* as in the phrase *es geht mir* 'it is my experience . . .' The second reason is because it demonstrates Heine's good ear for Jewish speech patterns and rhythms—even today an excited Ashkenazi Jew can talk in just such a series of questions and with just such an eloquent repetition of keywords.

'Gehen? Habe ich gesagt, daß sie gehen wird? Gehen Ihre Kompositionen? Es geht mir mit ihren Kompositionen, wie es Ihnen mit meiner Uhr geht. Sie gehen nicht.'

Heine did not often indulge his well-attested talent for mimicking Jewish speech to quite this extent in public.

The composer Jacques Fromental Halévy appears in *Lutezia* as a harmless nonentity. Meyerbeer need not fear him as he feared Rossini: Spontini is made to say that

Meyerbeer would even be prepared to pay his colleague Halévy simply for existing, as a rival in semblance only [*ein Scheinrivale*] who is quite incapable of doing him harm . . .[51]

In the French version, *Lutèce*, however, the poet adopts a friendlier attitude and even finds a good word to say about Halévy's opera *Il Lazzarone:*

C'est l'œuvre d'un grand artiste, et je ne sais pas pourquoi elle est tombée. M. Halévy est peut-être trop insouciant et ne cajole pas assez M. Alexandre, l'entrepreneur des succès et le grand ami de Meyerbeer . . . .[52]

M. Alexandre, in this last sentence, is Alexandre Gouin; and his presence here is most significant. Jewish composers such as Meyerbeer and Dessauer, Jewish entrepreneurs such as Schlesinger, know how to use a corrupt press and saleable organs of approbation for their own purposes. But this corruption is in no way a Jewish invention (the greatest of all press manipulators was Guizot!) nor are Jews the only ones to make use of it (Liszt, Gouin, and a host of other impeccable Christians are equally adept). And Heine takes good care to show his readers Jews who *disdain* such means of managing their reputations— that is one thing that can be said in favour of Jacques Halévy, of whom Heine tends otherwise to think as a bore. Of Jacques Halévy's brother Léon he is said to have remarked on one occasion: 'He is as dull as though his brother had composed him.'[53]

Compared with such a crew, Mendelssohn-Bartholdy looks better, in *Lutezia*, than he had done in Heine's earlier articles. The poet retains the comparison with Tieck that has already been quoted; but both Tieck and Mendelssohn-Bartholdy are now called 'masters', *Meister*, without any obvious irony; Mendelssohn is even said to be more gifted, *begabter*, than Tieck. These gifts, Heine adds, might well enable Mendelssohn to create works that would endure the test of time—but not, he reiterates, on the stage; for great drama and great opera demand a sustained truthfulness and passion such as neither Mendelssohn nor Tieck could command.[54]

To his discussion of Mendelssohn-Bartholdy Heine now subjoins another discussion of Ferdinand Hiller, in whom he continues to see a representative of German music worthy of the respect he has earned among discriminating Parisians. He repeats the charge of excessive intellectuality which he had already levelled at him in his *Morning Chronicle* account of 1831, but once again allows praise to outweigh blame.

Hiller is a thinking rather than a feeling musician and is charged, in addition, with having too much learning. It may indeed be true that the intellect and learning discernible in his compositions may occasionally have a somewhat chilling effect; but they are, for all that, invariably graceful, attractive, and beautiful. There is no sign of crooked-faced eccentricity; Hiller possesses an elective affinity with his compatriot Wolfgang Goethe. Like Goethe, Hiller was born in Frankfurt, where I saw his father's house when I last passed through—it is called 'At the Green Frog's', and the picture of a frog may be seen above the front door. Hiller's compositions, however, never remind one of such an unmusical beast; they recall only nightingales, larks, and other such birds of spring.[55]

The affinity with Goethe which Heine here ascribes to Hiller, whose music for *Faust* he had felt unable to praise in his essay of 1831, counteracts any temptation on the part of his readers to connect the 'intellectuality' of Hiller's art with his Jewish birth.

Executant musicians, virtuosi of the violin and (especially) the hated piano, are treated in *Lutezia* with the same distaste that had marked the original articles in the *Augsburg Gazette*.

Some expressions are modified: Heine puns on the name of Alexander Dreyschock, and hints at the Jewish origins of Josef Sina by warning his readers against confounding him with Mount Sinai.[56] The majority of the virtuosi caricatured in *Lutezia* are non-Jews, however, and we must keep this fact in mind when we come to Heine's ironic use of the Old Testament for their characterization and classification.

After Döhler Halle demands a special mention among the minor prophets; he is a Habakkuk of modest but true merit. I cannot forbear mentioning M. Schad as well—he occupies among pianist something like the rank Jonah has among the prophets. May no whale ever swallow him up![57]

Bible allusions continue to come easily to Heine, especially when his purpose is satirical—an amusing example is his use of Psalm 115 to describe the theatre and concert public in England: 'They have eyes, but see not; they have ears, but they hear not; noses have they, but they smell not . . .'[58] All this must be seen alongside such more serious passages as the poet's exegesis of the Judah and Tamar story, which represents his effort to defend the Bible's morality even when it relates incidents that might seem immoral by more modern standards.[59]

Spinoza also comes into view in the course of *Lutezia*, when Heine protests against attempts to make the French translation of his works more palatable to the French Catholic Church or to annex him wholly to the German tradition. He mocks misguided German patriots who want to annex everything worth while to their own nation, from Shakespeare to Jenny Lind; men for whom even Spinoza, in his innermost essence, can be nothing but a German.[60] But as we now know, Heine had come to think that there was indeed a profound affinity between the true Judaic and the true German spirit—a belief it is relevant to remember when we notice how constantly and consistently he presents himself, throughout *Lutezia*, as a German in exile.

The most famous passage in the whole work, the one that set out to answer the question why Heine had never become a naturalized Frenchman, culminates in the expression of his wish to see the words 'Here lies a German poet' engraved on his tombstone.'[61] The preface to the French edition, written in

March 1855, adopts quite consciously a kind of Atta Troll persona, the persona of a clumsy but well-meaning German bear in elegant Paris:

Ma belle Lutèce, n'oublie pas ma nationalité: bien que je sois un des mieux léchés d'entre mes compatriotes, je ne saurais pourtant pas tout à fait renier ma nature; c'est ainsi que les caresses de mes pattes tudesques ont put te blesser parfois, et je t'ai peut-être lancé plus d'un pavé sur la tête, dans la seule intention de te défendre contre les mouches . . .[62]

This is a perspective we must not ignore when we look at the Jewish figures Heine introduces, at such frequent intervals, into the work which he himself described as a history book in daguerreotypes (*ein daguerreotypisches Geschichtsbuch*).

To make these doleful accounts more gay, I interwove sketches from the realm of art and the sciences, from the dance-halls of high and low society; and if, on occasions, I drew, among such arabesques, the all too ridiculous face of some virtuoso or other, I did not do so in order to grieve some forgotten worthy of the pianoforte or the Jew's harp, but rather to give a picture of the time in its minutest nuances. An honest daguerreotype must represent a fly as faithfully as the proudest horse; and my reports are a history book in daguerreotype, in which each day has depicted itself. By combining such images the artist's co-ordinating spirit has provided a work in which what is represented documents its own authenticity. My book is therefore a product at once of nature and of art; and while it now satisfies, perhaps, the desires of the popular reading public, it will assuredly serve future historians as a historical source which, as I have said, guarantees its own truth to the facts of the day.[63]

Heine's imagery combines the work of the artist (especially the caricaturist and supplier of arabesques) with that of the photographer and that of the man who arranges the photographs in a meaningful sequence, but his image of the daguerreotype is seriously incomplete. He fails to draw attention to the importance which point of view, perspective, and selection assume in a photograph as they do in his literary accounts of life in Paris. He fails to take into account the way in which his reports are so constructed that they bring out the flow and change of life—his scenes, consequently, suggest the later snapshot rather than the posed daguerreotypes of the poet's own day. He fails, lastly, to tell us how heavily he retouched his earlier 'daguerreotypes' when he revised his newspaper articles of the 1840s for *Lutezia* and *Lutèce* in the 1850s.

One other passage in the Preface to *Lutèce* is of the utmost importance in helping us to evaluate the portraits with which the present book is concerned. Heine here reveals the strategies that included clothing opinions in the guise of facts, placing his own thoughts in the mouths of others, and adopting a tone of neutrality or indifference.

Il me fallait donc constamment songer à revêtir de la forme d'un fait tout ce que je voulais insinuer au public, l'évènement aussi bien que le jugement que j'en portais, bref, tout ce que je pensais et sentais; et dans ce dessein, je n'hésitais pas à mettre souvent mes propres opinions dans la bouche d'autres personnes, ou même je parabolisais mes idées. Voilà pourquoi mes lettres contiennent beaucoup d'historiettes et d'arabesques, dont le sens symbolique n'est pas intelligible pour tout le monde, et qui ont pu paraître aux yeux du lecteur superficiel comme un ramassis de jaseries mesquines et de notices de gobe-mouches. Dans mes efforts de faire toujours prédominer la forme du fait, il m'importait également de choisir pour mon langage un ton qui me permet de rapporter les choses les plus scabreuses. Le ton le plus avantageux à cet égard était celui de l'indifférence, et je m'en servais sans scrupule . . .[64]

This modifies what Heine had said about his 'arabesques' in the dedicatory preface of the German *Lutezia* and indicates the extent to which we must regard his anecdotes as parables: as stories chosen, and often invented, to convey truths that transcend the literal reportage of empirical facts. As for his tone of 'indifference'—he modifies that sufficiently to allow even this late French version of his *Augsburg Gazette* articles to term the Jews of modern times 'les descendants d'Israël, de ce peuple de prêtres pur et élu'.[65] That brief phrase constitutes an eloquent tribute to the *idea* of Israel which he had so often shown to have been compromised or perverted by fallible men; and notwithstanding his belief that the virtues of the ancestors may have become attenuated or perverted in many of their descendants, it suggests yet another reason why Heine could not follow Marx in believing that the best form of Jewish emancipation would be the emancipation of society from Judaism.

CHAPTER 15
'In My End is My Beginning'

'Je les tiens!', visitors to the sick-room of *l'homme enseveli*, as neighbours called the poet in his latter years, heard him exclaim after he had been working on notes for his memoirs. 'Look over there', he said to Alfred Meissner in 1854:

There lie my memoirs, in which for years now I have been gathering togethering caricature-portraits, repellent silhouettes [*fratzenhafte Porträts, abschreckende Silhouetten*] . . . Many a small bullfrog, many a perfidious snake, many intolerable tapeworms, and many a freak, have I caught, seized hold of, and preserved in spirit . . .[1]

Heine saw himself, Meissner goes on to report, as Apollo pulling Marsyas's skin over his ears, as an exterminator of vermin. Yet none of this actually appears in the *Memoiren*-fragment published after the poet's death. In fact, many earlier works considered in the present book—*Ideas. The Book of LeGrand*, for instance, or *Schnabelewopski*, or *Ludwig Börne*—introduce autobiographical material and caricatures of contemporaries that fit Heine's description to Meissner much more closely than anything in the fragmentary pages actually headed *Memoiren*. I shall refrain from speculating on the possible contents of lost portions and confine my comments to what (for the present at least) is all we have.

In the opening passage of a fragment usually prefixed to *Memoiren* and addressed, like *The Book of LeGrand*, to the shadowy outline of one particular female reader, Heine assumes responsibility for lacunae in the tale he will tell of his life, and warns future editors against any attempt to supply what is missing with the help of unpublished fragments, private letters, or other posthumous *inedita*.

Indeed, my dear lady, I have tried to set down the memorabilia of my time, in so far as I have myself come into contact with them as spectator or as victim, as truthfully, as faithfully as possible. Almost half of these notes, to which I gave the self-regarding title *Memoiren*, had, however, to be destroyed partly for some miserable family reasons, partly because of religious scruples. Since then I have tried to fill in the gaps, sketchily it is true; but I fear that considerations of posthumous duty will force me to subject my memoirs to a new *auto-da-fé* before I die, and that what is saved from these flames may never see the light of day . . .

This should not be read, however, as an invitation to others to supply the deficiency:

It is impermissible and immoral to publish a single line a writer has not himself destined for the public at large. That applies particularly to letters addressed to private individuals—whoever prints or publishes these is guilty of a felony that deserves contempt . . .[2]

His own effort, he assures his spectral reader as well as the public at large, will be directed towards selecting what he thinks significant and characteristic (*alles Bedeutsame und Charakteristische*); to exhibit the interaction of external events and what happens in the human soul (*die Wechselwirkung äußerer Begebenheiten und innerer Seelenereignisse*); and to trace in this way the 'signatures', *die Signatura*, of his being and his existence. He intends revealing his soul, with all its wounds, in the process of telling the reader whose ghostly presence he has summoned up the nursery-tale of his life: *das Märchen meines Lebens.*[3]

The phrase just quoted has obvious implications for the kind of memoirs we may expect from Heine. What he will not give us is a full and accurate, naturalistically detailed, 'objective' account of the events of his life. He will seek to select, to stylize, to impose shape and form, in order to highlight those elements which he had come to regard as the most formative and revealing. In describing his early education, for instance, he is at pains to stress its distance from the sort of education Jewish boys would have received in the ghettos of Europe; we therefore learn much that is interesting about his German High-School training, especially his contacts with Jesuit teachers, but nothing, not a single word, about the Jewish school or *kheder* run by a distant relative named Rintelsohn which we know him to have attended. We are aware that he could read and write non-cursive Hebrew letters, and that he had a fair knowledge of Jewish ritual, but he does not tell us how much of this he acquired in early childhood. We cannot look to him for authentification of tales about his boyhood told by others: tales of how he invoked or twisted the sabbath ordinances he had been bidden to obey in order to suit his own convenience and desire.[4] We do not even know for certain whether he actually went through that rite of passage which Jewish boys usually absolve at the age of thirteen, the *bar mitzvah*. What he does tell us about that crucial thirteenth year, however, has obvious implications for his attitude to Judaism.

Earliest beginnings explain latest phenomena. It is surely significant that in the thirteenth year of my life I already received instruction in all the systems of free thought, and that I received this from a venerable Christian clergyman who never neglected his sacerdotal duties in the slightest. From my early years, therefore, I saw how religion and doubt could walk side by side without hypocrisy. This produced within me, not just unbelief, but the most tolerant indifference.

Time and place are also of importance: I was born at the end of the sceptical eighteenth century, in a town which was governed, during my childhood, not only by Frenchmen, but also by the French mind and spirit.[5]

The maxim 'Earliest beginnings explain latest phenomena' can be inverted; 'late phenomena', Heine's subsequent development, and the stage it had reached at the time of writing, have governed the selection he has made from his memories of 'earliest beginnings'.

The controlling influence on his early development as he now depicts it—the force which ensured that he was given the best Gentile education his native city of Düsseldorf had to offer—was, undoubtedly, his mother, and a good deal of space is given to her efforts to procure her son a successful career in the wider world which Napoleon's conquests had made more accessible to Jews. There is not much talk, this time, of a possible career in the Catholic Church, and thoughts of military glory too are soon laid aside. The end of Napoleon's empire meant the end of dreams of *le rouge*; Heine's mother therefore turned, if her son's account can be believed, to dreams of a Jewish variant of *le noir*—the black-coated banker.

The house of Rothschild, whose chief my father knew, had already begun, at that time, its almost fabulous flowering; other princes of banking and industry had risen up in our vicinity and my mother maintained that the moment had now come in which a man of unusual intelligence could achieve the most incredible success in the mercantile line, and could attain the highest pinnacle of power. She therefore determined that I should become a mighty power in the world of money . . .[6]

When that bubble also burst, when dreams of 'my son the general' and 'my son the banker' had been thwarted, she turned towards dreams of 'my son the lawyer'—and these, as we know, determined the course Heine took in the universities of Bonn, Göttingen, and Berlin, and led to his doctorate in jurisprudence.

The portrait of his mother[7] which Heine draws in *Memoiren* brings out three significant features besides her driving ambition to ensure her sons' success in the Gentile world. He shows us, first, that she stemmed from a family which had perforce acquired a good deal of secular, non-Jewish knowledge because several of its members followed one of the few professional careers open to Jews in eighteenth-century Germany: that of the physician. The shadowy presence of these elder van Gelderns (*de* Geldern, Heine writes, as though the geographical particle were a predicate of nobility) looms behind the mother's portrait—a family once favoured by one of the Electors (*Kurfürsten*) of the Holy Roman Empire, but later reduced to comparative poverty. The second characteristic Heine brings into prominence is that without formally abandoning the religion into which she was born, his mother was a rationalist deist, whose educational principles had been gleaned from Rousseau's *Émile*. She is painted as being of the true rationalist temper: she abhorred romantic fantasies and had little sympathy with her Harry's wish to become a poet. This temper her father, Heine's maternal grandfather, would seem to have fostered: we learn that in her younger days she played the flute, but only secretly, in an attic, so as not to draw upon herself her father's wrath at such a 'sentimental waste of time'. Shades of Frederick the Great of Prussia! The third and last of the features foregrounded in this admiring but not wholly uncritical portrait is that his mother did not *love* money, but valued it for what it could do—whether it bought education, or helped its possessor dispense charity. As her grandmother had done before her, she sacrificed such jewels and trinkets as she had to help her sons finance their studies. Though Heine does not mention Judaism overtly while talking of his mother, and though he stresses that her self-sacrifice resembled that of the non-Jewish mother of the dramatist Christian Dietrich Grabbe, it is not difficult to recognize, in what he tells us of her history and her attitudes, traits she shared with other Jews of her time, place, and social position, with other descendants of the court Jews of eighteenth-century Germany. What Heine is doing here, in recounting the history of his mother's family, is very important: he is consciously dispelling simplistic notions—current even in our own day—of the lack of contact between Jews and Gentiles before the age of legal emancipation, of the Jews' alleged failure to absorb elements of Gentile culture before the pioneering efforts of Moses Mendelssohn.

'She is now', Heine concludes the fullest portrait he was ever to paint of the mother to whom he had paid so many tributes throughout his life, '87 years old, and her intellect has not been impaired by old age. She never tried to control the actual individual cast of my thinking [*meine wirkliche Denkart*] and has always been, with regard to me, the very personification of forbearance and love.'[8]

Another van Geldern comes next into view—Uncle Simon, a strange-looking little man, dressed in old-fashioned costume and wearing the outmoded pigtail; he is said to have been educated by Jesuits, to have amassed an excellent library which he allowed the young Heine to use, and to have had a writing-bug (*Wut des Schriftstellerns*) which may have turned Heine's own thoughts in the direction of literary experiment. Heine insists on the contrast between the somewhat ridiculous appearance of this little man and the nobility of his character:

This man had a sense of honour which recalled the rigorous code of the older Spanish drama—and his steadfast faithfulness also recalled that of the heroes of such plays.[9]

With this ethical rigour, Heine tells us, went a keen delight in the good things of this world—Uncle Simon loved fair-grounds, he loved to eat and drink well, but

all the fieldfare and all the delights life has to offer he would sacrifice with proud determination if some principle he had recognized as true and good was called into question. And he did this with so little ostentation, almost shamefacedly, that no-one noticed the secret martyr hidden beneath his droll exterior.

Heine does not suggest (though some of us might!) that this combination of devotion to ideas or principles with a keen delight in the good things of terrestrial life has anything speci-fically Jewish about it; he sees it, rather, as one possible way to unite 'Nazarene' and 'Hellenic' traits. Nor does his description of his uncle's somewhat grotesque exterior recall the caricatur-ists' Jewish stereotype—with the exception of the half-sentence which I have italicized in the quotation below.

He was an odd character of insignificant, even droll appearance. A small, roundish figure surmounted by a rather pale, severe face, in which the nose had the straight lines of the Greeks but *was, I am sure, a whole third longer than the Greeks used to wear their noses.*[10]

The humorous speculations which follow, embodying the sug-gestion that the uncle's nose might have acquired those extra inches by his habit of constantly pulling at it, deflect attention away from this gentler version of the stereotype which Heine had so crassly invoked in his description of Gumpelino's nose in *The Baths of Lucca*.

Heine had used the portrait of his mother to invoke the shadowy presence of two earlier generations behind her—giving us glimpses of her father and her grandmother. In just the same way he now uses his portrait of Uncle Simon to take us further back in time, back to an earlier Simon van Geldern, Heine's great-uncle, whose diary he discovered in Uncle Simon's attic. This great-uncle, nicknamed 'the Chevalier' or 'the man from the Orient', *der Morgenländer*, had been an intrepid traveller, an adventurer about whom many legends circulated in the family; legends which Heine now combines with his recollection of the diary to compose one of the most elaborate portraits in these fragmentary *Memoiren*.[11] He tells us of great-uncle Simon's voyages in the Middle East; his pilgrimage to Jerusalem, and the vision he is reputed to have had on Mount Moria; his sojourn with Bedouins who professed some sort of Mosaic religion, among whom he is said (without any historical justification) to have become a robber-chief; his occasional successes at various courts, where he was sought after as a reputed cabbalist and Cagliostro *à petit pied*; of his love-affairs; of his fall from grace at some court or other and his hurried departure for England, where he published his now lost oratorio, *Moses on Mount Horeb*—a romanticized version of a life whose more prosaic outlines we can still trace in Simon van Geldern's notebooks.[12] One of the most extraordinary episodes of Simon's life Heine fails to mention: his sojourn in France towards the end of his life, and his association with the Abbé Grégoire, whom he is said to have helped in the composition of a treatise that was to have far-reaching effects on Jewish emancipation in Revolutionary France and post-Revolutionary Europe.

Great-uncle Simon lived from 1720–88. He was thus nine years older than Moses Mendelssohn, who outlived him by twelve years; and in the economy of Heine's *Memoiren* his story serves to show a different kind of cultural contact between eighteenth-century Jews and non-Jews than that which had been so successfully established by Mendelssohn and Lessing. Heine even credits Simon with the ability to write in 'Arabic, Syrian, and Coptic' letters—a skill not illustrated in any surviving document. Did Heine perhaps mistake his great-uncle's cursive Hebrew for other Middle-Eastern scripts? It would be wrong, however, to see in Simon's story, as Heine remembered and told it, simply an episode in the history of Jewish-Gentile relations. The poet tries, rather, to place this romantic and romanticized story within a transitional period of European history, and to make it a starting-point for more general reflections on human character.

This great-uncle of mine was a puzzling phenomenon, difficult for us to understand. He led one of those strange lives which were possible only in the early and middle part of the eighteenth century. He was in part an enthusiast, a propagandist for cosmopolitan Utopias designed to make the world a happier place to live in, and in part an adventurer who, conscious of inner powers, broke through or overleapt the barriers of a decaying society. One thing, however, is sure: he was human through and through.[13]

One aspect of this humanity seems still to need an explicit commentary. Great-uncle Simon, Heine reflects, was a charlatan; a charlatan in grand style, perhaps, one who chose the courts of princes rather than country fairs as the field of his operations, but a charlatan nevertheless. This thought now receives a characteristic elaboration which leads one to ask oneself what sort of passages Heine can have consigned to flames (as we have heard him claim) for religious reasons.

Has there ever been any man of consequence who was not something of a charlatan? The end hallows the means. The Lord God Himself, when he proclaimed His law on Mount Sinai, made liberal use of thunder and lightning, although the law was so excellent, so divinely good, that it could well have dispensed with all these theatrical flashes and thunderous kettledrums. But the Lord knew his audience, which stood there at the foot of the mountain with its oxen and its sheep and its open mouths, and which was sure to be more impressed by some physical trickery than by all the miracles of eternal thought.[14]

Here Heine has made one of those sudden transitions which are so characteristic of his portraiture. Having firmly placed his subject in its historical setting—the eighteenth century, in this case, the age of Cagliostro and Casanova—he fastens on one characteristic that has trans-temporal significance, a characteristic that pertains as much to Heine himself and the epoch in which he wrote as to Simon van Geldern and the eighteenth century. Charlatanism, after all, the necessity of wooing a public whose discernment is questionable, is a problem which crops up in Heine's writings over and over again and which entered in ways already examined his portraits of such contemporaries as Meyerbeer and Schlesinger.

We need not be surprised, therefore, to find that in the rest of this haunting portion of the *Memoiren* great-uncle Simon's figure merges into that of Heine himself. He becomes a kind of *Doppelgänger* who invades the poet's dreams as well as his waking hours; a man with whom he identifies to such a degree that his father is led to exorcize the ghost with a characteristic mercantile quip. 'He hoped my great-uncle had not signed any bills which would one day be presented to me for payment.'[15]

The *Doppelgänger* is a symbolic figure that engaged Heine's imagination throughout his life; and recollection of his strange identification with a long dead great-uncle, which is said to have lasted for about a year, now leads him to speculate that those of his sentiments and actions which seemed to spring from a nature other than his own might perhaps be traced back to that early period of his life. This speculation, in turn, leads to thoughts about heredity and personal responsibility; about the meaning of the biblical saying that the sour grapes eaten by the fathers set the children's teeth on edge; and, as so often, about the humanity and good sense of Mosaic law. Heine's contrast between the 'philanthropic' laws of inheritance promulgated in the Pentateuch and the 'egoistic' *Erbrecht* of the Romans would have delighted Eduard Gans, had he lived long enough to read Heine's *Memoiren*. They constitute a lasting memorial to the lessons Heine learnt from Gans's life-work.

Another group of figures now occupies, for just a moment, the foreground of Heine's memoirs: ancient aunts and second cousins,

female bards who, day by day, chant the old family legends in an epic monotone for the benefit of the young brood, while the snorting of their noses does duty for the more usual obligato on the bagpipes.[16]

Düsseldorf, the poet tells us, held only bards competent to perpetuate the legends of his *mother*'s family; his father had come from elsewhere, and information about that side of his ancestry was scarce, especially since the father himself was anything but talkative. One day, however,

I took [a favourable] opportunity to ask who my paternal grandfather had been. My father answered this question half laughingly, half crossly: 'Your grandfather was a little Jew and had a long beard.'[17]

This information, Heine tells us, he imparted to his Gentile school-friends the next day and thereby caused a riot of mockery, in which animal noises and leaps were accompanied by the refrain: 'His grandfather was a little Jew and had a long beard.' The Jesuit teacher, entering the room and demanding an explanation, was told that the riot had been caused by young Heine, who received a sound hiding in consequence.

Along with the name of the man to whom I owed this first beating I retained its occasion in my memory; and whenever anyone spoke of little Jews with long beards, an uncanny recollection shuddered down my back . . . Since then, as everyone will readily understand, I have never felt greatly inclined to seek further news of this dangerous grandfather and his family tree, or to impart to a great public the information I once gave to a smaller one.[18]

Here we have for the first time a glimpse of the mockery young Jews in Gentile schools had to put up with as they prepared themselves for a career in the Gentile world of the early nineteenth century. The *Memoiren* afford us other such glimpses: the mockery of Heine's given name 'Harry' because it allegedly resembled the cry of a donkey driver, and the socially conditioned attacks on him by *Haluten*, Düsseldorf street urchins, who beat him with sticks and threw excrement at him.[19] No Jewish portrait gallery would be complete without the depiction of incidents of this all too familiar kind. They may help to explain—as the poet himself here suggests—the younger Heine's deliberate playing down, or concealment, of his Jewishness; but they may also tell us something of the psychological springs that drove him, again and again, to introduce Jewish figures and Jewish questions into his works. 'Never talk of Jewish affairs' ('niemals von jüdischen Verhältnissen sprechen'), is a jotting found among his papers after his death.[20] But we know by now that any kind of restriction—even if it was self-imposed—immediately triggered off in Heine the wish to transcend or transgress; a feeling to which he had once given memorable expression in one of his many poetic glosses on the Old Testament, the poem *Adam the First*, where the ostensible speaker is the biblical Adam, but the voice with which he speaks is unmistakably that of Heine himself. 'The poet,' Heine had said in *The Romantic School*, 'that little creative imitator, resembles God in this respect too: that he fashions his human figures in his own image.'[21]

It is not surprising, therefore, to find the *Memoiren* returning, after all, to the little Jew with the long beard whose mention had caused such a riot among Düsseldorf schoolboys. His paternal grandfather, Heine tells us, found a beautiful and wealthy wife in Hamburg:

I am led to suppose that the little Jew who took his beautiful bride from the house of her wealthy parents to his home in Hanover must have possessed very praiseworthy attributes besides his long beard, and must, indeed, have been worthy of great respect.[22]

He died early, we learn, and his widow returned to Hamburg with her six small boys before her own premature death. Her portrait hung in the bedroom of one of her sons, 'my uncle Salomon Heine in Hamburg' (here he is then, for a moment, the man whose depiction was to have been one of the centre-pieces of these *Memoiren*, where he was to have been drawn *con amore!*) But Heine focuses immediately on the portrait of his paternal grandmother, which he deliberately places in the greatest possible contrast with the Jewish stereotype evoked by his father's description of her husband.

Her features still showed traces of great beauty. They were at once mild and serious; the *morbidezza* of the skin colouring gave to the face a peculiar air of aristocratic distinction. If the artist had painted a great diamond cross at the lady's breast, one could have taken her portrait for that of the titled abbess of a charitable foundation for daughters of the Protestant nobility.[23]

Only two of her children, Heine continues, inherited her extraordinary good looks: his own father and (here he comes again) 'my uncle Salomon Heine, the head, now deceased, of the Hamburg banking house of that name'.

Heine now turns to his own father,[21] whose good looks are said to have had something too soft, too weak, almost feminine about it, while Uncle Salomon showed 'a manly handsome-ness; Salomon Heine was, altogether, a man whose strength of character showed itself in his nobly formed regular features in an imposing, sometimes even startling way. His children too'—and here Heine comes to a subject which engaged his emotions particularly deeply—'were delightfully good-looking; but death gathered them in before they had come to full flower, and from this fair bouquet only two blooms sur-vive today: the present head of the banking house and his sister . . .' What Heine's relations with Carl were, we know only too well: he had regarded him as a friend as well as a cousin, and felt that his confidence had been betrayed; his relations with Therese, however, are shrouded in surmise, and it is perhaps significant that at this point there appears the first obvious lacuna in the manuscript of this fragment of his memoirs. Whether the poet himself sacrificed the now missing passage, or whether someone else removed it after his death, or whether he perhaps left a gap to be filled in later, we may never known for certain. The most important aspect, however, is brought out when the text as we have it resumes:

I loved all these children, and I loved their mother too, who was also good-looking and who also died early; and they all caused me to shed many tears. In truth, at this moment I have to shake the bells on my fool's cap to make them ring out and drown my lachrymose thoughts.[35]

That is the nearest Heine can get, in these censored *Memoiren*, to a depiction of that poisoning of family affection, that perversion of potential love, which is one of the themes of *Castle Contumely* as of so many others among Heine's poems.

From this slippery and dangerous slope Heine scrambles back to the subject of his father. He speaks of his soft, rounded, rather feminine appearance (which did not, he hastens to add, betoken lack of virility): describes a pastel portrait which brought out to perfection the Watteauesque, rococo air his father had about him—he even powdered his soft fair hair after it had ceased to be fashionable to do so; and he tells us of the red uniform he wore on the painting already described, a uniform which denoted that he was quartermaster to Prince Ernest of Cumberland. Thoughts of little Jews with long beards are left far behind as Heine paints his affectionate portrait of an eighteenth-century court Jew *à petit pied*, whose appearance had nothing of the Jewish stereotype about it. We hear of his father's activities as a commissary officer or *officier de bouche* (disrespectfully dubbed *Mehlwurm*) during the wars that followed the French Revolution of 1789; of the favour he found with the Prince of Cumberland as a minor version of Beau Brummel; of the aristocratic proclivities these early experiences engendered in Samson Heine: love of uniforms and playing at soldiers, gambling, patronizing actresses, buying dogs and horses. When his master had no more need of his services he was dropped and never again admitted into the court orbit on whose periphery he had once moved; he set up in business in Düsseldorf, but even there, Heine tells us, he retained his passion for dogs and horses he could not longer afford to keep, and gratified his love of dressing up in uniforms by joining the Düsseldorf civil guard, entertaining his men lavishly whenever his turn came round to assume command. Fortunately Düsseldorf was a peaceful, law-abiding place, so that the havoc his father's gifts of wine caused among the guards did not endanger the city's safety.

Boundless delight in life was the dominant trait in my father's disposition; he was pleasure-loving and sunny-tempered. It was ever carnival time in his mind, and even when the music wasn't very loud, the violins were always being tuned up. Blue skies of cheerfulness, fanfares of lightheartedness were perpetually within him. He was carefree, always forgetting the day that had passed and refusing to think of the morrow to come.

This disposition stood in strange contrast to the gravity of his sternly tranquil face as well as his whole carriage and movement. Whoever did not know him and saw his serious, powdered head and imposing mien for the first time, might well have thought himself in the presence of one of the seven sages of ancient Greece. But closer acquaintance would soon reveal how far he was from being either a Thales or a Lampsacus [*sic*] pondering the question of the universe. His gravity was not deliberately assumed but it did remind one of those antique bas-reliefs which show a gay child holding a great tragic mask before his face.

And that's what he was: a big child, with a child's naïveté which unimaginative virtuosos of reasonableness might have taken for simplicity; but he occasionally betrayed, through some profound saying, the most extraordinary intuitive power.

With his mental feelers he would sense in a moment what cleverer men would only grasp slowly by means of reflection. He thought less with his head than with his heart—and his heart was the most lovable you could imagine. The smile which sometimes played about his lips and made an amusing, charming contrast with the gravity I have already described—that smile was the sweet reflection of the goodness of his soul.[26]

The reader will have sensed, by now, that all this is a transfiguration; that Samson Heine, the unsuccessful little merchant with his epileptic proclivities and his tendencies to melancholia is being seen through eyes of love which can distort just as much as eyes of hate. In a moving passage which follows soon afterwards, Heine makes this transfiguring love explicit.

Of all the men that have ever lived he was the one I loved most. He has now been dead for over 25 years. I never thought that one day I would lose him, and even now I can hardly believe that I really *have* lost him. It is so difficult to convince oneself that people one loves so dearly are truly dead. But then—they are not dead, they are alive within us, they live on in our souls.

There has not been a night in which I have not thought of my late father, and when I wake in the morning, I often think I hear his voice like the echo of a dream. And then I have the feeling that I must dress quickly and hurry down to my father who will be sitting in his large room, as he did when I was a boy.

My father was in the habit of rising early and applying himself to his affairs, in winter as in summer; when I came down I usually found him sitting at his desk and holding out his hand for me to kiss, without looking up. It was a beautiful, finely formed, aristocratic hand, which he always washed in almond powder. I can still see it in front of me, with every little blue vein traversing this dazzling white hand. The aroma of almonds seems to prickle in my nose, and my eyes fill with tears.

Sometimes there was more than kissing hands; my father would take me between his knees and kiss my forehead. One morning he embraced me with especial tenderness and said: 'Tonight I dreamt fine things about you and I am very pleased with you, dear Harry.' As he spoke these naïve words, a smile played about his lips, which seemed to say: 'However naughty Harry's conduct may be in reality, I shall always dream nice things about him so as to love him undisturbed.'[27]

What Heine's father is here described as doing with regard to his son is strangely analogous to what Heine himself is doing with regard to his father. And the transfiguration includes, once again, a deliberate departure from Jewish stereotypes: just as Samson Heine's tastes are depicted as those of the Gentile aristocracy with whom he associated during one impressionable but brief period of his life, so his speech and accent are presented as German pure and simple.

His voice, although it was manly and sonorous, had something childlike, something that recalled the warbling of woodnotes wild, a robin's song . . . The dialect he spoke was that of Hanover where . . . German pronunciation is at its best. This was a great advantage to me, for my father accustomed me to well-pronounced German from my earliest childhood, while in the town in which we lived they spoke the dreadful double Dutch of the lower Rhine regions . . .[28]

Such specimens of Samson Heine's *written* German as are extant hardly support this description, which is once again concerned to invert a stereotype. A Jewish household is being presented as an oasis of pure German in the midst of barbarous distortions of that language by the Gentile population all around! And even in respect of his trade, as an importer of velveteen from England, Samson Heine is made to transcend the stereotype of the Jewish businessman which Heine himself had helped to foster—though he had always made it clear that what he excoriated was business mentality *per se* and not something specifically Jewish.

[My father] had none of the calculating huckster's spirit, although he was always doing sums; business was just a game to him, as children play at soldiers or at cookery. He just kept himself continually occupied. Velveteen was his favourite doll, and he was happy when the great carts were unloaded and all the Jewish traders of the district filled the corridors of his warehouse. These Jewish merchants were his best customers—they not only bought his velveteen in large quantities, but they also appreciated its excellence.[29]

The stereotype of the Jew as cheapjack, as dealer in shoddy merchandise, is being quietly rejected. His father, Heine explains, was more interested in the quality of his goods than in the profit to be made from them; he always said that they brought in a good deal of money, but that he would have been willing to *lose* money as he directed his efforts to selling more velveteen of high quality than any of his competitors.

Velveteen was an import from England; and since (Heine tells us) one of his father's business correspondents in Liverpool signed his name as 'Harry', Samson Heine gave that name to his own son. What he does not tell us is that the name served as approximation and equivalent of the name *Khayim* (*Chaim*) borne by the poet's deceased grandfather, the little Jew with the long beard. He does tell us, however, that the English name became, during his schooldays, at least as great a cause of suffering as the genealogical information he had been so rash to impart to his non-Jewish schoolmates; for the name resembled all too closely the cry with which a local donkey driver encouraged his animal to move on. The schoolboy witticisms to which the resemblance between *Harry* and *Haarüh* gave rise would frequently, it is important to notice, take on a turn calculated to remind young Harry Heine of his Jewishness: 'For instance, someone would ask: "What is the difference between a zebra and the ass of Balaam, the son of Beor?" and he would receive the reply: "One speaks zebraic, the other Hebraic."'[30] The quip is harmless enough; but it does bring home to us that however assimilated, however committed to Germanic, Gentile ways he may have been, there was never a time in Heine's life in which he was not reminded by others that he was a Jew. Baptism did not alter this in any way—one only has to leaf through a collection of contemporary newspaper items about him to convince oneself that such was the case. Nor could Heine ever persuade the French that he was a German pure and simple. Lucien, in Balzac's *Lost Illusions*, reckons him among the Jews, along with Rothschild, Rachel Félix, and Meyerbeer; the first thing Vigny notes about him is that he is Jewish; Philibert Audebrand calls him 'un vrai fils de l'Orient égaré en Europe'; Gautier refers to 'la légère courbure hébraïque' of his nose, Edgar Quinet to his 'sourire judaïque'. Some remarked with astonishment that he did not look Jewish; others, like Hans Christian Andersen, when he met him in Paris, saw him as 'a little man of Israelitish appearance'. Heine thus experienced on his pulses the truth his old enemy Börne—baptized like himself—had proclaimed when he said that some people excoriated him for being Jewish, others forgave him for it, yet others even praised him for it; but no one could forget it. A magic circle, Börne had said, was drawn around the Jew, and people seemed unable to overstep its circumference.

Heine's fragmentary *Memoiren* return again to the beloved figure of his father. They show Samson Heine generously doling out alms to needy fellow townsmen of every persuasion (the Jews, this passage tacitly insinuates once again, do *not* look only after their own). The love of flattery imputed to Samson is shown as an amiable weakness which in fact stimulates charitable and other virtues—there is nothing wrong with seeking honour and reputation if the effects are so beneficial. Translated into words from the Jewish tradition which Heine does not here use: the quest for *koved* and *yikhes* may lead to *tsedaka* and the practise of other *mitsvot*.[31] The poet still tells his public nothing of his father's epileptic seizures, his melancholia, his bankruptcies, his being legally declared unfit to manage his affairs—instead, we take our leave of him, and of the *Memoiren*-fragment, with a glimpse of his *politesse de cœur* and his views on religious observance. The former shows up clearly when he makes it a point of honour to greet with punctilious courtesy a social outcast with whom his Harry had fallen in love.

Josepha told me that a distinguished-looking man with powdered hair had met her on the promenade, and when his companion had whispered something to him, he had looked at her kindly and had raised his hat in greeting.

When she described him further I realized that this could have been none other than my dear, kind father.

Then follows the modulation which changes the tonality of the *Memoiren* fragment into that of the *Confessions* (*Geständnisse*) of 1854.

My father did not show the same forbearance when gossips told him of some irreverent remarks I had made with regard to religion. They accused me of atheism, and my father admonished me in what must be the longest harangue he ever pronounced. 'My dear son!', he said. 'Your mother has got you studying philosophy with Rector Schallmeyer. That is her affair. I, for my part, do not love philosophy; it's all superstition, and I as a merchant have to keep my head clear for my business. You can be a philosopher as much as you like—but, please, don't proclaim publicly what you happen to be thinking! It would hurt my business if my customers came to hear that I have a son who does not believe in God; the Jews especially would stop buying my velveteen—and they are honest people, they are prompt in their payments, and they are absolutely right to stick to their religion. I am your father—that makes me older than you and, by the same token, more experienced; you may therefore take it from me that I know what I am talking about when I tell you that atheism is a great sin.[32]

The Gentile, aristocratic tastes Heine has projected on to his father help in giving that father's praise of Jewish business ethos an authority it might otherwise not have had; and the condemnation of atheism contained in this wryly humorous and deliberately 'unphilosophical' speech has behind it the weight of what we had earlier been told of Samson Heine's intuitive grasp of essential truths, as well as our recollection of Heine's own later denunciations of philosophical atheism. At the same time this complex passage introduces a problem which agitated Heine all his life and which the effort to write his memoirs raised with especial urgency. How far could one—and, what is more to the point, how far *should* one—give expression to everything that is in one's heart and mind? What sort of considerations should lead one to practise self-censorship, as opposed to the intolerable censorship exercised by others? Had he not perhaps, in hubristic years of good health, said things to encourage a contemporary atheism which he came to see, more and more, as a loathsome new orthodoxy?[33]

Whatever changes in his outlook Heine detected and depicted in his final years, there was one feature of his world-view which never changed, which in fact grew ever more pronounced as his life neared its end: his sympathy with the defeated, with those whom the world despised and cast out, with anyone he recognized as an underdog. Such sympathy animates the long passage in which Heine describes his early love for just such an outcast, the girl whom we have just seen his father treat with such courtesy.

Despite the infamy which clung to everyone who associated with these outcasts I kissed the public executioner's beautiful daughter. I kissed her, not only because of the tenderness I felt towards her, but also out of scorn for the old society and its dark prejudices. This moment ignited in me the first flames of those two passions to which my future life was dedicated: the love of beautiful women, and the love of the French Revolution, that modern *furor francese* which seized me too as I fought the servile champions of the Middle Ages.[34]

For all its playing down of the Jewishness of his early environment, the *Memoiren*-fragment leaves no doubt of the close connection between Heine's Judaism and his sympathy with the outcast, the underdog, and the apparently defeated whom a future time would vindicate and, where possible, raise again from the dust.

(ii)

The *Memoiren*-fragment shows Heine at his most touchingly affectionate; such distortions as one may find there are distortions dictated by love. The hatred and resentment he continued to feel towards those members of his family who had tried to gag him by applying financial sanctions found its expression in a number of terrifying poems, which contained such lines as

> Wenn ich sterbe, wird die Zunge
> Ausgeschnitten meiner Leiche ...
>
> [When I die the tongue
> will be cut from my corpse ...][35]

One poem even allows its lyric I to blame the family for the poet's miserable physical condition:

> Es schmilzt das Fleisch von meinen armen Rippen,
> Ich kann mich nicht vom Siechbett mehr erheben,
> Arglistig stahlen sie mein junges Leben—
> Das taten mir die Magen und die Sippen.
>
> [The flesh melts away from my poor ribs,
> I cannot rise again from my sick-bed,
> treacherously they stole away my life and my youth
> —my kith and kin did this to me.][36]

This same poem, a sonnet, ends with a sestet whose first part insists on the poet's Christian, baptized persona but then modulates, in the second part, to suggestions of quite unchristian vengefulness:

> Ich bin ein Christ—wie es im Kirchenbuche
> Bescheinigt steht—deshalb, bevor ich sterbe,
> Will ich euch fromm und brüderlich verzeihen.
>
> Es wird mir sauer—ach! mit einem Fluche
> Möcht ich weit lieber euch vermaledeien:
> Daß euch der Herr verdamme und verderbe!

[I am a Christian—in the Church Register
you'll see that certified—and thus, before I die,
I will offer you pious, brotherly forgiveness.

But I find this hard—ah! I would much prefer
to blast you with a curse:
may the Lord damn you and destroy you!]³⁷

Another of these 'kith and kin' poems features a Greek rather
than a Christian persona: the poet assumes the traditional guise
of Orpheus and descends into hell; not in order to retrieve
some lost Eurydice, however, but in order to tear the mask off
the man who had treacherously poisoned his life. The reader
of Heine's letters can find several names that might identify
this denizen of the infernal regions—beginning with Carl
Heine and Uncle Salomon himself. Yet another poem opens
with an unmistakably Jewish figure uttering a *klule*, a Jewish
curse:

> 'Nicht gedacht soll seiner werden!
> Aus dem Mund der armen alten
> Esther Wolf hört' ich die Worte,
> Die ich treu im Sinn behalten.
>
> Ausgelöscht sein aus der Menschen
> Angedenken hier auf Erden,
> Ist die Blume der Verwünschung—
> Nicht gedacht soll seiner werden!
>
> ['Let him not be remembered!'
> Out of the mouth of poor old
> Esther Wolf I once heard these words
> which I have faithfully preserved in my mind.
>
> To be blotted out from men's
> memory here on earth,
> that is the flower of all curses:
> Let him not be remembered!]

Yes indeed: if his relatives did not wish to have their deeds
remembered in the poet's work, then let their demands be met
in full:

Nicht gedacht soll seiner werden,
Nicht im Liede, nicht im Buche—
Dunkler Hund im dunkeln Grabe,
Du verfaulst mit meinem Fluche!

Selbst am Auferstehungstage,
Wenn, geweckt von den Fanfaren
Der Posaunen, schlotternd wallen
Zum Gericht die Totenscharen

Und alldort der Engel abliest
Vor den göttlichen Behörden
Alle Namen der Geladnen—
Nicht gedacht soll seiner werden!

[Let him not be remembered,
not in a song, not in a book—
obscure cur, in an obscure grave
you shall moulder with my curse.

Even on the day of resurrection,
when, wakened by the blowing
of the trumpets, the procession of the dead
tremulously approaches the judgement seat

and the angel up there reads out
before the divine authorities
all the names of those who have been summoned—
let him not be remembered!']³⁸

The curse comes from Jewish lips, the vision of the Last
Judgement from Christian traditions subtly, slyly adapted to
the procedure in modern courts of law. And as if to complete
the composite persona which speaks in these poems, chronicl-
ing the 'ridiculous crimes' committed against him (*die an mir
verübten/Lächerlichen Freveltaten*³⁹ the poet finds in Germa-
nic legend the closest parallel to the fate of this new Lazarus
betrayed by his kith and kin:

> Ach! Blutsfreunde sind es eben,
> Welche mir den Tod gegeben,
> Und die schnöde Meucheltat
> Ward verübet durch Verrat.

Siegfried gleich, dem hörnen Recken,
Wußten sie mich hinzustrecken—
Leicht erspäht Familienlist,
Wo der Held verwundbar ist.

[Alas—it is those bound to me by ties of blood
who have dealt me a death-blow;
the murderous deed was accomplished
with despicable treachery.

Like Siegfried, that impregnable warrior,
I was laid low by their cunning;
family guile easily spies out
where a hero is vulnerable.][40]

The power of these poems may be felt by anyone who reads them; but it will strike us even more strongly if we read them against the background of the family affection and family respect which animate the *Memoiren*-fragment.

(iii)

The principal butts of *Lutezia* also make their appearance in Heine's last poems. The imminent appearance of Meyerbeer's *Le Prophète* is greeted by a 'celebratory poem' (*Festgedicht*) built around two scabrous images: the celebrated composer in childbed, giving birth at last to an opus that had caused him colics for some thirteen years, and the artistic sweat accumulated in those thirteen years being poured out in one watery stream over the world's opera houses. The childbed scene introduces the composer's Jewish admirers when the silence of the room in which the *accouchement* has just taken place is suddenly shattered. The passage in which this happens offers an excellent example of Heine's manipulation of language for comic effect. Everything comes together here: rhythmic control, the play of sentence structure against line division, comic rhymes bringing the incongruous into illusory harmony, high-sounding compounds used to bathetic effect, and the taking apart of Meyerbeer's name only to recombine it into the absurd coinage *Beeren-Meyer*, fitter for a fruit merchant than a celebrated composer. In our special context we will be particularly alert to the poet's deliberate play with Jewish Messianic expectations: the Jews are still waiting for a prophet, but all they get is—Meyerbeer's *Le Prophète*.

> Doch die Kindbettzimmerstille
> Unterbricht ein laut Gebrülle
> Plötzlich—es erschmettern hell
> Die Posaunen, Israel
> Ruft mit tausend Stimmen: "Heil!"
> (Unbezahlt zum größten Teil)
> "Heil dem Meister, der uns teuer,
> Heil dem großen Beeren-Meyer,
> Heil dem großen Meyer-Beer!
> Der nach Nöten, lang und schwer,
> Der nach langen, schweren Nöten
> Uns geboren den Propheten!"

> [But the silence of the childbed chamber
> is shattered by loud yelling
> all of a sudden—there is a blare
> of trumpets, Israel
> shouts with a myriad voices: 'Hail!'
> (most of them have *not* been paid for these plaudits)
> 'Hail to the maestro so dear to us,
> Hail to great Berry-Meyer,
> Hail to great Meyer-Beer!
> Who, after labour long and hard,
> Who, after long and hard labour,
> Has given birth to our prophet!']⁴¹

The second part of this 'festive poem' isolates one speaker from the crowd of jubilant Israelites, while the third and last part lets us hear his speech of praise. The speaker turns out to be Louis Brandus, Maurice Schlesinger's successor in the music-publishing business; and the passage which introduces his advertising patter reinforces in several respects the Jewish atmosphere created by the introduction, in Part I, of the jubilant children of Israel. Schlesinger is called a 'Bedouin' to suggest Middle-Eastern origins, and the narrator uses the Ashkenazic Hebrew form of the name 'Moses':

> Aus dem Jubilantenchor
> Tritt ein junger Mann hervor,

Der gebürtig ist aus Preußen
Und Herr Brandus ist geheißen.
Sehr bescheiden ist die Miene
(Ob ihn gleich ein Beduine,
Ein berühmter Rattenfänger,
Sein Musikverlagsvorgänger,
Eingeschult in jeden Rummel),
Er ergreifet eine Trummel,
Paukt drauflos im Siegesrausche,
Wie einst Mirjam tat, als Mausche
Eine große Schlacht gewann,
Und er hebt zu singen an:

[From the midst of this jubilant chorus
a young man steps forwards—
he was born in Prussia
and his name is Brandus.
He has a modest mien
(although a famous bedouin,
a celebrated rat-catcher,
his predecessor in music publishing,
has taught him all the tricks of the trade).
He seizes a drum
and beats it wildly, in victorious exaltation,
as Miriam did, in former times, when Moses
won a great battle.
And he begins to sing . . .][42]

The 'song' introduced in this mock-heroic fashion takes up the
'Moses' image when Brandus is made to compare the immense
flood of Meyerbeer's sweated-out opus to the Red Sea:

Ja, er ist fast wie ein Meer,
Wie das rote, wo das Heer
Pharaonis mußt ersaufen,
Während wir hindurchgelaufen
Trocknen Fußes mit der Beute—

[It is almost like a sea,
like the Red Sea, where the army
of Pharaoh had to drown
while we ran through it
dry-shod, with our booty . . .][43]

The first person plural here used by Brandus clearly indicates that he is speaking to and for Jews; but when we respond to the sly reference to Israel's 'booty' we must not forget that the previous portions of Brandus's speech, not quoted here, had incorporated equally disrespectful jokes about Prussians and Poles. The whole speech, or 'song', culminates in the triumphant announcement that the Schlesinger-Brandus concern is publishing the *score* of *Le Prophète*:

> Und ich hab die Partitur!

So much for the impartiality of the praise lavished on Meyerbeer. In an epilogue appended to this poem, Heine compares himself to a sick lion who tried to cure himself by tearing a monkey apart and gobbling him up. 'I am not a lion', he adds, but leaves it open to us to continue seeing Meyerbeer as a cartoon ape.

The taking apart and absurd putting together again of Meyerbeer's name, which was so striking a feature of the 'festive poem' just analysed, is repeated in a complementary poem entitled *Paean (Pään)*. Here Heine uses the image of the excessive quantity of laurels heaped upon the composer, which we have already met in *Lutezia*, to compose a verbal cartoon: laurels dangle from Meyerbeer's head in such profusion that he can't hear the paeans of praise addressed to him unless he first sweeps them away from his ears. The absurdity of the image in heightened by the Byronic rhyme *Lorbeer/Ohr, Beer*:

> Streiche von der Stirn den Lorbeer,
> Der zu lang herunterbammelt,
> Und vernimm mit freiem Ohr, Beer,
> Was dir meine Lippe stammelt.
>
> Ja, nur stammeln, stottern kann ich,
> Trete vor den großen Mann ich . . .
>
> [Brush from your forehead the laurel
> that dangles down too low,
> and having freed your ear, Beer, listen
> to the stammering of my lips.
>
> Yes, I can only stutter and stammer
> when I stand before the great man . . .][44]

For the rest this 'stammering' poem brings a mock-devaluation of Rossini and Mozart (the latter's name is forcibly made to 'rhyme' with *Rotznas*, 'snot-nose') because their fame is based on the *merit* of their work rather than on 'political web-spinning' and 'exquisite calculation' like Meyerbeer's:

> Durch politische Gespinste
> Und die feinsten Rechenkünste . . .

After mock-praise comes mock-petition, as the poet 'humbly' begs the favour of the King of Prussia's mighty protégé. The 'stammering' the poet affects throughout is underlined by a sudden cessation of verse, in mid-sentence, followed by a deliberately conventional formula of devotion in plain prose.

The fable *The Bedbug* (*Der Wanzerich*), which belongs to this same satirical series, is a poem *à clef*. Its hero, the bug squatting astride a penny and boasting of having been in the beds of fine ladies is identifiable, by a reference to the *Dessauer Marsch* which closes its first part, as the composer and pianist Josef Dessauer. Heine had accused Dessauer, as we have already seen, of boasting that he had enjoyed the favours of George Sand; Dessauer, who denied this allegation, countered by accusing Heine of bearing him a grudge because he had refused the poet a loan. The first part of *The Bedbug* alludes to both these charges, while the second looks beyond Dessauer to other of Heine's *bêtes noires* and comic butts: to Meyerbeer, to Schlesinger, to venal journalists.

> Das Ungeziefer jeden Lands,
> Es bildet eine Heil'ge Allianz;
> Zumal die musikalischen Wanzen,
> Die Komponisten von schlechten Romanzen
> (Welche, wie Schlesingers Uhr, nicht gehn),
> Allüberall im Bündnis stehn.
> Da ist der Mozart der Krätze in Wien,
> Die Perle ästhetischer Pfänderleiher,
> Der intrigiert mit dem Lorbeer-Meyer,
> Dem großen Maestro in Berlin.
> Da werden Artikelchen ausgeheckt,
> Die eine Blattlaus, ein Mitinsekt,
> Für bares Geld in die Presse schmuggelt—

[The vermin of every country
has formed a Holy Alliance;
especially those musical bugs,
composers of rubbishy romances,
(which don't 'go', like Schlesinger's watch)—
they have allies everywhere.
In Vienna sits that Mozart of the itchy skin,
that pearl of aesthetic pawnbrokers,
who intrigues with laurel-crowned Meyerbeer,
the great maestro of Berlin;
they concoct little articles
which some journalistic vine bug, some fellow insect
smuggles into the papers in return for cash . . .][45]

Dessauer's Jewishness is unmistakably hinted at by the image
of the 'aesthetic pawnbroker' which the poet had once sug-
gested to Platen as an effective vehicle for anti-Semitic attacks
on Heine himself. But it's no good complaining, the fabulist
adds; if you squash insects like these in the way they deserve,
their foul smell poisons the sweet air, and their filth soils your
feet. You just have to let them bite.

It would be quite wrong to see this bitter fable as no more
than an expression of rage by one individual against another.
The bedbug is not just one obnoxious minor composer; he is an
image of the bourgeois *rentier* who thinks that everything can
be had for money.

Es saß ein brauner Wanzerich
Auf einem Pfennig und spreizte sich
Wie ein Rentier, und sprach: 'Wer Geld hat,
Auch Ehr und Ansehn in der Welt hat.
Wer Geld hat, ist auch lieblich und schön—
Es kann kein Weib ihm widerstehn . . .'

[A brown bedbug sat on a penny,
sprawling and giving himself airs
like a *rentier*. He said: 'If you have money
the world honours and respects you.
If you have money, you are handsome and charming—
No woman can resist you.][46]

That formulation, as the Marxist critic Gerhard Schmitz has
rightly pointed out, is strikingly close to certain formulations

in Marx's *Economic-Philosophical Manuscripts*, written at the very time at which Marx was often in Heine's company. However far the later Heine moved away from Marx, their perception of the failings of bourgeois society remained remarkably similar.

The poet's rage against Dessauer did not mean that his wrath was in any way deflected from Meyerbeer. In the late poem *A Contribution to Teleology* (*Zur Teleologie*) we find him looking at various organs of the body in a satiric survey of their usefulness—ending, of course, with the question why the organ of generation should also serve as a waste-pipe.

> Ohren gab uns Gott die beiden,
> Um von Mozart, Gluck und Hayden
> Meisterstücke anzuhören—
> Gäb es nur Tonkunst-Kolik
> Und Hämorrhoidal-Musik
> Von dem großen Meyerbeer,
> Schon ein Ohr hinlänglich wär!—

> ['God gave us our two ears
> So that we can listen to masterpieces
> by Mozart, Gluck, and Haydn.
> If there were nothing but the musical colic
> and haemorrhoidal compositions
> of the great Meyerbeer—
> then *one* ear would be ample!']⁴⁷

Heine's sick-chamber constantly obtruded bodily functions and functional disturbances on his attention; but the pleasure he appears to take in alluding to Meyerbeer's notorious digestive troubles seems to me one of his least-endearing traits.

One of the strangest works of Heine's last years purports to introduce a poem written by a Laplander. There is no such poem, and the portrait of the sick Laplander who has moved to St. Petersburg to enjoy the blessings of a milder climate is clearly a bitter self-caricature by the man who had gone from Germany to Paris in order to breathe a more liberal air.

Many of these sick exiles . . . contract, on top of their physical ailments, the moral diseases of the European civilization with which they come into contact. They occupy themselves with politics and religion. A reading of Marie de Maistre's *Soirées de Saint-*

Pétersbourg, which they mistake for a reliable guide to the capital, teaches them that the main pillar of civil society is the public executioner; but a reaction against this view is inevitable, and they then switch from de Maistre's *bourreaucracy* to the starkest form of communism; they declare that all reindeer and seals belong to the state, they read Hegel and become atheists; but as the disease takes firmer hold on their spinal marrow they become milder and topple over into a lachrymose pietism, they become zealots, sometimes even adherents of the 'Mother of Zion' . . .[48]

This is not straight autobiography, of course; it caricatures Heine's contemporaries along with certain aspects of himself, tendencies of his development that *might* have taken the extreme form depicted but never did so. After an excursus on the beliefs of the Christian 'Mother of Zion' sect in West Prussia, to which we have just seen him refer, Heine homes in on one figure that stands for himself more fully and obviously than the generalized 'exiles' in the earlier part of his essay.

Among the diseases to which Laplanders are subject, when they come to St. Petersburg to bask in a mild southern climate, is that of poetry. The poem that follows originated in a contagion of this kind: its author is a young Lapp who migrated to St. Petersburg because of an illness that affected his spinal marrow and who died there some time ago. He had a good deal of talent, made friends with the choicest spirits in the capital city which he now inhabited, and occupied himself a good deal with German philosophy. This brought him to the brink of atheism. Before it was too late, however, the special grace of Heaven saved him from the danger in which his soul stood. Before his death he came to recognize the existence of God. This scandalized those who had shared his unbelief; the high priests of atheism unanimously pronounced their anathema on this renegade from godlessness. In the mean time his physical sufferings increased as his finances decreased; soon he had eaten up all the reindeer that constituted his sole fortune. In the poet's last refuge, the charity hospital, he said to one of the two friends who had not seen fit to desert him: "Farewell! I am leaving this earth, where power is passing to money and to intrigue. Only one thing hurt me deeply: it hurt me to see that even fame could be acquired by means of such money and such intrigue; that these could make not only a small coterie of dupes proclaim you a genius, but the most gifted too—all your contemporaries, in fact, even to the uttermost corners of the earth." At that moment, under the hospital window, a barrel-organ could be heard grinding out

'Money is only a chimera'—the famous melody by Meyerbeer. The sick man smiled, covered his face, and died.[49]

At the end of this moving fable clearly based on Heine's own life, Meyerbeer has once again come into view. The passage leaves no doubt that Maestro Giacomo had become, for Heine, the symbol of a commercial world in which everything, including fame and reputation, has been turned into marketable commodity. Even the most gifted can be corrupted or deceived into becoming part of the advertising and propaganda machine! This last thrust goes particularly deep; Heine remembers his own earlier praise of Meyerbeer, his own acceptance of money and favours. Once again, therefore, an unacknowledged element of self-reproach informs the poet's attack on a composer he had once admired and lauded.

The bitterness that animates the Laplander piece appears also in Heine's sketch for a preface to the French edition of his writings on Germany and the Germans, *De l'Allemagne*. Written in the mid 1850s, this projected preface reflects once more on the sad lot of poets in a commercial society: would they not do better to let their inspiration go hang and use such talents as they have to become directors of gaslight companies?

Fame is a fine thing, but if you are rich you can buy that too. It's not as cheap a commodity as one might think; but anyone who has a million—especially a million Prussian *thaler*—can afford it. He can then buy himself a good solid fame, a reputation that spreads over the whole globe and survives the greatest geniuses—survives their bodies, that is, but not their works.

The old aristocracy, Heine continues, was arrogant and insolent enough; but at least it did not strain to outdo the geniuses on whom it thought itself entitled to look down.

But now things have changed. The insolence that genius has always had to put up with from the rich is now hideously compounded. Genius is cheated of the last possession left to it, that which once comforted it in its misery. For what value could fame retain in the eyes of a true genius when he sees that it can be bought by rich men with their money; when he has to share his fame with the unclean sons of Mammon?[50]

Ferdinand Friedland and Giacomo Meyerbeer are not named;

but there can be a few readers of Heine's later writings who would fail to sense their presence.

(iv)

The asperity of Heine's dealings with Meyerbeer and Dessauer is wholly absent from an amusing portrait-sketch of his erstwhile translator François-Adolphe Loève-Veimars, whose death occurred in 1854. He just hints at Loève-Veimars' Semitic ancestry by speculating that the 'Arabian knights of the desert' among whom he travelled might have been numbered among his forebears—the term 'Arabian', we remember, had served Heine as a periphrasis for 'Jewish' in the 1840s; and having defended him against various unfair attacks, he goes on to paint an amusing picture of the translator as dandy. The passage begins with a reference to the ten years (1838–48) which Loève-Veimars spent as French consul in Baghdad:

[His] outward appearance was less likely to impress Orientals who like to see great dignity of office represented by great corpulence, even by obesity. These advantages the French consul lacked: he was slightly built and not very tall, although he looked every inch a *grand seigneur*. He was not a baron, but deserved to be one, by reason of his character . . . His appearance suggested the nobleman: a dapper, dainty figure, smooth as an eel, aristocratic white hands whose diaphanous nails were smoothed with especial care, a gentle, almost feminine face with piercing blue eyes, cheeks whose rosy hue was more the result of art than of nature, and blonde hair, which covered his scalp but sparsely and was scrupulously kept in condition by all imaginable lotions,combs and brushes. With happy self-satisfaction Loève-Veimars would occasionally show his friends the box that contained his cosmetic apparatus: innumerable brushes and combs of every shape and size together with a multitude of large and small sponges. His joy at such exhibitions was the joy of a child showing off its toys—but is *that* a reason for the kind of intemperate abuse which was thrown at him? He never pretended to be a Cato, and our modern Catos have no right to demand of him the virtues in which they so conspicuously drape themselves in their republican journals. Loève-Veimars, not being an aristocrat by birth, did have democratic convictions; but his way of feeling was that of a *gentilhomme* . . .[51]

Nothing in this portrait of a blue-eyed, fair-haired little dandy suggests the Semitic affiliations at which Heine had hinted earlier on.

The poet does, however, make use of Jewish stereotypes in several of his later poems. We have already noticed this in *The Bedbug*, with its 'pawnbroker' associations; and we can observe it again in *Simplicissimus I*, where the supposedly Jewish antecedents of Georg Herwegh's wife are indicated by several references to the length of her nose. *Simplicissimus I* also contains a piece of adivce which Madame Herwegh is made to give her liberal husband on how to discharge at one fell swoop his duty to his country and his notorious debts.

> 'Denk an die Not des Vaterlands
> Und an die eignen Schulden und Nöten.
> In Frankfurt laß ich dich krönen, und Rothschild
> Borgt dir wie andren Majestäten.'

> [Think of your fatherland's distress,
> and of your own debts and distresses.
> Get yourself crowned at Frankfurt, and Rothschild
> Will lend money to you as to other royalty.']⁵²

The Rothschilds, on this view, will accommodate themselves to any post-revolutionary régimes willing to deal with them, as easily as they had once met the wishes of traditional monarchs.

To balance his caricatures of Jews Heine brings into his later poems caricatures of anti-Semites and their arguments. In *Atta Troll* he had ridiculed irrational anti-Jewish arguments by introducing their equivalent into the animal kingdom—and this device he used again, to excellent effect, in *An Election of Choice Asses*, where nationalistic anti-Semitism is humorously estranged, *verfremdet*, by making its spokesman a donkey. The characterization of this donkey as *ein Alt-Langohr*, which I translate below as 'a long-eared ancient', is of course a coinage designed to parallel *ein Altdeutscher*: a champion, that is, of the ancient virtues of the German people, and hence an opponent of such newfangled notions as civic equality for Jews and respect for French culture.

Als einer jedoch die Kandidatur
Des Rosses empfahl, mit Zeter
Ein Alt-Langohr in die Rede ihm fuhr,
Und schrie: "Du bist ein Verräter!

Du bist ein Verräter, es fließt in dir
Kein Tropfen vom Eselsblute;
Du bist kein Esel, ich glaube schier,
Dich warf eine welsche Stute.

Du stammst vom Zebra vielleicht, die Haut
Sie ist gestreift zebräisch;
Auch deiner Stimme näselnder Laut
Klingt ziemlich ägyptisch-hebräisch.

Und wärst du kein Fremdling, so bist du doch nur
Verstandesesel, ein kalter;
Du kennst nicht die Tiefen der Eselsnatur,
Dir klingt nicht ihr mystischer Psalter.

Ich aber versenkte die Seele ganz
In jenes süße Gedösel;
Ich bin ein Esel, in meinem Schwanz
Ist jedes Haar ein Esel.

[But when someone suggested that the horse
would be a good candidate, a long-eared ancient
interrupted him shrilly
and shouted: 'You are a traitor!

You are a traitor, in your veins
no drop of ass's blood flows;
you are no ass, I truly believe
some Latin mare must have foaled you.

Perhaps you are descended from the zebra, your skin
has some zebraic stripes;
and the nasal twang of your voice
sounds suspiciously Zebraic-Hebraic.

And even if you should turn out not to be a foreigner—you
    are still nothing but
a cold, merely reasoning ass.
You cannot fathom the depths of an ass's nature,
you are deaf to its mythical psalms.

But I have submerged the whole of my soul
in that sweet indistinction;
I am an ass, in my tail
every single hair is pure donkey.']53

How sad that this ridicule of Germanic racialism and nationalism could do nothing to arrest the progress of such ideas before they reached their murderous conclusion.

(v)

The Old Testament and its God are frequently invoked in Heine's last poems, often in strange contexts. The very title of *Song of Songs* (*Das Hohelied*), like the closing refrain of the poem usually known, because of its refrain, as *Halleluja*, proclaims that Heine is playing variations on biblical themes. *Halleluja* surveys God's creation with various degrees of irony, in tones that range from the mock-ecclesiastical to the street-singer mode familiar from the middle section of *The God Apollo*, while *Song of Songs*, a paean to the artist-God who made the female body, ends with a dissonant reference to the disease that prevents the poet, God's fellow artist, from studying that masterpiece as thoroughly as he would like.54 God, clearly, is not a transcendent being, an unknowable Other, revealed to the believer in a flash of religious illumination, nor is He the ultimate lawgiver Whose decree it is sinful to disobey. He is rather, as so often in Heine, a heavenly equivalent of earthly artists whose work can be criticized. God's humour, especially, appears somewhat heavy-handed, a 'sad jest', as the poem usually entitled *Miserere* proclaims in mock-reverential tones.

O Gott, verkürze meine Qual,
Damit man mich bald begrabe;
Du weißt ja, daß ich kein Talent
Zum Martyrtume habe.

Ob deiner Inkonsequenz, o Herr,
Erlaube, daß ich staune:
Du schufest den fröhlichsten Dichter und raubst
Ihm jetzt seine gute Laune.

Der Schmerz verdumpft den heitern Sinn
Und macht mich melancholisch,
Nimmt nicht der traurige Spaß ein End',
So werd' ich am Ende katholisch.

Ich heule dir dann die Ohren voll
Wie andre gute Christen—
O Miserere! Verloren geht
Der beste der Humoristen!

[O God, shorten my agony
so that I can be buried soon;
you know that I lack the talent
to be a martyr.

Permit me, Lord, to express astonishment
at your illogicality;
you created the merriest poet, and now
you rob him of his cheerfulness.

Pain dulls my gay serenity,
and makes me melancholy;
if this sad jest does not finish soon
I'll turn Catholic in the end.

Then I'll wail into your ears
like other good Christians.
O Miserere! the world is losing
the best of all humorists!][55]

Peter Guttenhöfer has documented the extent to which the
tone in which Heine speaks to his God is prefigured in the Old
Testament itself, by Abraham, by Jeremiah, by Job[56]—but
there is nothing in either the Old Testament or the New which
could prepare pious readers for this degree of ironic familiar-
ity.

The later Heine's addresses to God are not, then, those of a
pious soul communing with its creator. They presuppose an
alert reader, they draw him in, they ask him to respond with
some amusement to deliberately humorous touches which
often involve the commingling of different vocabulary regis-
ters—as when the poet assures his newly-found God that he
lacks 'talent' for martyrdom. Wilhelm Gössman is not alone in

feeling that theologically God is often more powerfully pre-
sent in Heine's last poems when He is *not* being addressed than
when He is: notably in the unforgettable 'Leave your sacred
parables . . .' [Laß die heil'gen Parabolen . . .] which ends with
a truly terrifying presentation of God's silence in face of man's
questioning:

> Woran liegt die Schuld? Ist etwa
> Unser Herr nicht ganz allmächtig?
> Oder treibt er selbst den Unfug?
> Ach, das wäre niederträchtig.
>
> Also fragen wir beständig,
> Bis man uns mit einer Handvoll
> Erde endlich stopft die Mäuler—
> Aber ist das eine Antwort?
>
> [What is to blame for this? Could it be
> that God is not quite all-powerful?
> Or does He make the mischief Himself?
> Ah—that would be dastardly.
>
> Thus we question without end,
> until a handful of earth
> is at last stuffed into our mouth to silence us—
> but is *that* an answer?[57]

The sudden substitution of assonance for an expected rhyme
hammers the incongruity home in a way possible only in
poetry.

Heine's last poems, not published in his own lifetime, also
contain reminiscences of Jewish ritual. In *Bimini*, for instance,
Juan Ponce de Leon's ship is decked out like a *Lauberhütte*, a
leafy tabernacle—a reference, not to German Whitsuntide cus-
toms as some commentators have thought, but to the *Succah*
which observing Jews are obliged to construct during *Succot,*
the Feast of Tabernacles.[58] There is an element of defiance in
this: for Heine, who had a keen memory for all intended
insults, will have remembered that August von Platen had
called him *Petrarch des Lauberhüttenfests*, the Petrarch of the
Feast of Tabernacles, in *The Romantic Oedipus*, the play that
had so incensed the poet and had led to his savage and self-

defeating retaliation in *The Baths of Lucca*. And then, in a dream-poem addressed to his last love, a poem which begins with the line 'I dreamt of a summer night' ('Es träumte mir von einer Sommernacht') and which is usually entitled *Für die Mouche*, the poet once more, for the last time, confronts the Hebrew and the Graeco-Roman heritage to which he owed so much. The figures of the Old Testament which he had so often invoked, sometimes seriously, more often with affectionate playfulness—Abraham and Isaac, Lot and his daughters, Moses and Aaron, Esther, Judith, Holofernes, the arch-enemy Haman, Balaam and his donkey—are now to be seen sculptured on a sarcophagus which also bears representations of the gods and heroes of classical antiquity. A passion-flower, reminiscent of the passion of Christ, bends over all. In the sarcophagus lies a dead man, the poet himself perhaps, communing with the flower in strange romantic converse, forgetful of the struggle between Greek and Hebrew which has raged within and without him. But such peace cannot last; the bas-reliefs come alive and renew the old quarrel.

> Spukt in dem Stein der alte Glaubenswahn?
> Und disputieren diese Marmorschemen?
> Der Schreckensruf des wilden Waldgotts Pan
> Wetteifernd wild mit Mosis Anathemen!
>
> Oh, dieser Streit wird enden nimmermehr,
> Stets wird die Wahrheit hadern mit dem Schönen,
> Stets wird geschieden sein der Menschheit Heer
> In zwei Partein: Barbaren und Hellenen.
>
> [Is this stone still haunted by ancient religious illusions?
> Can these marble wraiths carry on the old dispute?
> The wild god Pan's cry of terror
> Competes with the anathemata of Moses.
>
> This struggle, alas, will never end;
> truth will always quarrel with beauty,
> the host of mankind will always be divided
> into two parties: Barbarians and Hellenes.][59]

Our gaze comes to rest, in this late poem, not on Moses the humane and wise leader and guide, but on an enraged Moses thundering anathemata; and the Jews who look to him as the fount of wisdom are in possession of truth, certainly, just as the Hellenes are in possession of beauty—but such truth is paired, in this vision, with barbarism. There never was a time in which Heine could accept the Jewish heritage wholeheartedly and unquestioningly, any more than he could subscribe without qualification to other ancient beliefs whose illusory element the phrase 'der alte Glaubenswahn' now lights up for the last time. But the cries of the Great God Pan and the anathemata of Moses—figures we can respect and admire even if they frighten us or put us off—are drowned out in the end by the voice of Balaam's ass: not the charmingly gentle speech described in the Bible, but an ear-splitting 'Heehaw,' the bray of mindless stupidity which Heine had recently castigated in an *Open Letter to Jakob Venedey* (*Offenes Sendschreiben an Jakob Venedey*).[60] This is the final sound that assails the dreamer's ears before he too cries out, in horror and anguish, and wakes himself up.

To the last, we see, Heine refused to harmonize—whatever dissonances he heard, or thought he heard, in the world's symphony he had to share with his readers. This uncomfortable honesty, this endeavour to remain true to the tonality and the complexities of his experience, helps to make him—for all his stylizations, rearrangements, unfairnesses, and evasions—a witness whose voice we ignore at our peril.

FOURTH INTERMEZZO
Civilization of the Heart

(i)

Our examination of Heine's late writings will have served to confirm what Jeffrey Sammons has shown in his biography of the poet: how little he was concerned, in his years of sickness, with the objective truth of theological claims; how frequently his language betrayed the admission that he considered his 'return' to God a defeat; and how constantly he tried to demonstrate that his religious 'regression' had neither affected his rationality nor diminished his concern with political and social freedoms. All this is as true of his private as it is of his public pronouncements. A letter he wrote to François Mignet on 17 January 1849 is wholly characteristic of his tone and manner.

I must also confess to you that a great religious reaction has taken place in us. David [Friedrich] Strauß has avowed it in open court; as for me, it's still a secret that I confide to no one but my sick-nurse and some superior women. At the risk of being considered a blockhead I will no longer conceal from you the great event that has taken place in my soul: I have deserted German atheism and am on the verge of returning to the bosom of the most banal beliefs. I am beginning to appreciate that a tiny bit of God won't do a poor man any harm—particularly if he has to lie on his back for seven months and be racked by the most dreadful tortures. I don't, as yet, altogether believe in heaven; but I have had a foretaste of hell from the burns that the doctors have inflicted on my spinal column. There's progress for you—I can now consciously consign myself to the devil, and I thus have an advantage over my poor atheistic compatriots who have great need of the devil just now, especially at Berlin where the king has just proclaimed a constitution. It's a very good constitution, but it inspires a certain repugnance—the kind of repugnance one feels in face of a large cake that might just contain a little poison, just a tiny bit of Prussic acid.

'I have deserted German atheism'—it has been shown, by now, that Heine had no more been an 'atheist' in the true sense of the word than he had been a 'Hellene' or 'returned' to anything like orthodox Judaism. He told Alfred Meissner, who had always believed him to have a fundamentally religious nature, that some of his late poems should indeed be considered 'religious'—'blasphemously religious'. And how could one have the relief of blasphemy if one did not postulate a personal God? To Alexandre Weill he said that monotheism was the 'smallest possible dose' of religion, and he went on to speculate whether Jehovah—in whose name so many of the pleasant things of life were prohibited—might not find His own amusements in the way Jupiter was believed to find them. As for the bills of exchange on immortality which religion offered to suffering mankind—how could one be sure that they would be honoured? After all, they had not been signed by Rothschild! Ludwig Kalisch reports the poet as saying that pantheism was not a faith suitable to one in his condition—such sufferings called for a compensating life beyond the grave, and (above all) a personal God. He had not taken the road to this God through either Church or Synagogue, but had been well received nevertheless; the Lord had healed his soul—if only he would heal his body too! Caroline Jaubert remembers Heine asserting, on the contrary, that the God Who had struck him down was a barbarian god such as Egyptians might imagine; a Greek god would have killed him with a thunderbolt rather than letting him die piecemeal, limb by limb . . . Fanny Lewald reports that Heine repeated to her earnest conversations he had held with his new-found God in the course of his sleepless nights; the Lord had addressed him as 'Dear Doctor' and told him he might be a socialist, even a republican, so long as he was not an atheist. That was in 1848; two years later Adolf Stahr heard Heine say that opium was a religion too: 'When I cannot bear my agonies any more, I take morphine; when I cannot batter my enemies down, I look to Providence to take care of them; when I can no longer look after my own affairs, I leave them to the good Lord; only—he added with a smile—my money affairs I prefer to see to myself.' To other visitors he depicted his many charitable actions (and no one could be more charitable and generous than Heine when his back was not up!) by saying that he liked, from time to time, to leave his visiting-card with the good Lord.[1]

In his letters of the last eight years of his life he continued to say things like 'my ancestors belonged to the Jewish religion, and I have never taken pride in that origin' (to Saint-René Taillandier, 3 November 1851), and his references to God would, as often as not, seem blasphemous to orthodox Jews. God appears, at times, as a kind of celestial Uncle Salomon, at other times as a poet and satirist like Heine himself, at yet other times, as a sadistic tormentor. When the 1848 revolution broke out, the poet even suspects Him of having gone mad!

> I say nothing about what is happening in these times. What we have now is universal anarchy, disorder of the whole world, God's madness become visible! The Old One will have to be put under restraint, if things go on like that. It's all the fault of the atheists; they have made Him so angry that He's gone mad.
>
> (to Campe, 9 July 1848)

The Jewish tradition, it is true, can accommodate sitting in judgement on God Himself—*a din toire mit Gott*; but talk of 'putting Him under restraint' is another thing again. As a poet, Heine tells Georg Weerth on 5 November 1851, he does not *need* religion:

> I die as a poet who has no need of religion or of philosophy, and who has nothing to do with either of them. The poet understands the symbolic idiom of religion very well, as he does the abstract reasoning jargon of philosophy—but the men of religion and those of philosophy will never understand the poet, whose language will always be as Greek to them as Latin was to Professor Maßmann.

Just a week after writing the letter just quoted, however, Heine signed a last will and testament in which he speaks in a very different idiom. Having once again asked that there should be no religious ceremonies at his funeral, he continues:

> This desire is not dictated by atheistic aspirations (*quelque velléité d'esprit fort*). For the last four years I have abandoned all philosophic conceit and have returned to religious ideas and sentiments. I die believing in One Eternal God, Who has created the world and Whom I pray to have mercy on my eternal soul. I regret having sometimes spoken, in my writings, without due respect of sacred things; but it was more the spirit of the time than my own inclination that carried

me along. If I have, unwittingly, offended against good manners and against that morality which is the true essence of all monotheistic beliefs, I ask God and men to pardon me.[2]

'May one be pardoned and retain the offence?' asks Shakespeare's Claudius. Readers of Heine's writings after 1851 will often be inclined to echo that question, only to find that as far as God's pardon is concerned, the poet has his answer ready. 'Dieu me pardonnera', he is reported to have said; 'c'est son métier.'[3]

The will from which I have just quoted reiterates that the man who is making it has been baptized into the Protestant faith; but after his public presentation of himself, on 15 April 1849, as 'nothing but a poor Jew, sick unto death . . .', Heine will never again try to deny his connection with the Jewish people, in whose history he now takes frequent pride, despite the remark to Saint-René Taillandier already quoted in the present chapter. Perhaps one should now look at the whole passage in the original to obtain a better perspective:

Mes ancêtres ont appartenu à la religion juive; je me suis jamais enorgueilli de cette origine, moi qui me sentais déjà assez humilié, quand on me prenait pour une créature simplement humaine, pendant que Hegel m'avait fait croire que j'étais un Dieu!

(3 November 1851)

'Our forefathers', Heine had written to his brother Maximilian two years before this letter to Taillandier, on 3 May 1849, 'were fine, honest men; they humbled themselves before God and were stiff-necked and obstinate before men, before the powers of this world. I, on the contrary, confronted the heavens boldly but was humble and servile with men—and that is why I now lie on the ground like a crushed worm. Praise and glory be to the Lord on high!' One must not take either of these self-dramatizations too much *au pied de la lettre*. Whatever Heine might feel about himself in his despondent moments, his dealings with the powers of this world could hardly be called 'humble and servile'; he would have had an easier life had that been true. And a note of pride does, surely, sound through his appreciations of Jewish history:

A great civilization of the heart remained with them, an unbroken tradition of two thousand years. I think they were able to play a part in European culture so quickly because in respect of feeling they had nothing to learn: all they had to acquire was knowledge.

(to Joseph Lehmann, 5 October 1854)

When he looked at the Bible, he saw that 'civilization of the heart' everywhere; but he also found, as wrote to Laube on 25 January 1850, that the Pentateuch, 'the Mosaic documents', spoke to him forcibly and directly about the existence of God. Hegel, he tells Laube, has lost much of his credit with me, and old Moses's credit stands in full flower.' 'If only', he adds wrily, 'I had the *prophets* as well as Moses'—reminding his friend of the old student-slang term for 'the necessary cash': *Moses und seine Propheten*. He does not, in these late letters, identify himself with his 'favourite hero' Moses; as in the published works, it is Job, Lazarus, and Nebuchadnezzar reduced to eating grass with the beasts of the field who seem to offer more convincing parallels. Meissner reports that when Heine saw Kietz's portrait of him in July 1851, he commented: 'Yes, that is the true picture of Our Lord—after all, he was also a Jew.' Perhaps one should add, in view of the phrase 'Our Lord' (*unseres Herrn*) in Meissner's report, that Alexandre Weill claims to have heard Heine say: 'No Jew will ever believe in another Jew's divinity—not even Neander and Stahl, however much they might wish to deny it!'[4]

As for the 'grass' that Heine claims to have eaten when he was stricken down like Nebuchadnezzar among the beasts of the field: this included, once again, that *Schalet* or *tsholent* dish which he had once called the *ranz de vaches* of Judaism. 'My cook' he writes to his mother on 3 August 1850, concerned, as ever, to hide from her the desperate physical state into which he had fallen, 'is a genius; under the name "German noodles" she turns out a dish that is nothing more nor less than our Jewish *Schalet*. I eat it with delight.'

(ii)

Inevitably, in his confinement and his sleepless nights, Heine's thoughts turned to the past, to the childhood in which his father had not yet become a sick and broken man; in which his brothers had not yet become the boastful and quarrelsome fellows who jangled his nerves when they visited him and brought confusion into his affairs when they meddled with them in Hamburg or in Vienna; in which his mother was still a loved and respected companion, counsellor, and guide. Remembrance of his father brought with it recollections of Jewish ceremonial. 'I dreamt of our late father', he writes to Max on 11 September 1848, 'and of his naïve annoyance when he was not given a little knife at the ceremony you know about'. The ceremony Heine so pointedly does not mention is a funeral service; the 'little knife' is needed to perform the *keri'ah*, the ritual tearing of the mourner's garment. He affectionately remembers, too, his father's business terminology and its application to all spheres of life: 'Happy are they who finish with life quickly; *per acquit*, as dear father [*mein Vatterchen*] used to say. You turn around, you go to sleep, and you are quits.' (To Charlotte Embden and Betty Heine, 29 March 1849.) But if memories of his father brought with them recollections of rootedness in Jewish tradition, memories of his mother brought with them recollections of struggles against the Jewish environment which turned, at times, into downright hostility to fellow Jews. 'I have never desired to share your dislike of Jews', he writes to his mother on 7 May 1853, 'but they have made things damned difficult for me; Our Lord and Saviour must indeed have been divine if he could forgive such Pharisees their persecuting zeal.' His *Memoiren* suggest that he is acting in Betty Heine's spirit when he plays down the Jewish element in his early education—as he does even in a letter to his sister dated 16 July 1853. But he also saw in his mother, as he says to her in a letter of 19 August 1849, the very opposite of an atheist: 'a fine God-fearing woman, with true piety'. She, surely, of all people, will understand his struggle to find a way to God—even though she never appreciated his poetry. That there were strict limits to his mother's insight and intelligence he always saw clearly, but he related that to a generally unfavourable estimate of the female mind in which his alliance with Mathilde could only confirm him. This did not any way detract from the affection and respect Betty Heine inspired in his conscious mind. Whether there were or were not unconscious resentments that welled up in some of the images and situations of his poetry I must leave to others to determine; psychoanalysing the dead is not an activity I feel able to pursue with any degree of confidence.

'My dear, good, true and faithful mother—what are all the others compared with you? One should kiss the ground your feet have walked on.' (21 January 1850.) There was certainly not much else in his family to inspire lasting affection. Lotte was *Plapperlotte*, Max and Gustav were turning into caricatures of themselves, relations with Carl, with Cécile and with Moritz Embden, even when old quarrels were patched up, could never again be cordial, and though some satisfaction was to be gained from the neurotic afflictions of Uncle Salomon's sons-in-law (which in the case of Adolf Halle turned into certifiable madness) this was not a satisfaction conducive to warm family feeling. He did mellow just a little: 'I sympathize with the fate of this excellent man', he says of poor Dr Halle on 7 June 1851, but feels constrained to add immediately that his *idées fixes* were partly due to his avarice. Over this whole scene brooded the shadow of dead Uncle Salomon and what the poet regarded as his broken promises. This loomed large, not only in the letters, but also in successive drafts of Heine's last will and testament.

As long as my late Uncle S. H. lived, I did not think it necessary to secure the fortunes of my wife in any explicit way; for he was very fond of her and treated her like a father. To this must be added that I regarded the pension I derived from my uncle as interest on a sum of which he had made me a present; all he said on this subject conformed to this assumption. Later, when I married, I asked my uncle to arrange that half my pension should be paid to my wife, retaining for myself disposal of the other half. I thought, at the time, that I was proceeding towards a future in which I would have substantial means; for my uncle had on several occasions prophesied to me, when we spent an affectionate hour together, that one day I would be a rich man; he was generous and straightforward and wealthy enough to make that prophecy come true.

(Draft of last will and testament, 1851)[5]

Can we not hear the 'And yet he lied to me'—*und er hat mich doch belogen*—of *The Poet Firdusi*? But now Heine deflects responsibility away from the terrestrial uncle to the newly-found heavenly Father: 'The Lord determined otherwise. It was His high will that I should end in poverty and misery.'

Well, 'poverty' was something of an exaggeration—by most contemporary standards, as Michael Werner has shown in convincing detail, Heine was well off. The passage just quoted would not do, therefore; the poet deleted it, and tried again on another tack.

As early as 1846 I assigned what had up till then constituted my literary fortune—the copyright of my writings in German—to my Hamburg publisher for a very modest sum, in order to avoid, by means of this sacrifice, lawsuits which would have caused scandals annoying to my uncle Salomon, who was then still alive;

(nothing, but nothing supports this disingenuous explanation)

for Uncle Salomon, who promised to secure a splendid future for me in his will, had the right to expect that I would not use my talents like a businessman, for the mere earning of money, as I had done hitherto, but as a poet for the glorification of our family name.[6]

So much for the censorship the family had been trying to impose on Heine in an endeavour to see that the family name was not besmirched! But now a different sort of censorship has been added—that imposed by Heine's altered views on religion.

The manuscripts which I still possessed were, unfortunately, of a kind which compelled me to destroy a large portion of them; this compulsion was due to a change in my religious views and to my consideration for persons whom I must not injure by using expressions that might be misunderstood. Perhaps, in the end, I shall have to destroy them altogether; so that when I die my widow will lose that source of revenue too.[7]

The argument is clear: consideration for you, for my family, has led to a diminution of my literary earnings; it is therefore your duty to secure my wife's future after my death. The draft, ultimately abandoned, then sweetens the pill by acknowledging Carl Heine's generosity, and appeals to him to remember the love and kindness Uncle Salomon always showed to Mathilde.

A subsequent version of the will Heine made in 1851 was to have been accompanied by a letter in which the poet reverted once more to the understanding he had, or thought he had, with Uncle Salomon, and the terrible shock the terms of Salomon's testamentary dispositions were to him.

The clause in my uncle's will which left me merely a sum scarcely sufficient to cover the costs of sustenance in a single year posed me a riddle. Trying to find the solution of that riddle, and never succeeding, was bound to lead to darkest suspicions; my anger rose to its highest pitch, I tormented myself to the point of madness, and in this state of mind I spoke most harshly to those who deserved it least. With words as foolish as they were undignified I insulted the noblest and most affectionate of men, the friend of my youth. I have sufficiently atoned for this fault with sufferings extending over many years, but I cannot leave this world without solemnly expressing my repentance.

To secure his widow's financial future the poet here grovels before Carl in an embarrassing way. Heine was keenly conscious of his humiliation, and sought to compensate himself as much as possible—by venting his wrath on Salomon's and Carl's entourage.

The enemies who, indirectly, provoked my wrongdoing have also found ways to exploit it in order to ruin me. They did this with a cruelty that defied imagination. Yes: I had enemies in this world of the most bloodthirsty kind—male and female Shylocks, who thirsted after the satisfaction of cutting a piece of flesh from my heart, and succeeded (really succeeded!) in cutting a small piece away.[8]

The Shylock reference is not introduced lightly; it hints, if hints were needed, that these were *Jewish* enemies, enemies within his own family in the wider as well as the narrower sense. And from this spectacle of Shylocks more successful than ever Shakespeare's Shylock had been, Heine turns again to his newly-found or newly postulated God. He unloads on to Him all the resentments, all the anger that he dared not fully express towards His creatures, creatures that still had it in their power to harm, if not Heine himself, then his widow after his death.

I will not say that I forgive them; but even these enemies I will not accuse of being the ultimate cause of my misfortune. They are only blind tools of a higher will, only automata controlled in Heaven. You, O God, You alone are the true author of my ruin; those wretched human beings are not guilty of it. You, O God, willed my destruction, and I was destroyed. Praised be the Lord! He has cast me down from the pedestal of my pride, and I, who in my philosophical conceit believed myself a god and cherished feelings and practised virtues that belong only to a god—here I lie on the ground, wretched and miserable, writhing like a worm. Blessed be the Lord! I bear my torments with resignation, I drain the cup of humiliation to the last drop without shrinking. For I know

—and here, as so often, the old Heine reasserts himself, the Son of God parallel is evoked once more, as it had so often been in earlier times—

that I will be resurrected from this abasement, that I will arise justified, sanctified and celebrated.

Heine could never, for long, sustain the posture of the humble penitent even when he was making his last will; nor could he resist showing his claws when his reason told him that what was needed to achieve his purpose was a lamb-like bleat.

In one of his earlier letters (to Maximilian Heine, 9 January 1850) Heine had thought for a moment of applying to Carl the nickname he had secretly given to Uncle Salomon: 'Destiny', *das Fatum*. But Carl's unimpressive appearance and personality hardly warranted that; Uncle Salomon's other nickname, 'Reb Aaron', would do better. At other times the two eras, that of Salomon and that of Carl, are spoken of in biblical terms; Heine characterizes Carl's proceedings as

a base insult, miserly iniquity, which reminds me of so many events in the past, of similar happenings in Old Testament times . . .
(to Maximilian Heine 23 March 1850)

The new dispensation tends to parody rather than repeat the old—Carl's conduct towards his sick cousin is found, at one time, to exhibit 'a brutality such as I was hardly gratified with in my healthiest days by the Old Man' (to Maximilian Heine, 3 December 1848). The lump sum Salomon left him, in lieu of the secure income he thought he had been promised, seemed 'cursed'—though Heine mocks the superstition that leads him to think so (to Gustav Heine, January 1851). What is happening in Hamburg now, he surmises, is only a repetition of what happened at Uncle Salomon's court, where Aunt Hettie (*Tante Jette*), led the chorus of his detractors:

> They are influencing the Young Man against me in the way they once influenced the late Old Man. It's always the same baseness, the same Aunt Hettie-ism, the same stinking mess. What good is done is done only out of fear of being shamed by public opinion . . .
>
> (to Gustav Heine, 15 July 1851)

Constantly, when he thought of his present wrongs, the image of Uncle Salomon, 'a certain Reb Aaron', would spring to his mind (to Charlotte Embden, 26 June 1854). Even Carl's messengers become, in Heine's eyes, after-images of that Aaron Hirsch who had been Uncle Salomon's trusted factotum (to Maximilian Heine, 3 December 1848). But his true view of Carl Heine and his wife (the charmer Cécile with whom he had once been on such friendly terms) is best summed up by the nickname he derived for them from *schofel*, meaning petty, mean, and low: 'the young Schofelly' and 'Madame Schofelly'' (to Maximilian Heine, 12 August 1852).

It must not be overlooked, however, that a softer note could occasionally creep into the later Heine's letters when he talked about his family. In his eccentric and unhygienic cousin Hermann Schiff he saw a talented and amusing writer, and even Cousin Carl is occasionally credited with a good heart (to Betty Heine and Charlotte Embden, 6 May 1850). Of particular interest is the letter of condolence Heine sent to his cousin Hermann on 19 November 1855—a letter in which we may see more than a mere application of the principle *de mortuis nil nisi bonum*:

> The sad news has affected me deeply. My dear Uncle Henri was an excellent good man. His gentleness and benevolence amounted almost to a weakness, and that made him all the more lovable. He was polite and decent, had good manners, and never allowed a coarse word—let alone an insulting remark—to pass his lips. He never told lies, and softly insinuating villainy was as foreign to his heart as the coarsely insulting variety. And one word of praise he deserves above all: he was honest through and through!

It is impossible to read this paean without feeling that by praising Uncle Henri he is imputing to other members of the family the qualities Henri Heine is said to lack: coarseness,

prevarication, dishonesty, uncivilized manners. In what fol-
lows Heine makes this point crystal clear.

Such good qualities, dear Hermann, are unfortunately becoming rare
in our family; falseness and faithlessness are becoming dominant
traits, and where evil is sown, misfortune and destruction will be the
harvest.

And then, to complete the by now familiar pattern, Heine
turns to the God he so often invoked in these years, and to his
own suffering.

The tears of the insulted cry to God! His hand lies heavy on me too;
whether as punishment or visitation I do not know. I suffer greatly,
but I bear my misery with submission to God's inscrutable will.

Cousin Hermann will have found nothing in this letter to
suggest that the God of Whom Heine spoke to him was any
other than the Jewish God Whom rabbi and mourners had
addressed at his father's funeral.

The letters Heine wrote to his mother, his sister, and his
brother during the final years of his life abound with Judaeo-
German words and phrases: *Verbrengerin, mohlt euch, zehkel
a mohl, chappen, gannef, ketz, Scholem, Milchome*; with
idiomatic sayings current in Jewish families, like *ruf mich
Liberchen-Esser* (call me what you like—see if I care!'); with
puns like *Mistspoche* (*Mist:* 'garbage', 'manure', *Mishpokhe*:
'family'). He uses the Jewish calendar too, in computing his
mother's birthday, though he was not always successful in
working out which day of the Gentile calendar would corres-
pond to the day in question, Kislev 3, *Gimmel Kisselev*. In
small ways like this he recreated the linguistic ambience of his
youth and asserted a Jewish consciousness that had never left
him. Rutger Booß, who has studied this aspect of the poet's
vocabulary with especial care, makes an interesting point about
it. The Yiddish-Hebrew words of Heine's last letters do not
refer, as so many of their counterparts in the early letters did, to
Jewish religious ritual. Instead they recapture the linguistic
family ambience of Heine's youth by means of concepts that
recall the 'mattress-crypt' and its agonies. The *Schonim* (years)
pass, the *Chuschem* (powers) are failing, *Ketz* (the end) is
approaching, an end which involves *peigern*, to die like an

animal . . .'⁹ But though he might be dying, he was sure that his work would outlive him and that he would therefore be able to confer an unwelcome immortality on some, at least, of those who had been unwise enough to offend him. Alfred Meissner, in his interesting account of Heine's last period, describes the elation with which this thought filled him—an elation one occasionally feels in the letters too. On 7 April 1855, a year before his death, he exultingly reports to his mother that what she knew as 'the crooked corner' (*der schiefe Winkel*)—the coterie of the Leo family which had constituted a kind of gossip-exchange between Hamburg and Paris—would find French as well as German readers laughing at Heine's picture of their salon when *Lutezia* appeared in its French garb as *Lutèce*.

(iii)

Heine's disillusion with the younger generation of activists with whom he had once been allied was no less profound than his disillusion with Uncle Salomon, whose portrait he had once wanted to paint *con amore*. Of Karl Marx we have already heard him say, in a conversation with Moritz Carrière, that a man was little if he was nothing but a razor.¹⁰ It was Ferdinand Lassalle, however, who disappointed him most deeply.

My poor Ferdinand Lassalle! It breaks my heart to think of him, to see so many happy gifts of nature fall prey to demonic self-destruction. He has treated me with dreadful harshness because I refused to be dragged into his murky activities and countered his passion with cold reason.

(to Heymann Lassal, 16 April 1850)

What a face Ferdinand will make, he tells the same correspondent on 30 April 1850, when he hears 'that I have had my fill of atheistic philosophy and have returned to the common man's humble faith in God'. (The mind boggles: Heine and the common man's humble faith!) 'If Ferdinand still has some kind of inner calm, this news may induce some salutary reflections in him.' A few months later, Heine begins to fear that Lassalle might allow compromising letters from Heine to reach the public; his draft of a letter to Lassalle's sister shows him resorting to counter-threats:

I am in possession of letters which reveal the writer and all his machinations, and could put an end to those machinations . . . If only I could bring your brother to see reason, save his inner self, heal him, make him happy!

(October 1850)

In this same year, 1850, he was visited by Adolf Stahr and Fanny Lewald, who report that the poet had expressed his regret at having rejected, during his quarrels with his Hamburg relatives, the moderating counsels of Varnhagen von Ense:

I would have followed Varnhagen's well-meant advice if Lassalle had not ensnared and dominated me to such an extent that I sucked in his vindictiveness, as it were, and abandoned myself to the bitter, vengeance-seeking mood of the moment. With hindsight I am now sorry that I acted in this way . . .

When Heine writes to his brother Gustav in the following year, on 21 January 1851, there is no more talk of 'saving' Lassalle from himself. The letter throbs with disappointment in the man 'who figures in the scandalous strong-box affair of which, I am sure, you have read':

When he came here with Friedländer [Ferdinand Friedland], he was barely nineteen years old, and never has a young man made a more pleasing impression on me, by means of his knowledge, his personality, and, especially, his penetrating intellect joined with an energy lacking in my own more dreamy nature, than this young man Lassalle. When I had the damnable affair of the Frankfurt Jews around my neck he wrote an essay, without my prior knowledge, which manifested extraordinary intelligence and predisposed me greatly in favour of its unknown author. This made his arrival here an immediate pleasure . . . No one understood as well as Lassalle where the shoe pinched me: he knew that the injury to my financial interests were not the main thing at all, that my anger [with Uncle Salomon and his heir] had much deeper and older roots which I neither could nor would uncover in public . . . Even when it harmed me his passionate nature did me good; he poured oil onto the fire, egged me on to make the most egregious mistakes which would not, perhaps, have been mistakes if I had energetically followed his advice to the limit . . .

Does this last admission merely mean that the poet had been too eager to spare his family's feelings? Or is he now ready to concede Lassalle's contention that the poet's struggle against plutocratic relatives, and his own attempt, in the Hatzfeld affair, to help a woman to her rights against the opposition of a brutal aristocratic husband, were part of a wider social battle in which he and Heine were alike engaged? The former is more likely; for in the letter to his brother from which I have just quoted the poet's disillusion with Lassalle's character appears complete.

In his rapid development towards wickedness this man has become one of the most terrible evildoers. He is capable of everything: of murder, of forgery, and of theft; and he possesses an obstinate strength of will which borders on insanity. I don't want to start anything with such a man, and that is why I shall not attack his father, that old highwayman who is perhaps more cunning than all the rest because he knew how to preserve a reputation for honesty which his son lost when he first appeared on the scene.

He and Lassalle, Heine tells his brother, both hold documents that could seriously compromise the other. Not that Heine had done anything discreditable—but it was unwise to attack Lassalle just the same, for fear of what he might do or say. If, however, after the poet's death, Lassalle should come forward to claim that he had been his friend—as seemed only too likely after the *New Rhenish Gazette* (*Neue Rheinische Zeitung*) had published an earlier letter in which Heine had expressed his admiration of Lassalle—then Gustav was to come forward and expose the claim for the lie it was.

Gustav Karpeles, in a memoir of Heine written at the end of the nineteenth century, claims to have learnt from one of the poet's visitors that the latter had indignantly denied the claim that he had once 'recommended Lassalle to someone in Berlin by saying that he was the new Redeemer'. If he were that, Heine is said to have added, God help the redeemed! Karpeles also reports that in 1855 Heine said to Fanny Lewald that in Lassalle one could observe the best and the worst sides, the virtues and the vices, of the Jewish character—and that he would surely come to a bad end.[11]

By 1855 Heine had mellowed enough to allow his erstwhile

friend to visit him again. Towards the beginning of July we find Lassalle reporting his impressions to Karl Marx:

I have only visited Heine once so far. He is in a very bad way—but his intellect is as bright and as sharp as ever, though he does seem embittered against the whole world. He was very glad to see me, and after the first greeting he called out straightaway, pointing to his penis: ' What do you say to such ingratitude? The part for which I have done so much has brought me to this state.' He really is a dreadful sight . . .[12]

'He holds you in friendly remembrance', Lassalle tells Marx—thus suggesting that in making his peace with Lassalle, as his life drew to a close, Heine also summoned up warm recollection of another young friend of the 1840s with whose way of looking at the world he still, to some degree, sympathized.

Lassalle had warned Heine against indulging in financial speculations for which he had no aptitude; but part of the poet's rancorous feelings towards the Lassalle-Friedland family was unquestionably due to the ill success of Ferdinand Friedland's gaslight company and his fear that he would lose the capital he had invested in it. Poor Calmonius came in for a great deal of abuse in private letters to himself, his wife, and his father-in-law, and for many threats of public exposure. Yet through it all a note of affection can still be heard.

In exile, as Dante already complained in his *Divine Comedy*, one is exposed to the worst companions—and this Friedland was a means I had found for neutralizing worse company still. He was my favourite spy, and what made me even more disposed to receive him was that he amused not only me but my wife too. He is a man wholly without education, without understanding, a foolish fellow at bottom; but he has an inborn talent for finding things out, an almost instinctive understanding of the most diverse conditions, and an ability to put two and two together which could have made him an important man if he had not had the misfortune of also being the greatest liar—one who lies to himself even more than to others. He is a bad egg, but he is not wicked. Being of service is his passion; and in order to render a service of some kind to a man he does not even know he will, quite without pricks of conscience, betray those to whom he owes a debt of gratitude. An original, you see, one whom I always found an amusing puzzle.

Having thus begun, in this private letter, a complex character study of his own personal court Jew, Heine continues:

> He is the very personification of vanity; and crafty though he is, he can be made to do anything if there is hope of a decoration at the end of it. He knows the press for what it is, yet he fears it as one fears fire; and Meissner's essay on me, which contains some ungentle allusions to Friedland, has, I am sure, put the fear of God into him. The threat of exposing him in the press, combined with some dexterous flattering of his vanity, of his passion for self-aggrandizement, would enable me to obtain from him whatever I want. At the present moment he seems to be without money himself—otherwise I would have extracted from him some of the cash he lost for me. But the fellow is so without conscience, so gifted by nature for the tasks of the confidence-trickster, such a genius of roguery, that even if he is poor today, it is perfectly conceivable that he will cheat his way into new splendour tomorrow . . .
>
> (to Gustav Heine, 21 January 1851)

The last sentence just quoted is amplified later in this same letter: 'I am sure', Heine tells brother Gustav, 'that this man will cheat his way back into affluence: for he holds nothing sacred, and he knows the baseness of men.' He never breaks with Friedland, therefore, as he tried to break with Lassalle; he nurses him along, sends him copies of his works along with subtly threatening messages. For this reason he was gratified to learn from Joseph Lehmann, who visited him in 1854, that Friedland was reported to be doing well again, and he reports to Gustav, on 20 July of that year, that Lehmann had encouraged him to put new pressure on Friedland.

> As soon as I can catch my breath again I'll take the fellow by the throat; I'll reproach him with having deceived my poor tender-hearted, sensitive brother [Heine's irony at the expense of the blustering and insensitive Gustav is patent here!], with having manœuvred me into sparing him, by means of lies and pretexts; now, I shall say, I have waited for two years, long enough in all conscience—now I must have my money. You'll see, I'll squeeze something out of him; and that is very necessary, for my financial needs are enormous . . .

The poet's strategy paid off; the Lassalles and the Friedlands, it would appear, banded together to reimburse the poet, and though Heine never made anything like the profits he had hoped for, he did get his capital back, with modest interest, in the end. He was proved quite right, too, in prophesying that Friedland would bounce socially upwards in the end, and was able to write to him on 21 November 1854:

I congratulate you on your elevation to a knighthood—it was a great pleasure to hear that the Emperor had graciously conferred upon you the order of St. Joseph. It will look well on you, especially against the black of formal evening wear in a suitably illuminated drawing-room. For me, however, you remain what you always were. Despite your elevation we will, I hope, still be able to consort familiarly . . . I have remained favourably disposed towards you, despite all the misfortunes your recklessness brought upon my head . . .

Reproaches follow, and veiled threats to induce Friedland not to go back on his promise to make good the poet's losses; but there is no reason to doubt Heine's sincerity when he assures his newly splendid Calmonius 'that my inner feelings were always favourable to you, though the *idée fixe* of getting my money back never left me, so that the devil found it easy to take an occasional hand in the game.' In August 1855 Friedland and his wife visited the dying poet, who greatly enjoyed seeing them again and wrote to brother Gustav with unwonted warmth:

My friend Ferdinand Friedland from Prague, who was here in Paris, will probably pay you a visit in Vienna next week. He can give you excellent news about my financial position. He has shown himself an honest man and is paying me the whole sum he had guaranteed, along with the accrued interest. This means a significant augmentation of my budget. Friedland is more honest than many of those who boast of their heroic probity.

(17 August 1855)

Calmonius, it would appear, had brought home the goods—as Heine always thought he would.

In retaining his place in Heine's affections Friedland had a powerful ally: not his father-in-law, Heymann Lassal, in whom Heine saw only a commercial highwayman clever enough to retain a reputation for probity, but Heymann's daughter Friederike, who was Friedland's wife. She seems to have had the kind of physical presence to which Heine always responded warmly: 'my *bosom*-friend' (*meine Busenfreundin*)

he calls her, punningly, in a letter to his brother Gustav dated
21 January 1851; but the attraction was more than just physic-
al. 'She is a noble, passionate woman, capable of the loftiest
enthusiasm', he writes to her father on 16 April 1850, and adds
that to see her again would be his greatest joy. On 30 April he
sends another letter to the same addressee: 'I beg you to convey
my most cordial greetings to your daughter; not one of my
sleepless nights passes in which I do not see her defiant little
face. How white her skin is and how good her heart!' Yet
another missive to the same correspondent written early in
May 1850, elaborates the theme:

Give my most heartfelt, fiery greetings to your daughter; she can
have no idea how often she is in my thoughts, and how I long to see
her and to talk to her again. We needed no more than half a glance to
understand one another.

'And now, my dear friend', Heine adds, forgetting all rancour
against Heymann Lassal as, in the end, he forgot it against
Friedland, 'farewell and do not mock my religious illumina-
tion; if one's understanding is as clear as yours, one can, I am
sure, do without religion.' He also ventures a direct appeal to
the object of his devotions, Friederike Friedland.

Write to me soon or, even better, come to Paris! I am not long for this
world, and your most lovely apparition would help to cheer my final
days.

(October 1850)

The letter congratulating Friedland on his dizzying social
climb, from which I have already quoted, contains one last
glimpse of Heymann Lassal, 'that old robber-chief who has so
disgracefully led me by the nose'; but it also sends 'the most
amiable and affectionate greetings to my friend [Friederike]
Friedland. Her grace and high spirits, her generous way of
thinking, and also the glorious whiteness of her shoulders, are
ever in my mind.' (21 November 1854.) Friederike was thus the
last Jewish woman with whom the ever-susceptible Heine
conducted a flirtation.

(iv)

If Calmonius was the later Heine's court Jew, Ludwig Wihl and Alexandre Weill shared for a time the position of court fool and court jester. In 1839 Heine had indignantly repudiated Wihl as 'a fool and a liar' whom he would never admit to his intimacy (to Campe, 30 September 1839); but in the 1850s Heine was not quite so choosy. 'That arch fool Wihl visits me occasionally', he writes to his mother and sister on 21 January 1850, 'and he never fails to amuse me in one way or another.' Wihl, as we know, had published a collection of mediocre verse under the Goethean title 'West-easterly Swallows' (*West-östliche Schwalben*); and his melancholy Jewish appearance led Heine to confer on him the absurdly convoluted title: 'the sorrowing West-Eastern Swallows-Rabbi' (to Laube, 25 January 1850). 'You have no idea', he writes to Campe on 28 September 1850, 'how much worse the Germans to be seen around Paris have become. If I receive Wihl with real pleasure nowadays it is because he towers above the others in respect of sheer human decency. I have many a crass insult to make up for.' Heine's way of making up for crass insults, it would seem, was to rib Wihl unmercifully about his bad verses and (largely unrequited) love-affairs. The inevitable final break came in 1852. After joking about his copy of *West-Easterly Swallows*, which he pretends to have lent out again and again in the hope of losing it only to find that here was one book everybody insisted on returning, the poet tells Alfred Meissner 'I no longer see the father of these swallows here, thank God. My house has been swept fairly clear of this whole west-easterly rabble.' (1 March 1852.) But he still has an appetite for absurd anecdotes about the man he now despises for his vanity, his unprincipled gossip, his low intelligence, and his bad verses—as when he gleefully reports that Wihl is said to have fallen in love with a lavatory attendant and speculates on possible titles for the collection of verse this love is bound to inspire. *Violen und Kaktus*, perhaps? (To Meissner, 4 May 1854.)

Wihl kept Heine amused for a time; Alexandre Weill amused

Mathilde. On 15 September 1848, in a letter to L.-P. Véron, Heine can still describe him as 'mon ami Weill'; but it was not long before he too became intolerable. A letter to Meissner—one of Heine's most trusted confidants in these later years—complains of Weill's intrigues (1 March 1852); and on 7 May 1853 the poet complains to his mother and sister:

M. Wihl was good enough to throw himself out; and—thank the Lord!—an even filthier, viler, and more dangerous blackguard, the littérateur Weill, will also never again cross my threshold. Paris is full of this kind of rabble: people who run about, argue, and write notices for newspapers . . .

The 'rabble' of literati included Hebbel's friend, editor, and biographer Felix Bamberg, whose most constant preoccupation led Heine to coin a new verb, italicized in the first of the following quotations:

I occasionally see Herr Bamberg, whom you will surely remember; he *hebbels* worse than ever, especially if there is a new moon . . .
(to Heinrich Laube, 25 January, 1850)

The great Bamberg—I call him that in order to distinguish him from the little town that bears the same name—has come *hebbeling* to me again for a full hour a few days ago . . .
(to Laube, 7 February 1850)

A terrible person in these parts is Herr Bamberg, whose literary worth you have come to know to your cost. He calls himself the friend of Hebbel, and it is said that his visiting-cards bear this inscription. He is a great expert on music, and constantly makes music himself—through his nose. . . .
(to Campe, 28 September 1850)

M. Bamberg, the famous Hebbelist, has made a little stench around here and now stays away.
(to Laube, 12 October 1850)

The creeping bedbug that wrote the book on the February Revolution and whose name I don't want to mention here because of the smell—this insect, it would seem, has spread some malicious gossip about you, my friend, and about Élise of the large eyes, because he was annoyed at me and my wife . . .
(to Meissner, 1 November 1850)

The increasing acerbity of Heine's comments is explained by a letter to Georg Weerth, dated 1 November 1851, in which the poet once again parodies the Bible and quotes Dante in an attempt to convey that most complex of exile feelings, mistrust and the desire to unmask, which appears with such distressing frequency in his letters from Paris.

All is quiet around here, except that recently the Prefect of the Parisian Police, a second Herod, planned a monstrous child-slaughter among our innocent countrymen, instilling great fear into these little ones. They all had to present themselves at the police station to document their existence—and this caused some difficulty, for some of them had neither existence nor the means to sustain one. The new Herod was looking for a political Saviour hidden amongst us—and the information on which he acted emanated, alas, from someone not without education, a littérateur even . . . All this is gruesome, revolting. It makes me sick to think that for years such people were allowed to associate with me. What a terrible thing is exile! Among its saddest features I must reckon the bad company into which it precipitates us—company we cannot avoid if we don't want such rogues to band together against us. How moving, how sad, how angry are Dante's laments about this state of affairs in the *Divine Comedy*!

The 'littérateur' denounced in this bitter passage is undoubtedly Felix Bamberg, and the lament to which his conduct gives rise is heard many times in Heine's later correspondence. 'Alas,' he writes to Campe on 21 Ocotber 1851, 'those who are well disposed towards me, have some affection for me, and are, at the same time, people of some intellectual and spiritual worth, live far away—while my immediate surroundings contain only vulgarians who intrigue against me with envious hostility when they see that I am not willing to be exploited. I have dreadful tales to tell . . .' On 4 February 1852 he asked Bamberg to come to see him; we don't know what transpired at that meeting, but from then on he could see in Bamberg only an *agent provocateur*.

There is no lack of German spies here, and I have myself contributed to blowing the cover of one of these: I refer to a miserable German littérateur named Felix Bamberg . . .

(to Gustav Heine, 11 February 1852)

Among the police spies who now stand revealed for what they are a certain Bamberg or Bamberger stands out. He arrogates to himself the title Doctor of Philosophy and has very questionable antecedents . . .

(to Gustav Kolb, 13 February 1852)

M. Bamberg has become a common police spy; earlier on he was content with being a thief. Unfortunately I caused his cover to be blown, and now the fellow runs about everywhere spreading slanders about me; his companion, that great poet Hartmann, aids and abets him in this, adding that I wanted to play down his importance—out of envy, presumably . . .

(to Alfred Meissner, 1 March 1852)

That last quotation introduces another of the later Heine's butts, Moritz Hartmann, a German-speaking writer from Prague who inspired some of his most malicious sallies. To Heinrich Laube he wrote on 12 October 1850:

I saw [Meissner's] great compatriot Moritz Hartmann a few days ago; he is a very handsome man, and all the women are in love with him—except the Muses.

Heine professed annoyance when Laube made this joke public, but this did not stop him from indulging in further sallies—including a punning reference to Hartmann's circumcision:

I do wish Herr Hartmann had already succeeded in marrying money, as Herwegh did, and would not have to flog himself at every concert and every soirée . . . There is one thing he has overlooked, however: rich Jewish girls only want to marry great Christian poets, and in this respect your compatriot's wings are irremediably clipped [*beschnitten*]. Eight years ago, when he first honoured me with a visit, I already noticed that his patriotism and refugee status only served him as a means of advertising his tiny talent. He complained very ingenuously about his mother, who had, at that time, successfully petitioned for his return to the fatherland when all he wanted was the honour of being an exile . . .

(to Meissner, 1 March 1852)

His experiences with Laube induced him, on this occasion, to ask his correspondent not to repeat his jokes where Hartmann might get to hear them: 'Remember that I am lying here in bed, with my feet bound, and that in such a situation every bedbug can become troublesome.'

The 'bedbug' image recurs with disturbing frequency in Heine's last letters—we find it, for instance, in his complaint to J. H. Detmold, on 3 October 1854, about 'cowardly creeping creatures, bugs from those ancient bedsteads which we know so well'. Bamberg was one of those so designated, as was Alexandre Weill after he had fallen from favour. Its most elaborate application was the poem *The Bedbug* (*Der Wanzerich*) in which it characterized the composer Joseph Dessauer. Dessauer's accusation that Heine had become his enemy only because he had refused him a loan is glossed in the correspondence too. In a letter to his brother Gustav, in which Heine for the first time uses the epithet 'capitalist' as a term of abuse, he writes:

In 1842 my income was surely three times that of the affluent Herr Dessauer; but I might just have found myself in temporary difficulty and I might have applied to a musical capitalist who liked—old huckstering habits die hard!—to do a little profitable money-lending on the side. He did this as the secret *bailleur de fonds* of a philanthropic lackey who served in a music shop where he had opportunities to spy out the financial embarrassments of the artistic world, and who discounted bills of exchange for a dozen per cent less than their face value. I might have—but I didn't. Neither directly nor indirectly did I ever try to encroach on Dessauer's capital wealth. As for his charge that I threatened in the open street to use the power of my pen against him: this is so little my way of doing things that anyone can here recognize the invention, and the manner of expression, of people who know only two things—money and revenge. All this is so filthy, so clumsily conceived, so sticky, so smelly, that it can only have originated in an old bedbug's imagination. By this token I recognize my customers of the Old Covenant [*meine Pappenheimer vom alten Bunde*]. The first thing they always say is that people attack them because they refused to lend money. Go on then—vilify our motives for talking about your contemptible activities, slander the stick that hits your back; the stripes you bear will be no less visible, and will sting no less, for all that . . .

(to Gustav Heine, 17 August 1855)

Here we have one emancipated Jew writing to another in the mid-1850s and reviving the old Shylock syndrome of money and vengefulness—to say nothing of the associations summed up by the bedbug image. In case the reference to 'customers of the Old Covenant' should not be found sufficiently explicit, Heine adds, in this letter to his brother:

This Dessauer is a liar and an infamous Jew. He has a whole clique at the back of him; I don't care, let them call me what they like. If only I were well! Now that my books have appeared in French, my fame resounds all over the world.

The Jewish clique intrigues against me continuously. They have tried to influence Carl Heine—about that I'll tell you more when we next meet. I never said to Saphir that my family paid me no more than 3,000 francs. Send me the paper in which he says that, so that I can see whether chance, or error, or perfidy is involved. He is a creature of the infamous Meyerbeer.

Ever since the Strauß affair Heine had the feeling that a Jewish clique was conspiring against him in the way he had once thought aristocrats and clergy to be out for his blood; and just as he had picked the unfortunate Platen to atone for the sins of the rest, so he now picks Meyerbeer as focus for his hatred. Brooding over his wrongs, cut off from all but occasional contact with the world, he developed what can only be described as an access of persecution mania with regard to the German-Jewish composer whose works he had once lauded to the skies.

(v)

There can be no doubt that Heine's last letters are grossly unjust to Meyerbeer. What he complained of were either trivialities (as when the composer's agent sent Mathilde opera tickets which were not in the best part of the house) or figments of his imagination (as when he thought the ballet *Satanella*, performed in Berlin where Meyerbeer was Master of the King's Music, plagiarized his own *Doktor Faust* libretto). He sent Gustav Kolb a satiric *Paean* already quoted as an antidote to the universal praise Meyerbeer is said to have bought for himself:

Meyerbeer flourishes most of all; his new opera was performed last night, after everything unflagging intrigue and enormous wealth can do was called into action to puff this miserable opus as a prodigy of art . . .

(to Kolb, 17 April 1849)

How Heine could know that *Le Prophète* was a 'miserable opus' when he was unable to go to hear it and could not read a score defies human knowledge. The venomous utterances continue over the years.

Bacher [J. A. Pacher, impresario and agent] is a principal agent of Meyerbeer's intrigues . . . you cannot imagine how dangerous this purloiner of fame, this Meyerbeer, can be: for he knows how to use everyone after his kind, and to spin webs around those who might threaten them . . .

(to Gustav Heine, 21 January 1851)

Six days later Heine addresses himself directly to this 'principal agent' or 'private bravo' of the composer he had come to detest:

He is an egoist who has (perhaps) put such feelings as he can muster into his opera; as a human being, however, he is anything but a maestro. Time and bitter experience will bring you to see the truth of what I am now saying! You will come to realize how absurdly hypocritical he was when he told you how much he liked giving of his wealth to other artists and writers—he never gave anything that was not wrested away from his grasp. . . . But my main grounds of complaint have nothing to do with money. He has hurt me in the moral core of my existence, and wounds like that are more difficult to heal . . .

(to J. A. Pacher, 27 January 1851)

What Heine means by these moral wounds is not difficult to fathom: he feels that Meyerbeer has used him, Heine, as an instrument, has made him take part in the manipulation of public opinion which had become so distressing a part of cultural life. To the composer Michael Schloß whom he commissioned, along with others, to press his claims to the copyright of *Satanalla*, Heine hints that he might just feel able to take further part in Meyerbeer's public relations exercises by suppressing attacks on him if the composer honoured his claims, but that he would do so most unwillingly.

I feel the strongest urge not to deprive the world of my Meyer-

beeriana, and not to die like a muzzled dog. I must confess to you that
I cannot conquer this bad feeling; and dying men have no fear of the
weapons the great *Generalintendant* of music can command.

(4 May 1854)

Was it, perhaps, his bad conscience which made Heine demon-
ize Meyerbeer, unjustifiably and absurdly, into the kind of
force behind the scenes he had in earlier days located in clerics
and aristocrats?

You see, dear Campe, I am not wrong if occasionally I smell a rat, and
a very 'high' one at that, where you smell nothing but attar of roses.
You must remember that Meyerbeer, even if he remains silent him-
self, has a crew of bandits in his pay, and has one of his creatures in
the office of every journal—this is true of France, at least, but it
probably applies to Germany too. This crew lets nothing pass that is
directed against him, and constantly works to further his
interests . . .

(3 October 1854)

Heine was intrigued by the contrast he saw between Meyer-
beer's power (which he undoubtedly overestimated) and his
weak physical state. He was fascinated by anecdotes about the
composer's nervous stomach troubles and physical timidity. A
letter to Alexandre Dumas *père*, written on 8 February 1855,
speculates humorously that Meyerbeer's fears and phobias—
especially about cats—derived from subliminal memories of
some previous existence in which he had walked the earth as a
mouse; and many visitors reported on the verbal squibs against
Meyerbeer which the poet loved to let off from his sick-bed.
One such visitor had the temerity to remind the poet of the two
styles [*Stile*] he had himself attributed to Meyerbeer in earlier
years—a German style and an Italian one. Heine pretended to
have misheard. *Stühle*? Yes, indeed, Meyerbeer did have two of
those, two stools, and he fell neatly between them.[13] In one of
the very last letters he was ever to write, he returned to the
composer in more serious vein, designating him 'the soul of all
the intrigues that are conducted against me' (11 September
1855). Here, if anywhere, Heine came perilously close to
pathological delusions.

One particularly telling association of ideas comes out in a
letter Heine wrote to Meyerbeer himself on 9 June 1854—a

letter in which he can still speak of 'le respect que j'ai sans cesse [!] consacré, non pas à votre cœur, mais à votre génie':

Dans votre capitale de la conversion, dans votre grand vaisseau baptismal qu'on nomme Berlin, on a, à la vérité, fort bien su débaptiser mon Faust et nommer au lieu de Méphistophéla, je crois, Satanella, la femme endiablée ou le diable feminisé.

Resentment at the theft of his literary property, of which Heine unjustly accused Meyerbeer, mingles oddly with resentments at the baptism he had undergone many years ago in the hope of obtaining a post in Hamburg, or in Munich, or in that Berlin whose musical life was now dominated, in Heine's eyes, by Meyerbeer. We might once again recall, at this point, that the poet's hatred of the composer he had once praised so highly only began to show itself openly after the latter had entered the service of King William of Prussia.

Other musicians, literati, and publishers of Jewish origin fare better than Meyerbeer in Heine's last letters. Felix Mendelssohn-Bartholdy, in particular, has a subtle revenge: for the poet who had once needled Sir Charles Hallé by saying that he could find no melody in one of Mendelssohn's most tuneful compositions[14] now found himself haunted, on his death-bed, by the snatch of Mendelssohn's music which accompanied the words 'come soon', *Komme du bald*. A typical note to 'La Mouche', Heine's last love, runs: 'My brother is talking me to death—I suffer a great deal—*Komme du bald!*' (10 November 1855). After having shown Felix Bamberg the door Heine welcomed visits from another Jewish acolyte of Hebbel's, Siegmund Engländer, and he even attested that Engländer was among the few who really understood his own, Heine's, later work. He writes to Campe on 6 April 1852:

A German who is resident here, Herr Engländer, recently read me his review of *Romanzero*, which is among the best productions of its kind known to me. It is especially successful in refuting the unworthy insinuations of immorality which have been levelled against this book. The review was, I believe, written for publication in the Berlin *Nationalzeitung*; but I am sure it never actually appeared there. If you agree I shall persuade Herr Engländer to transform his essay into a pamphlet which you will, I am sure, honour with a decent fee—it would help the Collected Edition of my works which we have planned in an important way, for it would crush clumsy hypocritical lies about my alleged immorality and counter Pharisaical lamentations about my 'cynicism' . . .

In another letter to Campe, dated 28 September 1850, Heine expressed genuine pleasure at visits from Fanny Lewald, whose profile he admired and whom he declared good-looking—for a lady writer. This pleasure was in no way diminished by his amusement at her liaison with her fellow writer Adolf Stahr, to which he applied, after the pair's departure, a line from Schiller's *Wallenstein*:

> Und Roß und Reiter sah ich niemals wieder.

> [And I never saw the horse and its rider again.]
> (to Alfred Meissner, 1 November 1850)

Fanny was the daughter of a cousin of August Lewald, who had been his friend for many years. Lewald's name was always a recommendation in Heine's eyes; but when he came to look back on his friend's literary achievement, he found that it had not kept the promise he had once detected there. 'Lewald is a skilful journalist,' he said to the protesting Fanny; 'he has a certain talent for imitating what he sees; but he lacks the faculty of invention, and he cannot imagine anything he has not seen.'[15] The poet welcomed, in these final years, the prospect of a visit from Moritz Saphir, the professional humorist who had gone up in his estimate when Lewald had gone down:

> It will be a great pleasure to me if Herr Saphir would honour me with a visit; a few cheering moments are the best that can be offered to me in my wretched state, and these I will gratefully accept. Herr Saphir is one of the wittiest men in Germany, and we have many common enemies; he is also said to be very good-natured, and that is another quality that speaks in his favour . . .
> (fragment of a letter to one 'Steinitz', not otherwise known to fame, July 1855)

When the article Saphir published after the visit had taken place embroiled Heine with Joseph Dessauer, he bore Saphir no grudge: 'I have more important things to be annoyed about,' he wrote to his brother Gustav on 28 September 1855. When the bookseller and publisher G. F. Franckh, whom Heine tended to dismiss as a conceited ass, allowed himself to be cheated by Julius Campe's nephew F. E. Vieweg, Heine commented, in a letter to Campe dated 28 September 1850, that this could only happen because Franckh 'harboured the Jewish superstition that it's only the Jews who steal'. Heine himself had put such 'superstitions' firmly behind him, as he explained in a memorable letter to his old friend Joseph Lehmann:

The French version of my works is being published by Michel Lévy frères, who have been recommended to me. I had the choice between them and another publisher, a man who had been a *bonnetier*, that is to say, a manufacturer of cotton nightcaps; and I preferred the former, perhaps just because they belonged to the tribe of Levy. This affiliation does not make M. Lévy any less honest and trustworthy— and even if I were to be proved wrong in my estimation and sustained a great loss, I must not allow my actions to be guided by ancient prejudices against the Jews. I think that if one allows them to earn some money they will, at least, be grateful, and will not take advantage of one as much as their Christian colleagues would. An uninterrupted tradition of two thousand years has left them with a great civilization of the heart. I think the Jews were able to participate in European culture so quickly because in respect of feeling they had nothing to learn; all they had to acquire was knowledge. But all this you know better than I do . . .

(5 October 1854)

In the Lévy brothers, to whom he entrusted 'la mise en scène de mon immortalité' (to Philarète Chasles, 21 July 1855); in Joseph Lehmann; in Leopold and Adelheid Zunz, who, like Lehmann, renewed their old association with him in his sad final years; in Ludwig Marcus; in Salomon Munk; and, of course, in Adolphe Crémieux—in all these Jewish friends and acquaintances the dying Heine found again that 'civilization of the heart' which he so sadly missed elsewhere. It was also there in another old associate, now long dead and still lamented—in the woman he remembered, in his later years, not as Friederike Varnhagen von Ense, but as Rahel, as a woman whose Jewishness had always (despite her baptism) been as plain and as strongly marked as Börne's. 'I cannot imagine', Heine is reported to have said to Adolf Stahr and Fanny Lewald about this *Jewish* Rahel, 'that her appearance can ever have been even pleasing. She was small, fat, and almost ugly. When I came to know her she was old and sick, and her face was distorted by illness and by passion. But she was very witty and intelligent; she had the most brilliant ideas in conversation; and she was very good to me.'[16] Rahel's 'goodness', we must recall, had included a very clear view of Heine's faults and dangers, and an often expressed determination never to leave them unreproved. That educative purpose too sprang from a civilization of the heart which had made her physically unprepossessing person at least as dear to Heine as her wit and intelligence, and which caused him to cherish her memory until the very end of his life.

(vi)

All the qualities he remembered with gratitude and affection in Rahel were thrown into relief by the contrast her salon offered to that of the banker August Leo and his wife, the 'gossip-shop,' which he had ridiculed in *Lutezia* and which he recalled with loathing in his last letters.

Here they thought up the most vulgar insults to be flung at myself and my wife and sent abroad—especially to Hamburg, where these people had allies and fellow gossips linked to them by family relationships . . .

(to J. H. Detmold, 30 October 1854).

The Foulds, we know, were no better in Heine's eyes; but the poet was particularly disappointed by the conduct of the Péreire brothers, who had once been fellow Saint-Simonians and who now rebuffed him when he asked them to let him share, in a modest way, the profits they were making from railway stock. He appealed to Emile Péreire in a letter which is of great interest because Heine here speaks of the Jews as a race to which he himself belonged. Why, Emile Péreire will ask, do you not apply to your relatives, who have greater cause to support you than I have?

Vous avez raison, il serait parfaitement juste que je partageasse la bonne fortune de personnes qui, quelle que soit leur affection ou leur désaffection pour moi, ne m'en feraient pas moins partager leur sort ignominieux dans des jours de malheur et d'opprobre, sort qui suit quelquefois de très près la plus grande prospérité à des moments d'un mauvais réveil populaire, comme l'histoire de notre race nous montre assez d'exemples . . .

(27 November 1852)

What Heine is here appealing to is a Jewish sense of solidarity, a solidarity not affected by baptism; for once popular hostility has been aroused against the Jews, the difference between baptized and non-baptized counts for little. As for appealing to the Foulds and others linked to him by family ties:

je vous répondrai que je suis mal avec les personnes en question; elles sont aussi aveuglées que l'étaient leur pères qui jadis auraient donné des actions au pair à Barrabas plutôt qu'à notre Seigneur, si celui-ci dans son humilité leur en avait demandé . . .

(27 November 1852)

Again, we see, the Jewish connection is stressed in this hilarious transposition of nineteenth-century share dealings into New Testament times—with the ancestors of the unbaptized Foulds in the part of the Pharisees, while Heine and the Péreires acknowledge Jesus as 'notre Seigneur'. The poet ends his appeal with a challenge to the 'néo-millionnaires d'aujourd' hui' to show themselves more generous and more enlightened than 'les richards de la vieille école qui s'en va'. The response these *néo-millionnaires* made to his appeal was insulting and demeaning; and Heine turned with bitterness from 'these parvenus of Saint-Simonism, these *va-nu-pieds* of yore who have now become neo-millionaires and are filled to bursting with arrogant pride . . .' (to Betty Rothschild, 20 July 1855). How much better were the millionaires of the older dispensation! When he directed appeals to the Rothschilds in Paris or in Vienna, he was not rebuffed and not disappointed. Here he found again that 'civilization of the heart' which he thought fostered and enshrined by Talmudic precept—especially in the idea of *zaar baalei khayim*.

The Jews of former times, who were full of human feelings, believed that one should not partake of any delicacy in the presence of a child without letting that child have a share—they feared the child might otherwise lose a drop of its blood, and they prescribed *zaar lekhayim*, a term that means even more than *rakhmones*.

Your noble heart, M. le baron, seems to have remained faithful to this magnanimous superstition; and whenever fortune smiled on your colossal business operations with particular favour, you allowed not only the closest friends of your house, but also that great child the poet, to have a bite at the cherry. At this moment, when you are again taking the leading part in a tremendous enterprise and are emerging victorious and more millionaire than ever from the revolutionary storms, I take the liberty of reminding you that I have not yet died, although my condition hardly deserves to be called 'life' . . .

(to James de Rothschild, 15 January 1852)

The last sentence just quoted enshrines a covert reference to an archetypal Jewish joke—

'Why did you tell me the father of my son's intended was no longer living, when now I hear he is in prison?' Marriage broker: '*That* you call living?'

just as Heine's position *vis-à-vis* Rothschild recalls, not only that relationship between poor Jewish scholar and rich Jewish businessman of which Heine had once reminded Uncle Salomon, but also the proud stance of the Jewish beggar, the *Shnorrer*, who has a claim on the rich man's charity, who in fact confers a *benefit* on the rich man by giving him an opportunity to do the 'good deeds' enjoined by Judaism. As he nears the end of his life, Heine comes to value more and more the Rothschilds' sense of humour and proportion (they took no offence at what he said about them in *Lutezia*, for instance), and the tact with which they responded to his financial appeals. He writes to the head of the Viennese branch, Anselm von Rothschild, on 30 December 1855:

My most heartfelt thanks for your gift—I call it a gift, for I do not indulge in that petty pride of beggars which refuses to give things their proper names. I must confess, however, that the mercantile fiction in which you have clothed your gift has doubled my delight and my sense of obligation. I see in this a sign of respect for the poet and of reverence for the world of the spirit . . . How little the neo-millionaires of today understand the art of giving! If they deign to throw a piece of money in our direction they leave us with a hole in the head; for they cannot distinguish those finer heads which are easily wounded from the thick skulls of the mob which can bear anything. Yes, the art of fine giving is becoming ever more rare in our time, while that of coarse taking, of crude grasping, thrives everywhere. Once again, therefore, Herr Baron, I thank you for your gift and for the form in which you gave it, as well as for the compassion with my sad physical state which is so affectionately and feelingly expressed in your letter.

Allow me to assure you that no-one admires more steadfastly than I a family in which the younger members follow so faithfully in the footsteps of the old and which in this respect as in so many others is visibly blessed by God. Here the virtues of the fathers may truly be said to have built mansions—and what splendid mansions they are! Providence, I am sure, has intended your family to play a glorious part . . .

The letters to Betty Rothschild are, as always, particularly admiring and affectionate; and when he has to comfort the Baroness at a time of family affliction, he reminds her again of their common Jewish heritage.

Nothing is more loathsome to me than the usual condolences in which anyone who comes along is allowed, at any moment, to tear the bandage from our wounds, and to aggravate our pain with meaningless phrases . . . How truly human, in contrast, is the old Jewish custom of sitting down with the bereaved for a while and then going away again without saying a word . . .

(to Betty Rothschild, December 1855)

Camille Selden reports that Heine was appalled at a Gumpelino-like letter from Anselm von Rothschild, in which business affairs were decorated with quotations from Schiller.[17] But he was convinced, nevertheless, that all the Rothschilds with whom he had come into contact understood perfectly what the Péreires had so signally failed to grasp—that he, Heine, was in an important respect their ally:

Heaven knows that I never exploited [my influence as a publicist] for my own personal benefit; but I did use it to the advantage of persons who are dear to me and whom I regard as my natural allies in a battle that has lasted almost two thousand years. What I am claiming is no more, at bottom, than a subvention from an allied power.

(to Anselm von Rothschild, 16 December 1855)

The reference to a two-thousand-year-long battle suggests that Heine may want, on this occasion, to be seen as a champion of Jewish rights in a non-Jewish world. A letter to Michel Chevalier, on the other hand, suggests that the solidarity he felt with the Péreire brothers was rather that of common social ideals, the ideals of the Saint-Simonians:

Je priai donc M. Péreire de me procurer les moyens pécuniaires qui me donneraient les loisirs d'une année que je pourrais consacrer à un ouvrage dans lequel il trouvera un jour un contentement personnel, parce que des intérêts qui sont aussi les siens y seront traités d'une manière brillante et victorieuse, à la grande confusion de nos ennemis communs.

Oui, c'est précisément parce que nous avons des ennemis communs que je combats pendant que Péreire ne pense qu'à ses chemins de fer, que je croyais avoir le droit de lui demander un coup d'épaule, un service qu'il pouvait me rendre sans bourse délier. D'ailleurs, en détrônant Rothschild il m'a privé de ces profits que je tirais de lui à chacun de ses grandes entreprises où il m'intéressait toujours pour quelque chose . . .

(24 February 1855)

After his long, uneasy relationship with Uncle Salomon it is the record of his dealings with the Péreire brothers that seems best calculated to bring home to us the force of a line in his poem *Retrospect (Rückschau)*:

> Ich glaube sogar, ich mußte betteln.

> [I even think that I had to beg.]

What distinguished the Rothschilds from the Péreires was not least their consciousness of what rich Jews owed to those worse off than themselves, as well as a 'civilization of the heart' that enabled them to dispense largesse without humiliating the recipient.

(vii)

Besides Jewish financiers, needed to palliate the eternal consumption of his purse, Heine had a good deal of recourse in his final years to Jewish doctors: Drs Worms, Gruby, and Wertheim figure frequently in his correspondence. The last-named, in whom Heine had particular confidence, was physically assaulted by Mathilde on one unhappy occasion, and not unnaturally refused further attendance on a sick man guarded by such a termagant. Heine himself, for all the eagerness he showed to lure Wertheim back to his bedside, could not forbear playing a more delicate game with him than the forthright Mathilde, as becomes clear from a letter he wrote to the good doctor when the latter had been awarded a Spanish decoration.

I have learnt with great pleasure that you have become a Knight of the Order of Isabella. This order, which Queen Isabella founded to celebrate the expulsion of the Jews from Spain, is a very beautiful decoration, and I am very curious to see you wear this new adornment. . . . I have given up taking medicine; neither physician nor apothecary can help me now. The hand of God is heavy upon me—His sacred will be done.

(15 March 1850)

As the years went by, Heine was less ready to spurn the help of medicine, and became more insistent in his requests that Dr Wertheim should call; but Wertheim, after he had felt the sting of Mathilde's hand as well as that of the poet's tongue, came only rarely and unwillingly. Importuning him for another visit, Heine could not repress yet another allusion to that Order of Isabella which seemed to sit so strangely on a Jewish coat:

It is an eternity now that I haven't seen you. If this goes on, I won't even know what you look like any more. Even now I can't recall the colour of the riband you wear—the riband of the Order of Isabella!

(8 October 1852)

The irony of seeing Wertheim with this particular decoration sorts well with the irony the poet had once detected in Ignaz Gurowski's successful suit of a Spanish princess after he had been refused—so, at least, the Parisian rumour had it—the hand of the Jewish actress Rachel Félix.

(viii)

As many of the quotations in this chapter will have shown, Heine was increasingly conscious of an intellectual and spiritual Jewish heritage which no baptism could annihilate—but this in no way diminished his sense of also being a German. 'You see', he wrote to Gustav Kolb on 21 April 1851, 'I am a poor lamed German who cannot forget the day that has passed and who greets with dread the day that is coming.' To his French friends he liked to present himself as 'ce pauvre rossignol allemand qui a fait son nid dans la perruque de M. de Voltaire' (to E. Drouyn de Lhuys, July 1855). He examines with interest German stereotypes of the Jew: on 27 October 1853 we find him asking Campe for a copy of Eisenmenger's anti-Semitic compilation *Judaism Discovered* [*Entdecktes Judentum*] and tries them out on himself as well as on his acquaintances. The Shylock stereotype, as so often, is applied to relatives who have, in Heine's eyes, outdone Shakespeare's Jew in malice and success; Carl Heine's Parisian relatives, he reports to Gustav Heine on 15 November 1850, 'persecute me with the most sinister Shylockian rage and have cut many a pound of flesh from my breast.' The same correspondent is told that their brother Max has been trying to model himself on a more favourable literary image of the Jew:

You are wrong if you take him for a Tartuffe. His trouble is feebleness of soul, not hypocrisy; he has persuaded himself that he is Nathan the Wise.

(to Gustav Heine, 26 October 1852)

He adverts frequently on the 'cleverness' with which Jews are generally credited ('has there ever been a time in the whole of history', he asks Alfred Meissner, rhetorically, on 13 October 1852, 'in which the Jews were not *raffiniert*?'); but he finds that he himself does not fit that particular stereotype at all well:

I noticed long ago that I am, at bottom, rather stupid, and that I am therefore the dupe of a reputation for cleverness which my enemies, perhaps, have fostered . . .

(to Maximilian Heine, 23 March 1850)

The stereotype which occurs to him most often in a Jewish context is that of the dealer in old clothes. When he tells Campe that his newly-found belief in God has led him to destroy some of his writings, he claims to have heard Mephistopheles whisper to him:

God will pay you for these much better than Campe; and now you won't have to go through the tormenting process of getting them into print, nor will you have to haggle about them with Campe as though they were an old pair of trousers . . .

(1 June 1850)

The same stereotype recurs in a letter to brother Max, deputing him (unwisely, as it turned out) to negotiate with Campe on the poet's behalf: 'Bargain about these second-hand trousers as one usually does with such thieving rascals [*Ganoven*] . . .' (25 August 1852). The implication that in this process of haggling it is the non-Jew Campe rather than his partner in the bargain who fits the German stereotype of the overreaching Jew is spelt out in a particularly instructive passage of Heine's letter to Campe, dated 7 March 1854. Heine is offering his publisher important new material without extra charge while keeping steady the price he had originally asked for the unaugmented publication:

My experience here is that of Adolf, a friend I had in my university days. Adolf needed four thalers and wanted to sell Herr Abraham two waistcoats for that sum. Herr Abraham, however, persuaded him to hand over, in exchange for these four thalers, two coats, one of which was perfectly new. Adolf then boasted to me that in matters of money he never yielded a single groschen once he had fixed the price—and that he always got what he asked.

In this anecdote it is clear that Campe represents the Jew Abraham, and Heine the non-Jew Adolf. The stereotype has been neatly inverted.

(ix)

Alfred Meissner has noted how many of the visitors who came to see Heine in the last years of his life—visitors lumped together by Mathilde under the general designation *alle-mands*—were in fact Jewish or of Jewish descent.[18] It is no wonder, therefore, that in his last recorded conversations the poet is so often heard referring to his relations with, and attitudes towards, Jews, Judaism, and Jewishness. To Benno Goldschmidt he seems to have said, in October 1848, that he regretted his formal change of religion,[19] and to Ludwig Kalisch that he made no secret of his Jewishness 'to which I have not returned because I have never left it.'[20] He talked with pride of Jewish history[21]—particularly the symbiosis of Spanish and Jewish culture during the Middle Ages—and with loathing of Jeanette Wohl and her clique, who are charged, once again, with soiling his fame. Jeanette is now depicted as an ugly old witch who stepped into the path of his triumphal procession, causing him to start and let his laurel wreath slip from his head into the filthy street. 'Since then', the poet is said to have added, 'a revolting smell adheres to my laurels—a smell of which I cannot rid them now . . .'[22] Here as elsewhere, however, his sense of humour wins through. The Frankfurt clique, he tells his brother Gustav, showed greater interest in him than his professed friends ever did—for in disseminating slanders against him by means of paid insertions in French and German newspapers they actually spent money on him![23] Meissner reports conversations in which Heine is said to have spoken of Jewish cleverness and occasional sharp practice— but only in the context of a history of unprecedented martyrdom that had made Jews what they were. I do not write for one particular tribe or ethnic group, he is reported to have added, but for the whole of mankind.

It would be tasteless and petty to accuse me of ever having been ashamed of being a Jew; but it would be just as ridiculous if I maintained that I *am* a Jew.[24]

Fanny Lewald and Adolf Stahr report that Heine spoke to them of the great contrasts to be found among Jews:

Judas beside Christ; and beside [J. J.] Jacoby, whom you call selflessness personified, Ferdinand Lassalle, eminently gifted but selfishness incarnate.[35]

In other conversations Heine is made to deny, however, that Judas represents a Jewish type—Jews love haggling, it is true, but they are not greedy for money, and they are not given to betraying their friends (to A. Mels, October 1850).[26]

The character contrasts Heine is said to have painted for Lewald and Stahr have a counterpart in physical types too: 'Among the Polish Jews one finds a scale that leads from the most revolting ugliness to perfect plastic beauty.'[27] All the types of the Bible, Heine is reported to have said, can be picked out at German trade fairs frequented by Jews.[28] But one should never judge solely by appearances, Heine told his brother Gustav; the insanitary exterior which Jewish pedlars, *Schacherjuden*, present to the eyes of fastidious Germans 'often conceals a noble and generous disposition'. Jews, he is said to have added, drawing once again on his readings in medieval Jewish history, 'frequently hide this shining side of their character on purpose—just as, in an era of oppression, Jews hid their wealth behind a semblance of poverty in order to keep it safe from greedy eyes.'[29]

Visitors report that Heine's wit remained undimmed to the very end and that many of his quips concerned, in some way or other, the blending of German, French, and Jewish elements in his own cultural and psychological make-up. Mathilde, his French wife who spoke no German and seems to have had only the vaguest notion of Judaism, figured largely in such jokes. When Weill intoned synagogue melodies and Mathilde asked what these were, Heine is said to have answered: 'Our German folksongs.'[30] Saphir tells us that Heine taught Mathilde two Yiddish words with Hebrew roots, *nebbish* and *yofe*, and persuaded her that now she knew some German.[31] Saphir noted perceptively the reason why Heine had chosen these two words above all others: the first expressed his own sorry state, the second his sense of Mathilde's beauty. *Bons mots* about Jewish acquaintances figured largely in his conversation; many of these have already been cited, but two more may be added for good measure. Here is how he conveyed his dislike of the paintings of Heinrich Lehmann:

Heine was inclined to pardon Judaism's failure to cultivate the fine arts. The Jews, he said, had been idolators, and it was therefore necessary to prevent them from making images—otherwise there might have been even more backsliding into their bad old ways. Besides, Moses was a prophet: this means that he foresaw Lehmann would become a painter, and he did what he could to prevent that;[32]

and here is his final, less than generous, view of the most celebrated work his old adversary Börne had left to posterity:

I don't enjoy reading *Letters from Paris*; gall is not a pleasant drink.[33]

Heine's authentic voice can be recognized in many of these sayings, though they cannot, of course, be ascribed to him with absolute certainty. One must always remember his complaint about Adolf Stahr: 'I cannot understand how a man like Stahr can write articles about me in which I am made to say the exact opposite of what in fact I did say!'[34]

It used to be maintained by some of Heine's contemporaries that the jokes in his *Pictures of Travel* were appreciated most keenly in Jewish circles because they resembled the kind of jokes that Jews liked to tell about themselves and others. Börne too, it will be remembered, found something peculiarly Jewish about Heine's wit. It is highly interesting, therefore, to find Heine drawing, in conversation, on many time-honoured Jewish jokes and giving them an application of his own. We have met several specimens already; here is another, rather disreputable one, recorded by Gustav Heine after a visit to his brother's sick-bed in August 1851.

In the course of our conversation I took up a French journal and after glancing through its contents I asked Heinrich what he thought of public figures in France. 'Ah', he replied, 'here I can only say exactly what the old French sergeant-major said when army contractor Levy delivered a supply of oxen. This happened in the market-place of a little town where the army supply officer was stationed, before whom the oxen had to be paraded so that they could be counted. Having undertaken to deliver three hundred oxen Mr Levy found that he had only one hundred at his disposal. He therefore had the oxen filed past the supply officer one by one and then driven very quickly out of one gate, around the town, and back in at another gate—a stratagem which enabled him to get a receipt for three hundred oxen from the supply officer. An old sergeant-major, however, who was standing by, shook his head in astonishment, and said that it seemed to him as if the oxen were always the same ones.' 'Yes, my dear brother', Heinrich concluded, 'that's how it seems to me too: I always see the same horned beasts!'

Jews of the era of emancipation frequently took a self-torturing or prophylactic pleasure in applying to themselves the stereotypes evolved by their enemies—we have found evidence elsewhere that Heine was not exempt from this either before his baptism or afterwards. But, characteristically, the Jewish joke is only Heine's springboard to another joke—at the expense not of Jews, but of those who directed the fortunes of France in the early years of Napoleon III.

The poet's true voice also comes through, occasionally, in accounts of conversations in which wit and self-persiflage are not dominant. Among these I would reckon reports by Joseph Lehmann and Adelheid Zunz which speak of the spontaneous joy with which Heine received them, the delight he took in recalling the days in which they had worked for a common cause in the Berlin Society for the Culture and Science of the Jews, and his continuing interest in Jewish literature, culture, and history.

He spoke with [Leopold] Zunz about Kalir and other Jewish poets, showing love and interest for this subject; he talked about the Cabbala too and wanted to know who had written it; he spoke Judaeo-German and some Hebrew in between . . . He did not want to let us go, we were there for an hour and had to promise to come again frequently, a promise I shall keep . . .

(Adelheid Zunz to Julie Ehrenberg, 31 July 1855)[36]

'You are the only ones who have remained to me from a happy time in the past',[37] he is reported to have said to the Zunzes. It should not be thought, however, that such reunions were tearfully sentimental:

By and by he became gay, witty, spoke of the times in which we lived in close proximity . . . We could not stop laughing, and wondered how such a sick body could harbour such wit.

(Adelheid Zunz)[38]

In quick, lively fashion he passed in review the living and dead friends we had in common. Some he painted with the colours of a Titian or a Breughel, others . . . received most poetic last greetings.

(Joseph Lehmann)[39]

To Adolf Stahr and Fanny Lewald he talked of his family, dwelling in particular on his love for his father;[40] and Elise Krinitz, the 'Mouche' of his last days, he told of dreams in which his father seemed to come alive:

'On le coiffait; je l'appercevais comme à travers un nuage de poudre. Cependant, moi, tout joyeux de le revoir, je voulus me précipiter vers lui. Mais, chose bizarre, à mesure que je me rapprochais, les objets se brouillaient et prenaient une autre forme. Ainsi, quand je voulus embrasser les mains de mon père, je reculai, saisi d'un froid mortel: les doigts étaient des branchages desséchés, mon père, lui-même, un arbre dépouillé, et que l'hiver avait recouvert de givre . . .'[41]

Glimpses of the Jewish ambience of his childhood may occasionally be obtained from the conversations of his last years— as when he told Ludwig Kalisch of the Hebrew inspiration, mediated by the Passover Haggadah, that lay behind the early ballad *Belshazzar*.[42] And with his characterizations of Jews past and present which range from the grave to the gay, from the laudatory to the libellous, go characterizations of the enemies of the Jews and the martyrdom they caused. Meissner reports that Heine once said to him:

If Israel occasionally revenges itself on its tormentors with some minor dishonesty, it is only exacting a millionth part of what is really due to it by way of compensation and penance . . . If martyrdom ennobles, and patience, and faithfulness, and endurance of misfortune—then this people is more noble than many others. When we read the history of the Middle Ages, those classic times of alliance between clerics and knights, we cannot find a single year which did not hold torture, burning at the stake, beheading, and pillage, and massacre, for the Jews. And among the followers of Christ, who have been shaped by their religion, the Jews have suffered more than among the wildest and most savage peoples . . . What a tribute that is to the religion of love![43]

(x)

The authority which cannot be claimed for the sayings recorded by others does inhere in some of the jottings in the poet's own handwriting which he intended for future use and which were then found among his papers. A few of these have already been considered in earlier chapters; but we ought not to take leave of Heine without considering a few more.

'Rich Jews', one entry begins, only to continue with a parable of analogy from pig-keeping: 'The young swineherd, when he becomes rich, wants to guard his swine on horseback'.[44] Then comes the analogy with the people who have such an abhorrence of the animal mentioned, and who were therefore so often associated with it in the German mind: 'They have got on to their horse but they continue to engage in the same dirty business as before.' 'Swine-keeping', here, clearly stands for commerce and trade—those occupations for which the poet had himself been destined at one time, which he had cast off, and from which he had tried to wean other Jews in his Berlin days.

A characteristic sally acknowledges that there may be some danger in speaking as often and as publicly of Jewish affairs as we have seen Heine doing at various periods of his life.

One should never speak of Jewish circumstances and relationships [*von jüdischen Verhältnissen*]. The Spaniard who, in his dreams, talks every night with the Mother of God never touches on her relation to God the Father—out of delicacy: for even an immaculate conception *is* a conception . . .[45]

In the eyes of the world Jewish origins will often appear a blemish. Other jottings, however, show clearly why Heine chose to ignore his own warning. Jews, he noted in an aphorism we have met before, were 'the only people who retained their freedom of belief when Europe became Christian'; the laws of Moses respect human dignity and freedom, allowing women a much higher place than the other Oriental religions;[46] and the animating principle of Judaism is described in a way which leaves little doubt of its respectability in Heine's eyes. That principle, he jotted down, is *hope*: 'The Jews say to themselves: "We are in captivity, Jehovah is angry with us; but he will send us a redeemer.'[47] A later philosopher of Jewish extraction, Ernst Bloch, was to make that principle the lodestar of his philosophy.

Some of these jottings are exercises in paradox—as when Heine tries to discover affinities between revolutionary France and the Russia of Tsar Nicholas I. 'The scissors that cut off the beards of Russian Jews are the same as those which cut off Louis Capet's hair in the Conciergerie. They are the shears of revolution . . .'[48] The Tsar's endeavour to deprive Jews of their traditional beards and kaftans is experimentally seen as his attempt to 'give life to mummies'—to pull Russian Jewry into modernity by force. His means are terrible—but may not his will be noble?[49] In another, related fragment Heine descants on

Russian cruelty towards its Jews while himself making cruel fun of their beards, side-locks, and modes of dress in his least endearing manner.[50]

The poet's feeling of exile finds memorable expression in some of his jottings. 'My spirit', we read in one of them, 'feels exiled in France, banished into a strange language.'[51] And of course, inevitably the question of baptism crops up in these notes. The most famous of them all calls baptism 'the ticket of admission to European culture',[52] while another seeks to discover a historical chain of cause and effect which made baptism inevitable for Jews who wanted to play a full part in the civic and cultural life of Germany after the fall of Napoleon. 'That I became a Christian', he jots down, 'is the fault of the Saxons who suddenly changed sides at the Battle of Leipzig; or that of Napoleon, who did not, after all, *have* to go to Russia; or that of the geography teacher at Brienne who omitted to tell Napoleon that the winters are very cold in Moscow.[53] If the Napoleonic laws had still obtained in German-speaking countries after 1815, the necessity for Heine's baptism would never have arisen.

Yet in some other notes Heine does see a sort of logic in his baptism which goes beyond mere necessity. He tries to depict his step from Judaism to Christianity as a step from aristocratic to democratic principles.

Judaism: One God created the world and reigns over it, all men are His children, the Jews are His favourites, their land is His chosen dominion. The Jews are the nobility and Palestine is their entailed inheritance [*Majorat*]. God's exarchate—aristocracy.

Christianity: Democracy: one God Who has created everything and reigns over all, but who loves all men equally and protects all realms impartially. No longer a national god. Universalism . . .[54]

Another note speculates that the Germans only embraced Christianity in the first place because of their elective affinity, *Wahlverwandtschaft*, with the Jewish principle of morality, with the Judaism out of which Christianity had grown. 'Jews were the Germans of the Orient—and now Protestants in Germanic lands (Scotland, America, Germany, Holland) are nothing but Jews from the Orient of antiquity.' A complementary jotting calls ancient Judaea a 'Protestant Egypt'.[55]

Some of these jottings Heine worked into his published writings: his notion of an elective affinity between Jews and Germans, his idea that the Jews might be seen as a spectre set to guard a treasure (the Bible), or his reflections about the porcelain Jews were once forced to buy as part of the price of residence in Prussia, were incorporated into his work. Others however, like the following reflection on Jewish history, were never utilized in this way.

Jewish history is beautiful—but recent Jews detract from those of ancient times who—but for them—would be valued above the Greeks and Romans. I think that if Jews had ceased to exist and then someone demonstrated that somewhere a member of this people had somehow survived, men would travel for hundreds of hours just to see that survivor and shake him by the hand. But now they avoid us.[56]

Und jetzt weicht man uns aus. The *uns* of that sentence shows Heine identifying himself, in this private jotting, with the Jewish people.

Jewish self-definition, many of these notes serve to show, can never be independent of the image of Jews projected by their non-Jewish neighbours. 'T does not love the Jews', Heine writes, for instance. 'When I asked him why, he said that they are base without being graceful, and that they therefore inspired loathing of baseness, and that anyway, they did him more harm than good.'[57] This deliberate farrago exposes the 'logic' of vulgar anti-Semitism without overtly defending Jews. Other notes deal with the historical roots of anti-Jewish feelings, and discover that modern judaeophobia really begins 'with the Romantic School (delight in the Middle Ages, Catholicism, nobility; heightened by Teutomania; [Professor Friedrich] Rühs . . .).'[58] The notes also suggest, however, that some Jews may be more 'Jewish', or may come nearer the Jewish stereotype, than others: 'He looks like ten Jews, not like just one; he alone could constitute a *minyan*.'[59] That last expression refers to the requirement that ten adult males are required to make up a group which can engage in communal worship.

As the note just quoted may serve to show, Heine jotted down many *aperçus* that could be used as elements in his portraits of individuals—leaving him a fairly free choice of the particular individual to whom he might apply them. Some of these would be fictional, like the affecting image of the Jewish mother crazed by grief who cradles her dead child's memorial light.[60] In some cases, however, application would be predetermined. The jotting, 'Rachel—father rabbit, mother fish',[61] for instance, envisages Rachel Félix as an exemplum that would show how little we knew of a human being's nature and accomplishements if we looked only at his or her *ancestry*. That the ancestors themselves might be subject to the delusions this anecdote seeks to dispel is shown by another note about Rachel Félix.

Père Rachel preens himself with the success of his daughter. There he stands, in the stalls of the Théâtre Français—an old Jew—and thinks that *he* is Iphigenia or Andromache, that it is *his* declamation that has moved all hearts; and when the audience applauds, he blushes and bows.[62]

To ensure, however, that this Daumieresque caricature should not be taken to castigate only some specifically *Jewish* mode of self-glorification, Heine's note compares Rachel père in this respect with poets like Lenau and Freiligrath, who owe their success (in his view) more to the spirit of the age than to their individual genius.

Incredible as this may seem, these notes even contain shafts directed against Meyerbeer which Heine had not loosed against that unfortunate composer's head in his public or semi-public attacks on him. One jotting accuses him of introducing eclecticism into French musical tradition, while another proclaims:

Meyerbeer has become wholly a Jew. If he wants to go back to Berlin, to take up again his earlier relationships and appointments, he will first have to have himself baptized.[63]

Perhaps Heine did not use this particular sally because he remembered his own complaint about some of his Jewish enemies: when they wanted to insult him most, they proclaimed him one of themselves.

Rothschild, of course, also figures prominently in some of these sketches and jottings. One of them purports to enter his nightmares—the nightmare of the very rich: 'Rothschild dreams that he has given 100 000 francs to the poor, and that makes him ill;[64] while another shows him using a traditional riposte as he asserts his capitalist ethos against a communist who seeks to assail it.

The communist who wants Rothschild to share out his fortune of 300 million francs. Rothschild sends him his share, which comes to exactly 9 sous: "Now leave me alone!"[65]

Elsewhere the poet reflects more seriously on the enmities the House of Rothschild inevitably encountered:

The main army of Rothschild's enemies is made up of have-nots; they all think "what we don't have, Rothschild has". They are joined by the main force of those who have lost their fortune; instead of ascribing their loss to their own stupidity, they blame the wiles of those who managed to hold on to what they had. As soon as a man runs out of money, he becomes Rothschild's enemy.[66]

He speculates, too, on the inhabitants of Rothschild's Valhalla ('a pantheon of all the princes that have borrowed from him') and places the great financier not on a par with, but *above* the ruling princes of Europe.[67] At the other end of the scale we meet again our old friend *Nasenstern*, of whom it is wickedly suggested, in these notes, that he might have 'several' Jewish fathers (*daß er von mehreren Juden abstamme*).[68] This not very distinguished joke, which Heine suppressed with good reason, not only serves to call into question the legitimacy of its victim's birth, but also suggests, once again, that he has more of the traits generally thought of as 'Jewish' than most of his co-religionists.

The unpublished jottings preserved among Heine's papers include sketches of the salon of August Leo which make fun of the alleged social maladroitness and parsimony of the Leo family;[69] and a quip about Friedland/Calmonius which calls his craving for honours and decorations 'the tapeworm of his soul'.[70] Last of all we find a jotting particularly relevant to the Jewish Comedy examined in this book. 'When the Jews are good', the jotting reads, 'they are better than the Christians; when they are bad, they are worse.'[71] We know enough, by now, of Heine's historical sense, and have heard enough of his comments on Jews and Judaism, to realize that this *aperçu* cannot be meant as an absolute trans-temporal generalization;

but it does illuminate brightly what Heine himself felt about a particular moment of development. He saw 'Jewish' qualities produced by many centuries of history heightened and exaggerated by the social and political pressures of his own age—an age of struggle for full emancipation; an age in which Jews tried to integrate themselves in many different ways into a society that had for so long refused to accept them as equal members; an age of commercial, industrial and intellectual endeavour which offered great opportunities to talents the Jewish people had developed in post-exilic times. All this produced what Hans Mayer once called 'die berühmte und berüchtigte Intensität der Juden': a special kind of intensity which could push towards extremes in the intellectual and the aesthetic and occasionally in the moral sphere. The qualities that came to the fore in this age of transition Heine heightened still further, with a caricaturist's delight, to produce portraits of grotesque saints like little Samson or Ludwig Marcus, grotesque sinners like Gumpelino or Dessauer, and sharp-profiled mixed characters like Hirsch-Hyazinth or James de Rothschild.

CONCLUSION

I hope the material collected and examined in this book will have borne out the claim, made in the Prologue, that Heine's writings offer us a unique personal view of the Jewish population of early nineteenth-century Germany, supplemented by brief but telling glances, from the same point of view, at the Jews of Poland, England, and France. Though we found one Jewish landowner in Heine's early correspondence, and watched the Rothschilds negotiating for land purchase in Prussia, the social picture which emerges so vividly from his writings bears out what histories of economic life have more soberly documented: that while the Jews lacked equivalents of the nobility, gentry, and serf-peasantry in the early modern period, we do find among them equivalents of the urban patricians, the small producers (craftsmen) and middlemen (merchants), and the wage-earners and paupers of society at large. Heine's works and letters depict social and religious types that range from pious rabbis to atheistic revolutionaries, from fighters for the honour of Jehovah to devotees of Christ or of Buddha, from the cultural/religious traditionalists of the Synagogue to the reformers of the 'Temple', from pedlars to parliamentarians, from beggars to bankers, from commission agents to musical virtuosos and composers, from journalistic scribblers to poets and wits. We have found his pages crowded with doctors and lawyers too, with actors, sugar brokers, army contractors, industrial entrepreneurs, textile importers and dealers, cattle-merchants, lens grinders and spectacle sellers, wine-merchants, market Jews, pawnbrokers and money-lenders, lottery agents, second-hand furniture dealers and old clothes men. These figures are viewed against the background of contemporary Gentile society, and also, constantly, against that of Jewish figures from the past, ranging from the patriarchs of the Bible to Spinoza and Moses Mendelssohn. The pen which presents all this to us is that of a gifted caricaturist who fastens—in ways amply demonstrated above—on risible

features and exaggerates them, and who shows himself fertile
in the invention of symbolic situations that foreground comic
or reprehensible traits. He makes effective use of such tradi-
tional methods of comedy as *inversion*—the unexpected rever-
sal of roles—and *levelling*—the revelation of common human-
ity beneath the trappings of king and beggar, or Jew and
Gentile, alike. But caricature and comic business is not every-
thing in Heine; we have noted many deeply-felt, deeply se-
rious observations which enter as an essential ingredient into
his Jewish portraits. Serious points may be made comically;
comedy rests—as Heine explicitly tells us it always should—
on a foundation of seriousness.

Heine's writings exemplify the whole range of literary por-
traiture, from the cartoons and stereotypes of *The Hartz Jour-
ney* to the psychological realism of his 'iconic' presentation of
Börne. They seek to convey essential qualities of individuals at
various periods of history, of social types, and of groups of
varying size and time-span, from the Society for the Culture
and Science of the Jews to the people of Israel seen against the
surrounding non-Jewish world in biblical times. These convey
the full gamut of responses to the Jewish situation: defiant
encapsulation in traditional Judaism, militant opposition to
anti-Jewish attitudes, attempts at a synthesis of traditional
Jewish culture and the cultures of Gentile groups and societies,
servile aping of Gentile manners, neurotic over-reactions of
various kinds, living in 'masks' and camouflage, interiorization
of the enemy's charges, readiness to be of service, flattery,
clowning, making up and telling 'Jewish jokes' . . . These por-
traits and self-portraits bear out what Heine's fellow poet
Adelbert von Chamisso wrote about him to Hans Christian
Andersen on 21 June 1836: 'What [Heine] creates has life;
whatever is touched by him, be it a cat or a man, steps out
towards us from the paper and stands there, a target for laugh-
ter or contemplation.'

The 'cicerone' or 'gallery guide' persona which we have so
often seen Heine adopt reminds us of his inveterate habit of not
just *showing*, but drawing attention to the *act* of showing; of
portraying or caricaturing, not only the sitter, but also the
caricaturist or cartoonist. Our close scrutiny of just one small
corner of his crowded canvas will have served to illustrate this

along with other of his habits of thought and style: that of externalizing elements of his personality and projecting them on to others; that of converting what he experienced, heard, and saw, into metaphor, synecdoche, symbolic representation, animal fable, and imagined epiphany; that of accommodating refractory individualities and complex antinomies in various dualistic schemes of which the Nazarene/Hellene or Jew/Greek dichotomy proved especially important in our special context. Jeffrey Sammons, who has lucidly described and illustrated many of these habits in his biography of Heine, has also pointed to a danger the present book has sought at once to highlight and to avoid: 'We must not do Heine an injustice by reducing him to a comedian . . . [he was] a fierce and sometimes savage personality.'[1] The 'comedy' of our title therefore refers not only to Heine's key position in the history of the Jewish joke, but also to the Balzacian sweep of his social overview and the Dantesque vigour of his condemnations.

Heine never lived in a ghetto. He had spent his early years in a Jewish family atmosphere, where he came into contact with Jewish ceremonial and had the bare rudiments of a Jewish education. The main thrust of his education, however, was secular German. At school, where instruction was imparted mainly by believing Christians who did not ram their faith down their pupils' throats, he was occasionally reminded of his Jewishness by the rough jokes of other boys—but he came to feel that Jewishness made up only one small part of his complex identity. He strove to rid himself of this in various ways: by ostentatiously showing himself unfit for the kind of mercantile or banking career in which so many Jews (not least in his own family) had been signally successful; by adopting a flamboyantly German personality in his early poems—a personality expressed by the anagram SY FREUDHOLD RIESENHARF which he concocted for the anti-Jewish paper that published some of these poems; by steeping himself in German lore of all kinds; by seeking predominantly non-Jewish company at the universities of Bonn and Göttingen and subscribing to the duelling ethos of student fraternities. Eventually he took instruction from a Lutheran pastor and allowed himself to be baptized into the Protestant religion. For many years afterwards we find him adopting a Hegelian perspective and rejecting the Jewish religion as superseded, a fossilized relic of ancient Egypt that had little meaning for modern man. He espoused, for a time, the Saint-Simonian creed; he proclaimed his mission of fighting for the political and social emancipation of Germany and all mankind; he saw himself as Germany's cultural ambassador in France, dedicated to the task of mediating between the two countries, explaining the one to the other; he never felt at home in any language but German. We find him angrily rejecting the appellation 'Jew' when it was attached to him by friend or foe; devaluing Judaism as a 'sickness'; indulging in anti-Jewish abuse in his private correspondence, and making free use of stereotypes beloved by anti-Semites. Such stereotypes include physical clumsiness and gracelessness, the 'Jewish' nose, the insanitary appearance of Jews from Eastern Europe, Jewish pawnbroking and trade in cast-off clothing, the mercantile 'genius' of the Jews, the parvenu behaviour of Jewish *nouveaux riches*, the *Fresser* or guzzlers who despised the higher flights of the mind (particularly those of the poet), and Yiddish inflections of speech. All these have been documented in our examination of Heine's Jewish portraits.

Always, however, there were counter-currents—those stirred up by the many haters or despisers of Jews who turned on him at various stages of his career, and those that flowed from the depths of his own mind and soul. Baptism only confirmed that Christianity was not for him; his love-affair with Germany frequently turned sour; the Saint-Simonians disappointed him by their ridiculous behaviour in the early stages of their development and their materialism in the later stages. Heine's adoption of the Romantic creed, documented by an early essay written under the influence of A. W. Schlegel, is qualified by a sentence opposing exclusive nationalism and championing those 'to whom folly and guile would deny a fatherland'. In Berlin, Heine was soon drawn into a society which set itself to mediate between the scientific-Hegelian spirit of intellectual Germany and the traditions of Judaism—a mediation that included the systematic study of Jewish history, Jewish folklore, and Jewish literature. A visit to Poland confirmed Heine in his respect for the 'wholeness' of orthodox Judaism, though he himself opted for assimilation to Western-

European styles of living. Testimonies mount to the various 'pulls' that Judaism exerted on its renegade son: ranging from the remembrance of sabbath and Passover ritual (family life bound up with Jewish religious practice) to Jewish cookery, linked, once again, with the sabbaths and feast-days of the Jewish calendar. The attraction of the Old Testament, usually read in Luther's translation, is enhanced by remembrance of its Hebrew text, studied—however desultorily—in earliest youth; a remembrance in which the very look of the Hebrew letters played an important part. Yiddish and Hebrew words, sometimes in Hebrew script, flow into Heine's correspondence to the very end, creating and fostering a family atmosphere. He never ceased to feel that orthodox Judaism was intolerably restricting for a man like himself, and that Reform Judaism was neither fish, flesh, nor good red herring; yet whenever Jews were threatened—whether in Hamburg during the Hep-Hep riots or in Damascus at the time of the ritual murder accusation—Heine at once felt solidarity with his people, though he protested that he would have felt equal solidarity with any other group similarly threatened and oppressed. Heine is constantly drawn to Jewish personalities of the past, particularly the Sephardic Jews and Marranos of the Hispanic peninsula; this can lead to the kinds of identification and projection we noted in *Donna Clara*, the later portions of *The Rabbi of Bacherach*, and *Jehuda ben Halevy*. *Donna Clara* is only one of many documents that show Heine's concern to assert Jewish dignity in face of various anti-Judaic attitudes; and *Jehuda ben Halevy* has to be seen together with *The God Apollo* as Heine's fundamentally serious exploration of the dangers and possibilities confronting a poet of Jewish birth in the Diaspora.

Throughout his life, Heine was surrounded by Jewish-born associates of various persuasions and various degrees of congeniality: in Düsseldorf, in Hamburg, in Berlin, and more and more in Paris too. His loathing of Jewish commercialism was alleviated by reflections on its historical origins and by his conviction that it merely caricatured the commercialism of the Gentile world. Consciousness of historically conditioned faults is balanced, in his writings, by respect for Jewish traditions of support for the learned, Jewish loyalty to the sacred books, Jewish charities, and Jewish democratic traditions which gave the beggar, the *Shnorrer*, inalienable rights *vis-à-vis* his plutocratic co-religionists. Though he had mixed feelings about Jewish clinging to the past, about a historical imagination which continued to live in the time of the Exodus or the destruction of the Temple, he came to attach more and more value to Jewish steadfastness in the face of persecution, and to the people's ability to retain its identity by making the Bible its portable fatherland. He always valued strength and authenticity—and he found both amply documented in the history of the stiff-necked tribe into which his lot had ineluctably cast him. He came to appreciate more and more the force, and the poetic quality, of Jewish Jerusalem nostalgia—a longing for a lost but not irrecoverable homeland which he always associated with Psalm 137, the song of the Babylonian exile, and with the sound of the Hebrew word *Yerushalayim* or *Jeruscholajim*. These served to remind him of the indissoluble union between the Jewish people, the land of Israel, and the sacred Hebrew books. His speculative 'return' to God in his final years did not mean adherence to Jewish religious doctrine, whether 'reformed' or orthodox; but he spoke of God, to Jews, as 'the God of our fathers', and lent him features that clearly belong to Jehovah. His respect for Jesus was not the Christian's respect for the Son of God—that he often affronted with deliberate blasphemies; it was the respect, rather, for a reformer sprung from the Jewish artisan class who wanted to democratize the priest-ridden society of ancient Israel and to spread Jewish ethical teaching beyond the narrow frontiers of the ancient Hebrew nation.

In nineteenth-century Europe it was frequently those who *opposed* giving Jews full civil rights who spoke of modern Jewry as a 'nation'. 'Now that we have been granted the privilege of being accepted into the great French nation', the Jewish notables convened by Napoleon had declared in 1806, 'we Jews have ceased to form a nation and regard this as our political deliverance.' Heine too shows himself suspicious of the term 'nation' when applied to the Jews of modern times— he associated such talk, as the opening of the third chapter of *English Fragments* suggests, with the unthinking application of stereotypes. Though he was profoundly aware of the distinc-

tive contribution which the different peoples and nations of
Europe had severally made to their common cultural heritage,
the poet distrusted assertive nationalism of every kind, and
thought that in the nineteenth century division into 'parties'
(*Parteien*) was becoming more important than division into
nations. In his early years we found him speaking of Jews
collectively as 'the Jews', or 'adherents of the Old Testament',
or 'Israel', or 'the children of Israel', or 'the people who
understand arithmetic so well', and individually as 'a Jew' or
'the Mosaist'. Of Polish Jews he spoke in class terms, seeing
them as Poland's 'third estate'; German Jews he characterized
as 'stepchildren' when he made his narrator speak of Germany
as their 'stepfatherland' in a fragment intended for *The Hartz
Journey*. Very early on he ironically adopted the common
equation of 'Jew' and 'tradesman' in order to turn it against
those who generally make this equation by speaking of Gentile
traders as 'baptized Jews' and lumping them together with the
'unbaptized Jews' whose competition they feared. At the same
time he painted a fearful picture, in *Donna Clara*, of anti-
Jewish prejudices when he had the eponymous heroine dismiss
them first as akin to noxious insects, then as murderers of the
Christian savour, and at last as a group whose blood is tainted
and apt to corrupt those with whom it intermingles.

The later *Pictures of Travel* present Jews as a family ('a
family that has come down in the world') and as a people ('a
people out of Egypt'); but despite his own witty play with
popular stereotypes Heine deprecated attempts to present the
Jewish people as unchanging, with permanent and invariable
attributes. *The Rabbi of Bacherach*, indeed, is partly devoted
to showing that Jewry and Judaism demand to be studied
historically, comparatively, within the setting of the surround-
ing Gentile culture. The letters Heine wrote in the earlier 1820s
show that he knew about hopes for the ingathering of the
scattered people in a homeland of its own; such hopes were
roused by M. M. Noah's scheme for founding a Jewish mini-
state in North America, while in Eastern Europe various Mes-
sianic movements had raised expectations of a return to Jeru-
salem. The dream-visions, however, in which Heine speaks of
a new exodus, to 'Ganstown' in America or to Jerusalem, are
clearly satirical, and hold out no real prospect that the Jeru-

salem nostalgia which he knew so well and evoked so often would lead to any actual physical return. Though he seems to have advised others, on occasions, to emigrate to America, he saw himself as indelibly European. In his baptism he saw the purchase of an entry ticket to European culture. Nevertheless such phrases as 'wir sind ja im Gohles' (let us remember that we are in the Diaspora), have overtones of seriousness, leading one to understand the attraction which the legendary figure of the Wandering Jew, *der ewige Jude*, had for him.

Baptism brought home to Heine with renewed force that whatever Judaism was, it was not simply a religion, a *Konfession*, like any other. He now begins to speak of 'the mark of the Jew' which cannot be washed off in the baptismal font, and declares that no barber can shave off the Eternal Jew's self-rejuvenating beard. His tone is usally ironic when he speaks of the Jews as 'God's people' or 'God's chosen people'—he had little sympathy with such ethnic conceit; but he is wholly serious when he speaks of them as 'the people of the spirit' and 'the people of the book'. True, his comic creation Hirsch-Hyazinth can feel the Jewish religion to be a 'misfortune' and his 'lyric I' can speak of Judaism as a malady, a family affliction, in a poem of the early 1840s; he talks of the Jews haunting the world as 'the ghost of a people', a 'murdered people', 'the people that cannot die'; and when he finds himself classified as a Jew he is quick to retort that he does not adhere to the Jewish religion. In the religious sense he comes to see Judaism as a 'sect', subject to an *idée fixe* with which the Parisian Heine, the Heine of the 1830s and early 1840s, has little sympathy; but he continues to admire some Jewish ceremonial and synagogue poetry, he loves and reveres the Old Testament which he now characterizes as the Jews' 'portable fatherland', and he constantly experiences nostalgic longings for traditional Jewish cookery. While he is speaking the truth when he assures readers or listeners that he does not adhere to the Jewish religion, he does acknowledge it as that of his fathers, and he does see the history of the Jewish people as part of his own family history. From the 1840s onwards Heine expends a good deal of energy on demonstrating the universal validity of Jewish ethics and the universal message of Jewish Messianism. Jesus of Nazareth, whom the poet always regarded as a member of the

Jewish people, as his own 'cousin' and Börne's, made Jewish
ethics and Jewish Messianism accessible to all and thus gave the
whole world what Heine calls, in *Ludwig Börne. A Memorial*,
'the right of Jewish citizenship'. This is deliberately contrasted,
in the same book, with what Heine terms the 'egoistic national-
ism' of ancient Judaea as well as with the obstinacy of self-
styled German Christians who are unwilling to grant full civic
rights to the Jews in their midst.

Heine has now begun to speak of the Jewish people, not just
as a family, but as a *Stamm*—a word often translated as 'tribe'
which in Heine's usage points to common ancestry, common
descent. The image implied is that of the tree trunk and its
branches, familiar from genealogical trees or *Stammbäume*.
'Genealogical group' or 'ethnic group' or 'kinship group' ren-
ders its sense better than 'tribe'. Common ancestry implies a
blood relationship which enables Heine to say, figuratively,
that in his veins flows some of the same blood as that which
flowed in the veins of Jesus of Nazareth. And then, in the
1840s, we find Atta Troll, Heine's comic bear, characterizing
the Jews specifically as a 'race'. Heine himself, as we have seen,
occasionally uses the term 'race' in a value-free way: he sets up
no hierarchy of valuable or less valuable races, nor does he see
any virtue in keeping a human stock 'pure' or 'unmixed'. Men
are not horses, and human 'thoroughbreds' are worth no more
than those who stem from a less prestigious parentage. As for
the notion that the sexual congress of men and women of
aristocratic provenance results in more valuable infants than
that of commoners—we have heard Heine dismiss that notion
as an 'obscene joke'. The poet realized very early what a
dangerous weapon the 'race' and 'blood' concepts could
become in the hands of the Jews' enemies, and he seeks to
ridicule their arguments as fit for horse-traders and cattle-
breeders, but not for those who would understand and classify
human beings. At the same time he applies his distinction of
character types—variously defined as 'Jews' v. 'Greeks',
'Nazarenes' v. 'Hellenes', and in one of his last poems even
'Barbarians' v. 'Hellenes'—in a way that deliberately cuts
across religious, family, ethnic and class divisions and enables
him to call Gentiles who had attacked him as a Jew 'the Jew
Menzel', or 'the Jew Hengstenberg'.

In his very last years, the 'mattress-crypt' years 1848–56, Heine once again publicly speaks of himself as a Jew—'only a poor Jew sick unto death' we found him saying in *Confessions*; but this, as the word 'only' suggests, is felt as a defeat, a reduction, and it in no way implies acceptance of the Jewish religion.

'My ancestors belonged to the Jewish religion', he tells his readers, adding that he never thought this a matter for pride; but while continuing to castigate individual modern Jews who have made a 'caricature' of Judaism, he firmly believed that the caricature would vanish one day, since the ethical core of Judaism was so strong. He now descants freely and frequently on the glories of ancient Judaea and more modern Judaism in dispersion: their stern but admirable morality, their poetry, the great men and martyrs they produced. Despite the prevailing caricature, despite the extremes of money worship or abjectness to which individual Jews may be prone, Heine now attributes to the Jewish people 'a great civilization of the heart' and 'an unbroken tradition of 2,000 years'. To such traditions he acknowledges a loyalty that in no way conflicts with his German loyalties or his loyalties as a 'good soldier in the war of liberation fought by all mankind' whose duty it is to stand above sectarian quarrels and differences. In one way, of course, he does move closer to Judaism: he does posit, in his final years, the existence of a God who has many of the features of the biblical Jehovah. But this positing, as we have seen, is so pragmatic, so hedged around with mental qualifications, and so little accompanied by the love and awe observant Jews characteristically feel and express in their relations with the Deity, that one cannot help recalling Heine's own deliberate devaluation of death-bed conversions in happier days than those of the mattress-crypt.

Nevertheless it should now be clear that for all his many and varied attempts to distance himself from the Jews whom he lauded and derided with equal zest, there are aspects of his personality which remained Jewish even after 28 June 1825, the day on which Harry Heine, Khaim ben Shimshon, became Christian Johann Heinrich Heine by act of baptism. He was a Jew by birth. He was a Jew by circumcision—a reminder of his induction into the community of Israel was irreversibly carved into his flesh. He was a Jew by early upbringing: he had been taught the rudiments of Hebrew along with many ordinances and prohibitions which remained part of his consciousness even when he chose to disregard them. He was a Jew by family connection: unless he broke with every single member of his family, he would always be drawn back into a Jewish ambience. He was therefore in part a Jew by memory and feeling: the 'intimate culture' of the Jews, their Sabbath and festival customs, were inevitably subject to involuntary as well as voluntary recollection. He was and remained a Jew by decree of history: in the double sense that the very circumstances of his 'conversion' were part of the history of the Jewish people, and that he was aware of this history and his own place in it—that he had, indeed, studied this history in some depth and with a sense of his own involvement. He was a Jew by community of fate: he shared what was to become known as the Jewish *Schicksalsgemeinschaft* which impressed itself even more powerfully on his consciousness *after* his baptism than before. He was a Jew by common consent: one only has to leaf through any collection of contemporary comments about him to be left in no doubt on that score. All this ensured that he would also remain a Jew by introspection: what he admired and what he hated in Jews he often found in himself; in reacting against Judaism and Jewishness he often reacted against potentialities and dangers of his own personality. And what is by no means the same thing—he was also a Jew by conscience: when the Damascus affair broke, just fifteen years after his baptism, he at once felt personally involved and called to action, and he waxed volubly indignant at Jews and ex-Jews who failed to follow his example.

All this does not mean, of course, that Heine should be seen as a 'Jewish writer' in a narrow and exclusive sense. He wrote in the German language, and not in either Hebrew or Yiddish. When he first came to Paris, he went to the Bibliothèque Royale to look at a famous manuscript of a medieval German love-song, not at a copy of the Talmud. But he did remain ineradicably conscious of the common origin and life experience of modern Jewry—an origin and a life experience he shared with men he detested as well as with those he admired. External pressures, the growth of new forms of anti-Semitism out of the soil of ancient Jew-hatreds, helped to keep that consciousness vividly alive. He tried to mediate between the different aspects of his identity by stressing those aspects of the Jewish tradition which chimed in with modern democratic ideals, as well as those which it had in common with the best ethical traditions of Germany. This led to repeated assertions that through its absorption of Old Testament ethics and history, modern Europe had become, in a sense, Jewish, and that there was, in particular, a strong natural affinity between Jewish and German moral ideals, so that ancient Israel could be spoken of as the Germany of the Orient. In the teeth of those who asserted some radical incompatibility between the German and the Jewish spirit, Heine maintained that an elective affinity, a *Wahlverwandtschaft*, bound these two components of his personality solidly together. Jewish origins were fully compatible, in his eyes, with the highest German patriotism, with loyalties to France where he had made his home, with faithful adherence to democratic ideals, and with belief in the universal brotherhood of man. Nevertheless, as this book will have shown, there were inevitable tensions—between his Jewish and his German self, between his feelings as a scion of the ancient worshippers of Jehovah and those of an heir to the manifold civilization of Western Europe. Such tensions he frequently externalized in his portraits; and he gained relief from them through the kinds of wit which later generations recognized as a peculiar phenomenon of the nineteenth- and twentieth-century Diaspora. A good deal of this wit was directed at Jews, individually and as a group: in Heine's writings ethnic stereotypes function with regard to the group much as caricature-sketches function with regard to individuals.

The Jewish people, it has been well said, was not, from its origins, a people of comedians. There is some humour in the Old Testament, though it has to be searched for; the Talmud contains humorous tales and some satiric quips against the godless ('All joking', said Rabbi Nachman, 'is forbidden, except jokes about idol worship'); and like other peoples the Jews too had their tales about pranksters and fools. What we now know as the Jewish joke, however, with its self-criticism, its aggression anticipated and introjected, is the product of the age into which Heine was born, the age in which the ghetto walls were broken down and Western Jewry fought for its emancipation. Freud has demonstrated some (but by no means all) the mechanisms of Jewish jokes in *The Joke and its Relation to the Unconscious*—and it is no accident that Heine's quips occupy a central place in that demonstration. The jokes told by Jews about themselves differ from those made up about them by outsiders: they depend for their subtlest effects on the teller's and the hearer's consciousness of the high standards of honesty, decency, and hygiene enjoined by traditional Judaism, from which human weakness needs a temporary escape; and on the recognition of the necessary part played in the world's economy by the *yetser ha-ra*, man's evil inclination. They also, of course, act as a defence, by anticipating, voicing, and (apparently) interiorizing the charges of anti-Semites, thus robbing them of some of their sting. Behind Heine's humour lies the identity crisis inseparable from the process of Jewish emancipation; and the Jewish portraits examined in these pages often seem dedicated to the proposition that being Jewish in the nominally Christian world of Western Europe in the nineteenth century meant facing absurdity to the full. But then—did he not, in the end, come to see the whole world as absurd, a world in which it was so often the worse man who conquered the better? And did he not depict Judaism—in portraits that range from Moses Lump to Jehuda ben Halevy, in evocations of Jewish ritual, in positive evaluations of Jewish law and Jewish history and the character traits they fostered in those who did not become renegades—as a defence against the absurd, as a source of manly strength which those born into the Jewish community abandoned at their peril?

Heine used satire, wit, and irony as weapons with which to combat those whom he regarded as his enemies, and to pillory conditions he thought unworthy. He used it also to ridicule incongruity and pretence, to relieve pent-up aggressions, dissatisfactions with himself and others, and physical suffering. Like Dr Samuel Johnson, towards whom he was notably unjust, he tended to 'reduce' his enemies, sift them down to the lowest common denominator, in order to give drastic expression to his sense of human egotism and vanity. Much of what W. Jackson Bate has said of Dr Johnson applies to Heine too:

when he speaks, for instance, of the connection of Johnson's humour

with some of his most serious psychological problems—his attempts to gain 'distance', to curb or 'displace' aggression, and with his lifelong struggle for mental health and his ability, under the most trying circumstances, to retain his hold on reality. Humor, as Freud has said, is by far 'the highest of the defensive processes' against the psychological trials and anxieties of living, and in its genuine state, the most healthful. For in contrast to the common 'neurotic' forms of defence that cripple the psyche, humour does not rigidly repress or deny—thus 'quitting', says Freud, 'the ground of mental sanity'— but openly acknowledges threats and anxieties, and allows them to propel themselves by their momentum, while creatively steering and 'displacing' them into a new context.[2]

Heine's savage wit and gentler humour frequently show affinity with those of the great satirists who preceded him, from Aristophanes and Juvenal to Swift and Jean Paul Richter. Nothing could be further from the aims of the present book than to imprison him in a literary ghetto! Nevertheless we do find in his work many of the qualities which Freud, Theodor Reik, and Martin Grosjahn have described as characteristic of Jewish wit. Such qualities include exceptionally sharp self-criticism; prophylactic and experimental adoption of Jewish stereotypes that originate in the Gentile world; a democratic mode of thought that places rich and poor, aristocrat and simple man of the people on the same footing, without losing sight of regional differences and class rivalries within the Jewish communities; revolt against over-harsh and overplentiful precepts and prohibitions; a pervasive scepticism induced by a long history of exile and persecution which leads to witty demonstrations of the fragility of law and order in the human world; respect for learning coupled with delight in playing the card of common sense against it: and a fascination with intricate modes of thought, with a hypertrophied logic that leads to real or apparent absurdity.

The Jewish Comedy on which Heine brought his humour, his wit, his anger, and his compassion to bear was above all the tragicomedy of emancipation, assimilation, and acculturation, played out against the background of Jewish history from biblical times to those of Moses Mendelssohn. It is not too much to say that in the portraits we have examined every variety of Jewish response to the opportunities and perils attendant on the opening of the ghetto gates finds a real-life or imagined representative. At one extreme Heine shows us, with considerable sympathy, pious Jews who refuse altogether to change their traditional way of life and study; at the other extreme he brings before us men like August Neander, the convinced neo-Christian, Friedrich Julius Stahl, the no less convinced theorist of Prussian conservatism, and Karl Marx, doctor of the revolution, who thought he had put Jewishness behind him once and for all when he mistakenly and unhistorically equated the Jewish spirit with the spirit of capitalism. In between these extremes lie the points indicated in Heine's work by such figures as Rahel Varnhagen, Börne, Eduard Gans, Gumpelino, the Rothschild family, Hirsch-Hyazinth, Meyerbeer, Adolphe Crémieux, Ludwig Marcus, and Leopold Zunz—a sequence ranging from those who threw in their lot with the Christian world by act of baptism without attempting to deny their Jewish origins (even if, like Rahel, they had mainly negative feelings about these origins) to those who used the learning they acquired in the Gentile world to reveal to their fellow citizens, Christian as well as Jewish, the riches of the Jewish cultural tradition. The attitudes he depicted were not foreign to Heine himself, who in the course of his life approached many of the positions he portrayed without fully coming to rest on any of them. Even when he repudiated knaves and fools (or those whom he thought so) he was apt to dramatize temptations and possibilities he knew by introspection. No one was more intimately acquainted than he with what Philip Rahv once called 'the true irony, which implicates the person writing no less than other people, the subject as well as the object'.[3]

Throughout this book we have quizzed the Jewish scene through Heine's often tinted spectacles. Let us conclude by turning around for a moment in order to look at the poet's own part in the tragicomedy of emancipation through the eyes of two contemporary observers of similar origin. It is only just that Ludwig Börne should be the first of these. He is describing the civil marriage ceremony of an old acquaintance from Frankfurt who had established a medical practice in Paris—Dr

Julius (Jules) Sichel, whose walk-on part in Heine's Jewish comedy has occupied us in an earlier chapter.

> How strangely fate casts its dice! Here we have a baptized Jew from Frankfurt—the son of 'Salme Rappel', as old man Sichel used to be called because he was a little bit weak in the head—marrying a Christian girl from England, of God knows what ancestry; the marriage is performed in Paris, and the witnesses are a Christian, a Jew (Sichel's own brother), and two baptized Jews—and these last-named are the leading writers of their day, and ornaments of the German Confederation!
>
> (Börne to Jeanette Wohl, 25 October 1831)[4]

The 'two baptized Jews' to whom Börne refers in this letter are, of course, Heine and himself.

The second of our two observers is anonymous and mute. We know of him through the reminiscences of Heine's last love, Élise Krinitz, whom the poet called 'La Mouche' and who appeared before the reading public under the pen-name 'Camille Selden'. She was present at Heine's funeral; and as she watched this German poet of Jewish birth, whose baptismal certificate proclaimed him a Protestant, laid to rest in a French cemetery, she saw and recorded for posterity an almost imperceptible gesture that comments on the irony of the situation in a way Heine himself would have enjoyed:

> When we arrived at the cemetery gates, we left our coach to follow the hearse on foot. It is customary, when a corpse is carried by, to stop for a moment—just long enough to say a prayer—in front of a little chapel dedicated to the Holy Virgin which stands at the entrance. Our procession therefore halted in the usual way. At that moment a young man of Jewish appearance, with a gentle, intelligent, perhaps a little sceptical face, turned round to some men who were also part of the funeral cortège and, almost imperceptibly, shrugged his shoulders . . .[5]

It would not be right, however, to let our long scrutiny of Heine's Jewish Comedy come to a full close with a shrug. Better to end, therefore, with an observation by Isaac Rosenberg, the gifted Anglo-Jewish poet whose life and work were tragically cut short by the First World War. 'Heine, our own Heine . . .' Rosenberg wrote on August 1916; 'I admire him more for always being a Jew at heart than anything else.'[6] I hope to have shown that he was indeed a Jew at heart, as he was also a German and a European; and that much of the fascination exerted by his many portraits and caricatures of Jews and Judaism is due to the interplay of these identities, and the conflicts to which it occasionally gave rise. Heine felt such conflicts as keenly as his most sensitive contemporaries; and his poet's ability to express them, to externalize them in verbal portraits and cartoons, makes his work uniquely valuable as a contribution to intellectual and spiritual history. It is valuable for what it betrays—like Heine's not always conscious adoption of anti-Jewish charges and stereotypes; but it is even more valuable for what it expresses and reveals by means proper to literature. Like all caricaturists, like all satirists, Heine thrives on heightening and distortion. For all his patent unfairness, however, and all his disregard of facts and dates as he pursues his quest of symbolic anecdotes and 'signatures' of the time, Heine shows himself, in the portraits examined in the present book, an important historian as well as an important poet: a poet-historian who can give us insights into a past age that we would otherwise have lacked; who enables us to re-experience past feelings, attitudes, and opinions while reminding us, at the same time, of our own conflicts, our own difficulties, our own failings, and our own ability to rise above all these through laughter, through indignation not suppressed but given free vent, and through the pleasure we may take in a gifted poet's plain or distorted—but always recognizable—portrayal of fallible humanity. 'Who learns history from Heine?' Leopold Zunz is reported to have asked, implying that no one ever did.[7] I hope this book will have persuaded some of its readers that the answer to Zunz's rhetorical query is more complex and more positive than the distinguished questioner seems to have thought, and that an informed and critical contemplation of Heine's Jewish Comedy may bring understanding as well as delight.

NOTES

Prologue

1. A 'corn-cutter' is not a trained chiropodist, but a man who supplements his income by digging out corns from the feet of people prepared to trust his dexterity.
2. *B* III, 552.
3. *B* III, 330.
4. F. R. Leavis, *New Bearings in English Poetry*, London 1932, p. 13.
5. *B* VI(i), 640.
6. *B* IV, 644.
7. F. Hirth, *Heinrich Heine und seine französischen Freunde*, pp. 63–70.
8. *B* VI(i), 652.
9. cf. A. G. Lehmann, *Sainte-Beuve. A Portrait of the Critic, 1804–1842*, Oxford 1962, p. 295.
10. *B* V, 239.
11. e.g. *B* II, 23: 'Die Leute betrachten nicht das Gemälde, das ich leicht hinskizziere, sondern die Figürchen, die ich hineingezeichnet, um es zu beleben, und glauben vielleicht gar, daß es mir um diese Figürchen besonders zu tun war. Aber man kann auch Gemälde ohne Figuren malen, so wie man Suppe ohne Salz essen kann . . .'
12. e.g. *B* V, 230 and 187.
13. *B* IV, 102.
14. Werner-Houben, I, 589.
15. Sammons, op. cit., pp. 37–8.
16. cf. Michael A. Meyer, *Ideas of Jewish History*, New York 1974, p. 23. The same author's *The Origins of the Modern Jew. Jewish Identity and European Culture in Germany, 1749–1824* (Detroit 1967) contains an excellent chapter on the Society for the Culture and Science of the Jews. For the Hegelian connotations of *Wissenschaft* (here translated, inadequately, as 'science') see Shlomo Avineri, *Hegel's Theory of the Modern State*, Cambridge 1972, pp. 122–3: '*Wissenschaft* to Hegel relates to what can be known, it is the Greek *episteme*. Actuality can be known in this sense through a system of rigorous 'scientific' concepts needed to comprehend it, not through loose 'notions' and 'feelings'. What

characterizes *Wissenschaft* according to Hegel, is the unity of content and form, and it is this unity which distinguishes reason (*Vernunft*) from mere understanding (*Verstand*) which stops at the dichotomy between content and form and cannot overcome it.'

17. H. G. Reissner, *Eduard Gans. Ein Leben im Vormärz*, Tübingen 1965, p. 36.
18. *B* II, 20.
19. *B* II, 153.
20. *B* II, 284.
21. *B* I, 266.
22. *B* I, 210.
23. *B* II, 411–12.
24. J. L. Talmon, *Romanticism and Revolt. Europe 1815–1848*, London 1967, p. 125.
25. *B* II, 412.
26. *B* II, 477.
27. Reissner, op. cit., p. 158.
28. *B* II, 674.
29. *B* IV, 355.
30. Reissner, op. cit., p. 116.
31. *B* IV, 518.
32. *B* V, 179.
33. *B* V, 181–2.
34. *B* V, 182.
35. Ibid.
36. e.g. *B* VI(i), 471 ff.
37. 'servant-girl' is conjecture: what Heine writes is: 'Ueberlegt er noch des Morgens mit Male wen er des Tags über zitiren soll . . .' (*HSA* XX, 179).
38. Werner-Houben, I, 181.
39. Reissner, op. cit., p. 116.
40. Werner-Houben, I, 54.
41. Reissner, op. cit., p. 137.

Chapter 1: *Israel and Edom*

1. *B* II, 12.
2. *B* II, 23.
3. *B* II, 15.
4. H. H. Houben (ed.), *Gespräche mit Heine*, Frankfurt am Main 1926, p. 41.
5. 2(b) *B* II, 17–18.

6. *B* II, 36.
7. *B* II, 36–7.
8. *B* II, 40.
9. *B* II, 21.
10. *B* II, 32–3.
11. *B* I, 245.
12. *B* II, 34.
13. *B* II, 59.
14. *B* II, 59–60.
15. *B* II, 47.
16. *B* II, 48.
17. *B* II, 46–7.
18. *B* II, 71.
19. *B* II, 73.
20. *B* II, 90.
21. *B* II, 74–5.
22. Useful corrections may be found in J. K. Krzywon's *Heinrich Heine und Polen* and in the article by M. Grabowska cited in note 27 below.
23. P. F. Veit, 'Heinrich Heine and David Friedländer', *H-Jb* 19 (1980), pp. 227–34.
24. cf. K. Pabel, *Heinrich Heines Reisebilder*, Munich 1977, pp. 76–7.
25. E. J. Krzywon, *Heinrich Heine und Polen*, p. 160.
26. *B* II, 79.
27. M. Grabowska, 'Heine und Polen' in M. Windfuhr (ed.), *Internationaler Heine-Kongreß Düsseldorf 1972*, pp. 367, 360.
28. *B* I, 54–6.
29. *Werner-Houben*, II, 152.
30. Kircher, *Heinrich Heine und das Judentum*, p. 186 and *passim*.
31. *B* I, 317.
32. *B* I, 295.
33. *B* I, 284–5.
34. *B* I, 280.
35. *B* I, 310.
36. *B* I, 310–11.
37. *B* I, 337.
38. *B* I, 285, 282, 297.
39. *B* I, 321, 287.
40. *B* I, 296.
41. *B* I, 297, 288 f., 301, 298, 295.
42. *B* I, 276.
43. *HSA* XX, 29.
44. *HSA* XX, 19 (27 October 1816).

45. *B* I, 65–6.
46. *HSA* XX, 123 (6 November 1823).
47. *HSA* XX, 122.
48. HSA XX, 124.
49. *B* I, 156 f. cf. Kircher, op. cit., p. 195 f.
50. *B* I, 158.
51. *HSA* XX, 122.
52. *HSA* XX, 128.
53. *B* I, 34.
54. Ludwig Börne, *Sämtliche Schriften*, ed. I. and P. Rippmann, Düsseldorf 1964, I, 286.
55. *B* I, 271.
56. *HSA* XX, 177 (to Moser, 25 October 1824).
57. *HAD* (i), 526.
58. *B* I, 740.
59. *B* I, 159–62.
60. *B* I, 160.
61. F. Hirth, *Heinrich Heine. Bausteine zu einer Biographie*, pp. 97–100.
62. *B* V, 172.
63. *B* I, 462.
64. *B* I, 463.
65. *B* I, 464.
66. *B* I, 466, 467, 473.
67. *B* I, 472.
68. *B* I, 466.
69. *B* I, 470.
70. cf. Ruth L. Jacobi, *Heinrich Heines jüdisches Erbe*, p. 4.
71. *B* I, 471–4.
72. cf. W. Kanowsky, 'Heine als Benutzer der Bibliotheken in Bonn und Göttingen', *H-Jb* 12 (1973).
73. The singer was Karoline Stern—see Pierre Grappin's helpful note on this poem in *HAD* I (ii).

Chapter 2: *The 5,588 Years' War*

1. *B* II, 113–14.
2. *B* II, 133.
3. *Eos. Münchener Blätter für Poesie, Literatur und Kunst*, No. 132, 18 August 1828. cf. F. Hirth, *Briefe* IV, 182.
4. *B* II, 114–15.
5. *B* II, 119.
6. *B* II, 749.

7. *B* II, 127–9. For a full and accurate account of Saul Ascher, see Walter Grab's essay on him in *Jahrbuch des Instituts für deutsche Geschichte*, Tel Aviv. Vol. VI (1977).
8. *B* II, 127–8.
9. *B* II, 126–7.
10. M. A. Meyer, *The Origins of the Modern Jew*, p. 122 ff.; and Ellen Littmann, 'Saul Ascher: First Theorist of Progressive Judaism', *Leo Baeck Institute Year Book* V (1960), 107–21.
11. *B* II, 126.
12. Littman, loc. cit., p. 109.
13. *B* II, 147.
14. *B* II, 153.
15. *B* II, 161–2.
16. *B* II, 753.
17. *B* II, 107.
18. *HAD* VI, 229.
19. *HAD* VI, 232.
20. *B* II, 164.
21. e.g. *HAD* I (ii), 1031–2.
22. e.g. M. Pazi, 'Die biblischen und jüdischen Einflüsse in Heines "Nordsee"–Gedichten', *H-Jb* 13 (1974).
23. e.g. E. J. Krzywon, op. cit., pp. 153–58.
24. For documentation and critique, see William Rose, *The Early Love Poetry of Heinrich Heine*, p. 49 ff.
25. *B* I, 717.
26. *B* II, 133.
27. *HAD* I (ii), 1035–6.
28. *HSA* XX, 265 (to Moser, 8 July 1826).
29. see Pazi, loc. cit.
30. *E* II, 71.
31. *B* II, 224–5.
32. *E* III, 524; *HAD* II, 736.
33. *B* II, 804.
34. *HAD* II, 775.
35. *B* II, 223.
36. *HAD* II, 145 and 161.
37. *B* II, 215.
38. *B* II, 249.
39. *B* II, 253–4.
40. *B* II, 266.
41. *B* II, 287.
42. *B* II 268.
43. *B* II, 269. Heine coins the contemptuous terms *Dreigötterei* and

Eingötzentum to characterize the objects of Christian and Jewish worship.

44. *B* II, 284.
45. *B* II, 285–6.
46. *B* II, 294–5.
47. *B* II, 297.
48. *B* II, 300.
49. *B* II, 285–6.
50. *HAD* II, 811–12, 196.
51. *HAD* II, 801.

Chapter 3: *Jewish Emancipation and Gentile Cutlure*

1. *B* II, 426.
2. *B* II, 856.
3. *B* II, 380.
4. *B* II, 372.
5. Ibid.
6. *B* II, 376–7.
7. *B* II, 365.
8. *B* II, 12.
9. *B* II, 14.
10. *B* II, 397.
11. *B* II, 398.
12. cf. *B* VI(i), 651—last aphorism on the page.
13. Altman, op. cit., p. 143.
14. *B* II, 400.
15. *B* II, 401.
16. A. Strodtmann, *Heinrich Heines Leben und Werke*, 2nd rev. edn., I, 613; J. A. Kruse, *Heines Hamburger Zeit*, p. 81; P. F. Veit, 'Heinrich Heine and David Friedländer', *H-Jb* 19 (1980), pp. 227–34.
17. *B* II, 404.
18. *B* II, 407–8.
19. *B* II, 623.
20. *B* II, 623–4.
21. *B* II, 409.
22. *B* II, 414.
23. *B* II, 423.
24. *B* II, 624.
25. e.g. Werner-Houben, I, 204: 'hätt' er was gelernt, so braucht er nicht zu schreiben Bücher'.
26. *B* II, 424.

27. *B* II, 425.
28. Sigmund Freud, 'Der Witz und seine Beziehung zum Unbewußten', *Studienausgabe* Vol. IV, Frankfurt 1970, pp. 16 ff.
29. *B* II, 425–6.
30. *B* II, 625.
31. *B* II, 628–9.
32. *B* II, 430.
33. *B* II, 430–1. William Rose, *Heinrich Heine. Two Studies of his Thought and Feeling*, p. 135.
34. K. Pabel, op. cit., p. 200 ff.
35. *B* II, 440–1.
36. *B* II, 449.
37. *HSA* XV, 217.
38. *B* II, 467.
39. *B* II, 492.
40. *B* II, 630 f.
41. *B* II, 486.
42. *B* II, 489.
43. *B* II, 492–3.
44. *B* II, 500.
45. *B* II, 502.
46. *B* II, 512.
47. *B* II, 512–13.
48. *B* II, 515.
49. *B* II, 514–15. cf. Dolf Sternberger, *Heinrich Heine und die Abschaffung der Sünde*, Frankfurt 1976, p. 160.
50. *B* II, 510.
51. *B* II, 525.
52. *B* II, 634–5.
53. *B* II, 527.
54. *B* II, 905–7.
55. *B* II, 904. cf. Jeffrey Sammons, 'Heine and William Cobbett', *H-Jb* 19 (1980), pp. 69–77.
56. cf. Cecil Roth, *A History of the Jews in England*, Oxford 1964, p. 265; and Colin Holmes, *Anti-Semitism in British Society 1876–1939*, New York 1979, pp. 8–9.
57. *B* II, 585.
58. *B* II, 543.
59. *B* II, 557.
60. *B* II, 560.
61. *B* II, 544.
62. *Dichter über ihre Dichtungen: Heinrich Heine*, ed. N. and R.

Altenhofer, Munich 1971, p. 307 (*The Critic*, ed. John Crock-
ford, 1852). Cf. Werner-Houben, I, 299.
63. *B* II, 594.
64. *B* II, 595.
65. *B* II, 599.
66. *B* II, 601.
67. *B* I, 432.
68. *B* II, 647.
69. J. L. Sammons, *Heinrich Heine. A Modern Biography*, p. 136.
70. *B* II, 633.
71. *B* II, 667.

First Intermezzo: '*Will God be Strong in the Weak?*'

1. P. Grappin, 'Heines lyrische Anfänge', in M. Windfuhr (ed.),
   Internationaler Heine-Kongreß Düsseldorf 1972, pp. 67–70.
2. *Heinrich Heine. A Modern Biography*, p. 91.
3. Ibid., p. 90.
4. M. Meyer. *The Origins of the Modern Jew*, p. 180.
5. Werner-Houben, II, 394–5.
6. *B* I, 779.
7. *B* I, 265.
8. For Uncle Salomon's much-quoted observation that if his nephew
   had learnt something he wouldn't have to write books, see above,
   Chapter 3, Note 25.
9. Werner-Houben, I, 149.
10. Ibid., I, 163, 177, 230, 244, and *passim*.
11. *E* I, 531.
12. Werner-Houben, I, 153.
13. Op. cit., trans. J. Strachey, New York 1962, p. 57.
14. Werner-Houben, I, 140.
15. Ibid., I, 146.
16. *Life of Moscheles, with Selections from his Diaries and Corres-
    pondence, by His Wife*. Adapted from the Original German by A.
    D. Coleridge, London 1873, Vol. I, p. 197.
17. A. Lewald, *Aquarelle aus dem Leben*, Vol. II (Mannheim 1836),
    p. 96 f.
18. Werner-Houben, I, 59.
19. For this and the folllowing quotations, see *HAD* XI, 215–17.
20. Houben, *Gespräche* (1926), p. 191.

Chapter 4: *Philistines and Culture Heroes*

1. B III, 36.
2. Ibid.
3. B III, 37.
4. I. Zepf, *Heinrich Heines Gemäldebericht zum Salon 1831: 'Denkbilder'*, pp. 85–7.
5. Cf. 'Hillers Konzert', *B* V, 125 f.
6. *B* III, 272, 221.
7. *B* III, 150.
8. *B* III, 193.
9. *B* III, 175–6.
10. *B* III, 135.
11. *B* III, 224.
12. *B* III, 119, 229–30.
13. *B* III, 195–6.
14. *B* III, 91.
15. *B* III, 109.
16. *B* III, 15.
17. *B* IV, 333.
18. *B* I, 509.
19. *B* I, 513.
20. *B* I, 514–15.
21. *B* I, 527.
22. *B* I, 529.
23. *B* I, 537–8.
24. *B* I, 552.
25. *B* I, 543—4.
26. *B* I, 545.
27. *B* I, 549.
28. Ibid.
29. *B* I, 552.
30. *B* I, 555–6.
31. *B* III, 566.
32. *B* III, 584.
33. *B* III, 545.
34. *HAD* VIII (1), 690 (*B* III, 540).
35. *HAD* VIII (1), 34.
36. *HAD* VIII (1), 44 (*B* III, 551); *HAD* VIII (2), 698.
37. *B* III, 583.
38. *B* III, 563.
39. *B* III, 562.

40. *B* III, 562–3.
41. *HAD* VIII (2), 712.
42. *B* III, 562.
43. *HAD* VIII (1), 458.
44. *B* III, 565–6.
45. *B* IV, 325.
46. *B* III, 565.
47. *B* III, 620.
48. *B* III, 569.
49. *B* III, 546.
50. A. Altmann, *Moses Mendelssohn. A Biographical Study*, London 1973, p. 9.
51. *B* III, 583.
52. *B* III, 584–5.
53. *B* III, 583.
54. *B* III, 584. Heine later changed the name 'Grimbaldi' to the correct form 'Garibaldi' (Antonio Garibaldi, 1797–1853).
55. *B* III, 542.
56. *B* III, 590–1.
57. *B* III, 639 f.
58. *HAD* VIII (i), 454.
59. *B* III, 861.
60. *B* V, 19.
61. *HAD* VIII (i), 456.
62. *B* III, 423.
63. *B* III, 372. This is Heine's characteristic variation on Chapter 4 of the biblical Book of Ezra. In *Shakespeare's Girls and Women* Lessing is again compared to a temple builder: 'He brought the heaviest stone for a temple built to the glory of Shakespeare, the greatest poet of them all. And what deserves even higher praise: he laboured to clear accumulations of ancient rubble from the ground on which that temple was to be erected.' (*HAD* VIII (2), 1307).
65. *HAD* VIII (i), 472.
66. *B* III, 363.
67. *HAD* VIII (i), 482.
68. *B* III, 433–4.
69. *B* III, 456.
70. *B* III, 462.
71. *B* III, 409, 475, 440; Heinrich Heine, *Die romantische Schule*, ed. H. Weidmann, Stuttgart 1976, p. 194.
72. *HSA* XIV, 17.
73. Reeves, *Heinrich Heine. Poetry and Politics*, p. 108.

74. Ibid., p. 111.
75. *B* III, 21.
76. *B* III, 23.

Chapter 5: *Imperfect Sympathies*

1. *B* V, 141.
2. *B* V, 141–2.
3. *B* V, 142.
4. *HSA* XXI, 142.
5. *B* V, 38.
6. *B* V, 63.
7. *B* I, 569–70.
8. *B* I, 576.
9. *B* III, 702–3.
10. *B* I,10.
11. *B* III, 823.
12. Ibid.
13. *B* III, 826–7.
14. *B* III, 336.
15. *B* III, 337.
16. *B* III, 338.
17. Ibid.
18. *B* III, 338–9.
19. *B* III, 339 f.
20. *B* III, 342.
21. *B* III, 344.
22. *B* III, 345.
23. Ibid.
24. *B* III, 339.
25. *B* IV, 173.
26. *B* IV, 257.
27. *B* IV, 257–8.
28. *B* IV, 475.
29. *B* IV, 259.
30. *B* IV, 260–1.
31. *B* IV, 251.
32. K. J. Höltgen, 'Über "Shakespeares Mädchen und Frauen": Heine, Shakespeare und England', in M. Windfuhr (ed.), *Internationaler Heine-Kongreß Düsseldorf 1972*, p. 486.
33. *B* IV, 264–5.
34. *B* IV, 265–6.

Chapter 6: *Martyrs, Artists, and Plutocrats*

1. *HSA* X, 30.
2. *HSA* X, 32–3.
3. *HSA* X, 53.
4. *HSA* X, 36–7.
5 *B* V, 284.
6. *HSA* X, 25.
7. *HSA* X, 37: The most prominent of the 'young scholars' mentioned by Heine was the Orientalist Salomon Munk, whom we shall meet again in these pages.
8. *HSA* X, 38. The *Augsburg Gazette* substituted dots (. . .) for the names Romilly and Delmar.
9. *HSA* X, 45.
10. *HSA* X, 59.
11. Ibid.
12. *HSA* X, 52–3.
13. *HSA* X, 89.
14. *HSA* X, 89–90.
15. *HSA* X, 90.
16. *HSA* X, 197; *B* V, 215.
17. de Tocqueville, *Recollections*, ed. J. P. Mayer and A. P. Kerr, trans. George Lawrence, New York 1971, p. 70.
18. *HSA* X, 103.
19. Michael Mann, *Heinrich Heines Musikkritiken*, p. 89.
20. *HSA* X, 105.
21. *HSA* X, 104.
22. *HSA* X, 145.
23. *HSA* X, 191.
24. *HSA* X, 237–8.
25. *HSA* X, 190–1.
26. *HSA* X, 236.
27. *HSA* X, 149.
28. Cf. Michael Mann, op. cit., p. 126.
29. This quotation, and that immediately following, come from the *manuscript* of Heine's report dated 25 April 1844, which was not published until 1915. See F. Hirth, *Heinrich Heine. Bausteine zu einer Biographie*, pp. 86–90.
30. Richard Wagner, *Gesammelte Schriften und Dichtungen*, 2nd edn., Leipzig 1888, pp. 66–85.
31. *HSA* X, 229–30.
32. *B* V, 529. See the manuscript version detailed in note 29 above.

33. *HSA* X, 230.
34. *B* IV, 613.
35. *HSA* X, 190, 233.
36. *HSA* X, 189.
37. *HSA* X, 104; *M*, 165.
38. *HSA* X, 50, 82, 190; *M*, 143.
39. *HSA* X, 101–2.
40. *HSA* X, 187.
41. *HSA* X, 236.
42. *HSA* X, 101.
43. *HSA* X, 185.
44. *HSA* X, 112–13.
45. *HSA* X, 113.
46. *HSA* X, 9–10
47. *HSA* X, 18.
48. *HSA* X, 152.
49. *HSA* X, 25.
50. *HSA* X, 134.
51. *HSA* X, 156; and Lucienne Netter, *Heine et la peinture de la civilisation française 1840–1848*, Frankfurt and Bern 1980, p. 239.
52. *HSA* XIX, 52, 50.
53. *HSA* X, 123—November 1841.
54. *HSA* X, 196–7.
55. *HSA* X, 196.
56. *B* V, 451.
57. *HSA* X, 175.
58. *B* V, 424–5.
59. *HSA* X, 175.
60. *HSA* X, 208.
61. *HSA* X, 79.
62. *HSA* X, 152.
63. *HSA* X, 66.
64. *HSA* X, 199. 'Lorette' suggests ladies of easy virtue.
65. *HSA* X, 83, 208; *B* V, 391–2; *HSA* X, 242. The second quotation in this list comes from an article Heine contributed to *Zeitung für die elegante Welt*; the others were written for the *Augsburger Allgemeine Zeitung*.
66. *HSA* X, 209 (*Zeitung für die elegante Welt*).
67. *HSA* X, 92–3.
68. *HSA* X, 198.
69. *HSA* X, 195.
70. Werner-Houben, I, 236.
71. *HSA* X, 242.

Chapter 7: *A Fellow Exile and His World*

1. *B* V, 47.
2. *B* V, 48.
3. *B* IV, 47.
4. *B* IV, 19.
5. *B* IV, 108
6. *B* IV, 89.
7. *HAD* XI, 362, 364.
8. *B* IV, 118–19.
9. *B* IV, 23.
10. This phrase was used by Muslim jurists and statesmen to describe adherents of scriptural religions—Jews, Christians, and (for a time) Zoroastrians. For the economic and social implications of this, see N. Gross (ed.), *Economic History of the Jews*, New York 1975, p. 25.
11. *B* IV, 39–41.
12. *B* IV, 44–5.
13. *B* IV, 44.
14. *B* IV, 88.
15. These matters are fully discussed and illustrated in the exemplary critical apparatus of *HAD* XI.
16. cf. Louis Hay's contribution to *L'Enseignement et la littérature*, ed. S. Doubrovsky and T. Todorov, Paris 1971, p. 151.
17. *B* IV, 9.
18. *B* IV, 31.
19. *B* IV, 27.
20. *B* IV, 96, 110 ('Die listigen Worte, womit Menzel sein Deutschtum wie ein Hausierjude seinen Plunder anpreist . . .')
21. *B* IV, 28.
22. *B* IV, 13.
23. *B* IV, 32.
24. *B* IV, 68.
25. *B* IV, 140 ('. . . eine Radikalkur, die am Ende doch nur äußerlich wirkt, höchstens den gesellschaftlichen Grind vertreibt . . .')
26. *B* IV, 68.
27. *B* IV, 96.
28. *B* IV, 19.
29. See Heine's letter to Leopold Wertheim dated 22 December 1845 (*HSA* XXII, 177).
30. See Chapter 3, note 28 above.
31. *B* IV, 28.

32. *B* IV, 29.
33. *B* IV, 28 f.
34. *B* IV, 30–1.
35. *B* IV, 30.
36. *B* IV, 26–7.
37. *B* IV, 33.
38. Werner-Houben, I, 225.
39. *B* IV, 101.
40. *B* IV, 22.
41. *B* IV, 120–1.
42. Documented in Israel Tabak, *Judaic Lore in Heine*, and the critical apparatus in *HAD* XI.
43. *B* IV, 31.
44. *B* IV, 98.
45. *HAD* XI, 387–8.
46. *B* IV, 11.
47. *B* IV, 69.
48. *B* IV, 139.
49. *B* IV, 9–10
50. *B* IV, 13.
51. *B* IV, 13–34.
52. *B* IV, 11–12.
53. *B* IV, 34.
54. *B* IV, 17.
55. *B* IV, 35.
56. *B* IV, 61.
57. *B* IV, 98.
58. See Volkmar Hansen, *Thomas Manns Heine-Rezeption, passim.*
59. *HAD* IV, 110 and 113–14.
60. *B* IV, 93.
61. *B* IV, 67.
62. *B* IV, 132 f.
63. *B* IV, 130 f.
64. *B* IV, 128.
65. Reeves, *Heinrich Heine. Poetry and Politics*, Oxford 1974, pp. 61–2.
66. Gershom Scholem, 'Zum Verständnis der messianischen Idee im Judentum', *Judaica* I, Frankfurt 1963, pp. 12–13 *et passim*; M. Löwy, 'Jewish Messianism and Libertarian Utopia in Central Europe (1900–1933)', *New German Critique* 20 (Spring/Summer 1980), pp. 105–16.
67. *B* IV, 143, 758.
68. *B* IV, 18.

69. Spencer, *Dichter, Denker, Journalist. Studien zum Werk Heinrich Heines*, Bern 1977. For an authoritative assessment of the justice of Heine's portrait of Börne, and illuminating quotations from the latter's own work, see Inge Rippmann, 'Heines Denkschrift über Börne'', *H-Jb* 12, pp. 41–67.

Chapter 8: *The Shadow of the Ghetto*

1. *B* VI(i), 651.
2. *B* V, 84.
3. *B* IV, 366.
4. *B* IV, 481.
5. *B* I, 474–5.
6. *B* I, 486.
7. *B* I, 485.
8. *B* I, 480 f. and *B* IV, 331–2. For *Ludwig Börne*, see Chapter 7 above.
9. *B* I, 482–3.
10. *B* I, 484–5.
11. *B* I, 486.
12. *B* I, 483.
13. *B* I, 486–7.
14. *B* I, 488.
15. *B* I, 487.
16. *B* I, 487–8.
17. *B* I, 489–93.
18. *B* I, 494–5.
19. *B* I, 497.
20. *B* I, 498.
21. Ibid.
22. *B* I, 499.
23. *B* I, 499–500.
24. *B* I, 501.
25. *B* I, 473 and *B* VI(i), 54–5.
26. *B* I, 501.

Second Intermezzo: *Lions and Bed-Bugs*

1. Werner-Houben, I, 436–7.
2. Ibid., I, 357.
3. Ibid., I, 398.
4. Ibid., I, 317.
5. Ibid., I, 254.

6. A. Lewald, *Aquarelle aus dem Leben*, Vol. IV, Mannheim. 1837, p. 165.
7. Werner-Houben, I. 263; cf. O.L.B. Wolff's estimate, ibid. I, 296.
8. H. H. Houben (ed.), *Gespräche mit Heine*, Frankfurt 1926, pp. 335, 684.
9. Werner-Houben, I, 379.
10. Ibid., I, 410.
11. M. Werner, *Genius und Geldsack. Zum Problem des Schriftstellerberufs bei Heinrich Heine*, p. 100 ff.
12. Werner-Houben, I, 264.
13. J. Grandjonc, 'Die deutschen Emigranten in Paris. Ihr Verhältnis zu Heinrich Heine', in: M. Windfuhr (ed.), *Internationaler Heine-Kongreß Düsseldorf 1972*, p. 168.
14. R. Booß 'Dialekteigentümlichkeiten bei Heine', in M. Windfuhr (ed.), op. cit., p. 523.
15. Werner-Houben, I, 244–5.
16. Ibid., 326.
17. Ibid., 326–7, 327.

Chapter 9: *Kith and Kin*

1. Letter to Moser, 18 June 1823 (*HSA* XX, 97).
2. See Chapter 1, note 54.
3. *B* IV, 420–1.
4. But Brod nevertheless calls it 'one of his most beautiful as well as one of his most problematical poems' ('eines seiner schönsten und zugleich problematischsten Gedichte'). (*Heinrich Heine*, 'Non-stop Bücherei' edition, Berlin Grunewald n.d., p. 31.)
5. This has been well documented by Hannah Arendt in her perceptive biography *Rahel Varnhagen. The Life of a Jewess*, trans. R. and C. Winston, London 1957.
6. *Judaic Lore in Heine*, Baltimore 1948, p. 194.
7. This was a Romantic theme which held many attractions for Heine!
8. *B* IV, 319.
9. *B* IV, 426.
10. *E* I, 550.
11. *B* IV, 413.
12. *B* IV, 511.
13. Werner-Houben, II, 111.
14. *W*, p. 191.
15. *W*, pp. 119–20.
16. Ibid.

17. Ibid., pp. 120–1.
18. Heine's affinities with Grandville have been discussed by H. Thomke in *H-Jb* 17, and by W. Woesler in *Heines Tanzbär. Historisch-literarische Untersuchungen zu "Atta Troll"*, pp. 158–77.
19. *B* IV, 515.
20. *B* IV, 993.
21. *B* IV, 547–8.
22. *B* IV, 547.
23. *B* IV, 547–8.
24. MS in the Heinrich Heine Institut, Düsseldorf.
25. *B* IV, 532.
26. *Heines Tanzbär*, p. 225 *et passim*.
27. *E* II, 531.
28. *B* IV, 516–17; and MS Heinrich Heine Institut, Düsseldorf.
29. *B* IV, 992.
30. *B* IV, 522.
31. *B* IV, 573.
32. *B* IV, 637–8.
33. *B* IV, 605–6. The 'cousin' reference has disappeared from the French version—see *E* II, 544.
34. *B* IV, 641.
35. *B* IV, 585 and 1030.
36. Werner-Houben, I, 555.
37. *B* IV, 613.
38. E. Werner, *Mendelssohn. A New Image of the Composer and his Age*, New York 1963, pp. 36–8; M. Sklare and J. Greenblum, *Jewish Identity on the Suburban Frontier*, 2nd edn. Chicago 1979, pp. 292–3.
39. *B* IV, 601.
40. *B* IV, 1022.
41. *B* IV, 633; *E* II, 547.
42. *B* IV, 589.
43. *B* IV, 683.
44. *B* IV, 626.
45. *B* IV, 627.
46. *B* IV, 627–8.
47. *E* II, 546.
48. Ibid.
49. *Oxford German Studies* VII (1973).
50. N. Reeves, *Heinrich Heine. Poetry and Politics*, pp. 143–4; *HSA* II, 372–3. A political interpretation of this fragment may be found in *Impulse, Aufsätze, Quellen und Berichte zur Klassik*

und Romantik, ed. W. Dietze and P. Goldhammer, Berlin and Weimar 1978, pp. 236–7.

51. *B* IV, 483.

Chapter 10: *Figures in the Gathering Gloom*

1. *B* I, 176. Briegleb's Hanser edition cites this text in a form never authorized by Heine; I have therefore carefully collated it with the text and variant readings in Elster's edition, and with readings cited in the book specified in note 21 below.
2. *B* V, 176.
3. *B* V, 177.
4. Ibid.
5. *B* V, 177–8.
6. *B* V, 178.
7. *B* V, 179.
8. Ibid.
9. *B* V, 179–80.
10. *B* V, 180.
11. Ibid.
12. *B* V, 183.
13. *B* V, 183–4.
14. *B* V, 184.
15. 185–6.
16. *B* V, 187; *Bertolt Brechts Dreigroschenbuch: Texte, Materialien, Dokumente*, ed. S. Unseld, Frankfurt a.M. 1960, p. 80.
17. *B* V, 187.
18. *B* V, 188.
19. Ibid.
20. *B* V, 188–9.
21. These questions are authoritatively discussed by Michael Werner in his *Cahier Heine*, Paris 1975 ('Das "Augsburgische Prokrustesbett". Heines Berichte aus Paris 1840–47 [*Lutezia*] und die Zensur', pp. 42–65.
22. *B* V, 175–6.
23. *B* V, 185.
24. *B* V, 185.
25. *B* V, 186.
26. *B* V, 181.
27. *B* V, 201.
28. See Heine's contributions to the *Augsburg Gazette* discussed in chapter 6.
29. *B* V, 1025.

30. *B* V, 1025–6.
31. *B* V, 1026.
32. Ibid.
33. Ibid.
34. Jewish attitudes to history are authoritatively discussed and illustrated in the works by M. A. Meyer and L. Kochan listed in Section D of the Bibliography at the end of this volume.
35. *B* V, 94 ff.
36. *B* V, 166.
37. *B* V, 166–7.
38. *B* V, 167.
39. H. Becker, *Der Fall Heine-Meyerbeer*, Berlin 1958, p. 102.
40. *B* V, 524.
41. *B* V, 205–7. Cf. A. Weill, *Sittengemälde aus dem elsässischen Volksleben*, 2nd edn., 1852.

Third Intermezzo: *New Companions and Old Butts*

1. M. Werner, *Genius und Geldsack. Zum Problem des Schriftstellerberufs bei Heinrich Heine*, Hamburg 1978, p. 122. Heine's relations with Uncle Salomon, Carl Heine, and Cécile Furtado-Heine, are fully described and documented in L. Rosenthal's *Heinrich Heines Erbschaftsstreit. Hintergründe, Verlauf, Folgen*, Bonn 1982.
2. 'Heine and Cécile Furtado: A Reconsideration', *Modern Language Notes* 89 (1974), pp. 422–47.
3. *B* IV, 420.
4. See the work of Nigel Reeves, cited in notes 49 and 50 of Chapter 9, above.
5. *B* IV, 642.
6. *HSA* XXII, 180.
7. Werner-Houben, II, 25.
8. Alfred Meissner, *Geschichte meines Lebens*, Vienna 1884, I, 220–1.
9. Werner-Houben, I, 404.
10. Fedor Wehl, *Zeit und Menschen*, Altona 1889, I, 125.
11. Werner-Houben, I, 523.
12. *B* VI(i), 534 ff.
13. Werner-Houben, I, 589.
14. Werner-Houben, II, 15–16.
15. P. Audebrand, *Petits Mémoires du dix-neuvième siècle*, Paris 1892, I, 68 f.

16. M. Thomas, 'Heine Franc-Maçon', in M. Windfuhr (ed.), *Internationaler Heine-Kongreß Düsseldorf 1972*, p. 164.

Chapter 11: *Faibisch Apollo*

 1. *B* V, 109.
 2. Barker Fairley, *Heinrich Heine. An Interpretation*, Oxford 1954, *passim*. Cf. *B* III, 654 f.; I, 601; V, 390 f.; VI(i), 392.
 3. *Giselle* was first produced in 1841, with music by Adolphe Adam. It is based on the legend of the Willis, recounted by Heine in *De l'Allemagne*, 1835.
 4. *B* VI(i), 362.
 5. *B* VI(i), 376–7.
 6. *B* VI(i), 39.
 7. *B* VI(i), 40.
 8. H. H. Houben (ed.), *Gespräche mit Heine*, Frankfurt 1926, p. 878.
 9. *B* VI(i), 111.
10. *B* VI(i), 28–30.
11. *B* VI(i), 105–21.
12. *B* VI(i), 60.
13. *B* VI(i), 480.
14. *B* VI(i), 113.
15. *B* VI(i), 105 and 106.
16. *B* VI(i), 120.
17. *B* VI(i), 51.
18. *B* VI(ii), 51.
19. *B* VI(i), 18.
20. *B* VI(i), 105.
21. *B* VI(i), 34 f.
22. Cf. Herman Meyer, *Das Bild des Holländers in der deutschen Literatur (Forschungsprobleme der Vergleichenden Literaturgeschichte)*, Tübingen 1951, pp. 177–88.
23. *B* VI(i), 81.
24. Werner-Houben, II, 112–13.
25. *B* VI(i), 112.
26. see Gustav Karpeles, *Heinrich Heine und seine Zeitgenossen*, Berlin 1888, pp. 89–90.
27. *B* VI(i), 113.

Chapter 12: *Hebrew Melodies*

 1. *B* VI(i), 124; *B* II, 382.

2. *B* VI(i), 116.
3. *B* VI(i), 125.
4. 'Zur Judenfrage', in Karl Marx—Friedrich Engel, *Werke*, Institut für Marxismus-Leninismus beim ZK der SED, Berlin 1972, Vol. I, p. 372 f.
5. *B* VI(i), 126.
6. *B* VI(i), 127.
7. *B* VI(i), 128.
8. *B* VI(i), 129.
9. cf. Ruth L. Jacobi, *Heinrich Heines jüdisches Erbe*, p. 18.
10. The normal Hebrew form of this name is Yehuda Halevi or Yehuda ben Shmuel Halevi. Heine seems to have chosen the form 'Jehuda ben Halevy' for reasons of euphony.
11. *B* VI(i), 129–30.
12. *B* VI(i), 130.
13. *B* VI(i), 131.
14. *B* VI(i), 131–2.
15. *B* VI(i), 133–4.
16. *B* VI(i), 134.
17. *B* VI(i), 135.
18. *B* VI(i), 135–6.
19. *B* VI(i), 136–7.
20. *B* VI(i), 147.
21. *B* VI(i), 148–9.
22. *B* VI(i), 151.
23. *B* VI(i), 141.
24. *B* VI(i), 151–2.
25. *B* VI(i), 153.
26. *B* VI(i), 156.
27. *B* VI(i), 143–4.
28. *B* VI(i), 146.
29. The fullest and best exposition of the story behind the term *shlemihl* may be found in R. M. Copeland and N. Süsskind, *The Language of Herz's 'Ester'. A Study in Judaeo-German Dialectology*, Alabama 1976, p. 167.
30. *B* VI(i), 154–5.
31. *B* VI(i), 155–6.
32. *B* VI(i), 161.
33. *B* VI(i), 163.
34. *B* VI(i), 166–7.
35. *B* VI(i), 168.
36. *B* VI(i), 169.
37. *B* VI(i), 170.

38. *B* VI(i), 172.
39. I am grateful to Professor Gilman for letting me read his essay 'Nietzsche, Heine and the Otherness of the Jew' before publication.
40. *B* VI(i), 182 f.
41. *B* VI(i), 182.
42. *B* VI(i), 185–6.
43. *B* VI(i), 185.
44. cf. Ruth Wolf, 'Versuch über Heines Jehuda ben Halevy', *H-Jb* 18 (1979), p. 91.
45. cf. Gerhard Sauder, 'Blasphemisch-religiöse Körperwelt. Heines "Hebräische Melodien"', in W. Kuttenkeuler (ed.), *Heinrich Heine. Artistik und Engagement*, pp. 118–143.
46. J. L. Sammons, *Heinrich Heine. The Elusive Poet*, p. 387.

Chapter 13: *Moses, Nebuchadnezzar, and Job*

1. *B* IV, 405.
2. *B* IV, 406.
3. *B* VI(i), 277–8.
4. *B* III, 510.
5. *B* III, 511.
6. *B* III, 511–12.
7. *B* III, 512.
8. Ibid.
9. *HAD* VIII(i), 500–1.
10. *HAD* VIII (2), 1606.
11. *HAD* VIII (1), 501–2;
12. *HAD* VIII (2), 1612.
13. *HAD* VIII (2), 1595.
14. *HAD* VIII (2), 1596, 1601.
15. J. Carlebach, *Karl Marx and the Radical Critique of Judaism*, London 1978, pp. 190–2.
16. *B* VI(i), 445.
17. *B* VI(i), 446.
18. *B* VI(i), 455.
19. *B* VI(i), 456–7.
20. cited in E. J. Krzywon's *Heinrich Heine und Polen*, p. 28.
21. *B* VI(i), 471–2.
22. *B* VI(i), 472.
23. *B* VI(i), 473.
24. *HSA* XVII, 172. In this version *Geständnisse* is called *Aveux de*

l'auteur; the earlier version in the *Revue des deux mondes* had borne the title *Aveux d'un poète* (15 September 1854).

25. *B* VI(i), 478–9.
26. See note 59 below.
27. *B* V, 223–7.
28. *B* VI(i), 480.
29. *B* VI(i), 481.
30. Ibid.
31. *B* VI(i), 481–2.
32. *B* VI(i), 483–4.
33. *B* VI(i), 484.
34. *B* VI(i), 486.
35. Ibid.
36. *B* VI(i), 488.
37. *B* VI(i), 487.
38. *B* VI(i), 491.
39. *B* VI(i), 499.
40. *B* VI(i), 499–500.
41. P. Guttenhöfer, *Heinrich Heine und die Bibel*, pp. 53–6 *et passim*.
42. Op cit., p. 157.
43. W. Gößmann, 'Die theologische Revision Heines in der Spätzeit', in M. Windfuhr (ed.), *Internationaler Heine-Kongreß Düsseldorf 1972*, p. 320 f.
44. *B* VI(i), 447.
45. *B* VI(i), 496.
46. *B* VI(i), 498.
47. *B* VI(i), 189 and 239.
47. *B* VI(i), 189.
49. *B* VI(i), 191.
50. *B* VI(i), 213.
51. *B* VI(i), 200.
52. *B* VI(i), 206.
53. *Die Audienz*, *B* VI(i), 231.
54. *B* VI(i), 230.
55. *B* VI(i), 224.
56. *B* VI 358–9.
57. *B* VI(i), 208.
58. *B* VI(i), 413.
59. Cf. E. Weidl, *Heinrich Heines Arbeitsweise. Kreativität der Veränderung*, p. 114.
60. *B* V, 189.
61. *B* V, 189–90.

62. *B* VI(i), 201.
63. *B* V, 190–1.

Chapter 14: *Valkyries and Weather-Frogs*

1. *B* V, 319.
2. *B* V, 425 and 424.
3. Most modern edition spell this *Lutetia*; I have preferred to retain Heine's own spelling.
4. *B* V, 322.
5. *HSA* XIX, 85.
6. *HSA* XIX, 51.
7. *B* V, 354.
8. Ibid.
9. *B* V, 355.
10. Ibid.
11. *B* V, 356.
12. *B* V, 452.
13. *B* V, 452–3.
14. *B* V, 453.
15. Ibid.
16. Ibid.
17. *B* V, 454–5.
18. *HSA* XIX, 193.
19. *B* V, 455–6.
20. *B* V, 456.
21. *B* V, 287f.
22. *B* V, 284.
23. *B* V, 287–8.
24. *B* V, 290.
25. *B* V, 456.
26. *B* V, 451.
27. Ibid.
28. *B* III, 510.
29. *B* V, 200.
30. *B* V, 466.
31. Marx's 'indulgent attitude' to Heine is well documented and described in Nigel Reeves's *Heinrich Heine. Poetry and Politics*, pp. 152–9.
32. Werner-Houben, II, 289.
33. *B* V, 440.
34. *B* V, 469–70.
35. *B* V, 470.

36. M. Mann, *Heines Musikkritiken*, pp. 51–2, 60, 104–5 *et passim*; P. U. Hohendahl, 'Kunsturteil und Tagesbericht. Zur ästhetischen Theorie des späten Heine', in W. Kuttenkeuler (ed.), *Heinrich Heine. Artistik und Engagement*, pp. 227–8.

37. *B* V, 542.

38. *HSA* X, 49.

39. *B* V, 291.

40. *B* V, 292.

41. *B* V, 296–7.

42. *B* V, 363.

43. *B* V, 363–4.

44. *B* V, 364.

45. Ibid.

46. *B* V, 547–8.

47. *B* V, 444.

48. *B* V, 446.

49. *B* V, 444.

50. *B* V, 444–5.

51. *B* V, 492.

52. *HSA* XIX, 228.

53. H. H. Houben (ed.), *Gespräche mit Heine*, Frankfurt 1926, p. 485. The source is Varnhagen von Ense.

54. *B* V, 529–30.

55. *B* V, 530.

56. *B* V, 439.

57. *B* V, 535.

58. *HSA* XIX, 72.

59. *B* V, 482 f. and 1020 f.

60. *B* V, 510.

61. *B* V, 546.

62. *B* V, 219–20.

63. *B* V, 239.

64. *HSA* XIX, 14.

65. The corresponding German version reads: 'die Nachkömmlinge Israels, des reinen auserlesenen Priestervolks'. *B* V, 285.

Chapter 15: '*In my end is my Beginning*'

1. Werner-Houben, II, 511. For the most authoritative account of the nature and status of the *Memoiren*-fragment and the prologue editors usually prefix to it, see M. Werner's 'Les *Mémoires* de Heine. L'Histoire d'un manuscrit et le manuscrit d'une histoire' in *Cahier Heine II: Écriture et Genèse*, Paris 1981, pp. 39–59.

2. *B* VI(i), 555; *L* 3. My translations follow the text in *L*.
3. *B* VI(i), 556; *L* 4.
4. Werner-Houben, I, 24–5.
5. *B* VI(i), 557; *L* 6.
6. *B* VI(i), 560; *L* 12.
7. *B* VI(i), 559 f.; *L* 11 f.
8. *B* VI(i), 562; *L* 14.
9. *B* VI(i), 567; *L* 27.
10. *B* VI(i), 566; *L* 26.
11. *B* VI(i), 571 f.; *L* 35 f.
12. The evidence has been fully presented in Ludwig Rosenthal's *Heinrich Heines Großoheim Simon von Geldern. Ein historischer Bericht.*
13. *B* VI(i), 572–3; *L* 35–6.
14. *B* VI(i), 574; *L* 36.
15. *B* VI(i), 574–5; *L* 40.
16. *B* VI(i), 576; *L* 41–2.
17. Ibid.
18. *B* VI(i), 577–8; *L* 43.
19. *B* VI(i), 589 f. 591 f.
20. *B* VI(i), 413.
21. *B* III, 394.
22. *B* VI(i), 578; *L* 44.
23. *B* VI(i), 578; *L* 44–5.
24. *B* VI(i), 579 f; *L* 45 f.
25. *B* VI(i), 579; *L* 45.
26. *B* VI(i), 583–4; *L* 53–4.
27. *B* VI(i), 586–7; *L* 58–9.
28. *B* VI(i), 584; *L* 54–7.
29. *B* VI(i), 587; *L* 60–1.
30. *B* VI(i), 590; *L* 64.
31. *B* VI(i), 593; 88–9. *Koved* is honour, *yikhes* family reputation, *tsedaka* is charity, and *mitsvot* are meritorious acts.
32. *B* VI(i), 593; *L* 89.
33. e.g. *B* VI(i), 466–7: 'Wir haben jetzt fanatische Mönche des Atheismus, Großinquisitoren des Unglaubens . . .'
34. *B* VI(i), 608; *L* 86.
35. *B* VI(i), 325.
36. *B* VI(i), 322.
37. *B* VI(i), 322–3.
38. *B* VI(i), 324.
39. *B* VI(i), 325.
40. *B* VI(i), 325.

41. *B* VI(i), 296.
42. *B* VI(i), 296–7.
43. *B* VI(i), 297.
44. *B* VI(i), 298.
45. *B* VI(i), 300.
46. *B* VI(i), 299.
47. *B* VI(i), 302–3.
48. *B* VI(i), 528.
49. *B* VI(i), 529–30.
50. *HSA* XVI, 214.
51. *B* VI(i), 527.
52. *B* VI(i), 281.
53. *B* VI(i), 287.
54. *B* VI(i), 312–13.
55. *B* VI(i), 332–3.
56. P. Guttenhöfer, *Heine und die Bibel*, p. 160.
57. *B* VI(i), 201–2.
58. *B* VI(i), 262
59. *B* VI(i), 349.
60. *B* V, 116–17.

Fourth Intermezzo: *Civilization of the Heart*

1. H. H. Houben, *Gespräche mit Heine*, Frankfurt 1926, pp. 896, 814, 668–9, 596, 609, 712–13, 901; Werner-Houben, I, 269.
2. *B* VI(i), 541–2.
3. H. H. Houben, *Gespräche mit Heine*, 2nd edn., Potsdam 1948, p. 1064. The source is Alfred Meissner.
4. H. H. Houben, *Gespräche mit Heine*, Frankfurt 1926, pp. 802, 813.
5. *B* VI(i), 543.
6. *B* VI(i), 546. A reliable calculation of Heine's income in the course of his life, including the considerable sums he received from his Hamburg relatives, can be found in Michael Werner's *Genius und Geldsack. Zum Problem des Schriftstellerberufs bei Heinrich Heine.*
7. *B* VI(i), 546.
8. *B* VI(i), 548–9.
9. R. Booß, 'Dialekteigentümlichkeiten bei Heine', in M. Windfuhr (ed.), *Internationaler Heine-Kongreß Düsseldorf 1972*, pp. 520–1.
10. Werner-Houben, II, 289.
11. Houben, *Gespräche*, 1926, pp. 626, 772, 954.

12. Werner-Houben, II, 396.
13. Houben, *Gespräche*, *1926*, *p. 837*.
14. Werner-Houben, I, 213.
15. Houben, *Gespräche*, 1926, p. 611.
16. Ibid., pp. 735–6.
17. Ibid., p. 976.
18. Ibid., pp. 646–7.
19. Werner-Houben, II, 117.
20. Ibid., II, 155.
21. Ibid., II, 185–6.
22. Ibid., II, 125.
23. Ibid., II, 272.
24. Ibid., II, 175.
25. Ibid., II, 215.
26. Ibid., II, 231.
27. Ibid., II, 230–1.
28. Ibid., II, 230.
29. Houben, *Gespräche*, 1926, p. 805.
30. Werner-Houben, II, 176.
31. Ibid., II, 401.
32. Ibid., II, 236.
33. Ibid., II, 126.
34. Houben, *Gespräche*, 1926, p. 792.
35. Werner-Houben, II, 273.
36. Ibid., II, 395.
37. Ibid.
38. Ibid.
39. Ibid., II, 347.
40. Ibid., II, 243.
41. Ibid., II, 441.
42. Ibid., II, 152.
43. Ibid., II, 174.
44. *B* VI(i), 618.
45. *B* VI(i), 639.
46. *B* VI(i), 622.
47. Ibid.
48. *B* VI(i), 634.
49. *B* VI(i), 635.
50. *B* VI(i), 635.
51. *B* VI(i), 634.
52. *B* VI(i), 622.
53. *B* VI(i), 639.
54. *B* VI(i), 652.

55. *B* VI(i), 642 and 659.
56. *B* VI(i), 653 and 652.
57. *B* VI(i), 651.
58. *B* VI(i), 652.
59. *B* VI(i), 641.
60. *B* VI(i), 668.
61. *B* VI(i), 658.
62. *B* VI(i), 664.
63. *B* VI(i), 665.
64. *B* VI(i), 633.
65. *B* VI(i), 665.
66. Ibid.
67. *B* VI(i), 660. Both these suggestions were used in works Heine saw through the press.
68. *B* VI(i), 667.
69. *B* VI(i), 650.
70. *B* VI(i), 667.
71. *B* VI(i), 666.

Conclusion

1. J. L. Sammons, *Heinrich Heine. A Modern Biography*, p. 348.
2. W. J. Bate, *Samuel Johnson*, New York 1977, p. 480 f.
3. P. Rahv, *Essays on Literature and Politics 1932–1972*, ed. A. J. Porter and A. J. Dvosin, Boston 1978, p. 319.
4. Werner-Houben, I, 245 (letter to Jeanette Wohl, 27 October 1831).
5. Werner-Houben, II, 483 (letter to Alfred Meissner, 7 August 1856).
6. *The Collected Works of Isaac Rosenberg*, ed. I. M. Parsons, London 1979, p. 242.
7. Cited by E. R. Malachi, *Mekubolim in Erets Yisrael*, New York 1928, p. 83. I owe this reference to Professor S. L. Gilman.

SELECT BIBLIOGRAPHY

For full bibliographical information see Gottfried Wilhelm and Eberhard Galley: *Heine-Bibliographie* (Weimar 1960); Siegfried Seifert: *Heine-Bibliographie 1954–1964* (Berlin and Weimar 1968); and the annual bibliographical supplement of the *Heine-Jahrbuch*.

A. Principal Editions Consulted

Heinrich Heine. Historisch-Kritische Gesamtausgabe der Werke (Düsseldorfer Ausgabe), ed. M. Windfuhr *et al.*, Hamburg 1973 ff. (in progress) (*HAD*).

Heinrich Heine. Säkularausgabe, ed. Nationale Forschungs- und Gedenkstätten der klassischen deutschen Literatur in Weimar and Centre National de la Recherche Scientifique in Paris, Berlin and Paris 1970 ff. (in progress) (*HSA*).

Heinrich Heine. Sämtliche Schriften, ed. K. Briegleb *et al.*, Munich 1968–76 (*B*).

Heines Sämtliche Werke, ed. E. Elster, Leipzig and Vienna 1887–90 (*E*).

Der Prosanachlaß von Heinrich Heine, ed. E. Loewenthal, in *Heines Werke in Einzelausgaben*, ed. G. A. E. Bogeng, Vol. 12, Hamburg 1925 (*L*).

Heinrich Heine: Atta Troll. Ein Sommernachtstraum, ed. W. Woesler, Stuttgart 1977 (*W*).

Heinrich Heine: Deutschland. Ein Wintermärchen, ed. W. Gössmann and W. Woesler (*Politische Dichtung im Unterricht*), Düsseldorf 1974.

Heinrich Heine: Zeitungsberichte über Musik und Malerei, ed. M. Mann, Frankfurt a.M. 1964.

Heinrich Heine: Briefe, ed. F. Hirth, Mainz 1950–51.

Gespräche mit Heine, ed. H. H. Houben, Frankfurt a. M. 1926

Begegnungen mit Heine. Berichte der Zeitgenossen. In Fortführung von H. H. Houbens "Gespräche mit Heine", ed. M. Werner, 2 Vols., Hamburg 1973 (Werner-Houben).

Dichter über ihre Dichtungen: Heinrich Heine, ed. N. and R. Altenhofer, Munich 1971.

Heinrich Heine: Confessio Judaica. Eine Auswahl aus seinen Dichtungen, Schriften und Briefen, ed. H. Bieber, Berlin 1925.

B. *Some English Versions of Heine's Writings*

The Prose and Poetical Works, C. G. Leland, 20 vols., New York 1900.

Prose and Poetry, trans. T. Martin and others, ed. E. Rhys, London 1934.

Heinrich Heine: Self Portrait and other Prose Writings, trans. F. Ewen, Secaucus, N. J., 1948.

A Biographical Anthology, trans. M. Hadas, ed. H. Bieber, Philadelphia 1956.

Religion and Philosophy in Germany. A Fragment, trans J. Snodgrass, Boston 1959.

Heine. Selected Verse, ed. and trans. P. Branscombe, Harmondsworth 1967.

Selected Works, trans. H. M. Mustard and M. Knight, New York 1973.

The Sword and the Flame: Selections from Heinrich Heine's Prose, ed. A. Werner, New York 1960.

Lyric Poems and Ballads, trans. E. Feise, Pittsburgh 1961.

The Poetry of Heinrich Heine, ed. F. Ewen, trans. A. Kramer, L. Untermeyer, E. Lazarus, et. al., New York 1969.

The Lazarus Poems, trans. A. Elliot, Manchester 1979.

The Complete Poems of Heinrich Heine. A Modern English Version, trans. H. Draper, Boston and Oxford 1982.

C. *Heine's Portraits of Jews and Judaism*

Abels, K, 'Zum Scharfrichtermotiv im Werk Heinrich Heines', *Heine-Jahrbuch* 12 (1973) (*H-Jb*).

Adorno, T. W., 'Die Wunde Heine', in *Noten zur Literatur* I, Frankfurt 1958.

Altman, S., *The Comic Image of the Jew. Exploration of a Pop-Culture Phenomenon*, Cranbury, N. J. 1971.

Arendt, D., 'Parabolische Dichtung und politische Tendenz. Eine Episode aus den "Bädern von Lucca"', *H-Jb.* 9 (1970).

Becker, H., *Der Fall Heine-Meyerbeer. Neue Dokumente revidieren ein Geschichtsurteil*, Berlin 1958.

Becker, K. W., *et al.*, (eds.), *Heinrich Heine. Streitbarer Humanist und volksverbundener Dichter*, Weimar 1973.

Betz, A., *Ästhetik und Politik. Heinrich Heines Prosa*, Munich 1971.

Betz, L. P., *Heine in Frankreich. Eine literarhistorische Untersuchung*, Zurich 1895.

Bienenstock, M., *Das jüdische Element in Heines Werken*, Leipzig 1910.

Bloemerz, W., *Die Personenschilderungen in Heines journalistischen Berichten*, Düsseldorf 1909.

Börne, Ludwig, *Sämtliche Schriften*, ed. I. and P. Rippmann, Düsseldorf 1964 f.

Borries, M., *Ein Angriff auf Heinrich Heine. Betrachtungen zu Karl Kraus*, Stuttgart 1971.

Brod, Max, *Heinrich Heine*, Amsterdam 1934.

Brummack, J., *Satirische Dichtung. Studien zu Fr. Schlegel, Tieck, Jean Paul und Heine*, Munich 1979.

Brummack, J. (ed.), *Heinrich Heine. Epoche—Werk—Wirkung*, Munich 1980.

Clarke, M. A., *Heine et la Monarchie de Juillet. Etude sur les "Französische Zustände" suivi d'une étude sur le Saint-Simonisme chez Heine*, Paris 1927.

Cohn, H., *Heinrich Heine: The Man and the Myth* (Leo Baeck Memorial Lecture, 2), New York 1959.

Dresch, J., *Heine à Paris (1831–1856)*, Paris 1956.

Eisner, F. H., 'Einige Rätsel in Heines Leben', *H-Jb* 7 (1968).

Fairley, B., *Heinrich Heine. An Interpretation*, Oxford 1954.

Feuchtwanger, Lion, *Heines "Der Rabbi von Bacherach". Eine kritische Studie*, Diss. Munich 1907.

Fingerhut, K.-H., *Standortbestimmungen. Vier Untersuchungen zu Heinrich Heine*, Heidenheim 1971.

Finke, F., 'Zur Datierung des "Rabbi von Bacherach"', *H-Jb* 4 (1965).

Fuhrmann, A., *Recht und Staat bei Heinrich Heine*, Bonn 1961.

Freud, Sigmund, *Der Witz und seine Beziehung zum Unbewußten*, Leipzig and Vienna 1905 (reprinted in *Studienausgabe*, Vol. IV, Frankfurt 1970).

Galley, E., *Heinrich Heine*, 4th rev. edn., Stuttgart 1976.

Galley, E., and A. Estermann (eds.), *Heinrich Heines Werk im Urteil seiner Zeitgenossen*, Vol. I, Hamburg 1981.

Gößmann, W., *et al.* (eds.), *Geständnisse. Heine im Bewußtsein heutiger Autoren*, Düsseldorf 1972.

Großklaus, G., *Textstruktur und Textgeschichte. Die "Reisebilder" Heinrich Heines*, Frankfurt a. M. 1973.

Grubačič, S., *Heines Erzählprosa*, Stuttgart 1975.
Guttenhöfer, P., *Heinrich Heine und die Bibel*, Diss. Munich 1970.

Hansen, V., *Thomas Manns Heine-Rezeption*, Hamburg 1975.
Hatfield, H., *Clashing Myths in German Literature from Heine to Rilke*, Cambridge (Mass.) 1974.
Heinrich Heine und die Zeitgenossen. Geschichtliche und literarische Befunde, ed. Akademie der Wissenschaften der DDR, Zentralinstitut für Literaturgeschichte, and Centre National de la Recherche Scientifique, Centre d'Histoire et d'Analyse des Manuscrits Modernes, Berlin and Weimar 1979.
Hengst, H., *Idee und Ideologieverdacht. Revolutionäre Implikationen des deutschen Idealismus im Kontext der zeitkritischen Prosa Heinrich Heines*, Munich 1973.
Hermand, J., *Streitobjekt Heine. Ein Forschungsbericht 1945–75*, Frankfurt a.M. 1975.
Heymann, F., *Der Chevalier von Geldern. Eine Chronik der Abenteuer der Juden*, Köln 1963.
Hinderer, W., 'Nazarener oder Hellene. Die politisch-ästhetische Fehde zwischen Börne und Heine', *Monatshefte* 66 (1974).
Hirth, F., *Heinrich Heine und seine französischen Freunde*, Mainz 1949.
Hirth, F., *Heinrich Heine. Bausteine zu einer Biographie*, Mainz 1950.
Höllerer, W., *Zwischen Klassik und Moderne. Lachen und Weinen in der Dichtung einer Übergangszeit*, Stuttgart 1958.
Holub, R. C., *Heinrich Heine's Reception of German Graecophilia. The Function and Application of the Hellenic Tradition in the First Half of the Nineteenth Century*, Heidelberg 1981.
Hörling, H., *Heinrich Heine im Spiegel der politischen Presse Frankreichs von 1831 bis 1841*, Frankfurt a.M. 1977.

Immerwahr, R., and H. Spencer (eds.), *Heinrich Heine. Dimensionen seines Wirkens. Ein internationales Heine-Symposium*, Bonn 1979.

Jacobi, R. L., *Heinrich Heines jüdisches Erbe*, Bonn 1978.
Jacobs, J., 'Zu Heines "Ideen. Das Buch LeGrand"', *H-Jb* 8 (1969).
Johnston, O. W., 'Signatura Temporis in Heines "Lutezia"', *The German Quarterly* 47 (1974).

Käfer, K.-H, *Versöhnt ohne Opfer. Zum geschichtstheologischen*

Rahmen der Schriften Heinrich Heines, 1824–1844, Meisenheim 1978.

Kanowsky, W., *Vernunft und Geschichte. Heinrich Heines Studium als Grundlegung seiner Welt und seiner Kunstanschauung*, Bonn 1975.

Karger, I., *Heinrich Heine. Literarische Aufklärung und wirkbetonte Textstruktur. Untersuchungen zum Tierbild*, Göppingen 1975.

Karpeles, G., *Heinrich Heine: Aus seinem Leben und aus seiner Zeit*, Leipzig 1899.

Kaufmann, D., *Aus Heinrich Heines Ahnensaal*, Breslau 1896.

Kaufmann, H., *Heinrich Heine. Geistige Entwicklung und künstlerisches Werk*, Berlin and Weimar 1967.

Kircher, H., *Heinrich Heine und das Judentum*, Bonn 1973.

Koopmann, H. (ed.), *Heinrich Heine (Wege der Forschung)*, Darmstadt 1975.

Kreutzer, L., *Heine und der Kommunismus*, Göttingen 1970.

Kruse, J. A., *Heines Hamburger Zeit*, Hamburg 1972.

Kruse, J. A., ' "Ein Abkömmling jener Martyrer . . .", Heinrich Heine und das Judentum', *Emuna* 12 (1977).

Kurz, P. K., *Künstler Tribun Apostel. Heinrich Heines Auffassung vom Beruf des Dichters*, Munich 1967.

Kuttenkeuler, W., *Heinrich Heine: Theorie und Kritik der Literatur*, Stuttgart 1972.

Kuttenkeuler, W. (ed.), *Heinrich Heine. Artistik und Engagement*, Stuttgart 1977.

Krzywon, J. K., *Heinrich Heine und Polen. Ein Beitrag zur Poetik der politischen Dichtung zwichen Romantik und Realismus*, Cologne and Vienna 1972.

Lasher-Schlitt, D., 'Heine's Unresolved Conflict and "Der Rabbi von Bacherach"', *Germanic Review* 27 (1952).

Lea, C. A., *Emancipation, Assimilation and Stereotype. The Image of the Jew in German and Austrian Drama (1800–1850)*, Bonn 1978.

Lefebvre, J.-P., *Heine et Hegel. Philosophie de l'histoire et histoire de la philosophie*, Diss. Paris 1975.

Lehmann, U., *Popularisierung und Ironie im Werk Heinrich Heines. Die Bedeutung der textimmanenten Kontrastierung für den Rezeptionsprozeß*, Frankfurt and Bern 1976.

Lehrmann, C. C., *Heinrich Heine: Kämpfer und Dichter*, Bern 1957.

Loeb, E., *Heinrich Heine. Weltbild und geistige Gestalt*, Bonn 1975.

Loewenthal, E., *Studien zu Heines Reisebildern* (Palaestra 138), Berlin and Leipzig 1922.

Loewenthal, E., ' "Der Rabbi von Bacherach" ', *H-Jb* 3 (1964).

Lukács, G., 'Heine und die ideologische Vorbereitung der 48er Revolution', in *Text + Kritik* 18/19 (new edn. 1971).

Lüth, E., *Der Bankier und der Dichter. Zur Ehrenrettung des großen Salomon Heine*, Hamburg n.d.

Lüth, E., *Hamburgs Juden in der Heine-Zeit*, Hamburg 1961.

Maier, W., *Leben, Tat und Reflexion. Untersuchungen zu Heinrich Heines Ästhetik*, Bonn 1969.

Mann, M., *Heinrich Heines Musikkritiken*, Hamburg 1971.

Marcuse, L., *Heinrich Heine. Ein Leben zwischen Gestern und Morgen*, Berlin 1932.

Marcuse, L., *Essays, Porträts, Polemiken*, ed. H. v. Hofe, Zürich 1979.

Mayer, H., *Von Lessing bis Thomas Mann. Wandlungen der bürgerlichen Literatur in Deutschland*, Pfullingen 1959.

Mayer, H., *Außenseiter*, Frankfurt a. M. 1975.

Mende, F. (ed.), *Heinrich Heine. Chronik seines Lebens und Werkes*, Berlin 1970.

Möller, D., *Heinrich Heine: Episodik und Werkeinheit*, Wiesbaden and Frankfurt a. M. 1973.

Na'aman, S., 'Heine und Lassalle. Ihre Beziehungen im Zeichen der Dämonie des Geldes', *Archiv für Sozialgeschichte* IV (1964).

Netter, L., 'Heine, l'affaire des juifs de Damas et la presse parisienne' *H-Jb* 11 (1972).

Oesterle, G., *Integration und Konflikt. Die Prosa Heinrich Heines im Kontext oppositioneller Literatur der Restaurationsepoche*, Stuttgart 1972.

Ott, B., *La Querelle de Heine et de Börne. Contribution à l'étude des idées politiques et sociales en Allemagne de 1830 à 1840*, Diss. Lille, n.d.

Pabel, K., *Heines Reisebilder. Ästhetisches Bedürfnis und politisches Interesse am Ende der Kunstperiode*, Munich 1977.

Paucker, H.-R. *Heinrich Heine. Mensch und Dichter zwischen Deutschland und Frankreich*, Bern 1970.

Pazi, M., 'Die biblischen und jüdischen Einflüsse in Heines "Nordsee"-Gedichten', *H-Jb* 13 (1974).

Plotke, G. J., *Heinrich Heine als Dichter des Judentums. Ein Versuch*. Leipzig 1913.

Prawer, S. S., *Heine's Buch der Lieder*, London 1960.

Prawer, S. S., *Heine: The Tragic Satirist. A Study of the Later Poetry, 1826–1856*, Cambridge 1961.

Preisendanz, W., *Heinrich Heine. Werkstrukturen und Epochenbezüge*, Munich 1973.

Puetzfeld, C., *Heinrich Heines Verhältnis zur Religion (Bonner Forschungen. Schriften der literarhistorischen Gesellschaft*, Neue Folge 3), Bonn 1912.

Radlik, U., 'Heine in der Zensur der Restaurationsepoche', in: *Zur Literatur der Restaurationsepoche 1815–1848*, ed. J. Hermand and M. Windfuhr. Stuttgart 1970.

Raphael, J., 'Heines Marchese Gumpelino', in: *Text + Kritik* 18/19 (new edn. 1971).

Reeves, N., *Heinrich Heine. Poetry and Politics*, Oxford 1974.

Reich-Ranicki, M., *Über Ruhestörer. Juden in der deutschen Literatur*, Frankfurt 1977.

Rippmann, I., 'Heines Denkschrift über Börne. Ein Doppelportrait, *H.-Jb* 12 (1973).

Rose, M. A., 'Über die strukturelle Einheit von Heines Fragment "Der Rabbi von Bacherach"', *H-Jb* 15 (1976).

Rose, M. A., *Die Parodie. Eine Funktion der biblischen Sprache in Heines Lyrik*, Meisenheim 1976.

Rose, W., *Heinrich Heine. Two Studies of his Thought and Feeling*, Oxford 1956.

Rose, W., *The Early Love Poetry of Heinrich Heine. An Enquiry into Poetic Inspiration*, Oxford 1962.

Rosenthal, L., *Heinrich Heine als Jude*, Frankfurt a.M. 1973.

Rosenthal, L., *Heinrich Heines Großoheim Simon von Geldern. Ein historischer Bericht*, Kastellaun 1978.

Rosenthal, L., *Heinrich Heines Erbschaftsstreit. Hintergründe, Verlauf, Folgen*, Bonn 1982.

Sammons, J., 'Heine's Rabbi von Bacherach: The Unresolved Tensions', *The German Quarterly* 37 (1964).

Sammons, J., *Heinrich Heine. The Elusive Poet*, New Haven and London 1969.

Sammons, J., *Heinrich Heine. A Modern Biography*, Princeton 1979.

Sandor, A. I., *The Exile of Gods. Interpretation of a Theme, a Theory, and a Technique in the Work of Heinrich Heine*, The Hague and Paris 1967.

Schmitz, G., *Über die ökonomischen Anschauungen in Heines Werken*, Weimar 1960.

Schnee, H., *Heinrich Heines Ahnen als Hofjuden deutscher Fürstenhöfe*, Munich 1944.

Schulte, K. H. S., 'Das letzte Jahrzehnt von Heinrich Heines Vater in Düsseldorf', *H-Jb* 13 (1974).

Seeba, H. C., 'Die Kinder des Pygmalion: Die Bildlichkeit des Kunstbegriffs bei Heine. Beobachtungen zur Tendenzwende der Ästhetik', *Deutsche Vierteljahrsschrift* 50 (1976).

Selden, Camille [= Krinitz, E.], *Les Derniers Jours de H. Heine*, Paris 1884.

Sengle, F., *Biedermeierzeit. Deutsche Literatur im Spannungsfeld zwischen Restauration und Revolution, 1815–1848*, Stuttgart 1971 ff.

Siegrist, C., 'Heines Traumbilder', *H-Jb* 4 (1965).

Simon, M., 'Hebräisches und Jüdisch-deutsches Sprachgut bei Heine', *Yediot Khadashot*, 25 March 1956, p. 6.

Spann, M., *Heine*, London 1966

Spencer, H., *Dichter, Denker, Journalist. Studien zum Werk Heinrich Heines*, Bern 1977.

Steinhauer, H., 'Heinrich Heine', *The Antioch Review*, Winter 1956–7.

Steinhauer, H., 'Heine and Cécile Furtado: A Reconsideration', *Mod. Lang. Notes* 89 (1972).

Stern, J. P., *Reinterpretations. Seven Studies in Nineteenth-Century German Literature*, London 1964.

Stern, J. P., *Idylls and Realities. Studies in Nineteenth-Century Germany Literature*, London 1971.

Sternberger, D., *Heinrich Heine und die Abschaffung der Sünde*, Hamburg and Düsseldorf 1972 (augmented paperback edn. Frankfurt 1976).

Storz, G., *Heinrich Heines lyrische Dichtung*, Stuttgart 1971.

Strodtmann, A., *Heinrich Heines Leben und Werke*, 2nd (rev.) edn. Berlin 1873–74.

Tabak, I., *Judaic Lore in Heine*, Baltimore 1948.

Thomke, H., 'Heine und Grandville', *H-Jb* 17 (1978).

Untermeyer, L., *Heinrich Heine: Paradox and Poet*, New York 1937.

Veit, P. F., 'Fichtenbaum und Palme', *Germanic Review* 51 (1956).

Veit, P. F., 'Rätsel um Heines Geburt', *H-Jb* 1 (1962).

Veit, P. F., 'Heine and his Cousins. A Reconsideration', *Germanic Review* 47 (1972).

Veit, P. F., 'Heine: The Marrano Pose', *Monatshefte* 66 (1974).

Veit, P. F., 'Heinrich Heine and David Friedländer', *H-Jb* 19 (1980).

Victor, W., *Marx und Heine*, Berlin 1970.

Wadepuhl, W., *Heine-Studien*, Weimar 1956.
Weidl, E., *Heinrich Heines Arbeitsweise. Kreativität der Veränderung*, Hamburg 1974.
Weigand, H. J., 'Heine's Return to God', *Modern Philology* 18 (1920).
Weinberg, K., *Henri Heine, "Romantique défroqué": Héraut du Symbolisme français*, New Haven and Paris 1954.
Weiss, W., *Enttäuschter Pantheismus. Zur Weltgestaltung der Dichtung in der Restaurationszeit*, Dornbirn 1982.
Werner, M., *Genius und Geldsack. Zum Problem des Schriftstellerberufs bei Heinrich Heine*, Hamburg 1978.
Werner, M. (ed.), *Cahier Heine*, Paris 1975.
Werner, M. (ed.), *Cahier Heine II: Écriture et Genèse*, Paris 1981.
von Wiese, B., *Signaturen. Zu Heinrich Heine und seinem Werk*, Berlin 1976.
Windfuhr, M., *Heinrich Heine. Revolution und Reflexion*, 2nd rev. edn., Stuttgart 1976.
Windfuhr, M. (ed.), *Internationaler Heine-Kongreß Düsseldorf 1972: Referate und Diskussionen*, Hamburg 1973.
Woesler, W., *Heines Tanzbär. Historisch-literarische Untersuchungen zu "Atta Troll"*, Hamburg 1978.
Wolf, R., 'Versuch über Heines "Jehuda ben Halevy"', *H-Jb* 18 (1979).

Zagari, L., and P. Chiarini, *Zu Heinrich Heine*, Stuttgart 1981.
Zeitschrift für deutsche Philologie 91 (1972): *Heine und seine Zeit* (Sonderheft).
Zeldner, M., 'Heinrich Heine, the German-Jewish Poet', *Jewish Frontier*, March 1973.
Zepf, I., 'Exilschilderung in Heines Prosaschriften', *Emuna* 10 (1975).
Zepf, I., *Heinrich Heines Gemäldebericht zum Salon 1831. Denkbilder. Eine Untersuchung der Schrift "Französische Maler"*, Munich 1980.
Zohn, H., 'Heinrich Heine. A Reassessment', *Jewish Perspectives*, ed. J. Sonntag, London 1980.

D. *Jewish History in and up to Heine's Time*

The *Encyclopaedia Judaica*, the *Jahrbuch des Instituts für deutsche Geschichte* (Tel Aviv), and above all the Year Books and Bulletins of the Leo Baeck Institute, are treasure-troves of essays on all aspects of German-Jewish history into which I have had constant occasion to delve. The Leo Baeck Institute Year Books also contain, from 1956 onwards, annual Bibliographies of Post-War Publications on German Jewry. Among other books I have consulted with profit are the following:

Adler, H. G., *Die Juden in Deutschland. Von der Aufklärung bis zum Nationalsozialismus*, Munich 1960.

Altmann, A., *Moses Mendelssohn. A Biographical Study*, London 1973.

Arendt, H., *Rahel Varnhagen. The Life of a Jewess*, trans. R. and C. Winston, London 1957.

Arendt, H., *The Jew as Pariah. Jewish Identity and Politics in the Modern Age*, New York 1971.

Baron, S. W., *A Social and Religious History of the Jews*, New York 1958 f.

Basnage, J., *L'histoire et la religion des Juifs depuis Jésus-Christ jusqu' à présent*, The Hague 1706–11.

Böhm, F., W. Dirks, and W. Gottschalk (ed.), *Judentum. Schicksal, Wesen und Gegenwart*, Wiesbaden 1965.

Cahnmann, W., 'A Regional Approach to German-Jewish History', *Jewish Social Studies*, V, 3 (1943).

Carlebach. J., *Karl Marx and the Radical critique of Judaism*, London 1978.

Carmely, C. P., *Das Identitätsproblem jüdischer Autoren im deutschen Sprachraum. Von der Jahrhundertwende bis zu Hitler*, Königstein/Taunus 1981.

Drewitz, I., *Berliner Salons. Gesellschaft und Literatur zwischen Aufklärung und Industriezeitalter*, Berlin 1965.

Dubnow, S., *Weltgeschichte des jüdischen Volkes*, Berlin 1920–23.

Eichstädt, V., *Bibliographie zur Geschichte der Judenfrage*, Vol. I, Hamburg 1938.

Eisenberg, J., *Une Histoire du peuple juif*, Paris 1974.

Gilbert, F., *Bismarckian Society's Image of the Jew* (Leo Baeck Memorial Lecture 22), New York 1978.

Glatzer, N. N. (ed.), *Leopold and Adelheid Zunz. An Account in Letters*, London 1958.

Select Bibliography 815

Grab, W., 'Saul Ascher', *Jahrbuch des Instituts für deutsche Geschichte*, 6 (1977).

Graetz, H. H. , *Geschichte der Juden von den ältesten Zeiten bis auf die Gegenwart*, rev. edn., Leipzig 1897—1911.

Gross, N. (ed.), *Economic History of the Jews*, New York 1975.

Hess, M., *Rom und Jerusalem*, Leipzig 1862.

Hertzberg, A., *The French Enlightenment and the Jews. The Origins of Modern Anti-Semitism*, New York 1968.

Jost, I. M., *Neuere Geschichte der Israeliten von 1815 bis 1845*, Berlin 1846–7.

Katz, J., *Tradition and Crisis. Jewish Society at the End of the Middle Ages*, New York 1961.

Katz, J., *Jews and Freemasons in Europe, 1723–1839*, Cambridge (Mass.) 1970.

Katz, J., *Emancipation and Assimilation. Studies in Modern Jewish History*, Farnborough 1972.

Katz, J., *Out of the Ghetto. The Social Background of Jewish Emancipation, 1770–1870*, Cambridge (Mass.) 1973.

Kedourie, E. (ed.) *The Jewish World. Revelation, Prophecy and History*, London 1979.

Kochan, L., *The Jew and His History*, London 1977.

Krohn, H., *Die Juden in Hamburg 1800–1850. Ihre soziale, kulturelle und politische Entwicklung während der Emanzipationszeit*, Frankfurt, 1967.

Leschnitzer, A., *Saul und David. Zur Problematik der deutsch-jüdischen Lebensgemeinschaft*, Heidelberg 1954.

Liebeschütz, H. and A. Paucker (eds.), *Das Judentum in der deutschen Umwelt. Studien zu Frühgeschichte der Emanzipation, 1800–1850*, Tübingen 1977.

Liptzin, S., *Germany's Stepchildren*, Philadelphia 1944.

Mahler, R., *A History of Modern Jewry, 1780–1815*, London 1971.

Meyer, M. A., *The Origins of the Modern Jew. Jewish Identity and European Culture in Germany, 1749–1824*, Detroit 1967.

Meyer, M. A. (ed.), *Ideas of Jewish History*, New York 1974.

Mosse, G. L., *Towards the Final Solution. A History of European Racism*, London 1979.

Poliakov, L., *The History of Anti-Semitism*, Vol III: *From Voltaire to Wagner*, trans. M. Kochan, London 1975.

Pollack, H., *Jewish Folkways in Germanic Lands (1648–1806). Studies in Aspects of Daily Life*, Cambridge (Mass.) 1971.

Reichmann, E. G., *Hostages of Civilisation. The Social Sources of Anti-Semitism*, London 1950.

Reissner, H. G., *Eduard Gans. Ein Leben im Vormärz*, Tübingen 1965.

Richarz, M., *Der Eintritt der Juden in die akademischen Berufe. Jüdische Studenten und Akademiker in Deutschland, 1678–1848*, Tübingen 1974.

Richarz, M. (ed.), *Jüdisches Leben in Deutschland. Selbstzeugnisse zur Sozialgeschichte 1780–1870*, Stuttgart 1976.

Rivkin, E., *The Shaping of Jewish History*, New York 1971.

Rühs, F., *Über die Ansprüche der Juden an das deutsche Bürgerrecht*, Berlin 1816.

Rürup, R., *Emanzipation und Antisemitismus. Studien zur Judenfrage der bürgerlichen Gesellschaft*, Göttingen 1975.

Sacher, A. L., *A History of the Jews*, 5th rev. edn., New York 1979.

Sachs, M., *Die religiöse Poesie der Juden in Spanien*, Berlin 1845.

Scholem, G., *Judaica*, Frankfurt a. M. 1983 ff.

Scholem, G., *The Messianic Idea in Judaism and Other Essays on Jewish Spirituality*, London 1971.

Schudt, J. J., *Jüdische Merkwürdigkeiten*, Frankfurt a. M. 1714–17.

Sombart, W., *Die Juden und das Wirtschaftsleben*, Leipzig 1911.

Sterling, E., *Judenhaß. Die Anfänge des politischen Antisemitismus in Deutschland 1815–1850*, Frankfurt a. M. 1960.

Stern, S., *The Court Jew. A Contribution to the History of the Period of Absolutism in Central Europe*, Philadelphia 1950. (see also Täubler-Stern, S., below.)

Talmon, J., *Romanticism and Revolt. Europe 1815–1848*, London 1967.

Talmon, J., *Israel Among the Nations*, London 1971.

Täubler-Stern, S., 'Der literarische Kampf um die Emanzipation in den Jahren 1816–19', *Monatsschrift für Geschichte und Wissenschaft des Judentums*, N. F. 47 (1963).

Thieme, K. (ed.), *Judenfeindschaft. Darstellungen und Analysen*, Frankfurt a.M. 1963.

Toury, J., *Die politischen Orientierungen der Juden in Deutschland*, Tübingen 1966.

Toury, J., *Der Eintritt der Juden ins deutsche Bürgertum. Eine Dokumentation*, Tel Aviv 1972.

Toury, J., *Soziale und politische Geschichte der Juden in Deutschland, 1847–1871*, Düsseldorf 1977.

Wallach, L., *Liberty and Letters. The Thoughts of Leopold Zunz*, London 1959.

Wilhelm, K. (ed.), *Wissenschaft des Judentums im deutschen Sprachbereich*, I, Tübingen 1967.

Wirth, Louis, *The Ghetto*, Chicago 1928.

Wohlwill, I., 'Über den Begriff einer Wissenschaft des Judenthums' *Zeitschrift für die Wissenschaft des Judenthums*, I, Berlin 1823.

Zunz, L., *Die gottesdienstlichen Vorträge der Juden. Ein Beitrag zur Alterhumskunde und biblischen Kritik, zur Litteratur- und Religionsgeschichte*, Berlin 1832.

INDEX